BERKSHIRE

Encyclopedia of China

中华全书

BERKSHIRE

Encyclopedia of China

中华全书

*Modern and Historic Views of the
World's Newest and Oldest Global Power*

跨越历史和现代，审视最新和最古老的全球大国

VOLUME **5**

Berkshire Publishing Group
Great Barrington, Massachusetts

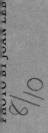

Digital editions

The *Encyclopedia* is also available through most major e-book and database services (check with them for pricing). With every print sale Berkshire provides a free one-year individual license to subscription version of the *Encyclopedia of China* with all photographs in full color (send proof-of-purchase to receive your login information).

For information, contact:
Berkshire Publishing Group LLC
120-122 Castle Street
Great Barrington, Massachusetts 01230-1506 U.S.A.
info@berkshirepublishing.com
Tel +1 413 528 0206
Fax +1 413 541 0076

Photo credits: See page 2666

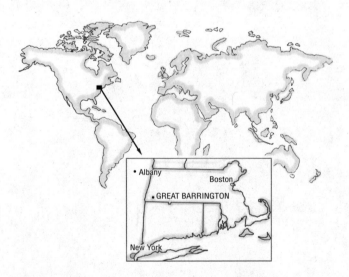

Library of Congress Cataloging-in-Publication Data
Berkshire encyclopedia of China: Modern and historic views of the world's newest and oldest global power/general editor, Linsun Cheng ; associate editors, Kerry Brown . . . [et al.].
    p. cm.
  Includes bibliographical references and index.
  ISBN-13: 978-0-9770159-4-8 (hardcover : alk. paper)
  ISBN-10: 0-9770159-4-7   OCLC 310171885
  1. China—History—Encyclopedias.   2. China--Social conditions—Encyclopedias.
I. Cheng, Linsun, 1951– .   II. Brown, Kerry, 1967– .
  DS735.A2B47 2009
  951.003—dc22   2009007589

Contents

List of Entries

BERKSHIRE

Encyclopedia of China

中华全书

Tangshan Earthquake, Great

Tángshān Dà Dìzhèn 唐山大地震

The Great Tangshan Earthquake of 1976 lasted only fifteen seconds but was one of the worst natural disasters of all time. The earthquake, possibly the deadliest in recorded history depending on the source consulted—the central government did not release death toll figures for three years—is considered symbolic of the end of Mao's era in Chinese history.

The Great Tangshan Earthquake of 1976 killed 255,000 people and injured more than 160,000 in the city of Tangshan in northern China's Hebei Province. The earthquake, with a magnitude of 7.5, occurred directly under Tangshan at a depth of 8 kilometers at 3:42 a.m. on 28 July. Over 90 percent of Tangshan's buildings were flattened, and economic losses were estimated at 3 billion yuan (US $375 million). The earthquake lasted only about fifteen seconds. It was followed by an aftershock of magnitude 7.1 about fifteen hours later. The tremors caused damage in cities as far away as Beijing, Qinhuangdao, and Tianjin. The Chinese government did not report a death toll until 1979, after economic reform had begun.

Although the U.S. Geological Survey (USGS) lists the official death toll at 255,000, it estimates that the death toll may have reached as high as 655,000. That figure would make the Tangshan earthquake the deadliest in modern times and the second deadliest in recorded history. The 2004 Sumatra earthquake in Indonesia killed 283,106, and the Kanto earthquake in Japan killed 142,800 in 1923. The earthquake of 12 May, 2008 in Sichuan Province is

TABLE 1 Most Destructive Earthquakes on Record

Rank	Name of Earthquake	Country	Year	Deaths	Magnitude
1	Shaanxi	China	1556	830,000	8
2	Sumatra	Indonesia	2004	227,898	9.1
3	Tangshan	China	1976	255,000	7.5
4	Aleppo	Syria	1138	230,000	*
5	Damghan	Iran	856	200,000	*
6	Ningxia, Gansu	China	1920	200,000	7.8
7	Ardabil	Iran	893	150,000	*
8	Kanto	Japan	1923	142,800	7.9
9	Ashgabat	USSR	1948	110,000	7.3
10	Chihli	China	1290	100,000	*

*Magnitude unknown.

NOTE: *Although the 1556 Shaaxi earthquake is estimated to have killed 830,000 people, figures from this period are hard to verify.*

Source: United States Geological Survey. (n.d.). Most destructive known earthquakes on record in the world. Retrieved March 28, 2008, from http://earthquake.usgs.gov/regional/world/most_destructive.php

estimated to have killed 87,000 people and was the nineteenth deadliest in recorded history.

Aid Refused

In 1976 the chief members of a radical political faction of the Chinese Communist Party (CCP), known as the "Gang of Four," considered natural disasters a domestic issue and regarded the refusal of aid and sympathy from the international community as an opportunity to "display the socialist system's superiority of being self-reliant" (Rong, 2006).

The Chinese government has changed its attitude after more than three decades of economic reform. When the SARS (severe acute respiratory syndrome) epidemic rocked China and the rest of the world in 2003, the Chinese government joined with worldwide medical and scientific experts to prevent and control the killer disease. China received international aid of $37.5 million, including medical equipment and epidemic prevention materials, from nearly thirty countries, international organizations, and foreign companies. On 12 May 2008, during the Great Sichuan Earthquake, which killed near 70,000 people, the Chinese government also made a great effort to receive international aid and to allow the media the freedom to report the disaster.

After the Tangshan earthquake the Chinese government's efforts at relief were criticized as inadequate. The government also was criticized for having ignored scientists' warnings of the need to prepare for an earthquake. Even today earthquake prediction is far from accurate.

The Tangshan earthquake was one event in what came to be referred to in China as the "Curse of 1976." At the time any extraordinary natural phenomenon, whether snow in summer or droughts in spring, earthquakes or insect plagues, was interpreted as a sign of the displeasure of heaven, indicating that the Mandate of Heaven, which bestowed legitimacy on the Chinese ruling group, might be withdrawn. Enormous political significance was attached to the Tangshan earthquake. In the early 1970s the chaotic Cultural Revolution (1966–1976) had placed the country in a state of social and ideological anarchy. The leadership took great pains to explain away any political significance that might be attached to expressions of cosmic displeasure. For many Chinese the Tangshan earthquake indicated that important developments were about to take place. Many people in Tangshan reported seeing strange lights (so-called earthquake lights) the night before the earthquake. The "Curse of 1976" was also identified with the deaths of Premier Zhou Enlai (1898–1976) in January, Communist military leader and statesman Zhu De (1886–1976) in July, and CCP leader Mao Zedong (1893–1976) in September, and with the arrest the Gang of Four in October. The power struggle between Mao's chosen successor, Hua Guofeng, and CCP leader Deng Xiaoping (1904–1997) began in 1976 as well.

From Rubble to Recovery

Today more than 7 million people live in the 134,720-square-kilometer Tangshan municipal area, including an urban population of 3 million. By 2006 Tangshan's gross domestic product had increased to 236.2 yuan, ranking first in Hebei Province. In 2006 the per capita disposable income for urban residents was 12,376 yuan ($6,514) and 5,155 yuan ($2,713) for rural residents.

On 28 July 2006 President Hu Jintao visited Tangshan to commemorate the thirtieth anniversary of the earthquake. In July 2007 the Chinese government, along with the Architectural Society of China, decided that a memorial park would be built on the earthquake ruins; as of 2008, applications for design ideas were still being accepted. The park will cover about 40 hectares around the ruined site of the Tangshan Rolling Stock Plant. The park will be a museum of earthquake science and will provide a place for the public to pay tribute to earthquake victims.

Unryu SUGANUMA

Further Reading

(2006, July 28). China marks Tangshan earthquake. *BBC News.* [Television broadcast]. London: British Broadcasting Corporation.

Li Jinfang. (1991). *Social responses to the Tangshan earthquake.* Unpublished manuscript. University of Delaware Disaster Research Center.

Liu Huixian, Housner, G. W., Lili Xie, & Duxin He. (2002). *The great Tangshan earthquake of 1976* (Monograph). Pasadena: California Institute of Technology.

Rong Jiaojiao. (2006, July 27). 30 years after Tangshan earthquake, China's attitude toward int'l aid changes. *Xinhua General News,* 1.

Tangshan City Government (2008). Zhongguo Tangshan [Chinese Tangshan]. Retrieved July 31, 2008, from http://www.tangshan.gov.cn/

United States Geological Survey. (n.d.). *Most destructive known earthquakes on record in the world.* Retrieved December 29, 2008, from http://earthquake.usgs.gov/regional/world/most_destructive.php

Wang Wenlan. (2006). Tangshan earthquake: Unforgotten history. *China Daily.* Retrieved August 20, 2007, from http://www.Chinadaily.com.cn/china/2006-07/26/conent_649955.htm

TAO Yuanming

Táo Yuānmíng 陶 渊 明

365–427 CE   *Jin period Poet*

Tao Yuanming was one of the most eminent of pre-Tang poets, effortlessly blending poetic expression with the Confucian and Daoist ideals of simplicity. He was a recluse who rejected the life of the court in favor of that of the country; his poetry exhibits a great concern for the small delights of everyday life. A little over a hundred of his poems survive.

One of the foremost poets of the Jin period (265–420 CE) of the Southern and Northern Dynasties (220–589), Tao Yuanming 陶淵明 or Tao, also known as Tao Qian, was a recluse, preferring rustic settings to courtly splendor and fineries. He was born in Jiujiang in Jiangxi Province to a family that had long served the emperors but had fallen into poverty.

Trained as a scholar-official, Tao was given various minor posts at court, but he could not bring himself to agree with the way things were done by his superiors; he was known for being outspoken and critical. When he lost his sister to an illness, his priorities changed, and at the age of 30, he resigned his post, sold his house, and retreated to the country to do those things that he deemed important in his life—farming and writing poetry—stating famously that he would not humble himself for a few measures of grain. (The salaries of court officials were calculated in measurements of grain.)

At court he saw himself as a caged bird or as a fish in a small, artificial garden pond. During this period of seclusion a theme emerged in his poetry that would define it: bucolic ease. Linguistically he abandoned all things courtly and expunged from his verse all artificially ornate expressions that represented the grave excesses of a life rooted in the rituals and concerns of the court. He chose instead to write about simple pastoral pleasures, such as drinking or appreciating rural landscapes, developing an austere and simple style that reflected the essence of his rural life.

Perhaps in an effort to describe the peace and tranquility he had achieved by escaping from the constraints of the court, he wrote his renowned *Peach Blossom Spring* (*Tao Hua Yuan*, 桃花源記), a utopian description of pastoral life in which the virtues of living harmoniously with nature and with fellow human beings are extolled. The story tells of a fisherman who drifts along a stream in his boat and finds himself in an enchanted and unknown valley, where the inhabitants know nothing of the outside world's ills and are concerned solely with living in harmony with nature. When the time comes for the fisherman to return home, he carefully marks his path so that he might visit the valley again, but when he tries to find it he fails; the charmed place is lost to him, and he must live the rest of his life with the knowledge that he briefly lived in a paradisiacal place to which he can never again return.

Tao died on his farm, which he had made into his own utopia. Tao Yuanming is not remembered for his erudition, but rather for his poems that are so intimate and so well crafted that they become perfected reflections on

Tao Yuanming Returning to Seclusion, **a Chinese handscroll painting on silk, from the late Northern Song Dynasty, early twelfth century. This handscroll is inscribed with a poem by the Song Dynasty scholar Li Peng (c. 1060–1110) titled "Returning Home"; it honors the fourth-century poet Tao Yuanming, also known as Tao Qian.** FREER AND SACKLER GALLERIES OF WASHINGTON D.C.

the individual as he seeks a place within the flow of history. This placing of the infinitesimal within the infinite marks his verses, making their appeal transcendent of both time and space.

Nirmal DASS

Further Reading

Acker, W. (1952). *T'ao the hermit: Sixty poems.* London: Thames and Hudson.

Hightower, J. R. (1970). *The poetry of T'ao Chi'en.* Oxford Library of East Asian Literatures. Oxford, U.K.: Clarendon Press.

Hinton, D. (1993). *The selected poems of T'ao Chi'en.* Port Townsend, WA: Copper Canyon Press.

Tan Shilin (Ed. and Trans.). (1992). *The complete works of Tao Yuanming.* Hong Kong: Joint Publishing (H.K.) Co. Ltd.

Tian Xiaofei. (2005). *Tao Yuanming and manuscript culture: The record of a dusty table.* Seattle: University of Washington Press.

Tarim Basin

Tǎlǐmù Péndì　塔里木盆地

Known for its sparse vegetation and extreme climate, the Tarim Basin is located in the northwestern corner of China and will play a major role in China's oil and energy production in the coming century. It is one of the largest endorheic basins in the world, meaning that rivers that flow into it dry up rather than flowing on to the sea.

The Tarim Basin is located in Xinjiang Uygur Autonomous Region in northwestern China between the Tian Shan and Kunlun Shan mountain ranges. The basin encompasses 906,500 square kilometers (a little over half the size of the state of Alaska) of mostly shifting sands, undulating expanses of arid terrain, and dry lake beds. Rivers that flow into it off the surrounding mountains dry up into the earth or evaporate rather than flowing on to the ocean. (The Great Basin in the American west is an example of another such "endorheic" basin.)

The Taklimakan Desert, which is the fifteenth-largest nonpolar desert in the world and the world's second largest sand desert, occupies the lower basin of the Tarim. The Silk Roads—a network of trade routes that connected eastern, southern, and western Asia with the Mediterranean area, including northern Africa and Europe—threaded the region and was split into two routes. The northern route ran along the northern edge of the Taklimakan Desert, and the southern route ran along the southern edge.

An Uygur Muslim cemetery in northwest China, Tarim Basin, Turfan, Xinjiang Uygur Autonomous Region. The Uygurs, a Turkic minority people, have inhabited the basin region for two millennia.
PHOTO BY JOAN LEBOLD COHEN.

Tarim Basin, Subashi city in Xinjiang. The Han Chinese wrested control of the basin from the Xiongnu people at the end of the first century. PHOTO BY JOAN LEBOLD COHEN.

The term *tarim* describes a river that either flows into a lake or meanders amid desert sands. The desert climate has temperature extremes of −20° to 50° C and precipitation of just 50–100 millimeters a year. The snow on K2, the world's second-highest mountain, flows into glaciers that creep down valleys to melt. This melted water forms rivers that flow into the Tarim Basin. Vegetation is sparse except for riparian (relating to the bank of a natural watercourse) stands of wormwood and poplar and willows, Ural licorice, sea buckthorn, and Indian hemps.

The Han Chinese wrested control of the basin from the Xiongnu people at the end of the first century under General Ban Chao (32–102). Today the basin is sparsely settled by Tajiks and Uygurs and other Turkic peoples. Oasis agriculture in far-flung and small settlements produces cotton, fruits, grains, wool, and silk. Khotan jade, a nephrite jade that occurs in a variety of colors, is mined, and tourism is increasing in importance. Recent discoveries of oil and natural gas will make these an important source of China's energy supplies in the next century.

Since the 1980s archaeologists have discovered remains of bodies dating back almost four thousand years in the eastern and southern parts of the basin. Dating from 1800 BCE–200 CE, some of the mummies have been linked to Indo-European Tocharian languages in the basin, although evidence is not conclusive. The cemetery at Yanbulaq yielded twenty-nine mummies, which have dated from 1100–500 BCE. The mummies have both Mongoloid and Caucasoid characteristics, suggesting ancient contacts between East and West. Their clothing indicates a common origin with Indo-European Neolithic (8000–5500 BCE) textile techniques. Many of the mummies are in excellent condition because of the desiccation of the corpses caused by the dryness of the desert.

Nuclear tests have been conducted at Lop Nur, a saline, marshy depression at the east end of the basin. Although once an important stop along the Silk Road, the lake, which has a tendency to shift its location due to blowing sands, has mostly dried up, mostly because of human activity.

Stephen F. CUNHA

Further Reading

Blackmore, C. (1996). *The worst desert on Earth: Crossing the Taklamakan*. London: John Murray.

Mallory, J. P., & Mair, V. H. (2000). *The Tarim mummies: Ancient China and the mystery of the earliest peoples from the West*. New York: Thomas and Hudson.

Rudelson, J. J. (1997). *Oasis identities: Uyghur nationalism along China's Silk Road*. New York: Columbia University Press.

Taxation and Taxes

Shuìshōu yǔ shuìzhǒng　税收与税种

China's tax system is probably the most ancient and, at the same time, the most recent in the world. While records of land taxes go back almost four thousand years, the current tax structure did not come into existence until after 1980. Despite the Western influences of China's current tax system, it remains compatible with China's culture and politics.

The Chinese tax system looks like other tax systems in many ways. It consists of income taxes, consumption taxes (similar to sales taxes), property taxes, and other miscellaneous taxes. The functions of taxation are to raise revenue, to stimulate economic growth, and to facilitate social and political stability. China's current system is the result of major reforms since the 1980s.

Tax Reforms

Soon after the People's Republic of China came to power in 1949, the Communist Party reconstructed the economy. Private capital was nationalized, and foreign investment gradually left China. A type of sales tax and a property tax were introduced and administered by the general tax bureau. The reconstruction was more or less complete by 1956. From 1956 to 1978, a strict Soviet-type economy was practiced, and the private sector almost vanished. Industry and commerce were controlled by publicly owned enterprises. State-owned enterprises delivered all their profits to the government, and sales taxes were generally used to facilitate the transfer of funds from enterprises to the government's coffer. At the peak of the political and economic turmoil during the Cultural Revolution (1966–1976), law and order were in disarray, the role of taxation was disregarded, and the tax department existed only in name.

In 1978, under the leadership of Deng Xiaoping, the Communist Party changed its policy from political struggle to economic development. Deng made it clear that the need for economic development prevailed over the pursuit of the party's socialist ideals. Economic reforms changed the relationship between the state and the market, allowing for the creation of a tax policy.

The new economic policy had two objectives: opening up China to the outside world and reforming the domestic economic system. Establishing a modern tax system was considered critical to the success of the economic policy. To facilitate the transition, a two-track tax system was introduced so that a Western-style tax system would apply to foreign firms and individuals and another system would apply to Chinese firms and citizens.

The foreign track was created first and consisted of the individual income tax, targeted at foreign individuals (1980); the equity joint ventures income tax (1980); and the foreign enterprise income tax, applicable to foreign-owned enterprises and other foreign entities doing business in China (1981). An earlier tax—the consolidated industrial and commercial tax—remained applicable to foreign investors because it was the only tax in effect before 1980.

The domestic track was created in 1983 and 1984. State enterprises became subject to taxes, a reform commonly referred to as *li gai shui* (taxation replacing profit delivery). Separate taxes applied to the emerging collective enterprises and private enterprises; sales taxes applicable to domestic enterprise were introduced; and numerous miscellaneous taxes on property and transactions were reintroduced.

More substantive reforms began in 1986. In 1991 the foreign track was consolidated to create the enterprise income tax on foreign investment enterprises and foreign enterprises (FIE tax). In 1994 the three domestic enterprise income taxes were replaced by a one consolidated domestic enterprise income tax. The foreign track merged with the domestic track in the areas of sales tax and individual income tax. The 1994 reform also resulted in a new tax assignment between the central government and local governments as well as a new system of tax administration. Overall, the foreign track is a more Western-style tax. Because China wanted to follow the international tax norm, the FIE tax addresses international issues. The domestic track has more features from the old Soviet-style economy and is much less detailed than the FIE tax is. With respect to deductible expenses, FIEs may deduct the cost of wages, salaries, and employee benefits, whereas domestic enterprises can deduct only the amount of wages in accordance with the standard set by the government.

As of 1 January 2008, China implemented a fundamental enterprise income tax reform that adopts a lower general tax rate and unifies the tax rules applied to all enterprises. This new Enterprise Income Tax (EIT) replaced FIE tax and domestic enterprise income tax. It is a hybrid of international tax norms and China's indigenous rules. For example, the new tax legislation provides anti-avoidance rules such as transfer pricing rules and thin capitalization rules, which seem to be the most direct adoption from international tax rules and are designed to prevent multinational corporations from shifting profits away from China without paying Chinese taxes. On the other hand, the legacies of economic transition and Chinese culture find their ways into this legislation. For instance, there are still a number of "residual" clauses authorizing the government to determine "other" amounts or issues in the new tax system.

Current Tax Structure

The State Administration of Taxation (SAT) is responsible for administering tax laws in China. Its national head office is in Beijing. Local tax bureaus collect local taxes and some taxes shared between the central government and local governments. Although they are part of the local government, they fall under the SAT in terms of tax law interpretation and policy.

Four types of taxes are collected in China: consumption taxes, income taxes, property taxes, and miscellaneous taxes.

CONSUMPTION TAXES

Consumption taxes (*liu zhuan shui*) generate more than two-thirds of the total tax revenue. A consumption tax is a type of sales tax.

The value added tax (VAT) is the most productive source of revenue—generating about 37 percent of total tax revenue in recent years (e.g., 36.7 percent in 2006 and 37.5 percent in 2005). This tax applies to the sale of goods and certain services. The standard rate is 17 percent; a lower rate of 13 percent applies to necessities, certain culture products, agricultural supplies, and certain other goods. Small suppliers are taxed at 6 percent. Exports are not taxed. The business tax is imposed on business activities that are not subject to the VAT, mostly services. The tax rate is 3 percent for transportation, construction, postal communication, and cultural and athletic activities; 5 percent for banking, insurance, services, and the transfer of intangible property and immovable property; and 5 percent to 20 percent for entertainment (the applicable rate is determined by the local government).

The consumption tax is imposed on the sale and importation of luxury goods, such as tobacco, liquor, cosmetics, fireworks and firecrackers, gasoline, diesel, tires, motorcycles, and automobiles. The tax rates range from 1 percent on nonluxury cars to 45 percent on top-quality cigarettes. This tax is imposed in addition to the VAT.

The resource tax is imposed on the production and sale of crude oil, natural gas, coal, nonferrous metals, ferrous metals, and salt. The amount of tax payable is determined by the Ministry of Finance according to the mining or production conditions of the taxpayer.

INCOME TAXES

Income taxes are the second major source of revenue, generating about 22 percent of total tax revenues. Income taxes have been growing faster than consumption taxes since the late 1990s. For example, VAT grew by 22 percent in 2000, while FEI tax grew 50 percent, individual income tax grew 59 percent (SAT http://www.chinatax.gov.cn).

The individual income tax is a *schedular tax*; that is, different types of income are subject to different tax rates, and certain deductions are allowed. Income from employment is taxed monthly at progressive rates ranging from 5 percent to 45 percent. Income from the business of industrial and commercial activities and enterprise leasing and management are taxable annually at progressive rates ranging from 5 percent to 35 percent. Income from personal services is subject to a 20 percent flat rate tax. Investment income, incidental income, and capital gains are taxed at a flat rate of 20 percent. In computing the taxable amount, a deduction for actual expenses is allowed only in the case of business income. A standard deduction is allowed in the case of employment income, income from services, rents, and royalties. Interest, dividends, and incidental income are taxed on a gross basis. Taxes are withheld at the source. Enterprise Income Tax now applies to all enterprises (any business or organization that is not a sole proprietorship or partnership).

PROPERTY TAXES

A large number of taxes are imposed on property, transactions, and other real estate activities, generating about 8 percent of total tax revenues. Taxes on real estate are the most significant. A real estate gains tax was introduced in 1993 to regulate the growing real estate market in China. It applies to gains from the transfer of land-use rights, buildings (other than residential housing), and other structures on the land at progressive rates ranging from 30 percent to 60 percent. The urban real estate tax is imposed on the owners of real estate in urban areas. The deed tax is levied on the transfer of land-use rights and the sale, gift, or exchange of houses and buildings.

MISCELLANEOUS TAXES

The stamp tax applies to the signing or issuing of commercial contracts and documents. For example, loan contracts are taxed at 0.005 percent of the loan amount, and technology contracts are taxed at 0.03 percent of the contractual price. Taxpayers pay the tax by purchasing and affixing tax stamps.

The banquet tax is levied at 15 percent to 20 percent of the cost of each banquet costing over 250 yuan (about $37). The tax is withheld by the restaurant.

Tax Revenue Sharing

A key function of taxation is raising revenue. Since the 1980s, taxation has become a main source of government revenue. Most taxes in China are collected by the use of consumption taxes. Compared to income taxes, consumption taxes are easier to administer. These taxes are collected from enterprises, not consumers, thereby reducing the cost of administration and compliance. The tax mix has been favorable for generating revenue. Sharing the revenue from taxes between the central government and local governments is an enormous challenge.

China's financial system is highly decentralized. Expenditures by local governments account for 71 percent of government expenditures. The central government has exclusive taxing powers in terms of legislation. All taxes are introduced by the central government. However, revenue from specific taxes is assigned to local governments. Overall, local governments receive about 50 percent of total tax revenues.

Under the current revenue-sharing system, local governments are entitled to the revenue from the following taxes: 100 percent of property and transaction taxes; 25 percent of the VAT; business taxes (with minor exceptions); domestic enterprise income taxes (other than those paid by centrally owned enterprises, local banks, financial institutions, and railway, banking and insurance companies that pay income tax centrally through their head office); FIE taxes (other than those paid by foreign banks); and resource taxes (other than those paid by off-shore oil companies).

Tax Expenditures as Policy Instruments

Using tax expenditures as policy instruments is consistent with China's previous practice of central planning, the need to accommodate local economic conditions of different regions of the country, and the desire to compete with other developing countries in attracting foreign direct investment. International competitiveness has always been a key concern in Chinese tax policy.

China has used tax expenditures extensively in both the income tax system and consumption tax system. Every major tax contains tax expenditure provisions. For example, the VAT exempts contraceptive medicines from taxation. The business tax exempts child care, education, and medical services. The individual income tax exempts a large variety of items from taxation. They include awards from the government, settlement fees to military personnel, and salaries of foreign experts sent to work in China international organizations.

The new enterprise income tax law provides a general low tax rate and unified tax incentives to both domestic and foreign investment enterprises. The nominal enterprise income tax rate is 25 percent, which is internationally competitive. The new tax incentives are designed to achieve tax equity between domestic enterprises and FIEs, to reduce administration and taxpayer compliances costs, as well as to achieve an overall, long-term, sustainable development of Chinese economy. They favor high-tech, industry-oriented or environment-oriented investments, and nonprofit organizations, or small, low-profit enterprises. These eligible enterprises obtain tax preferences based on the nature of their investments, other than the form of ownership or special locations.

Tax Policies and Development

Development in any country has three broad dimensions: economic, legal, and social, which are generally interrelated. Since the 1980s, China's tax policies have had varying effects on development.

TAX POLICIES AND ECONOMIC DEVELOPMENT

In many ways China's experiment with economic development has been unique. China is a socialist country governed by a single party. The economy is highly fragmented and in transition toward a socialist market economy. China had no modern tax system until the 1980s. Chinese leadership has always resisted the advice of international experts to go for "big-bang" economic reforms in favor of a more gradual, pragmatic approach.

China's development goal has been to build up a relatively well-off (xiaokang) society in which people generally are not rich but have adequate food, clothing, and other material goods necessary for a decent life. Economic development is a precondition for reaching this goal.

According to the National Bureau of Statistics, China's gross domestic product (GDP) grew from 362 billion yuan in 1978 to 21.18 trillion yuan in 2006. In 2006, China was the world's fourth largest economy measured by the size of GDP, the third largest trader, and one of the largest recipients of foreign direct investment.

UNEQUAL DEVELOPMENT

But amid its rapid economic development, China has achieved social development only in certain areas. Poverty has been noticeably reduced. The unemployment rate for 2007 stood at 4 percent in urban areas though it was much lower in rural areas. China's human development index has improved continuously since the 1990s, according to United Nations reports on human development. China's global ranking rose from number 101 in 1991 to number 81 in 2007.

On the other hand, there have been increasing income disparities, regional disparities, and urban and rural disparities in China. In the early 1990s, for instance, the top 10 percent of the population held 40 percent of the savings in China. In 2006, saving deposits in urban and rural areas were 161.58 trillion yuan; the top 5 percent of the population owned about 50 percent of the national savings. Some parts of the country, typically the southeast coastal areas and provincial capital cities, are more developed.

Disparities also exist between women and children and men, and between racial minorities and the more dominant ethnic groups. The Chinese tax system disproportionately benefits men because they are generally the higher income earners. In China women make up a smaller proportion of the white-collar workforce than men do, and the ratio of female-to-male earnings is about 0.82.

The regional disparities and shortages of financial resources at the local level also have had significant adverse effects on women and ethic minority groups. Ethnic minority groups generally live in less-developed regions. A lack of resources at the local level often results in a lack of funding for hospitals, schools, housing, and other public works. Thus local service providers have to charge for their services. Local schools, for example, charge what are high fees for peasants. This has led to a dramatic shift in educational opportunities for women in rural areas. A son is the future "retirement plan" for his parents. A daughter is someone's wife and will help support the husband's parents. Thus, in the rural areas and minority areas where the one-child policy is not strictly applied, the daughter is often required to work to pay for the schooling of her brother. The results are that many fewer girls than boys are going on to higher education. Tax policies have played no significant role in income redistribution. By its very design, the tax structure in China cannot play a key role in alleviating inequality in income and wealth. In developed countries, the income tax, especially the personal income tax, has been used as the main instrument for redistributing income. But in China the role of the individual income in redistribution remains largely symbolic. This tax accounts for about 6 percent of total tax revenues. It is progressive only with respect to employment income and business income. Other types of income are taxable at a flat rate. The fraction of population paying the tax grew from 0.1 percent of all wage earners in 1986 to about 32 percent of all wage earners in 2001 and the average amount of annual tax paid by each wage earner was 314 yuan (less than $40) in 2002. More than one-third of the total individual income tax on employment income was collected from workers at foreign investment enterprises. Given the current situations in China, the individual income tax cannot be a meaningful tool of redistribution.

Some provisions of the sales taxes have some progressive features. For example, the consumption tax is imposed on luxury goods and services at progressive rates. This tax is presumably borne by high-income earners. The VAT is slightly progressive with a lower rate on certain necessities, such as grain, edible oil, and running water. Overall, however, these taxes worsen the urban/rural disparities because low-income rural residents must pay these taxes. In many poor rural areas, these taxes are the only taxes collected.

Tax Policies and Social Development

Compared with the wide variety of tax preferences for economic development, tax expenditures for social development have been fewer in number and less in amount. Most of the tax expenditures under the individual income tax relate to disaster relief, family planning, payments to military personnel, and retired cadres. These measures are largely in response to other policy decisions and are not designed to promote any social activities.

Arguably, tax expenditures on social development are as important as those for economic development during an economic transition. At a time of increasing income gaps, the economic reforms smashed the "iron rice bowl" style of social security (which was tied to lifetime employment at a work unit) when state-owned enterprises were transformed into "economically efficient" entities. Redundant workers lost their jobs as well as their welfare system, which typically consisted of subsidized housing, medical insurance, and retirement income. The government has not introduced any meaningful tax subsidies for housing, education, charitable donations, child care, medical care, family support, or retirement savings. No specific tax expenditure has been designed to create jobs or workers' training or relocation. Although the government has flirted with the idea of tax-subsidized retirement plans, no concrete tax policy has yet been enacted.

Retirement income security is a significant social and political issue in China. The Chinese population is aging at an accelerating rate owing to three possible factors: the baby boom in the 1950s and 1960s; the single-child policy, which has produced the four-two-one family structure (four grandparents, two parents, one child); and the increasing longevity of the Chinese people. The percentage of individuals aged sixty and older in the Chinese population was 10 percent in 1999 and is expected to be 20.4 percent in 2030. All this means that there will be fewer young people in the future to pay taxes that can adequately support the elderly.

Since the early 1990s, the Chinese government has regarded employer-sponsored retirement plans as an important pillar in the retirement system and the tax policy as a key instrument for supporting retirement plans. Employer-sponsored retirement plans are expected to supplement the public retirement pillar, which is designed to provide a basic retirement of up to 40 or 45 percent of the average salary at the time of retirement. It is estimated that retirement funds in China could exceed $160 billion by 2030 and become the world's third largest retirement market. Many enterprises created retirement plans for their workers in order to attract and retain workers in an increasingly competitive labor market. The government introduced regulatory measures in 2004 to require that all retirement plans be defined as contribution plans and be managed in accordance with market principles. Under existing tax legislation, contributions made by an enterprise into a privately funded retirement plan are generally not deductible.

Tax Policies and the Law

Taxes and taxation are complex and create the need for rules, regulations, and laws to oversee implementation and collection, protect taxpayers' rights, and prohibit abuses by taxing agents. Although China does not have the rule of law, it has enacted a number of tax laws.

China's primary tax policy objectives are revenue, efficiency, and international competitiveness. Establishing a system of taxation based on clear rules is important in achieving these objectives because tax rules are written to govern not only the relationship between taxpayers and the government but also relationship between the State Administration of Taxation (SAT) and local tax offices and the relationship between the tax administration and other government departments.

In terms of promotion of economic development, predictable and clear tax rules are undoubtedly important. Taxpayers need these rules to arrange their affairs and even to decide whether to invest in China. One reason for the two-track enterprise income tax system was to create a tax system that would be perceived as predictable and fair by international investors. The two-track system is highly discriminative now, but its original rationale was sound in the 1980s. China has always been sensitive to its international image, and creating a rule-based system was considered to an important part of projecting a positive image. This sensitivity helps explain why the foreign track of the tax system is regulated by laws enacted by the National People's Congress.

SOURCES OF TAX LAWS

Tax laws in China include not only statutes (laws) enacted by the legislature but also administrative regulations authorized by the State Council and administrative rules introduced by the SAT. China has three major tax laws (the Individual Income Tax Law, the Enterprise Income Tax Law, and the Tax Administration and Collection Law), thirty or so administrative tax regulations, and about fifty administrative rules. Administrative policies and documents that have no force of law in Western countries have the status of legislation in China. Court decisions do not have the force of law in China.

Since the 1980s, tax legislation has become more detailed and comprehensive. The trend has been to elevate administrative rules to administrative regulations or to tax laws. For example, tax collection and administration had been governed by administrative regulations until 1991 when the Tax Administration and Collection Law (TACL) was enacted. The TACL, with 94 articles, modernized the collection system, set clear standards on the collection of taxes at both the national and the local levels, and established penalties for various violations of the law. It also provided the framework to allow tax authorities more access to taxpayer information and to better define the rights and responsibilities of both tax officers and taxpayers. The implementation rules for the TACL, 113 articles, provided detailed implementation guidance for the supervision and administration of tax collection in China. The TACL, along with the implementation rules, has been acclaimed as a breakthrough in China's tax administration system.

THE ROLE OF THE JUDICIARY

In the area of taxes, the role of the court is limited to adjudicating tax disputes between taxpayers and the tax administration. There are generally two types of disputes. One involves the interpretation of tax legislation to determine tax liability. The other involves taxpayers bringing tax officials to court for wrongful or illegal administrative actions. Because administrative appeals are available to taxpayers in the case of the first type of disputes, most taxpayers resort to administrative appeals. Judicial appeals on matters of interpretation are virtually nonexistent in China. With respect to the second type of disputes, more and more taxpayers bring their lawsuits in accordance with the Administrative Procedures Law. Local tax offices are generally named as defendants in such cases for assessing tax penalties, enforcing tax collections, or other unlawful actions. In such administrative cases, taxpayers have won more than two-thirds of the cases.

The judiciary's role is limited for several reasons. First, the courts do not have the exclusive power of interpretation: The body that introduces the law has the final power to interpret it. As such, the legislature, the State Council, or even the State Administration of Taxation has the sole power to interpret the meaning of statutory provisions. Since most of Chinese taxes are governed by regulations or rules introduced by the State Council or the SAT, the SAT has the sole power of interpretation in most cases. Even with tax laws enacted by the National People's Congress (the highest state legislative body) the legislation is vaguely worded, leaving the tax administration with broad powers of interpretation. In the case of entitlement to tax preferences, the legislation generally requires taxpayers to apply to the tax administration for approval before they can enjoy the preferences. This makes it difficult for the court to challenge the administrative interpretation.

Another reason for the limited role of the judiciary is the lack of tax expertise in the judiciary. Tax expertise is concentrated within the tax administration. Although some tax officials have joined private practice, none has become a judge. The small number of tax cases makes it difficult for judges to develop tax expertise. There is a general lack of confidence in the judiciary in treating taxpayers equally in interpretative matters.

Finally, the court and the local tax bureaus are part of local governments. The payroll and benefits of judges and tax officials are determined by the same government. Local protectionism is a serious problem. Local tax bureaus may treat local taxpayers differently than they treat outsiders, whose tax revenue belongs to the central government. The courts' decisions are sometimes influenced by the local government. Promoting local interest may prevail over the strict application of the law. Personal relationships between a judge and tax officials may also make it hard for the judge to overturn officials' interpretations.

TAX ADMINISTRATION

The administration of taxes has been increasingly governed by rules and procedures. In addition to the TACL, there are rules governing invoice management, tax administrative reviews, tax audits, internal inspections, assessments of tax penalties, and tax litigation. The administration of taxes has progressed in providing services, becoming more transparent, and respecting taxpayers' rights.

At the beginning of the economic transition in China in the 1980s, a direct assessment system was necessary because taxpayers were unfamiliar with the tax laws. With the continuing of the transition, direct assessment was gradually replaced by taxpayer reporting. By 1997 a three-part administration system was established: filing of returns by taxpayers coupled with taxpayer services, utilization of information technology, and centralization of tax collection and targeted tax audits and inspections. Taxpayers file tax returns at tax-service centers. Tax collectors are no longer directly involved in establishing a taxpayer's tax liability. There is less face-to-face contact between taxpayers and tax officials who assess their tax liabilities and thus fewer opportunities for dishonest taxpayers and tax collectors to collude in cheating on the tax system.

Taxpayer services have been improving. Tax officials are required to smile at taxpayers or just be polite and put themselves in the shoes of taxpayers. The move to self-assessment has been accompanied by computerization and information technologies. Opportunities for corruption have been reduced greatly after the computerization of taxpayer records and initial selection of targets for audit.

The level of transparency in the tax administration has also improved over the years. During the early years of reform, many tax documents were labeled "Confidential," out of reach to taxpayers. Now the SAT publishes tax legislation, interpretation documents, rulings, and other types of information on its website or in print through the China Taxation Press. The SAT is also developing an advance ruling system, especially in the area of transfer pricing. The process of negotiating advance pricing agreements is governed by certain implementation rules.

Taxpayers' rights are specified in the TACL and Implementation Rules. Taxpayers (and withholding agents) have the following rights: to request that the tax authorities treat the information provided as confidential; to apply for tax reductions, exemptions, and refunds according to the relevant tax laws; to make a statement or to defend themselves against the decision of the tax office; to resort to the process of administrative and judicial review and to request compensation for damages incurred; and to use and disclose illegal activities conducted by the tax authorities and tax officials. In addition, taxpayers have the right to deny a tax inspection if tax officials fail to present a tax inspection certificate and tax inspection notice and to request an extension to file returns and to make tax payments.

Tax authorities and tax officials are required by the TACL to be independent and impartial in enforcing tax laws, to act with integrity and courtesy, to respect and protect the rights of taxpayers and withholding agents, and to avoid conflicts of interest when carrying out collections or investigations. If taxpayers' rights are unlawfully infringed upon or violated, taxpayers can sue for damages. Tax officials may be sued for inappropriate conduct, such as withholding or seizing taxpayers' accommodations (including residential property), misusing daily living necessities in enforcing tax collections, or abuse of power. Penalties are enforced on tax officials who show favoritism; commit malpractice; fail to report criminal acts to lawful authorities; retaliate against taxpayers for reporting tax officials' wrongdoing; intentionally delay, advance, or allocate revenue quotas; or wrongfully collect taxes.

To secure revenue, the SAT has worked hard to introduce rules to clarify the obligations and rights of taxpayers as well as those of local tax offices and other government agencies. The head office of the SAT does not actually collect any taxes, the SAT requires clear tax rules to guide and monitor the work of local offices. Clear rules also enable the SAT to fend off the interference of local governments with tax collection. In principle, national taxes are collected by the local offices of the SAT, and local taxes are collected by local tax bureaus. For example, income tax owed by state-owned enterprises under the control of the central government is collected by the SAT, while other types of domestic enterprises pay taxes to the local tax bureaus. Under the previous central planning model, enterprises were managed by different level of governments. This legacy has continued into the current tax system. Since the SAT has only a weak supervisory role, and there is no effective system for distributing and enforcing common policy, the SAT sometimes has to rely on more clear and authoritative legislative rules to carry out its policies.

To ensure productive cooperation between the SAT and other government departments (such as the police, the People's Bank, and the courts), the TACL specifically provided the obligations of these agencies in enforcement. In the absence of legislative rules, departmental conflicts or noncooperation could be a serious problem. A lack of support from the police has been a main reason for the SAT to request a special tax-police force and a specialized tax court. To regulate departmental relations, the rules must come from a superior body, the State Council or the National People's Congress. That is why the TACL is one of three pieces of taxing statues enacted by the NPC.

The excessive use of tax expenditures as policy instruments threatens not only revenue collection but also the effectiveness of tax policy and respect of the SAT and tax legislation. There is a misconception that the tax system is about obtaining preferences as opposed to collecting taxes. Once these preferences are considered tradable commodities, they breed corruption and disrespect for the tax system. Because most tax preferences are granted at local levels, they provide opportunities for local protection. More centralized rules are expected to deal with these problems.

The number of tax professionals who assist taxpayers

in tax planning, compliance, and dispute resolution has been growing. At present, tax practice is dominated by accountants. On average, 30 percent of the revenue of accounting firms is from tax work. Lawyers are also engaged in tax practice but on a much smaller scale. There are also more than 62,000 certified tax agents, including 20,000 active practitioners who assist taxpayers with compliance, dispute resolution, and other dealings with the tax administration.

A Homegrown System

Overall, the Chinese tax policy is generally compatible with China's culture and politics. The best tax policy is one that suits local conditions, and China's tax policy is largely homegrown. At the same time, international influences have helped shape China's tax policy. The Chinese have always used foreign ideas to meet Chinese needs.

Development is a universal issue, but the path to development is unique for every country. As an instrument of social development, the tax policy has not been used much in China. Redistribution of income has been minimal. Social spending through tax expenditures is insignificant. On the other hand, China's tax policy has spurred economic development and contributed to major changes in the legal system.

Ultimately in China everything is political. All reforms, changes, and development have taken place within the confines of socialism and under the leadership of the Communist Party. This distinct model of development defines China's distinct tax policy.

LI Jinyan and HUANG He

Further Reading

Brean, D. J. S. (1998). *Taxation in modern China.* New York: Routledge.

United Nations Development Programme. (2008). Human Development Report 2007/2008: Fighting Climate Change: Human Solidarity in a Divided World. New York: Palgrave Macmillan.

Li Jinyan. (1991). *Taxation in the People's Republic of China.* New York: Praeger.

Li Jinyan. (2005). Relationship between international trade law and national tax policy: A case study of China. *Bulletin for International Fiscal Document,* 59(2), 77–87.

Li Jinyan. (2006). China's individual income tax: A 26-year-old infant. *Tax Notes International,* 3(4), 297–302.

Li Jinyan. (2007). Fundamental enterprise income tax reform in China: Motivations and major changes. *Bulletin for International Taxation,* 61(12), 519.

Lipsher, L. E. (2007, January 17). China's new era goals: More transparency, less income disparity. *Tax Notes International,* 149–151.

Tan, S., Lu, D., & Kadet, J. (2008, May 5). China outlines criteria for high–tech companies. *Tax Notes International,* 369–373.

Wang Zhenhua. (2007, April 2). Corporate tax reform in China: Background, features and impacts. *Tax Notes International,* 97–103.

Tea and Tea Culture

Chá hé cháwénhuà 茶和茶文化

Drinking tea—traditionally a brew made from the leaf, bud, or twig of the *Camellia sinensis*—is today universal in East Asia and much of the world, but the beverage took a long time to catch on. The precise form of tea consumed has also varied over time and by culture, reflecting different times and different tastes.

Tea is a drink made from the leaf, bud, and twig of the *Camellia sinensis* plant, which was probably first domesticated in Southeast Asia, although a number of possible sites have been named, including some in south China. Several varieties exist; some, such as Assam tea from India, are quite distinctive. Tea is cultivated at moderate altitude in China in tropical and semitropical areas, usually in marginal soils not suited to growing highly productive food crops such as rice. This fact was a major reason for tea's economic importance. During Song dynasty (960–1279) China, for example, tea could be cultivated on a broad scale without limiting food production in any way. At the time it became an economic powerhouse and a primary basis for the prosperity of the dynasty.

Initially tea was grown in hilly areas of Fujian Province and neighboring Jiangxi Province, but its cultivation was later expanded to other suitable areas. It cultivation was later established in Yunnan Province, for example, when Yunnan definitely became a part of China during the Yuan dynasty (1279–1368) and Ming dynasty

(1368–1644). Fine tea, including some of the most famous varieties, is still grown there.

Tea Drinking

Tea drinking arose in China around the beginning of the first century CE but was at first a localized practice confined to the south. Tea, at first brewed from green leaves, was originally more a medicinal than a recreational beverage. By the Tang dynasty (618–907 CE) the practice had become common in the south and north, and during the Song dynasty tea drinking became the rage, as it has continued to be to the present. Song dynasty tea was a product greatly in demand, not only in China but also in Tibet and other neighbors of China, later even in the far West.

Although the first teas were made from leaf, the preferred form of tea during Tang times was brick tea. This tea used large square bricks of pressed tea leaves boiled for long periods of time to produce a strong and thick beverage, consumed with milk and cream in central Asia. Later, particularly during the Song dynasty, powdered teas became common and were the form of tea later taken over by Japan as the basis for its tea ceremony. By late Song times carefully selected leaf teas had also become common, and these were associated with a substantial connoisseurship. More recently oxidized leaf and pressed teas, known incorrectly as "fermented teas" (although some teas were fermented), have been popular and were long the preferred tea for the European and U.S. export market. The story that a shipload of tea rotted and that Europeans, not knowing any better, liked the flavor of

A woman picks tea leaves at the Dragon Well Tea Commune in Hangzhou, 1978. PHOTO BY JOAN LEBOLD COHEN.

the rotten tea, although entertaining, is folklore. Some of the oxidized teas are even highly regarded in China to this day.

Culture of Tea

China never had a tea ritual comparable with the Japanese tea ceremony, but China had a distinct culture of tea beginning during the period of disunity (third to sixth centuries CE) and continuing many centuries thereafter. Playing a key role in the development of this tea culture were Buddhist monasteries and monks. Like the Sufis (Muslim mystics) of the Islamic world, who helped introduce their favorite beverage of coffee to the Islamic world, Buddhist monks seem to have enjoyed tea as a stimulant during dull monastic work or meditation. Probably because of this practice, tea drinking became a formal part of monastic rituals, which helped stress the elegance, simplicity, and introspection involved. Because monasteries were never isolated from the secular world in medieval and early modern China, laymen soon became involved both in monastic tea culture and their own varieties of it. These varieties were developed outside monasteries but incorporated much of the ritualized content of monastic tea consumption. Tea drinking thus became an important link between the literati and the monastic culture of Zen in particular and was an earmark of Song dynasty culture.

Outside both literati culture and the monastery, strictly speaking, was another area of the Song dynasty's concern with tea: the tea house. Restaurants, as they exist today, and, for that matter, tea houses, first appeared in China. Places where one could go, eat a few snacks, drink tea, and enjoy the company of others, especially females, were noticed by, among others, the Venetian traveler Marco Polo. He expressed amazement that one could go, rent a space—on the West Lake of Hangzhou, no less, famed for its beauty—and be served, individually or as a group, wonderful delicacies and be provided entertainment. Tea houses were more specialized than restaurants, and from the beginning the society of the tea house was associated with prostitution, but this did not make them any less popular. Tea houses were already present in the Tang capital of Chang'an in large numbers in the eighth century. During the Five Dynasties period (907–960 CE) and Song dynasty, tea houses were associated not only with female entertainment but also with a particular form of poetry, the *ci*. The verses of *ci* were set to popular melodies and usually sung by the women of tea houses and the formal houses of prostitution. During the period the most famous literati wrote *ci*, although they did not originate the form, and through their verses we know a great deal about the popular tea houses of the Southern Song capital of Hangzhou, for example.

The more elegant tea houses had well-kept gardens. One could enjoy fine teas not only in repose but also in the most beautiful surroundings. Chinese teas houses became the eventual model for tea houses in the West.

Today Portland, Oregon, for example, has a fine tea house with scores of wonderful varieties of teas available in a beautiful garden closely modeled on the classic Chinese gardens of Hangzhou and Suzhou.

Literature of Tea

Going along with a distinct culture of tea was a distinct literature of tea. The most famous work in this genre is the *Chajing* (Tea Classic) of Lu Yu from the late eighth century. His ten-volume work is a compendium of tea lore, including its Daoist connection as a magic herb, the medical qualities of tea itself, its food value, even tea bowls. Other important books on tea were the *Chalu* (Record of Tea) of *Tsan Xiang* (1012–1067) and the *Daguan chalun* (Discussion of Tea of the Daguan Period) by Song Emperor Huizong (reigned 1101–1125),

who was known for his painting, calligraphy, and refined tastes.

Porcelain

Porcelain tea bowls, created in special shapes, textures, and colors, and made just for tea drinking, became a key component of tea culture during Song times. Porcelain differs from other potteries in its raw materials and high firing temperatures. Although not invented during the Song dynasty, porcelain reached its first high point then. Most famous of Song porcelains were its celadons. They were created in a blue-green color by applying a thick glaze to a relatively delicate base. Celadon was the preferred porcelain of the court, but the Song period is also known for its blackware, including Jian tea bowls. On these bowls a black glaze was intended to contrast with

Tea House in the older district of Shanghai. PHOTO BY JOAN LEBOLD COHEN.

Picked tea leaves are brought inside to dry at the Dragon Well Tea Commune in Shanghai, 1978. PHOTO BY JOAN LEBOLD COHEN.

the green color of the tea consumed in them. The body of the bowl, relatively thick, helped maintain the temperature of the beverage. Although considered a popular ware, such bowls were still used at court, by the literati, and at monasteries. Song porcelain was imitated throughout East Asia and beyond, and fine examples continue to be highly prized today.

Mongolian Tea

Although brick tea was already exported to Tibet during the Tang dynasty, tea drinking began much later as a general central Asian practice. The earliest reference to traditional Mongolian tea, long-boiled (later brick) tea with thick milk or cream, for example, dates only to the fourteenth century, where an apparent recipe is found in the imperial dietary for Mongol China, the *Yinshan*

zhengyao (Proper and Essential Things for the Emperor's Food and Drink). In addition to its early recipe for Mongolian tea—in this case a powdered tea boiled with liquid butter and mentioned in the dietary under a Turkic name, suggesting that the Mongols may have borrowed it from local Turks—that same source mentions the following kinds of tea as being drunk at court: jade mortar tea, made from tea and roasted rice; golden characters tea, a presented powdered tea from the south; Mr. Fan Tianshuai's tea, a tribute bud tea from south China; purple shoots sparrow tongue tea, made from new shoots; another variety of swallow tail tea; Sichuan tea; clear tea, made with tea buds; Tibetan tea, made with liquid butter and highly bitter and astringent; roasted tea, tea buds fried in butter oil and orchid paste; and a powdered tea, flour, and liquid butter made into a paste and boiled in water as a kind of *tsampa* (a Tibetan staple foodstuff). The central Asian interests of the text are obvious, although one cannot be sure that the teas in question are purely central Asian. The same source also lists a number of herb teas from various sources and even rates fresh waters.

With these beginnings, tea caught on in Mongolia in a big way, as witnessed by the position of tea in the Ming dynasty's trade with the north. Similar to the Tibetans, who were Song China's source of horses, Ming China traded masses of tea to the Mongols for ponies. In Mongolia itself tea quickly became a way of life. Not offering a visitor tea became unthinkable, and Mongols, like Tibetans, added barley and other ingredients to their tea, along with butter, to provide a hot staple that is still consumed today.

Tea in the West

Not only the central Asian peoples but also the Iranian west, then the Turkish world, and finally Europe became fond of Chinese tea. In Iran, where tea was first a medicinal (as in China) from as early as the ninth century, it has now become the drink of choice and has many local variants, although black teas are preferred. In Turkey tea drinking took hold, but after the sixteenth century coffee became the beverage of choice. Because Chinese tea bowls were preferred over cups with handles in many areas of the West, the tea cultures of Iran and Turkey were not that different from that of China. Even the tea gardens were similar.

Europeans were exposed to tea (and coffee) drinking by those in the Islamic world, but Europe still obtained most of its tea from China, as did the North American colonies. Although Britain tried to push the teas of India, where tea was domesticated and developed independently of China, Chinese teas continued to be imported both to Britain and elsewhere in Europe, leading to a vast trading crisis as European silver went east to pay for Chinese tea, the first true mass commodity of the European trading system, if one excludes slaves. The attempt by Britain to substitute Indian opium for silver to cut its costs ultimately led to a series of wars with China, but the tea trade continued, right down to the present when Chinese teas are making a comeback on the world market. This is the case in spite of the fact that coffee has been of growing importance in Europe and the United States since the eighteenth century. Coffee simply lacks the delicacy of tea, and coffee drinking lacks the simplicity and elegance of tea drinking, thus tea enjoys a continued importance throughout the world.

Paul D. BUELL

Further Reading

Buell, P. D., Anderson, E., & Perry, C. (2000). *A soup for the Qan: Chinese dietary medicine of the Mongol era as seen in Hu Szu-hui's Yin-shan Cheng-yao.* London: Kegan Paul International (Sir Henry Wellcome Asian Series).

Ludwig, T. (1981). Before Rikyu, religious and aesthetic influences in the early history of the tea ceremony. *Monumenta Nipponica, 36*(4), 367–390.

Suzuki, D. T. (1959). *Zen and Japanese culture.* Princeton, NJ: Princeton University Press (Bollingen Series LXIV).

No wind, no waves.

无风不起浪

Wú fēng bù qǐ làng

Television

Diànshì 电视

China's television industry is a latecomer, by international standards, but it has become an important political and cultural apparatus. Although controlled by the state—as is all mass media in China—television offers a wide variety of programming, both domestic and foreign, to some 1.29 billion viewers, the largest TV audience in the world.

Compared to most industrial countries in the world, China has a much shorter television history. Television was not available until the late 1950s, more than a decade later than in most industrial nations. Since television emerged in China, the medium has experienced various drastic changes and has now become one of the largest and most advanced, sophisticated, and influential television systems in the world.

Short but Convoluted History

The country's first TV station, Beijing Television, began broadcasting on 1 May 1958. Within just two years, dozens of stations were set up in major cities like Shanghai and Guangzhou. Most stations had to rely on planes, trains, or cars to send tapes and films from one to another.

The first setback for Chinese television came in the early 1960s when the former Soviet Union withdrew economic aid to China. Many TV stations closed. In a short time, the number of stations was reduced from twenty-three to five. The second setback derived from an internal factor, the Cultural Revolution of 1966 to 1976. Beijing Television's regular telecasting was forced to a halt in January 1967 by the leftists of the Chinese Communist Party (CCP) led by Mao Zedong (1893–1976). All other local stations followed its lead. Television stations were criticized for their bourgeois direction and changed to a new, revolutionary direction as a weapon for class struggle and anti-imperialism, anti-revisionism, and anti-capitalism campaigns both at home and abroad.

Beginning in the late 1970s, and the start of the country's reform, television became the most rapidly growing medium. On 1 May 1978, Beijing Television changed to China Central Television (CCTV). As China's only national network, CCTV had the largest audience in the world. From the 1980s through the 1990s, television developed swiftly. The number of TV stations once exceeded 1,000, with one national network, thirty-six provincial and major city networks, and several hundred regional and local networks. The government deregulated the development of television when it became somewhat chaotic in the late 1990s.

Since the early 2000s, China's television industry has further substantially expanded. By the end of 2006, there were 296 national, provincial, and regional stations; 46 educational stations; and 1,935 local radio/television stations. In addition, there were 44,620 radio-TV transmitting-and-relaying stations and 2.2 million satellite-TV receiving-and-relaying stations. At the same time, China had 400 million TV sets, becoming the country with the most TV sets in the world. Statistically, there were two television sets for each Chinese family. By the end of 2007, the penetration rate of television reached 97 percent, reaching 1.29 billion people. Among households with TV, 40 percent, or 153,246,800 households, had cable TV. Shanghai and Beijing had the highest cable TV penetration rates in the nation at 96 percent and 71 percent. In the same year, households with digital TV reached 26,860,500, which reflected a 112 percent increase from 2006.

Television broadcasting technology has also developed quickly. Most major stations use such technologies as virtual-field production and high definition. CCTV opened its Webcast service in 1996 to a worldwide audience, providing text, audio, and photographic and video images. Digital broadcasting has been set as one of the priorities of China's National Development Plan. Based on a twenty-year digital television development plan, by 2015 all television programming in China will be transmitted via digital technology.

Ideological Basis

Despite the many changes since the reforms launched in the 1970s, all media is still state owned. Neither privately owned nor foreign-owned television is allowed. Receiving foreign TV programming via satellite is prohibited without government permission. There are no license fees for owning a TV set and no charge for viewing broadcast television. Until the late 1970s, television was not allowed to carry advertising; it was completely financed by the government.

Political theories undergirding the organization and uses of television flow directly from Marxis-Leninist doctrine. Mao embellished Marx's idea of the importance of the superstructure and ideological state apparatus and Lenin's concept of the importance of propaganda and media control, stressing that media must be run by the Communist Party and become the party's loyal eyes, ears, and mouthpiece. The current leadership of the CCP inherited this concept and requires broadcasting to be kept in line with party doctrine and serve the party's purposes voluntarily, firmly, and appropriately.

Under these guidelines, television is regarded as part of the party's overall political machine. Television is used, to the greatest extent, by the party and state to impose ideological dominance on society. The party and the central government set the tone of propaganda for television at all levels. Although TV stations provide news, entertainment, and education, television's first and most important function is to popularize party and government policies and motivate the masses in the construction of Communist ideology.

A tightly controlled administrative system has been used to run television. The CCP is the ultimate owner, manager, and practitioner of television. TV stations are under the dual jurisdiction of the Communist Party's Propaganda Department and the government's State Administration of Radio, Film, and Television. The Propaganda Department sets propaganda policies, determines programming content and themes, and issues operational directives. Technological, regulatory, and administrative affairs are generally the concern of the Radio-Television-Film Bureau of the State Council. As media are crucial political organs of the CCP, virtually no independence of media is allowed or envisioned. Except for several years in the 1980s—which were criticized later by the party as the period of "Western liberalization" and "bourgeois spiritual pollution"—neither open and large-scale debates on ideology nor serious criticisms of the party, government policies, or high-ranking officials has been permitted, unless organized by the party to meet certain political needs. The self-censorship policy has been long and extensively used. Routine broadcasting material does not require approval from party authorities, but important editorials, news stories, and sensitive topics all require official endorsement before their dissemination.

Programming

Television programming in China consists of six categories: news , documentary and infotainment, variety and entertainment, TV plays , advertising and service, and sports and other programs. In 2007, 14,546,700 hours of TV programming were broadcast, a 7 percent increase over the previous year's hours. The bulk of programming, 45 percent, was TV dramas and movies, followed by advertising (13 percent), news (12 percent), variety (11 percent), services (10 percent), and entertainment (9 percent).

Before the 1970s, most entertainment programs were old films of revolutionary stories, with occasional live broadcasts of modern operas about model workers, peasants, and soldiers. Newscasts from that era were mostly what the CCP's official newspaper, *The People's Daily,* and official news agency, the Xinhua News Agency, reported. Production capability was low; production quality was poor; equipment and facilities were simple; and broadcasting hours, transmitting scales, and channel selections were limited. Television broadcasted usually three hours a day.

Part of the explosive development of TV since the late 1970s is a result of the CCP's new move toward openness and reform. Many taboos were eliminated, restrictions lifted, and new production skills adopted. Entertainment programs in the form of TV plays, soap operas, Chinese traditional operas, game shows, and domestic and foreign feature films have become routine. News programs have also changed substantially and expanded enormously. International news coverage and live telecasts of important news events are now often seen in news programs. Educational programs in particular have received special treatment from the government. Production capability has been enhanced as well.

CCTV expanded from two channels in 1978 to sixteen channels in 2006. Channel 1, the main channel, focuses on news; Channel 2, economy and finance; and Channel 3, culture, arts, and music. Channel 4 is dedicated to overseas Chinese and international audiences. Channel 5 shows sports; Channel 6, movies; Channel 7, social programs; and Channel 8, TV plays and series. Channel 9 is an English-language channel that broadcasts twenty-four hours a day, targeting an international audience. Channel 10 focuses on science; Channel 11, Chinese opera; Channel 12, law-related programs; Channel 13, news; Channel 14, children's programs; and Channel 15, music. Channel 16 is a Spanish-language and French-language channel aimed at audiences in Spanish-speaking and French-speaking nations.

Most provincial and major city networks have also increased the number of their broadcasting channels and offer more programs. In 2006 alone, 546 TV plays with 18,133 episodes were produced. In contrast, during the two decades from 1958 to 1977, only 74 TV plays were produced. TV broadcasting hours have increased considerably as well. In an average week of 1980, 2,018 hours of programs were broadcast. The number went up to 7,698 in 1985, 22,298 in 1990, 83,373 in 2000, and 261,538 in 2006.

Internationalization and Commercialization

The most important indication of the internationalization of China's television industry is the change in the importing of programming. Before the late 1970s, TV imports were quantitatively limited and ideologically and politically oriented. From the late 1950s to the late 1970s, only the national network was authorized to import TV programs. During those years programs were imported almost exclusively from socialist countries, and the content usually concentrated on the Soviet Revolution and the USSR's socialist economic progress. Few programs were imported from Western countries, and they were restricted only to those that exemplified the principle "Socialism is promising, capitalism is hopeless."

In the early 1970s, imported programming accounted for less than 1 percent of programming nationwide. That figure jumped to 8 percent in the early 1980s, to 15 percent in the early 1990s, to around 25 percent in 2000, and remained at 20 percent in recent years. Although they still face various kinds of restrictions, central, provincial, regional, and even local television stations are looking to other countries, mostly Western nations, for programming. The government now stipulates that, unless special permission is obtained, no imported programming is allowed to be shown during prime time (7–10:30 p.m.) and that imported programming cannot fill more than 15 percent of prime time.

Another sign of TV's internationalization is the effort to expand the exporting of China-produced TV programs. Major Chinese TV stations have produced programs for the global market and have even become main programming suppliers of some television stations in other Asian countries. CCTV and a few major city networks have set up offices in the United States, the United Kingdom, France, Belgium, Russia, Egypt, Japan, Hong Kong, Macao, India, Thailand, and Australia to promote business. In addition, CCTV and a few other major Chinese TV stations have established joint-venture businesses with television stations in North America, South America, Europe, Asia, and Oceania to broadcast programs via satellite. CCTV's international and English-language channels are now broadcast via China's own satellite and are available in most countries. In 2006 CCTV alone exported 6,000 episodes, more than 4,000 hours of television programs. CCTV's Channels 4, 9, and 16 are now watched in eighty-six countries by 68 million household subscribers.

Another significant change in China's television industry since the reforms is commercialization: the resurrection of advertising on television and its impact on programming. Economic reforms have revived the importance of market forces and the power of advertising. Both foreign and domestic advertising have been resurrected. Since the early 1980s, revenue from advertising has increased at an annual rate of 50 to 60 percent.

By the 1990s television had become the most commercialized and market-oriented medium in China and attracted a large portion of advertising investment from both domestic and foreign clients. For the hundreds of television stations across the country, advertising and other commercial activities now constitute the majority of programming revenue, ranging from 40 percent to 90 percent. All television stations are now supported by advertising revenue.

While media advertising accounts for 70 percent of China's total advertising expenditure, television advertising alone accounts for 80 percent of total media advertising expenditures. Over the last several years, advertising revenues for almost all other media have been declining, but television advertising has continued to increase. In 2006 advertising revenue for the broadcasting industry reached 527 million yuan (approximately $75 million at the time). Some 453 million yuan was from television advertising revenue, a 12 percent increase from 2005. In 2007 advertising revenue for the broadcasting industry reached 601 million yuan (approximately $86 million). Advertising revenue in the television industry alone reached 519 million yuan, a 15 percent increase from 2006.

The television structure in China is quite different from that in most Western nations, where national networks usually are the biggest advertising revenue makers. In China, by contrast, in 2007 provincial TV stations reaped 57 percent of the total of TV advertising revenues, followed by 21 percent for the regional and county-level TV stations, and only 11 percent for the national networks. Over the last several years the top three commodities of China's TV advertising have been cosmetics, medicine, and food, occupying 21 percent, 16 percent, and 14 percent of the total television advertising in 2007. The top-ten list of television advertising also included ads for telecommunication devices (mobile phones and computers),

Chinese liquors and beverages, entertainment and leisure activities, the service industry (hotels), and transportation (cars and domestic/foreign airlines). This list is quite similar to the top-ten list of television advertising in developed nations, a reflection of China TV's move toward a Western model.

The telecasting of the Beijing 2008 Olympic Games was one of the biggest events not only in China's TV history but also in the history of world television. More than 4 billion people across the world watched the televised games, a new record in world TV history, surpassing the audience for the 2000 Sydney games (3.4 billion) and the 2004 Athens games (3.9 billion). The Beijing Olympics opening ceremony was said to have hit a record high TV rating: more than 90 percent of TV audiences across the world watched the event. Thanks to the 2008 games, China's total advertising revenues in 2008 were estimated to have increased 29 percent over 2007 revenues. For CCTV alone, its advertising revenues during the seventeen days of the games were estimated to have reached 2 billion yuan (approximately $300 million). The Beijing Olympics also made many global companies very interested in China's huge media market. The biggest foreign sponsors of the telecasting of the Beijing Olympics included Coca-Cola, McDonald's, Adidas, and Johnson & Johnson. In 2008, because of the Beijing Olympic Games, Coca-Cola's advertising expenditure in China increased 24 percent; Visa's, 30 percent; Kentucky Fried Chicken's, 39 percent; Adidas's, 100 percent; and Nike's, 143 percent.

Internet Viewing

Watching television on a computer or mobile device is increasingly popular in China, as it is in the United States and Western countries. In fact, Westerners looking for their favorite programs sometimes watch pirated versions, in English with Chinese subtitles, on Chinese websites. This unstructured and uncommercialized Internet viewing is even said to have cut into the market for pirate DVDs in China. Volunteer groups download popular U.S. televisions show such 24, *American Idol, Survivor,* and *Battlestar Galactica* from BitTorrent, a peer-to-peer file-sharing site, immediately after new episodes are broadcast in the United States. They locate closed-captioned English scripts, made for the hearing-impaired, and translate them into Chinese. Perhaps in future a commercial version like the U.S. Hulu.com will compete, but that would be possible only if the Chinese government allowed the distribution of more Western programming.

Future Direction

Under the modernization plan, the open door policy, the transformation from a state economy to a market economy, and the tendency toward lessening controls since the late 1970s, television in China has become a very popular medium, a very technologically advanced broadcast system, and a highly professionally performed service. Television's function has evolved from a single-purposed one for political and ideological propaganda to a multipurposed one for serving both the party/government and the society/public.

However, by and large, television in China is still a state-owned and party-controlled political and ideological instrument, despite its having evolved to fulfill other purposes. Television, like all other mass media in China, is required to run in the socialist track, but, at the same time, it is forced to operate in a Western way, the capitalist way. This conflict has brought about many unprecedented problems to television.

No signs of change in the character of television are seen for the near future. As long as the country's political system does not change, the Marxist-Leninist-Maoist doctrine on the media, including television, will not change. This obstacle will not be overcome until fundamental changes in the political system occur. It is certain that television's internationalization and commercialization will continue, despite fluctuations that may occur as a result of the change of the political climate and the ideological needs of the Communist Party. But it is unlikely in the foreseeable future that television, along with all other media in China, will become an independent social mechanism, nor will it become truly free from the control of the party and government.

Television in China has developed unevenly. For historical and economic reasons, most TV stations in China—especially those that have larger audiences and, therefore, are more influential—are in the eastern coastal areas or central section of the country, places such as Beijing, Shanghai, Guangdong, Tianjin, Jiangsu, Zhejiang, and Hunan. For example, in 2007, 22 percent of the total TV advertising revenue was from Beijing alone, 47 percent from the eastern coastal areas, and 21 percent from the central part, whereas only 11 percent was from the western section of the nation, which has more than 50 percent of China's total geographic area and population. All of the top ten provincial TV stations of China's television advertising were in the eastern coastal area or central part, with Guangdong first, Jiangsu second, and Shanghai third.

Since the beginning of the twenty-first century, China's television industry has undergone a profound shift toward conglomeration as China aims to become more competitive in the global television arena. New ways of doing business and new technologies will help the television industry thrive and be an important part of Chinese culture.

Junhao HONG

Further Readings

Chan, J. (1994). Media internationalization in China: Process and tensions. *Journal of Communication, 44*(3), 70–88.

Hong, Junhao. (1994). The resurrection of advertising in China: Developments, problems, and trends. *Asian Survey, 24*(4), 70–88.

Hong, Junhao. (1997). Changes in China's media function in the 1980s: A new model in a new era. In M. Bailie & D. Winseck (Eds.), *Democratizing communication: Comparative perspectives on information and power* (pp. 288–306). Cresskill, NJ: Hampton Press.

Hong, Junhao. (1998). *The internationalization of television in China: The evolution of ideology, society and media since the reform.* Westport, CT: Praeger.

Hong, Junhao. (2000). China's dual perception of globalization and its reflection on media policies. In G. Wang et al. (Eds.), *The new communications landscape: Demystifying media globalization* (pp. 70–88). London: Routledge.

Hong, Junhao, Yanmei, L., & Zou Weining. (2008). CCTV in the reform years: Setting up a new model for China's television. In Ying Zhu & C. Berry (Eds.), *TV China: A reader on new media* (pp. 40–50). Bloomington: Indiana University Press.

Huang, Y. (1994). Peaceful evolution: The case of television reform in post–Mao China. *Media, Culture, and Society, 16,* 217–241.

Lull, J. (1991). *China turned on: Television, reform, and resistance.* London: Routledge.

Television–Dramas and Reality Shows

Diànshìjù yù zhēnrén jìshíxiù

电视剧与真人纪实秀

Everyone likes a good story, and China's TV viewers are no different. Dramatized retellings—with added embellishments—of the exploits of ancient officials and emperors, and fictionalized accounts of modern revolutionary heroes are among the most popular entertainment on Chinese TV. At the same time, reality-based programs, so popular in the United States, are also gaining an audience.

The most widely viewed television show in the world is the New Year's extravaganza that China Central Television (CCTV) presents each year. But television dramas and Chinese equivalents of *American Idol* and other reality shows are also hugely popular.

Rise of Drama

Entertainment programs dominate Chinese television, but dramas have consistently garnered the highest share of ratings since 2000. In 2004 television dramas accounted for 29.4 percent of all program ratings, followed by news programs (16.8 percent), variety shows (7.9 percent), special features (7.7 percent), sports (7.0 percent), and films (5.6 percent). In 2004, 505 television dramas, with 12,265 episodes, were shown. In that same year, 156 channels operated by 33 city television stations aired 1,598 dramas totaling 183,123 episodes.

The average television drama in the early 2000s ran for twenty episodes. Since 2004, that figure has increased to twenty-six, with many dramas having as many as fifty to sixty episodes. Each episode runs about thirty-eight minutes. Among all types of TV programs, dramas have garnered the largest amount of television advertising revenue. In 2004 receipts from television dramas accounted for 44.1 percent of all television advertising revenue. In that year television advertising revenue amounted to over 150 billion yuan ($22 billion). By comparison, box office revenue for the Chinese film industry in 2004 was 360 million yuan ($53 million). This includes domestic revenue of 250 million yuan ($37 million)—of which 100 million yuan ($15 million) came from television broadcasting—and 110 million yuan ($16 million) in international revenue. The number of television dramas produced and broadcast and the advertising revenue generated indicate that television drama, not film, is the top form of entertainment in China.

Dramas' Run

The first Chinese TV drama was a thirty-minute play called *A Veggie Cake* (*Yikou cai bingzi* 一口菜饼子), the bitter story of a starving peasant family under the old regime. It was aired live on the Beijing television station on 15 June 1958. From 1958 to 1966, nearly two hundred single-episode dramas were performed and telecast live. Television drama production—along with much other TV productions—ceased during the Cultural Revolution and did not resume until 1978. In the early 1980s, Chinese television stations began to broadcast foreign television serials, or soap operas, from Japan and the United States. But domestic television drama arrived in 1990 with the fifty-episode *Yearning* (*Kewang* 渴望). *Yearning* entranced thousands of millions viewers with its melodramatic portrayal of the lives and struggles of ordinary citizens during the Cultural Revolution.

Popular Dramas

Modern television dramas not only amass the highest ratings but also covers a rich diversity of subject matter and genres. In 2004 the most popular genres were romance, domestic drama, martial arts, romantic and youth idol drama, crime, revolutionary drama, and history.

Drama genres can be classified in various ways. Romance, for example, can include fictional historical drama, the most popular genre. Within this genre themes from the Qing dynasty (1644–1912) are extremely popular. Examples include *Prime Minister Hunchback Liu* (*Zaixiang Liu luoguo* 宰相刘罗锅) (1996), the story of a legendary witty and honest Qing prime minister who fights imperial officialdom and corruption, and *Iron-Toothed Ji Xiaolan* (*Tiechi tongya Ji Xiaolan* 铁齿铜牙纪晓岚) (2001), a comic tale about a Qing scholar who bravely challenges the treachery of the emperor. Stories like these touch on popular sentiments against corruption and age-old expectations of honorable officials (*qingguan* 清官). Also popular are romantic stories that place actual historical figures—such as Qing emperors, princes, and princesses—in totally fictional situations. One such romance, *Princess Pearl Returned* (*Huanzhu gege* 还珠格格) (1999), with its mischievous and rebellious teenage heroine, is enormously popular. Although taking place in the distant past, it reflects radically changed social stereotypes and expectations of modern Chinese girls.

Also popular are historical dramas about famous Chinese emperors that recapture China's past imperial glory, such as *The Great Han Emperor Wudi* (*Han wu dadi* 汉武大帝) (2004); *Yongzheng Dynasty* (*Yongzheng wangchao* 雍正王朝) (1999); and *Kangxi Dynasty* (*Kangxi diguo* 康熙帝国) (2003). Revolutionary dramas, such as *Years of Burning Passions* (*Jiqing ranshao de shuiyue* 激情燃烧的岁月) (2002), remind TV viewers of the revolutionary legacy that is part of modern history. Other popular subgenres

include adaptations of Chinese classical novels—such as *Dream of the Red Chamber* (*Hong lou meng* 红楼梦) (1987), *Journey to the West* (*Xi you ji* 西游记) (1986), and *Romance of Three Kingdoms* (*Sanguo yanyi* 三国演义) (1995)—and adaptations of the popular martial arts novels of Jin Yong, such as *Dragon's Eight Tribes* (*Tianlong babu* 天龙八部) (2004).

In recent years television dramas from Korea have become popular creating a Korean cultural boom among urban youth. This trend has caused some concern among officials of the State Administration of Radio, Film, and Television and among domestic television drama producers. China's imports of television dramas have remained quite small (only about 5 percent of all dramas in 2004), but more cultural and media exchanges are likely to increase the import and export of television dramas.

Spring Festival Gala

One television program stands out among all the rest and attracts the largest audience in the world: the Spring Festival gala, or celebration show, produced by CCTV. The gala, which has been an annual event since 1983, is a spectacular variety show. It includes dance and musical performances, sketch comedy, and appearances by national celebrities and is broadcast live on Chinese New Year's Eve from 8 p.m. till after midnight on New Year's Day. The program boasts of ratings of more than 90 percent, or approximately 1 billion viewers. It is so popular that it has become a new custom of the Chinese New Year celebrations.

Each year the gala's producers try to work in new forms of popular culture to go along with traditional folk forms and Beijing Opera while satisfying the Chinese Communist Party's demand to make the show a comprehensive representation of mainstream, official ideologies. But the most popular part of the show is the comic sketches, often mild satires of modern life. For example, in the 2009 show, Jiang Kun, a popular actor, made the audience laugh with his routine on China's new look after thirty years of reform and opening up. "In the past," he said during his skit, "we had no traffic jams and no highways. Now we have congestion everywhere, even though we have so many highways."

Because of its large scale and the tremendous advertising revenue it generates, the gala is often troubled with scandals and power struggles. Zhao An, a former director of the gala, was sentenced to ten years in prison in 2004 for taking bribes. In recent years, criticism of CCTV's monopoly on New Year's television shows has increased, as the CCTV gala now has to compete with a greater variety of entertainment forms, some of which were unavailable when it first started. However, as a cultural ritual with widespread appeal, the gala remains the highest rated television program in the world.

New Developments

Challenges to CCTV's monopoly on reality programs have surged in recent years. Hunan Satellite TV has captured the hearts of young, especially teenage, viewers with its enormously successful program *Super Girl* (*Chaojinusheng* 超级女声), which debuted in 2004. Modeled after *American Idol*, *Super Girl* is a blend of reality show, singing and dancing contest, and beauty pageant. Viewers can vote for contestants by cell phone (more than 300 million viewers cast their votes by cell phone in 2005), and thousands of millions of teenage girls and their families participate. A *Super Girl* craze swept China in 2005, ending in the selection of three winners. Two of the three—Li Yuchun, the first-place winner, and Zhou Bichang, the second-place winner—were widely regarded as amateurs with poor singing skills and music talent. But their alternative and often defiant and androgynous style attracted fans. As expected, mainstream and academic circles have criticized *Super Girl* for its vulgarity and bad-taste sensationalism and populism.

CCTV has refused to allow any of the *Super Girl* winners to appear on its programs. Nevertheless, because of the huge popularity and enormous profitability of the show, many local television stations have introduced copycat shows. In 2005 Dragon TV, the satellite TV channel of Shanghai Media Group, introduced *My Hero* (*Hao nan'er* 好男儿), a male version of *Super Boy*, with only male contestants, and *My Show* (*Wo xing wo Show* 我型我*), which included both male and female contestants. Since 2006, there has been fierce competition for music talent contest show. Even CCTV has introduced such programming But in 2007 the central government issued a series of directives to all TV stations to tone down such music contests and reality shows and to uphold high moral and educational standards. Consequently, *Super Girl* and its clones have lost much of their momentum.

The consistent high ratings of television dramas and the popularity of shows like *Super Girl* indicate that entertainment is playing a vibrant role in the Chinese television industry, with far-reaching implications for the future of Chinese mass media. Chinese television, despite being caught between political pressure from the Chinese Communist Party and market competition, has rapidly developed into a cultural indicator as well as a profitable industry.

LIU Kang

Further Reading

Canaves, S., & Ye, J. (2009, January 29). Imitation is the sincerest form of rebellion in China. *The Wall Street Journal*, p. A1.

Liu Kang. (2008). Media boom and cyber culture: Television and the Internet in China. In K. Louie (Ed.), *Cambridge companion to modern Chinese culture* (pp. 318–338). Cambridge, U.K.: Cambridge University Press.

Ying Zhu. (2008). *Television in post-reform China: Serial dramas, Confucian leadership and the global television market.* London: Routledge.

Ying Zhu, Keane, M., & Ruoyun Bai (Eds.). (2009). *TV drama in China.* Hong Kong: Hong Kong University Press.

Zhang Mingyu. (Ed.). (2009). *China's Spring Festival annual TV gala mixes humor, history.* Window of China. Retrieved February 18, 2009, from http://news.xinhuanet.com/english/2009-01-26/content_10722216.htm

Television–News

Diànshì xīnwén　电视新闻

Television news in China has been broadcast since TV became available in the country in the late 1950s. China Central Television (CCTV)—the national network owned and managed by the government (and the standard for all TV news stations in China)—has begun to offer several popular "news magazine" shows that cover everyday events or touch on a wide range of hot topics in China and the world.

After dramas, news bulletins are the most popular TV shows with Chinese viewers. Broadcast news in China is ubiquitous, popular, and influential. The government stipulates that each television station must have a comprehensive channel to broadcast important news. The people of China are well informed—up to a point. The power of the press belongs to those who own the press. In China the Chinese Communist Party (CCP) owns and manages TV news, along with all other mass media.

News Policy

China Central Television (CCTV), the country's first TV station, is the only national network and the standard for all other TV networks. CCTV has eighteen channels. CCTV-News, launched in 2003, broadcasts news twenty-four hours a day. CCTV's domination of news programming is shown by its prime-time *Network News* (*Xinwen lianbo*), a program that began broadcasting in 1978, and which still runs daily from 7 to 7:30 p.m. The government requires all local stations to broadcast this program simultaneously.

The editorial board of *Network News* consists of senior officials of CCTV, overseen by the network's president. *Network News* is the model for Chinese television news programs. It serves as one of the most important news outlets for the CCP, in addition to the People's Daily (Renmin ribao) and the Central People's Radio Station (Zhongyang renmin guangbo diantai). *Network News* adheres to CCP media theory and guidelines: Television's first purpose is to serve as the "mouthpiece" of the government and the party, and should mainly cover political and economic successes and the positive aspects of government, and not spread negative thinking or foster low morale. This media policy is part of the political and ideological agenda of the CCP. And there are no signs that the CCP will relinquish its firm hold on the media in the foreseeable future.

Program Format

The format of *Network News* has remained unchanged since its first day of broadcasting. Any radical changes in the format are unlikely, and any changes are incremental and gradual. There are two presenters, one male and one female. Two or three pairs of presenters rotate daily. These presenters are merely announcers and have no editorial power to determine the selection of news.

Network News always begins with the public activities

of the top leaders, in order of their rankings in the highest political body, the Standing Committee of the Political Bureau of the CCP. The first appearance is reserved for the general secretary of the CCP. Conferences, meetings with foreign visitors, tours, and speeches involving the top leaders usually take up the first ten minutes, or a third of the program. The next ten-minute segment covers economic news from across China. Some segments are prerecorded and produced weeks or even months in advance. Most news stories are produced by local television stations and cover positive reports of growth, development, and technological advances.

Other News Programming

As part of reforms in news programming, CCTV launched two news magazines in 1993, *Oriental Horizon* (*Dongfang shikong*) and *Focus* (*Jiaodian fangdan*).

Oriental Horizon is a one-hour program broadcast at 7 a.m., before most of the audience goes to work or school. It features coverage of events in the daily lives of ordinary citizens, portraits of well-known figures, and in-depth reports on a single issue. The program is hugely popular, and some observers claim that it has caused a silent revolution in daytime television.

Focus is a thirty-minute current affairs program broadcast at 7:30 p.m., prime time. It touches on a wide range of hot topics in China and the world, with background analysis, on-the-spot reporting, and in-studio interviews. *Focus* usually covers issues of significant social impact and of considerable interest to both the government and the public. Sensitive issues—such as corruption, injustice, and rising social disparities—are approached using an investigative reporting style. This kind of tough reporting has made *Focus* extremely popular. It usually trails only Network News in the ratings.

In 1996 CCTV launched the news magazine, *News Probe* (*Xinwen diaocha*), a forty-five-minute weekly program that provides in-depth investigative reporting of sensitive social issues. It is broadcast on CCTV-1 first at 10:30 p.m. on Mondays and then repeated on CCTV-News the following Tuesday, Saturday, and Sunday, all during off-peak times. The issues exposed and the criticism of social problems on *News Probe* are sometimes more distressing or controversial than those covered on

Focus, partly because it is aired during off-peak hours. The editorial board reckons that because fewer people watch the show, its impact is less widespread.

News programs like *Focus* and *News Probe* are governed by a complicated and difficult process of selection, negotiation, framing, and censorship. A former director of *Focus* admitted that for each program he had to carefully weigh the question of its possible negative effects on political stability, in general, against the resolution of the problems it uncovered, in particular. To satisfy the government and meet the public's demand to know the truth behind incidents, crimes, and disasters, journalists and editors need to walk a fine line. Their work in recent years reflects a trend toward more accurate, balanced, and fair news reporting in an increasingly open society.

In October 1998 then-premier Zhu Rongji met with *Focus* editors and reporters, and left a written message that paid tribute to the program. Zhu expressed the hope that *Focus* would function as a leader in reform, the government's mirror, and the "people's mouthpiece." Observers noted that the change from the party's mouthpiece to the people's mouthpiece was a significant shift, especially when articulated by a top leader. Although no substantial reorientation occurred at CCTV after this visit, local television stations took the cue from Zhu in their efforts toward reform.

A trend toward a diverse range of television news programs and news magazine shows continued on local television stations into the early 2000s. These programs devote more attention to local issues that have direct impact on the everyday lives of ordinary citizens. On 1 January 2002, Jiangsu Television's City Channel launched the prime-time news program *Nanjing Zero Distance* (*Nanjing lingjuli*), which airs from 6 to 7:30 p.m., overlapping with CCTV's *Network News*. (City Channel's sister channel Jiangsu TV-1 obligingly airs *Network News*.) *Nanjing Zero Distance* ushered in a new way of covering the news of people's lives (minsheng xinwen), dealing mostly with the everyday events and issues that concern the residents of Nanjing. Because Nanjing is the provincial capital of one of the most prosperous provinces on China's east coast, events in the city have implications for all of Jiangsu Province. The program's ratings soon soared, and it attracted the highest Nielson rating (17 percent) of all television programs in Nanjing and vicinity, an area of more than 6 million people.

China Today, a news program on CCTV, is also broadcast in English.

More than ten programs of this type emerged in Jiangsu and Nanjing alone over the next few years and have dominated television broadcasting and ratings. Across China, similar programs have appeared on provincial and city television stations, creating a sort of TV war for programming on people's lives. Such local news programs meet the needs of a public with ever-growing concerns about issues that affect the rights and well-being of individuals. In addition, such programs are in keeping with the government's policy priority of building a harmonious society.

LIU Kang

A CCTV Focus report, with a reporter at Tiananmen Square.

Further Reading

Chan Tsan-kuo. (2002). *China's window on the world: TV news, social knowledge and international spectacles.* Cresskill, NJ: Hampton Press.

de Burgh, H. (2003). *The Chinese journalist.* London: RoutledgeCurzon.

Li Xiaoping. (2001). *Significant changes in the Chinese television industry and their impact in the PRC: An insider's perspective* [Monograph]. Washington, DC: Center for Northeast Asian Policy Studies, the Brookings Institution.

Zhao Yuezhi. (1998). *Media, market, and democracy in China.* Urbana. University of Illinois Press.

Temple of Heaven

Tiāntán 天坛

The Temple of Heaven was the imperial site of prayer to Heaven during the Ming (1368–1644) and Qing (1644–1912) dynasties. The Temple's most spectacular structure is The Hall of Prayer for Good Harvest 祈年殿, 38 meters (125 feet) tall, built entirely of wood without using a single nail.

The Temple of Heaven, or Altar of Heaven, was built between 1406 and 1420 in Beijing during the reign of Zhu Di 朱棣, the Yongle emperor (reigned 1402–1424). Zhu Di is also credited for overseeing the planning and construction of the Forbidden City. The Temple of Heaven served as the prayer site for the emperors of the Ming (1368–1644) and Qing (1644–1912) dynasties in China. It is regarded as a Daoist temple, although Heaven worship was practiced before the rise of Daoism.

Every year, on the fifteenth day of the first lunar month, the emperor would come to the Hall of Prayer for Good Harvest (祈年殿 Qi Nian Dian) to pay homage to Heaven and pray for a good harvest. He would honor his ancestors as well, as he was regarded as the Son of Heaven. In early winter the emperor would come again to thank Heaven for the good harvest. If a drought plagued China during the summer, the emperor would come to the temple to pray for rain. Accompanying the emperor on these visits would be his entourage of officials, all wearing special ceremonial robes. Ordinary Chinese were not allowed to view the emperor's procession from the

View of the Temple of Heaven, the imperial site of prayer to Heaven during the Ming and Qing dynasties.

Forbidden City to the Temple of Heaven or the ceremonies that followed.

The temple grounds cover 2.7 square kilometers (1.5 square miles). On the site are three imperial sacrificial

2223

sites: the Imperial Vault of Heaven, the Circular Mound Altar, and the Hall of Prayer for Good Harvest. Within the Imperial Vault of Heaven is the Echo Wall, a marvel of acoustical engineering that can carry sounds across long distances. The Circular Mound Altar is the altar proper. It is comprised of three rounded white-marble platforms. The bottom platform represents Hell; the middle, Earth; and the top, Heaven.

The Hall of Prayer for Good Harvest lies at the center of the grounds and is the most spectacular building on the site. It is a tripled-gabled circular building 38 meters (125 feet) tall, built entirely of wood with no nails. It is considered a masterpiece of traditional Chinese architecture. The hall was designed with many symbolic features. Of the twenty-eight pillars that support the domed structure, the four large ones represent the four seasons, the twelve inner pillars represent the months in the lunar calendar, and the twelve outer pillars represent the twelve two-hour periods of a day.

The Temple of Heaven became a United Nations Educational, Scientific, and Cultural Organization (UNESCO) World Heritage Site in 1998. Today the temple grounds are a popular exercise park for locals and visitors alike.

Jian-Zhong LIN

Further Reading

Yu Chen (Ed.) (1999). *Great sites of Beijing.* Beijing: Beijing Arts and Crafts Publishing House.

Terracotta Soldiers

Bīngmǎyǒng 兵马俑

The uncovering of thousands of clay statues that were buried in 210 BCE during the Qin dynasty has taught archaeologists and other scholars about classes of soldiers, beliefs of the period, and skills of craftspeople. The clay army, originally painted in vivid colors to distinguish different groups of soldiers and featuring individual facial features, is one of China's most iconic images.

One of the most spectacular archaeological finds of the twentieth century is the army of nearly eight thousand life-size terracotta soldiers and horses that guards the tomb of China's first emperor, Qin Shi Huangdi (d. 210 BCE), whose name means First (Shi) Emperor (Huangdi) of the Qin dynasty (221–206 BCE), a short-lived and authoritarian dynasty.

The army was discovered beginning in 1974 by peasants digging a well, and is located twenty-two miles east of Xi'an (formerly Ch'ang-an) in Shaanxi Province and about one mile east of the unexcavated mausoleum of the ruler. The figures are distributed over three pits (a fourth was found to be empty) built of rammed earth. The buried army yields more complete and detailed information on Qin military science than the fragmentary texts from the period can provide.

Today, the soldiers are part of a large complex known as the Museum of the Terracotta Army, which opened in 1979 outside of Xi'an. More recently, the burial army was made accessible to an audience outside of China when the British Museum mounted a ground-breaking exhibition in London in 2007. Among the 120 objects on display—the largest number of material related to China's First Emperor ever to be shown outside China—were twelve complete soldiers and artifacts excavated from around his tomb, which highlighted the achievements of this short but important period in China's history.

At about 14,300 square meters, Pit 1 is the largest of the pits and contains nearly six thousand figures, primarily armored and unarmored infantry, including archers and charioteers. The pit also contains terracotta horses, the remains of six chariots, and bronze weaponry such as swords, crossbows, halberds, and long and short daggers. Rectangular in form and dug to a depth of five meters, Pit 1 arranges the soldiers in precise military formation in eleven corridors separated by earthen walls. The extreme left and right corridors consist of archers who face outward as if anticipating a flank attack. In the nine wider corridors soldiers stand four abreast with a chariot and four horses at the head of six corridors. Three corridors of unarmored soldiers with bows and crossbows take up the front and the rear. Each corridor is paved with bricks, and has wooden rafters and crossbeams above. Woven matting was used to absorb any moisture that seeped in; on top of the matting the builders put a layer of clay. The pit was originally covered with a mound of earth.

At about six thousand square meters, Pit 2 is smaller than Pit 1, and held the cavalry. It contains around a thousand figures that include cavalry men and their horses,

2225

eighty-nine chariots each drawn by four horses, and some archers and foot soldiers. Pit 3 is 520 square meters in area and most likely represents the command unit. It contains sixty-eight officers, four horses, and one chariot. Together, these three pits represent a single army composed of an infantry unit, a smaller and more mobile mounted unit, and a command post to oversee operations.

Realistic, Colorful, and Armored Soldiers

The figures were made with local clay and fired in kilns that would have been set up close to the mausoleum. It was generally thought that these kilns were made in an upright pit, but research suggests that the process was

Terracota soldier from the tomb of Qin Shi Huangdi (d. 210 BCE). Each terracotta soldier was sculpted with individual features and armor suited to their position in the army. PHOTO BY YIXUAN SHUKE.

much more complicated. The figures were hand built and had solid legs for stability but hollow torsos. The heads were made with molds, but facial features and details such as hair and headgear were added by hand.

The realism of each soldier's face, individually modeled to show age as well as the multicultural backgrounds of the emperor's soldiers, and the meticulous detail paid to the clothing are remarkable. Originally, the figures were brightly painted, but much of the pigment has flaked off. The colors were used to distinguish between the different units of the army. For example, Pit 1 had two color schemes. One group had green robes with lavender collars and cuffs, dark blue trousers, and black shoes with red laces; its armor was black with white rivets, purple cords, and gold buttons. The other group had red tunics with pale blue collars and cuffs; its armor was dark brown with red or light green rivets and orange cords.

The terracotta army yields valuable information on armor and weaponry in early China. Eight different styles of armor were used, falling into two categories: armor made by fastening rectangular scales to a base layer and armor constructed by stringing scales together without a support layer. These scales were probably made of lacquered leather—no metal plates from this period have yet been found—and were probably attached to one another by knotted leather strips to allow movement with the body. The armor was slipped over the head and buckled with a right front closure.

The armor in both categories ranges from simple to complex. In all cases the armor was adapted to the rank and weaponry of the individual warrior. The most basic armor of the first type covered only the front of the wearer and was held in place by straps crossed in back. In contrast, the commanding officers wore the most distinctive and complex protection: the front portion of each piece of their waist-length armor had a flexible triangular extension in front that covered the lower abdomen. The wide-sleeved undergarment and the intricate threading of the armor plates signified the overall high rank of the wearer. In addition to the armor, some wore a bright, tasseled cape at the shoulders.

Cavalry, infantry, and charioteers wore armor of the second type. Cavalry wore a short vest, which was suitable for riding because it was trim and efficient. Charioteers wore more substantial and complex armor than any other soldier. Covering more of the body, it included

An excavated section of the archaeological site where the terracotta soldiers were discovered. A cover has been built over the site to protect the soldiers from the elements.

PHOTO BY YIXUAN SHUKE.

a neck guard and articulated sleeves, which covered the arm to the wrist. More than three hundred intricately arranged plates allowed for freedom of movement while protecting the wearer.

Technical Know-How

The pits also indicate that the Qin metalworkers had a high degree of technical know-how and produced a wide range of bronze weaponry, including swords, daggers, halberds, crossbow mechanisms, and arrows. More than ten thousand finely made weapons were found, and many of them were inscribed, indicating where and when they were cast. Even after two thousand years underground, many of the weapons showed little signs of corrosion.

The terracotta soldiers and the mausoleum they were to protect were designated by the United Nations Educational, Scientific, and Cultural Organization (UNESCO) in 1987 as a World Heritage Site. A museum established at the site covers approximately 16,300 square meters and includes Pits 1, 2, and 3, each covered by large hangar-like structures. Visitors to Pit 1, for example, can view nearly 1,000 restored soldiers and horses arranged in battle formation as well as watch the on-going excavations at the site.

Catherine PAGANI

Further Reading

Cotterell, A.(1981). *The First Emperor of China: The greatest archaeological find of our time.* New York: Holt, Rinehart and Winston.

Guisso, R. W. L., & Pagani, C. (1989). *The First Emperor of China.* Toronto: Stoddart Publishing.

Li Xueqin. (1985). *Eastern Zhou and Qin civilizations.* New Haven, CT: Yale University Press.

Portal, J. (Ed.) (2007). *The First Emperor: China's terracotta army.* London: The British Museum Press.

Wood, F. (2007). *China's First Emperor and his terracotta warriors.* New York: St. Martin's Press.

Terrorism

Kǒngbù zhǔyì 恐怖主义

Before the events of September 11, 2001, international terrorism was a remote concern for China. But now that terrorists have attacked in Asia—and the East Turkestan Islamic Movement is a threat on China's own soil—the Chinese government is no longer willing to sit on the sidelines. As an increasingly large player in global strategic affairs, China has joined the international antiterrorism coalition.

The spread of international terrorism in Asia is of particular concern to China, since terrorism threatens China's efforts to modernize economically, establish social stability, and improve relations with its neighbors. The September 11, 2001, terrorist attacks on the United States put antiterrorism at the top of Asia's political and security concerns, creating an unusually strong consensus among Asian nations in support of antiterrorism action on all levels—bilateral, regional, and international. China had its own political reasons for joining the U.S.-led war on terror—specifically, the elimination from the Xinjiang Uygur Autonomous Region of its main terrorist threat, the separatist East Turkestan Islamic Movement (ETIM), supported by al-Qaeda. But China's cooperation and leadership in the war on terror underscored a more important strategic decision by China to abandon its traditional position of noninterference in other countries' internal affairs as well as its opposition to multilateralism. In other words, China's efforts to combat international terrorism indicate that a much broader strategic role is emerging for China in the world and may well elevate China to the ranks of the great powers.

Background: Terrorism in the 1990s

Before September 11 international terrorism was a rather remote concern for China and did not figure prominently in its foreign policy. Its exposure to terrorism was limited, and China had been basically on the sidelines in the fight against international terrorism. Although China had signed and ratified most of the international conventions and treaties against terrorism, the participation of China in international counterterrorism activities had been minimal, generally. International terrorism was considered mainly a scourge of the developed world, since the vast majority of terrorist acts were committed in Europe or the Middle East. China and East Asia were largely untouched by terrorism throughout the later years of the Cold War, allowing the region to concentrate more on developing its economies and maintaining internal stability. Furthermore, China was more concerned about its position in the strategic balance of Asia than about conflicts or antiterrorism far removed from China's sphere of influence.

Of course, some violent and terrorist activities, mostly with economic motivations, did occur in China—for example, kidnappings, bank robberies, and armed drug trafficking. Most kidnappings and robberies took place in the eastern coastal regions, where the economy and overseas connections were more developed, while drug trafficking generally originated in the northwest (for example, in Afghanistan and Xinjiang) and in the southwest. To be sure, terrorism of a political nature—such as the occasional hijacking of airplanes to Taiwan—also occurred. Yet even these hijackings were often simply a way to escape prosecution for economic crimes committed on the Chinese mainland. On the whole, the Chinese government treated these activities as ordinary criminal acts rather than acts of terrorism.

China became concerned about international terrorism in the early 1990s, after terrorist acts in Xinjiang by the separatist group ETIM; they were the most significant terrorist attacks to occur within the borders of China in modern times. These attacks, which involved bombings and armed attacks that targeted Chinese police and security facilities and personnel, compelled Chinese authorities to formulate an antiterrorism strategy for combating East Turkistan separatist groups—particularly the ETIM, which had gained the support of the Taliban and al-Qaeda in Afghanistan—and for ensuring the security and stability of Xinjiang. In this context, an antiterrorism corps was organized in Xinjiang with the support of the central government. Moreover, because the East Turkistan movement crossed borders, the Chinese authorities recognized that antiterrorism would need to include mechanisms for international cooperation.

But the problem of terrorism was not nearly as acute or pressing in East Asia as it was for the West during the immediate post–Cold War period and was overshadowed both on the international front and in China itself by globalization and the economic and political consequences of the collapse of the Soviet Union, bringing to an end the strategic rivalry between the two superpowers. For most of the 1990s, Chinese scholars and government officials remained focused on keeping up with the rapid pace of global change and the transformation of China's economic system, while scholars of security and strategic issues were also busy tracking and analyzing the episodic crises on the Taiwan issue, tensions on the Korean peninsula, the break-up of the Soviet Union, and China's strategic relationships with the United States, Japan, and the European Union. The importance of these international economic and strategic issues to China's development and role in the world pushed the subject of international terrorism to the background.

Impact of September 11

It was only near the end of the 1990s that Chinese scholars and policy makers began to take more interest in the problem of international terrorism—particularly, that of militant Islamic groups, which were migrating to South Asia, Central Asia, and Southeast Asia. Terrorism was no longer a distant threat; it was actually approaching China's doorstep. The danger became even greater after the September 11 terrorist attacks on the United States. China's sense of security was profoundly shaken by September 11 (as was that of the whole international community), causing a rapid shift in Chinese foreign policy toward Central and South Asia to meet the direct threat of al-Qaeda.

Antiterrorism became an urgent consideration in China's relations with its Asian neighbors—particularly, countries to the west—after the September 11 attacks. Although al-Qaeda and its brand of Islamic extremism were a known and gathering terrorist threat to China's western frontier prior to September 11, the al-Qaeda terrorist network's long reach into Southeast Asia, unearthed after U.S. forces went into Afghanistan, was cause for considerable concern, as it might undermine the progress made in regional cooperation and might derail China's agenda for regional economic integration and development. Thus, antiterrorism cooperation joined regional and global economic cooperation as top Chinese diplomatic goals.

Since the September 11 terrorist attacks, based on its new security concept, China has been actively promoting international antiterrorism cooperation on all levels. On the international level China has spoken out in favor of giving the United Nations the leading role in international efforts against terrorism, arguing that the organization provides an international legal framework for antiterrorism activities and that the Security Council—particularly, the Counter-Terrorism Committee (CTC)—is the best mechanism for coordinating counterterrorism activities. On the regional level, China has made antiterrorism cooperation a priority issue in the Shanghai Cooperation Organization (SCO), Asia Pacific Economic Cooperation forum (APEC), Asia-Europe Meeting (ASEM), and the Association of South East Asian Nations Regional Forum (ARF).

In the immediate aftermath of the September 11 terrorist attacks, China led the push to strengthen antiterrorism

East Turkistan Islamic Movement (ETIM)

The East Turkistan Islamic Movement (ETIM) is a small Islamic extremist group based in China's western Xinjiang Uygur Autonomous Region. It is the most militant of the ethnic Uygur separatist groups pursuing an independent "Eastern Turkistan," an area that would include Turkey, Kazakhstan, Kyrgyzstan, Uzbekistan, Pakistan, Afghanistan, and the Xinjiang Uygur A. R. of China. ETIM is linked to al-Qa'ida and the international mujahedin movement. In September 2002 the group was designated under EO 13224 as a supporter of terrorist activity.

ACTIVITIES

ETIM militants fought alongside al-Qa'ida and Taliban forces in Afghanistan during Operation Enduring Freedom. In October 2003, Pakistani soldiers killed ETIM leader Hassan Makhsum during raids on al-Qa'ida–associated compounds in western Pakistan. US and Chinese Government information suggests ETIM is responsible for various terrorist acts inside and outside China. In May 2002, two ETIM members were deported to China from Kyrgyzstan for plotting to attack the US Embassy in Kyrgyzstan as well as other US interests abroad.

STRENGTH

Unknown. Only a small minority of ethnic Uygurs supports the Xinjiang independence movement or the formation of an Eastern Turkistan.

LOCATION/AREA OF OPERATION

Xinjiang Uygur Autonomous Region and neighboring countries in the region.

EXTERNAL AID

ETIM has received training and financial assistance from al-Qa'ida.

Source: Sabasteanski, A. (Ed.) (2005). *Patterns of global terrorism.* Great Barrington, MA: Berkshire Publishing Group.

---

cooperation with its Central Asian neighbors and Russia through the SCO. Three days after September 11 in Alma-Ata, Kazakhstan, the SCO member states issued a joint statement that strongly condemned the attacks and renewed their determination to combat the "three evil forces"—separatism, terrorism, and extremism—as detailed in the Shanghai Convention on Combating Terrorism, Separatism and Extremism. Chinese premier Zhu Rongji also proposed in Alma-Ata the creation of an SCO antiterrorism center, which was formally agreed to at the SCO's St. Petersburg summit in June 2002 and established in Tashkent, Uzbekistan, in October 2003. In other regional organizations such as APEC, ASEAN, and ASEM, China has pushed for greater antiterrorism cooperation in areas such as finance, shipping and transport, and intelligence. At the ASEM Copenhagen summit meeting in September 2002, Zhu helped forge an antiterrorism statement and cooperation plan. A year later an ASEM antiterrorism conference was held in Beijing. At the sixth summit meeting of China and ASEAN in November 2002, China agreed to expand its cooperation with ASEAN countries on nonconventional security issues like drug trafficking to include antiterrorism cooperation.

In October 2001 China, at the request of the United States, sealed its border of over ninety kilometers with Afghanistan to coordinate with American military actions in that country. After the United States captured some East Turkistan terrorists of Chinese nationality in Afghanistan, Chinese security officials were invited to join the interrogation of the detainees. In August 2002 the U.S. State Department formally included the ETIM on its list of terrorist organizations. This act was followed by a similar move on the part of the U.N. Security Council through the joint efforts of China, the United States, Afghanistan, and Kyrgyzstan. China-U.S. antiterrorism cooperation has become institutionalized through a number of expert-level working groups that exchange information and methods on terrorist financing, security of container ships, and intelligence. Significantly, the FBI now runs an office in Beijing, which also facilitates bilateral cooperation against drug trafficking, weapons smuggling, illegal immigration, and various other cross-border crimes. Similar bilateral consultation and cooperation mechanisms have been set up with Russia, India, and Pakistan. China has also had a series of bilateral dialogues and negotiations on antiterrorism with the United Kingdom, France, and Germany.

On the Domestic Front

The September 11 terrorist strike, which shocked the world, also reinforced the determination of Chinese leadership to come up with a domestic antiterrorism mechanism for China. Shortly after September 11 China established the National Anti-Terrorism Coordination Group (NATCG) headed up by Hu Jintao. The National Ministry of Public Security also set up an antiterrorism bureau, which is responsible for the research, planning, guidance, coordination, and implementation of national antiterrorism efforts and for all counterterrorism investigations and enforcement. The antiterrorism bureau works closely with other ministries including foreign affairs, national defense, state security, customs, finance, and the People's Bank of China, as well as with provincial and municipal antiterrorism bureaus, to improve China's domestic counterterrorism capabilities.

The antiterrorism mechanism developed by the NATCG has four elements: (1) an early-warning and prevention system, which monitors the activities of terrorist groups in order to preempt terror attacks well in advance and to cut off their sources of funds; (2) a rapid-response system, which is designed to quickly remove terrorist threats or to contain the fallout of terrorist attacks (in almost every provincial capital China has deployed armed rapid-reaction antiterrorism troops); (3) an emergency control-and-management system, which focuses on the control of both physical and human losses in the wake of terrorist attacks or during their development (striving to contain the destructiveness of terrorist attacks and to restore order, China has drawn on New York City's experience of September 11 and has increased coordination of police, fire fighters, armed troops, emergency rescue and medical personnel in emergency cases); and (4) a mass education and mobilization system, which increases the general public's awareness of the government's antiterrorism efforts and policies.

China has also expanded and clarified provisions related to terrorism in Chinese administrative, financial, criminal, and national security laws so as to more rigorously and effectively combat terrorism at home and abroad. The most extensive antiterrorism provisions can be found in the Chinese criminal code. In 1997 the Standing Committee of the eighth National People's Congress amended the criminal code to include a specific antiterrorism provision—Article 120:

> Whoever organizes, leads or actively participates in a terrorist organization shall be sentenced to fixed-term imprisonment of not less than three years but not more than ten years; other participants shall be sentenced to fixed-term imprisonment of not more than three years, criminal detention or public surveillance.
>
> Whoever, in addition to the crime mentioned in the preceding paragraph, commits other crimes of homicide, exploitation or kidnapping shall be punished in accordance with the provisions on combined punishment for several crimes.

After September 11 the Chinese government adopted another criminal-law amendment that is even more specific and detailed on terrorist crimes and brought the criminal code into conformity with counterterrorism obligations and requirements of international conventions on terrorism and relevant U.N. Security Council resolutions, particularly, resolution 1373.

Long and Difficult Fight Ahead

The priority target of the Chinese antiterrorism campaign is four East Turkistan organizations: the ETIM, the East Turkistan Liberation Organization, the World Uygur Youth Congress, and the East Turkistan Information Center. While the government has had some success in thwarting terrorist attacks by these groups in 2007 and early 2008, it has not been able to stop them totally as demonstrated by the terrorist attacks in the Xinjiang towns of Kashgar on 4 August 2008 and Kuqa on 10 August 2008, despite the extraordinary security measures for the 2008 Beijing Olympics. China recognizes that it has a long and hard fight ahead in overcoming the Xinjiang insurgency and will have to strengthen its antiterrorism cooperation, regionally and globally, to win.

China's war on terrorism is not restricted to battling the ETIM in Xinjiang and Central Asian terrorist groups that support and supply the ETIM. China is well aware that the global networks of terrorists and other international criminal organizations are a significant threat to the international system and to China's national strategic and economic interests, which have progressively expanded beyond the Asia–Pacific region. Hence, it is not surprising that China has been very active in the international antiterrorism coalition. The war on terrorism has involved China in global strategic affairs at a much higher level than ever before, testing China's power and influence in the world. Beijing is acutely aware of how much is at stake and that the price of failure will be high. So far, China has demonstrated that it has the capacity and capability to play a leading role in the international antiterrorism coalition alongside the other great powers.

James P. MULDOON Jr.

Further Reading

Bolt, P. J., Su Changhe, & Cross, S. (Eds.). (2008) *The United States, Russia, and China: Confronting global terrorism and security challenges of the 21st century.* Westport, CT: Praeger Security International.

Chung Chien-peng. (2006). Confronting terrorism and other evils in China: All quiet on the western front? *The China and Eurasia Forum Quarterly 4*(2), 75–87.

Hu Shuli. (2008). Fighting terrorism over the long haul. *Caijing Magazine,* 216. Retrieved September 5, 2008, from http://english.caijing.com.cn/2008-08-19/100077365.html

Malik, M. (2002). *Dragon on terrorism: Assessing China's tactical gains and strategic losses post-September 11.* Carlisle, PA: US Army War College Strategic Studies Institute.

Muldoon, J. P. (2003). *International conference on international terrorism and counter-terrorism cooperation: A conference report.* Shanghai: Shanghai Academy of Social Sciences.

Muldoon, J. P. (2004). The impact of 9/11 on Chinese regional security cooperation. *China Brief 4*(12), 7–9.

Pan Guang. (2006). East Turkestan terrorism and the terrorist arc: China's post-9/11 anti-terror strategy. *The China and Eurasia Forum Quarterly 4*(2), 19–24.

Shen, S. (Ed.). (2006) *China and antiterrorism.* Hauppauge, NY: Nova Science Publishers.

Wayne, M. I. (2007). *China's war on terrorism.* London: Routledge.

Textile and Clothing Industry

Fǎngzhī fúzhuāngyè　纺织服装业

China became a major textile manufacturer beginning in the early 1980s. Its industry quickly expanded to become a top producer and, by the late 1990s, China had become the world's leading textile-exporting nation. Today, expansion into technical textile products reflects a general trend toward innovation and higher-value products for the domestic as well as export markets.

Textile production has played a key role in the initial stages industrial development in China and its East Asian neighbors. Because it is labor intensive and does not require a large amount of capital, the textile and clothing industry is well-suited to developing economies that have little capital and plenty of low-wage labor. As the industry matures, exports generate foreign capital, mechanization and production techniques become more sophisticated, and wages rise. This leads to a shift toward more capital-intensive and higher-value industries.

Textile Industry in the Newly Industrializing Economies

The newly industrialized economies (NIEs) of Hong Kong, Taiwan, and South Korea began developing their textile and clothing industries in the 1950s and 1960s. Production and exports steadily increased throughout the 1970s as did their export share in the Japanese, U.S., and European markets. As their industries matured, they shifted toward more high-value products, such as manmade fibers. By the end of the 1970s and into the 1980s, the quality of synthetic fibers coming from the Asian NIEs had improved enough to be competitive with other exporting countries.

Hong Kong became the world's leading clothing exporter from 1973 to 1977 and again from 1980 to 1985. Taiwan's industry peaked in the 1980s, briefly becoming the leading apparel exporter to the U.S. market and the second leading producer of manmade fibers (after the United States). Throughout the 1980s, the textiles industry played a critical role in South Korea's exports, consisting of US$11.9 billion, or 19.6 percent of total export earnings. In 1989, the total value of South Korea's textile exports reached US$15.34 billion, an 8 percent increase over the previous year.

By the late 1980s, the low-wage advantage that the Asian NIEs held in the labor-intensive clothing segment began to dwindle as their industries advanced and labor costs increased. Their textile exports, accompanied by a shift to synthetic fibers, remained at around a quarter of total world trade in the 1990s, while their share of garment exports fell steadily from around a quarter in the 1980s and early 1990s to 16 percent by 1999.

A common response to this situation was for the NIEs to upgrade their technology and the quality of their products. Production was upgraded through automation, mechanization, and computer-aided design. Emphasis was placed on producing upmarket and high-fashion apparel. Taiwan and South Korea increasingly moved away

A Tianjin carpet factory, 1980s. Automation has since changed textile production methods. PHOTO BY JOAN LEBOLD COHEN.

from the production of textiles and clothing to manufacturing value-added products such as electronics and semiconductors. In addition, as the NIEs and Japan increasingly outsourced the labor-intensive manufacturing of such items as clothing to China and other low-cost producers, they were able to devote more resources to higher value-added activities while still maintaining demand for their textile exports.

Trade Barriers and Market Shifts

Throughout their development, East Asian textile exporters confronted challenges that pushed the industry to undergo structural reform. First, considerable trade barriers existed in the global textile trade. In 1974, the Multi Fibre Arrangement (MFA) was adopted by the United States, Canada, and Europe. The arrangement set quotas on the imports of textiles and clothing to the United States, Canada and the European Union. It was intended to prevent textile and garment industry jobs in developed nations from moving to developing nations where manufacturing and labor was cheaper.

The effects of the MFA in East Asia were complex. For example, limits on exports for Japan and Hong Kong led to greater export opportunities for Taiwan and South Korea. When quotas were placed on exports from Taiwan and South Korea, Thailand and Indonesia reaped the benefits. This created a shift in the market in which investment in textile production spread throughout the region and often to those countries not yet limited by the MFA. What had been an attempt to limit exports sometimes resulted in greater exports from countries that otherwise might not have attracted the capital and expertise to develop a textile industry of their own.

In 1995, the World Trade Organization (WTO) adopted the Agreement on Textiles and Clothing, which called for a 10-year phaseout of the MFA. And in 2005, the MFA ended, giving all WTO members unrestricted access to the U.S., Canadian, and EU markets.

A second challenge faced by East Asian nations was the increase in labor and production costs that accompanied the expansion of their textile industries. As costs increased, their textile industries became more vulnerable to competition from low-cost producers. In many cases, this resulted in relocation of manufacturing facilities to the very countries that housed their low-cost competitors. Hong Kong, for example, relocated factories to China on a large scale beginning in the 1980s, bringing to the mainland the benefits of massive investments and training. Japan also began moving its manufacturing operations offshore in the late 1980s and early 1990s. China received the bulk of these investments, seeing new Japanese-backed plants go from 23 to 187 in the late 1980s while spending rose from US$16 million to US$120 million.

Third, the formation of regional trade blocs, such as the European Union in 1993 and the North American Free Trade Agreement in 1994, threatened market shares of the NIEs in Europe and North America. Hong Kong was hit especially hard, for example, by the erosion of its U.S. market share to lower-cost Mexican and Canadian producers.

China's Textiles and Clothing Industry

China became a major player in the world textile market after it initiated market reforms in the early 1980s. The production value of its textile and clothing industry grew at an annual rate of 15.6 percent from 1986 to 1995, while exports increased from US$8.5 billion to US$38 billion. In 1991, China surpassed Italy to become the economy with the biggest trade surplus in textiles and clothing. In 1999,

A shirt factory at the Yangzhou Commune in the 1970s. The textile industry in China would begin to see market reforms in the 1980s, and China became a major player in the world textile market. PHOTO BY JOAN LEBOLD COHEN.

after a decade of 13 percent annual growth, China's clothing sector captured 16.2 percent of world trade, while Hong Kong garnered 12 percent. In 1997, and again in 1999, China passed Germany as the world's top textile exporter.

However, as a socialist economy undergoing market reforms, China's economy suffered from the burden of money-losing state-owned enterprises (SOEs). The SOEs dominated the textile industry but were plagued by labor redundancy, high pension and benefit costs, and outdated equipment. Reform of these enterprises took precedence in government efforts to transform the state-owned sector in 1998. As a result, money-losing factories were closed by the hundreds, 1.16 million workers were laid off, and 9.6 million antiquated cotton spindles were taken out of production by 1999.

After China joined the WTO at the end of 2001, it began upgrading its textile and clothing manufacturing equipment. In 2002, it imported US$3.5 billion worth of advanced equipment, mainly from Western textile producers who had outsourced production to lower-cost producer nations such as China and India. With this new equipment, Chinese textile manufacturers improved their productivity and the quality of their textile exports.

China's textile industry also saw an increase in investment from internationally renowned corporations, such as Toray Industries and Asahi Chemical Industry of Japan, DuPont of the United States, BSF of Germany, and others from Hong Kong, Taiwan and South Korea. Enterprises from other sectors, such as coal, steel, and chemical manufacturing, also stepped into China's textiles industry with big investment projects. This influx of funds helped finance upgrades in textile and clothing manufacturing equipment.

In 2003, the industry saw its exports reach US$80.4 billion, a jump of 27 percent over the previous year, accounting for 18 percent of the country's total export value. But with the surge in exports came problems in the form of trade friction with Western nations, especially the United States. Claiming that Chinese imports were creating a disruption in the U.S. market, the U.S. Department of Commerce announced in 2005 that it was imposing temporary quotas on cotton shirts, cotton trousers, and underwear from China. The announcement came just five months after the lifting of quotas under the Multi Fibre Arrangement.

In 2007, China's textiles and apparel exports reached US$171 billion, a rise of 16 percent year on year, but 8.5 percentage points lower than the previous year. In the first two months of 2008, China's exports of textiles and clothing grew by 8.19 percent, a drop of 30.9 percentage points over the previous comparable period. Factors contributing to the slowdown included a higher-valued Chinese currency, cuts in export tax rebates, rising raw materials costs, and higher wages. Since 2003, China's average wages have risen more than 50 percent, and the value of the yuan has gained about 18 percent against the U.S. dollar since lifting the unit's peg in 2005. This has made Chinese textiles more expensive and has taken away their cost advantages compared to products from Vietnam, Bangladesh, Pakistan, and India.

Although some in China's textile and apparel industry have appealed to the government for help, such as adjustment of the export tax rebate, many experts and industry insiders realize that a slowing of the industry offers a good opportunity for restructuring. Many see China's industry shifting away from production capacity to innovation and product upgrades. For example, the China National Textile and Apparel Council (CNTAC) urged the country's textile manufacturers to focus on innovation, environmentally friendly production methods, and high-end apparel for the international market. The council supports a strategy of developing Chinese brands and targeting overseas markets with high-end, China-made fabrics and Chinese-designed clothing. Innovation and technological advancement are the two primary directions for the industry at this time, according to the council.

Meanwhile, the government has established a Textile Industry Technical Advancement and Development Program as part of its Eleventh Five-Year Plan, and set up a fund of $180 million to drive technological development and innovation. Many textile factories have continued to upgrade their equipment. According to the German Engineering Federation, China is one of the largest buyers of German textile machines. The Chinese government is seeking faster modernization and higher value, the federation said in a recent report.

Future Trends in the Industry

One of the most promising areas for the future of the textiles industry is technical textiles, which includes those products used for their performance or functional

In the global economic meltdown, inventory stockpiles are a threat to all industries.
PHOTO BY JOAN LEBOLD COHEN.

characteristics rather than for their aesthetics. Technical textiles account for about one-third of the world's annual consumption of fibers, both natural and manmade. Volume growth in developing countries is expected to average between 4 percent and 5 percent annually to 2010, with a large portion of production coming from China and India. China imported nearly 500,000 tons of technical textiles in 2004, and its consumption has averaged 11 percent a year since 1998.

As China has developed into a consumer society, its demand has grown for technical textile products, such as diapers and feminine hygiene items. Higher standards for medical care have led to an increase in demand for disposable bed sheets, surgical drapes, gowns, and caps. The microelectronics industry has also spurred growth through demand for clean-room (protective) clothing. And the rise in car ownership has resulted in a sharp jump in demand for technical textiles in the auto manufacturing sector.

Chinese companies have increasingly expanded into specialty areas previously occupied by producers in developed countries. And its strategy of innovation and self-sufficiency is likely to be applied to the technical textiles segment. Success in this area will likely help it turn the tables to become a major exporter of technical textile products in the future, although the global financial meltdown of 2008 makes predicting future trends difficult.

The financial meltdown is likely to affect China and its Asian neighbors adversely in the near future: even number-one China has experienced a drop of 10.7% in the growth rate of its textile and garment exports in 2008 as compared to 2007. The State Council announced on 4 February, 2009 a comprehensive national plan to reinvigorate China's textile industry by increasing the tax rebate rate for textile and garment exports to 15%, providing financial assistance for technology upgrades and branding, promotion of the domestic market, and other measures.

Robert Y. ENG

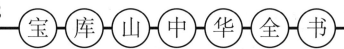
Further Reading

Berkowitch, J. E. (1996). Trends in Japanese textile technology. Retrieved July 12, 2008, from http://www.technology.gov/Reports/textile/textile.pdf

China: 2003 textile exports top US$80.4 billion. Retrieved on July 13, 2008, from http://findarticles.com/p/articles/mi_qa5358/is_200404/ai_n21348248

China's textile exports hit hard by the yuan's appreciation. Retrieved on July 14, 2008, from http://www.chinastakes.com/story.aspx?id=286

China's textile industry becoming less competitive. Retrieved on July 14, 2008, from http://www.financialexpress.com/news/Chinas-textile-industry-becoming-less-competitive/259175/

China's textile industry struggles to survive. Retrieved on July 14, 2008, from http://www.impactlab.com/2008/04/19/chinese-textile-industry-struggles-to-survive/

Diao, Ying. Worry creases in textile industry. (2008, May 9). *China Daily* online edition. Retrieved on July 14, 2008, from http://www.chinadaily.com.cn/bizchina/2008-05/09/content_6672281.htm

Division of Research Cooperation, Economic Research Institute, Economic Planning Agency of Japan. (1993). Trade and Industrial Interdependence in the Pacific Region: Textiles and Clothing. In *Dynamic Interdependence among the Asia-Pacific Economies* (pp. 37–66). Retrieved July 12, 2008, from http://www.esri.go.jp/jp/archive/bun/bun130/bun129b-e.pdf

Faehnders, T. (2007). China's textile industry strives to shake off cheap image. Retrieved on July 14, 2008, from http://www.monstersandcritics.com/news/business/features/article_1281264.php

Growth of China's textile industry slows. Retrieved on July 14, 2008, from http://www.chinadaily.com.cn/bizchina/2007-03/21/content_833242.htm

Gupta, S. (2008). Technical textiles and nonwoven sectors growing in Asia. Retrieved on July 15, 2008, from http://www.fibre2fashion.com/industry-article/13/1236/technical-textiles-and-nonwoven-sectors1.asp

Li, Qian. Textile industry urged to reform. (2007, Sept. 14). *China Daily* online edition. Retrieved on July 14, 2008, from http://www.chinadaily.com.cn/china/2007-09/14/content_6107992.htm

Luo, Lan. Review of textile industry after WTO entry. Retrieved on July 13, 2008, from http://info.hktdc.com/report/indprof/indprof_040301.htm

Meyanathan, S. D. (Ed.). (1994). *Managing Restructuring in the Textile and Garment Subsector: Examples from Asia*. Edi Seminar Series. Washington, DC: World Bank.

Savada, A. M., & Shaw, W. (Eds.). (1990). Industry. In South Korea: A Country Study. Retrieved on July 12, 2008, from http://countrystudies.us/south-korea/50.htm

Textile industry overview. (2004). Retrieved July 12, 2008, from http://en.j-cast.com/2004/11/01000091.html

Textiles Intelligence. (2001, January). Trends in World Textile and Clothing Trade. *Textile Outlook International, 46*–88.

Textiles Intelligence. (1997, July). World Textile Trade and Production Trends. *Textile Outlook International, 9*–37.

The phase-out of the Multifiber Arrangement. (2004). Retrieved July 13, 2008, from http://www.cleanclothes.org/publications/04-04-somo.htm

Thun, E. (2001). Growing up and moving out: Globalization of "traditional" industries in Taiwan. MIT globalization study. Special working paper series. Retrieved on July 12, 2008, from http://ipc-lis.mit.edu/globalization/globalization%2000-004.pdf

Zhang, Face. (2008). Pessimism in the Chinese textile industry. Retrieved on July 14, 2008, from http://ezinearticles.com/?Pessimism-in-the-Chinese-Textile-Industry&id=1229313

Textiles

Făngzhīpǐn 纺织品

Ancient Chinese trade routes through central Asia are collectively called the "Silk Roads," indicating the importance that textile has long had for China's economy. Textile designs, created by weaving, embroidery, or fabric printing, often reflect symbology important in Chinese religious and official life: dragons are symbols of imperial power; fans are motifs in Daoist philosophy.

Chinese textiles reflect many centuries of technology, trade, government, religion, and art. They provide continuing evidence of the Chinese culture's rich heritage. Although the best known and most highly valued fabrics are of silk, the earliest people relied on reindeer skins, gut, and sinew before beginning to use fibers from stems of plants, such as hemp and ramie, silk, and cotton.

Archaeological Evidence of Early Cloth Production

Loom pieces from Hemudu, an early Neolithic site that dates to over six thousand years ago, are the earliest evidence of cloth production. The Hemudu culture lived in modern-day Zhejiang Province, on the southeast coast. A cut-open cocoon of the silkworm moth (*Bombyx mori*) in Xiyingcun and parts of equipment for reeling silk at Qianshanyang point to the cultivation of mulberry trees for raising silkworms at this time. Other early examples of textile production include parts of backstrap looms at Liangzhu and Yunnan provinces from the second century BCE. Actual silk fabric fragments surviving at a number of late Neolithic sites are the best evidence of the early development of yarn and fabric construction in early China.

Developing Technology and Trade

As looms evolved, so did structures of weaving and ways of creating woven motifs. The addition of shed sticks to looms allowed weavers to incorporate warp patterns into cloth. Early examples of this technology have survived in Scythian burial mounds in the Altai Mountains. The atmosphere of the Han dynasty (206 BCE–220 CE) supported an unprecedented growth of the arts. Surviving figured, pile, and gauze weaves testify to the magnificence of Han fabrics, which made up much of the trade along the famed Silk Road, an interconnecting network of caravan trails across Asia extending to the Mediterranean Sea. A new, complex draw loom in the Tang dynasty (618–907 CE) produced many weft-faced patterned damasks and brocades, slit tapestries, and crepes for the court and for export. Motifs in some of these cloths reflect trade with the Persian Sasanid dynasty (224/228–651 CE) just as Sasanian patterns show eastern influence.

Embroidery also developed into a highly skilled method of decorating fabrics. Traders included the exquisite embroideries that incorporated a great variety of stitches and silk yarns into packs for the Silk Road trade. Like woven cloths, high quality embroideries still play an important role in Chinese life and trade, as do so-called "resist" methods of printing cloth, including batik and tie-dye, that produce stylized and abstract designs on silk and cotton fabrics.

From a practical standpoint, the Chinese have used textiles for bed hangings and bed covers; on screens, walls, chairs, and tables; for cushion covers, boxes, cases and books; for garments, purses, hats, shoes, and gloves; for banners, curtains, canopies, and as altar coverings for commemorative and religious ceremonies. The rich history of cloth documents its past use as currency, tax payments, tributes, bribes, and dowries. The extensive trade in textiles has sustained the economy and has introduced Chinese design and technology to faraway places, but this trade venue has also brought foreign ideas and customs into the country.

The Power of Design in Dragon Robes

Patterns in woven and embroidered Chinese fabrics reflect governmental efforts to create an orderly universe as well as the philosophical and religious thought of Chinese culture. Dragons, probably the most famous and ubiquitous of Chinese motifs, denoted imperial authority and power.

Dragon robes of the Qing dynasty (1644–1912) are among the most frequently held Chinese textiles in private and public collections. Bright yellow robes reserved for the emperor and empress have eight dragons woven into or embroidered on them. Four of the dragons surround the wearer's head with positions at each shoulder, at the center front, and at the center back. A pair of dragons set in clouds facing each other in a mirror image decorates the front and back of the robe's lower section.

The Manchu added twelve ancient symbols of imperial authority among the clouds to the emperor's garments in the mid-eighteenth century. They include a sun with a three-legged cockerel and a moon and rabbit with the elixir of life on the left and right shoulders, respectively. The other ten symbols had specific positions on the robe and were not present on the robes of the heir apparent.

A Manchu-Style Dragon Robe (metal-wrapped core yarns couched on yellow silk satin used to produce the dragons and universe motif).
SOURCE: UNIVERSITY OF RHODE ISLAND HISTORIC TEXTILE AND COSTUME COLLECTION.

Strong diagonal lines representing water topped by waves decorate the bottom of many dragon robes and on many other textiles. Rising out on the water on the sides and the center front and back—the four cardinal compass points—are representations of land. These distinctive spikes move up into the cloud-covered sky where the dragons writhe. This frequently used composite represents the emperor's rule over the universe.

Creating Order with Rank Badges

Textile collections also often have rank badges that reflect attempts to maintain an orderly society in the four hundred years before the twentieth century.

Conferred by the emperor, a civil official's rank designated his level of achievement on rigorous tests. In the

A Fourth-Rank Wild Goose Surrounded By Clouds (created by couching metallic-covered core yarns onto a satin surface; late nineteenth or early twentieth century, when various shades of blue became popular). SOURCE: UNIVERSITY OF RHODE ISLAND HISTORIC TEXTILE AND COSTUME COLLECTION.

Ming (1368–1644) and Qing dynasties, a round or more often square badge incorporated a specific bird that represented each level of achievement. Since the civil officials supplied the badges for themselves and their wives to place on the front and back of their robes, the methods of construction and quality varied greatly. The most expensive rank squares have the bird, clouds, and other motifs incorporated into the tapestry or patterned weave or embroidered design. Others have motifs surrounding a blank center to which a pre-embroidered bird was appliquéd. Upgrading to a higher level would be easier and less costly with the generic ground.

Military officials also had hierarchical badges, but with an animal rather than a bird. Today, these are rarer than civilian squares, especially ones of the lowest ranks. If one of a pair of rank squares is cut in half vertically, the official intended it for a Han-style robe that opened at center front; solid squares fit Manchu-style robes that fastened on the right side. Made of narrow-width silk fabrics, the agrarian Han garments opened in the center front and had a center-back seam. Manchu-style robes, based on a leather tradition and appropriate for horseback riding, originally had large front and back pieces. After taking over (and establishing the Qing dynasty) in the

early seventeenth century, the Manchu switched to narrow woven silk fabrics that required center seams, but the silhouette of the garment did not change.

Reflections of Philosophy and Religion in Textile Designs

For over four thousand years printers, painters, embroiderers, and weavers have incorporated symbols representing Chinese culture into their products for individuals, homes, and temples. Many long-established motifs may have represented Confucian philosophy, which became a major influence on the customs and thought of the Chinese people during the Han dynasty. Ancient motifs include stylized pearls, coins, books, scrolls, rhinoceros horns, leaves, clouds, coral, bats, and designs representing the opposites—yin and yang. Even then, these motifs mixed with those of Daoism and Buddhism.

The Chinese often have ordered symbols in groups of eight or four. Eight motifs symbolizing Daoist philosophy and beliefs in textiles and other art forms include a fan, sword in a sheath, pilgrim's staff and gourd, castanets, a flower basket, a tube holding two rods, a flute, and a lotus blossom. Many textile patterns depict one or more of eight Immortals often holding one of these specific Daoist symbols.

Two Daoist Immortals (reversible slit tapestry weave [*kesi*]; nineteenth or early twentieth century). SOURCE: UNIVERSITY OF RHODE ISLAND HISTORIC TEXTILE AND COSTUME COLLECTION.

Buddhist Conch (satin stitch and outline couching of metallic covered core yarn; late nineteenth or early twentieth century). SOURCE: UNIVERSITY OF RHODE ISLAND HISTORIC TEXTILE AND COSTUME COLLECTION.

Buddhism, the third major Chinese religion, came from India during the last half of the Han dynasty. Eight Buddhist symbols represent specific beliefs of the religion, but interpretations have changed over the centuries, and original meanings sometimes become obscure. These symbols, whose meanings are often related to happiness and well being, include the following: a protective canopy; an ever-changing wheel; a sacred vase; a fish or a pair of fish with the latter possibly representing yin and yang; a lotus representing purity; an endless knot or mystic diagram; a conch that called worshipers to prayer; and a parasol. Particularly by the nineteenth century, artisans mixed the motifs from the three religions along with patterns of other symbolic groupings.

Patterns for Ceremonies and Expressions of Nature

Symbols of indefinite origin support special ceremonies, such as weddings, which also incorporate the color red or red-orange. A bride's robe may contain motifs such as a pomegranate with some exposed seeds (symbolizing fertility), ducks (because they mate for life), and phoenixes (reserved for the empress and brides who became an empress for a day). Wishes for a marriage to produce many children are reflected in numerous "hundred children" or "thousand children" designs that depict colorfully dressed children playing a variety of games.

Many designs in Chinese textiles reflect nature and familiar scenes, often incorporating architectural features.

Beautifully executed colored blossoms and butterflies decorate skirt panels, robes, and sleeve bands. Many textile collections have women's robes with embroidered bands sewn on the bottom edge of wide sleeves. Collections also may hold sleeve bands not sewn to a robe. Sometimes these bands are decorated only in the areas that are exposed to a viewer when the wearer holds her bent arms in front of her body. The surface of the band on the side of the sleeve toward her is undecorated since this area would be subject to abrasion.

Worldwide Influence of Chinese Textile Design

Occasionally the design in Chinese textiles has reflected outside influence, such as roundels with a pair of affronted mounted warriors from the Sasanid dynasty in Persia, but more often textiles in other parts of the world contain Chinese motifs. That these patterns have been such an inspiration to other cultures speaks for their strength, beauty, and appeal, even without their symbolism. The entire world is enriched by the heritage of China's textiles.

Margaret T. ORDOÑEZ

Scene on Sleeve Band (embroidered; late nineteenth century). SOURCE: UNIVERSITY OF RHODE ISLAND HISTORIC TEXTILE AND COSTUME COLLECTION.

Mandarin Ducks on Bride's Red Robe (embroidered; twentieth century). SOURCE: UNIVERSITY OF RHODE ISLAND HISTORIC TEXTILE AND COSTUME COLLECTION.

Further Reading

Haig, P., & Shelton, M. (2006). *Chinese Textiles: Ming to Ch'ing*. Atglen, PA: Schiffer.

Hall, A. J. (1974). A lady from China's past. *National Geographic* 145(5), 660–81.

Vollmer, J. E. (1980). *Five colours of the Universe: Symbolism in clothes and fabrics of the Ch'ing Dynasty (1644–1911)*. Edmonton, Canada: Edmonton Art Gallery.

Vollmer, J. E. (1977). *In the presence of the dragon throne: Ch'ing Dynasty costume (1644–1911) in the Royal Ontario Museum*. Toronto: Royal Ontario Museum.

Wilson, V. (1996). *Chinese dress*. London: Weatherhill.

Wilson, V. (2005). *Chinese textiles*. London: V & A Publications.

Wood, F. (2002). *The silk road*. Berkeley: University of California Press.

Third Front Policy

Dàsānxiàn　大三线

The Third Front policy, a response to the perceived threat of U.S. and Soviet aggression at the height of the Cold War, refers to an ambitious but ultimately wasteful program for the military-industrial development of China's remote mountainous hinterland.

The large scale of "Third Front" or "Third Line" (*da sanxian*) policy, a reaction to China's vulnerability to U.S. and Soviet aggression during the Cold War, entailed massive investment in developing a military-industrial complex, including mining, metallurgy, machine building, and transportation that could serve as the basis for continued military capability in the event of an invasion of China's capital, coastal cities, and core territories. Although the most intense period of investment and construction was brief, from 1964 to 1971, the effort had a strong negative impact on China's economic development and provided few lasting benefits.

Origins of Third Front Policy

The term "Third Front" was first used by Lin Biao in a speech in January 1962 to refer to a redoubt (fortification, in this case military-industrial) in Anhui Province in the event of the need to retreat from Shanghai. By the time Mao Zedong revived the program and incorporated it into the revised Third Five-Year Plan in 1964, the area defined as the "Big Third Front" included a vast swath of territory stretching from Beijing in the north to Hainan Island in the south. Much of this area is rugged mountainous terrain 500 meters or more above sea level, including the provinces of Guizhou, Sichuan, and Yunnan in the southwest, Gansu and Qinghai in the northwest, and parts of the provinces of Shaanxi, Hubei, and Hunan. It was hoped that this region, distant from both the coast and the northern plains, might serve as a base for a continued war of resistance in the event of an invasion from the north or the Pacific. As the economist Barry Naughton puts it, through the "Third Front" strategy, "China was preparing to fight a 'people's war' ... in which the 'people' were equipped with the products of modern industry" (Naughton 1988).

There was no precedent for the massive effort to build up advanced industrial capacity and the accompanying infrastructure in this mountainous region. During the Japanese invasion from 1937 to 1945, the Nationalist government retreated to southwest China, moving an impressive amount of industrial capacity, including armaments factories, into Sichuan and Yunnan provinces. But this was a temporary emergency measure and not an attempt to build up a permanent industrial base.

From 1963, as China was recovering from the disasters of the Great Leap Forward (begun in 1958), Chairman Mao and Lin Biao, who became Minister of Defense in 1959, actively promoted the Third Front policy. There would seem to have been a strong consensus in favor of the policy among the party's top leadership in the years leading up to the Cultural Revolution (1966–1976). China's nascent nuclear program, which successfully tested its first atomic weapon in 1964, was also located in the western provinces of Qinghai and Gansu. There were also considerable mineral and hydropower resources available in the southwest and northwest, including steel and aluminum. The Third Front policy was also broadly consistent with the economic policies implemented since 1949. In the 1950s, the government consistently transferred resources, including plant, capital, and personnel, from the industrial centers of the east coast and Manchuria to inland provinces and rural areas in order to distribute the benefits of economic development more evenly throughout the country. Similarly, the emphasis on heavy industry such as mining, metallurgy, and machine building was consistent with the investment policies of the First Five-Year Plan (1953–1957) and the Great Leap Forward. Nonetheless, the attempt to develop a massive military-industrial complex in some of the most remote and mountainous terrain in China was extraordinary, and was motivated primarily by international and strategic concerns.

Policy Implementation

The initial impetus for the first phase of Third Front projects was the intensification of U.S. involvement in the war in Vietnam following the Gulf of Tonkin incident in August 1964. That year, the government of the People's Republic of China initiated a program of railroad construction and development of heavy industry in the southwestern provinces of Guizhou and Yunnan that was intended to facilitate both Chinese defense of the region and support for the Communist forces in Vietnam.

It soon became apparent, however, that while the U.S. was taking great pains to avoid conflict with China, China's relationship with the Soviet Union had reached a crisis. In January 1966, the USSR signed a mutual defense pact with Mongolia and stationed large forces there. By 1969, the two socialist giants had fought several border skirmishes, and Soviet actions in Czechoslovakia and the announcement of the Brezhnev Doctrine (that the Soviet Union had the right to intervene to preserve the socialist system in other countries) made China's leaders apprehensive. By the autumn of 1969, Lin Biao had ordered the evacuation of the party's top leadership from Beijing, and China's leaders were expecting and prepared for an apocalyptic final conflict between socialism, imperialism, and revisionism.

The amount of resources invested in Third Front projects reflects the urgency and importance of this defense-related program. From 1965 to 1970, the "third front" received more than half of all state investment, and an even higher proportion of investment in capital resources. Third Front projects also received the most advanced industrial equipment and some of the most skilled personnel China possessed. Initially, the Third Front was centrally managed, and "general command headquarters" for construction were established at key project sites. These projects also enjoyed direct and priority access to funds and materials through supply offices and branches of the Construction Bank established at various project sites. As the planning system broke down during the Cultural Revolution, however, control over these projects devolved to local authorities.

Changes in the international and strategic context are reflected in shifts in Third Front investment, and the Third Front policy can be divided into three phases. In the first phase, from 1964 to 1969, investment and construction was focused mainly in the southwestern provinces of Guizhou, Yunnan, and Sichuan. The first task was to connect the railroad lines feeding into the region from Shaanxi and Guangxi provinces with the French-built line from Vietnam. The link from Chongqing to Guiyang was completed in October 1965 by mobilizing hundreds of thousands of laborers and shifting funds from the national rail network to this single priority project. The centerpiece of the project was the massive iron and steel combine built at Panzhihua, on the mountainous border between Yunnan and Sichuan. The first phase in the southwest also developed mining operations and hydroelectric power to supply the new heavy-industrial base. Armaments and machine-building factories were established in the area of Chongqing and northern Guizhou, including facilities for aluminum smelting and stamping, rubber, precision instruments, and optics. Hundreds of factories throughout China, including the famous Anshan Iron and Steel Complex in Manchuria, sent skilled personnel and equipment to support Third Front projects in the southwest. In some cases, entire plants were relocated, along with their employees, to remote valleys from coastal cities like Shanghai.

The second phase, from 1969 to 1972, was partly a response to the worsening of Sino-Soviet relations and the threat of invasion from the north. Second phase projects were located mainly in the mountainous region where the borders of Shaanxi, Henan, Hubei, Sichuan, and Hunan provinces meet. Like the first phase, the second phase included rapid and large-scale development of railways, hydroelectric power, and metallurgical and machine-building industries. An effort to build a steel complex at Wuyang in Henan Province, smaller than but similar to the one at Panzhihua, was ultimately unsuccessful. The second phase continued the high rates of investment and mobilization of hundreds of thousands of workers to build three new railway lines, which were completed in less than four years. Construction of what was then China's largest dam, at Gezhouba, was also initiated in 1970, but the project was not completed until the 1990s.

Machine-building industries, mainly for military uses, dominated the second phase projects, especially the Number Two Automobile Plant at Shiyan in the mountains of Hubei Province, which was built to produce two-and-a-half-ton trucks. More than 140 factories, including the Number One Auto Factory in Changchun, provided assistance in the form of personnel and equipment. This reflected an effort to remove productive capacity from the northeast, which was vulnerable to Soviet attack, into the mountain vastness of northwestern Hubei. Nearly all of the equipment installed in the plant was designed and produced in China, which had only begun producing its own trucks with Soviet equipment in 1957. Like many Third Front projects, however, the plant suffered from flaws in design and inefficiencies born of perceived defense requirements. Subsidiary factories were built in mountain valleys, and even caves, dispersed across 32 kilometers. This naturally created transportation difficulties and dramatically increased production costs.

Throughout the same period, several projects in the northwest provinces of Gansu, Ningxia, and Qinghai were also included in the Third Front. Railways and military industries, including China's nuclear program, were built up in this region from the 1950s. From 1964, these projects were accelerated and supported with massive investment from the central government. Projects designed to supply specialty steel and hydroelectric power to the nuclear program in Gansu Province were given top priority from 1965. As in other Third Front regions, these projects were supported by the transfer of resources from other parts of China, and factories were dispersed and built into sites that were naturally fortified but difficult to access.

The year 1972 marked a sudden and dramatic reversal of the Third Front policy and the beginning of the third and final phase of the program. Most Third Front projects were discontinued by 1973 and many construction crews were transferred to new projects in eastern China. There were several reasons for the reversal of policy, but with the death of Lin Biao, one of the policy's most ardent advocates, as well as the beginnings of rapprochement with the United States, the sense of military urgency was reduced.

Most importantly, however, the dramatic inefficiencies and tremendous waste inherent in the effort to establish a modern industrial base in China's mountainous hinterland had become apparent to central leaders. The levels of investment required could not be sustained given China's level of economic development. When Premier Zhou Enlai regained control of the organs of government in 1972, following the peak years of chaos and violence during the Cultural Revolution, he quickly ordered a reduction in the rate of investment. Third Front projects were particularly inefficient. The entire program was so massive that it was clearly impossible to complete most of the individual projects in a timely fashion. The push for immediate accomplishments and practices such as simultaneously designing, constructing, and operating new plants produced many design problems. Poor design and siting necessitated wasteful redundancies.

Despite these many obvious problems, however, and the need to reduce the rate of investment, from 1972 to 1978 some Third Front projects continued to receive support from central planners. Continued concern with the Soviet threat was one motivation. But the simple fact that so much manpower and resources had already been invested in these projects inclined the party's leaders to continue to develop certain key projects, such as the Panzhihua iron and steel complex. By 1979, however, it had become clear that even these key projects were unworkable. Following China's brief war with Vietnam in 1978, military preparedness became less of a priority and the Third Front program was finally abandoned.

Implications of Third Front Policy

In the short term, the Third Front probably did enhance China's capacity to withstand a major conventional invasion. But this event was unlikely even at the height of

China's strategic isolation, and the threat passed well before most of these projects came on line. The goal was far more ambitious than previous attempts to remove industry to the interior during a military crisis as the Third Front aimed to establish a comprehensive industrial sector from mining and electric power provision to metallurgy to machine building. Only 20 percent of Third Front investment went to specifically military industries. The rest was for transportation or dual-use industries such as steel making.

The program was too massive and ambitious, however. It would take too long to complete and would require more resources than China possessed at the time. It is furthermore doubtful that these installations were that much more protected than any other part of the country considering the developments in military technologies such as intercontinental ballistic missiles (ICBMs), long-range bombers, and nuclear weapons. In any case, much of this investment in China's defense was wasted and many projects were left uncompleted. Only one of the four large steel plants included in the Third Front was operating near capacity by the 1980s. In some locations, such as Wuyang, advanced equipment and skilled personnel were wasted because insufficient supplies of ore and poor transportation made the plant's efficient functioning impossible.

The total costs of the Third Front projects are still unknown, but it is clear that the central government invested tens of billions of yuan, most of it never recovered and left to rust in the form of disused or inefficient plants located in remote mountain valleys. According to Barry Naughton's estimates, China's industrial output in the 1980s was 10 to 15 percent below what it would have been if China's leaders had not pursued the Third Front policy.

Most economists similarly agree that the Third Front projects, in contrast with other efforts at developing inland industries, provided little or no benefit to the national economy. Not only were many projects abandoned before completion, they were often located in the most inaccessible areas, which prevented them from fostering the development of industries supplying inputs in the immediate neighborhood. For example, the construction of Number Two Auto in northwestern Hubei could have spawned a whole string of support industries. But the plant's remote location prevented it from serving as an engine for further industrialization. By the mid-1980s, this problem led to the removal of 121 factories (and their personnel) from their rural mountain locations to urban centers such as Chongqing.

Even the construction of a railway network in China's mountainous regions, perhaps the most positive legacy of the Third Front, exhibited many problems. Priority development of Third Front railway lines diverted resources for the maintenance and expansion of the rest of China's national rail network, and the costs per kilometer of track were five or six times higher than average. Nonetheless, the expansion of rail service to remote hinterland areas is one of the few positive legacies of this otherwise wasteful and misguided project.

Robert CLIVER

Further Reading

Bramall, C. (2003). Path dependency and growth in rural China since 1978. *Asian Business and Management, 2,* 301–321.

Naughton, B. (1988, September). The Third Front: Defense industrialization in the Chinese interior. *The China Quarterly, 115,* 351–386.

Naughton, B. (1991). Industrial policy during the Cultural Revolution: Military preparation, decentralization, and leaps forward. In W. Joseph, C. Wong, & D. Zweig, (Eds.). *New perspectives on the Cultural Revolution.* Cambridge, MA: Harvard University Press.

Dali Yang. (1990, June). Patterns of China's regional development strategy. *The China Quarterly, 122,* 230–257.

Thirteen Ming Tombs

Míng Shísānlíng 明十三陵

Built between 1409 and 1644, the Thirteen Ming Tombs is the largest imperial burial compound in the world, with thirteen emperors and twenty-three empresses entombed. Dingling 定陵, the only excavated mausoleum of the compound, is known as the Underground Palace. On display in the Palace are the emperor's intricately woven gold crown and the empress's phoenix crown laden with pearls and precious stones.

Situated in Tianshou Mountains (Heavenly Longevity 天寿山) in Beijing's northwestern suburb of Changping (Prosperity and Peacefulness, 昌平), the Thirteen Ming Tombs is the largest complex of imperial burial grounds in the world, covering an area of more than forty square kilometers (15 square miles).

Emperors' Resting Place

In these mausoleums, about fifty kilometers from Beijing, rest thirteen emperors, twenty-three empresses, two princes, more than thirty concubines, and one eunuch of the Ming dynasty (1368–1644). The construction of the mausoleums started with Changling (Perpetuity Mausoleum 长陵) in 1409 and ended with Siling (Remembrance Mausoleum 思陵) in 1644.

Of the sixteen Ming dynasty emperors, thirteen constructed their last dwellings in the Tianshou Mountains. The Thirteen Ming Tombs has the densest population of former emperors anywhere in the world.

Chronologically, the mausoleums and their respective emperor occupants are as follows:

1 Changling 长陵 (Emperor Chengzu 成祖)
2 Xianling 献陵 (Renzhong 仁宗)
3 Jingling 景陵 (Xuanzong 宣宗)
4 Yuling 裕陵 (Yingzong 英宗)
5 Maoling 茂陵 (Xianzong 宪宗)
6 Tailing 泰陵 (Xiaozong 孝宗)
7 Kangling 康陵 (Wuzong 武宗)
8 Yongling 永陵 (Shizong 世宗)
9 Zhaoling 昭陵 (Muzong 穆宗)
10 Dingling 定陵 (Shenzong 神宗)
11 Qingling 庆陵 (Guangzong 光宗)
12 Deling 德陵 (Xizong 熹宗)
13 Siling 思陵 (Sizong 思宗)

Architectural Wonder

Closely observing Chinese feng shui guidelines, architects of the Ming mausoleums sought harmony between architecture and nature, and between Heaven and human. Each mausoleum stands by a mountain, which enabled the builders to integrate the mountain landscape with the underground space of the mausoleum. Each mausoleum is square in the front and circular in the back, corresponding to the ancient Chinese concept of "circular heaven and square earth."

Listed as a United Nations Educational, Scientific, and Cultural Organization (UNESCO) World Heritage Site in 2000, the Thirteen Ming Tombs is a popular tourist attraction. To date, only two of the mausoleums have been opened to visitors: Changling and Dingling (Stability Mausoleum), the latter being the only excavated mausoleum of the complex.

About 120,000 square meters (100,890 square yards), Changling is the mausoleum of Chengzu, the third emperor of the Ming Dynasty, and his Empress Xu. As the first mausoleum built in the complex, Changling is the centerpiece of the Ming tombs. A ruler for twenty-two years, Chengzu started constructing the mausoleum in the sixth year of his rule and saw it completed five years later. With walls, gates, buildings for ceremonies, security, storage, and cooking, the mausoleum looked like a functional small imperial palace. Its layout influenced the designs of other mausoleums in the years that followed.

Marble Gateway, the entrance to the mausoleums, was added as part of Changling in 1540. On the grand five-arched Gateway are carved auspicious symbols such as dragons, clouds, lions, and *qilin* (a mythical animal). Changling's ten-kilometer-long (6 miles) Divine Path 神路 has served as the main path to all the mausoleums. It is flanked by twenty-four stone sculptures of animals and twelve stone sculptures of imperial officials. To the left of the Divine Path stands the Dragon Hill while the Tiger Hill crouches on the right, matching the Daoist preference in placing dragons on the left and tigers on the right for beneficial positioning.

While each mausoleum has a Ling'en Hall (Hall of Most Imminent Favor) for memorial services, Changling's Ling'en Hall is exceedingly magnificent, measuring 1,956 square meters (1,644 square yards), almost as large as Taihe Hall (Supreme Harmony 太和殿), the largest structure at 2,377 square meters (1,997 square yards) in the Forbidden City, where emperors met their ministers to discuss state affairs. Most impressive in the hall are the thirty-two precious nanmu wood pillars with diameters up to 1.12 meters (4 feet). These majestic one-piece wood pillars came from nanmu trees that grew in China's southwest. They are even more precious today, as no one is able to find nanmu trees of similar sizes any more. During the Ming and Qing dynasties, Changling's Ling'en Hall was the designated location where shrines of deceased emperors and empresses stood and where emperors held memorial services for family members.

Located at the foot of Zi Jin Shan (Purple & Golden Mountain) in an eastern suburb of Nanjing, Jiangsu Province, these two elephants guard the Sacred Way that leads to the Tomb of the first Ming Dynasty Emperor Hongwu (reigned 1368–1398) and Empress Ma. Nanjing was the capital of Ming China during this period. PHOTO BY JOAN LEBOLD COHEN.

Kneeling Camel sculpture, one of a pair of the guardians along the Sacred Way, the path leading to the Ming Tombs that lie in a valley outside of Beijing. The Sacred Way is lined with many animal and human guardian couples on both sides of the road, to repel evil spirits from entry to the imperial tombs. PHOTO BY JOAN LEBOLD COHEN.

Dingling Mausoleum

In power for forty-eight years (1572–1620), Dingling's occupant Shenzong was the longest ruling emperor of the Ming dynasty. It took six years to build the mausoleum of 182,000 square meters (152,941 square yards) at the cost of over eight million ounces of silver—the equivalent to two years' taxes collected by the central government. Excavation of Dingling, which lasted from May 1956 to July 1958, unveiled the mystery that had shrouded the mausoleums. An all-stone underground palace lies 17 meters (56 feet) below the ground. The underground vault, free of beams and pillars, is 87.34 meters (287 feet) long and 47.28 meters (155 feet) wide, divided into five halls with a total area of 1,195 square meters (1,004 square feet).

In the central hall are three thrones for the emperor and his two empresses, all carved out of stone. Images of dragons are carved on the emperor's throne while those of phoenixes are on the empresses' thrones. In front of each throne is a large porcelain container, originally filled with oil, which was meant to provide lighting for the emperor and the empresses.

The three coffins are placed in the rear hall. Twenty-six wood trunks, lacquered in red and filled with sacrificial objects, lie next to the coffins. Among the more than three thousand unearthed artifacts are the emperor's 24-centimeter-high gold crown with images of two dragons at play, which is woven with extremely fine gold thread, and the empress's phoenix crown, adorned with 3,500 pearls and 150 precious stones.

Jian-Zhong LIN

Further Reading

Paludan, A. (1981). *The imperial Ming tombs.* New Haven, CT: Yale University Press.

Paludan, A. (1991). *The Ming tombs.* New York: Oxford University Press.

Yu, C. (Ed.). (1999). *Great sites of Beijing.* Beijing: Beijing Arts and Crafts Publishing House.

Three and Five Antis Campaigns

Sānfǎn Wǔfǎn 三反五反

The Chinese Communist Party's Three Antis Campaign of 1951–1952 targeted waste, corruption, and bureaucratism. The party's Five Antis Campaign, launched soon afterward, targeted bribery, tax evasion, theft of state assets, cheating on government contracts, and theft of capital. Both campaigns led to mass suicides, as well as placing many hitherto private industries in the hands of the government.

In the early years after the People's Republic of China was founded in 1949, the Chinese Communist Party (CCP) launched two political campaigns to reinforce party control over the population over 1951–1952. Both campaigns targeted mainly urban dwellers and people who worked in the modern business sector.

First, the CCP launched the Three Antis Campaign against waste, corruption, and bureaucratism. The campaign targeted cadres in industry and government, especially those who had become (or were thought to have become) overly acquainted with China's capitalists. Second, the party launched the Five Antis Campaign against bribing, evading taxes, stealing state assets (that is, state property and economic information), cheating on government contracts, and stealing capital. This campaign

targeted capitalists themselves. Some of the blacklisted capitalists were left to function as government employees; many were simply eliminated and disappeared. Estimates vary, but it is thought that upwards of 200,000 disgraced or displaced people committed suicide during the two campaigns (Chow 1980, 115 and 133, quoted in MacFarquhar 1997, 37).

The Five Antis Campaign also had a hidden agenda: It seized factories and capital from the blacklisted capitalists and placed them under government control. Through these efforts the CCP expanded its influence over China's modern economic sectors. At the same time the campaign helped the party to identify people who could be recruited into the party, thereby consolidating the party's grip over every aspect of Chinese society. Between 1947 and 1953 membership of the CCP increased from 2.7 million to 6.1 million.

Stephanie CHUNG

Further Reading

Chow Ching-wen. (1960). *Ten years of storm: The true story of the Communist regime in China*. New York: Holt, Rinehart and Winston.

Goldman, M. (1981). *China's intellectuals: Advice and dissent*. Cambridge, MA: Harvard University Press.

MacFarquhar, R. (1997). *The politics of China: The eras of Mao and Deng*, 2nd ed. Cambridge, U.K.: Cambridge University Press.

Three Fundamental Bonds and Five Constant Virtues

Sāngāng Wǔcháng　三纲五常

The Three Fundamental Bonds and the Five Constant Virtues are separate Confucian terms for the most important human relations and social virtues. In early Confucianism, one who perfectly fulfilled these relationships and manifested these virtues was the highest form of human—a sage. The neo-Confucians combined these two terms into a single cosmological principle that stood for human social order.

The expression *Three Fundamental Bonds and Five Constant Virtues* sums up a Confucian doctrine that was designed to guide people's behavior and aspirations in traditional China. The Three Fundamental Bonds deal with traditional society's most fundamental social relationships: father and son, lord and retainer, and husband and wife. As essential relationships, these three serve as shorthand for all human relationships. The Five Constant Virtues mean the Confucian virtues of benevolence (*ren* 仁), righteousness (*yi* 義), propriety (*li* 義), wisdom (*zhi* 智), and trustworthiness (*xin* 信). As with the Fundamental Bonds, these five virtues are the most significant ones and thus serve as shorthand for all the Confucian virtues. In other words, the Three Fundamental Bonds designate the social relationships that are essential for structuring human social life, while the Five Constant Virtues are the values needed to live a moral life.

For late imperial neo-Confucians the Three Fundamental Bonds and Five Constant Virtues (*sangang wuchang* 三纲五常), or the shorter Bonds and Constants (*gangchang*), was the heart of Confucianism. Zhu Xi 朱熹 (1130–1200), the great synthesizer of Neo-Confucian thought, criticized the teachings of Buddhism and Daoism in the following manner:

> [It] is unnecessary to analyze them to understand that they both abandon the Three [Fundamental Bonds] and Five Constant Virtues. Just this one [omission] earns them a reputation for committing a grave crime. It is unnecessary to say anything else about them.

In other words, if a teaching did not promote the Fundamental Bonds and constant virtues, then not only was it of no account, but, even worse, it was guilty of promoting disorder. Zhu Xi believed that humans could become sages by perfecting these three relationships and realizing these five virtues. Interestingly though, in terms of China's long history, these concepts of the Three Fundamental Bonds and the Five Constant Virtues did not have an ancient pedigree: they were creations and expressions of the unified Han empire (206 BCE–220 CE). Hence, one could cynically argue that the guides and virtues were Confucianism in the service of the state. The full four-character term *sangang wuchang* was not commonly used until the tenth century CE.

Three Fundamental Bonds

Searching the Confucian classics for a reference to the Three Fundamental Bonds, one encounters Confucius's conditions for a well-ordered society: "Let the lord be lordly, the retainer loyal, the father fatherly, and the son sonly" (*Analects* 12.11, *Lúnyǔ* 論語). Here though, Confucius presents only two relationships: lord and retainer, and father and son. In the *Mencius* (*Mèngzǐ* 孟子) one finds five rather than three principal human relationships (*renlun* 人倫); moreover, the text stresses their reciprocal basis: "Father and son have love [for each other]; lord and retainer have obligations [to each other]; husband and wife have distinct [spheres]; senior and junior have precedence; and friends have faith [in each other]" (*Mencius* 3A.4). Although clearly a strong sense of hierarchy pervades each set of relationships, both Confucius and Mencius underscore that everyone, whether a superior or an inferior, has obligations to properly fulfill his or her role. As the Confucian scholar Hsü Dau-lin has pointed out, the first text that more overtly promotes what would become the Three Fundamental Bonds is one of the later chapters of the Legalist text written by Han Fei Zi 韓非子. The chapter, which probably dates from the beginning of the unified Han empire, states: "A retainer serves his lord; a son serves his father; a wife serves her husband. If these three principles are followed, then all-under-Heaven is well-governed; if these three principles are betrayed, then all-under-Heaven is in chaos" (Chapter 51). What is striking is that no mention is made of mutual obligations.

The first person to label these relationships was Dong Zhongshu 董仲舒 (197–104 BCE), the great Han dynasty Confucian philosopher and statesman. Dong called them the Three Cardinal Guides or Bonds (*sangang*). For him, these relationships are not social constructions; instead, they are natural expressions of the cosmological principles of yin and yang. He tells us in *The History of the Han* (*Han shu* 漢書):

> The lord is *yang* 陽, the retainer is *yin* 陰; the father is *yang*, the son is *yin*; the husband is *yang,* the wife is *yin*. The way of *yin* cannot proceed anywhere on its own. . . . Therefore, the retainer depends on his lord to gain merit; the son depends on his father; the wife on her husband, *yin* on *yang,* and the Earth on Heaven. . . . The Three [Fundamental Bonds] of the kingly way can be sought in Heaven. (Chapter 53)

Since for Dong yang is superior to yin, lords are superior to their retainers, fathers to their sons, and the

The three-year-old Prince Bu Yi, throne name Xuantong, on the right. On the left is his father, Prince Zhun, the Regent, holding a younger brother, 1909. The Confucian influence of the Three Cardinal rules applied even to the highest levels of Chinese society. LIBRARY OF CONGRESS.

husband to his wife. In other words, Dong accepts Han Fei Zi's formulation of these relationships as entirely vertical and one sided. That Dong was living in a centralized empire and serving a powerful monarch undoubtedly helps explain his view.

The most extensive formulation of the concept behind the Three Fundamental Bonds is found in *Baihutong* 白虎 ("Comprehensive Discussions in the White Tiger Hall") by Ban Gu 班固 (32–92 CE). The book devotes an entire chapter to a discussion of this notion. Interestingly though, here the Three Fundamental Bonds are not matched up with the Five Constant Virtues but rather with the Six Rules (*Liuji* 六紀), which are relations with one's paternal uncles, brothers, clansmen, maternal uncles, teachers, and friends. The Three Fundamental Bonds and Six Rules thereby incorporate all the most important social relationships that constitute society. Without them society falls apart. This same book tells us: "In past times, the Three Fundamental Bonds and the Six Rules did not yet exist; as a result, people only knew the identity of their mother, not their father" (Chapter 2). That is to say, without these fundamental relationships, civilized social order cannot exist.

The Five Constant Virtues

Even though the Five Constant Virtues (benevolence, righteousness, propriety, wisdom, and trustworthiness) were articulated as such only in the Han dynasty, the idea of five interrelated virtues appears earlier. The fourth-century BCE Confucian text known as the *Wuxing* 五行 ("Five Types of Action") argues that there are five types of favorable behavior: benevolence, righteousness, propriety, wisdom, and sagacity (*sheng* 聖). The person who harmonizes and enacts four of these actions, is good. The person who realizes all five of these actions is a sage (*shengren* 聖人), in accord with heaven. Here, four of the Five Constant Virtues are articulated, and sagacity substitutes for trustworthiness. The *Mencius* sets forth four of Five Constant Virtues, leaving out sagacity. In an argument about whether human nature is intrinsically good, Mencius notes: "Benevolence, righteousness, propriety, and wisdom are not welded onto me from the outside. They are that which I have always had" (*Mencius* 6A.6). In other words, these four virtues are inherent in all people.

Once again, Dong Zhongshu, the Confucian statesman and philosopher, was the first person to unambiguously use the term *wuchang* to designate the Five Constant Virtues. He relates:

> Benevolence, righteousness, propriety, wisdom, and trustworthiness—i.e., the Way of the Five Constant Virtues—should be that which the king cultivates. If the king cultivates the Five Constant Virtues, then he will receive blessings from Heaven and will enjoy the spiritual efficacy of the spirits; moreover, his virtue will extend across the world and will reach all creatures. (*The History of the Han* 56.2504)

Many scholars believe that Dong added the fifth virtue, trustworthiness, to Mencius's four-virtue formulation so that it would be in accord with the Five Phase (*wuxing*) cosmological theory that was in vogue during the Han dynasty.

The *Baihutong* provides the first extensive discussion of the Five Constant Virtues. It states:

> What are the Five Constant Virtues? They are benevolence, righteousness, propriety, wisdom, and trustworthiness. Benevolence means not being able to endure (seeing others suffer), loving others, and aiding all living things. Righteousness means doing what is proper. In making judgments one hits the mark. Propriety means to enact. That is, to realize the way and perfect the refined. Wisdom means knowledge. One has a special understanding and can know things before hearing about them. He is not befuddled by matters and can discern the subtle. Trustworthiness means sincerity. One cannot be deterred from his purpose. Therefore, people are born and respond to the Eight Trigrams, thereby obtaining the five energies (qi 氣) that are the Constant Virtues. (Chapter 30)

In other words, the five virtues are inherent in us and consist of qi (energy, ether, psychophysical matter). The *Baihutong* further equates the Five Constant Virtues with the Five Viscera; hence, benevolence resides in the liver, righteousness in the lungs, propriety in the heart, wisdom in the kidneys, and trustworthiness in the spleen. Similarly, because of the existence of the Five Constant Virtues, there are also the Five Musical Notes, the Five Classics, and the Five Cardinal Directions.

The Neo-Confucian Interpretation

From the Han dynasty on, scholars and politicians made frequent mention of the Three Fundamental Bonds and Five Constant Virtues, but usually separately, not together. However, by the Song dynasty (960–1279), these two lists were often fused. In fact, for Zhu Xi, the Three

Fundamental Bonds and Five Constant Virtues became cosmological principles:

> Within the cosmos there is but one eternal principle. Heaven, by getting hold of it, becomes heaven. Earth, by getting hold of it, becomes earth. All things which live between heaven and earth, by getting hold of it, become what they are. Expanded, it becomes the "three bonds." Elaborated, it becomes the "five constants." All these are this principle in operation. Wherever one goes, it is there. (Hsü, 1970–71, 32)

Rather than naming humankind as the third element of the cosmos (which is the common formulation), Zhu Xi puts the Three Fundamental Bonds and Five Constant Virtues in that place. Hence, heaven, earth, and the Three Fundamental Bonds and Five Constant Virtues compose the universe. Clearly these human relationships and virtues were the most important characteristics of mankind. Chen Chun (1159–1223), Zhu Xi's student, thought that the Five Constant Virtues were so important that he devoted a whole chapter of his book *Beixi ziyi* 北溪字義 (Neo-Confucian Terms Explained) to explaining them. He believed that all good stemmed from these virtues: "Generally speaking, in human nature there are only the four virtues of humanity, righteousness, propriety, and wisdom. All the ten thousand good deeds are produced from them. In reality, they are a summary of the ten thousand good deeds" (Chan 1986, p. 85). Goodness is born out of these virtues, so to become a sage it is essential that one practices them. Likewise, since the Three Fundamental Bonds constitute the most significant human relationships, Zhu Xi believed that perfecting them would also lead to sagacity. As Hsü Dau-lin indicates, though, in making the Three Fundamental Bonds a cosmological principle, the neo-Confucians enshrined the guides' emphasis on the hierarchical rather than the reciprocal duties inherent in the relationships. As a consequence, Zhu Xi stressed that parents could never be wrong, while another neo-Confucian philosopher, Cheng Yi (1034–1106), emphasized that a woman could never remarry.

By late imperial times, the Three Fundamental Bonds and Five Constant Virtues had been transformed from being general Confucian concepts about social structure and virtues to being a specific term that designated all social relationships and values and, by extension, human social order itself. To not adhere to these Confucian norms and virtues was to threaten both social and cosmological order. Hence, particularly in the late imperial period, Three Fundamental Bonds and Five Constant Virtues was a concept of immense significance.

Keith N. KNAPP

Further Reading

Ames, R. T. & H. Rosemont, Jr. (1998). *The analects of Confucius.* New York: Ballantine Books.

Chan Wing-tsit. (Trans. & Ed.). (1986). Neo-Confucian terms explained. (The *Pei-his tzu-i*) by Ch'en Ch'un, 1159–1223. New York: Columbia University Press.

Csikszentmihalyi, M. (2004). *Material virtue: Ethics and the body in early China.* Leiden, The Netherlands: Brill.

Fung, Yu-lan. (1953). *A history of Chinese philosophy: Volume II The period of classical learning.* D. Bodde (Trans.). Princeton, NJ: Princeton University Press.

Holloway, K. (2005). The five aspects of conduct: Introduction and translation. *Journal of the Royal Asiatic Society 12*(2), 17–198.

Hsü Dau-lin. (1970–71). The myth of the "Five Human Relations" of Confucius. *Monumenta Serica, 29*, 27–37.

Lau, D. C. (1970). *Mencius.* London & New York: Penguin Books.

Som, Tjan Tjoe. (1949). *Po Hu T'ung: The comprehensive discussions in the White Tiger Hall.* 2v. Leiden, The Netherlands: Brill.

Svarverud, R. (1998). *Methods of the way: Early Chinese ethical thought.* Leiden, The Netherlands: Brill.

Tu, Wei-ming. (1998). Probing the 'Three Bonds' and the 'Five Relationships' in Confucian Humanism. In W. H. Slote and G. A. DeVos, (Eds.), *Confucianism and the Family* (pp.121–36). Albany: State University of New York Press.

Three Gorges Dam

Chángjiāng Sānxiá Dàbà　长江三峡大坝

The Three Gorges Dam project, the world's largest engineering venture, will harness the mighty Yangzi (Chang) River and supply China much needed hydroelectric power. But the costs of the project—financial, environmental, political, and cultural—have many people questioning its true worth to China and the world.

The Three Gorges Dam project is the world's largest engineering feat and the largest in China since the building of the Great Wall. Electricity generated by the dam will meet almost 10 percent of China's requirements. But the project has forced the relocation of 1.3 million people, drowned valuable farmland, and destroyed ancient settlements of historical and cultural importance. Declining water quality resulting from submerged industrial sites, increased landslide risk, biodiversity decline, and accumulating silt are unresolved problems. The full impact of the dam on China is yet to be realized.

Old Dream

For centuries Chinese emperors and dictators dreamed of building a great wall across the Yangzi (Chang) River. This cradle of Chinese civilization originates in perpetual snows of the lofty Qinghai–Tibet Plateau. It flows southward across treeless plains before dropping 4,000 meters (13,123 feet) into the deep valleys that separate Sichuan from Tibet. Near Yibin the river enters the fertile Sichuan Basin, where the Minjiang, Tuojiang, Jialing, and Wujiang Rivers—just four of more than seven hundred tributaries—swell its size. Beyond the industrial city of Chongqing, the Yangzi slices through limestone strata of the Wushan Mountains to create a spectacular 200-kilometer (124-mile) section of narrow and precipitous gorges: Qutang, Wuxia, and Xiling. Beyond these celebrated Three Gorges, the river spills onto the fertile Yangzi Plain at Yichang and meanders to the Pacific Ocean. At 6,276 kilometers (3,900 miles), the Yangzi is China's longest river and the third longest in the world, behind the Nile and Amazon. The watershed covers 19 percent of China's total landmass.

As one of Asia's most emblematic landscapes, the Three Gorges of the Yangzi River figure prominently in Chinese cultural lore. Although local water diversions date to the Han dynasty (206 BCE–220 CE), modern China's revolutionary founder, Sun Yat-sen, first proposed damming the river in 1919. During the 1940s the United States Bureau of Reclamation cooperated with the Chinese to explore potential dam sites and evaluate costs and benefits. The Chinese civil war (1945–1949) derailed these plans until the 1950s, when the victorious Mao Zedong, leader of the Chinese Communist Party, revived the idea, although political and economic problems again trumped construction. In 1992, with the urging of Chinese Premier Li Peng, a trained engineer, the National People's Congress approved the plans by the smallest margin in the history of that normally compliant legislative body. Construction on the $25 billion project started in 1994 at a site below the Three Gorges in central Hubei Province.

A view of the Three Gorges Dam, the world's largest feat of engineering, which will supply China with much-needed hydroelectric power when fully operational in 2009.

The World Bank declined support, citing major environmental and human rights concerns. The closing of diversion gates in 2006 promoted nationalistic pride. The government predicts that the full hydropower complex will operate by 2009.

The concrete gravity dam at Three Gorges is the world's largest engineering feat and the largest in China since the Great Wall. It consumed record amounts of soil, steel, and concrete. It also forced relocation of a record 1.3 million people. The project continues to generate unprecedented domestic and international controversy, fanned by the concurrent evolution of digital communications and emerging supranational environmentalism. The controversy stems from environmental and human rights concerns.

Environmental Challenges

Declining water quality in the Three Gorges Reservoir quickly emerged as a major problem. The rising waters submerged 1,600 industrial enterprises (factories, mines, and waste dumps) that retained tons of unmitigated hazardous waste and other pollutants. Added to this waste is ongoing waste from municipal, agricultural, and industrial enterprise that continues to flow unrestricted into the reservoir. Whereas the free-flowing Yangzi once diluted and transported pollutants downstream, trapped chemicals now trigger algal blooms that contaminate municipal drinking water and kill fish. A recent bloom in Fengdu County, for example, tainted domestic water for fifty thousand people.

Landslides are another major problem. The rising waters exert pressure on unstable hillsides that encircle the 5,300-kilometer (3,293-mile) shoreline. Seepage into rock joints weakens the steep slopes. Hundreds of slides occur each month, although Chinese officials overseeing the project insist the new reservoir does not promote instability. In 2007 a landslide just upstream from the Three Gorges Dam crushed railroad workers and a bus, killing more than thirty people. More slides are expected as the reservoir rises to a maximum expected height of 175 meters (574 feet) in 2012.

Trapped silt behind the static reservoir waters presents two problems. Silt deposited during floods in the lower Yangzi Basin now settles in the reservoir floor. Accumulating silt is already reducing the hydropower capacity of tributary dam projects, and planners expect sedimentation to become an issue within twenty years near the city of Chongqing at the upper end of the reservoir. Furthermore, although the dam should reduce catastrophic downstream flooding, it will also block much of the silt that has enriched the lowland soils for centuries and was the source material for the natural levee system.

As a result agricultural productivity in the lower Yangzi basin may suffer from the loss of flood-deposited silt.

Scientists are also monitoring riparian (relating to the bank of a natural watercourse) and aquatic biodiversity loss resulting from the changes in the flood regime, water temperature, and water chemistry.

The potential for an earthquake-induced failure of the dam itself also exists although the dam has been build to withstand large earthquakes. The dam survived the massive 7.9 Richter scale quake in May 2008 and the subsequent aftershocks. But there is some speculation that the dam itself may have caused the quake. A phenomenom known as reservoir-induced seismicity occurs when the sheer weight of water in a reservoir causes tetonic plates to shift, resulting in an earthquake.

Human Cost

The Three Gorges reservoir inundated 17 cities, 109 towns, and more than 1,500 villages, forcing permanent relocation of a 1.3 million people. Resettlement began in 1997 and is four times greater than any prior infrastructure resettlement program in world history. The government was not prepared to manage or mitigate the three-pronged humanitarian crisis resulting from forced displacement, labor dislocations, and the more recent unanticipated dislocation of people fleeing landslides. Moreover, this ancient and densely populated land offered few places for resettlement, especially of farmers, who comprised half the number. As population density in resettlement zones increased to double the national average, farmers pushed higher into steep and less fertile hillsides where forest clearing contributed to slope instability. Resettled people had little involvement in policymaking and relocation decisions. Many were forced to change livelihood and move far away from their former homes. Those resettled face unemployment and poverty rates higher than those of people who were not removed, and one-third live in severe poverty. Insufficient government compensation for this loss of land and livelihood is magnifying the crisis although an effective state security apparatus minimized both refugee flight and

Boats on the river at the Three Gorges Dam, which forced the resettlement of more than 1.3 million people.

vocal resistance. In 2007 the Chongqing municipal government decided to relocate an additional 4 million people as a result of new slope instability problems.

The reservoir is also destroying thousands of cultural and archaeological sites, including temples, hanging tombs, and historic landmarks. Evidence of human habitation in the area dates to the Paleolithic era (2 million–10,000 BCE). Many sites in newly depopulated areas are looted before underfunded government teams arrive to catalog and remove the artifacts.

Benefits versus Risks

The government believes that the benefits of the Three Gorges Dam exceed the environmental and social challenges. When the twenty-six generators reach full operational capacity in 2009, the 8,200 megawatts of power will meet almost 10 percent of current Chinese requirements and be the largest source of clean, renewable energy in the world. It may also temporarily curb the millennia-old problem of downstream flooding, such as the 1998 event that killed thousands. The placid reservoir now allows 10,000-metric ton freighters to safely navigate 2,250 kilometers (1,398 miles) inland from Shanghai, free of the treacherous shoals and strong currents of the once-untamed Yangzi River.

The project gave birth to a nascent Chinese environmental movement. An unexpected twist occurred in June 2007 when Chinese Premier Wen Jiabao publicly announced that solving the environmental problems created by the Three Gorges Dam should be a national priority. It remains to be seen how the government and the Chinese people will adjust to the economic, environmental, and social changes—good and bad—of the world's largest engineering project.

Stephen F. CUNHA

Further Reading

Dai Qing, Thibodeau, J., & Williams, P. (Eds.). (1997). *The river dragon has come: The Three Gorges Dam and the fate of China's Yangtze River and its people* (Ming Yi, Trans.). Armonk, NY: M. E. Sharpe.

Heggelund, G. (2004). *Environment and resettlement politics in China: The Three Gorges project.* Surrey, U.K.: Ashgate Publishing.

Heggelund, G. (2006). Resettlement programmes and environmental capacity in the Three Gorges Dam project. *Development and Change (37)*1, 179–199.

Stone, R. (2008). China's environmental challenges: Three Gorges Dam: Into the unknown. *Science* 321: 5889, 628–632.

Zorn, B. (2006). *Three Gorges.* [Photographs]. St. Simon' Island, GA: Flat Edge Press.

Three Obediences and the Four Virtues

Sāncóng Sìdé 三从四德

The Three Obediences and the Four Virtues describe precepts for womanly behavior that derive from Confucian ideals of harmony and order. The first century CE book *Lessons for Women* states that the proper role of a woman is to be a submissive daughter, wife, and mother who restrains her speech, dresses in a pleasing manner, and manages her household.

The role and function of women in Chinese society has long been defined by the Confucian moral precept of the Three Obediences, or Submissions, and the Four Virtues. The Three Obediences seek to give stricture to the entirety of a woman's existence, and accordingly state that the woman, in her youth, should be obedient to her father and her older brothers; in married life, she should be obedient to her husband; and as a widow she should be obedient to her son. The Four Virtues, on the other hand, impart rules of propriety, whereby a woman may be able to govern her life and her conduct. The first virtue is the ability of a woman to know and adhere to a submissive place in society and to modulate her behavior accordingly. The second virtue consists of restraining speech, since a talkative woman is not only considered impolite but even tiresome. The third virtue instructs a woman to dress and adorn herself in order to please a man. The last virtue states that a woman must know the proper management of her household and she must cheerfully do all the work needed in the home.

Origins

The idea of defining and instilling a mode of conduct for women may be traced back to the first half of the Han Dynasty (206 BCE–220 CE), during which time the scholar Dong Zongshu (179–104 BCE), who was instrumental in making Confucianism the state religion, formulated his Three Cardinal Guides and Five Constant Virtues, through which he sought to describe the ethical relationship that existed between humankind and heaven. The Three Guides consisted of axiomatic formulations on the proper correlation between the individual and institutional power. Thus it was stated that (1) a prince was the guide of his ministers; (2) the father was the guide of his sons; and (3) the husband was the guide of the wife. These Three Cardinal Guides led to the Five Constant Virtues, which consisted of mercy, correctness, propriety, wisdom, and trustworthiness. The guarantor of both the Virtues and the Guides was heaven itself, which required obedience in order to ensure that human society functioned well, and in order to bring about a consistent ethical balance, or harmony, in the world. Therefore, to go against the Virtues and the Guides was to go against the will of heaven itself. For women, the stipulation of being obedient to the husband meant that the state of being a mother and a wife was deemed the highest achievement, which brought about an ethical stability of sorts, in which all persons knew their place in society.

The perception of women as wives and mothers is intimately related to the Confucian understanding of the two essential principles that govern both the world and the universe: the yin–yang (shady/sunny), and the *nei–wai* (inner/outer). Care must be taken to ensure that these principles are not interpreted as mutually exclusive or even oppositional; rather, they are to be seen as complementary opposites, in that the one principle finds completion in the other; nor can the one exist without the other or come into a position of dominance; and both are required to achieve harmony and balance. Whereas the yin–yang principle defines the characteristics of men and women, the *nei–wai* elaborates the realm in which each of them functions.

The Four Books for Women

It was within this Confucian context that the earliest woman historian of China, Ban Zhao (45–116 CE), composed her small but influential book *Lessons for Women*, in which she expounded the precept of the Three Obediences and the Four Virtues. The book received wide acclaim and was often entirely memorized by women to serve as a convenient vade mecum (Latin for "manual") of proper behavior and comportment. The book consists of seven chapters: "Humility," in which the female is described as being humble by nature; "Husband and Wife," in which a woman is instructed to do all she can to serve and attend to her husband; "Respect," in which a man is given the nature of hardness, while a woman is soft and yielding—therefore, a husband and wife are to treat each other with respect; "Female Virtues," in which the Four Virtues and their benefits are stipulated; "Devotion," in which a wife is advised to be entirely devoted to her husband; "Obedience," in which the Three Obediences are outlined and explained; "Harmony among Younger In-Laws," in which a wife is advised to work towards creating harmony among in-laws that are younger than she, as if she were their mother.

These various moral precepts sought to describe the ideal station for a woman in the world, namely, that of a wife and mother. Wisdom for a woman, therefore, resided in her ability to gain the knowledge that would ensure the achievement of her place in society. In other words, the realm of the woman was the house; that of men was the public sphere. But a woman did not naturally come by such domestic wisdom; she had to be taught it, just as men had to be taught the ways of the world. This brought about a concern to create and establish a system of education

for women that would inculcate in them the spirit and willingness to become good mothers and good wives. Indeed, it was argued that just as men brought order into the world, so women brought order into the family and to the house; and an orderly family led to an orderly society. By the time of the latter Ming period (1368–1644), a specialized educational system for women was firmly established. Just as men studied the Four Books (*The Analects, The Mencius, The Doctrine of the Great Mean,* and *The Great Learning*), women were provided with their own four books, the first of which is *Lessons for Women.* The other three are *The Women's Analect* by Song Ruoxin, the eldest of the famed Song sisters, in which the proper behavior of a woman is outlined: how she may educate

Historical illustration of a noblewoman who is a wife and mother. Her life would likely have been modeled after the Confucian ideals of Three Obediences, or Submissions (to the men in her life), and the Four Virtues (a code of moral conduct for women).

Historical illustration portraying the husband of a noblewoman. Women in China have historically been expected to obey the wishes of their husbands, fathers, brothers, and sons.

which would provide tangible examples which other women could imitate in order to become worthy themselves. However, these biographies of sorts do not simply relate the lives of good mothers and wives; rather, they show women involved in the entire breadth of Chinese society. For example, there are women who are both virtuous in the Confucian sense, as well as women who exist outside this traditional definition, namely, demonic and power-hungry women who act for their own benefit and advancement, and women who are skilled in debate, argumentation, and intellectual and cultural activities. Further, these biographies in no way show women to be docile creatures, who submit to the will of fathers, husbands, and then sons; rather, they show women who seek to fulfill their destinies as they will them to be, entirely outside the demands and wishes of men. Thus we read of women admonishing and shaming their husbands into action, of women defiantly mutilating their faces in order to avoid having to marrying a man they cannot respect or love. In effect, these biographies seek to define what the realm of a woman is in Chinese society; they do not seek to demarcate that realm. It may even be stated that when we read of such active and engaged women, we are being presented with the various possibilities available to them, rather than simply reading about the reification of the docile and submissive woman. But these examples may also be seen as the chaos that results when a woman does not follow the precepts that have been laid down for her.

Women and Universal Harmony

The Confucian ideal of womanhood was closely related to notions of order and disorder, in that personal behavior reflected universal harmony. Thus, a disobedient woman who acted without virtue created chaos in the sphere assigned to her, namely, the home; this chaos extended outwards to disrupt the world and society. Since women were inseparable from domesticity, they had no right to divorce or separate from a husband. But a husband could divorce his wife if she failed to obey and serve her in-laws, if she bore no son, if she talked too much, if she stole, if she was libidinous, or even if she became ill with some disease. The only time a husband could not divorce his wife was if he had married her when he was poor and had eventually

herself in womanly virtues, how she is to bring up her children, how she is to treat her husband and her in-laws, and how she is to observe the various religious rituals. Then, there is *Domestic Lessons,* written by the Empress Xu, wife of the Ming Emperor Ch'engtsu (1360–1424), in which the courtly behavior of women is delineated: the rules of proper conduct, the need for restraint and moderation, and the pursuit of those things that will bring honor in her dealings with those around her. Lastly, there is *The Traditions of Exemplary Women,* by Liu Xiang (77–6 BCE), in which the traditional Three Guides and the Five Virtues were made relevant to women living in the domestic sphere by way of examples drawn from the past.

The Traditions of Exemplary Women brought about a subgenre of books for women in which the lives of women deemed worthy were recounted, the reading of

Historical illustration of two Chinese girls caring for their younger siblings. Being a mother and wife was traditionally viewed as the highest achievement a woman could reach.

got rich, if she had given birth within a given year, if she had no family to return to, or if she had officially mourned the passing of one or both of her husband's parents.

The strength of this tradition is still prevalent in China, despite Maoist teachings to the contrary, and the old adage that men are in charge of external things and women are in charge of internal things is very much part of Chinese society.

Nirmal DASS

Further Reading

Ayscough, F. (1975). *Chinese women: Yesterday and today.* New York: Da Capo Press.

Behnke, K. A. (2003). *Lienü zhuan: The traditions of exemplary women.* Retrieved February 19, 2009, from http://www2.iath.virginia.edu/xwomen/

Bernhardt, K. (1999). *Women and property in China, 960–1949: Law, society, and culture in China.* Stanford, CA: Stanford University Press.

Cass, V. (1999). *Dangerous women, warriors, grannies and geishas of the Ming.* Lanham, MD: Rowman & Littlefield.

Chang, Pang-Mei Natasha. (1996). *Bound feet and western dress: A memoir.* New York: Doubleday & Company.

Chung, Priscilla Ching. (1981). *Palace women in the Northern Sung, 960–1126.* Leiden, The Netherlands: Brill.

Cole, R. A. (1998). *Mothers and sons in Chinese Buddhism.* Stanford, CA: Stanford University Press.

Croll, E. (1984). *Chinese women since Mao.* Armonk, NY: M. E. Sharpe.

Cusack, D. (1986). *Chinese women speak.* North Pomfret, VT: Trafalgar Square.

Davin, D. (1980). *Woman-work: Women and the Party in revolutionary China.* New York: Oxford University Press.

Ebrey, P. B. (1991). *Confucianism and family rituals in imperial China: A social history of writing about rites.* Princeton, NJ: Princeton University Press.

Ebrey, P. B. (1993). *The inner quarters: Marriage and the lives of Chinese women in the Sung period.* Berkeley: University of California Press.

Eunson, R. (1975). *The Soong sisters.* Danbury, CT: Franklin Watts.

Fan Hong. (1997). *Footbinding, feminism, and freedom: The liberation of women's bodies in modern China.* London: Frank Cass.

Gross, S. H. (1980). *Women in traditional China.* Saint Paul, MN: Upper Midwest Women's History Center.

Hoe, Susanna. (2001). *Chinese footprints: Exploring women's history in China, Hong Kong and Macau.* Hong Kong: Roundhouse Publications.

Jaschok, M. (1988). *Concubines and bondservants: The social history of a Chinese custom.* London: Zed Books.

Johnson, K. A. (1985). *Women, the family and peasant revolution in China.* Chicago: University of Chicago Press.

Ko, Dorothy. (1994). *Teachers of the inner chambers: Women and culture in seventeenth-century China.* Stanford, CA: Stanford University Press.

Kristeva, J. (1986). *About Chinese women* (A. Barrows, Trans.). New York: Marion Boyars. (Original work published 1977)

Ling, Amy. (1990). *Between worlds: Women of Chinese ancestry.* New York: Teachers College Press.

Lee Yao, Esther S. (1983). *Chinese women: Past and present.* Irving, TX: Ide House.

Lee, Lily. (1994). *The virtue of yin: Essays on Chinese women.* Honolulu: University of Hawaii Press.

Tsai, Kathryn A. (1994). *Lives Of the nuns: Biographies of Chinese Buddhist nuns from the fourth to sixth centuries.* Honolulu: University of Hawaii Press.

TIAN Han

Tián Hàn 田汉

1898–1968   Dramatist

Tian Han was a founder of the Chinese spoken drama (*huaju* 话剧) and a prolific writer who produced a large body of plays, operas, and film scripts. His death during the Cultural Revolution 文化大革命 (1966–1976) represented the tragic fate of many Chinese intellectuals caught up in this political upheaval.

Tian Han 田汉 was a founder of the Chinese spoken drama (*huaju* 话剧) movement, a reformer of traditional Chinese opera, and a playwright with more than sixty spoken dramas and twenty operas to his credit. He was also a pioneer in China's film industry as well as a poet, best remembered for the lyrics he wrote to *March of the Volunteers,* which became the national anthem of the People's Republic of China.

A native of Hunan Province, Tian Han followed the trend of his time to study in Japan. During his stay in Japan from 1916 to 1921 Tian discovered the works of many Western dramatists, which inspired him to devote his life to drama. In 1921 he and his fellow students, Guo Moruo 郭沫若 and Yu Dafu 郁达夫, established the Creation Society (*Chuangzao She* 创造社) to promote romanticism in literature and the arts.

His Early Plays: In Search of the Self

After his return to Shanghai in 1922, Tian Han organized the Southern Drama Society (*Nanguo She* 南国社), which became an important training school for actors as well as a production company for the performance of modern plays, including Tian's own works. Representative plays of his early period, *Night in a Café* (*Kafei dian zhi yiye,* 咖啡店之夜, 1922), *The Night a Tiger Was Captured* (*Huo hu zhi ye,* 获虎之夜, 1924), and *Death of a Famous Artist* (*Mingyou zhi si* 名优之死, 1927), all deal with adverse effects of social environment on love and artistic fulfillment. They also reflect Tian's own search for the meaning of life and art.

His Proletarian Dramas: Art to Serve Politics

His agonized search ended in 1930 with publication of his article "Our Self-Criticism" (*Women de ziwo piping* 我们的自我批评), in which he criticizes the petty bourgeois sentiments in his and other dramatists' writings. In the same year he joined the League of Left Wing Writers. These events marked a turning point in his career. The romantic tone of his early plays would be replaced by realism; his belief in art for art's sake would shift to that of art serving political goals; and his Southern Drama Society would henceforth produce proletarian dramas. During the War of Resistance against Japan (1937–1945, known outside of China as the Second Sino-Japanese War and fought in the context of World War II) Tian Han wrote a number of patriotic plays such as *The Song of Beautiful Women* (*Liren xing* 丽人行, 1947), which depicts the suffering of the Chinese people under Japanese occupation. He also tried to reform traditional opera by incorporating modern stage techniques and injecting new meaning into old plays. In his Beijing Opera (Jingju, a style of opera known for its spare stage sets evoking the Ming dynasty) adaptation of *The Legend of the White Snake* (*Baishe zhuan* 白蛇传, 1950), for example, the "snake monster" is transformed into a brave young woman who fights for her right to love and happiness.

His Historical Plays: Using the Past to Criticize the Present

After the founding of the People's Republic of China in 1949, Tian Han's creative output decreased, but he did produce two historical dramas worthy of note: the spoken drama *Guan Hanqing* 关汉卿 (1958) and the Beijing Opera *Xie Yaohuan* 谢瑶环 (1961). The first play tells the story of the Yuan dynasty (1279–1368) dramatist Guan Hanqing, who wrote the play *Injustice Done to Dou E* (*Dou E yuan* 窦娥怨) about a young woman wrongly accused of murder by corrupt officials. The courageous Guan who spoke out for the people could be Tian Han's self-image, and the oppressive rule of the Mongols depicted in the play could also be a reflection of the current situation in China. In *Xie Yaohuan,* Tian Han created another character who dared to speak out for the people—a woman official in the court of Empress Wu Zetian of the Tang dynasty (618–907 CE).

Tian Han's use of the past to criticize the present (*iie gu feng jin* 借古讽今) was, of course, recognized by the authorities. After the outbreak of the Cultural Revolution (1966–1976), a political campaign launched by Mao Zedong against his enemies, Tian was arrested and died in prison in 1968. Like many other writers and artists who perished during this upheaval, Tian Han became a victim of the Communist revolution that he had supported for forty years.

Shiao-ling YU

Further Reading

Chen Xiaomei. (2006). Reflections on the legacy of Tian Han: 'Proletarian modernism' and its traditional roots. *Modern Chinese Literature and Culture, 18*(1), 155–215.

Dong Jian. (1996). *Tian Han zhuan* [A biography of Tian Han]. Beijing: Shiyue wenyi chubanshe.

Dong Jian, & Tu An. (Eds.). (1998). *Tian Han daibiao zuo* [Tian Han's representative works], 2 vols. Beijing: Zhongguo xiju chubanshe.

Kaplan, R. B. (Trans.). (1994). The night a tiger was captured. *Asian Theater Journal, 2*(1), 1–34.

Lu Wei. (1995). *Tian Han juzuo lun* [A critical study of Tian Han's dramatic works]. Nanjing, China: Nanjing Daxue chubanshe.

Tian Benxiang, Wu Ge, & Song Baozhen. (1998). *Tian Han pingzhuan* [A critical biography of Tian Han]. Chongqing, China: Chongqing chubanshe.

Tien, H. (1961). *Kuan Han-ching.* Beijing: Foreign Languages Press. (This translation is reprinted with several scenes omitted in Gunn, E. M. (Ed.). (1983). *Twentieth-century Chinese drama: An anthology.* Bloomington: Indiana University Press. Another partial translation can be found in Hsu, Kaiyu (Ed.). (1980). *Literature of the People's Republic of China.* Bloomington: Indiana University Press.

Tung, C. (1968). Lonely search into the unknown: Tian Han's early plays, 1920–1930. *Comparative Drama, 2*(1), 44–54.

Wagner, R. G. (1990). *The contemporary Chinese historical drama.* Berkeley and Los Angeles: University of California Press.

Tian Shan

Tiānshān 天山

The Tian Shan range, located mainly along the border between China and Kyrgyzstan, is 2,414 kilometers long and covers more than 1 million square kilometers. Oil and gas extraction, mining of nonferrous metals, and tourism are all important industries. The highest point in the range is 7,439 meter Pobeda Peak, famous among mountaineers.

The great arc of the Tian Shan range and its intervening valleys stretches 2,414 kilometers east to west along China's frontier with Kyrgyzstan and southeastern Kazakhstan and the Xinjiang Uygur Autonomous Region of southwestern China. The range is 320 to 480 kilometers wide and covers 1,036,000 square kilometers. The Pamir ranges lie to the southwest, the Dzungarian and southern Kazakhstan plains lie to the north, and the Tarim Basin lies to the southeast.

A central cluster of tall peaks reaches 7,439 meters on Pobeda Peak, which is also the highest point in Kyrgyzstan and lies on the border with China. The second-highest peak of the Tian Shan is Khan Tengri (Lord of the Spirits). At 7,010 meters it lies on the Kyrgyzstan-Kazakhstan border. These two peaks are known among mountain climbers as the two most northerly mountains

The Tian Shan range, even from a distance, dominates the landscape.
PHOTO BY JOAN LEBOLD COHEN.

of more than 7,000 meters, although whether or not Khan Tengri qualifies as a 7000m peak is a matter of debate: its geographical elevation is 6995m, but its glacial cap brings the peak to 7010m.

At 154 meters below sea level the Turfan Depression is the lowest elevation in the Tian Shan and the lowest point in central Asia. Issyk-Kol, in western Tian Shan, is the ninth-largest lake in the world by volume.

The Silk Roads that linked China and Southwest Asia to the Mediterranean world followed the southern edge of the Tian Shan. To early travelers of the Silk Roads these "heavenly mountains" (*tian* is Chinese for "sky" or "heaven") offered an alpine respite from the steppe (a vast, usually level and treeless tract in southeastern Europe or Asia), forests, and glacial lakes. The interior continental location of the Tian Shan produces short, cold winters that are followed by long, hot summers. Winds of Gulf of Arabia and Mediterranean origin bring moisture to the windward western and northwestern slopes (up to 800 millimeters annually) but leave the eastern and interior regions in an arid rain shadow (less than 100 millimeters annually). Common fauna include bear, snow leopard, wolf, fox, wild boar, mountain goat, Manchurian roe, and mountain sheep.

Mount Tian Safari Park, located north of Liumu Lake, covers 63 square kilometers and is part of the Bogeda South Foot Conservation Area. It is home to sixty-nine species of animals. The United Nations Educational, Scientific, and Cultural Organization (UNESCO) is considering naming the western Tian Shan to its World Heritage List.

The Kyrgyz people predominate in the western Tian Shan; Uygurs predominate in the eastern Tian Shan. Ethnic Kazakhs, Tajiks, Russians, Chinese, and Tartars also settle the periphery. The economy revolves around irrigated agriculture (in the lowlands) and livestock herding (in the uplands). Oil and gas extraction, mining of nonferrous metals, and tourism are also important.

The eastern Tian Shan contains an autonomous county for Mongols, who remain Buddhists. Sunni Islam

Snow on Mount Tian, 1755, Palace Museum, Beijing. This painting by Hua Yan (sometimes considered one of the Eight Eccentrics of Yangzhou) is reproduced in *Three Thousand Years of Chinese Painting.*

Roof tiles found on the shores of a lake at the foot of the Tianshan mountains.

predominates among the Uygur and Kyrgyz communities, whereas small Russian Orthodox Christian and Jewish communities are settled in and around Ürümqi in the Xinjiang Uygur Autonomous Region.

Stephen F. CUNHA

Further Reading

Howard-Bury, C. (1990). *Mountains of heaven: Travel in the Tian Shan Mountains, 1913.* London: Hodder & Stoughton.

Khan Tengri. (2006). Retrieved February 25, 2009 from http://www.summitpost.org/mountain/rock/150339/khan-tengri-tengi-tag.html

Poole, R. M., & Nebbia, T. (1988). Tian Shan & Pamir. In *Mountain worlds.* Washington, DC: National Geographic Society.

United Nations Educational, Scientific, and Cultural Organization (UNESCO). (2007). Sub-regional meeting on the nomination of the West Tien-Shan as Transboundary Natural Heritage Site. Retrieved February 25, 2009 from http://whc.unesco.org/en/events/415/

Tiananmen Square

Tiān'ānmén Guǎngchǎng　天安门广场

Events in Tiananmen Square, at the heart of Beijing, have shaped modern China, and the People's Republic of China's sixtieth anniversary celebrations in October 2009 will again bring the world's attention to the largest public open space in the world. The student protests of 1989, which took place there and elsewhere in China, significantly influenced China's diplomatic relations with the United States and other nations and continue to symbolize the Chinese government's determination to control the pace and focus of social change.

Tiananmen Square 天安门广场 is located in the center of Beijing, the capital city of the People's Republic of China (PRC). Originally designed and built in 1651, the square was enlarged fourfold in 1958 to cover 100 acres, making it the biggest public square in the world. It is best known in the West for the "Tiananmen Incident" (*Guang chang shi wei* 天安门广场示威) of 1989.

The square is named for the Tiananmen Gate (Gate of Heavenly Peace), which is on the northern side of the square. Outside the gate are two marble pillars called the *huabiao*. The *huabiao* are said to date back to the sage kings of Yao and Shun in China's mythical times. Originally wooden, they served as the notice boards, or "wood of direct speech" (*feibang zhi mu*), which stood just outside the court for the purpose of soliciting public criticism. They were replaced during the Han dynasty (206 BCE–220 CE) by stone pillars, eventually becoming elaborately sculpted columns in traditional Chinese architectural style and a common sight on the grounds of imperial palaces. But they still symbolize people's right to speak up against official injustice.

The Presence of Mao

The posthumous presence of Mao Zedong (1893–1976) is visually and physically prominent at the square. The official portrait of the former chairman of the Chinese Communist Party (CCP) has hung on Tiananmen Gate since 1949. It is flanked by two slogans: "Long Live The Unity of the Peoples of the World!" and "Long Live The People's Republic of China!" Mao is also the only permanent resident of the square: In a mausoleum on the south side, the body of Mao lies in a crypt covered in a crystalline sarcophagus surrounded by flowers. The body is retired after public viewing hours to an earthquake-proof chamber deep in the bowels of the square. An Ancestral Hall of the Revolution contains relics of other first-generation revolutionary leaders like Liu Shaoqi (1898–1974), Zhu De (1886–1976), and Zhou Enlai (1898–1976).

In the center of the square, a marble obelisk known as the *Monument to the People's Heroes* commemorates those who died for change and revolution in China from 1840 on. Every morning at daybreak a ceremonial guard facing it hoists the five-star red flag of the PRC. To the east, the Museum of History and the Revolution has more often than not been "closed to the public" due to the constant

Soldiers stand before the southern Gate of Tiananmen Square, early in the morning. Each morning, tourists from all over China visit the heart of Beijing to see the national flag raised.

vacillation of party policy and the rewriting of Chinese history. Instead, it has been used for exhibiting official and avant-garde artwork, contemporary fashion shows, and so forth. To its west is the Great Hall of the People, which, with its ten thousand seats, is the annual meeting site of the National People's Congress. All major plenums of the CCP and government are held there as well.

The Tiananmen Incident

On 15 April 1989, students gathered in Tiananmen Square to mourn the death of reformist CCP general secretary Hu Yaobang. When government officials refused their petitions at the Great Hall of the People, the students clashed with police. The party mouthpiece, *People's Daily*,

published an editorial on 26 April accusing a "handful of plotters" of creating "turmoil" with the object of overthrowing the regime. The next day, 200,000 students from over forty universities marched to the square in protest. Hundreds, then thousands, of Beijing University students began a hunger strike on 13 May around the *Monument to the People's Heroes*. Premier Li Peng (b. 1928) and moderate officials affiliated with General Secretary Zhao Ziyang (b. 1919), who was later dismissed, failed to defuse the situation before the arrival of Soviet leader Mikhail Gorbachev (b. 1931) for a summit with Deng Xiaoping (1904–1997), China's paramount leader. The welcoming ceremony at the square for Gorbachev was abandoned: Chinese president Yang Shangkun (b. 1907) later gave Beijing's loss of face and international prestige as one reason for the crackdown. On 20 May, martial law was declared, but for two weeks the students, now joined by workers, reporters, army personnel, and civil servants—numbering at one point over 2 million—blocked the advance of 150,000 troops toward the city. On 3–4 June, army tanks rolled in, clearing the square and killing an undisclosed number of civilians.

The term "pro-democracy" would oversimplify description of a student-led movement that made a complex set of demands, which included dialogue with the government, crackdown on official corruption, vague political reforms, greater funding for education, a freer press, and so forth. The students used the word "democracy," but they were short on specifics. They stressed the need to improve the existing system, not to overthrow it. Many acknowledged party leadership and believed that an American-type democracy was unsuitable for China. It may also be argued that they were not sufficiently versed in liberal democratic traditions to represent their interests and aspirations. They did, however, think that by playing to the international news media (over one thousand foreign journalists had converged in Beijing for the Deng-Gorbachev summit), they could gain Western sympathy and thereby advance their cause. This partly explains why, on 30 May, students unveiled the ten-meter-high *Goddess of Democracy* statue in the square. Ironically, Deng himself had been misled by Premier Li to believe that the demonstrators wanted to overthrow the party government.

This was not the first time Chinese students demonstrated against government policies in the twentieth century, but it was certainly one of the biggest demonstrations and the focus of huge international media attention. The Tiananmen Square protests represented a debate between young, liberal, and progressive-minded students and an older generation of political leaders attempting to maintain control even while considerable economic and social transitions were underway. There were repercussions within the government itself: Some leaders took a more sympathetic approach; others were committed to a strong and swift response, including military action against the students.

In the aftermath of the 1989 incident, the CCP organized Young Pioneers parades to show that the "revolutionary successors to the Communist enterprise" had taken back the square from protestors.

Today Tiananmen Square remains a source of tension for Chinese officials, with a considerable police presence, as it is thought to be a focal point for some activist groups. Security concerns often focus on such events as the twentieth anniversary of the Tiananmen Square protests in June 2009. Western media companies were, after lengthy discussion with Chinese Olympics officials, allowed to broadcast live from the Square during the 2008 Olympic Games. The Square remains, nonetheless, a major tourist attraction and venue for public events. Kite flying is common during the day. Tens of thousands celebrate Labor Day (1 May) and National Day (1 October) with fireworks and floats, and flood into the Square for the early morning flag-raising ceremony, arriving at 3:30 a.m. to get a good spot. This ceremony is similar in pomp and popularity to the changing of the guard at Buckingham Palace in London. The sixtieth anniversary of the PRC on 1 October 2009 will again draw the world's attention to the Square.

Anthony Alexander LOH

Further Reading

Fewsmith, J. (2001). *China since Tiananmen: The politics of transition.* Cambridge, U.K.: Cambridge University Press.

Liu, M. (1989). Beijing spring: Loss of the Mandate of Heaven. In David C. Turnley (Ed.), *Beijing Spring*, New York: Stewart, Tabori & Chang, 25–43.

Ming Pao News reporters and photographers. (1989). *June Four: A chronicle of the Chinese democratic uprising*, Zi Jin & Qin Zhou (Trans.). Fayetteville: University of Arkansas Press.

Nathan, A. J., & Link, P. (Eds.). (2001). *The Tiananmen papers.* New York: Public Affairs.

Spence, J. D. (Ed.). (1990). The gate and the square. In *Children of the dragon*, Human Rights in China. New York: Collier, 16–37.

Unger, J. (Ed.). (1991). *The pro-democracy protests in China: Reports from the provinces.* Armonk, NY: M. E. Sharpe.

Wu, Hung. (1991, Summer). Tiananmen square: A political history of monuments. *Representations 35*, 84–117.

Tiangan Dizhi

Tiāngān dìzhī 天干地支

An ancient system for dating events, *tiangan dizhi* was replaced after the end of the Chinese imperial system by the Gregorian calendar. But some Chinese people still rely on the sixty-year cycle of *tiangan dizhi* to determine where and when to plan events both momentous and mundane in the course of their lives.

*T*iangan dizhi is a cyclical time-measuring system used in China since antiquity. The system juxtaposes two parallel sequences: the sequence of heavenly stems (*tiangan* 天), which consists of ten equal-length named units, and the system of earthly branches (*dizhi* 地支), which consists of twelve equal-length named units. Specifically, the calendrical system identifies major time units, principally a year or a day, by pairing one stem and one branch.

Because of the difference in the number of stems and the number of branches, it takes sixty counts before the original pairing reappears, thus forming the sexagesimal, or sixty-year, cycle in Chinese time reckoning. Enumerated below are the sixty pairings that occur as the heavenly stems, numbered here 1 through 10 for the purpose of illustration, pair with the heavenly branches, coded here A through L for the purpose of illustration. (The actual *tiangan dizhi* system does not use numerals and letters; the system uses Chinese characters to stand for the ten branches and twelve stems.)

1A, 2B, 3C, 4D, 5E, 6F, 7G, 8H, 9I, 10J,
1K, 2L, 3A, 4B, 5C, 6D, 7E, 8F, 9G 10H,

1I, 2J, 3K, 4L, 5A, 6B, 7C, 8D, 9E, 10F,
1G, 2H, 3I, 4J, 4K, 6L, 7A, 8B, 9C, 10D,
1E, 2F, 3G, 4H, 5I, 6J, 7K, 8L, 9A, 10B,
1C, 2D, 3E, 4F, 5G, 6H, 7I, 8J, 9K, 10L,
1A (the beginning of a new cycle) . . .

History of *Tiangan Dizhi*

Scholars generally agree that this sexagesimal system began during the Shang dynasty (1766–1045 BCE), when the kings attached the names of the heavenly stems to their personal names. The paired names also appeared on oracle-bone inscriptions (called *jiaguwen*, 甲骨文 which means "words carved on tortoise shells or cattle scapulars" and which were used by Shang kings for divination purposes). The paired names carved on bones were used to indicate the day but not the year when a spiritual quest was to be performed. The late historian Derk Bodde believed that it was not until the Han dynasty (206 BCE to 220 CE) that this sexagesimal system was used to date both years and days.

This sequential system had been complicated in the late Zhou dynasty (1045–256 BCE), when other cosmological signs or beliefs were correlated with *tiangan* and *dizhi* to map space and time. The ten heavenly stems were split into the duality of yin and yang: 1, 3, 5, 7, 9 belong to yang and 2, 4, 6, 8, 10 belong to yin. The ten heavenly stems were further paired to correlate with the five elements (wuxing, 五行) or the "five movements—wood bending (1, 2), fire rising (3, 4), soil growing (5, 6), metal molding (7, 8), and water sinking (9, 10)—and the five cardinal directions—east (1, 2), south (3, 4), center (5, 6), west (7, 8), and north (9, 10).

In the same manner, the twelve earthly branches were categorized into the yin–yang dichotomy: yang—A, C, E, G, I, K; yin—B, D, F, H, J, L. They were further correlated with the twenty-four solar terms (*jieqi* 节气) in a solar year, the twelve zodiac animals representing the years (rat, ox, tiger, hare, dragon, serpent, horse, sheep, monkey, rooster, dog, and boar), the twelve lunar months in a year (the Chinese months are called by their numerical order), and, lastly, the twelve two-hour units (*shicheng* 时辰) in a day.

These two greatly enriched sequences in post–Han China (after 220 CE) thus constituted a composite cosmological order of space-time configuration for interpreting the existence and meanings of ephemeral human lives, from the nature and affairs of the emperor to individual mundane existences. For example, unlike the followers of the lineal Gregorian calendar, which extends from the time of Christ's alleged birth to infinity and represents a year by a number in sequential order, the Chinese typically chronicled and named years following this sexagesimal cycle of each reign, such that the Gregorian 1840 CE was chronicled as the 1G year of Emperor Daoguang. Besides chronicling the yearly order for the entire state, the court astronomers also determined the auspicious time and place for the emperor to visit, the proper direction of the main gate of the court, the spatial allocation of household furniture—all based on the calculation of this *tiangan dizhi* system. At the time of the emperor's death, the court astronomers also prescribed the most auspicious time and location for the funeral, the physical construction of the coffin and the tomb, and the direction of the cemetery.

Tiangan Dizhi Today

With the downfall of the imperial court in 1912, the sexagesimal system was replaced with the Gregorian calendar system. Except for respected scholars who still date important events by using the traditional and formal *tiangan dizhi* names, few people today use *tiangan dizhi* to name the years.

Other parts of the *tiangan dizhi* system are better preserved and widely in use in daily life. For instance,

people may figure out the unique characteristics of a specific space-time period, or node, and arrange activities (such as scheduling a haircut, launching a new business, taking a trip, and so on) accordingly. This practice has persisted throughout Chinese history, down to the twenty-first century. A newborn baby's birth characters called *shengcheng bazhi* (生辰八字 the eight characters of birth)—for the birth year, month, day, and hour— are still carefully recorded according to the designated characteristics of the paired heavenly stems and earthly branches. Fortune-tellers use these eight birth characters to predict the ebb and flow of an individual's life cycle. It is a common practice for parents to bring the eight birth characters of a prospective bride and groom to a fortune-teller to see if the two sets are compatible. At the time of death, a fortune-teller or a Daoist priest will analyze the eight birth characters of the deceased in order to pick the proper time and location for the funeral.

HUANG Shu-min

Further Reading

Bodde, D. (1975). *Festivals in classical China: New year and other annual observances during the Han dynasty, 206 BC–AD 220*. Princeton, NJ: Princeton University Press.

Cooper, E. (2000). The annual round of agricultural tasks in Dongyang county: Synoptic illusion or symbolic capital? *Asian Folklore Studies, 59*, 239–264.

de Bary, W. T. & Bloom, I. (2000). *Sources of Chinese tradition*. New York: Columbia University Press.

Fung, Yu-lan (1948). *A short history of Chinese philosophy*. New York: MacMillian.

Henderson, J. (1984). *The development & decline of Chinese cosmology*. New York: Columbia University Press.

Needham, Joseph. (1956). *Science and civilization in China (Vol. 2) History of scientific thought*. Cambridge: Cambridge University Press.

Siven, Nathan (1986). On the limits of empirical knowledge in the traditional Chinese sciences. In J. T. Frazer, N. L. & F.C. Haber, (Eds.). *Time, science and society in China and the West*. Amherst: University of Massachusetts.

Tsai, J. (2006). Eye on religion: By the brush and by the sword: Daoist perspectives on the body, illness and healing. *Southern Medical Journal, 99*, pp. 1452–1453.

Tianjin

Tiānjīn 天津

11.15 million est. 2007 pop

Tianjin 天津 is one of the four Chinese municipalities that reports directly to the State Department. It is important for its role as the economic center of China. It is the third largest city in China after Shanghai and Beijing (which it is linked to by a new high-speed rail), and serves as the gateway to the capital city, 120 km away. It is a port city and an economic powerhouse.

Tianjin, China's third largest city, is one of China's four province-level municipalities (the others being Beijing, Shanghai, and Chongqing). It is a relatively young city by Chinese standards. The city received its current name (which translates literally as "ford of heaven") from the Ming emperor Zhu Di (r. 1403–1424), who marched through the area with his army on his way south to dethrone his nephew in 1400 CE. To commemorate that auspicious event, Zhu created a walled garrison next to a settlement called Zhigu in 1404, bestowing on the new walled city the name Tianjin. Located at the confluence of the many navigable rivers of the North China Plain, the Grand Canal, and the Haihe, which drains into the Bohai Gulf (an arm of the Yellow Sea), the city's commerce began to prosper.

Tax collectors soon followed, joined by the Changlu commissioner and his sprawling bureaucracy, who supervised the production, collection, transportation, and distribution of salt as a state monopoly and were responsible for the collection of the gabelle (salt tax), a major source of revenue for the central government behind land tax. Wealthy salt merchants were joined by traders importing goods from central and south China through a vibrant coastal junk trade, as well as by native bankers specializing in long distance remittance banking.

Recognizing Tianjin's economic importance, the city was promoted in 1725 from a guard station to a department and became the seat of Tianjin Prefecture in 1731. By the nineteenth century, if not earlier, the city served as the economic center of north China (as opposed to Beijing's cultural and political centrality), with a commercial hinterland that stretched from the coastal plain over the Taihang Mountains and into the steppes beyond.

The arrival of foreign imperialism altered Tianjin's developmental path. In the aftermath of the Second Opium War (1858–1860), the city was declared a treaty port, and foreign concessions were established. The city suffered xenophobic incidents such as the Tianjin Massacre in 1870, during which foreigner missionaries and residents were killed, and the Boxer movement in 1900 which resulted in the occupation of the city by the Allied Expeditionary Force until 1902.

In the aftermath of the destruction, Chinese reformers began to promote industrial development and modernization, stimulating Tianjin's early industrialization, led by the Beiyang arsenal, the telegraph service, and flour and cotton-spinning mills, and followed by heavy industries such as the Kailuan Mining Administration and Yongli Chemical Industries. Before the Second World War, the city was the country's third largest industrial center (after Shanghai and Wuhan) and the largest in

north China, while serving as the provincial capital for Hebei Province.

Under Beijing's shadow, after 1949, the role of Tianjin changed yet again. State investment largely bypassed Tianjin, while the city served the capital as a transportation hub with railroad and ocean links. The post-Mao economic reforms created an even larger gap between the city and growth centers such as Shanghai, Canton, and Shenzhen.

The 2006 master plan for the city finally made it the core of the Bohai economic region. With the construction of a high-speed rail link between Tianjin and Beijing, Tianjin and the capital are becoming one, supported by a ring of cities to form a circum-Bohai economic region. In 2008, the central government authorized Tianjin as the site for new land use and financial policies. Utilizing the new high-speed rail, it served as a venue of soccer events for the 2008 Beijing Olympics at the newly created

The First China-born Olympic Medalist

Eric Liddell—the runner portrayed in *Chariots of Fire*—who refused for religious reasons to run on a Sunday, was the first Olympic gold medalist born in China.

Liddell, known in China as Lee Airui, was the son of Scottish missionaries and grew up in Tianjin, a city southeast of Beijing. At in the 1924 Olympics in Paris, Liddell, a devout Christian, found himself unable to participate in the preliminary heats for his own event, the 100-meter race. Instead, he made a last minute switch to the 400-meter contest. He not only won the race but set a new world record, and became a symbol of personal faith as well as athletic brilliance.

Returning to China, he became a coach at the Xinxue School in Tianjin, a mission school that is now Tianjin's Middle School #17. During World War II he was imprisoned by the Japanese in north China. He died there, in the land where he was born, and today a plaque in Tianjin commemorates the home of Lee Airui, China's first Olympic medalist.

Source: Fan Hong, et al. (2008). *China gold: China's quest for global power and Olympic glory.* Great Barrington, MA: Berkshire Publishing.

Tianjin Olympic Center Stadium, and has become a host city for many international conferences. A new exchange for over-the-counter (OTC) trading of equity securities and corporate bonds, together with direct access to the Hong Kong stock market, ensured that the city would reclaim its place as the economic center of north China, while Beijing would continue as the political and cultural center of the country.

KWAN Man Bun

Further Reading

Kirk, M. (Ed.). (2009). *China by numbers 2009.* Hong Kong: China Economic Review Publishing.

Kwan Man Bun. (2001). *The salt merchants of Tianjin.* Honolulu: University of Hawaii Press.

Rolgaski, R. (2004). *Hygienic modernity: Meanings of health and disease in treaty port China.* Berkeley: University of California Press.

Tianjinshi defangzhi bianxiu weiyuanhui, comp. (1996). *Tianjin tongzhi.* Tianjin: Tianjin shehui kexueyuan chubanshe.

Tiantai

Tiāntái 天台

The first truly Chinese school of Buddhist thought, Tiantai, was founded in the sixth century. With its Chinese perspective on an Indian religion, Tiantai spread through East Asia, establishing itself in Japan and Korea.

Geographically, Tiantai refers to a mountain as well as a mountain range in Zhejiang Province; historically, this mountain became home to a school of thought that came to revolutionize Buddhism in China, imbuing it with a uniquely Sinitic approach that broke away from a continued dependence upon India as the place of authority for all things Buddhist. Therefore, Tiantai philosophy gave the Far East (China as well as Japan and Korea) its own form of Buddhism.

The infiltration of Buddhism into China depended on the sporadic appearance of texts and traditions retrieved by travelers to India. Consequently, the result was a plethora of teaching and practices that were both divergent and even at times contradictory. For example, some prescribed strict observance of rituals, others denied such practices entirely. More importantly, however, the Chinese worldview was most unlike the Indian Buddhist one, for the former gave eminence to the development and nurturing of the individual and the body while the Indian view regarded the body and the person as only a brief illusion. In effect, China was strongly Confucian and Daoist; that is, Chinese culture was intensely "humanistic," concerned with understanding how to live in the world and how to achieve a just society through good governance. Buddhism, on the other hand, was antihumanistic, for it cared for neither of these things and privileged the search for nonexistence as the chief end of human existence: The body was a barrier that needed to be overcome in order for the soul to be free from suffering. Thus, the real source of the varieties and disparities of Buddhism in China was the result not only of divergent texts, but also of divergent cultures. China was not northern India, and the process of inculcating Buddhism was not simply a matter of transplanting what had worked in India and Central Asia. The process of translation of an entire worldview required the creation of a new set of ideas and ideals. Indeed, translation is not only a linguistic act, it is also a philosophical one.

It was the monk and philosopher Zhiyi (538–597 CE), who came to a Buddhist retreat at Tiantai Mountain around the year 587 and began to address the twin problems facing Buddhism this far from its place of origin: First, how to make the faith relevant to China, and second, how to synthesize and unify Buddhist teachings so there would not be confusion and disparity.

The immediate need was for synthesis, and Zhiyi took an innovative approach. Rather than seeking to refute each and every text that contradicted another, he instead provided a methodology to understand the contradictions, and he did not deny that the Buddha himself was the source of these contradictions. In this way, Zhiyi avoided creating conflict among the various followers of these contradictory traditions, each of whom believed in the verity of what they taught and practiced. He stated that the various approaches, texts, and scriptures found in the China of his time were certainly teachings of the

2277

Buddha, but they were only partial ones, because over his lifetime the Buddha realized that a person could not encompass the entirety of the enlightenment process in one attempt; rather she or he had to achieve this state gradually. Therefore, each of the many teachings and texts that appeared contradictory were in fact small steps towards enlightenment; or in the words of his famous dictum, "All was One, and One was All." In effect, the model he used was that of the student who proceeds from an initial, preparatory stage, to a beginning stage, to a middle stage, and finally to an advanced one. The many teachings represented each of these stages, and each was important for it brought the student to the highest, most accomplished state. Once this highest state was reached, the student had no more need for the other stages. Thus, each stage was utilitarian and not complete in itself. Accordingly, the many teachings would ultimately be abandoned once they had fulfilled their function. Truth, implied Zhiyi, is revealed a little at a time; once it is known in its fullness, partiality or semi-concealment is no longer possible. For example, the experience of reading a book for the first time can only be undertaken once, a page at a time. Once the book is entirely read, nothing remains hidden. This is what Tiantai philosophy refers to as "Round Teachings," or that approach which encompasses everything so there is no room for contradiction or conflict.

For Zhiyi, the highest state of all was explained in one text only, the *Lotus Sutra*, which is a very significant Mahanyana sutra that takes the form of a dialog with the Buddha and which consists of parables that seek to explain skillful means, or those skills through which an individual may terminate suffering and also acquire the ability to teach others in the path of the Buddha. It became the central work for Tiantai philosophy. The purpose of this sutra is to expound on the nature and purpose of those means that will allow a person to reach the highest state, that is, the end of personal suffering. Importantly for Zhiyi, the sutra also hints at the notion that the teaching found in it replaces all other Buddhist teachings. This brought authority to Zhiyi's notion of the various stages.

Further, Zhiyi gave precision to the definition of phenomena, or, things that are observed. He saw their nature as threefold: Things are empty because they contain nothing intrinsically their own; things exist solely because they are the result of external causes and are therefore impermanent; and things are middle, meaning that things are both empty and temporary, and thus their true reality is ultimately unknowable. This epistemology led Zhiyi to conclude that each phenomenon is one with true emptiness (the state of being devoid of absolute identity, the complete lack of permanence, the entire erasure of the self). And on a more pragmatic level, he found room for all activity; even deluded thoughts are initial, preparatory steps towards achieving enlightenment. This guided Zhiyi to formulate various methods of contemplation or meditation to allow the individual to observe his or her mind in order to continue climbing upwards into enlightenment.

This approach makes Tiantai philosophy uniquely Chinese and forever ruptures its connection to India. By equating things to provisional instances of enlightenment, the phenomenal world acquires significance and this in turn leads to a uniquely Chinese Buddhist position: The erasure of the self is not self-negation but the acquisition of bliss, permanence, and purity. Perhaps it may even be said that in China the purpose of meditation is to confront the world and seek to solve its problems because the process is a step towards enlightenment. This broadening of perspective allowed Buddhism to extend easily throughout China and into Japan and Korea. Tiantai is still important in China, but in Korea and Japan it has lost its Chinese perspective and has been made more indigenous, such as Nichiren Buddhism in Japan.

Nirmal DASS

Further Reading

Chan, W. T. & Moore, C. A. (1947). *The essentials of Buddhist philosophy.* Honolulu: University of Hawaii Press.

Donner, N. & Stevenson, D. B. (1993). *The great calming and contemplation: A study and annotated first chapter of Chih-i's Mo-ho-chih-kuan.* Honolulu: University of Hawaii Press.

Hurvitz, L. (1963). *Chih-I (538–597): An introduction to the life and ideas of a Chinese Buddhist monk.* Brussels, Belgium: Imprimerie Sainte-Catherine.

Gregory, P. N. (1986). *Traditions of meditation in Chinese Buddhism.* Honolulu: University of Hawaii Press.

From the *Lotus Sutra*

The Lotus Sutra *is by far the most popular and influential of Mahayana scriptures. This excerpt translated by Kumarajiva in 406 CE illustrates one of the main doctrines of the text: that the* Lotus Sutra *itself embodies the Buddha's truth.*

At that time Sakyamuni Buddha saw the Buddhas that were his emanations all assembled, each sitting on a lion seat, and heard all these Buddhas say that they wished to participate in the opening of the treasure tower . . .

Sakyamuni Buddha with the fingers of his right hand then opened the door of the tower of seven treasures. A loud sound issued from it, like the sound of a lock and crossbar being removed from a great city gate, and at once all the members of the assembly caught sight of Many Treasures Thus Come One seated on a lion seat inside the treasure tower, his body whole and unimpaired, sitting as though engaged in meditation. And they heard him say, "Excellent, excellent, Sakyamuni Buddha! You have preached this *Lotus Sutra* in a spirited manner. I have come here in order that I may here this *sutra*.

At that time the four kinds of believers, observing the Buddha who had passed into extinction immeasurable thousands, ten thousands, millions of *kalpas* in the past speaking in this way, marveled at what they had never known before and took the masses of heavenly jeweled flowers and scattered them over Many Treasures Buddha and Sakyamuni Buddha.

Source: Source: de Bary, W. T., & Bloom, I. (1999). *Sources of Chinese tradition, vol. I.* New York: Columbia University Press, 453.

Swanson, P. L. (1989). *Foundations of T'ien'T'ai philosophy: The flowering of the two truths theory in Chinese Buddhism.* Berkeley, CA: Asian Humanities Press.

Wright, A. F. (1959). *Buddhism in Chinese history.* Stanford, CA: Stanford University Press.

Wu, J. (1993). *T'ien-T'ai Buddhism and early Madhyamika.* Honolulu: University of Hawaii Press.

Zhiyi & Saso, M. R. (Trans.). (2000). *Zen is for everyone: The Xiao Zhi Guan text by Zhi Yi.* Carmel, CA: New Life Center.

Ziporyn, B. A. (2000). *Evil and/or/as the good: Omnicentrism, intersubjectivity, and value paradox in Tiantai Buddhist thought* (Harvard-Yenching Monograph Series No. 51). Cambridge, MA: Harvard University Press.

Ziporyn, B. A. (2004). *Being and ambiguity: Philosophical experiments with Tiantai Buddhism.* Chicago: Open Court.

China changes constantly, and the *Encyclopedia of China* will change and grow, too. Berkshire's authors and editors welcome questions, comments, and corrections: china.updates@berkshirepublishing.com.

Tibet (Xizang) Autonomous Region

Xīzàng Zìzhìqū 西藏自治区

2.84 million est. 2007 pop. (this figure is debatable)   1.22 million square km

Tibet—"the Roof of the World"—is one of China's five autonomous regions. A distinction is made between "political" Tibet, the area governed by the Lhasa government before 1950, and "ethnic" or "cultural" Tibet, the area inhabited by mainly Buddhist people of Tibetan origin. Tibet has been the focus of international attention because of calls for increased autonomy or independence, and at the same is being developed as an international tourist destination.

Tibet—since 1965 officially known as the Tibet (Xizang) Autonomous Region (TAR)—is made up of the central Asian landmass between the Kunlun mountain range to the north, the Himalayan Mountains to the south, and the Karakoram range to the west. It is one of China's five autonomous regions (areas dominated by one or more of China's fifty-five officially recognized minority ethnic groups: in this case, the Zang people).

On the east Tibet is bounded by a region of three great rivers: the Yangzi (Chang), Mekong, and Salween. With most of its territory located above 4,500 meters and its capital, Lhasa, located at 3,607 meters, Tibet has been called "the Roof of the World." The total Tibetan population remains uncertain, and is a highly-politicized issue, particularly given the movement of Han Chinese into the TAR over the last five decades. While around 130,000 Tibetans live in exile in India and elsewhere, estimates of the Tibetan-speaking population of China range between 2 and 5 million.

Although the degree to which Tibet was a part of China in earlier eras is disputed, Tibet certainly has been a part of China since the Chinese Communist invasion in 1950 and exists today only in the much-reduced area of the TAR. A Tibetan government-in-exile, headed by the Dalai Lama (the spiritual and temporal leader of the Tibetan people), has been established in India, and significant Tibetan exile communities exist in the United States and Switzerland. The Tibetan government in exile continues to campaign for self-determination for Tibet, and the ongoing Sino-Tibetan dispute invests facts and figures regarding Tibet with political implications. However, a distinction historically has been made between "political" Tibet, the area governed by the Lhasa government before 1950, and "ethnic" or "cultural" Tibet, the area inhabited by mainly Buddhist people of Tibetan origin.

Geographic Features

"Political" Tibet had an estimated population of 1.8–3 million, around half of whom were seminomadic yak herders. The settled urban and agricultural populations were concentrated in the river valleys, particularly in the triangle formed by the major settlements of Lhasa, Gyantse, and Shigatse (Xigaze). Today the TAR population includes a large number of Han Chinese immigrants, and with the completion of a railroad connecting Lhasa with other Chinese cities, the Han Chinese are now believed to form a majority of the Lhasa population.

Although Tibet is located at a latitude similar to that of Algeria, the location and altitude of the Tibetan plateau produces a cold and generally dry climate, although southeastern Tibet includes tropical jungle. The western Tibetan area around the Gangdise (Kailas) mountain range and Lake Mapam Yumco (Manasarowar) is the source of four great rivers: the Indus, Brahmaputra, Ganges, and Sutlej. Mount Everest, located on the Tibet-Nepal border, at 8,848 meters is the world's highest mountain.

Tibet's climate limits its sedentary agriculture. Barley is the major crop and, in its roasted form as *tsampa,* comprises, along with yak meat and tea (a traditional import from Sichuan and other parts of China), the staple diet of most of the Tibetan population.

Origins

The origins of the Tibetan peoples appear to be linked to central Asian nomadic tribes such as the Yue Zhi (Tokharians) and Qiang. The first unified Tibetan state was a tribal confederacy formed in the seventh century under the rule of King Songtsen Gampo (or Srong-brtsan Sgampo (c. 608–650 CE), who established his capital at Lhasa. The introduction of a Tibetan script and Buddhist teachings is among the innovations attributed to his reign. His dynasty lasted until the assassination of King Langdharma around the year 842.

During this period Tibet was a formidable military power, constantly warring with neighboring powers and strong enough to sack the Chinese capital of Xi'an in 763. At its zenith the Tibetan empire reached as far west as Samarqand in modern-day Uzbekistan. Buddhism became

A Tibetan girl in traditional dress stands in a courtyard with intricately painted pillars.

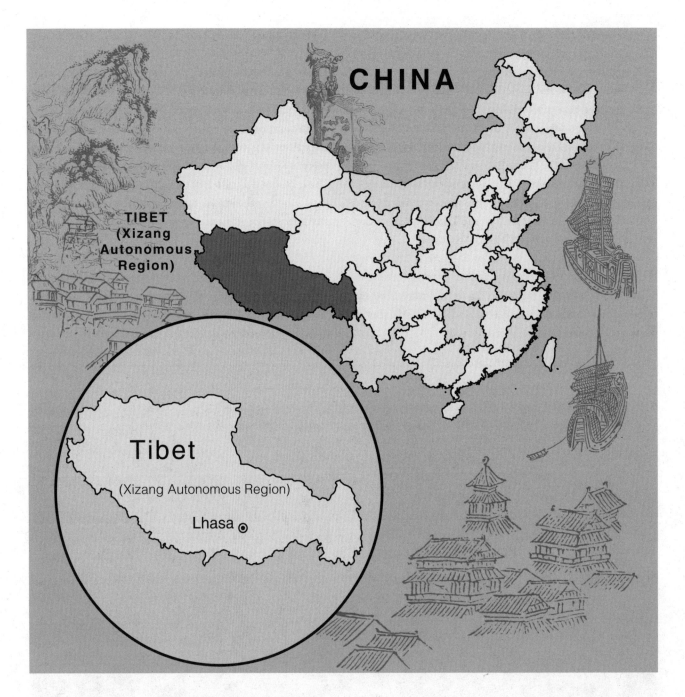

CHINA

TIBET
(Xizang
Autonomous
Region)

Tibet

(Xizang Autonomous Region)

Lhasa ◉

increasingly important, particularly in the court, and the first monastery in Tibet was established at Samye around 779. However, there was considerable opposition to the new religion among aristocratic factions associated with followers of the indigenous Tibetan belief system, which was later identified with the Bon faith but probably at that time was an unsystematized tradition that included elements of divine kingship and sacrifice.

During the eleventh and twelfth centuries Buddhism became firmly established when Indian Buddhist texts were translated into the Tibetan language. Of the four major sects of Tibetan Buddhism that developed on the basis of these teachings, the Gelugpa sect eventually emerged as prominent, and from the sixteenth century onward Tibet was ruled by a line of incarnate Gelugpa monks with the title of "Dalai Lama." Religious factions in Tibet tended to seek Mongol or Chinese patronage, and in the eighteenth century China became increasingly involved in events in Tibet. Thus, from 1793 until 1911–1912 China exerted at least nominal suzerainty (dominion) over Lhasa.

The British imperial government of India in 1903–1904 dispatched a mission to Lhasa that forced Tibetans to accept British representatives and effectively opened the country to Western influences. However, despite some modernization during the next couple of decades, Tibet remained an essentially conservative religious society and strongly resisted change. The thirteenth Dalai Lama (1876–1933), a strong nationalist leader, led Tibet to independence after the Chinese revolution in 1911, and Tibet survived as a de facto independent state until the Communist Chinese invasion in 1950. However, its independence was not officially recognized by any major powers, with China continuing to claim Tibet.

Society

In spite of the continuing existence of the Bon faith and its many cultural manifestations, the outstanding feature of Tibetan culture generally is considered to be its unique

An elderly Tibetan woman with a prayer wheel.
PHOTO BY YIXUAN SHUKE.

form of Buddhism, a synthesis of the Mahayana and Tantric forms of the faith. Buddhism influenced virtually all aspects of traditional society. An estimated 20 percent (although some estimates place the figure as high as 50 percent) of the male population were monks, and more than six thousand monasteries were located throughout the Tibetan cultural world. These were important economic and political centers as well as guardians of Tibetan artistic and cultural expression. Aside from the monasteries, pilgrimage to sacred cities and mountains was an especially significant religious expression for all classes of people.

A small aristocratic class enjoyed considerable privilege, although the Tibetan peasantry, in comparison with their contemporaries in neighboring states, were tolerably well treated. Women also enjoyed greater-than-average freedom, particularly in the economic and social spheres, although they were almost entirely excluded from religious power.

Cultural influences from both India and China were present, but Tibetan culture was strikingly distinct from the culture of its neighbors. This was particularly true in such areas as literary traditions (in particular the Gesar of Ling epic), language, and art and architecture, with buildings such as Lhasa's Potala Palace and Jokhang Temple, as well as the regional monasteries, being of striking originality. Some of this culture has been destroyed in the TAR, but much is remembered or preserved in exile, and the Chinese government has in recent years focused on developing Tibet as a domestic and international tourist destination. The Qinghai-Tibet railway links the Tibetan capital of Lhasa with Beijing and is the world's highest railway line, with nearly 1000 km of track at an altitude of more than 4,000 meters above sea level.

Alex McKAY

Further Reading

Coleman, G. (Ed.). (1993). *A handbook of Tibetan culture: A guide to Tibetan centres and resources throughout the world.* London: Rider.

International Commission of Jurists (1959). *The question of Tibet and the rule of law.* Geneva: International Commission of Jurists.

Kirk, M. (Ed.). (2009). *China by numbers 2009.* Hong Kong: China Economic Review Publishing.

Lustgarten, A. (2008). *China's great train: Beijing's drive west and the campaign to remake Tibet.* New York: Times Books.

McKay, A. (Ed.). (2002). *The history of Tibet* (3 vols.). Richmond, U.K: Curzon Press.

Mikel, D. (2004). *Buddha's warriors: The story of the CIA-backed Tibetan freedom fighters, the Chinese invasion, and the ultimate fall of Tibet.* New York: Penguin.

Richardson, H. (1984). *Tibet and its history.* Boston: Shambhala Publications.

Richardson, H. (1998). *High peaks, pure Earth: Collected writings on Tibetan history and culture.* London: Serindia Publications.

Samuel, G. (1993). *Civilized shamans: Buddhism in Tibetan societies.* Washington, DC: Smithsonian Institution Press.

Snellgrove, D., & Richardson, H. (1968). *A cultural history of Tibet.* London: Weidenfeld and Nicolson.

Stein, R. A. (1972). *Tibetan civilization.* Stanford, CA: Stanford University Press.

Tarthang, T. (Ed.). (1986). *Ancient Tibet: Research materials from the Yeshe De Project.* Berkeley, CA: Dharma Publishing.

Tucci, G. (1980). *The religions of Tibet.* London: Routledge & Kegan Paul.

Tibetan Uprising of 1959

1959 nián Xīzàng Qǐyì　1959 年西藏起义

In 1959 Tibet, now an autonomous region of China, revolted against Chinese rule. Many Chinese were surprised when they were not welcomed as liberators following the 1949–1950 invasion, viewing their takeover of Tibet as succor from a feudalist system. The Tibetans were greatly outnumbered and ill-equipped for revolt. Their uprising was crushed, and the Dalai Lama, the Tibetan spiritual and temporal leader, was forced to flee to India.

The status of Tibet, located in southwestern China, has long been disputed. Tibet enjoyed de facto, if not legally recognized, independence during the era of Republican China (1912–1949), but the Chinese, in their period of turmoil, oddly claimed that Tibet was still part of their territory and that the Tibetans were one of the "five races" that made up China. They continued to claim Tibet as part of China in such forums as the Simla Convention of 1914—at which British India and Tibet agreed on the Indo-Tibetan frontier and various trade issues, but China's participants refused to sign—and at the 1922 Washington conference, a meeting between nine nations to decide post–World War I policy in the Far East.

The Communist takeover in China in October 1949 was an obvious threat to Tibetan self-determination because the Chinese Communist Party (CCP), led by Mao Zedong (1893–1976), was prepared to use military force to take over Tibet, for Mao, like his Republican predecessors, considered Tibet to be a part of China lost as a result of the actions of the European imperial powers. During 1949–1950, Communist forces took over Tibetan-speaking areas such as Amdo, and gathered on the frontiers of the Lhasa-controlled regions of Kham (eastern Tibet). After attempts to arrange negotiations on neutral territory failed, in October 1950 Chinese military forces invaded Tibet from the north-east and east and quickly conquered the largely demilitarized Tibetan state after the commander of their garrison at Chamdo, Ngawang Jigme Ngapo, fled and was captured by the Chinese.

During the 1950s China applied with increasing force policies designed to transform traditional Tibetan society and to integrate Tibet into the Communist system. As a result, Tibetan resistance to the assault on their culture and religion quickly increased, culminating in the nationalist revolt of 1959. However, the Tibetans were greatly outnumbered and ill equipped for armed conflict. Their resistance was crushed, and the fourteenth Dalai Lama (b. 1935), Tibetan spiritual and temporal leader, was forced to flee into exile in India. Since then China has continued to rule Tibet by military force, and the Dalai Lama, who was awarded the Nobel Peace Prize in 1989, remains leader of the Tibetan government-in-exile in northern India.

Events of 1950–1958

In January 1950, when India formally recognized the new Communist government in Beijing, China informed India of its plans to peacefully "liberate" Tibet from its traditional monastic rulers and from foreign powers. To the Communists the Tibetans were an oppressed people living at the mercy of a feudal elite, and the Chinese expected to be welcomed as liberators. When Sino-Tibetan negotiations failed, China launched a full-scale military invasion of Tibet on 7 October 1950. An appeal by El Salvador on behalf of the Tibetan Government-in-exile to the United Nations went unanswered because of Tibet's ambiguous status under international law. Tibet had an army of only eight thousand men, and within days Chamdo, the main Tibetan administrative center in Kham Province, fell to the invaders.

Kham was home of the Tibetan-speaking Khampa peoples, who, although loyal to the Dalai Lama as head of their Tibetan Buddhist faith, had considerable autonomy and did not necessarily view themselves as subjects of either Lhasa or Beijing. The Khampas had a strong martial tradition, and Kham became the center of armed opposition to China.

After the invasion by China the Tibetan National Assembly asked that the young Dalai Lama assume full secular power in Tibet several years earlier than planned. Meanwhile, China forced a Tibetan delegation to sign the Sino-Tibetan Agreement of 1951 (known as the "Seventeen Point Agreement"), by which Beijing absorbed Tibet into its territory. China soon breached guarantees of Tibetan autonomy and religious freedoms in that agreement as China began to absorb the Tibetan administration and to usurp functions of the Tibetan government. Chinese soldiers and settlers moved into Tibet in increasing numbers, especially after completion of a drivable road to Lhasa through eastern Tibet in 1954. Many Chinese Communists had sincerely expected to be greeted as liberators by the people they saw as feudal masses; they were surprised by Tibetan opposition to their presence.

In 1954 the Dalai Lama went to Beijing, where he met Mao Zedong, and in 1956 the Dalai Lama was allowed to travel to India for celebrations of the 2,500th anniversary of the enlightenment of the Buddha. While he was there the Indian government advised him to accept Chinese control of Tibet, and, with China hinting at compromise, the Dalai Lama returned to Tibet hoping to reach a solution through discussion with the Communist leadership.

The years 1955 and 1956 brought a quick acceleration of the transition to Communism throughout China, climaxing in the disastrous Great Leap Forward policy in 1958. Tibet experienced an accelerated program of collectivization, the widespread institution of "class struggle," especially against monastic authorities, and attempts made to render the large Tibetan nomadic population sedentary.

These Chinese policies triggered a strong reaction by Tibetans. By 1956 a guerrilla movement, the Chushi Gandruk (Four Rivers, Six Ranges) was active in eastern Tibet. The Dalai Lama's policy of nonviolence meant he was not able to offer his personal support to the guerrillas, and he continued to attempt to mediate a peaceful solution to the crisis until his departure from Tibet. However, many elements of the Tibetan government supported the guerrillas, who were then defending primarily Tibetan Buddhism and the Tibetan social system rather than explicitly trying to create a nationalist movement.

Tibet's resistance to the Chinese Communists attracted the intention of the intelligence services of various countries, including the U.S. Central Intelligence Agency (CIA). By 1958 CIA aid began to reach the guerrillas.

Uprising and Exile

By 1959 the turmoil in eastern Tibet had created a sizable influx of refugees entering Lhasa, which worsened food shortages created by the large numbers of Chinese troops stationed there. By early March of 1959 the population of Lhasa was further increased by the large crowds who gathered for the Monlam Chenmo (Tibetan New Year) celebration, traditionally an unruly period when the monastic powers dominated the secular structures of state.

Contributing to the instability in Lhasa was an invitation to attend a theater performance issued to the Dalai Lama by the Chinese military commander in Lhasa. On 9 March the Dalai Lama was instructed by the Chinese to come to the military barracks the next day without his usual armed escort. The Tibetan public interpreted his invitation as a Chinese attempt to seize the Dalai Lama.

A crowd estimated at thirty thousand people (Lhasa's population in 1950 was around twenty thousand) gathered around Norbu Lingka, the Dalai Lama's summer palace. The primary goal of the crowd was to prevent the Dalai Lama from accepting the Chinese invitation, but the apparently spontaneous demonstration took on a nationalist character as the crowd also began to protest Chinese presence in Lhasa and to demand Tibetan independence. A showdown became inevitable.

On 17 March Chinese troops fired artillery shells into the grounds of the Norbu Lingka, apparently in an attempt to frighten the Tibetans into submission. That night a plan was put into operation whereby the Dalai Lama, disguised as a Tibetan soldier, was smuggled out of the palace. His escape was kept secret for several days, and with a small group of supporters he traveled south through the mountains to India. Eighty to a hundred thousand Tibetans joined him in India, and a Tibetan government-in-exile was established at Dharmsala in northern India.

Meanwhile, in Lhasa the Chinese began a full-scale military crackdown. Exact figures are difficult to ascertain, but thousands of Tibetans were killed or executed, with Chinese army intelligence reports admitting that Chinese forces "eliminated" 87,000 of their opponents in Lhasa and surrounding areas in March–October 1959 alone.

Forgotten Footnote

The Communist invasion of Tibet stimulated a sense of Tibetan national identity, and in the eyes of Tibetans and much of the world, the uprising of March 1959 was a nationalist uprising against the rule of a foreign power. Tibetan resistance subsequently coalesced around the Dalai Lama, whose insistence on nonviolent resistance has meant that armed Tibetan resistance to China has been largely forgotten. The uprising of 1959 remains a historical division between traditional and modern Tibet and with events in 1989 and 2008 is often referred to by those who are involved in campaigns for Tibetan autonomy or independence.

Alex McKAY

Further Reading

Ali, S. M. (1999). *Cold war in the high Himalayas: The USA, China and South Asia in the 1950s.* Richmond, U.K.: Curzon.

Barnett, R., & Akiner, S. (Eds.). (1994). *Resistance and reform in Tibet.* London: C. Hurst.

Goldstein, M., Siebenschuh, W., & Tsering, T. (1997). *The struggle for modern Tibet: The autobiography of Tashi Tsering.* Armonk, NY: M. E. Sharpe.

Richardson, H. (1984). *Tibet & its history.* Boston: Shambhala.

Shakya, T. (1999). *The dragon in the land of snows: A history of modern Tibet since 1947.* Washington, DC: Columbia University Press.

Smith, W. (1996). *Tibetan nation: A history of Tibetan nationalism and Sino-Tibetan relations.* Boulder, CO: Westview.

Carry out an execution before seeking the decree.

先 斩 后 奏

Xiān zhǎn hòu zòu

Comprehensive index starts in volume 5, page 2667.

Tibetans (Zang)

Xīzàngrén 西藏人

Living in the highest mountainous region in the world, the Zang people of Tibet arrived from India over two thousand years ago. Numbering around 5.4 million people in the 2000 census, they are one of China's fifty-five officially recognized ethnic minority groups.

The Zang ethnic minority of China, or Tibetans, mainly live in the Tibetan Autonomous Region and in Qinghai, Gansu, Sichuan and Yunnan provinces. Their population in the 2000 census was around 5.4 million, although statistics can be unreliable. The Zang's ancestors, known as Ch'iang, were nomads from India who herded sheep and cattle. They moved westward, climbing the Himalayan mountain chain along the Yarlung Zangbo River over 2,000 years ago. Zang live in the highest mountainous region in the world, about 7,000 meters above sea level, which is remote and inaccessible, with virtually uninhabited high mountains and plains of intense cold, and abundant mineral resources.

Zang people developed two basic ways of life: one agricultural, settled in the warmer river valleys, and the other nomadic, which spread north and east into mountainous steppe grasslands also inhabited by Mongolian tribes.

Today Zang people live in three main regions: U-Tsang (west and central Tibet), Kham (Qinghai, Sichuan and Yunnan provinces), and Amdo (northeast and Gansu Province), and speak regional dialects of a Tibeto-Burman non-tonal language. They have their own writing system, based on the Devanagari script similar to Sanskrit, which was developed in the 600s under the great Tibetan warrior king Srong-btsan sGam-po (620–650? CE) who unified the country. He is credited with introducing Buddhism to Tibet and building the Jo-Khang temple in the capital of Lhasa, influenced by Nepalese and Chinese

A Tibetan man wearing a traditional fur hat.

Tibetan women at a market in Xiao Zhongdian, a rural area known for its breathtaking scenery.
PHOTO BY JOAN LEBOLD COHEN.

wives. The Chinese Princess Wencheng cemented an alliance with the Tang Dynasty (618–907 CE).

Zang have been known for their great devotion to religion. Tibetan Buddhism or tantric lamaism is a mixture of Mahayana Buddhism and the Tibetan nativist religion of Bon, a kind of animistic shamanism. It has a number of schools emphasizing different traditions, and, until the era of the People's Republic of China (PRC), many Tibetan males (estimates vary between 20 and 50 percent of the male population) lived as monks in thousands of monasteries. During the Cultural Revolution (1966–1976) it is claimed that 6000 monasteries were destroyed, and hundreds of thousands of religious killed or forcibly laicized. In recent decades, the government of the PRC has rebuilt many of the destroyed monasteries and permitted some monks to return.

The Tibetan kingdom from the 660s to 1200 was powerful and independent until the rise of the Mongols. After envoys of Chinggis Khan (1162–1227) demanded Tibetan submission in 1207, the Mongols and the Tibetan Buddhist sect of Sa-skya developed a Patron-Priest relationship with the Mongolian army installing its grand lama as the religious leader of Tibet in exchange for support of Mongolian military and political power in Tibet. The 'Phags-pa Lama (1235–1280) became the tutor of Khubilai Khan (1215–1294), who introduced Tibetan lamaism

to his court during the Yuan Dynasty (1271–1368). With the end of Mongol rule in China, Tibet degenerated into political and religious turmoil.

Tsong-kha-pa (1357–1419) was a great Buddhist reformer who established the dGe-lugs-pa ("Yellow Hat") sect of reincarnating lamas. The highest reincarnation was called the Dalai Lama. This system rose to religious and then political supremacy in Tibet through the support of Western Mongol leaders, particularly Altan Khan (1507–1582), who created the title of Dalai Lama and renewed the Patron-Priest alliance between Tibet and Mongolia of Khubilai's period that competed against the Ming Dynasty (1368–1644). A Mongol army invaded Lhasa to install the 5th Dalai Lama (1617–1682), the first to combine religious and secular power in Tibet and the builder of the Potala Palace (the largest structure in Tibet). During the Manchu Qing Dynasty (1644–1912), Tibet closed itself off from foreigners, who were not allowed to enter the capital of Lhasa under pain of death. In 1720s the Kham and Amdo regions of Tibet were incorporated into the Qing Empire and Chinese high commissioners (*ambans*) were posted in Lhasa. The Qing emperors financially supported lamaism and engineered the selection of the Dalai Lamas by the drawing of lots in Beijing.

The twentieth century was a turbulent one for the Zang. The British Younghusband expedition of 1904 invaded

The central room of the Wong family's house in the Tibetan village of Shan Qiao. PHOTO BY JOAN LEBOLD COHEN.

Tibet to temporarily occupy Lhasa. Chinese armies invaded in 1905 and in 1910, but retreated during the decades of civil war and Japanese invasion, although neither the Republic of China nor the PRC ever renounced claim to control over Tibet. In 1951 Tibetan and PRC authorities signed an agreement affirming Chinese sovereignty. In 1959 an anti-Chinese rebellion spread to Lhasa and the 14th Dalai Lama (b. 1935) fled to Dharamsala in north India where he still lives with his government in exile; in 1989 the Dalai Lama was awarded the Nobel Peace Prize. In 1965 U-Tsang and western Kham were made an autonomous region, monastic estates were disbanded, and secular education introduced. The regional government today includes Han Chinese as well as members of the Zang ethnicity. Since 1980, economic development has accelerated, most religious freedoms have been restored, and Tibet has been opened up for tourism, although the situation of the Zang is a sensitive issue for the PRC and the outside world, and violent demonstrations are not uncommon.

Tibetan culture and customs are unique. Its Buddhist iconography, epitomized by *thankha* painting, is vividly colored with elaborate religious representation. The palace and temple architecture consists of massive wooden structures with flat roofs and multiple windows, and ornate interiors. Homes are made from rocks, wood, and cement, while nomads live in yak-hide tents. Zang men and women have plaited hair. Women wear long-sleeved wrapped gowns over white blouses with colorfully stripped woolen aprons, while nomadic men wear trousers covered by a long-sleeved gown. Zang often exchange *khatas,* a long, usually white, ceremonial silk scarf.

Tibetan cuisine is distinctive, utilizing the main agriculture crop, barley. *Tsampa,* the main staple of Tibetan cuisine, is barley flour that is roasted and rolled into dough; barley is also made into meat-filled dumplings called *momo.* Yak, goat, and mutton meat, cheese, yogurt, and buttered milk-tea are common. Tibetan wool rugs, a Tibetan calendar, and Tibetan medicine are renowned. Zang celebrate many religious festivals and the Tibetan New Year's festival.

Alicia CAMPI

Further Reading

R. A. Stein. (1972). *Tibetan civilization.* Stanford, CA: Stanford University Press.

Snellgrove, D., & Richardson, H. (1995). *A cultural history of Tibet.* Boston & London: Shambhala.

Goldstein, M. C., & Beall, C. M. (1990). *Nomads of western Tibet.* Berkeley: University of California Press.

Comprehensive index starts
in volume 5, page 2667.

Tigers

Lǎohǔ 老虎

Once a royal symbol of war, tigers have become a casualty of both traditional Chinese medicine and environmental destruction in modern China, fading into extinction. The most endangered species of tiger, the South China Tiger, has not been spotted in the wild since the 1960s, and only a few dozen survive in captivity, making it "functionally extinct."

Deeply ingrained in Chinese culture as a fierce symbol of war, tigers were, for millennia, the emblems of the highest ministers of defense in China, second only to the dragon and the phoenix of the emperor and empress. The Asian equivalent of the lion as the "king of the jungle," the strong and elegant tiger has also been an important icon as the White Tiger of the West, one of the Four Constellations of Chinese astronomy, and a prevalent image in Buddhist lore and martial arts such as Shaolin.

Although the Indochinese tiger (*Panthera tigris corbetti*) is found in China, Cambodia, Laos, Myanmar (Burma), Thailand, and Vietnam (the International Union for Conservation of Nature and Natural Resources estimates that only 630 survive), the South China or Amoy Tiger (*Panthera tigris amoyensis*), is the indigenous species with which most Chinese relate. With no official sighting since 1964, the Amoy has faded into "functional extinction" since the 1950s, when at least four thousand

A paper cut-out depicting Wu Sung, the folk hero from the famous Chinese novel *Water Margin*, who was revered for killing the tiger that had terrified the people living on Mount Ching Yang.

remained in the wild forests and grasslands of central and southeastern China. Now one of the world's ten most endangered animals, the dilemma of the South China tiger is three-fold: first, the dried bone of the tiger has been a coveted ingredient in Chinese traditional medicine (TCM) for thousands of years; second, agricultural expansion has put it at odds with farmers and herders upon whose cattle, pigs and goats it naturally preys, qualifying it as an official "pest" in the anti-pest campaigns of the 1950s and 1960s; and third, China's burgeoning population has converted much of its wooded habitat and previous range. By 1982 it was estimated that only 200–300 of these tigers remained; domestic trade of traditional medicines and "tiger wines" made from tiger bones was outlawed in China in 1993. Other preservation efforts have included the establishment of nature reserves by China's State Forestry Administration in the 1990s. Nevertheless, by 1996 the Amoy tiger population had been reduced to less than one hundred animals, with less than fifty in the wild.

Today, about sixty-five individuals live in zoos and on breeding preserves, all located within China. However, since 2002 an organization called Save China's Tigers has sponsored a project in coordination with the Chinese government in which several Amoy have been exported to a South African preserve, with some breeding success. The hope is that a wild population can be developed there for eventual repatriation to China. But some genetic research suggests that all of these captive tigers are descended from only a few animals, making the genetic pool too small to prevent eventual attrition from inbreeding.

The South China Tiger (*Panthera tigris amoyensis*) is thought to be the original "stem" tiger from which all tiger subspecies evolved, and it is considerably smaller than its Siberian cousins. In addition to wild populations which some scientists and farmers insist still exist, it is as endangered as the panda and even more of an historic cultural symbol. Yesterday the tiger embodied China's fierce power of conquest, and today it is an emblem of China's modern environmental controversy.

Nicole MUCHMORE

Further Reading

Alderton, D., & Tanner, B. (1998). *Wild cats of the world.* New York: Sterling.

Thapar, V. (1992). *The tiger's destiny.* London: Kyle Cathie.

IUCN-World Conservation Union. (2000). The 2000 IUCN red list of threatened species. Retrieved January 18, 2009, from http://www.redlist.org

World Wide Fund for Nature (WWF). (6 December, 2006). Traditional Chinese medicine experts speak against captive breeding of tigers. Retrieved February 25, 2009 from http://www.wwfchina.org/english/loca.php?loca=416

Tofu

Dòufu 豆腐

The Chinese food staple tofu, made from soybeans, is ancient. The discovery of how to process soybeans in order to derive food value from them was a breakthrough in human nutrition.

Tofu (bean curd) serves as a protein- rich meat substitute, and is an inexpensive and popular staple of Chinese cuisine. PHOTO BY J. SAMUEL BURNER.

S cholars are not sure when the food tofu was first made, but the technology was well known in China by early medieval times and possibly as early as the Han dynasty (206 BCE–220 CE). Scholars have cited imitation of cheese making in the Altaic region—between Mongolia and China and between Kazakhstan and Russia—as one possible source of the technology. Regardless, one of the great breakthroughs in human nutrition was the discovery of how to process soybeans, which are difficult to digest, into nutritious tofu (*doufu*). To make tofu one soaks soybeans overnight, grinding them finely with water, boiling them into a slurry, and filtering the slurry to produce soy milk. The milk can then be precipitated (caused to separate from solution or suspension) using settlers, commonly magnesium salts, and pressed into slabs.

Recently tofu has become a staple of Chinese cooking as a readily available and inexpensive source of protein. Tofu is less well represented in early recipe books, but this status might be because of tofu's common origins. Other tofu products include the fermented *choudoufu* ("stinking bean curd," an acquired taste) and the "skin" (*doufupi*), which is skimmed off and dried.

Paul D. BUELL

Further Reading

Anderson, E. N. (1988). *The food of China*. New Haven, CT: Yale University Press.

Huang, H. T. (2000). *Biology and biological technology: Science and civilisation in China series*. Cambridge, U.K.: Cambridge University Press.

Huang, H. T. (2001). *Fermentations and food science: Science and civilisation in China series*. Cambridge, U.K: Cambridge University Press.

Shurtleff, W., & Aoyagi, A. (1975). *The book of tofu*. Berkeley, CA: Ten Speed Press.

Tongdian

Tōngdiǎn 通典

Tongdian 通典 **is an encyclopedia compiled in the Tang Dynasty (618–907 CE) by the prominent scholar-official Du You** 杜佑 **(735–812 CE). A survey of the social, political and cultural institutions of Chinese history, the** *Tongdian* **served as a longstanding model for the compilation of Chinese encyclopedias.**

The *Tongdian* (*Survey of Institutions*) is an historical encyclopedia of two hundred chapters that was presented to the court in 801 by Du You (735–812 CE). Widely revered for his broad learning, Du was a successful official and influential figure in politics of the Tang dynasty (618–907 CE), serving mostly in provincial posts with occasional appointments in the central administration. Drawing upon a wide range of sources for his compilation, Du took thirty-six years to complete the *Tongdian*.

During this period the empire partially recovered after the disastrous An Lushan Rebellion (755–763 CE), an era of great cultural and intellectual foment. Scholars such as Du You felt that a considered analysis of the social, political, and cultural institutions of Chinese history was crucial to understanding and addressing the challenges of his era. In his writings Du You held to the traditional Confucian view that the past serves as a guide for the present. In a rather non-Confucian stance, however, Du argued that the emulation of high antiquity is insufficient and that social and political institutions need to change with the times. Only by carefully examining the evolution of human institutions in history can proper administrative practices be determined. The *Tongdian* reflected these concerns and was designed as a broad reference guide for the scholar-officials of the realm.

The *Tongdian* is composed of quotations from varied sources, arranged in topical order, and punctuated with the compiler's own comments and observations. The materials included traced the institutions from the dawn of Chinese history up to the Tianbao reign (742–755) of the Tang dynasty, just before the An Lushan Rebellion. Du You intermittently added comments about changes made between that time and his own day. The inspiration for the *Tongdian* was an earlier work, the thirty-five-chapter *Zhengdian* (Institutions of Governance), compiled by Liu Zhi, the son of the famous Tang historian Liu Zhiji (661–721). The *Zhengdian* is no longer extant, although the *Tongdian* quoted liberally from this work. In fact, so much of this earlier text was incorporated into the *Tongdian* that it is frequently difficult to discern Du's own views from those that apparently came from the *Zhengdian*.

Social and Political Focus

Although the *Tongdian* makes frequent references to Confucian moral cultivation and harmony, the focus of the text is social and political, economic, and pragmatic rather than philosophical or doctrinal. Du You did not include extended accounts of cosmology, metaphysics, or moralistic historical judgment. The *Tongdian* presents a view of human history shaped largely by its social and political institutions. The bottom-line value in this encyclopedia is social and political order and the institutional formulations necessary to achieve it. In his opening chapter on economic matters, Du You observed that the first priority in governance is the edification of the people. That edification depends upon first making sure that the people have sufficient food and clothing.

Beyond these basic human needs, however, the *Tongdian* strongly emphasized ritual: the ceremonies and protocols of the court and society. One hundred chapters—half of the encyclopedia—are devoted to ritual prescriptions from earliest times down to the eighth century. Included here are important commentaries on early ritual texts that are no longer extant elsewhere. A large portion of the ritual section of the *Tongdian* dwells on current prescriptions. Much of this part was taken directly from the official Tang ritual code, the *Kaiyuan Li* (Rituals of the Kaiyuan Reign), compiled in 732.

Organization

The *Tongdian* is organized by a number of chapters grouped in categories and subcategories.

- **Economics (*Shihuo*, chapters 1–12).** A broad survey of economic management issues, including land tenure and organization, population fluctuation and registration, different forms of taxation, money and coinage, canal transportation, and the government salt and iron monopolies.

- **Civil Service Selection (*Keju*, chapters 13–18).** A description of the systems of selecting officials, dynasty by dynasty, followed by summaries of the various debates on civil service selection.

- **Bureaucracy (*Zhiguan*, chapters 19–40).** A survey of the various official positions and bureaus, the changing meaning of titles in different periods, and the allocation of rank and compensation for service. This section includes both the civil and military bureaucracy and both central and provincial administrations.

- **Ritual (*Li*, chapters 41–140).** A broad summary of the ritual ceremonies and the protocol obligations of the imperial family, the court and top officials, and families throughout the empire. Prescriptions include ritual performances, clothing and ornamentation, transportation, seasonal timing of activities, and arrangements for birth, marriage, illness, death, and the veneration of ancestors.

- **Music (*Yue*, chapters 141–147).** A description of theories of music and its place in society, music offices in different dynasties, the twelve tones of music, instrument calibration, song, and ceremonial music.

- **Warfare (*Bing*, chapters 148–162).** A survey of military theory and strategy.

- **Punishments (*Xing*, chapters 163–170).** A description of the theories of punishment and its uses and a survey of penal systems through the dynasties, followed by a summary of debates on the subject.

- **Administrative Districts (*Zhoujun*, chapters 171–184).** An overview of the administrative units of China, with a description of the evolution of each prefecture and county.

- **Border Frontiers (*Bianfang*, chapters 185–200).** A description of the tribes and kingdoms of the four directions.

Model for Later Works

The *Tongdian* was one of the first encyclopedias of its kind and served as a model for many future compilations. A two hundred-chapter sequel to the *Tongdian*, the *Xu Tongdian*, was commissioned by Emperor Taizong (reigned 976–997) of the Song dynasty (960–1279), although that work is no longer extant. Another 150-chapter work by the same name was ordered in 1767 by the court of Emperor Qianlong (reigned 1736–1795) of the Qing dynasty (1644–1912). The *Tongdian* was regarded as one of the "Three Surveys" (Santong), the other two being Zheng Qiao's (1104–1162) *Tongzhi* (Survey Monographs) and Ma Duanlin's (1254–1324) *Wenxian tongkao* (Survey of the

Du You's Preface to the *Comprehensive Institutions*

In his preface to the "Food and Goods" section of the Comprehensive Institutions (Tongdian), Du You explains why he believes that satisfying the people's material needs is a prerequisite to educating them.

Although I engaged in the study of books from an early age, because I was a dullard by nature, I did not succeed in mastering the arts of number or astrological sciences, nor was I good at literary composition. Thus my *Comprehensive Institutions* actually amounts to no more than a compilation of various records that, if used in dealing with human affairs, might be helpful in governmental administration.

The first priority in ordering things according to the Way lies in transforming the people through education, and the basis of education lies in providing adequate clothing and food. The [*Classic of*] *Changes* [*I Ching*] says that what attracts people is wealth. The "Grand Model" [chapter of the *Classic of Documents*] lists eight administrative functions, of which the first is food and the second provision is goods. The *Guanzi* says: "When the storehouse is full, then people can understand rites and good manners; when there is a sufficiency of food and clothing, people can understand the difference between honor and shame." The Master [Confucius] spoke of enriching people first and then educating them. All these saying express the same idea.

To carry out education one must first establish offices; to establish offices, one must recruit people with the requisite talents; and to recruit talent one must have an examination system, establish proper rites to rectify popular customs, and have music to harmonize people's minds-and-hearts. These were the methods employed by the early sage kings to establish proper governance.

It is only when there has been a failure in education that one resorts to laws and punishments, to commanderies and prefectures for local administration, and to fortifying the borders against barbarians. Thus "Food and Goods" come first; official recruitment next, offices next after that; then rites, music, punishments, and local administration, with border defenses last. Anyone who reads this book should keep in mind my reasons for arranging things in this order.

Source: de Bary, W. T., & Bloom, I. (1999). *Sources of Chinese tradition, vol. I.* New York: Columbia University Press, 655–656.

Literary Record). In 1936 Commercial Press in Shanghai published a compilation of the "Ten Surveys" (Shitong), including the three aforementioned and seven other works that were designed in the same format.

Peter B. DITMANSON

Further Reading

Twitchett, D. (1992). *The writing of official history under the T'ang.* Cambridge, U.K. and New York: Cambridge University Press.

Tourism

Lǚyóu 旅游

Tourism in China has experienced revolutionary change, growing from its most basic level to a strategic industry in China's evolving socialist market economy. Two decades of development have brought positive experiences and presented some challenges, both with an impact on local attitudes, culture, and practice.

Before the economic liberalization that accompanied China's open door policy in 1978, the country really did not have a modern tourism industry. Even after opening and normalization, change in the tourism industry was slow. The structure of China's tourist industry remained relatively simple, although gradual changes could be noted as China moved more and more toward trade and commerce.

Not until the 1990s did an increase in the Chinese people's annual income and improvements in public transportation infrastructure result in a considerable increase in domestic tourism. The number of domestic tourists increased from 300 million in 1991 to 629 million in 1995. Travel was becoming fashionable in China.

A 1998 survey on domestic tourism showed that the main motivations of Chinese tourists were sightseeing and visiting family and friends, accounting for 46.9 percent and 27.2 percent of the total, respectively. But such leisure travelers represented only the wealthiest portion of the Chinese population—even in 1998 the vast majority of people in China did not "vacation." Rather, the only

In the harbor of Macao, an international tourist destination because of its famous casinos, a cruise ship approaches the dock.
PHOTO BY JOAN LEBOLD COHEN.

Every morning at dawn thousands of Chinese tourists flock to Tiananmen Square to watch the flag raising ceremony and listen to lectures and musical performances.
PHOTO BY TOM CHRISTENSEN.

travel periodically done by the masses was for business, academic, health, and religious reasons.

Reformed Gold Weeks

The introduction of the reformed "Gold Weeks" holiday policy allowed the concept of leisure travel to really take hold in China, and the country began to experience an unprecedented travel boom. The Chinese government in September 1999 introduced a new holiday policy that extended three major public holidays—the Spring Festival (Chinese New Year), which occurs in January or February, International Labor Day (1 May), and National Day (1 October)—such that each became a week long.

Zhu Rongji, prime minister at the time, hoped that this holiday policy would quicken development of the tourism industry in China, increase domestic demand, and stimulate economic growth. The new policy had an immediate effect. During the first Gold Week in October 1999, 28 million Chinese went on holiday, which earned 14.1 billion yuan ($1.8 billion) for China's tourism industry. Experts have said that the institution of the Gold Weeks was probably the most effective policy ever introduced in China. Called "gold" because of the great economic benefits they would bring, not only did these holiday periods stimulate the development of the tourism industry, but also they had a great impact on Chinese lifestyle and culture. More Chinese, especially young people, have become willing to spend money on their holidays, traveling to tourist destinations inside or outside China. The word *leisure* has become a part of the Chinese vocabulary.

Travel and Leisure

Leisure, formerly a concept known only to the wealthy, now encompasses the masses in China. Farmers have embraced the concepts of travel and leisure, with more farmers traveling every year.

The holiday policy has had a direct impact on some of the most valued and prominent traditions in China. This impact is seen most poignantly by the nationwide debate of how to spend time during the Spring Festival, the most important festival in China—as important as Christmas is in the Western world. The festival traditionally is a time for families to reunite and to celebrate the New Year. But today more and more people are traveling elsewhere during the Spring Festival rather than returning home to their families. This option has created conflict. Generally speaking, the older generation insists that people respect the traditions of Spring Festival and return home for the holiday, whereas the younger generation insists that tradition is outmoded. For the young travel is a good alternative.

Mixed Opinion

Public opinion in China is varied regarding the impact of tourism. Whereas many people enjoy the benefits that the tourism industry offers, others point to the negative ways it has affected the lives of people, especially those living in tourist areas.

Tourism promotes interaction between people in the tourist destinations and the outside world. Travelers to remote areas bring new technology and ideas, which in turn can promote social development of the local community. Thus, most local communities appreciate the

People traverse the Great Wall. The Great Wall remains one of the most popular tourist destinations in the world.
PHOTO BY JOAN LEBOLD COHEN.

opportunities given them by tourism, including knowledge of other languages, lifestyles, and ideas, as well as the chance to share their own culture with others.

But many people believe that this exposure has been a corrupting influence, damaging the local culture of the people—often minorities—who live in remote areas, which include many of China's tourism destinations. With development of the tourism industry, many of these peoples have begun to adopt the language, clothing, and cultural values of tourists.

The development of domestic tourism in China has created a number of other problems, most notably problems of environment and heritage protection. Travel in China, extremely congested during the Gold Weeks, placed a great burden on most tourist destinations during those times. Lacking sustainable practices, many tourist destinations, especially natural and heritage sites, are suffering the impact of mass visitation.

For example, at the Dunhuang Caves, a United Nations World Cultural Heritage site in Gansu Province in northeast China, carbon dioxide and water vapor from the breathing of the great number of visitors during the Gold Weeks discolored the caves' centuries-old murals. Implementation of sustainable practices has often taken a backseat to recovery measures; people working with these attractions spend all year recovering damaged works.

Travel safety was always an issue from the time the Gold Weeks were first declared. The Traffic Control Bureau of the Ministry of Public Security always reported an increase of traffic incidents and fatalities during these times. According to its statistics, 1,107 people were killed in a total of 3,358 traffic accidents during the Spring Festival peak tourist season in 2007, although the death toll dropped by 36.5 percent and the number of injured people decreased by 56.7 percent fewer than the same period of 2006. As a result of the traffic and other problems Gold Weeks presented, National Day, along with Labor Day, was reestablished as a one-day holiday in December 2007.

Travel Abroad

As domestic tourism has increased, the Chinese have had a growing perception that the quality of their trips is declining significantly. Overcrowding and deterioration of attractions are having an adverse effect on the tourism experience during the Gold Weeks to the point that inbound tourists have learned to avoid travel to China during these times.

Chinese authorities in recent years sought solutions to these problems, such as introducing compulsory annual leave to ensure that workers had chances to travel during times other than the Gold Weeks. In the meantime a large middle-class population with disposable income has become more dissatisfied with traveling inside China, and outbound tourism has been increasing rapidly since the beginning of the twenty-first century. China's outbound tourists totaled 20.2 million in 2003, overtaking Japan's total for the first time. Around 100 countries or areas are open to Chinese tour groups with the USA receiving its first leisure tour groups in 2008. Also in July 2008, direct leisure flights from mainland China to Taiwan increased significantly.

What the increase in outbound tourism will mean is yet to be learned, but as with the increase in domestic tourism, the cultural and heritage implications are certain to include both positive and negative effects.

Peiyi DING and Noel SCOTT

Further Reading

China National Tourism Administration. (2001). *Zhongguo luyouye fazha "shiwu" jihua he 2015/2020 nian yuanjing mubiao gangyao* [The 10th five-year plan and long-term goal outlines up to 2015 and 2020 for tourism development in China]. Beijing: China Tourism Publishing House.

Ding Peiyi & Craig-Smith, S. (2004). International tourism potential in Inner Mongolia: A marketing appraisal. In Tian Chen (Ed.), *Inner Mongolia tourism master plan and project report* (pp. 173–193). Beijing: Commercial Press.

Lew, A. A., & Yu, Lawrence. (Eds.). (1995). *Tourism in China: Geographical, political, and economic perspectives.* Boulder, CO: Westview Press.

Wall, G., & Stone, M. (2003). Ecotourism and community development: Diaoluoshan National Forest Park, Hainan, China. In M. Ranga & A. Chandra (Eds.), *Tourism and hospitality management in the 21st century* (pp. 20–52). Delhi: Discovery Publishing House.

Township and Village Enterprises

Xiāngzhèn qǐyè 乡镇企业

Township and village enterprises (TVEs) were businesses designated to operate in the countryside or in small and medium-size towns. These enterprises created a large number of jobs from the late 1970s to the 1990s, and are responsible for a huge proportion of China's economic development. In recent years, their contribution has become more limited, and as more people move to urban areas the wealth gap between countryside and cities is increasing again.

The growth of township and village enterprises (TVEs) is linked to the first wave of China's economic reforms from the late 1970s to the beginning of the 1980s. The implementation of the household responsibility system (HRS) and the decentralization program of the 1980s fueled the growth of TVEs and the industrialization of the countryside. The HRS revealed much underemployment in rural areas, possibly 100 to 150 million people, and part of this redundant labor force found jobs in TVEs.

The growth of TVEs can be divided into at least three phases. During the first phase (from 1978 to about the end of the 1980s) the scale of growth was unexpected, and academic and political debates emphasized the advantages of either the Wenzhou (city) model (i.e., the development of private enterprises) or the Jiangsu (Province) model (based on the importance of collective enterprises).

During the second phase (from the end of the 1980s to the mid-1990s) growth accelerated further. Scholars then shifted to the debate over whether local governments or populations were more important in the course of local development. Finally, during the mid-1990s specialists began to question if the growth of rural enterprises was sustainable in the long term as the development of China became more urban driven.

Definition and Statistics

The amount of research generated by the growth of TVEs during the 1980s and 1990s has led to the proliferation of definitions of TVEs. Yet, the definition itself affects the interpretation one can have of this phenomenon (for example, whether or not individual enterprises are included). The most expedient solution is to refer to the official definition.

This definition has two major dimensions. The first is historical and geographical. Originally the term *TVEs* (in Chinese *xiangzhen qiye* 乡镇企业, or literally "town and township enterprises") applied *only* to enterprises that were under the ownership of the People's Commune and the Brigade of Production. They were collective in nature and anchored in the countryside. The second dimension includes details of the mode of property. With the HRS individual activities were greatly stimulated and resulted in the creation of "individual businesses" (of fewer than eight workers) and, since 1988 (officially), private enterprises (of eight workers or more). When such enterprises are located at the county (*xian*) level or at any administrative unit under this level (towns and townships), they are also TVEs. Finally, TVEs also comprise enterprises created by several households, various forms of joint ventures, and so forth. In short, the official definition of a TVE incorporates any type of enterprise that is located at the county level or lower other than state-owned enterprises. This categorization had to be gradually adjusted since the end of the 1990s because of a multiplication of the types of property, but the theoretical differences between the collective and private sectors remain. This is an important point because most TVE scholars have ignored the private economy (especially individual enterprises).

Indeed, a large part of TVE growth can be attributed to the private sector, which in 1990 employed more workers than the collectives for the first time. All in all, this growth has been impressive: In 1978 only 28 million people were working for TVEs, all of which were in collective enterprises. By 1996 the number of TVE workers reached 135 million, but since then the growth has slowed, inching up to 142 million by 22.5 million enterprises by 2005. That year total net TVE profits were RMB¥1,069 billion (US$ 133.63 billion) and the taxes they paid were RMB¥518 billion (64.75 billion).

Wenzhou Model versus Jiangsu Model

The origins of the TVEs are twofold. The first dates back to the collective era at the time of the promotion of rural industries. Even though this experience was not successful (especially during the Great Leap Forward), it gave the local cadres the experience of managing industrial ventures (particularly after the development of the "five small industries" during the 1970s). With the 1980s decentralization policies that placed resources in their hands, these cadres were able to make use of their experience and develop collective enterprises—mostly for local taxation income. The second origin relates to the long existence of nonagricultural activities in the Chinese countryside, a phenomenon already noted by John Buck, the then- renowned specialist of China agriculture during the 1920s, but which were banned during the collectivization period. The HRS revived these activities, especially small commercial and industrial businesses that did not require a substantial amount of capital.

During the 1980s the coexistence of these two forms of rural enterprise raised concerns among the Chinese leadership and academia alike. They perceived the growth of TVEs as a tool for keeping people in the countryside or in small and medium cities instead of having them move to large metropolises (in accordance with the strategy elaborated by Fei Xiaotong 费孝通, the sociologist at the roots of the rural reforms in China). However, questions arose over the respective roles of the private and collective sectors within the national economy—sometimes over the very existence of the private sector itself. The debate converged on the mode of development of the two regions, which were especially successful in terms of TVE growth. The first mode one was in the Wenzhou area of Zhejiang Province, where the private economy was especially large; the other was in the Wuxi area of Jiangsu Province, which is famous for its collective sector. This debate was, of course, not only academic but also political because it questioned the role of the private sector in a socialist economy. Deng Xiaoping 邓小平 definitively settled this matter in 1992 with his highly publicized tour in the south, during which he gave explicit support to the private sector.

Government Intervention or Private Initiative

Therefore, beginning at the end of the 1980s the previous debate had to shift. The reasons for this shift were not only the definitive acceptance of the private sector and the conceptualization of the "socialist market economy" but also the appearance of multiple property forms in which private and collective sectors were tightly intertwined— making the distinction between them somewhat blurred. An increase in foreign investment (in particular in the coastal provinces) also contributed to the confusion. Therefore, after ten years of TVE growth, an assessment of the various roles of the private and collective sectors in this growth was necessary. Similarly, the reasons for the evolution of the mode of property and their complexity had to be analyzed.

Private enterprise (mainly in the form of individual enterprises) started in 1978 or even earlier, usually by people with little social and financial capital: A large proportion of these genuine entrepreneurs was demobilized soldiers, "educated youth," former political prisoners, people with a "bad" class origin, the unemployed, and so forth. They offered services that were no longer provided in the countryside (such as small restaurants, tailors, etc.) or made simple goods that the planned economy did not provide. For example, in the Wenzhou area households started producing buttons for clothes. By the end of the 1980s Wenzhou's button market became famous in China and beyond.

During the mid-1980s the economic success of these entrepreneurs stimulated a host of imitators, among them local cadres or their relatives. This second wave of entrepreneurs was much better connected and could access resources such as raw materials, information, technology, bank loans, and so forth. At the same time, to find enough financial resources for the development of their counties, local authorities also continued to stimulate the collective sector in order to reap the profits of and the taxes paid by these enterprises: Despite national regulations the separation between the budgets of the collective enterprises and the local budget was rather thin. Little by little the two waves of entrepreneurs started to merge into a single category while maintaining strong relationships with the local bureaucracies. Therefore, these enterprises were regarded, at the local and national levels, as a tool to promote the development of the local economy, not only through the employment they created but also through the taxes and the resources they generated.

In addition, the decentralization process put local authorities in control of major resources, such as raw materials, technological and marketing information, networks, and so forth, located in their areas. It was therefore necessary for private entrepreneurs to cultivate good relationships with the local authorities, who could either help them or ruin them (by refusing to issue the necessary authorizations or confiscating their ventures for example). Scholars such as Jean C. Oi described the phenomenon as "local state corporatism," in which local governments act as corporate firms (Oi, 1996). Other scholars, such as Daniel Kelliher, emphasized the role of private initiative.

Whatever the position adopted, the collusion between private entrepreneurs and local authorities was patent and generated negative externalities (corruption, for example). On the other hand, the system generated confusion between the different modes of property, which stimulated growth: The collective made use of the flexibility of the private sector, while the private sector got protection from the collective. For example, during the economic downturn of 1988–1990 many private enterprises registered as collectives while keeping their original management structure because the private sector did not have much political momentum at the time. Similarly, many collective enterprises lost money because of poor management and were contracted to the private sector in order to be more competitive. Still others were sold to management teams or to the workers (under the so-called cooperative system) while officially remaining under the collective banner. In this last case the decisions might have rested with the local cadres.

This system shaped a development pattern that was controlled by the local authorities and in which a strong bond existed between the private and collective sectors, so it was difficult to draw a border between the two property modes. Whether or not this arrangement is still suitable for the future development of China's economy and TVEs remains to be seen.

TVEs as a Factor for Development

In 2001 out of 21 million TVEs, 18.5 million were individual enterprises employing more than 60.2 million people (46 percent)—an average of three people per enterprise. Another 2 million private TVEs employed an average of eighteen people per enterprise. This meant that nearly all TVEs (20.5 million), totaling 97 million workers (or nearly 75 percent or the TVEs' labor force), were small businesses. A more recent breakdown is unavailable, but partial statistics confirm the previous trend.

These enterprises have been instrumental in creating employment, lowering the revenue gap between rural and urban areas, and offering a partial solution to unemployment. Nevertheless, despite their overwhelming statistical importance, these enterprises do not constitute a solution for China's long-term development because most have not increased in size or provoked organizational or technological changes. Their contribution to investment, for example, remains extremely limited. This is why most TVE scholars mistakenly omit them in their analysis.

In fact, few TVEs have played a major role in transforming the countryside, apart from those in selected rural areas (the Pearl River delta in Guangdong Province, for example). These enterprises have built connections with local authorities, as described earlier. Nevertheless, their functioning mode has also cast a shadow on their potential for sustainable development because the opportunities to benefit from both the collective and private systems in the short term are offset by the confusion over the property system. To give one example, enterprises that have been contracted to private hands have to return to collective management at the end of the contract (typically five years). However, in practice contractors and local governments have held endless debates over this setup, especially when the contractors have invested a significant amount of money (which is usually the case) in the venture. Signs indicate that the mode of development based on local government control of their resources has provoked waste and duplicated infrastructure, while corruption feeds growing discontent in the countryside. This is why Beijing now aims, with difficulty, to recentralize.

China's development based on TVEs has lost momentum since the end of the 1990s. The wealth gap between rural and urban areas has increased again, showing that the full potential of TVEs to provide jobs and be a tool for development has been reached. In recent years urban areas have generated most of China's economic growth, which has provoked a shift in the interest of researchers. The development of TVEs, however, remains an important experience and demonstrates to the developing world the potential of the countryside.

Louis AUGUSTIN-JEAN

Further Reading

Ahmad, E., et al. (2002). *Recentralization in China?* (IMF Working Paper WP/02/168), New York, International Monetary Fund. Augustin-Jean, L. (1997, June 1). Rural enterprises and the law. *China News Analysis 1586*, 1–10.

Augustin-Jean, L. (2006). The local economy in the context of globalization: Local organization versus WTO principles: An overview from Zhangpu and Yong'an Districts, Fujian Province. In K. Y. Chen, A. Androuais, & L. Augustin-Jean (Eds.), *Asian economies in the age of globalization* (pp. 165–179). Hong Kong: Centre for Asian Pacific Studies.

Buck, J. L. (1937). *Land utilization in China.* Nanjing, China: University of Nanking.

Byrd, W. A., & Lin, Q. S. (Ed.). (1990). *China's rural industry: Structure, development and reform.* Washington, DC: World Bank.

Fei, X. T. (1989). *Rural development in China: Prospect and retrospect.* Chicago: University of Chicago Press.

Kelliher, D. (1992). *Peasant power in China: The era of reform (1979–1989).* New Haven, CT: Yale University Press.

Nolan, P., & Dong, F. R. (Eds.). (1990). *Market forces in China, competition and small business: The Wenzhou debate.* London: Zed Books.

Odgaard, O. (1992). Entrepreneurs and elite formation in rural China. *The Australian Journal of Chinese Affairs 28*, 89–108.

Oi, J. C. (1989). *State and peasant in contemporary China: The political economy of village government.* Berkeley and Los Angeles: University of California Press.

Oi, J. C. (1992). Fiscal reform and the economic foundations of local state corporatism in China. *World Politics 45*, 99–126.

Oi, J. C. (1999). *Rural china takeoff: Institutional foundations of economic reforms.* Berkeley and Los Angeles: University of California Press.

Walder, A. (Ed.). (1996). *China's transitional economy.* Oxford, U.K.: Oxford University Press.

Whiting, S. H. (2001). *Power and wealth in rural China: The political economy of institutional change.* New York: Cambridge University Press.

Wong, P. W. C. (1988). Interpreting rural industrial growth in the post-Mao period. *Modern China, 14*(1), 3–30.

Young, S. (1995). *Private business and economic reform in China.* New York: M. E. Sharpe.

Toy Industry

Wánjù hángyè 玩具行业

Since its beginnings in the 1920s, China's toy industry has grown to become the largest in the world. Though faced with accusations of poor working conditions and taking the blow of recent recalls, the toy market in China remains the leading toy market today.

China is the world's largest toy maker and exporter with more than 8,000 toy manufacturers producing around 30,000 kinds of toys. The country's toy exports in 2005 totaled $15.18 billion, accounting for 70 percent of the world toy market. But the industry suffered a blow in 2007 with a series of recalls that dented the industry's reputation but did not alter predictions for continued growth, especially in the country's expanding domestic market.

Growth of China's Toy industry

Toy making in China began to take shape with the arrival of tin-can manufacturing around Shanghai in the 1920s and 1930s. Western influences in the area led to the manufacture of Western tin-plate toys that became quite popular. War-related toys, such as fighter planes, tanks,

An American boy looks at a store window display of toys, including a Chinese Checkers game, a policeman's accessory set including a toy pistol and handcuffs, Ring Toss, and a pastry set, 1942. Toys produced in China were finding their way onto the shelves of American toy stores as early as the 1920s. LIBRARY OF CONGRESS.

and soldiers, dominated the market around the time of the Japanese invasion of China in the mid-1930s. After the Communist Revolution of 1949, toys became a vehicle for propaganda, especially during the Cultural Revolution (1966–1976) when dolls in Mao suits and cars painted with political slogans flourished.

By the early 1980s, Hong Kong had become the world's largest toy exporter, but rising labor and land costs pushed the colony's toy manufacturers to relocate across the border to China. In 1984, China designated Shenzhen, Guangdong Province, its first special economic zone (SEZ), offering foreign investors a tariff-free environment with low-cost labor and cheap factory space. Hong Kong toy manufacturers moved more and more production into China while leaving in Hong Kong the value-added work, such as product design, production planning, quality control, management, and marketing.

Drawn by the incentives of the SEZs, multinational toy companies began to set up shop in China, especially in the Pearl River delta region of Guangdong. China developed a solid network of supporting industries and services, such as logistics, communications, and component manufacturing, which helped international companies to strengthen productivity, reliability, and delivery.

By 1993, China had become the world's largest toy manufacturer and leading exporter, reaching an export volume of $8 billion. China's accession to the World Trade Organization in 2001 strengthened its domestic industry, and its exports rose sharply. In 2006, China exported 22 billion units of toys worth $7.5 billion. By the end of the year, Chinese toys accounted for 75 percent of world output.

Trade Friction

Throughout the 1990s, China was confronted with allegations of dismal working conditions and human rights violations. Labor unionists and human-rights activists cited low wages, failure to provide social insurance, appalling safety and working conditions, and restrictions on workers' freedoms to call for the elimination of China's most-favored-nation (MFN) trading status.

The U.S. toy industry argued against such demands, saying that without MFN status, toy importers would face price increases of 10 percent to 30 percent. The industry

trade group Toy Manufacturers of America estimated that U.S. toy consumers would see prices rise up to 50 percent, and 25,000 jobs in the American toy industry would be lost.

After much pressure from both sides of the controversy, President Clinton renewed China's trade privileges in 1994, saying that the United State needed to see its relations with China in a "broader context" than simply human rights. He renewed China's trade privileges annually until 2000, when the U.S. Congress voted to grant China permanent Normal Trade Relations status.

Economic Challenges

By 2005, many toy factories faced difficult challenges that threatened to impact the structure of the industry. Powerful foreign buyers demanded lower prices while the cost of labor and raw materials increased. In addition, U.S. and European brands increased pressure on China's toy companies to meet their high labor standards. This caused some manufacturers to leave Guangdong for second border locations or even the Chinese hinterland. Other Chinese manufacturers blamed Western corporations for squeezing their margins so tightly there wasn't enough money to improve worker conditions. Bama Athreya, director of the International Labor Rights Forum, testified before the U.S. Congress in 2005 that "Wal-Mart bears a lion's share of responsibility for pushing the [Chinese] toy industry to a place where worker health and safety are basically nonexistent" (Written testimony, 2007).

China's toy industry also faced increasing scrutiny of its product safety. The Chinese government responded in 2006 with the China Compulsory Certification (CCC) scheme, which allowed only those toys that meet CCC standards to be exported to foreign markets or sold domestically. Later the same year, the government, responding to an EU report that many "problematic imported products" were toys from China, signed a draft Guide for the Strengthening of Sino-EU Cooperative Action for Toy Safety. A month later, China and the EU held a toy-safety forum on enforcing stricter quality and safety standards.

Despite the persistent quality and safety issues, foreign buyers remained confident in China's toy manufacturing industry. Besides, international toy companies and China's manufacturers had become so intertwined

A selection of modern toys manufactured in China. COURTESY OF THE PULVER FAMILY.

over the years that neither could easily survive without the other. "China has a very systematic toy production system involving layers of suppliers in screws, paint, electronics, and other components. No other countries have this cutting edge," said Ben Lau, technical director of toys and premiums at Specialized Technology Resources, an international safety and testing lab, in an interview with a *Forbes* magazine reporter. "There is no alternative to China, no contingency plan. If you shift production to other countries, you'll face similar problems or even worse" (Shen 2007).

The Year of Recalls

Problems for China's toy industry escalated in mid-December 2006, when the first warning in what was to become a spate of recalls was issued by the U.S. Consumer Product Safety Commission (CPSC). Chinese-

made products, such as bell rattles, Christmas lights, and four other types of toys, were listed as having parts that posed a choking risk to children. High lead content and leaking batteries were given as other reasons for the warnings. Several retail outlets in the United States recalled the toys. The EU also issued warnings around the same time for a list of fifteen toys made in China.

In February 2007, the CSPC and international toy maker Hasbro recalled nearly 1 million China-made Easy-Bake Ovens because the door could trap children's fingers, causing serious burns. In June of the same year, the CSPC and RC2 Corporation recalled 1.5 million Thomas & Friends railway toys because the paint on the toys contained unsafe levels of lead.

In July, the CSPC and Hasbro recalled another 1 million Easy-Bake Ovens, citing an additional 77 cases of children's hands or fingers getting stuck in the door. In one case, a 5-year-old girl suffered serious burns that required the partial amputation of fingers.

In August, Mattel twice announced recalls of China-made toys due to unsafe levels of lead and magnets that could be swallowed by children. In September, Mattel recalled another 844,000 toys because of high lead levels. In all, Mattel recalled about 20 million toys. The scandal cost the Dali Toy Limited Company, a Mattel supplier in Guangdong, a devastating $30 million and drove CEO Zhang Shuhong to commit suicide.

Mattel apologized for the recalls, but the damage was done. With the toy scandals combining with earlier recalls of tainted seafood, toxic toothpaste, and poison-laced dog food, U.S. and European consumers were losing faith in the "Made in China" label.

The Chinese government responded by setting up a task force led by a well-known trade official, Wu Yi, to get a handle on product quality and food safety. The General Administration of Quality Supervision, Inspection and Quarantine promised to check every shipment of goods leaving the country. And new rules were put into effect that required Chinese companies that manufacture defective products to cease production and sales until the problems are resolved.

Some analysts suggested that the recalls underscored the problems facing toy makers and other manufacturers in China. Pressure to keep prices low in the face of rising costs for labor, raw materials and transportation, as well as an appreciating yuan, pushed some manufacturers to cut corners and use cheap and illegal substitutes.

Despite the recalls, China's toy exports grew in the first 10 months of 2007, reaching $7.07 billion, a 20 percent increase over the previous comparable period. The United States and EU bought 67.6 percent of those toys.

Outlook for China's Toy Industry

Many analysts see economic changes in the U.S. and China as the real threat to China's toy industry. In China, efforts to improve safety checks have caused shipment delays and product rejections. In 2007, the yuan appreciated 7 percent against the dollar, migrant-labor wages increased at least 17 percent, and new environmental controls all helped to push up the cost of production.

In the United States, a slowing economy resulted in slower retail sales of toys. An industry report released in February 2008 said that U.S. retail sales for toys were down 2.2 percent in 2007, a downward trend that has continued into 2009.

Nevertheless, toy companies don't see a realistic alternative to China as a producer nation. Its infrastructure and manufacturing costs still give it an edge over alternative locations. Philip Shoptaugh, owner of the Oakland, California-based Shoptaugh Games, quoted in an article posted on the Green Options blog, wondered whether consumers would pay more for toys produced in other locations. "Are you going to spend twice as much for a doll because it's not made in China? The thing is you cannot make these things in the United States and have them be competitive on the shelf" (Lance 2008).

Meanwhile, China-based toy makers are looking at the potential of its domestic market. By some estimates, China has a population of 300 million children in the under eight-year-old age group compared to 50 million in that group in the United States. Industry experts also stress the importance of the Chinese toy industry to undergo innovation-oriented reforms and create its own brands.

The global financial meltdown of 2008 has made the reorientation towards the domestic market and the upgrading of quality a matter of urgency for the toy industry, which suffered the closing of 49 percent of its export-oriented companies by early 2009.

Robert Y. ENG

Further Reading

Barboza, D. (2007, October 13). No flinching from recalls as China's exports soar. *The New York Times* online edition. Retrieved July 16, 2008, from http://www.nytimes.com/2007/10/13/business/world business/13trade.html

Barboza, D, & Story, L. (2007, August 14). Mattel issues new recall of toys made in China. *The New York Times* online edition. Retrieved July 16, 2008, from http://www.nytimes.com/2007/08/14/business/15toys-web.html?_r=1&adxnnl=1&oref=slogin&pagewanted=print&adxnnlx=1216316302-ZNDkBVqoUboMo+h7xiXzmQ

Battles in toyland—industry fights in favor of China trade status. (1991, June 12). *The Seattle Times* online edition.

Retrieved July 16, 2008, from http://community.seattle
times.nwsource.com/archive/?date=1991 0612&slug=
1288604

Chakraborty, B. & Govind, S. (2008). Troubled times
for the Chinese toy industry. The ICFAI Center for

**Historical illustration of a wandering toy-man.
A selection of inexpensive toys fills his cart.**

Management Research. Retrieved July 16, 2008, from
www.icmrindia.org

Chinese Toy Making: Where the Furbies Come From.
(1998, December 19) *The Economist.*

Chinese Toy Making: The Worker. (1998, December 19)
The Economist.

Greenlees, D. (2008, January 9). Toy industry tries to regain parents' trust. *International Herald Tribune* online
edition. Retrieved July 16, 2008, from http://www.iht.
com/articles/2008/01/09/business/toys.php

Lance, J. (2008). The latest news on toy safety. Retrieved
February 25, 2009, from http://greenoptions.com/
tag/toy-safety

Shen, S. J. (2007, August 21). Trapped in the Chinese toy
closet. *Forbes* online edition. Retrieved July 16, 2008,
from http://www.forbes.com/2007/08/21/china-
toy-industry-markets-equity-cx_jc_0821 markets1_
print.html

Written testimony submitted by Bama Athreya, Executive
Director International Labor Rights Forum, before
the Committee on Commerce, Science, and Transportation, United States Senate. (2007). Retrieved
February 27, 2008, from http://commerce.senate.
gov/public/_files/BamaAthreyaTestimony_Senate
CommerceILRFTestimonyOct2007FINAL.pdf

Trading Patterns, China Seas

Zhōngguó hǎiyù màoyì xíngwéi

中国海域贸易行为

The China Seas, a term coined by European navigators and cartographers, comprise five bodies of water adjacent to the country's 14,000-kilometer-long coastline. Although the Chinese were not generally seafarers, throughout much of China's history the major ports of the China Seas have been important in coastal, regional, and long-distance trading patterns.

D uring most of its long history Chinese civilization turned its back to the sea and looked inward, towards fertile river basins in which most of its people lived. As a general rule the Chinese were not seafarers. Only a small fraction of the population derived its livelihood from maritime activities—fishing, overseas trade, piracy, or naval warfare. Chinese mariners, with the notable exception of Admiral Zheng He (c. 1371–1433), attempted few long-distance voyages, and China never ruled any of the major oceanic waterways. However, having a coastline of 14,000 kilometers makes maritime defense a major part of any government's security policies, despite the fact that historically, most threats to China came from the north. Even more important, port cities developed along that coastline, many of them in the river estuaries of south and central China. The main economic function of these cities was to organize exchange with commercial communities across the China Seas.

Three Functions of the China Seas

China Seas is a summary term coined by European navigators and geographers. The term is rarely used in China. Chinese maps and geographic manuals distinguish between five expanses of water adjacent to the Chinese coast: the Gulf of Zhili, called in Chinese "Bohai," south of Manchuria; the Yellow Sea, called "Huanghai," between north China and the Korean peninsula; the Strait of Taiwan, called the "Taiwan Haixia," separating that island from Fujian Province; the East China Sea, called "Donghai," into which the Yangzi (Chang) River discharges its waters; and, finally, the South China Sea, called "Nanhai," which is the maritime "foreland" of the southernmost Chinese province, Guangdong.

These five maritime spaces are clearly separated from the high seas of the Pacific Ocean and the Indian Ocean. Yet in an important way they form a connection between both: For centuries after the arrival of European shipping in East Asia, the main route from India into Pacific waters led through the Strait of Malacca and the South China Sea and then around the northern tip of the Philippine archipelago.

This fact points to the triple function of the China Seas, considered in terms of economic geography. First, the China Seas serve as an avenue for China's coastal trade. Coastal trade has always been vital for the integration not only of the various seaboard districts but also of all of China's eastern provinces. Before the advent of the railroad coastal trade was indispensable for transporting bulky goods in a north-south direction. Second, the China Seas are the arena in which regional trade between China, Japan, and the countries of Southeast Asia transpires. No other function is more vital than this one. The China Seas gave rise to and still support a thick network of commerce connecting different economic systems that in many ways complement one another. Third, access to the oceans necessarily leads through the China Seas. In the long run the China Seas' transit function is probably their least important, assuming major importance only with the rise of the Canton (Guangzhou) trade in the early eighteenth century. But at least for modern times, it forms part of the complete picture. By definition the predominant emporia (places of trade) are those that combine all three functions. These major ports are pivots of coastal, regional, and long-distance traffic and commerce.

Trade from the Fourteenth to the Eighteenth Century

Modern scholars have reconstructed the great achievements of Chinese nautical engineering for epochs even earlier than the establishment of the empire in 221 BCE. Only with the Ming dynasty (1368–1644), however, does a comprehensive picture of maritime trade emerge. The basic type of ship, in use for many centuries, had already been developed during the tenth century. This "Fujian ship" (*fuchuan*) was safe, spacious, fast, and admirably suited to the trading conditions in the China Seas. It later evolved into the cheap and popular "shallow-water ship" (*shachuan*), an even more advantageous flat-bottomed watercraft. Southeast Asian shipbuilders also provided technical innovation. The result was the ubiquitous junk (the word *junk* probably originated in Javanese but later was applied mainly to Chinese ships), which shaped European perceptions of the Asian maritime world.

Extended trading networks covering the South China Sea emerged as a result of two developments that occurred in the fifteenth century. First, the Chinese government dispatched several huge fleets under the aforementioned Admiral Zheng He to establish contact with numerous countries in Southeast Asia and on the Indian Ocean. Although the government soon discontinued this policy, several of the links formed by these naval missions were maintained as "tribute" relationships, in which ritual,

diplomacy, and commercial interest interacted in a complicated way. The best example of a tribute relationship with a strong economic content was the Sino-Siamese (Thai) tribute trade, conducted officially between the Siamese royal court and imperial representatives in South China. Its material underpinnings were the complementary structures of the two economies: Siam produced rice, which was needed to feed the rapidly growing population of the southern provinces of Guangdong and Fujian. The Chinese demand for rice, in turn, was partly the result of the conversion of rice paddies into fields for cotton, tea, and mulberry trees for silk—all commodities used at home and in trade. In the opposite direction Siam imported copper from mines in the Chinese province of Yunnan. This trading pattern persisted until the middle of the nineteenth century.

Second, during the fifteenth century emigration from Guangdong and Fujian seems to have increased. Chinese merchant communities settled in various parts of insular and continental Southeast Asia. The Ming dynasty viewed them with suspicion, and after the Chinese authorities restricted maritime commerce much of their trading activity was considered illegal. This ban did not prevent a flourishing trade in spices, silk, timber, copper, tin, skins, gold, medicinal materials, and other goods. Apart from Chinese merchants, many local groups, Arab traders, Indian businessmen (many of them from Gujarat), and even Japanese ships participated in these commercial transactions, many ultimately driven by demand in an increasingly thriving Chinese market. For example, the famous pepper trade to Europe found its equivalent in vast exports of pepper from Sumatra and other islands to China.

The arrival of European ships altered the established trading patterns within the region without overturning them. The main advantage of Europeans lay in the size and armament of their ships. After a brief period of intrusive violence, the Portuguese understood the wisdom and even the necessity of partially adapting to Asian trade. The Dutch and later the British developed their own forms of "country trade," conducted by private European trading firms along intraregional trading routes. European traders were closely dependent on indigenous producers, merchants, and providers of credit. Long-distance trade to Europe remained in the hands of the European chartered companies. Whereas the East

Container ship in the South China Sea. For centuries after the arrival of European shipping in East Asia, the main route from India into Pacific waters led through the Strait of Malacca and the South China Sea and then around the northern tip of the Philippines.
PHOTO BY JOAN LEBOLD COHEN.

India Company (EIC) preferred direct contact with Chinese merchants in Guangzhou and other south Chinese ports, the Dutch Verenigde Oost-Indische Compagnie (Dutch East India Company or VOC) relied on Batavia (present-day Jakarta) as its central emporium and collecting point in the East. Thus, Batavia served as a link between the various Eastern networks and the transoceanic shipping routes.

Little statistical evidence exists for the scope of trade in the China Seas in the early modern era. Data on maritime customs revenue collected at ports in south China, however, indicate that the volume of trade multiplied between the 1500s and the 1820s. The expansion of foreign trade facilitated regional specialization all around the China Seas and thus had a huge effect on economic activity in the entire region. The rise of port cities, with their cosmopolitan communities of sailors and traveling merchants, contributed greatly to social differentiation. Yet China made no steady progress in opening up to the world. Japan's Tokugawa shogunate, the military government in power from 1600/1603 to 1868, drastically limited Japan's foreign trade from the 1630s onward, and although Chinese maritime commerce flourished after about 1720, many noncolonial entrepôts (intermediary centers of trade and transshipment) in Southeast Asia lost their dynamism at about the same time. Trade in the China Seas not only constantly changed its patterns in space but also went through long-term as well as short-term cycles of expansion and contraction. These cycles were partly driven by political and military factors because the market economy of maritime Asia in early modern times operated under conditions set by rulers and nations.

Treaty Ports, Steam Ships, and the Global Market

The opening of China and the establishment of the earliest treaty ports (ports designated by treaty for trade) in 1842 were soon followed by the introduction of steam shipping to Chinese coastal and riverine traffic. Although Chinese-type sailing vessels proved remarkably resilient and were completely superseded hardly anywhere, steamers had advantages that had a great impact on trading patterns. Their carrying capacity was virtually unlimited; they could easily operate on the sea as well as on major rivers; and their deployment could be organized by large-scale capitalist enterprises. In the China Seas, especially in the south, steam and sail continued to coexist. The most dynamic lines of business, however, were captured by modern forms of transportation.

From the 1820s through the 1870s illegal and, from 1858, legalized shipments of opium from India to China dominated China's foreign trade. This trade used the South China Sea for transit but hardly affected Southeast Asia, where different networks of drug traffic existed. An important change occurred with the economic development of the European colonies in that area of the world during the last quarter of the nineteenth century. The introduction of large-scale plantations and of mechanized mining as well as the intensification of peasant production for export integrated Southeast Asia much more into the world economy than ever before. Expatriate entrepreneurs of Chinese origin were pivotal in forging these connections. By this time an impoverished China was no longer the promising market it had been. China now became important as a supplier of cheap labor. Chinese emigrants took advantage of the agricultural and mining opportunities in insular and continental Southeast Asia and beyond. The migration of contract labor from southern China to various overseas destinations, termed the "coolie trade" by contemporaries, was largely organized by Chinese recruiting firms, although transport remained in the hands of European-owned steamship companies.

A structural hallmark of Chinese foreign trade between the First Opium War (1839–1842) and the establishment of the People's Republic in 1949 was that indigenous shipping companies secured a substantial share of the market in coastal and inland transport but never succeeded in entering overseas shipping. China's lack of a merchant navy was symbolic of the country's subordinate position in the international economy. Another new feature of the early twentieth century was incipient industrialization. British sugar factories in Hong Kong and Japanese sugar factories in colonial Taiwan exported their products to countries around the China Seas. Part of the factories' raw sugar came from the Dutch East Indies.

Fall and Rise of Maritime Commerce

The Great Depression of the 1930s, along with Japanese aggression against China and the Western colonies in Southeast Asia, severely strained the trading networks in the region. Exports of conventional commodities fell sharply during the Depression as demand fell in Asia, Europe, and the Americas. Chinese emigration, formerly a mainstay of steam traffic in the South China Sea and also between north China and southern Manchuria, declined. After the Japanese occupation of Manchuria in 1931, the activities of Japanese shipping companies became ever more imperialistic. The formation of a Japanese-dominated trading sphere known as the "yen bloc" was a bid for autarky (self-sufficiency) and protected export markets. In the early 1940s the Japanese restructured large segments of long-distance trade according to the needs of their war economy. The United States' petroleum embargo against Japan, imposed in July 1941, made it clear to the Japanese that a self-sufficient empire unaffected by the world market was an impossibility; economic factors such as this contributed to Japan's aggression on all fronts of war in the Pacific (the War of Resistance against Japan, often called the Second Sino-Japanese War) and World War II itself.

The collapse of the Japanese empire in 1945, the Chinese revolution of 1949, and the disappearance of European colonial rule in Southeast Asia after World War II ruled out a return to prewar patterns of maritime commerce.

Only Hong Kong survived as a first-rate emporium, now with a substantial industry of its own. A large part of the People's Republic of China's trade with Southeast Asia and Europe was channeled through Hong Kong. At the same time the Communist government in China began the long-term process of reestablishing China's lost military sea power and mercantile presence in the China Seas and on the world's oceans. Today that process continues.

Jürgen OSTERHAMMEL

Further Reading

Chaudhuri, K. N. (1985). *Trade and civilisation in the Indian Ocean: An economic history from the rise of Islam to 1750.* Cambridge, U.K.: Cambridge University Press.

Chaudhuri, K. N. (1990). *Asia before Europe: Economy and civilization of the Indian Ocean from the rise of Islam to 1750.* Cambridge, U.K.: Cambridge University Press.

Chaudhury, S., & Morineau, M. (Eds.). (1999). *Merchants, companies and trade: Europe and Asia in the early modern era.* Cambridge, U.K.: Cambridge University Press.

Cushman, J. W. (1993). *Fields from the sea: Chinese junk trade with Siam during the late eighteenth and early nineteenth centuries.* Ithaca, NY: Cornell University Press.

Deng, G. (1999). *Maritime sector, institutions, and sea power of premodern China.* Westport, CT: Greenwood Press.

Dermigny, L. (1964).. *La Chine et l'Occident: Le commerce à Canton au XVIIIe siècle 1719–1833* [China and the Occident: The Canton trade in the eighteenth century, 1719–1833] (Vols. 1–3). Paris: S.E.V.P.E.N.

Gaastra, F. S. (1991). *De geschiedenis van de VOC* [The History of the Dutch East India Company]. Leiden, The Netherlands: Walburg Press.

Gardella, R. (1994). *Harvesting mountains: Fujian and the China tea trade, 1757–1937.* Berkeley and Los Angeles: University of California Press.

Greenberg, M. (1951). *British trade and the opening of China, 1800–42.* Cambridge, U.K.: Cambridge University Press.

Guillot, C., Lombard, D., & Ptak, R. (Eds.). (1998). *From the Mediterranean to the China Sea: Miscellaneous notes.* Wiesbaden, Germany: Harrassowitz.

Heine, I. M. (1989). *China's rise to commercial maritime power.* New York: Greenwood Press.

Lombard, D. (1990). *Le carrefour javanais: Essai d'histoire globale* [The Javanese crossroads: An essay on global history] (Vols. 1–3). Paris: Éditions de l'École des Hautes Études en Siences Sociales.

Osterhammel, J. (1989). *China und die Weltgesellschaft. Vom 18. Jahrhundert bis in unsere Zeit* [China and the world since the eighteenth century]. Munich, Germany: C. H. Beck.

Ptak, R. (1999). *China's seaborne trade with South and Southeast Asia (1200–1750).* Aldershot, U.K.: Ashgate Variorum.

Ptak, R., & Rothermund, R. (Eds.). (1991). *Emporia, commodities and entrepreneurs in Asian maritime trade, c. 1400–1750.* Stuttgart, Germany: Steiner.

Reid, A. (1988–1993). *Southeast Asia in the age of commerce, 1450–1680* (Vols. 1–2). New Haven, CT: Yale University Press.

Wiethoff, B. (1963). Die chinesische Seeverbotspolitik und der private Überseehandel von 1368 bis 1567 [The politics of Chinese maritime trade prohibitions and private overseas trade from 1368 to 1567]. Wiesbaden, Germany: Harrassowitz.

Wills, J. E., Jr. (1998). Relations with maritime Europeans, 1514–1662. In J. K. Fairbank & D. Twitchett (Eds.). *The Cambridge history of China: Vol. 8* (pp. 333–375). Cambridge, U.K.: Cambridge University Press.

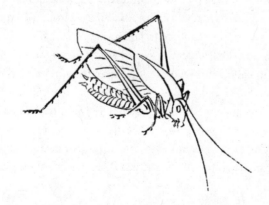

Transfer Gas from West to East Program

Xī qì dōng shū 西气东输

As an increasingly important energy source in China, natural gas needs to follow the rule of balance between supply and demand. But the supply of natural gas, mainly from western parts of the country, and the demand for natural gas, mainly from eastern parts, are not balanced; this created the background of the project "Transfer Gas from West to East."

In 2003 China surpassed Japan to become the second largest energy consumer in the world after the United States. China's consumption of natural gas has been increasing with amazing speed through the years. During the tenth Five-Year Plan (2000–2005), the annual consumption of natural gas was 13 percent of total energy consumption, and this number increased to 20 percent in the past two years. In response China launched the Transfer Gas from West to East Program (the Program) in 2002.

Supply and Demand

China's supply of natural gas comes from west China. Some 77 percent of China's natural gas is located in the Talimu Basin (which stores 22 percent of China's total natural gas reserves), E'erduosi Basin, Sichuan Basin, Chaidamu Basin, Yingqiong Basin, and East Sea Basin. The first four basins mentioned store 60 percent of China's total natural gas deposits.

The demand for natural gas, the other side of the energy story, comes largely from east China, in which the Yanzgi River delta stands out as an example; 85 percent of the energy used in the delta, including natural gas, comes from outside the area. Experts predict that natural gas consumption in the Yanzgi River delta will only continue to rise. The area consumed 4 billion cubic meters of natural gas in 2002 and 10 billion cubic meters in 2005 and is projected to use 20 billion cubic meters in 2010.

The economic law of supply and demand is the theoretical foundation of the Transfer of Gas from West to East Program. In addition, sending what is needed to areas of high demand will do more than provide a balance between supply and demand. It will also stimulate related industries, further activate the industrial base in the west, and reduce pollution. This program, therefore, is extremely important in one of China's preeminent national strategies: the Great West Development Plan.

The Program's Impact

The first phase of the Transfer of Gas from West to East Program involved building a 4,000-kilometer gas pipeline network stretching from the west to the east of China. The pipeline starts at the Talimu oilfields in Lunnan; continues through Xinjiang, Gansu, Ningxia, Shanxi, Shaanxi, Henan, Anhui, Jiangsu, Zhejiang, and Shanghai; and terminates in Baihe town in Shanghai. The pipeline is the first world-class pipeline designed by China. Construction began in February 2002, and the pipeline began to transport natural gas on 1 October 2004. It is estimated that the gas pipeline can transfer at least 12 billion cubic meters of natural gas per year.

The Program, however, undertakes more than setting a balance between gas supply in the west and gas demand in the east. The Program will help promote related industries—such as steel, cement, and machinery—which will form a new industrial growth belt. The pipeline project itself used 1.74 million tons of steel 5,100 tons of welding rods, and many air pumps and other hand tools and precision instruments, along with enormous amounts of water and timber. Some 67 percent of the gas pipeline runs through the west of China, which greatly stimulates local economies and connections between the west and the east. In Xinjiang, for example, the Program attracted more than 20 billion Chinese yuan in investments. The Xinjiang part of the Program also created large tax revenues for local governments and created employment opportunities for local peoples.

China's energy consumption structure will be largely upgraded by the Program. Natural gas can be widely used not only for people's daily needs but also for fueling industry by generating electricity. And compared to coal, natural gas is a much more environmentally friendly choice of fuel, especially in areas of rapid economic development. The development of the gas pipeline should actually help improve the environment.

Improving the Environment

Natural gas is much more effective than coal is in terms of thermal efficiency, cost, and negative impact on the environment. Coal is a heavily used source of energy in China, accounting for 72 percent of China's total energy consumption. Although burning coal creates power, it also creates sulfur dioxide (SO_2), nitrogen oxide (NOx), carbon dioxide (CO_2), and dust, which are all harmful to the environment. China exceeds the United States in SO_2 emissions, and is now Number 1 in the world. China ranks second in CO_2 emissions, right behind the United States.

Twelve billion cubic meters of natural gas—the amount the pipeline can transfer annually—is equivalent to 9 million tons of coal. At these amounts, using natural gas instead of coal would eliminate 135,000 tons of SO_2, 153,000 tons of NOx, and 270,000 tons waste-smoke emissions and dust from the environment. While producing the same amount of thermal efficiency, the ratio of dust emissions from burning coal to natural gas is 148:1; the ratio of SO_2 emissions is 700:1; and the ratio of NOx emissions is 29:1. The ecosystem of east China is fragile and can no longer afford the pollution burden from burning coal. Moreover, Shanghai and Jiangsu suffer from a high frequency of acid rain.

In many ways it appears that utilizing natural gas from the west of China is an effective choice for minimizing environmental pollution without significantly sacrificing the country's drive toward economic development.

The construction of the west-to-east natural gas pipeline is only the first stage of the Program. A planned project based on market forces is making a success of the Project Transfer of Gas from West to East, and this combination of markets and government planning is going to speed up both economic development and environmental protection in China. With the success from Project Transfer Gas from West to East, more similar projects started, to boost commodities exchange, smooth supply and demand and further apply the rules of market economy.

ZHOU Guanqi

Further Reading

Chen Lixiang. (2006). *Xi Qi Dong Song Yu Sheng Tai Ti Xi An Quan* [Projects of Transfer of Gas from West to East and ecological system security]. Beijing: Science Publishing.

Chen Xiushan. (2006). *Xi Bu Da Kai Fa Zhong De Ju Xing Xiang Mu* [Mega projects in the Great West Development Plan]. Beijing: Renmin University.

Hou Jinwu. (2005). *Xi Qi Dong Song Yu Di Zhi An Quan* [Project of Transfer of Gas from West to East and geographic hazards]. Beijing: Dadi Publishing.

Hu Xin. (2005). *Zhong Guo De Jing Ji Di Li* [Economic geography in China]. Beijing: Lixin Accounting Agency.

Wang Junhao. (2002). *Zhong Guo Long Duan Chan Pin De Ding Jia Ti Xi* [The pricing system of monopoly products in China]. Beijing: China Economics Publishing.

Transportation Systems

Yùnshū xìtŏng 运输系统

As China expands its economy, increases its population, and opens up to the outside world, its political leaders and urban designers face increased pressure to create more efficient and environmentally friendly transportation systems.

China, with its enormous and increasingly urbanized population, faces unprecedented challenges and opportunities in the way in which it transports its people and goods. The country's recent rapid economic growth will continue for the foreseeable future, placing increased pressure on its political leaders and urban designers to create more efficient and environmentally benign transportation systems.

Roads

The main focus of upgraded transportation systems has been on China's road and vehicle network. China's light industry and agricultural sectors rely heavily on road-based transportation. China has roughly 88 motor vehicles per 1,000 people, compared with approximately 765 motor vehicles per 1,000 people in the United States. The number of motor vehicles in China more than tripled between 1985 and 2000; by 2007 some 118 million vehicles were traveling the nation's roads. As of early 2009, China is on the verge of surpassing the U.S. to become the world's largest vehicle market (Kurtenbach 2009).

More foreign automobile companies are entering China to meet the demand for new vehicles. Volkswagen began manufacturing automobiles in Shanghai in 1985. Other major companies have also begun manufacturing

In the last two decades China has built many super highways—but every Chinese wants to own a car and traffic is fierce. While China produces its own makes of cars, joint ventures with international car makers and foreign car–imports offer potential car buyers a choice. PHOTO BY TOM CHRISTENSEN.

for the Chinese market, including Daihatsu, Citroen, Peugeot, General Motors, and Daimler-Chrysler. Most vehicles are built in the Shanghai region and near Dalian in the northeastern province of Liaoning.

China has enlarged its road system such that now all towns can be reached via the highway system. Approximately 1.3 million kilometers of roads stretch across the country. In 1998 alone 37,000 kilometers of highways were built; of those, 1,487 kilometers were expressways. The central government's eleventh Five-Year Plan (2005–2010) calls for investing $700 billion in highway infrastructure, with the goal of building 2.3–2.5 million kilometers of new roads, including 55,000 kilometers of expressway, which are being built to connect cities with populations of 200,000 or more.

A consequence of China's growth in motor vehicles is increased use of energy (mostly oil). If China achieved U.S. levels of vehicle ownership, it would have more than 900 million vehicles—nearly 50 percent more than the total number of vehicles in the world in 2001. China would need to consume more oil than is currently produced throughout the world.

Commuters wait for the train in a subway station. Many of the densely populated cities have developed or plan to develop commuter rail transportation systems involving subways and light rail.
PHOTO BY TOM CHRISTENSEN.

Rail

China has an extensive rail network, with Beijing being the hub for the north-south line to Shanghai and Guangzhou (Canton). Rail lines also extend to the west and connect China to Europe. New lines are being built, particularly in southern China and other industrial areas. In 2006, China opened a new 1,100 kilometer railroad from central China across the high Tibetan plateau to the Tibetan capital of Lhasa.

China's first subway was constructed in Beijing in 1969. Many of the densely populated cities have developed or plan to develop commuter rail transportation systems involving subways and light rail. These include the cities of Shenyang, Changchun, and Harbin in the northeast and other major cities, including Shanghai, Guangzhou, Nanjing, Shenzhen, and Chongqing.

In April of 2008 China opened a new 120 km high-speed rail line linking the cities of Beijing and Tianjin in time for the Beijing Olympics; three trains initially operated at speeds of up to 300 km per hour, cutting travel time from 80 minutes to 30 minutes between the two cities. According to the Xinhua news agency, fifty-seven high-speed trains (reaching speeds up to 350 km per hour) are expected to be in commercial operation by the end of 2009.

In 2004 the length of China's rail system was approximately 75,000 kilometers. By 2020 it is expected that 100,000 kilometers of rail transit systems will have been built at a construction cost of more than 130 billion yuan ($15.7 billion).

Air

Since 1970 China has constructed and expanded numerous airports, mainly to handle increasing tourist traffic and to link remote areas. As of 2007 there were 148 airports open to civil airplanes. Beijing is the hub of domestic air travel from which airlines reach all provinces, autonomous regions, and municipalities. The other two international gateway airports are in Guangzhou and Shanghai. Around thirty Chinese airlines serve the domestic market. China has a fast-growing fleet of Western aircraft and is one of Boeing's top three customers.

Travelers in the 1980s wait in Shanghai Airport. In the period since 1970, China has constructed and expanded numerous airports, mainly to handle increasing tourist traffic and to link remote areas. PHOTO BY JOAN LEBOLD COHEN.

In 2009, China hopes to launch new airport hubs in Chengdu, Xi'an, and Guangzhou, and plans to invest over 200 billion RMB Yuan (about 28.6 billion USD) into the building of over forty regional airports.

Water

Because China has a coastline of more than 18,000 kilometers and 110,000 kilometers of navigable inland waterways, it is easy to understand why water transport has a long history in the country. Countless boats transport goods along rivers and the coast. The major inland navigable rivers are the Yangzi (Chang) (known as the "golden waterway" of China's inland river transport, and much altered by the new Three Gorges Dam, expected to be fully operational by 2009), Huang (Yellow), Pearl, Heilongjiang, Huai, Qiantang, Minjiang, and Huangpu, as well as the Grand Canal between Beijing and Hangzhou. The volume of passenger transportation is approximately 12 billion trips per year. Around seventy major inland river ports have more than five thousand berths. China has twenty large ports for international shipping, with Shanghai Harbor being one of the largest in the world.

Historical illustration of junks on a river. Water transport has a long history in China, which has a coastline of over 18,000 kilometers and 110,000 kilometers of navigable inland waterways.

Transport Options

China is presented with enormous dilemmas concerning the most appropriate mode of development as the country continues its economic growth. The mode it chooses will significantly affect numerous countries. China's transportation policies will increasingly influence the world energy market and transboundary environmental deterioration, particularly a reduction in regional air quality and an increase in greenhouse gases if there are

Young men ride bicycles along a sun-dappled street. Cars are quickly replacing bicycles as the preferred mode of personal transportation.

increased emissions of gasoline-driven vehicles. China's transportation policies will also affect the health of its citizens because the emissions from gasoline-driven vehicles are detrimental to people's health. However, China can focus on less environmentally harmful alternatives, such as vehicles powered by natural gas or batteries, as well as electric hybrids and fuel-cell vehicles powered by nonpolluting and renewable hydrogen. China is relatively unhindered in developing these options because the country is not heavily dependent on oil. It has few petroleum vehicle-related investments, such as are common in many Western countries, and it can base its transport infrastructure on cleaner fuels. China is particularly interested in vehicles powered by natural gas because natural gas is abundant in several provinces.

China is investigating cleaner fuel technologies through institutions such as the Institute of Natural Gas Vehicles in Beijing. Currently China's transportation policy is focused both on developing "cleaner" vehicles and on increasing investment in mass transportation systems in the cities. China's latest Five-Year Plan focuses on coordinating economic development among different regions and between urban and rural areas. The plan increases the priority given to environmental protection and indicates that China will attempt to pursue less environmentally harmful transportation systems than were favored by

many Western countries at a similar stage of economic development.

Warwick GULLETT

Further Reading

Cannon, J. S. (1998). *China at the crossroads: Energy, transportation, and the 21st century.* New York: Inform.

China unveils its fastest train. (12 April, 2008). Retrieved February 27 from 2008http://www.thaindian.com/newsportal/health/china-unveils-its-fastest-train_10037229.html

Kurtenbach, E. (2009, February 10). China tops U.S. in monthly auto sales for 1st time. Retrieved February 11, 2009, from http://www.manufacturing.net/News-China-Tops-US-In-Monthly-Auto-Sales-For-1st-Time-021009.aspx

MacArthur, P., & Low, J. (1994). *Tapping into China's transport infrastructure market.* Canberra: Australian Government Publishing Service.

Research Report on China's Civil Airport Industry, 2008-2010 (November 2008). China Research & Intelligence. Retrieved February 27, 2009 from http://www.researchandmarkets.com/reportinfo.asp?report_id=687112

World Bank. (1985). *China: The transport sector.* Washington, DC: International Bank for Reconstruction and Development, World Bank.

Treaty of Tianjin

Tiānjīn Tiáoyuē 天津条约

One of the most important of the "unequal treaties," the Treaty of Tianjin developed as an outcome of the Second Opium War (1856–1860) and greatly expanded foreign rights and foreign control over the China coast.

The Treaty of Tianjin, signed in June 1858, was the chief diplomatic outcome of the Second Opium War (1856–1860, also called the *Arrow* War). Actually four separate Tianjin treaties were written with England, France, United States, and Russia. The British were the main force behind the war and the treaties. Lord Elgin, high commissioner to China, had been sent to China to force the Chinese government to agree to an expansion of foreign rights and to honor rights granted in the Treaty of Nanjing (1842), especially the right to trade in Guangzhou (Canton). For Elgin the most important rights were the right of residence for foreign ministers in Beijing and the right of Britain and the other powers to conduct relations with China on the Western model of diplomatic equality rather than as part of the Chinese tribute system (the traditional method of dealing with foreign relations).

Elgin was particularly concerned that China be willing to permanently accept whatever agreement was reached, which led him both to ignore some of the broader demands of British merchants in China and to be willing to use force to impress the Chinese court with the necessity of coming to a permanent accommodation with the foreigners.

After initial fighting around Guangzhou, a joint Anglo-French expedition sailed north and seized the Dagu forts and forced the negotiations that led to the Treaty of Tianjin. The treaty expanded the number of treaty ports—ports open to foreign trade and residence—from five to sixteen and opened the Yangzi (Chang) River to foreign navigation. The treaty also was to make travel outside the treaty ports easier for foreigners. The British and French each were to receive a large indemnity, which was to be guaranteed by the revenues of Chinese Customs. Foreign legations also were to be established in Beijing.

The Chinese court was unhappy with the treaty even after it was agreed to. Although officials in charge of dealing with the foreigners were convinced that China had no option but to accept the terms, the Xianfeng emperor (reigned 1851–1861) was convinced by more conservative advisors that diplomatic equality in particular could not be granted. The British fleet coming to exchange the final ratification of the treaty was driven off when it attempted to force a passage at the Dagu forts in June 1859, and the court took advantage of this unexpected victory to abrogate the treaty. A large Anglo-French force was sent to Tianjin in the summer of 1860. The foreign troops defeated the Qing dynasty (1644–1912) armies, and the emperor was forced to flee Beijing. The foreigners burned the imperial Summer Palace outside Beijing in retaliation for the killing of foreign prisoners, and the Qing court was forced to accept the terms of the treaty.

The Treaty of Tianjin, along with the end of the Taiping Rebellion, ushered in an era of rapid growth of foreign influence on the China coast. Foreign economic activity increased, and the number and geographical spread of

China's Unequal Treaties

For the Qing dynasty, the signing of the Treaty of Tianjin was merely an expedient to get the foreigners to withdraw troops threatening Beijing. But waiving foreign taxation in exchange for the abandonment of the aggressors' other demands proved to be merely an illusion that "failed to move the barbarian chieftains." The imperial negotiators even tried to convince Emperor Xianfeng that signed treaties were not binding. One of the Chinese negotiators, Gui Liang, wrote:

At present, the treaties of peace with Britain and France cannot be taken as real. These few sheets of paper [the treaties] are simply a means to get foreign troops and warships to leave the coast [of Tianjin]. In the future, if Your Majesty desires to break these agreements and the peace, Your Majesty needs only to punish your slave [Gui Liang] for mismanagement. [Those treaties] can henceforth be treated as rubbish.

Source: Dong Wang. (2005). *China's unequal treaties.* Oxford, U. K.: Lexington Books, 17.

foreign missionaries, merchants, and military forces grew. The Treaty of Tianjin fully established the treaty port system. Although the treaty did not explicitly legalize opium, the Qing court did legalize domestic opium production in the aftermath of the treaty. After the treaty China also established the Zongli Yamen (the equivalent of a modern foreign ministry) to deal with diplomatic relations with Westerners and began its program of self-strengthening to begin borrowing foreign technology.

Alan BAUMLER

Further Reading

Fairbank, J. K. (1978). The creation of the treaty system. In D. Twitchett & J. K. Fairbank (Eds.), *The Cambridge history of China* (Vol. 10), (pp. 213–263). Cambridge, U.K.: Cambridge University Press.

Morse, H. B. (1910). *The international relations of the Chinese empire.* London: Longmans Green.

Wong, J. W. (1998). *Deadly dreams: Opium and the Arrow War (1856–1860) in China.* Cambridge, U.K.: Cambridge University Press.

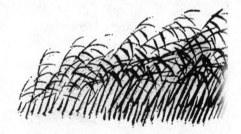

Treaty of Wangxia

Wàngxià Tiáoyuē 望厦条约

The 1844 Treaty of Wangxia set a pattern for Sino-American relations, as United States diplomats sought to build upon British imperialism and to stand apart from it, to establish principles, and to maximize profit. Chinese usually point to the 1844 treaty as proof that the United States had joined the ranks of the imperialists.

Before the 1840s, the Chinese, then led by the Manchu-dominated Qing dynasty (1644–1912), did not see the United States as important, particularly in the context of British naval power and wealth. The United States was a minor player in the Canton (Guangzhou) System, a monopoly of Chinese merchants created by the Qing to limit trade and contact with the West. The Chinese placed the United States in the context of the traditional tribute system and did not seek the establishment of formal diplomatic ties.

British victory over China in the First Opium War and the subsequent Treaty of Nanking spurred Americans to take more aggressive action. In response to lobbying by merchants, President John Tyler dispatched Caleb Cushing, a Massachusetts lawyer and former congressman, as commissioner to China. Cushing met with Qiying (Ch'i-ying), who represented the Qing dynasty as governor-general of Guangdong and Guangxi, and as superintendent general of trade and foreign intercourse of the five ports. The treaty itself was signed at Wangxia near Macao on 3 July 1844 but was not ratified and in effect until December 1845. The 1844 agreement was modeled on the 1842 Treaty of Nanking and included the right to trade in five treaty ports, extraterritoriality, and most-favored nation (MFN) status. Extraterritoriality gave Americans in China immunity from Qing criminal and civil law. The Qing, reflecting a traditional Chinese expectation that outsiders would more effectively police themselves, initially accepted extraterritoriality. Westerners portrayed China's criminal procedures as barbaric and biased, and extraterritoriality became one of the most humiliating provisions of the unequal treaties. MFN meant that United States merchants and diplomats would enjoy whatever privileges or benefits were granted in future treaties with other nations. Although the MFN provision would devastate China over the next century, at the time the Qing hoped that it would spur competition among the Western powers to the dynasty's benefit. Other provisions were less onerous to the Chinese. The treaty enabled Americans to benefit from future military conflicts initiated by the British or other European powers. The treaty stated that any ports closed to belligerents would remain open to American merchants with "full respect being paid to the neutrality of the flag of the United States." Wangxia also called for diplomatic equality in official correspondence, in effect undermining the traditional Chinese practice of treating foreigners as "barbarians" because of their lack of knowledge of Confucianism and Chinese culture. Finally, the 1844 treaty outlawed the hated opium trade, although enforcement remained sporadic at best.

This agreement would be further expanded to the advantage of the United States in 1858, which occurred as a

From the Treaty of Wangxia

A clause from Article II of the first treaty between the United States and China, signed on 3 July 1844, reads:

Citizens of the United States resorting to China for the purposes of commerce will pay the duties of import and export prescribed in the tariff, which is fixed by and made a party of this Treaty. They shall, in no case, be subject to other or higher duties than are or shall be required of the people or any other nation whatever … And if additional advantages of privileges, of whatever description, be conceded hereafter by China to any other nations, the United States, and the citizens thereof, shall be entitled there upon, to a complete, equal, and impartial participation in the same.

Source: Ji, Zhaojin. (2003). *A history of modern Shanghai banking.* Armonk, NY: M. E. Sharpe, 26.

result of another unequal treaty obtained by the British after the Second Opium War (1856–1860, also called the *Arrow* War. While Americans would dream of a special, benevolent relationship with China, Chinese usually point to the 1844 treaty as proof that the United States had joined the ranks of the imperialists.

Steven PHILLIPS

Further Reading

Hunt, M. (1983). *The making of a special relationship: The United States and China to 1914.* New York: Columbia University Press.

Latourette, K. S. (1964). *The history of early relations between the United States and China, 1784–1844.* New York: Kraus Reprint.

A sly rabbit will have three openings to its den.

狡 兔 三 窟

Jiǎo tù sān kū

Tribute System

Cháogòng zhìdù 朝贡制度

In premodern China foreign relations were both hierarchical, with all foreign rulers paying tribute to the Chinese emperor as their superior, and systematic, conducted through a single set of bureaucratic rules and institutions. The forms taken by these relations varied greatly over the centuries; only from about 1425 to 1550 were all foreign relations actually managed through a single set of rules and institutions.

The premodern Chinese tended to conduct their foreign relations hierarchically, with all foreign rulers paying tribute to the Chinese Son of Heaven, the emperor considered to be the sole supreme ruler of the world, and to manage foreign relations systematically via a unilaterally developed set of bureaucratic rules and institutions. In the long span of China's history as an empire, only for a little more than a century during the Ming dynasty (1368–1644), circa 1425–1550, did China's rulers seek to manage all of their foreign relations through a unified set of institutions centered on the tribute embassy, a tribute system in the full sense of the term.

The use of the tribute system idea as a master concept for all of China's premodern foreign relations has made it hard to keep in focus early Han dynasty (206 BCE–220 CE) equal relations with the Xiongnu people, mid-Tang dynasty (618–907 CE)hazardous negotiations with neighboring great powers, the multistate involvements of the Song dynasty (960–1279), or Qing dynasty (1644–1912) relations with Inner Asia and with maritime Europe, which were not centered on tribute embassies. The use of this misleading master concept owes something to European obsession with ceremonial equality from the time of the Macartney Embassy—sent by King George III of England from 1792 to 1794 under George Lord Macartney—on, and more to the scholarship of John King Fairbank and others reading Qing bureaucratic compendia and noting the hierarchic thinking of nineteenth-century Qing officials. The concept is little used but little questioned in English-language writing today. Interest in it in China, Taiwan, and Japan reflects a sense of east Asian superiority in the management of asymmetric relations as compared with European-U.S. delusions of absolute sovereign equality.

The concept of tribute (gong) appears in the classics, most importantly in the "Tribute of Yu" (Yu gong) section of the Classic of Documents (Shu Jing). There it refers to gifts of representative products of various areas to the central sovereign as symbolic acknowledgments of his sovereignty. Such tribute from areas of foreign or "barbarian" nature is a small part of this picture. In another section of the same classic it takes the form of gifts of exotic animals, a theme that would recur in the lore of tribute embassies down to the elephants sent by Siam (modern Thailand) and the lion sent by Portugal to Qing-ruled Beijing. In the centuries of political transformation and bureaucratic unification from the Warring States period (475–221 BCE) to the Qin dynasty (221–206 BCE)and Han dynasty (206 BCE–220 CE), there was much discussion of the differences between civilized and barbarian peoples but little focus on the ceremonial subjection of the latter; on the inland frontier it was all the Chinese rulers could do to keep the dangerous nomads at bay by building walls and buying peace with gifts and imperial princesses given in marriage. In the reign of Emperor Wu, 141–87 BCE, more assertive policies toward the Xiongnu had some success, especially when rival Xiongnu groups could be turned against each other, and the more submissive groups were required to leave hostage princes in the imperial capital. The mid-Han turn toward ceremonialism produced some disastrous attempts to give all foreign rulers titles inferior to the emperor's under Wang Mang and some spectacular collections of homage-paying foreigners at the New Year in the early years of later Han dynasty.

It is instructive to follow the thread of ceremonial practice through the dynastic records of foreign relations. It is not at all surprising that the most elaborate set of ceremonies for receiving foreign envoys is recorded for the Tang dynasty. Envoys were received and banqueted and their presents displayed before the emperor, all in one dazzling ceremony. For powerful and threatening Inner Asian rulers, extra layers of splendor could be added. All this was in the service of the survival of the Tang dynasty in a polycentric world of powerful empires—Tibetan, Uygur, Turkic. The Tang rulers were not as distant in culture from their Inner Asian challengers as the Song and Ming rulers were and were quite capable of facing down an invading nomad army in person or, in desperate straits, of granting equality to the Uygur ruler with an imperial *wansui* (ten thousand years). The immense impression that the splendors of court and capital made on Korean and Japanese envoys was an important facet of the spreading influence of Chinese culture in those countries. In south coast ports, beginnings can be seen of the use of tribute embassies as instruments of marginal advantage for foreign traders.

The even more dangerous Inner Asian world faced by the Song dynasty (960–1279) was reflected in the differentiation of ceremonies for contemporary embassies—the Liao dynasty was most favored, then Koryo and Xi Xia, then all the rest. The treatment of the Liao as near-equals may have been a realistic solution to a dangerous confrontation but was criticized by many officials. The various acknowledgments of equality or even inferiority to the Jurchen Jin dynasty from 1142 on were widely resented and contributed to unrealistic calls for reconquest of the north; foreign relations were an important facet of the emergence of the moralistic Learning of the Way (Daoxue), or Neo-confucianism, in this period. Maritime trade to southern ports under the guise of tribute embassies flourished and became an important facet of the power and prosperity of such Southeast Asian states as Šrivijaya on Sumatra and Champa in what is now southern Vietnam.

Rulers Summoned

In the early Ming dynasty the example of wide conquests and lavish court ceremonies of the Mongol-ruled Yuan dynasty (1279–1368), resentment of the cultural alienness of the Mongol rule, and the mutual co-optation of an uncouth despot and some very able Daoxue literati produced visions of systematic institutional perfection in many aspects of government, not least foreign relations. Messages were sent to all known foreign rulers, ordering them to come and pay homage to the new dynasty. An early spectacular result was the parading through the streets of Nanjing, the first Ming capital, of elephants—forty in one year and forty-two two years later—from Champa. Fears of Japanese pirates and their Chinese allies, some left over from the rivals of the Ming founder, led to the prohibition of all maritime trade in Chinese shipping and the limitation of foreign shipping in Chinese ports to that in connection with tribute embassies. Maritime rulers, often advised by émigré Chinese, made the most of the loophole; the kingdom of the Ryukyu Islands was among the most successful.

The usurping Yongle emperor, a great warrior needing all the legitimation he could get, sent envoys and expeditions out in all directions to summon foreign rulers to present tribute; the maritime expeditions of Zheng He are the most famous of these expansionist efforts. The assembly of rulers and ministers paying homage at the new capital of Beijing in 1421 was without parallel since the early Tang dynasty. However, the elaborate ceremonies of the embassies of the founding reign already had been somewhat reduced, and after the Yongle reign there were many limitations on the size and frequency of embassies. Of course, there also was only one more maritime expedition. Efforts to control the Mongols by giving them titles and trade in connection with embassies were not successful. Management of relations among Hami, Turfan, and more distant Muslim city-states in Inner Asia was incoherent. The Jurchen people became experts in manipulating the privileges of the tribute system, sending oversized embassies that threatened mayhem in the streets of Beijing if they did not like the terms of trade or the quantities of gifts they received.

The succession of the Jiajing emperor in 1524 was accompanied by intense discussions of many facets of the imperial ceremonial tradition, the publication in the *Da Ming huidian* (*Collected Statutes of Great Ming*) of 1530 of the most comprehensively idealized picture of a millennial tribute system ever produced, and a major effort to enforce all the rules and restrictions of the system, which

An early Qing dynasty illustration portrays nomadic representatives offering tribute to Chinese officials.

often had been violated in the previous reigns. The results included an epidemic of sham ambassadors from Inner Asian kingdoms and the growth of out-of-control piracy and smuggling networks along the coast. There were no more embassies from Japan after 1548. The Ryukyu tribute window was decrepit long before the Satsuma conquest of those islands in 1609. The trade agreement with Altan Khan, de facto ruler of the Western tribes of the Mongols, in 1570 used tribute rhetoric but did not allow the Mongols to come to Beijing. The Portuguese were allowed to settle at Macao without establishing any kind of place in the tribute system. Tribute rhetoric would live on, and the precedents of the full-fledged system would remain in place for later statesmen and the Qing conquerors to consult, but never again was the tribute embassy the center of a system for the management of all foreign relations.

The Manchu rulers were descendants of one branch of the Jurchen people who had been the most adept and cynical exploiters of the Ming tribute system. They understood its rules very well and had the Ming precedents on hand to use as starting points in working out their policies, but, being themselves outsiders with their own language and culture, they could scarcely be expected to go along with the culturally sinocentric rhetoric of the tradition. The Dutch sent three embassies in the early Qing dynasty and the Portuguese two. They were treated as tribute embassies and conformed to all the ceremonial routines but accomplished little for those who sent them. Court literati wrote poems about a lion brought all the way from Mozambique by the Portuguese embassy of Bento Pereira de Faria in 1678, and it gave the Kangxi emperor a chance to show favor to his court Jesuits and to Macao. But in 1684 the Qing dynasty moved to open trade in its ports to all foreigners regardless of their relation to the tribute system. This was the origin of the famous Canton (Guangzhou) trade of the eighteenth century; despite occasional pictures of Europeans in compendia on tributaries, their trade was institutionally completely separated from the tribute embassy matrix.

Unbending Resistance

Two more Portuguese embassies in the eighteenth century were received as tribute embassies and accomplished nothing for the beleaguered Catholic missions.

Detail of a Dunhuang cave painting, most likely portraying the monk Xuanzang returning from India with the white elephant given to him by Emperor Harsha. Exotic animals were often given as tribute to the Chinese rulers.

The famous embassy of Lord Macartney in 1793 was a British initiative, an effort to enlighten China concerning the wonders of open trade and European science. The ambassador's resistance to the required ceremonies, especially the three kneelings and nine prostrations of the *ketou* (kowtow), became iconic in European-U.S. perceptions of a China mired in tradition and self-regard. The Qing dynasty was glad to find more compliant Europeans in the Dutch embassy of Titsingh and Van Braam in the years from 1794 to 1796 and in dealing with several more British and Russian embassies was anxious not to give any openings for Macartney-style resistance to the accustomed ceremonies.

The amazing widening of Qing control in Inner Asia in the course of the eighteenth century was a result of activist organization and leadership that owed much to the Manchus' Inner Asian heritage and very little to the institutions and attitudes of the tribute system. Garrisons and resident administrators, assignment of grazing territories, and management of legal cases reaching all the way up to Beijing were key mechanisms; Inner Asian subordinate rulers might pay symbolic tribute, often of fine horses, to the emperor, but this was not the focus of their relation to the Qing dynasty.

The tribute system continued to be central in management of relations with Korea, Ryukyu, Annam (modern Vietnam), Siam, and Burma (modern Myanmar). Korea sent several embassies every year; it, Ryukyu, and Annam all had genuine affinities with Chinese elite culture, and their ambassadors exchanged poems in classical Chinese while they were in Beijing. No regular formal communication existed between Qing China and Tokugawa (1600/1603–1868) Japan. The Siamese connection, astutely managed by émigré Chinese, facilitated the import to south China of substantial quantities of Siamese rice, exempted from import duties. When both Siam and Annam experienced major collapses of order in the late eighteenth century, the tribute system provided a matrix for reestablishment of normal relations. This was especially striking in the Annam case, where the Qing dynasty launched an ill-advised intervention in support of the collapsing Lê dynasty in 1788 and then had to accept the victorious T̩y Sı̄n rebels as the new kings of Annam and then their conquerors, the new Nguyễn dynasty. Émigré Chinese advisors again were important, especially in the later, Nguyễn phase of the transition. Thus, in these cases a tribute connection seemed to have been of real use and to have revived under the new dynasty of foreign rulers, but the difficulties of the Annam changes probably also contributed to the anxiety with which the Qing rulers confronted the resistance to traditional ceremonies by Macartney and those who came after him. The distant tribute relation with the rulers of Burma does not seem to have either hindered or helped the Qing dynasty in its inept and costly ventures across the Yunnan frontier.

In the nineteenth century the heritage of regional hegemony (influence) embodied in the tribute system led the Qing dynasty into unsuccessful resistance to French conquest in Vietnam and Japanese conquest in Korea. Siam made its own transition to modern diplomatic standards and stopped sending embassies. The Ryukyus were fully incorporated into the Japanese state. European nations and the United States established resident diplomatic missions in Beijing after 1860 and were intensely opposed to any bit of language or protocol that might be a distant echo of the days when all foreign envoys reaching the capital would prostrate themselves in the great court before the Taihe Hall of the Palaces.

John E. WILLS Jr.

Further Reading

Fairbank, J. K. (Ed.). (1968). *The Chinese world order.* Cambridge, MA: Harvard University Press.

Fairbank, J. K., & Teng, S. Y. (1960). *Ch'ing administration: Three studies.* Cambridge, MA: Harvard-Yenching Institute Studies. (Reprinted from On the Ch'ing tributary system by J. K. Fairbank & S. Y. Teng, 1939, *Harvard Journal of Asiatic Studies, 4,* 12–46.)

Hevia, J. L. (1994). *Cherishing men from afar: Qing guest ritual and the Macartney embassy of 1793.* Durham, NC: Duke University Press.

Wills, J. E., Jr. (1984). *Embassies and illusions: Dutch and Portuguese envoys to K'ang-hsi, 1666–1687.* Cambridge, MA: Fairbank Center for East Asian Research (distributed by Harvard University Press).

Wills, J. E., Jr. (1999, Spring). Did China have a tribute system? *Asian Studies Newsletter, 44*(2), 12–13.

Yü Ying-shih. (1967). Trade and expansion in Han China: A study in the structure of Sino-barbarian economic relations. Berkeley and Los Angeles: University of California Press.

Tujia

Tǔjiāzú 土家族

The Tujia are a large minority ethnic group in central China, numbering 8 million in the 2000 census. The Tujia language, with no written form, belongs to the Tibeto-Burman subfamily of the Sino-Tibetan family. With a long history of involvement in China's national politics, the Tujia have striven to maintain their traditional culture along with their efforts to develop modern education.

The Tujia are the eighth-largest ethnic group in China. Numbering 8,028,133 in the fifth national census (2000), they are more numerous than the better known Mongols and Tibetans. Settlements of the Tujia are distributed over western Hunan, western Hubei, and northeastern Guizhou provinces, as well as in several autonomous counties under the jurisdiction of the Chongqing municipality.

Tujia Language

Some linguists consider the Tujia language to be part of the Yi language branch of the Sino-Tibetan language family. According to others, however, although the Tujia language shares some characteristics with the Yi languages, those characteristics are not enough to make the Tujia a member of that branch. Nonetheless, it is beyond question that the language, like those in the Yi branch and some others, belongs to the Tibeto-Burman subfamily of the Sino-Tibetan family. The language has no written form.

Chinese is the dominant language used by the Tujia. Many Tujia speak nothing but Chinese. Some are bilingual, speaking both Chinese and Tujia. A number also speak the language of the Miao (known outside of China as the Hmong), one of their immediate neighbors. Fewer than 200,000 Tujia still rely on the Tujia language as their major means of communication.

Tujia Names

In their own language, the Tujia call themselves Bi-dzih-ka. Throughout history they have been called various names by their neighbors, based on perceived ethnic markers or distinguishing signs, such as their totem (the white tiger, at one time the totem of their chief), or names of rivers or places where they lived. The name *Tujia* came into being in the late seventeenth century when a large number of Han Chinese (the Chinese ethnic majority people) migrated into the Tujia area. The term, which means "aboriginal families" in Chinese, was coined to distinguish the natives from the immigrants. This name did not become official until October 1956, when the Tujia were granted the status of unitary ethnic group (*danyi minzu*) by the Chinese government.

The Tujia are accomplished in textile arts including embroidery, knitting and weaving. PHOTO BY PAUL AND BERNICE NOLL.

Tujia History

The early history of the Tujia is a matter of dispute. Based on clues in Chinese historical literature, some scholars believe that the Tujia are descendents of the Ba, a tribe extinguished by the Qin Dynasty (221–206 BCE). Based on linguistic characteristics and some customs that are close to the Yi's in Yunnan, other scholars think that the ancestors of the Tujia are the *wuman,* or black barbarians, who lived in southwestern China. The fact that in the 1970s two significant Neolithic sites were found in Tujia area suggests that those regions were inhabited as early as the prehistoric period.

The picture since the Later Han dynasty (25–220 CE) is clearer. Located close to the great historical powers, the Tujia have a longer history of involvement in China's national politics than do many other Chinese minorities. As early as the tenth century, so-called bridled-and-tethered prefectures (*jimi fuzhou*), or native tributary administrations, were established in the area. The establishments were converted into a system of native chieftains (*tusi zhidu*) in the thirteenth century. Under this system minority areas in the Chinese empire were ruled by families of native chieftains instead of officials appointed by the central government. This system lasted in the Tujia area until 1723.

Conflict was the keynote of the recorded early history of interactions between the ancestors of the Tujia and Chinese society. With the establishment of the tributary system and the subsequent system of native chieftains, the Tujia became increasingly assimilated into the greater Chinese culture. During the Ming (1368–1644) and Qing (1644–1912) dynasties, a considerable number of Tujia soldiers, called different names at different times, were sent to coastal areas to fight against the Japanese and British invaders.

In the meantime, many upper-class Tujia received a Confucian education and entered the gentry-scholar rank. Some accomplished poets and scholars of the Tujia gained national reputations. When the native-chieftain system was abolished in the eighteenth century, some Tujia customs and conventions were condemned as corrupted or ugly and were reformed by force. As a result the Tujia were further assimilated, and many of their ethnic characteristics were lost.

Tujia Culture

Love-based marriage was a tradition among the Tujia. In recent centuries until the early 1950s, however, parental approval had become a norm, and wealth and social status became decisive factors. Cross-cousin marriage (a preferential rule requiring marriage between cross-cousins: mother's father's brother or father's sister's daughter if such a person is available) and levirate (the custom whereby a man marries the widow of his deceased brother) are commonly practiced among the Tujia. In some areas maternal-parallel-cousin marriage (a convention in which one marries an opposite-sex child of one's mother's sister) is also practiced.

Seniority of age is highly venerated by the Tujia. Elderly men and women are respected and treated well while alive, and elaborate funerals are held at their death. Mortuary rituals are also held for people who die at a younger age, but with less care and expense. No ceremony is held for the death of a child.

There is no organized religion among the Tujia. Their faith—a mixture of animism, ancestor worship, and worship of deified deceased chiefs and heroes—has apparently been influenced by the folk religion of the neighboring Han Chinese.

The Tujia have a long tradition of sophisticated folk arts. More than seventy prescribed movements are available for dancers of the popular *bai shou wu* (hand-waving dance) to depict such things as hunting, agricultural activities, battling, and feasting. Legends tell about the genesis and migration of their ancestors as well as their aspirations for and fantasies about the ideal life. Almost every Tujia is an accomplished singer of improvised or traditional ballads, which cover all aspects of daily life and feeling.

The traditional Tujia economy is diversified. Agriculture in narrow strips of terraced fields is complemented by logging, hunting, fishing, and growing or working on cash crops. The Tujia are also known for their traditional weaving, knitting, and embroidery. A variety of light and heavy industries has been developed in the Tujia area, and Jishou University was established there in 1958. In the past two decades, more than 95 percent of Tujia children have received at least a primary education.

Chuan-kang SHIH

Further Reading

Brassett, C. & Brassett, P. (2005). *Imperial tiger hunters: An introduction to the Tujia people of China*. Chippenham, U.K.: Antony Rowe.

Brassett, C., Brassett, P. & Meiyan Lu. (2006). *The Tujia language*. Münich, Germany: Lincom Europe.

Duan Chao. (2000). *A Cultural History of the Tujia*. Beijing: Minzu Chubanshe.

Shih, Chih-yu. (2002). *Negotiating ethnicity in China: Citizenship as a response to the state*. London: Routledge.

Twelve Muqam

Shí'èr Mùkǎmǔ　十二木卡姆

The Twelve *Muqam* are a suite of songs of the Uygur people of northwestern China's Xinjiang Uygur Autonomous Region. The pieces may be sung, danced, or instrumental, and may be performed individually or in small groups. Their lyrics are drawn from many sources, including Persian, Turkic, and folk poetry, although the actual origins of the *Muqam* are hazy. The lyrics are often infused with Sufi imagery.

The Uygur* people of northwestern China's Xinjiang Uygur Autonomous Region are closely identified with the Twelve *Muqam,* a suite of songs drawn from several Central Asian traditions that may be sung either individually or in small groups. The Twelve *Muqam* are related to the Arabo-Persian *maqam* system; the term *muqam* is the Turkic-language variant of this Arab term, and many names of suites are also drawn from Arabic. However, musically the *Muqam* are more closely related to central Asian art-music traditions, such as the Bukharan *Shashmaqam* (music of Tajikistan and Uzbekistan). Unlike the Arabo-Persian traditions, which involve some improvization

in performance, each of the Uygur Twelve *Muqam* is basically a tripartite (divided into three parts) suite consisting of (1) *chong naghma* (great music)—a series of vocal and instrumental pieces beginning with a meditative, unmetered *bash muqam* (introduction); (2) *dastan* (stories)—slower metered pieces; and (3) *mashrap* (festival)—fast dance pieces.

Rhythmic formulas marked out by the hand-held *dap* (drum) characterize the pieces. Each of the Uygur Twelve *Muqam* has a defining pitch range and mood, but the modulation of the notes played is so frequent that it is hardly possible to link a *Muqam* to one mode, or range of notes (as compared to a Western classical piece, for example, which generally stays in one key throughout the course of the piece).

The Twelve *Muqam* lyrics are attributed to the great Persian and Turkic poets or drawn from folk poetry. They are imbued with Sufi (Muslim mystic) imagery and ideals. Said to have originated in the fifteenth-century Kashgar court (an oasis city on the old Silk Roads, now in Xinjiang Uygur A. R.), their current form is more realistically traced back to the nineteenth century. *Muqam* may be performed by one singer with a bowed or plucked lute (*satar* or *tanbur*) and a drum or with a small group of supporting voices and instruments. Men, women, beggars, and religious men may practice this tradition for religious purposes or for enjoyment. The Twelve *Muqam* have an important place in Uygurs' affections and are often referred to in terms of moral authority and spiritual necessity.

Rachel HARRIS

*The author uses the spelling "Uighur" in her publications, rather than Uygur; changes have been made to reflect encyclopedia style, both in the article and in the accompanying sidebar.

Heartbreak in the Twelve *Muqam*

The Twelve Muqam, *an epic suite of songs of the Uygur people, often contain lyrics of heartbreak and loss, such as these from "Rak Muqamining Uchinchi Dastani."*

[UYGUR]	[ENGLISH]
Ey yaranlar qedirdanlar	Dear friends
Bugun qiyamet qayum dengler	Today is the end of the world you say
Ishqi otida koydi janler	Love's fire has consumed my life
Ne boldi yarim kelmidi.	Why does my lover not come?
Kilurmen dep wede qildi	I will come she promised
Kilur muddetidin ashti	But the time of arrival has come
Kozum yoligha telmurdi	My eyes on the road hoping
Ne boldi yarim kelmidi.	Why does my lover not come?
Ygen ashim zeher boldi	The food I eat is poison
Keygen tonum kepen boldi	My clothes are a winding sheet
Chirayim zepireng boldi	My face is sallow like a (flower?)
Ne boldi yarim kelmidi.	Why does my lover not come?
Chushtin keyin bolur peshim	What I did in the afternoon
Yarning kongli bek ewrishim	My love is so soft and fine
Ewrishimdek boylaring'gha	Like silk her figure
Chirmeship olsem kashki.	Entwined with her I am happy to die

Source: Li Bai (n. d.). *Ancient air.* Retrieved March 13, 2009, from http://www.chinese-poems.com/lb19.html

Further Reading

During, J., & Trebinjac, S. (1991). *Introduction au Muqam Ouigour* [Introduction to the Uyghur Muqam]. Bloomington: Indiana University Press.

Mackerras, C. (1985). Traditional Uyghur performing arts. *Asian Music, 16,* 29–58.

Trebinjac, S. (2000). *Le Pouvoir en chantent: L'Art de fabriquer une musique chinoise* [The power in singing: The art of composing a Chinese music]. Nanterre, France: Societé d'ethnologie.

Recordings

La Route de Soie, Chine, Xinjiang [The Silk Road, Xinjiang, China] [Recorded by Anderson Bakewell] (1992). On *Recordings by Anderson Bakewell* [CD]. Boulogne, France: Playasound PS.

Turkestan Chinois/Xinjiang: Musique Ouigoures [Turkestan Chinese/Xinjiang: Uyghur Music] [Recorded by Sabine Trebinjac and Jean During]. (1990). [CD]. France: Ocora.

Uyghur Musicians from Xinjiang (2000). Music from the Oasis Towns of Central Asia [CD]. London: Globestyle.

Twenty-One Demands

Èrshí Yī Tiáo Yāoqiú 二十一条要求

The economic and political ultimatums presented to China by Japan in 1915 are called the "Twenty-One Demands." They marked the beginning of Japan's emergence as the most aggressive foreign power pressuring China.

In January 1915 the Japanese government presented the Chinese government with a diplomatic ultimatum that came to be known as the "Twenty-One Demands." Many of these demands were fairly specific, aimed at expanding Japan's economic and political influence in China, especially in south Manchuria and eastern Inner Mongolia. The Japanese were particularly interested in the right to build railways in China and to deny other powers the right to do so. Specific demands also aimed at increasing Japanese control over the Hanyeping mines in central China, Japan's most important source of coal and iron. China was also to allow Japan to keep the German concessions it had recently seized in Shandong Province.

Most troubling to the Chinese government was the fifth set of demands, requiring the Chinese to hire Japanese political, financial, and military advisors and to allow joint Japanese-Chinese administration of certain districts in China. All of the other demands were expansions of Japan's existing position in China; the fifth set suggested that the Japanese were moving toward turning China into a protectorate.

From the Japanese point of view the Twenty-One Demands were a way of taking advantage of World War I to increase Japanese influence in China. Japan had been expanding its formal and informal empire in China ever since the First Sino-Japanese War (1894–1895), but rivalry between the powers had limited the expansion of Japanese control. With the coming of World War I Japanese imperialism was no longer constrained by the balancing interests of other imperialist powers. The Japanese were not entirely sure what to do with this newfound freedom of action, as reflected in the mixed goals of the demands.

Yuan Shikai's Chinese government realized that it could neither risk a war with Japan nor accept the demands as given, and so it attempted to negotiate a compromise. Yuan conducted these negotiations as publicly as possible. As expected, these public negotiations led to popular outcry among Chinese both in China and overseas. Anti-Japanese boycotts were organized, mass rallies were held, and citizens donated money to national salvation funds to prepare for war. Yuan's attempts to resist the demands briefly increased his popularity, and Sun Yat-sen's refusal to denounce them further isolated him from possible supporters. Yuan Shikai's government was able, partially because of support from England and the United States, to get the Japanese to agree to withdraw the fifth set of demands and accepted the modified demands on 9 May. This result was unacceptable to almost everyone involved. Yuan himself called the agreement a "national humiliation" and the date was later remembered as National Humiliation Day. The Kato government in Japan eventually fell because it had not secured enough from the Chinese. The long-term effects were limited. The popular anti-Japanese movement quickly died out, although Chinese became increasingly

Japan's Demands on China

Translations of documents given to Chinese president Yuan Shikai by Japanese minister Hioki Eki on 18 January 1915.

The Japanese Government and the Chinese Government being desirous of maintaining the general peace in Eastern Asia and further strengthening the friendly relations and good neighbourhood existing between the two nations agree to the following articles:

Article 1. The Chinese Government engages to give full assent to all matters upon which the Japanese Government may hereafter agree with the German Government relation to the disposition of all rights, interests and concessions, which Germany, by virtue of treaties or otherwise, possesses in relation to the Province of Shantung [Shandong].

Article 2. The Chinese Government engages that within the Province of Shantun and along its coast no territory or island will be ceded or leased to a third Power under any pretext.

Article 3. The Chinese Government consents to Japan's building a railway from Chefoo or Lungkow to join the Kaiochow-Tsinanfu Railway.

Article 4. The Chinese Government engages, in the interest of trade and for the residence of foreigners, to open herself as soon as possible to certain important cities and towns in the Province of Shantung as Commercial Ports. What places shall be opened are to be jointly decided upon in a separate agreement.

Source: Wood, Ge-Zay. (1921). *The Twenty-One Demands.* New York: Fleming H. Revell Company, 108–109.

unlikely to take Japan as a model for Chinese development after 1915. The Twenty One Demands were a harbinger of things to come because in the following decades Japan would be the chief imperialist power attempting to expand its power in China, and China would attempt to resist by mobilizing public opinion and seeking aid from the United States and England.

Alan BAUMLER

Further Reading

Chi, M. (1970). *China diplomacy 1914–1918.* Cambridge, MA: Harvard East Asian Research Center.

Dickenson, F. R. (1999). *War and national reinvention: Japan in the Great War 1914–1919.* Cambridge, MA: Harvard University Press.

Zhitian, L. (1993, May). National humiliation and national assertion: The Chinese response to the Twenty-One Demands. *Modern Asian Studies, 27*(2), 297–319.

United Front Strategy

Tŏngyī zhànxiàn cèluè sīxiǎng

统一战线策略思想

The United Front strategy in China and Korea was the implementation of the theory that Communist groups should form a united front with Nationalists to win their liberation before beginning their socialist revolutions.

The United Front strategy developed from a belief of the Soviet Comintern (the international organization of Communist parties) that Communist groups in nations subject to foreign subjugation should form a united front with nationalists to win their liberation before beginning their socialist revolutions. The Russian Communist leader Vladimir Lenin expressed this tenet succinctly: "Hostile classes are united by a common interest in opposing foreign exploitation" (Schram 1969, 134). The strategy was first used in China and, after a successful start there, was adopted by Korea. In the end both attempts were unsuccessful, and the societal divisions that emerged linger in the divided Korean Peninsula and in the politically divided governments of China and Taiwan.

In China until the Communist purge in 1927, the union of the Communists and the Guomindang (Chinese Nationalist Party) led to the formation of a government with Communist participation; one Russian adviser even noted that members of the right-wing Guomindang were moving toward the left. This observation was premature, with the brutal purge of the Communists by Chiang Kai-shek's (1887–1975) Nationalist group ending any hope of a strong united front to challenge Japanese imperialism in China.

In Korea the United Front strategy was intended to create "a broad national revolutionary front that included handicraftsmen, the intelligentsia, and the petty and middle bourgeoisie along with the workers and peasants" (Scalapino and Lee 1972, 95). The structure for this united front was the Korean National Party (KCP), which was formed in early 1926, organized by Korean Communists in an attempt to form an alliance with Korean nationalists. It thus placed Korean Communist Party members at its core. This effort was weakened by the roundup of many KCP leaders by the Japanese after the funeral of former Emperor Sunjong in June 1926.

Formation of the Singanhoe (New Korean Society) in 1927 was Korea's best chance to unify rival factions. The society accommodated a variety of groups ranging from the moderate to the radical and soon established a national network of 386 branches with more than seventy-five thousand members. The beginning of the end for the New Korean Society came in 1929 when its leaders were rounded up by Japanese police and charged with supporting the student riots in Kwangju in 1929. The society's subsequent move to the right caused many leftist members to quit, resulting in its demise in 1931 and ending hope for a Korean united front against Japan.

These efforts by the Soviets to create united fronts in China and Korea failed because of the political differences facing the leaders of the respective nationalist and conservative parties. In both nations these differences eventually erupted into civil wars, deepening divisions that persist into the twenty-first century.

Mark E. CAPRIO

Further Reading

Eckert, C. J., Lee, Ki-baik, Lew, Young, Robinson, M., & Wagner, E. W. (1990). *Korea old and new: A history.* Cambridge, MA: Korean Institute, Harvard University.

Scalapino, R. A., & Lee, Chong-sik. (1972). *Communism in Korea, Vol. 1: The society.* Berkeley and Los Angeles: University of California Press.

Schram, S. R. (1969). *The political thought of Mao Tse Tung.* New York: Praeger Press.

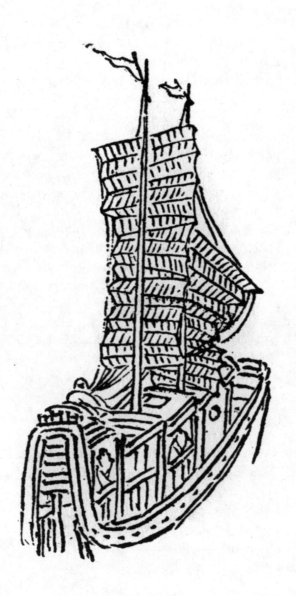

A foot can be shorter while an inch can be longer.

尺短寸长

Chǐ duǎn cùn cháng

United Kingdom–China Relations

Yīng-Zhōng wàijiāo guānxì 英中外交关系

China and the United Kingdom have a long history of relations—some contentious, some collaborative—with Hong Kong at the center. In the twenty-first century, both countries look toward cooperation.

China and the United Kingdom, two nations that have greatly affected regional and world affairs for centuries, seemed destined by history to interact on a grand scale. Relations between the two nations since the eighteenth century have, in turn, helped and hindered China.

Empire to Empire

For a major seafaring and exploring nation, Britain was a late arriver in China. The main European interests in China in the sixteenth and seventeenth centuries were from the Portuguese and to some extent the Dutch. But Britain's interests, when they became more substantial in the eighteenth century, concentrated on trade. Britain sourced tea, silk, and spices in China and was part of what was largely viewed by the court of Emperor Qianlong (reigned 1735–1796) as unwelcome commercial foreign encroachment.

To defend its interests, Britain sent a trade mission in the late 1780s, which was aborted due to the illness of its main emissary. Britain sent a more successful and well-known mission under Lord Macartney in 1793.

Macartney, a respected diplomat and statesman, was given tasks by the government of King George III of opening up the Chinese market and establishing some kind of embassy in Beijing. Summoned from Beijing to the emperor's summer residence in Jahol, 100 kilometers (about 62 miles) northeast of the city, Macartney spent huge amounts of time and effort in negotiations with the Qing court on how he should kowtow before the emperor, finally agreeing to bow on one knee and not abase himself fully. In an early example of how an event is given "spin," the Chinese account says that even having agreed to this, Macartney still fell to his knees when in the presence of the emperor, so overcome by awe was he. Conflicts regarding trade (and imperial protocol) were to become commonplace over the next two centuries and escalated when Britain's requests were rebuffed. Qianlong famously responded that China had no need of Britain's manufactures. This typified the empire's inward-looking and somewhat conservative stance.

Britain's interests in the next half century continued to be based on trade, but they would become increasingly fractious. The most highly industrialized and economically powerful nation at the time, Britain was keen to address what it saw as trade imbalances in China. Britain, part of the carefully controlled foreign presence in the open ports of Guangzhou (Canton), through its companies (particularly Jardine Matheson) became involved in the thriving opium trade, importing immense amounts into China. Dissatisfaction with this led to the Chinese government's military opposition in 1839.

This First Opium War (1839–1842) escalated to full military conflict, which Britain, with its superior army

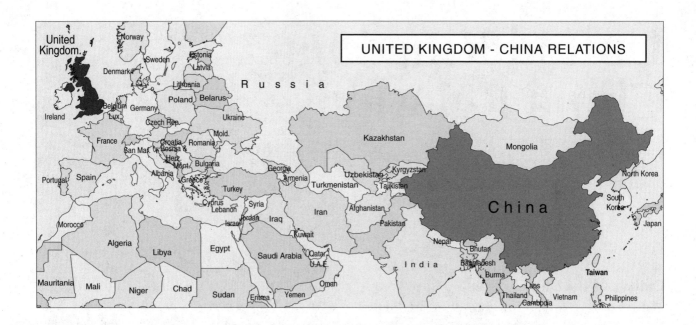

UNITED KINGDOM - CHINA RELATIONS

and firepower, easily won. The Treaty of Nanjing in 1842, what has come to be called the first of the unequal treaties imposed on China, granted the island of Hong Kong to the British to house their warehouses and allowed them to continue trading in opium and other goods more freely.

Continued tensions over the freedoms granted to trading culminated in a second war in the early 1860s, which, like the first, resulted in China's defeat and the granting to Britain of further land in Hong Kong (the Kowloon peninsula) and further trading privileges. In 1898 a ninety-nine-year lease was given for the rest of the Hong Kong area. British and the other European powers were attacked during the Boxer Rebellion in 1900, resulting in massive reparations that financially crippled the Qing court. By 1911 the Qing era was over, although the emperor did not abdicate until 1912.

Modern Concerns

In the early part of the twentieth century, Britain was the largest investor in China, with massive interests, mostly headquartered in Shanghai, in energy and mining. Companies like British American Tobacco and Shell were already active. Britain controlled almost 70 percent of China's energy supply through coal and electricity production. The British concession in Shanghai was the

home to British entrepreneurs, intellectuals, and, to an increasing extent as the century went on, artists. This era of openness in China's history was to result in a tragic outcome, however, when the war with Japan in 1937 created massive refugee issues and swept away much of the business community. By 1949 and the establishment of the People's Republic of China (PRC), most of the business infrastructure (including banks) had been either eradicated or dramatically scaled down.

Britain was one of the first countries to recognize the PRC, in 1950, if only to preserve its key interests in Hong Kong, which remained under British control. For the next half century, this protectorate remained Britain's priority, and Hong Kong became one of the world's important business centers, something that the increasingly radical government of the PRC was to tolerate in view of the economic lifeline it gave to the rest of the world. By the late 1960s, even with the Cultural Revolution spilling over into Hong Kong and causing disruption and riots there—notably the sacking of the British Embassy Office by the Red Guards in 1967, when the Chinese demanded that the British release individuals convicted of perpetrating terrorist attacks in Hong Kong—the importance of this trade link was still recognized by Beijing. In 1971 Hong Kong–related trade accounted for almost all of the PRC's foreign business. The visit by President Nixon in 1972, reopening relations between the United States and

China, was quickly followed up by a visit from British prime minister Edward Heath, who also upgraded relations to the ambassadorial level.

New "Lease on Life" for Hong Kong

While the issue had been put on hold during the uncertainties of the 1970s, the arrival of a more liberal leadership under Deng Xiaoping (1904–1997) in 1974 raised the question of what would be done about the ninety-nine-year lease agreed on Hong Kong in 1898. Tentative enquiries in the early 1980s by British officials about the possibility of simply extending the lease by another ninety years were met with firm rebuttals. Deng suggested a one country, two systems arrangement, whereby Hong Kong's unique political and economic structure be respected and the region be returned to Chinese sovereignty in 1997. The Basic Law, which acted as a de facto constitution, was promulgated in the late 1980s. The shock of the Tiananmen Square riots in 1989, while causing panic and consternation in Hong Kong, did not prevent the final agreement for the full return of Hong Kong on time on 30 June 1997. The final five years under the reforming governorship of British politician Chris Patten, with whom the Chinese had strained relations, had not derailed the agreement. With the return of Hong Kong to China, one of the largest and most contentious issues between Britain and China had been resolved.

Since 1997, the government in Beijing has kept its side of the agreement, interfering very little in Hong Kong, allowing it to govern itself, and acting only in foreign affairs and military issues.

Trade Relations

In the meantime, Britain's main interests in China have reverted to trade. Britain has continued to be China's main investor from Europe, with more than 6,000 joint ventures with Chinese companies and almost $25 billion of contracted investment in every province and autonomous region. The largest British companies investing in China include energy companies BP and Shell, telecommunications company Vodafone, the Royal Bank of Scotland, and retailers like Tesco, B and Q, and Marks and Spencer.

Since 2003, China has also increased its investments in the United Kingdom, with more than 350 companies now active there, ranging from the Bank of China to the telecommunications giant Huawei. China has also invested through its State Administration for Foreign Exchange in more than 100 London-listed companies and bought a 3 percent stake in Barclays Bank. China's role

Ferry pier on Hong Kong Island, central Hong Kong is on the left. Hong Kong, having been under British rule since 1842, was returned to Chinese sovereignty in 1997. PHOTO BY JOAN LEBOLD COHEN.

The owner of a Chinese clothing store poses with former British prime minister Tony Blair and his wife. This photo is proudly displayed in the window of her shop. PHOTO BY TOM CHRISTENSEN.

as an investor in the United Kingdom is likely to increase dramatically in the years ahead.

Nevertheless, Britain shares with the rest of Europe and the United States concerns over the trade imbalance with China. In June 2008, while it increased its exports to China to $800 million a month, this still ran at a massive deficit, with China exporting back to the UK over $2 billion worth of goods. Britain undertook most of its negotiations on the trade deficit through the European Union.

Education Exchange

Chinese students have been attending British universities in increasing numbers, rising from 3,000 in 1998 to more than 70,000 in 2007. The British universities of Liverpool and Nottingham have set up educational joint ventures in China, with Nottingham having the only foreign university campus in Ningbo, Zhejiang Province.

Britain remains one of the key international centers for the study of both ancient and modern China, with large, thriving academic centers at Oxford, Cambridge, London, Leeds, Edinburgh, and Nottingham.

Toward an Understanding

While relations have remained warm since 1997, history continues to leave a stain. Arguments within and outside China continue over the role that Britain played during what has been labeled China's century of humiliation. Some historians argue that the Qing empire was complacent and that it overreacted to foreign overtures for greater links. If China had been sharper and more sensible in its reaction, it might have used these links to make itself more secure and stronger. Others argue that economic and social development in China, particularly in Hong Kong, was established and expanded by the Chinese with little help from the British.

In one particular area, Tibet, Britain's colonial past still reverberates: Britain is the only country in the world that does not recognize Chinese sovereignty in the region.

In spite of, or because of, past connections, Britain and China have expressed the desire for continued relations. Britain has become a destination for large numbers of Chinese tourists, though the fact that it is not yet part of the European Schengen visa zone (and unlikely to be one for the foreseeable future) has kept these numbers limited. In 2007 British prime minister Gordon Brown and Chinese premier Wen Jiabao agreed to joint efforts in further developing Sino-British cooperation in economic, educational, and cultural matters.

Kerry BROWN

Further Reading

Carroll, J. M. (2007). *A concise history of Hong Kong.* Lanham, MD: Rowman & Littlefield Publishers.

Hoare, J. E. (1999). *Embassies in the East: The Story of the British and their embassies in China, Japan and Korea from 1859 to the present.* London: Routledge.

Cradock, P. (1994). *Experiences of China.* London: John Murray.

Bickers, R. (1999). *Britain in China: Community, culture and colonialism.* Manchester: Manchester University Press.

Welsh, F. (1997). *A history of Hong Kong.* London: Harper Collins.

United Nations–China Relations

Liánhéguó hé Zhōngguó de wàijiāo guānxì

联合国和中国的外交关系

China is a founding member of the United Nations and, as a permanent member of its Security Council, holds veto power over resolutions brought before the U.N. Due to political unrest in China during the years following the U.N.'s founding in 1945, China's representation in the U.N. became a source of unresolved domestic strife and international conflict for over two decades.

The United Nations was established as an international peacekeeping organization on 26 June 1945, several weeks after the conclusion of World War II in Europe, when representatives of fifty nations, including China, met in San Francisco to sign the U.N. charter. As one of the "Big Five" Allied nations (along with the United States, the Soviet Union, France, and Great Britain), China participated in negotiations leading to the U.N.'s creation at the Teheran (1943), Dumbarton Oaks (1944), and Yalta (1945) conferences. China is not only a founding member but also one of the five permanent members of the U.N.'s Security Council.

The charter-signing ceremony was staged with great fanfare and publicity. Since each delegation signed in English alphabetical order, the Chinese were first and contributed to the pageantry by preparing fresh ink for traditional brush calligraphy. In 1945 the U.N. enjoyed support from the major political organizations in China. The ten-member delegation in San Francisco was comprised of high-ranking officials representing diverse political views but all officially appointed as delegates by Republic of China (ROC) president Chiang Kai-shek (Jiang Jieshi) (1887-1975). The ROC's ruling Guomindang (Nationalist Party) sent four representatives: T. V. Soong (Soong Ziwen), minister of foreign affairs; Ambassador V. K. Wellington Koo (Gu Weijin); Defense Council Minister Wang Chung-hui (Wang Conghui); and Ambassador Wei Tao-ming (Wei Daoming). Dong Biwu was sent by the Chinese Communist Party (CCP). The State Socialist Party sent historian Carson Chang (Zhang Junmai), and Li Huang represented the Nationalist Youth Party. Also in attendance were philosopher Hu Shih (Hu Shi), Ginling College president Wu Yifang, and Hu Lin. After ratification by the ROC's People's Political Council, the charter was signed by President Chiang Kai-shek on 24 August 1945. Soon, however, cooperation and goodwill among political rivals in China disappeared as civil war led to a CCP victory and the fleeing of Chiang and the Guomindang government to Taiwan. Within five years of the charter's signing, China's representation in the U.N. would be a source of domestic strife and international conflict that would not be resolved for over two decades.

PRC-ROC Conflict over U.N. Membership

The founding of the People's Republic of China (PRC) on 1 October 1949 set in motion a controversy over which government, Beijing or Taipei, should occupy China's seat. On 18 November 1949, Beijing's premier Zhou Enlai

(1898–1976) communicated to U.N. authorities that the PRC was the sole legal government of China and the legitimate representative of the Chinese people. He further notified the president of the General Assembly that his government repudiated the legal status of the U.N. delegation headed by Ambassador T. F. Tsiang (Jiang Tingfu) (1895–1965) and called for the immediate expulsion of Guomindang representatives. However, during the 1950s and 1960s Cold War politics prevailed when the U.S. government worked to keep its ally, the ROC headed by Chiang Kai-shek, in the U.N. while the Soviets and many Third World nations called for the PRC's admission. Beijing's Ministry of Foreign Affairs has blamed hostility to China's new government and "deliberate obstruction," mainly by the United States, for preventing the PRC from assuming China's seat despite "unremitting efforts" by the CCP beginning in 1950.

In September 1950 the U.N. General Assembly first considered the question of China's membership when it rejected resolutions supporting the PRC sponsored by the USSR and India. The General Assembly then set up a special committee to review China's representation, during which time the ROC held China's seat. In 1951 the USSR repeated attempts to secure Beijing's admission by putting forward proposals to place the question of China's representation on the General Assembly agenda. At the time, PRC forces were fighting U.N. troops in the Korean War. After Soviet efforts failed the General Assembly approved a resolution sponsored by Thailand to postpone any review of China's representation. Meanwhile, on 1 February 1951, the U.N. voted to condemn China as aggressor in Korea and initiated a global embargo of shipments of war materiel, further isolating the PRC from the international community. From 1951 to 1960, during

A delegation from the National Committee on United States–China Relations visits the United Nations in 1973. COURTESY OF NCUSCR.

each session of the United Nations, the General Assembly approved U.S.-sponsored motions to keep the question of China's representation off the agenda. As a result, effective deliberation of the representation question was thwarted while the CCP openly condemned certain U.N. member states, particularly the United States, for what the Chinese referred to as subversive manipulation.

Despite Beijing's failure to secure a U.N. seat, throughout the 1950s CCP leaders maintained a positive public outlook toward the U.N. CCP representatives occasionally participated in U.N. discussions on an ad hoc basis on issues of concern to China, including talks on the agenda item entitled "Complaint of Armed Invasion of Taiwan (Formosa)" (1950) as well as Security Council debate on the Korean War. In 1955 Premier Zhou Enlai told delegates at the Afro-Asian (Bandung) Conference that the Chinese people supported the purposes and principles of the U.N. Charter. In addition, many of the bilateral treaties signed by the Beijing government cited U.N. principles. By the end of the decade, however, CCP leaders began to question the value of the U.N. as a vehicle to promote international peace and openly criticized its actions, claiming, for example, that the U.N. had begun to serve the goals of "imperialism" and "neocolonialism."

The 1960s were years of transition for Beijing's official position toward the U.N. As more Asian and African nations won independence and joined the U.N., many of their governments called for the PRC's admission as the legitimate government of China. In response, supporters of the ROC successfully sponsored resolutions in the General Assembly to consider China's representation as an "important question," thereby requiring passage by a two-thirds majority vote of member states. Such procedural changes made Beijing's case problematic into the next decade. As a result, the PRC apparently abandoned hope of replacing the ROC, publicly accused member states of departing from the charter's intentions, and refused to participate in ad hoc deliberations on issues involving China. In 1965 the CCP called for revisions to the U.N. Charter and proclaimed its support for the establishment of an alternative "revolutionary" United Nations organization.

Beijing's position was influenced by two issues during the 1960s: the Sino-Soviet dispute and the development of the Cultural Revolution (1966–1976). China's open break with its former ally, public by 1960, led to assertions by the Chinese that both the United States and the USSR were conspiring to keep Beijing out of the U.N. The power struggle within the CCP and turmoil associated with the Cultural Revolution kept the government focused on domestic issues. The PRC press during these years avoided the topic of China's U.N. seat and advocated that third-world nations either not join or drop out of the U.N. By 1969, however, CCP leaders acknowledged the dangers of international isolation and the potential threat of the USSR, causing them to take another look at U.N. membership. A more moderate tone toward the U.N. was apparent in an October 1969 speech by Premier Zhou Enlai honoring Premier Alfred Raoul of the Congo, in which Zhou thanked that country for taking up China's cause in the U.N. and advocating the expulsion of the Guomindang delegation.

The early 1970s were characterized by significant changes in China's foreign policy that coincided with a shift in the U.N. vote on China's representation. In 1970 General Assembly members who supported Beijing's claim outnumbered the opposition for the first time. The ballot question on China's resolution sponsored by eighteen member states resulted in fifty-one nations voting for the PRC and forty-nine voting against, with twenty-five abstentions. Apparently emboldened by the more widespread support, the Chinese government began to adopt new strategies aimed at winning the U.N. seat. A multi-faceted campaign promoted a more pragmatic approach to foreign policy. Abandoning the antiforeign polemics associated with the Cultural Revolution, the CCP began courting the goodwill of dozens of nations through improved relations, increased contacts, and aid programs. After the visit of U.S. National Security Advisor Henry Kissinger to China in July 1971, Beijing's success seemed assured, causing U.N. Secretary-General U Thant to predict the likelihood of a solution to the representation conflict in favor of the PRC. At the General Assembly's twenty-sixth session in 1971, 131 nations voted on Resolution 2758, the question of China's seat. Seventy-six voted pro-PRC, thirty-five opposed, and seventeen abstained. PRC representatives arrived in New York and replaced those of the ROC on 11 November 1971.

Beijing's first delegation was an experienced team. Vice Foreign Minister Qiao Guanhua (1912–1983) served as delegation head until 1976. He had represented China at several international conferences and had been present at the U.N. in 1950 when he spoke for the PRC as ad hoc participant during Korean War debates. The vice chairman and permanent representative to the Security Council, Huang Hua, also had considerable diplomatic experience and served as advisor to Premier Zhou Enlai. Huang was the PRC's ambassador to Ghana and Egypt during the 1960s. Other delegates included Fu Hao, Chen Chu and U.S.-educated Xiong Xianghui, all of whom held high rank within the Foreign Ministry.

Champion of the Third World

In his first speech before the U.N. General Assembly in November 1971, Ambassador Qiao Guanhua outlined the theme for China's role in the U.N. He announced that "like the overwhelming majority of the Asian, African and Latin American countries, China belongs to the Third World," pledged Beijing's support for "oppressed peoples and nations," and condemned "the power politics and hegemony of big nations bullying small ones or strong nations bullying weak ones." During the early 1970s the PRC occasionally used the U.N. as a stage to air its grievances against the two "imperialist superpowers," the United States and the USSR, but, for the most part, the Chinese advanced their national interests with a pragmatic approach to U.N. politics aimed at improving relations with member states worldwide.

China's early voting record revealed, for the most part, Beijing's adherence to its stated goal of championing Third World initiatives. Throughout the 1970s China's votes were more consistent with those of poorer Third World nations than with those of either the Western or Communist worlds. The PRC garnered favor with Asian, African, and Latin American nations by supporting, for example, resolutions on the "Declaration of the Indian Ocean as a Zone of Peace," demands by Latin American governments to extend territorial seas to 200 nautical miles, enlargement of the Economic and Social Council so as to include more developing nations, and relocation of Security Council meetings from New York to an African city. Moreover, China's delegates were known to mingle informally with Third World colleagues, a practice in which the United States and Soviet Union participated infrequently. In addition, the U.N. became the platform for China's critique of U.S. and Soviet positions on several contentious issues, including Middle Eastern politics and arms control, that promoted, in China's view, "superpower hegemony."

Veto Power

As a permanent member of the Security Council, China is one of five nations that holds the power to veto resolutions coming before the U.N. China's use of the veto has been selective compared with that of the other permanent members, which together already have cast 254 vetoes. Since the founding of the U.N. China has used the veto six times, including the 1955 veto of Mongolia's admission by the ROC on the grounds that Mongolia is a province of China. The five resolutions that the PRC vetoed are admitting Bangladesh (1972); calling (with the USSR) for a ceasefire during the Yom Kippur War (1973); sending 155 ceasefire observers to Guatemala (1997); extending the U.N. Preventative Deployment Force in Macedonia (1999); and criticizing (with Russia) Myanmar (Burma) on its human rights record (2007). Beijing used the veto to promote China's foreign policy goals as well as to challenge many U.N. initiatives that the Chinese deem to be violations of sovereignty or territorial integrity. For example, the Beijing government vetoed the sending of U.N. peacekeeping forces to Guatemala and Macedonia because the two governments accorded diplomatic recognition to the government of Taiwan and not the PRC at the time. Pressure by China in the U.N. bore some success for Beijing as Guatemala resolved to stop pressing Taiwan's interests in the U.N., resulting in the PRC's lifting the veto within weeks. The Republic of Macedonia opened bilateral ties with Beijing in 2001. With the remaining three vetoes China took unpopular stands on several contentious issues.

The PRC cast its first veto on 25 August 1972, when it refused to support a Security Council resolution granting Bangladesh U.N. membership. China's blocking the admission of a new Third World nation appeared to contradict its aim of promoting the rights of poorer nations. The Chinese, however, had argued for postponement of the vote because issues involving Bangladesh's independence from Pakistan had not been resolved, including the status of over ninety thousand Pakistani prisoners of war held by India. The Chinese accused the Soviets of

Generalissimo Chiang Kai-shek as a representative for China signing the United Nations Charter on 24 August 1945.
COURTESY OF NCUSCR.

attempting to embarrass Beijing by introducing the measure prematurely, forcing the Chinese to take an apparently hypocritical stand. China's veto was in support of Pakistan, its ally since the 1962 invasion of China by India. Bangladesh gained a U.N. seat in September 1974 with no opposition from China.

The October 1973 Arab-Israeli War was the occasion for China to cast a negative vote along with the Soviets on a resolution calling for a ceasefire, presumably in protest of the United States' sponsorship of Israel. After the cessation of hostilities the Chinese vigorously denounced what they deemed Soviet-U.S. manipulation of the Security Council when a U.N. emergency force (UNEF II) was deployed in the Sinai Peninsula. The Security Council representative, Huang Hua, referred to UNEF II as "an attempt to occupy Arab territories." China, however, never blocked the establishment of U.N. peacekeepers for the Middle East and either abstained or was absent from Security Council votes on the issue.

The 2007 veto of a U.S.-sponsored Security Council resolution criticizing the government of Myanmar for its human rights record is consistent with Beijing's view that the U.N. should not interfere in the internal affairs of member states. The resolution garnered support from nine Security Council members. Russia and South Africa also cast negative votes, while three others abstained. Beijing has maintained that the U.N. has no mandate to sanction governments for actions within their own borders.

Abstentions as Policy

Beijing's sparse use of the veto since 1971 does not necessarily reflect China's approval of Security Council actions that passed because the Chinese delegation failed to cast a negative vote. The Chinese have abstained or chosen not to participate in votes on many controversies. The strategy of abstaining is consistent with Beijing's unwillingness to approve U.N. initiatives, such as peacekeeping forces or sanctions, that infringe upon a nation's sovereignty or that could alienate China's friends in the international organization. By not using its veto, China does no damage to its relations with either side in the conflict and also allows the U.N. to act.

The PRC has been critical of U.N. peacekeeping forces, claiming that they violate a nation's sovereignty. The use of sanctions, the Chinese argue, can be a "double-edged sword" that harms innocent civilians along with the target government. The Chinese have not, however, consistently upheld these principles. Beginning in 1990 the Chinese have deployed military personnel to thirteen U.N. peace-keeping operations. China did not veto Security Council Resolution 1333, which placed sanctions on Afghanistan in 2000, nor did China veto any of the Security Council proposals since 2004 that imposed sanctions on Sudan, a state with which China has close economic ties.

China's actions during the first Persian Gulf War are another example of the strategic use of the abstention. The U.N. has authorized the use of force only twice—in 1950 in the Korean War and in 1990 against Iraqi forces in Kuwait. China approved the eleven Security Council resolutions condemning Iraq's aggression during the first Persian Gulf War, including the imposition of sanctions, but condemned the use of U.N.-sponsored military force against Iraq. Nevertheless, the Chinese chose not to veto military intervention. China's selectivity in its use of the veto has caused many Third World leaders to question whether China's interests will continue to coincide with those of poorer nations.

Millennium Challenges

On 8 September 2000, the U.N. overwhelmingly approved the Millennium Declaration, whose objective is to promote peace, security and disarmament. It also pledged to reduce by half the number of people with incomes of less than one dollar a day by 2015. With its phenomenal economic growth, China is on target to meet the economic targets established by the U.N., but other challenges for the twenty-first century may not be so easily resolved.

Since 1991 the government of Taiwan has indicated its desire to return to the United Nations. In 2004 Taiwan's president, Chen Shui-bian, made the provocative claim, "Taiwan is a sovereign state, and should join the United Nations by the name Taiwan." As a result, the controversy of China's representation has been revisited. Taiwan's allies have attempted to put the question of Taiwan's inclusion on the General Assembly's agenda but have failed to procure the required votes. Beijing remains steadfast in its position that Taiwan is part of China. Since the PRC can veto any resolution that acknowledges Taiwan's sovereignty, the likelihood of Taiwan's gaining a seat in the U.N. is dim.

Beijing has also promised to veto efforts to enlarge the Security Council. In 2005 four nations referred to as the "Group of Four" (G-4)—India, Germany, Japan, and Brazil—have called for increasing the Security Council from its present fifteen members to twenty-five. The G-4, moreover, has demanded the veto. The Chinese claim that the proposal fails to uphold the interests of most developing nations. It also diminishes the clout of the original "Big Five" founders of the United Nations. As China's rise as a global power continues, China's role in the United Nations will evolve.

June GRASSO

Further Reading

Chai, T. R. (1980). Chinese politics in the General Assembly. *The Public Opinion Quarterly, 44*(1), 23–34.

Chai, W. (1970). China and the United Nations: Problems of representation and alternatives. *Asian Survey, 10*(5), 397–409.

Chiu, H., & Edwards, R. R. (1968). Communist China's attitude toward the United Nations: A legal analysis. *The American Journal of International Law, 62*(1), 20–50.

Embassy of the People's Republic of China. (2004, May). Struggle to restore China's lawful seat in the United Nations. Retrieved July 8, 2008, from http://www.chinaembassy.ee/eng/zggk/xzgwjjs/t110281.htm

Fravel, M. T. (1996). China's attitude toward U.N. peacekeeping operations since 1989. *Asian Survey, 36*(11), 1102–1121.

Kim, S. S. (1979). *China, the United Nations, and world order.* Princeton, NJ: Princeton University Press.

Mclaughlin, D. (1995, September). Signing the charter. *UN Chronicle.*

Ogden, S. (1979). China's position on U.N. Charter review. *Pacific Affairs, 52*(2), 210–240.

Shichor, Y. (2006). China's voting behavior in the UN Security Council. *China Brief, 6*(18).

United States–China Relations

Měi-Zhōng wàijiāo guānxì 美中外交关系

China and the United States have recently forged close economic ties, but relations between the two nations have often been marred by political tension. Beginning in the eighteenth century when the U.S. emerged as a nation during China's Qing dynasty, through the Nationalist period, and for much of Chinese Communist Party rule, the two nations often clashed.

*I*n February 1784 the *Empress of China* left New York harbor on its historic voyage to China's southeastern port of Guangzhou (Canton). In August it became the first U.S. ship to trade in China at a time when Europe had already dominated the China trade for decades. By the turn of the nineteenth century an average of twenty-five U.S. vessels arrived in Guangzhou annually, and continued to grow even during the periods of upheaval which typified the twentieth century. At the beginning of the twenty-first century China became the United States' number one trading partner, surpassing European Union nations and powerful neighbors such as Japan. The development of U.S.-China relations, however, has not always been smooth, and political entanglements continue to complicate relations. Both economic and political conflicts have been the source of controversy for the governments of both nations, but throughout much of the comparatively brief history of the United States, commercial relations have played a paramount role in U.S.-China relations.

Competition with the British for Opium Trade

U.S. traders arrived in China in the late eighteenth century as relative newcomers who benefited from inroads made by their European counterparts. Like the Europeans, U.S. traders had few commodities to sell to the self-sufficient Chinese, so they had to use silver, primarily Spanish silver dollars, to pay for Chinese tea and silk until they, like the British earlier, turned to selling opium. Before 1820 U.S. traders had a profitable monopoly in Turkish opium that allowed them to take a small share of Guangzhou's market from the British East India Company, which sold opium originating in India, a British colony. However, when British "free" or private traders began competing for Turkish opium sources, the U.S. traders found themselves at a competitive disadvantage because U.S. ships were prohibited from carrying opium directly from British India to China. Nevertheless, U.S. dealers became adept at procuring opium stocks from a variety of sources, and in the years leading up to the First Opium War one U.S. company, Russell & Company, was ranked third among foreign firms dealing in Indian opium in Guangzhou.

Attempts by the Qing dynasty (1644–1912) at halting opium sales led to war and consequently the "unequal treaties" that permitted foreign merchants and missionaries in China's coastal cities. Still in the shadow of the Europeans, U.S. traders gained advantages from the terms of the treaties. The "most favored nation" clause in the Treaty of Nanjing ending the First Opium War granted foreign powers in China a share in whatever concessions

2351

were granted to any one of them. Extraterritoriality, a legal provision that allowed foreigners to ignore China's laws, made trade in opium possible without fear of prosecution. U.S. citizens and Europeans in China during the decades after the opium wars engaged in commercial and missionary activities, but, unlike the Europeans, the U.S. government did not seek territory in China. That difference in policy would influence U.S.-China relations into the twentieth century.

Burlingame Mission and Its Consequences

The Second Opium War concluded with China's defeat by the British and French, who then demanded that the Qing rulers establish permanent foreign embassies in Beijing. The Treaties of Tianjin, signed with several European states and the United States, forced the opening of Beijing to foreign residence. In response the Chinese government created the Foreign Office (Zongli Yamen) to handle diplomatic matters. The first U.S. minister sent to Beijing was Anson Burlingame, appointed in 1861 by President Abraham Lincoln, who expected Burlingame to ensure U.S. interests by defending China's territorial integrity in the face of European colonial expansion. In 1867, in an unusual move, Burlingame was recruited by the Foreign Office to head China's first delegation abroad, serving as an official representative of the Qing throne. The three-year-long Burlingame mission featured visits to foreign capitals and other points of interest. One accomplishment included the negotiation of an amendment to the Treaty of Tianjin, called the Seward-Burlingame Treaty (1868), asserting that the United States did not have territorial designs on China and providing freedom

for citizens of both nations to emigrate and trade without discrimination.

The Seward-Burlingame Treaty was denounced by members of the U.S. Congress from western states who, responding to intense nativism, worked to curtail Chinese immigration into the United States. In 1880 the treaty was revised when both Beijing and Washington agreed that the U.S. government could suspend but not prohibit Chinese immigration. Congress responded in 1882 by passing the first of the Chinese "exclusion laws" that suspended Chinese immigration for a decade. In 1892 California congressman Thomas Geary proposed an extension of the law for another ten years in the Act to Prohibit the Coming of Chinese Persons into the United States, also known as the "Geary Act." Despite protests by the Qing throne and Chinese-Americans, the Geary Act passed and was upheld by the U.S. Supreme Court in 1893. In 1902 Congress renewed the exclusion act with no terminal date and included the requirement that all Chinese in the United States possess a certificate of residence or face deportation. (The exclusion laws were not repealed until the passage of the Magnuson Act in 1943.) The restrictions placed on Chinese by the United States were in stark contrast to simultaneous attempts by the U.S. government to protect U.S. interests in China.

Open Door Policy

By the close of the nineteenth century the Qing dynasty faced increasing pressure from imperialist powers, especially after China's defeat in the Sino-Japanese War (1894–1895). The years from 1895 to 1900 have been referred to as the time of the "Slicing of the Melon" when China was carved into spheres of influence by Europe and

Japan. In 1899 the U.S. government responded to China's situation with the concept of an "open door" aimed at protecting U.S. trade by promoting equality of economic opportunity in China. In 1899 U.S. Secretary of State John Hay sent the Open Door Notes to governments with interests in China, including Great Britain, France, Russia, Germany, and Japan. Hay was successful in securing tacit acceptance of the principles of free and open markets throughout China, but within a year the outbreak of the Boxer Rebellion (Yi Ho Tuan Movement) threatened to negate the agreements. As foreign armies fought their way inland to rescue their citizens in Beijing, Hay feared that the creation of colonies throughout China would follow the defeat of the Boxers and their supporters in the Qing royal family. In the Open Door Circular (1900) Hay reiterated the need to maintain open access to markets and emphasized that all nations should respect the "territorial and administrative integrity" of China. The Open Door agreements were not binding but were upheld by the United States over the next several decades.

When the Open Door policy was initiated, the United States had just begun to expand into the Pacific with the annexation of Hawaii (1898) and the acquisition of the Philippines and Guam from Spain (1899). Access to China's markets served U.S. interests at a time when other powers, such as Russia and Japan, threatened to close their territories in China to foreign trade. After the Qing

dynasty collapsed in 1911, the Open Door policy expanded to include the goal of preserving China's independence. In 1915 Secretary of State William Jennings Bryan announced the Non-Recognition Doctrine after Japan attempted to colonize China with the Twenty-One Demands presented to President Yuan Shikai. Because of its commitment to the Open Door policy, the U.S. government refused to recognize any Sino-Japanese treaty that violated its principles.

The conclusion of World War I in 1918 brought new challenges to U.S.-China relations. Because China was an ally of the United States, many Chinese assumed that their country would benefit from having contributed to the victorious side. In particular, Chinese intellectuals counted on an international commitment to President Woodrow Wilson's Fourteen Points, one of which guaranteed "national self-determination." But the terms of the Treaty of Versailles were disappointing; Japan won former German possessions in Shandong. The failure of the United States to uphold China's territorial integrity reflected the complexity of the international situation, including Japan's secret treaties with European powers, Wilson's focus on Japan's joining the League of Nations, and the timing of a joint British-U.S.-Japanese invasion of Siberia. The Chinese, however, responded to the rebuff with the widespread, violent antiforeign demonstrations of the May Fourth Movement (1919). Some of China's

Chinese meet with American congressman and diplomats in the American Embassy, Beijing. PHOTO BY JOAN LEBOLD COHEN.

intellectuals then rejected U.S.-style democracy and turned to Bolshevism for a new model.

Ties to the Guomindang

The absence of political unity characteristic of the warlord decade (1916–1927) was relieved to some extent with the defeat by the Guomindang (Chinese Nationalist Party) of southern warlords and the establishment of the Republic of China's (ROC) new capital at Nanjing in 1927. China's new government, headed by the Guomindang's Chiang Kai-shek, immediately sought to improve relations with Western nations. The close ties that Chiang forged with the United States produced an alliance that lasted for decades.

In 1927 Chiang embarked on a quest to alter China's image from that of hapless victim of imperialism to that of a united and modern nation. He undertook a personal image change when he divorced his wives and married U.S.-educated Meiling Soong in a Christian ceremony in December 1927. Known as "Madame Chiang," Soong was a political asset and a passionate advocate for an independent, Guomindang-controlled China. Beginning in the 1930s she raised money and lobbied for support from wealthy U.S. citizens and the U.S. Congress. Fluent in English, Christian, modern and attractive, Soong

President Richard Nixon meets with China's Communist Party leader, Mao Zedong, 29 February 1972. NATIONAL ARCHIVES.

symbolized what many in the United States hoped would be China's future. In 1937 Chiang and Soong were named *Time* magazine's "Man and Woman of the Year."

Despite U.S. support, Chiang's government faced insurmountable challenges during the 1930s as Japan colonized Chinese territory, and the Chinese Communist Party (CCP) became the Guomindang's primary enemy. Although the U.S. government approved of the Guomindang's anti-Communist posture, concern over Japanese aggression in Asia took precedence for U.S.-China policy. The 1931 Japanese invasion of Manchuria and subsequent creation of the puppet state of Manzhouguo led the United States to reemphasize the Doctrine of Non-Recognition. When Japan's large-scale military operations in China began in 1937, U.S. secretary of state Cordell Hull offered that the United States serve as a neutral ground for representatives from Nanjing and Tokyo to address the conflict. After Tokyo ignored the gesture, Hull announced the Doctrine of Non-Intervention aimed at keeping U.S. forces out of international conflicts while heaping condemnation on Japan for its aggression in China.

Japan's attack on Hawaii's Pearl Harbor in December 1941 and subsequent U.S. entrance into World War II caused President Franklin D. Roosevelt to strengthen ties to the Guomindang. In 1943 the United States negotiated a treaty on equal terms with the ROC that relinquished U.S. extraterritorial privileges and provided the United States with bases in China to facilitate the fight against Japan. Roosevelt pushed to elevate China's international standing, making Chiang one of the "Big Five" Allies. Nevertheless, U.S.-China cooperation during World War II was troubled.

In March 1942 U.S. Army Lieutenant General Joseph W. Stilwell, Roosevelt's choice to command the China-Burma-India theater of war, arrived in Chongqing, China's wartime capital. Stilwell was initially welcomed by Chiang and appointed chief of staff, but their relationship soon became strained. For Stilwell conditions in the Guomindang army were cause for dismay. Civil conflict, tentative control over warlord forces, corruption, erratic supply lines, and overwhelming Japanese strength made the outlook bleak. Despite assistance from the American Volunteer Group, the Flying Tigers, who flew supplies to Chinese forces, the United States could not provide the logistical support needed to make the Guomindang army effective. As the war wore on, Stilwell opposed Chiang's tactics that he deemed defensive and criticized deployment of forces against Communist strongholds. In September 1944 Roosevelt urged Chiang to put Stilwell in command of Chinese ground units. When Chiang refused, Stilwell was replaced with Major General Albert C. Wedemeyer, but relations between Roosevelt and Chiang cooled.

Japan's defeat was followed by the repatriation of more than 1 million Japanese troops and the airlift of a half-million Guomindang forces to cities throughout China by the U.S. military. Then the United States stepped in to avert civil war by sending General George Marshall to mediate between Chiang and the CCP. The Marshall mission attempted to create a coalition Guomindang-CCP government with Chiang as head, but after talks broke down in 1946 civil war began. The United States sent to the Guomindang aid worth more than $2 billion, not including the nearly $2 billion in aid delivered during World War II. In 1948 the defeated Chiang and his government fled to the island of Taiwan.

Recognition for the Republic of China

The establishment of the People's Republic of China (PRC) in October 1949 was a blow to those in the United States who expected victory for their wartime ally, but the administration of President Harry Truman, aware of Chinese conditions, had predicted a CCP victory. In the State Department's white paper on China released in August 1949, Secretary of State Dean Acheson wrote: "The unfortunate but inescapable fact is that the ominous result of the civil war in China was beyond the control of the government of the United States." In the months after the CCP victory, Truman adopted a "wait and see" policy, assessing whether the United States would recognize Chinese Communist Party leader Mao Zedong's government and establish commercial ties, as it had in 1948 with the Communist head of Yugoslavia, Josip Broz Tito. Many factors, however, worked against possible conciliation. An intense "Red scare" had reemerged in the United States. Provoked by Senator Joseph McCarthy's allegations of Communists within the State Department, conservatives in Congress vehemently denounced the Truman administration for being "soft" on Communism. When

Henry Kissinger meets 11-year-old Li Lianjie (Jet Li) at the 1974 Wushu Delegation, while National Committee on United States–China Relations representative Jan Berris looks on. COURTESY OF NCUSCR.

the CCP signed the Sino-Soviet Treaty of Friendship, Alliance, and Mutual Assistance in February 1950, Truman's critics rushed to exaggerate his failures.

For Truman China's entrance into the Korean War (1950–1953) ruined any chance for normal relations with Beijing and assured continued recognition of the ROC. The Korean War caused Truman to declare a national state of emergency, increase draft calls, urge the United Nations (U.N.) to condemn China as an aggressor nation, and station the U.S. Seventh Fleet in the Taiwan Strait. Premier Zhou Enlai denounced the action as "armed aggression against the territory of China." Meanwhile, Moscow's efforts to seat the PRC in the U.N. were blocked by the United States. In December 1950 the United States announced a total trade embargo on the PRC that would last for twenty-one years.

For two decades the United States recognized the ROC while adhering to the official position that "the regime in Peiping" (Beijing) was not China's government. Beginning in April 1951 the United States resumed direct military aid to the Guomindang. In 1954 the United States signed a mutual defense treaty with Taiwan, followed by the passage of the Formosa [Taiwan] Resolution (1955), which guaranteed protection against armed attack. U.S.-China relations became inextricably tied to the intensification of the Cold War. U.S. policies were aimed at stopping the spread of Communism, while China policies focused on supporting the "revolutionary struggles" of former colonial peoples. In 1965 People's Liberation Army commander Lin Biao described the United States as "the most rabid aggressor in human history" in his essay "On People's War."

Ping-Pong Diplomacy

The unlikely champion of opening ties with the PRC was President Richard M. Nixon, once a hard-line anti-Communist associate of Senator Joseph McCarthy. Nixon's historic journey to Beijing in 1972 opened a dialogue when both sides saw advantages to ending the decades-long feud. China's aging leaders, Mao Zedong and Zhou Enlai, in the years after the violent and divisive Cultural Revolution (1966–1976) and the failed coup attempt by Lin Biao (1971), began to moderate their views, even reappointing to government positions once-jailed associates such as Deng Xiaoping. Moreover, hostilities with Moscow made China increasingly isolated and vulnerable. On the U.S. side Nixon began sending positive signals to Beijing as early as 1969 when he sought to reevaluate U.S. policy in Asia and end the conflict with China's ally Vietnam. The first break came in 1971 with the start of "people's diplomacy" after the Chinese invited the U.S. table tennis team to Beijing. U.S. national security advisor Henry Kissinger followed up with a secret trip to China, arranging Nixon's future visit and announcing that the United States would no longer block Beijing's entrance into the U.N. In February 1972 Nixon and Zhou Enlai issued a joint statement, the Shanghai Communiqué, outlining the provisions for establishing diplomatic and commercial ties. Because no agreement could be reached on the future of Taiwan, separate statements summarized each government's position. Full diplomatic relations between the United States and China were officially restored in January 1979, but Congress responded by passing the Taiwan Relations Act (April 1979), which encouraged continued economic, cultural, and military ties with Taiwan.

Two Superpowers Cooperate and Compete

Beginning in 1978 economic reforms by Premier Deng Xiaoping opened China's markets to the world. Soon China's economy boomed from exports and foreign investment. U.S. citizens were quick to take advantage of opportunities once denied them and embraced new possibilities while ignoring, for the most part, the reality of the CCP's strict authoritarianism. U.S.-China commercial ties, including joint ventures and buyouts of U.S. firms, rapidly expanded, and by 2005 China became the United States' number one trading partner. But with closer economic ties came conflict. Citing complaints of closed markets, rampant infringement of copyright laws, and government crackdowns on dissidents, the United States blocked China's initial bid to join the World Trade Organization in 1997. Eventually China's entrance in 2001 gave Chinese greater access to member states' markets and contributed to a trade surplus with the United States of nearly $300 billion in 2007.

With the Cold War's conclusion the United States became the sole superpower, but China's ascendance as a potential rival in east Asia is apparent. As China reaches superpower status, it will challenge U.S. hegemony (influence) in the Pacific. U.S.-China relations can be described as both cooperative and competitive. On the one hand, for example, Beijing was successful in curtailing North Korean nuclear proliferation after Chinese president Hu Jintao led six-nation talks that proved more effective at reining in North Korea than had earlier U.S. threats. On the other hand, unresolved issues, such as Taiwan's future, continue to loom. The United States remains committed to defend Taiwan from military attack. The outlook for the twenty-first century appears to be characterized by close commercial ties, political disagreements, and strategic rivalry for the United States and China.

Recent events that continue to influence public opinion in China include the accidental 1999 bombing of the Chinese Embassy in Belgrade by the United States and

China's women's basketball team visited the United States in 1974 and was photographed with President Gerald Ford and Secretary of State Henry Kissinger at the White House.
PHOTO BY THE NATIONAL COMMITTEE ON UNITED STATES–CHINA RELATIONS.

the forced landing of a U.S. spy plane on Hainan Island on 1 April 2001, as well as U.S. and other Western protests during the Beijing Olympic torch relay, all of which provoked a nationalist backlash both in China and from Chinese people living overseas. The U.S. plan to sell $6.5 billion of advanced weaponry to Taiwan announced in October 2008 also caused negative reactions in China, even though tension over Taiwan, the most important challenge to U.S.-China relations since 1949, had eased after PRC-Taiwan relations began a new phase with the election of Taiwanese president Ma Ying-jeou in March 2008.

During the U.S. elections of 2008, the trade deficit and job outsourcing were prominent in the public discussion, and product and food safety were much commented on in the press along with extensive coverage of human rights and Tibet-related protests before the Olympic Games.

These issues and differences of perspective continue to affect U.S.-China discussions.

The thirtieth anniversary of the "normalization" of U.S.-China relations was on 1 January 2009, and 1 March 2009 marked thirty years since the U.S. Embassy reopened in Beijing. Many celebratory events were held in the United States and in China to bring together those who were involved in the events leading to normalization with younger leaders in the diplomatic, academic, and business communities. Initiatives such as the the Strategic Economy Dialogue started under President George W. Bush draw support from a broad spectrum because both countries and leaders around the globe recognize that in spite of differences the cooperation of the United States and China on the global economic crisis, climate change, and terrorism is essential to future global stability.

But tensions between the two countries escalated again just one week after the celebratory events on 1 March. An American surveillance ship, the USNS *Impeccable,* and five Chinese ships were involved in a military confrontation 60 miles off the coast of Hainan Island in the South China Sea on 8 March 2009. Director of Naval Intelligence Donald Blair called it the "most serious" dispute since the April 2001 EP-3 incident. Both sides have insisted their actions were justified; U.S. military leaders and policymakers met soon after the incident to discuss its ramifications on U.S.-China relations.

June GRASSO

Further Reading

Biggerstaff, K. (1936, July). The official Chinese attitude toward the Burlingame Mission. *The American Historical Review, 41*(4), 682–702.

Fifield, R. (1965). *Woodrow Wilson and the Far East. The diplomacy of the Shantung Question.* Hamden CT: Archon Books.

Fairbank, J. K. (1976). *China perceived: Images and policies in Chinese-American relations.* New York: Vintage Books.

Fairbank, J. K. (1983). *The United States and China.* Cambridge, MA: Harvard University Press.

Hexter, J. & Woetzel, J. (2007). *Operation China: From strategy to execution.* Boston: Harvard Business School Press.

Khalizad, Z. M. (1999). *The United States and a rising China: Strategic and military implications.* Washington, D.C.: RAND.

Schaller, M. (2002). *The United States and China: Into the twenty-first century.* New York: Oxford University Press.

Stelle, C. C. (1941, March). American trade in opium to China, 1821-39. *The Pacific Historical Review 10* (1), 57–74.

Stelle, C. C. (1940, December). American trade in opium in to China, prior to 1820. *The Pacific Historical Review, 9*(4), 425–444.

U.S. Department of State. *Secretary of State John Hay and the open door policy in China, 1899–1900.* www.state. gov/

University Education

Dàxué jiàoyù 大学教育

China's university system, the world's largest, has the fifth-largest international-student enrollment in the world. Once funded solely by the state, today universities must raise an increasing proportion of their operating funds from such sources as tuition fees, research grants, endowment gifts, and income from university-run enterprises.

As China's economy has liberalized and grown, enrollments in China's institutes of higher education have been shooting up, with an unprecedented expansion just in the past decade. In 1990, only 3.4 percent of the age cohort between eighteen and twenty-two benefited from any form of higher education. This percentage reached 7.2 percent in 1995, 12.5 percent in 2000, 15 percent in 2002 (thus reaching the internationally acknowledged threshold of higher education for that age cohort), and 23 percent in 2007, with roughly 27 million students enrolled in 2008 in what has become the world's largest higher education system. The expansion of access to higher education in all subjects is an essential component to developing skilled workers who will be able to contribute to China's global ambitions. In fact, China is unique in educational history as it simultaneously pushes for rapid enrollment growth, institutes new governance structures, and seeks to build world-class universities.

Decentralization & Diversification

This rise in China's higher education system in the twenty-first century is qualitatively different from the rise it experienced in the 1950s under Soviet tutelage. The growth back then occurred within the parameters of detailed planning for a socialist economy and resulted in highly specialized institutions that trained personnel for each sector of the economy. The whole system was regulated from above, with minimal autonomy given to individual institutions or regions. Now the Chinese government has been gradually moving away from a centralized model of governance, in which it controlled the detailed operations of higher education institutions. As the numbers of institutions and students grew, it became increasingly difficult for the state to exercise control in a way that was compatible with the growing market economy.

As a result, the government began to develop the legal framework that would designate universities as independent legal entities and to establish the mechanism on which the universities' managerial autonomy could rest. The legal framework would allow universities to set their own strategic goals and define their own academic focus (including the establishment of new specializations) in order to respond to the increasing competition, and also to control their own resources. The architecture for a less centralized higher education system began to emerge in the late 1990s and was enshrined in the Higher Education Law that took effect on 1 January 1999.

A new and decentralized higher education structure, in which provincial governments play principal roles, has taken shape in China. The boundaries among different types of institutions have blurred, with universities now being allowed to add programs of their own choice. A result of these changes is the impulse toward more comprehensive patterns of knowledge, with all higher education institutions seeking to broaden their curricular coverage. This has involved quite a remarkable development of social sciences and humanities programs in institutions originally designated to teach highly specialized technical subjects. The rationale of current reform seems to be to make "comprehensive universities" the norm, and to a large extent this trend has been driven by market forces that reward expanded enrollments.

The diversification also has implications for the financing mechanisms of higher education. Chinese universities used to be solely funded by the state, but today they must raise an increasing proportion of their operating funds from such non-governmental sources as tuition fees, research grants, services, endowment gifts, and income from university-run enterprises. Strategically, the state now concentrates resources on a small number of elite universities, while encouraging all other institutions to mobilize local resources through student fees and income-generating activities.

The Ambition for World-Class Status

This dramatic change in the size of China's higher education system also has qualitative dimensions. The Chinese government launched programs, such as Project 21/1 in 1993, to enable one hundred top universities to reach world-class (elite) standards in the twenty-first century. Since 1998, Project 98/5 has been providing additional funding to a smaller number of top institutions. (It was named for the date of the centennial anniversary of Peking University, May 1998, since the project was announced shortly after that event.) The universities included in Project 98/5 were initially nine in number and have expanded to thirty-nine in 2009. The country's two top universities, Peking University and Tsinghua University, are exclusively funded by the central government (getting ¥1.8 billion each for the first three-year cycle of the program), while the rest are funded by the Ministry of Education with matching funds from multiple sources at lower levels. The top echelon universities of the system enjoy significant advantages from the extra resources provided under the elite-university development projects and carry out most of the graduate education and research across the whole higher education system.

Chinese higher education institutions are being structured in a hierarchical way according to their functions and goals. On the top are the national elite universities that focus on research, mainly those in Project 21/1 and particularly those in Project 98/5. They educate the majority of doctoral students, in addition to master's- and bachelor-degree students. They are designated to function as the "national team" that will move China's capacity for innovation to a higher level, play a leading role in performing research activities that are of great importance to national development and security, and to collaborate in international research efforts as well. The universities at the second rank are oriented to both research and teaching, mainly educating master's and bachelor students, with doctoral students only in a few specific disciplines. The universities at the third rank are those that are fundamentally teaching-oriented, training mainly undergraduates. Finally, at the bottom of the hierarchy is a new tier of institutions, the higher vocational college, providing only two-to-three-year sub-degree programs. Their number has grown rapidly since 1999, when the central government delegated authority over approving and establishing such colleges to local governments at the provincial level.

The last two categories constitute the majority of China's higher education institutions, and they have increased their enrollment dramatically, taking on the main burden of enrollment expansion while the elite universities have played a mainly symbolic role. The deliberate policy of creating a hierarchical structure of higher education, combined with the integration of curricular offerings, serves China's needs to address both global competition and domestic demands. With this approach China seems to be able to maintain the world's largest higher education system, and nurture a few players at a global level.

Academic Autonomy

Recent reforms have made possible a higher degree of autonomy than has been seen since the revolution of 1949. University autonomy is usually viewed as an important condition for the protection of academic freedom, and there can be little doubt that academic freedom has also increased greatly in recent years in China. Nevertheless, China's socialist government is still intensely concerned about maintaining "stability" in the face of the rapid economic transformation under way, and it still exercises considerable control over China's press and publishing industry. For their part, Chinese scholars have never found it easy to limit themselves to critical comment in their fields of study; academic criticism tends to overflow into political and social arenas, as happened in the tragedy of Tiananmen Square in 1989. Given these opposing tendencies, the road to academic freedom is likely to be an arduous one.

In spite of the constraints on academic freedom that the government places on them, China's universities have become global actors, capable of holding their own in international circles of research and scholarship in many fields of the natural sciences as well as in some social and professional areas of knowledge. They already have well-established patterns for offering support to countries in Africa through the training of students and through bilateral projects, and they have recently begun a series of dialogues with leading scientists and intellectuals in India to share ideas and perspectives on Asian responsibility for global development. It remains to be seen when they will be accepted as genuinely equal partners with universities in Europe and North America.

Characteristics of an Emerging Chinese University Model

Despite controversies around quality and equity issues in the rapid expansion of Chinese higher education, as well as some continuing constraints on academic freedom, a number of characteristics can be detected that might signal the emergence of a Chinese model of the university.

China has a rich history of education, and some aspects of its traditional education philosophy and pedagogy are evident in its contemporary methods of teaching. As more and more Chinese universities organize their curriculum around a core of basic subjects and emphasize interdisciplinary education, they are deliberately connecting reform to their own educational traditions.

China is perhaps one of the first systems to take a bold step to concentrate public research resources in an effort to create world-class universities. Its world-class university development plans, Project 21/1 and Project 98/5, might be seen to have triggered a worldwide competition. Related to this competition, the *Academic Ranking of World Universities,* launched by China's Shanghai Jiao Tong University since 2003, has quickly gained international prominence. It is now widely viewed as providing a legitimate evaluation of universities worldwide.

Chinese universities exhibit a high level of engagement with national and local development and thus can be seen as providing services for economic and community development. This can be regarded as a legacy from the planned economy, which formed self-enclosed higher education "systems" that related to various sectors in the economy, but it turns out to be a strength in the market context. The recent expansion in size has dramatically enhanced the capacity at both the institutional and system level to have an impact on national and local social development and economic growth. Most Chinese universities are engaged in unique industry–university relations or the so-called integration of production, teaching, and research, which enables the universities to contribute directly to building China's capacity for innovation capacity and its infrastructure. In particular, top universities are facilitating a transformation of the national economy from one with a solely industrial focus to a more knowledge-based economy through a variety of ways, including the creation of a series of science and technology parks in their proximities, which combine education, research, and industry. The most famous of these, Zhongguancun Science and Technology Zone, which is often called "China's Silicon Valley," surrounds China's two most renowned universities, Peking and Tsinghua, in northwestern Beijing.

In addition, China has been extremely active in internationalizing higher education. The past thirty years witnessed 1.2 million Chinese students and scholars studying

Art Education Student at Tsinghua University. PHOTO BY JOAN LEBOLD COHEN.

abroad, among whom nearly 320,000 have completed their study programs and returned to China, with the result that the majority of leaders and many faculty in top universities have had international academic exposure. China has also recently become the world's fifth-ranking destination for international students. Chinese universities have responded to globalization in other ways as well, such as through active participation in international university consortia. For instance, Peking University is an active member of the prestigious International Alliance of Research Universities (IARU), along with the Australian National University, ETH Zurich, the National University of Singapore, the University of California at Berkeley, Cambridge University, the University of Copenhagen Oxford University, the University of Tokyo and Yale University.

Qiang ZHA

Further Reading

Chen, H., & Xu, Y. (1999). Juguo zhumu xin zheda, renzhong daoyuan chuang yiliu [The new Zhejiang University has attracted attention from all over the country, and it is a heavy responsibility to make it a first-class university]. *China's Higher Education, 1999*(1), 16–20.

Cheng, Chung-Ying, & Bunnin, N. (Eds.). (2002). *Contemporary Chinese philosophy.* Oxford, U.K.: Blackwell.

Edmonds, R. (2002/2003). The growth of contemporary China studies and *The China Quarterly.* In *Issues and Studies, 38*(4) and *39*(1), 320–326.

Franklin, U. (2001). Art, technology and knowledge transfer. In R. Hayhoe and J. Pan (Eds.), *Knowledge across cultures: A contribution to dialogue among civilizations* (pp. 243–248). Hong Kong: Comparative Education Research Centre, University of Hong Kong.

Friedman, T. (2000). *The Lexus and the olive tree.* New York: Anchor Books.

Gillespie, S. (2001). *South-south transfer: A study of Sino-African exchanges.* New York and London: Routledge.

Hall, D. L., & Ames, R. (1999). *The democracy of the dead: Dewey, Confucius and the hope for democracy in China.* Chicago and Lasalle, IL: Open Court.

Hayhoe, R. (1989). *China's universities and the Open Door.* New York: M.E. Sharpe.

Hayhoe, R. (1999). *China's universities 1895–1995: A century of cultural conflict.* Hong Kong: Comparative Education Research Centre, University of Hong Kong.

Hu, D. (2001). He er butong: Gaodeng jiaoyu mianxiang shijie de zhongyao yuanze [Harmonious co-existence within diversity: A cardinal principle of higher education facing the world]. *China's Higher Education, 22*(22), 15–17.

Knight, J. (1997). Internationalisation of higher education: A conceptual framework. In J. Knight & H. D. Wit (Eds.), *Internationalisation of Higher Education in Asia Pacific Countries* (pp. 5–19). Amsterdam: The European Association of International Education.

Law, Wing-Wah (Ed.). (1999). New rules of the game in the education in the People's Republic of China: Educational laws and regulations. *Chinese Education and Society: A Journal of Translations,* May–June.

Urban Geography

Chéngshì dìlǐ　城市地理

Urban geography addresses the development of cities—from their origins and organizational principles to their evolving infrastructures and policies. China's urban development has been most dramatically affected by shifts in its economic strategies, from a focus on national self-sufficiency to an increasingly active participation in the free market.

China boasts the largest urban population in the world (516.57 million in 2005) and a long history of urban development; its earliest city can be traced back at least 4,000 years. China also has more officially designated urban centers than any other country: 661 cities and close to 20,000 towns in 2005.

Cities in the Pre-Socialist Era

The earliest Chinese cities were built as administrative centers and were hierarchical in nature, with the national capital at the top, then several province/prefecture-level administrative centers at the next level down, followed by many local centers, and then, finally, by outposts such as county towns. After a period of significant commercialization of agriculture and coastal trade in South China in the tenth and eleventh century, commerce-based urban centers emerged and grew rapidly, adding another layer of cities to the preexisting administrative cities. In the vast countryside of the more developed regions, large numbers of market towns, either permanent or periodic, came into being as a result of the rise in agricultural productivity. These cities were organized based on the economics of trade.

Some of world's largest cities of the time, such as today's Hangzhou, emerged in China in the thirteenth century. Most preindustrial Chinese cities, however, were smaller in size and population and were set up largely as extensions of the rural economy. Unlike medieval cities in Europe, traditional Chinese cities never developed into autonomous political entities but remained seats of the centralized imperial power. Chinese cities were where government officials, wealthy landlords, merchants, and their families and servants lived. The cities also housed other service personnel such as artisans, sojourning traders, and entertainers. In general, different social groups lived in segregated quarters of the city.

A different genre of cities and towns (about 100 in total), called treaty ports, came into existence or grew rapidly in size in the nineteenth and early twentieth centuries in response to a new set of political and economic imperatives. These port cities (including Shanghai, Guangzhou, Shantou, Xiamen, and Hankou) were forced open for international trade under various unequal treaties whose terms were dictated by Western powers and Japan in this era of imperialism and colonialism. Hong Kong had a different political fate as a ceded territory to Britain, but the nature of its growth was very similar to many other treaty ports.

In the late nineteenth and early twentieth centuries, these cities also became the locus of modern China's industrialization and Westernization. Extraterritorial

2363

concessions controlled by Western countries were set up in many of them—a reflection of foreign dominance. The concessions were totally outside China's legal and often administrative control. With a large foreign and domestic migrant population and a greater diversity of economic activities, the spatial social structure of the treaty ports was quite different from that of the "indigenous" cities.

Urbanization from 1949 to 1978

The industrialization strategy China adopted following the Communist victory in China's civil war had tremendous impact on the urban geography of the country. The new government pursued an autarkic development strategy (one geared at national economic self-sufficiency) that put emphasis on promoting domestic industry—especially heavy industry—at the expense of agriculture; it also gave priority to production over consumption in an attempt to build a strong defense industry and catch up with the West in modernization. Achievement was often measured in terms of the physical output of steel and other industrial and military products. As part of this strategy, urbanization was curtailed in the 1960s and 1970s through the household registration (*hukou*) system, and other mechanisms tied to employment

and housing. As a consequence, while China had a high industrial growth rate from 1950 to 1980, the rate of urban growth was comparatively low. Similarly, relative to China's level of industrialization, its percentage of urban population was low by world standards.

This approach substantially curtailed the development of the service sector in cities and turned many cities into "producer cities," cities heavily skewed toward manufacturing. The approach also fostered the emergence or growth of a large number of mining- and manufacturing-based cities, many of which were located in interior regions. The Third Front industrialization program in the period between 1965 and 1975 also pushed industrialization and the associated urbanization further inland. Inevitably, these producer cities became highly polluted. China's command economy also reinforced the hierarchical nature of its cities. For example, provincial capital cities, as the centers of regional administration and economies, increased their dominance and became "primate cities" in the regional economy.

During this period, many elements of the urban landscape were designed to serve a specific political purpose and/or to showcase the grandeur of socialism. In almost all large and medium-sized cities, government buildings dominated the city center, large public squares were designed mainly for political gatherings, and statues of Mao were erected in the middle of traffic roundabouts in the

A worker at a-Heavy Machinery Plant in Beijing. Although China's industrial production increased rapidly during the beginning of the Communist era, China's Urban centers remained relatively small. PHOTO BY JOAN LEBOLD COHEN.

View of Suzhou Creek, Shanghai, 1979. Crowded public housing and older housing built in the foreign concession areas are visible. PHOTO BY JOAN LEBOLD COHEN.

city center. Chinese city centers during this period usually had a low residential population density.

In this era, the *danwei* (work unit) was the constituent unit of urban society and economy. A *danwei* is a state-owned enterprise or an institution, such as a government agency, university, hospital, or military office, but it functioned more like a comprehensive cellular economic and social unit. A large *danwei* often occupied a walled compound, with one or more normally guarded gates, and were divided into workplace and residential areas. The residential structure was typically composed of rows of functionally and visually homogeneous low-rise buildings. Basic facilities and services, such as hospitals or clinics, grocery stores, cinemas, and dining halls, were also set up near the residential area.

The *danwei* served as a mechanism through which the state provided social services such as child care, education, employment, marriage, housing, health care, and retirement benefits. The state also exercised its social and political control through the *danwei*. Even leisure activities, which consisted largely of political studies, sports, and watching movies, were organized by the *danwei*. It is not an exaggeration to say that every urban worker was tied to the *danwei* from the cradle to the grave. Urban land was owned by the state and was assigned to the *danwei* at no charge. Urban housing was considered to be a welfare benefit, which was mainly provided at a nominal rent by

work units and local housing authorities. Urban residents had few housing choices and had to wait for subsidized public housing, which they received based on a set of criteria, such as seniority, job rank, and marital status.

Without competition from a private real estate market, the state had little incentive to invest much in building new residential housing, and a severe housing shortage developed as China's population increased. The quality and maintenance of urban housing were also very poor; the average per capita living space in the late 1970s was below four square meters. Cities remained compact, and there was not much suburbanization.

Even though the official ideology was to construct a socialist society with a uniform spatial and social organization, and the physical settings might have appeared to be similar, the social space varied considerably because work-units were ranked according to status and access to resources. This social differentiation was reflected in many aspects of life, such as the quality of housing, schools, and medical benefits.

Urban Geography in the Reform Era (1978–present)

The late 1970s saw a significant change in China's economic strategy. The autarkic approach was finally abandoned in

Beijing city at night. The central Chinese government established economic development policies that favor coastal cities such as Beijing. PHOTO BY TOM CHRISTENSEN.

favor of producing goods for export. By the end of the twentieth century, China rose to become the "world's factory." At the same time, measures to marketize the economy were also gradually introduced, though even today the government still plays a decisive role in running the economy. With China's rapid economic growth, cities have also grown and changed, one major change being the higher rates of rural-urban mobility (mostly in the form of "temporary" migration). By the 1990s, many large cities became increasingly cosmopolitan and diverse socially and culturally, and marked by unbridled consumerism.

"LETTING SOME PEOPLE AND SOME PLACES GET RICH FIRST"

Different regions and cities have fared differently in the reform era, depending on their development history and, more importantly, government policies. Under Deng Xiaoping's principle of "letting some people and some places get rich first," China's development focus shifted to the coastal cities. Shortly after the beginning of the reform, four cities (Shenzhen, Zhuhai, Shantou, and Xiamen) on the south coast were established in 1980 as special economic zones; Hainan joined this category in 1998. In

1984, fourteen cities on the east coast were designated as "coastal open cities." The central government established economic development policies that favored these cities in an effort to attract foreign investment. Their good location and access to the international market and human resources has led to booming economic growth for these coastal cities.

THE WESTERN DEVELOPMENT PROGRAM

The development gap between the coastal zone and the interior has widened and become a major public and policy concern. In 1999, the government announced its Western Development Program, which was designed to channel more attention and resources to the Western provinces in order to reduce these regional gaps. At present, the core of the Chinese spatial economy is concentrated in three major regions centered on several large cities: the Pearl River Delta region (including the cities of Guangzhou, Shenzhen, Dongguan, and Zhuhai), the Changjiang Delta region (based on the cities of Shanghai, Kunshan, Suzhou, Wuxi, Nanjing, Hangzhou, and Ningbo), and the Bohai Gulf region (Beijing, Tianjin, and Dalian). Despite the establishment of the Western Development Program, the western region and its cities are not an economic center, and the devastation wrought by the earthquake in May 2008 has created a further setback.

LOCAL AUTONOMY

Fiscal decentralization since the 1980s has granted local governments (cities) more economic and political autonomy, and they have played a greater role in the national economy. Indeed, some have argued that local autonomy has brought *de facto* competitive federalism to China, but that is not an accurate reading of the situation. The hierarchical system of urban administrative jurisdictions means that local governments are evaluated by their supervisory units. Because the governments directly participate in the economy and because economic growth (fairly narrowly defined) is the prime objective of the central government, the criteria by which local cities are evaluated are necessarily heavily tilted to this set of rather parochial economic indices, such as various GDP indices, budgetary revenue, and foreign investment. To reach those targets, individual local governments adopt practices and policies that often sacrifice other public goods (such as the environment and labor welfare) and the broader regional and even national interests.

The pursuit of parochial interests within a small jurisdiction often leads to local protectionism as well as costly duplications. The hierarchical nature of the architecture of the administrative system is not congenial to horizontal cooperation. Answerable only to upper-tier governments and lacking a means to deal with neighboring jurisdictions, local governments often have to appeal to the upper-level governments to resolve interjurisdictional conflicts.

THE TRANSFORMED LANDSCAPE

Rapid urban and economic growth has not only changed the spatial relations between regions and cities, it has also altered the internal structure of individual cities. There has been a parallel process of urban expansion and renewal. Economic growth in the urban sector has led to suburbanization and establishment of urban-type activity at the perimeter of urban zones. Cities push their administrative boundaries outward to include large amounts of farmland and many villages. Factories are relocated to the city outskirts, and new housing estates have mushroomed, encroaching on the farmland. At the same time, every major city has undertaken large-scale inner city (city center) redevelopment, striving to become an international economic and cultural center. Land development and sales are also important to local government finance.

Housing reform and urban land-use reform initiated in the late 1980s have contributed greatly to the transformation of the urban landscape. The urban land reform and land leasing system have commercialized urban space, which has gradually morphed into more discernible commercial, industrial and different grades of residential zones. The reform has opened households to more choices in housing location and tenure type. The traditional *danwei* have gradually declined, but they have not totally disappeared. Separation of workplace and residence has become increasingly common. However, the lack of coordination and governments' and developers' pursuit of short-term monetary benefits mean that the development is often piecemeal: Urban structure in Chinese cities is fragmented and multimodal, with mixed densities.

Many large Chinese cities now have a more Western look, with high-rise office towers, suburban housing estates, large shopping centers, special economic and technical zones, science parks, and college districts. These new, "modern" capitalist-type elements are juxtaposed, at times uncomfortably, with the large socialist-style public squares and uniform apartment buildings left from the prereform era. For example, the city center often contains both dilapidated lodging for the urban poor, new high-end apartment complexes, and skyscrapers hosting financial and commercial companies. In the suburbs, "economical" housing for low-income families are often put up next to luxury villas, and new industrial zones can be adjacent to residential neighborhoods and farmland. With continuing expansion and inner-city redevelopment, living in the city center has become more and more expensive. The suburbs and outlying areas have thus become a more important area for those who need to relocate, but many of these areas still lack quality facilities such as schools and shops.

Being gradual, adaptive, and partial in nature, economic reforms have resulted in a dual system of urban land and property development involving both market and administrative mechanisms that are still fraught with problems, including corruption and disputes between displaced residents and developers and governments. At the urban periphery one finds many "villages in the city" that are often occupied by migrant workers who can only afford this type of low-end housing (they are not eligible for low-income public housing because they are not considered as "locals" under China's *hukou* system). Many migrants congregate in enclaves based on their place of origin. A famous example is the Zhejiang Village in south Beijing. But the ambiguity of ownership makes these "villages" a headache for city planning and management; the common problems are overcrowding and the illegal installation of utilities infrastructure.

Even though the housing reform has improved people's living conditions and granted them tenure, not everyone has benefited from it; new housing is too expensive for many urban residents, particularly rural-urban migrants, who have no association with the formal state sectors, and those who occupy the lower rungs of the employment hierarchy, such as laid-off workers from the state-owned enterprises. Due to increasing income and housing disparities, residential segregation, a term that was once alien to Chinese society, has become more frequently used within the lexicon of recent China scholarship.

Looking Forward: Accomplishments and Challenges

It is commonly acknowledged that China's spatial environment and social space changed drastically after the reforms that began in 1978. Many big Chinese metropolises look much more cosmopolitan than their counterparts in other developing countries; as a whole, the national economy has grown rapidly, and many people's living standards have been greatly improved. But these achievements have not been without costs and the improvement has not been equitably shared. In addition to the burden on the environment, there has been widening inequality among China's population, due partly to the newly arrived market and partly to the many unreformed socialist

institutions in the country. These pose serious challenges to the long-term sustainability of China's development and urbanization model.

Kam Wing CHAN and Man WANG

Further Reading

Chan, Kam Wing. (1994). *Cities with invisible walls.* Hong Kong: Oxford University Press.

Chan, Kam Wing. (2007). "Misconceptions and Complexities in the Study of China's Cities: Definitions, Statistics, and Implications." *Eurasian Geography and Economics, 48*(4), 383–412.

Chan, Kam Wing, Henderson, V., and Tsui, Kai Yuen. (2008). Spatial dimensions of Chinese economic development. In L. Brandt and T. Rawski (Eds.), *China's Great Transformation* (pp. 776–828). Cambridge, U.K.: Cambridge University Press.

Chang, S. D. (1970). Some observations on the morphology of Chinese walled cities. *Annals of the Association of American Geographers, 60*(1), 63–91.

Gaubatz, P. R. (1995). Urban transformation in post-Mao China: Impacts of the reform era on China's urban form. In D. Davis, R. Kraus, B. Naughton, & E. Perry (Eds.) *Urban Spaces in Contemporary China* (pp. 28–60). Cambridge, U.K.: Cambridge University Press.

Li, Si-Ming. (2005). China's changing urban geography: A review of major forces at work. *Issues and Studies, 41*(4), 67–106.

Ma, Laurence J. C. (2002). Urban transformation in China, 1949–2000: A review and research agenda. *Environment and Planning A, 34*(9), 1545–1569.

Pannell, C. W. (1990). China's urban geography. *Progress in Human Geography, 14*(2), 214–236.

Rozman, G. (1973). *Urban networks in Ching China and Tokugawa Japan.* Princeton, NJ: Princeton University Press.

Skinner, G. W. (Ed.). (1977). *The city in late imperial China.* Stanford, CA: Stanford University Press.

Solinger, D. (1999). *Contesting citizenship in urban China.* Berkeley and Los Angeles: University of California Press.

Wang, Ya Ping. (2004). *Urban poverty, housing and social change in China.* New York: Routledge.

Wu Fulong. (2004). Urban poverty and marginalization under market transition: A case of Chinese cities. *International Journal of Urban and Regional Research, 28*(2), 401–423.

Urbanization

Chéngshìhuà 城市化

Because of its agrarian nature and socialist control over cities, until the 1980s China's level of urbanization remained low. Since then, rapid rural-urban migration and aggressive reclassification have quickly transformed China into an increasingly urban society. Urbanization, now seen as a tool for economic development, has given rise to problems of inequality, social stratification, environmental degradation, and loss of arable land.

*U*rbanization is defined as the increase in the proportion of the overall population living in cities. It refers also to the social and economic changes that occur as a society becomes more urbanized. In the twenty-first century, China is being transformed from a predominantly rural economy to one that is predominantly urban.

The Level and Speed of Urbanization

For most of its history, China has been an agrarian society. Its earliest cities, created during the Shang dynasty (1766–1045 BCE), served mainly administrative, political, and ceremonial purposes. From those early days to recent decades, for thousands of years, the vast majority of China's population was primarily rural; the urbanization level was extremely low.

At the time of the People's Republic of China's (PRC's) first national census in 1953, only 13 percent of its population lived in urban areas, which was considerably lower than the world's average (about 30 percent) and lower than the levels in most Asian developing countries, including India, Thailand, and the Philippines. Between the 1950s and early 1980s, China's level of urbanization increased, albeit at a slow speed. (See table 1.) Urbanization accelerated from the 1980s onward and gained an average of more than one percentage point annually between 1990 and 2007, a rate faster than that of most Western industrialized economies at their respective stages of urbanization. In 2007, 44.9 percent—just shy of 600 million—of China's population lived in urban areas. It is projected that by 2030, China's level of urbanization will reach 60 percent, surpassing the world's average.

TABLE 1 **China's Level of Urbanization in Selected Years**

Year	Level of Urbanization (percent)
1953	13
1982	21
1990	26
2000	36
2007	45
2030 (United Nations' projection)	60

NOTE: *Except for the year 2030, all data are from China's National Bureau of Statistics.*

New construction spurred by urban population growth. PHOTO BY TOM CHRISTENSEN.

The Process and Measurement of Urbanization

Urbanization results from one or more of the following processes: migration, natural population increase in urban areas, and reclassification. As is true of most other countries, China's urbanization is mainly due to the internal movement of people from rural areas to urban areas. Natural population increase in urban areas leads to urban growth, but in most countries, including China, population growth is slower in urban areas than it is in rural areas and is not an important factor in urbanization. Reclassification refers to an administrative change whereby a formerly rural area is redefined as urban, thus accomplishing "in-situ" urbanization. This is usually a result of rapid population growth, increased population density, intensification of urban activities, annexation by an adjacent city, or a combination of the above. Since the 1980s, many previously rural places in China have been reclassified as urban areas.

The measurement of urbanization in China is complex and hotly debated. For example, it is difficult to accurately estimate rural-urban migration, and reclassification often incorporates a large number of rural people into a newly defined urban area. These issues obscure the documentation of urban areas and urban population, a task delegated primarily to China's National Bureau of Statistics. In the 1982 census, the urban population was defined as the total population found within the administrative boundaries of cities and towns. During the 1980s, however, the criteria for establishing cities and towns were significantly relaxed, and as a result, the number of cities and towns increased dramatically. Counting all the population in cities and towns as urban would have resulted in a grossly inflated level of urbanization. Therefore, in the 1990 census, a new and more restrictive set of criteria, focusing on population within cities' urban districts and towns' residents' committees, was used. The 2000 census employed additional criteria of population density, population size, and the extent of built-up areas. Most scholars consider the definition used in the 2000 census more realistic and desirable than those in previous censuses. However, definitional changes from one census to the next have complicated comparison of urbanization levels over time.

Researchers have warned against taking Chinese urban statistics at face value. A common mistake is to neglect the role of reclassification when interpreting the number and population size of cities. The number of Chinese cities increased from 193 in 1978 to 655 in 2007. This rapid increase reflects not only rural-urban migration and urban natural growth but also aggressive efforts by rural and town governments to seek reclassification into cities, as reclassification would increase their autonomy and access to resources. At the same time, large cities have actively pursued annexation of adjacent counties and cities so that the latter's land could be put to revenue-generating uses. The city of Guangzhou in southern China, for example, incorporated Huadu County and the city of Panyu in 2000 and as a result more than doubled the amount of land under its jurisdiction. Chongqing became a municipality in 1996, and during that process incorporated a large span of rural areas. The total population of Chongqing in 2006 was close to 32 million, which has led some to consider it the largest city in the world, but in fact two-thirds of its population was rural.

While reclassification leads to an inflated picture of urbanization, the opposite occurs when only the resident population is considered and migrants are ignored. For cities that have received a large number of migrant workers, the difference can be enormous. For example, the number of permanent residents in Shenzhen in 2005 was less than two million, but if all migrants were included, then the city's total population would have been more than 11 million.

Socialist Control

During the Maoist period (1949–1976), China followed a socialist model of development, one that emphasized industrialization, defined cities as sites of production rather than consumption, and discouraged rural-urban migration. Although rural-urban migration did exist —especially during the 1950s when rural collectivization, poverty, and crop failures pushed peasants to seek opportunities and survival in cities—the *hukou* (household registration) regulations that were promulgated in 1958 severely limited rural people's ability to survive in urban areas and became a powerful tool for curbing rural-urban migration. The *hukou* system, which entailed state subsidies for urban dwellers, was also intended to accelerate city-based industrialization. Extending these subsidies to rural people would have bankrupted the state coffer, and thus controlling rural-urban migration became a necessity. Paradoxically, the state limited the growth of cities—interpreted by some as anti-urbanism—but its policy, in essence, privileged urban people and disadvantaged rural people.

The PRC inherited a spatial pattern of urban and industrial development that favored the eastern, coastal region. Not only did coastal cities enjoy geographical advantages such as good accessibility, but many had benefited in terms of trade and industrial development from their experience as treaty ports from the mid-nineteenth century onward. Policies and programs during the Maoist period, however, sought to undermine urban growth, especially the growth of cities in the eastern region. For example, the majority of state industrial investment during the First Five-Year Plan (1953–1957) went to the inland region. Convinced that the coastal area would be vulnerable if China were attacked, the state launched the Third

"Fully engage in the movement to increase production and to practice economy to set off a new upsurge in industrial production" propaganda poster from 1965, created by artist Yang Wenxiu. During the Maoist period, cities were defined more by production than consumption. COLLECTION STEFAN LANDSBERGER.

City of Shanghai at night, 2003. PHOTO BY TOM CHRISTENSEN.

Front program (1965–1971), which involved moving factories and industrial workers from the coastal regions to remote and mountainous areas inland. Finally, justified on ideological grounds, the rustication movement during the Cultural Revolution (1966–1976) sent millions of urban youths, cadres, and intellectuals "up to the mountains and down to the countryside" to learn from the peasants. Some stayed in those remote locations for decades before finally returning to their urban homes.

Until the late 1970s, therefore, the pace of urbanization was kept slow and the size of cities was strictly controlled. The urban hierarchy—defined as the array of cities from largest to smallest—of China was rather flat, unlike most industrializing Third World countries, where one or two large cities (e.g., Jakarta, Mexico City) dominated the urban system. China's development under Mao was therefore quite unique and has been aptly described as "industrialization without urbanization," "industrialization with controlled urbanization" and "underurbanization," in contrast with the "overurbanization" found in many developing countries, where massive rural-urban migration has given rise to acute problems of urban slums and unemployment.

Renewed Urbanization and Urbanism

Even after the economic reforms of 1978, China continued to adhere to a policy of controlling the size of large cities, moderately developing medium-sized cities, and actively promoting the growth of small cities and towns, a policy inherited from the Maoist period. What is new in the first decade of the twenty-first century is that the Chinese state now sees urbanization as a powerful tool to modernize the nation and accelerate economic growth. But in order to avoid problems of overurbanization, the state pursues a strategy of steady, not speedy, urbanization. For example, the Eleventh Five-Year Plan (2006–2010) has as its target for increase of urbanization only 0.8 of a percentage point annually.

Chinese urbanization during the reform period has been pursued via two tracks: city-based urbanization and "urbanization from below." City-based urbanization depends on the rationale that large cities and agglomerations are more efficient than smaller places. Thus cities, especially large cities, are repositioned as the nation's economic nodes. Special economic zones such as Shenzhen have been transformed from rural places or small cities into full-fledged, globalizing urban centers. Large investment is pumped into "city-building" projects; often foreign elite architects are invited to design landmark districts and buildings, such as the Pudong New District and the "bird's nest" Olympic stadium, in order to transform Shanghai, Beijing, and other large cities into truly international metropolitan centers.

The economic bases of these cities, meanwhile, are shifting from industries to services. Western-style malls, promenades, and business districts have mushroomed across Chinese cities, a clear indication of rapidly increasing urban consumption. The internal structure of cities has changed as well. While the center of Beijing, with Tiananmen Square and other monuments and structures, still symbolizes a political and historical hub of power, the rest of the city is rapidly expanding outward and vertically. Work-unit (danwei) compounds used to be where most urbanites lived, but today new high-rise condominium buildings and gated complexes are proliferating in the city and its fringes, thanks to the housing reform of the late 1980s that boosted the housing market and promoted home ownership. Rapid urban transformation, however, has jeopardized historical and cultural landscapes such as Beijing's hutongs, the narrow alleys between traditional courtyard residences, and the associated neighborhoods.

"Urbanization from below" describes urban development that is driven by industrialization of small cities and towns and often based on local entrepreneurship and resources rather than state investment or initiatives. Related concepts such as "rural urbanization" and desakota (combining the Indonesian terms desa for village and kota for town) have been used to describe the juxtaposition of agricultural and industrial activities in rural spaces and on urban margins. The Pearl River Delta in south China, for example, is characterized by a large number of industrial enterprises in small and medium-sized cities, towns, and even villages, that are supported by foreign investment, social networks with overseas Chinese, and a large influx of rural migrants. By connecting to the world market and global commodity chains, some rural places in China are industrializing and urbanizing rapidly and as a result enjoying remarkable economic growth.

Challenges

The recent path of urbanization in China has given rise to new challenges of national and global significance. China's rural-urban income gap has widened since the economic reforms and is larger than that in most other developing countries. In 2005, real rural income per capita was only 39 percent of real urban income per capita. Inequality within urban areas has increased as well, with the urban poor comprising mainly laid-off workers (from state-owned enterprises), the elderly, and the disabled. Social stratification has intensified, and residential segregation and heterogeneity is increasingly seen in Chinese cities. Migrant enclaves, for example, can be found not far from secluded complexes of mansions for the newly rich. Social, economic, and rural-urban polarization is a major reason for the surge in protests across China in recent years.

Increase in urban consumption, in conjunction with a growing middle class, is exerting severe pressure on China's energy supply and urban infrastructure. Ownership of passenger vehicles more than doubled between 2001 and 2005, and in 2006 China surpassed the United States as the leading emitter of carbon dioxide. Water scarcity, waste management, and urban transport are among the pressing problems facing Chinese cities. Finally, urban sprawl is taking place at the expense of rural land and the environment. Loss of arable land is most serious at urban margins and in rural areas that are urbanizing. These are also the places where the border between urban and rural jurisdictions tends to be blurry and where environmental

The relatively few pedestrians on this urban street in China belie statistics that indicate just how rapidly the country's populace is making the change from rural to city life. PHOTO BY TOM CHRISTENSEN.

regulations may not be strictly enforced, thus permitting sustained pollution. Addressing the challenges of urbanization in China, therefore, requires commitments not only from urban governments but also from authorities at various levels from the countryside to the city and from the local to the national.

C. Cindy FAN

Further Reading

Chan, Kam Wing. (1994). *Cities with invisible walls: Reinterpreting urbanization in post-1949 China*. Hong Kong: Oxford University Press.

Chan, Kam Wing, & Hu Ying. (2003). Urbanization in China in the 1990s: New definition, different series, and revised trends. *China Review, 3*(2), 48–71.

Friedmann, J. (2005). *China's urban transition*. Minneapolis: University of Minnesota Press.

Goodkind, D., & West, L. A. (2002). China's floating population: Definitions, data and recent findings. *Urban Studies, 39*(12), 2237–2250.

Lin, G. C. S. (1997). *Red capitalism in South China: Growth and development of the Pearl River Delta*. Vancouver, Canada: University of British Columbia Press.

Logan, J. (Ed.). (2008). *Urban China in transition*. Malden, MA: Blackwell.

Ma, Laurence J. C. (2002). Urban transformation in China, 1949–2000: A review and research agenda. *Environment and Planning A, 34*(9), 1545–1569.

Ma, Laurence J. C., & Wu, Fulong. (Eds.). (2005). *Restructuring the Chinese city: Changing society, economy and space*. London and New York: Routledge.

McGee, T. G., Lin, George C. S., Martin, A., Wang, Mark Y. L., & Wu, Jiaping. (2007). *China's urban space: Development under market socialism*. London and New York: Routledge.

Pannell, C. W. (2002). China's continuing urban transition. *Environment and Planning A, 34*(9), 1571–1589.

Wu Fulong. (Ed.). (2007). *China's emerging cities*. London and New York: Routledge.

Wu Fulong, Xu, Jiang, & Yeh, Anthony Gar-On. (2007). *Urban development in post-reform China: State, market, and space*. London and New York: Routledge.

Yusuf, S., & Saich, T. (Eds.). (2008). *China urbanizes: Consequences, strategies, and policies*. Washington, DC: The World Bank.

Zhou, Yixing, & Ma, Laurence J. C. (2005). China's urban population statistics: A critical evaluation. *Eurasian Geography and Economics, 46*(4), 272–89.

U.S.-China Business Council

Měi-Zhōng Màoyì Quánguó Wěiyuánhuì

美中贸易全国委员会

The U.S.-China Business Council is a nonprofit trade association representing over 250 major U.S. corporations. It has promoted economic engagement since its founding, as the National Council for United States–China Trade, Inc., in 1973.

The U.S.-China Business Council (USCBC) is a private, nonprofit organization of more than 250 major U.S. corporations that do business with China. Founded in 1973 as the National Council for United States–China Trade, Inc., USCBC has offices in Washington, D.C., Beijing, and Shanghai. It provides information, advisory, and advocacy services to its membership; working with its counterpart organization, the China Council for the Promotion of International Trade (CCPIT 中国国际贸易促进委员会), USCBC's mission is to develop commercial relations with China to the benefit of members and, more broadly, the U.S. economy. The council focuses on rules-based trade, investment, and competition, and on developing a commercial environment in China that is predictable and transparent to all parties.

Member companies include American Express, Anheuser-Busch, Apple, AT&T, Coca-Cola, Walt Disney Company, Time Warner, and more than two hundred others. USCBC is governed by a board of directors composed of corporate leaders; its 2007–2008 chair was W. James McNerney Jr., chairman, president, and chief executive officer of Boeing, a company at the forefront U.S.-China relations after President Richard Nixon's historic trip to China in 1972, when trade with China resumed and the United States sold 10 Boeing 707 aircraft to China. Andrew N. Livernis, chairman and chief operation officer of Dow Chemical Company, took office as board chair on 1 June 2008.

USCBC History

The concept of turning to a private U.S. organization to encourage the development of trade relations through initiatives such as commercial missions and trade exhibitions arose from a report to Congress by House Majority Leader Hale Boggs and Minority Leader Gerald Ford. Reporting on their June–July 1972 China trip, *Impressions of the New China,* Boggs told the House that "until we have normal state relations with China, a quasi-public body" could lay a basis for U.S. trade with the PRC. Boggs urged private efforts to enlarge trade and business with China, and identified the China Council for the Promotion of International Trade (CCPIT) as the PRC's channel for fostering trade relations "where lack of diplomatic relations might otherwise be a barrier to international contact." Ten members of the board of the newly founded National Council for U.S. China Trade, which would become known as the UCSBC in 1988, traveled to Beijing in early November 1973 as the first formal U.S. trade mission to China since the People's Republic of China was founded in 1949. Board members included the leaders of John Deere & Co.; JC Penney Co., Inc.; Manufacturers Hanover Trust Co.; and Westinghouse Electric Corp.

2375

USCBC Today

USCBC hosts events featuring senior officials from the U.S. and Chinese governments. USCBC has received the following Chinese officials: President Hu Jintao, Premier Wen Jiabao, Vice Premier Wu Yi, and others from central and provincial governments. Recent U.S. public figures to meet with USCBC members in the United States and China have included Treasury Secretary Henry M. Paulson Jr., Commerce Secretary Carlos M. Gutierrez, former U.S. secretary of state James A. Baker III, Lieutenant General Brent Scowcroft, and numerous specialists on U.S.-China affairs from the executive branch of government. Other USCBC events include forums on green business practices and meetings on labor issues.

The council produces the *China Business Review* and *China Market Intelligence* in addition to books and reports aimed at helping business people understand China and facilitating business with Chinese companies. USCBC also produces policy reports and advocacy statements regarding labor, economy, trade, human rights, and politics. The council collaborates on programs and events with other organizations such as the National Committee on U.S.-China Relations, which, for example, cosponsored a luncheon held in New York in September 2008 for Premier Wen Jiabao, who, while in the United States, also addressed the United Nations and was interviewed on television by U.S. journalist Fared Zakaria.

The USCBC has been criticized for a pro-business, free-trade perspective that is insufficiently attentive to issues such as human rights, product safety, and child

The first U.S. business delegation to China, led by the National Council for U.S.-China Trade (as the USCBC was then known), at the Great Wall in November 1973. Council President Christopher Phillips is the tallest man in the middle of the back row. Eugene Theroux is fifth from the left, also in the back. PHOTO BY THE U.S. CHINA BUSINESS COUNCIL.

America's First Trade Mission to "the New China"

China's market has been a magnet for U.S. merchants since the 1784 voyage of the U.S. ship, Empress of China. That vessel left New York and sailed east around the southern tip of Africa, across the Indian Ocean, into the Pacific, and up the Pearl River to Canton (Guangzhou), one of the Middle Kingdom's thriving southern ports. The venture launched a trade that would grow and flourish until World War II.

In his report to U.S. Secretary of Foreign Affairs John Jay in 1785, Major Samuel Shaw, soon to be the U.S. Consul at Canton, explained how he got the Chinese interested in commerce with the United States:

"By the map," he related, "we conveyed to them an idea of the extent of our country, with its present and increasing population," adding that the Chinese "were highly pleased at the prospect of so considerable a market for the production of their own empire." And how "considerable" a market it would become—the two countries recorded $386.7 billion in bilateral trade in 2007 alone!

Source: Theroux, G. (2008). America's first trade mission to "the New China." *The China Business Review.* Retrieved March 5, 2009, from http://www.chinabusinessreview.com/public/0811/theroux.html

labor, and for government lobbying that focuses on the requirements of multinational corporations rather than small and medium-sized enterprises. As an established trade association it must continue to meet the needs of traditional members while attracting fast-growing, cutting-edge new businesses; it must also provide leadership in the midst of continued debate about trade restrictions, currency valuation, and cooperation as businesses and countries alike face the global economic challenges that began in 2008.

The Editors

Further Reading

US-China Business Council. (2008). Retrieved December 26, 2008, from http://www.uschina.org

Comprehensive index starts
in volume 5, page 2667.

U.S.-China Education Trust

Zhōng-Měi Jiàoyù Jījīn　中美教育基金

The U.S.-China Education Trust provides China's future leaders with resources to learn about U.S. society in the context of the political, cultural, and economic forces that have given rise to the United States and its values.

The U.S.-China Education Trust (USCET) is a program of the F. Y. Chang Foundation, a private, nonprofit organization founded in 1998 by Ambassador Julia Chang Bloch, the first Asian-American to be appointed U.S. ambassador to Nepal (in 1989). The foundation, established to commemorate Chang Fu-yun, the first Chinese graduate of Harvard Law School (1917), supports subsequent generations of China's Harvard Law graduates. USCET, the foundation's largest program, supports activities in China and in the United States designed to promote U.S.-China relations.

USCET provides China's scholars, professionals, and future leaders with resources to understand U.S. society in the context of the political, cultural, and economic forces that have given rise to the United States and its values. USCET projects are aimed at building confidence, basic understanding, and trust between China and the United States through support for U.S. studies programs at academic and policy institutions in China. Thirty-three Chinese institutions are affiliated with USCET through its American Studies Network (ASN), which provides a platform for members in China to communicate and share ideas..

The trust sponsors the Congressional Practicum, its first initiative in China, which includes elections seminars, training sessions, and lectures focused on teaching Chinese professionals, officials, and students about the U.S. legislative and political process through the use of hands-on-training, case studies, and interactive exchanges between Chinese and U.S. experts. USCET also runs media programs that explore the role of a free press and free speech in a free society and provides resources so that media professionals and students from both the United States and China might learn from each other. Its flagship Journalist-in-Residence program sends Pulitzer Prize winners to campuses across China. Other endeavors include the Financial Media Institute, a certificate program for undergraduate and graduate journalism students; symposia on international economics; fellowship programs; and the Greenberg/Starr Scholarships, which provide funding for poor Chinese students to attend universities in China.

USCET is a nonprofit organization founded with funding from the Starr Foundation, established in 1955 by Cornelius Vander Starr, an insurance entrepreneur and philanthropist, and with contributions from other organizations.

USCET successfully completed its inaugural session of the All China Summer Institute for the Study of the United States. From 5 July 5 to 2 August 2008 twelve Chinese professors from ten universities in China were invited to attend the institute to study American history and politics (in Washington D.C.) and American society and culture (with travels to Kansas City; Reno, Nevada; and San Francisco). And in October 2008 the USCET, in partnership with its American Studies Network and supported by

Ambassador Chang-Bloch students at the USCET's Summer Institute graduation lunch.
PHOTO COURTESY USCET.

the Henry Luce Foundation, published for the first time in English the *All-China American Studies Directory: An Overview of American Studies in China,* edited by the USCET founder Julia Bloch. The directory lists over thirty institutions offering American studies in China and provides detailed information about each institution's programs, resources, faculty, course work, and mission.

Chris GAUTHIER

Further Reading

Starr Foundation. (2008). Retrieved September 9, 2008, from http://www.starrfoundation.org/index.html

US-China Education Trust. (2008). Retrieved September 9, 2008, from http://www.uscet.net////about/index.cfm

Uygurs

Wéiwú'ěrzú　维吾尔族

Uygurs are a Turkic group in Xinjiang Uygur Autonomous Region. During most of the past ten centuries they lived under the control of Mongolian peoples. After the Uygur rebellion of 1931–1934 the Chinese government granted the Uygurs the status of a minority people.

U ygurs are the largest of the Turkic groups who live in Xinjiang Uygur Autonomous Region, with an estimated modern population of 8 to 15 million in 1997. Uygurs account for almost half of the population of the area, with an additional third represented by the Han Chinese and members of other minority ethnicities accounting for the rest. During most of the past ten centuries these people lived under the control of Mongolian peoples. The Uygurs live in the Tian Shan range as nomads (although the nomadic population is decreasing). They herd sheep, cows, horses, goats, and camels. In oases near the Taklimakan Desert they farm with the help of irrigation canals or underground waterways to run melt-water. Popular crops are wheat, cotton, corn, and fruit (grapes, watermelons, and muskmelons). Trade is conducted across borders in the southwestern cities, where people weave traditional carpets.

The Uygurs today are Sunni Muslims, but earlier in their history they inclined to Manichaeanism (since the eighth century) and then Buddhism (since the tenth century). Before that they practiced shamanism and believed that heaven (*tengri*) gives order, power, and wisdom to people. Archaeologists have uncovered fragments of many kinds of texts on Manichaeanism, Buddhism, and Nestorian Christianity at archaeological sites in Uygur areas. Islam came to Uygur territory along the Silk Roads, and almost all Uygurs had become Muslims by the end of the fifteenth century, replaced Manichaeanism and Buddhism.

The Chinese government during the reform era (since 1978) has maintained an appeasement policy regarding religious expression, supporting the revival of religious activities, including reconstruction of mosques and religious schools and supporting publication of books in Uygur in an effort to promote reform and an open-door policy. This policy is an attempt to mend the damage done by the Cultural Revolution (1966–1976), when much of the culture of the pre-Communist period was destroyed. Muslim Uygurs hope that this policy will lead to a resurgence of religious and ethnic autonomy, but their optimism is cautious. They fear that their cultural and ethnic sovereignty will be overwhelmed by the region's burgeoning Han Chinese population. China, for its part, is sensitive about issues affecting its sovereignty over the Xinjiang Uygur Autonomous Region.

Early History

The term *Uygur* originally was the name of one of the Nine Tribes (Tokuz Oghuz), a confederation of Turkic nomads that first appeared in the annals of Chinese history in the early seventh century. A clan of the Uygur tribe, the Yaghlakar, founded a state (744–840 CE) in what is now Mongolia. This state's most noteworthy contribution was the military rescue of the Chinese Tang dynasty (618–907 CE)from the crises created by the rebellion of General An Lushan (703–757). In return, the Chinese emperor gave the Uygur state a large monetary award each year. The Uygurs strengthened their relationship with the Sogdian merchants (Sogdians were a people who lived in Transoxiana, now Uzbekistan), who traded horses from the Uygur state for silk from China. In 763 the Uygurs allowed the Sogdians' to perform Manichaean missionary work. The city of Ordubalik (Town of the Palace), located on the Orkhon riverside and later named "Karabalghasun," enjoyed its greatest era during this time. The Sogdians traded with their colonies along the Silk Roads leading to China and the Uygur state.

The ruling classes of the Uygurs attempted to strengthen economic and social relations with the Sogdians, an attempt that caused unrest among nomadic Uygurs, who were suffering from famine and pestilence, and, in 839, from heavy snowfall. Probably recognizing the chance to take advantage of the situation, a large number of Kyrgyz—a Turkic tribe in the upper Yenisey Valley—allied with a discontented Uygur general and invaded and burned Ordubalik, bringing down the Uygur government in 840. Both Uygur nomads and nobles of the ruling classes emigrated, settling eventually in the area from the Tian Shan range to Gansu Province in northwestern China. Immigrant Uygurs established at least two new states—the Uygur kingdom of Ganzhou (890–1028) and the West Uygur kingdom (early tenth century–1284). Descendants of the Ganzhou Uygurs may be the Yugur in Gansu, traditionally known as the "Yellow Uygurs."

Chinggis Khan

The Tangut people (herders from the Ordos Desert area of northern China) absorbed the Uygur kingdom of Ganzhou into their Xi Xia kingdom in 1028. In the 1130s the West Uygur kingdom fell under the control of the Kara Khitan. In 1209, unable to bear the tyranny of the local Kara Khitan magistrate, the king of the Uygurs had him killed. The king no doubt was emboldened by the promise of protection from a new and more powerful overlord: the Mongol conqueror Chinggis Khan (often spelled Genghis Khan). The king surrendered the West Uygur kingdom to Chinggis Khan in that same year; it survived as a Mongol vassal state until 1284. The Uygurs originally were supposed to provide military service for the Mongol empire but ended up holding higher positions in government.

Uygur couple on donkey cart head to market with produce in baskets. Turfan, Xinjiang. PHOTO BY JOAN LEBOLD COHEN.

Xinjiang Urumqi Market, Xinjiang Uygur Autonomous Region.
PHOTO BY JOAN LEBOLD COHEN.

At the end of the thirteenth century a dispute over succession among the Mongol khans turned the Uygur lands into a battlefield, and by the early fourteenth century the castle towns in the Turfan Basin were devastated by war. The Uygur royal family and its subordinates found refuge in Gansu in 1284, and the Uygur lands came to be ruled by the descendants of Chagatai Khan, son of Chinggis Khan. When the Kashgar Khojas, Islamic nobles, gained power in the seventeenth and eighteenth centuries, Islam and Islamic culture—for example, the Naqshbandiya order of sufi (Islamic mystics)—spread among the Uygur people. Galdan Khan (1645–1697), leader of the Oirats of western Mongolia, occupied the land of the Uygurs for seventy years after an invasion in 1679. During the first half of the eighteenth century under Galdan's successors, many Uygur farmers (later called "Taranchis") of southern Xinjiang were forcibly relocated to the Ili Valley on the northern border.

Chinese Rule

In 1760 the Uygur territory was conquered by military expeditions of the Chinese Qing dynasty (1644–1912). In 1881 approximately forty-five thousand Uygurs relocated to Semirechie in Kazakhstan. The Uygur people in the oases around the Taklimakan Desert came under Chinese rule in 1884 when Xinjiang Province was established there. After the Uygur rebellion of 1931–1934 the Chinese government granted the Uygurs the status of a minority people at last, which provided them with national recognition, various rights to promote their own culture, and, in the modern era, the right to disregard China's one-child policy.

The Uygurs, with China's Kazakh minority, founded a state (the East Turkistan Republic) in northern Xinjiang in 1944–1949, but the newly founded People's Republic of China absorbed it in October 1949.

In 1955 the Chinese opened an administrative office in the Xinjiang Uygur Autonomous Region at Urumchi. About sixty thousand people, including Uygurs and Kazakhs, emigrated to Kazakhstan in 1962. Today more than two hundred thousand Uygurs are citizens of Kazakhstan.

Uygurs gained a certain amount of international attention in 2008 due to several violent incidents in western China by Uygur nationalists on ethic Han Chinese, resulting in fatalities. While the Uigurs have had nationalist movements since the establishment of the PRC in 1949, it is since the attacks of September 11, 2001 that the government of the People's Republic of China has used new techniques to encourage harmonious relationships between the Uygur minority population and the rest of China, and has focused on promoting all minority groups in the new face of China's ethnic milieu.

Juten ODA

Further Reading

Allsen, T. T. (1983). The Yuan dynasty and the Uighurs of Turfan in the 13th century. In M. Rossabi (Ed.), *China among equals: The middle kingdom and its neighbors, 10th–14th centuries* (pp. 243–280). Berkeley and Los Angeles: University of California Press.

Gansu Province Statistical Bureau. (Ed.). (1998). *Gansu yearbook: 1997*. Beijing: Zhongguo tongji chubanshe.

Mackerras, C. (1990). The Uighurs. In D. Sinor (Ed.), *The Cambridge history of early inner Asia* (pp. 320–342). Cambridge, U.K.: Cambridge University Press.

Warikoo, K. (1998). Ethnic religious resurgence in Xinjiang. In T. Atabaki & J. O'Kane (Eds.), *Post-Soviet central Asia* (pp. 269–282). Leiden, The Netherlands: Tauris Academic Studies in association with the International Institute for Asian Studies.

Xinjiang Uygur Autonomous Region Statistical Bureau. (Ed.). (1998). *Xinjiang statistical yearbook: 1997*. Beijing: Zhongguo tongji chubanshe.

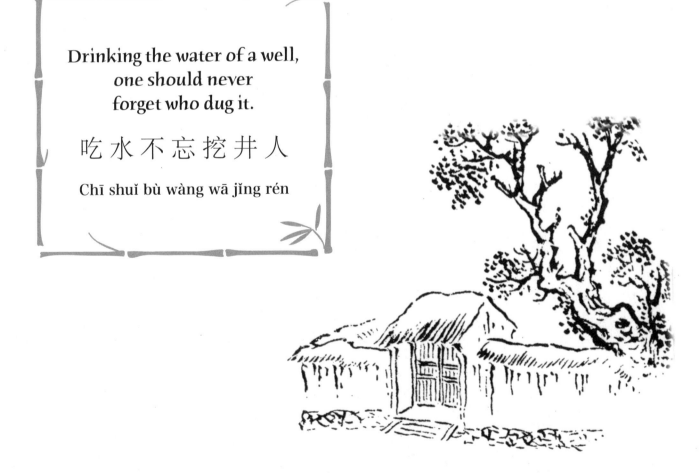

Drinking the water of a well, one should never forget who dug it.

吃 水 不 忘 挖 井 人

Chī shuǐ bù wàng wā jǐng rén

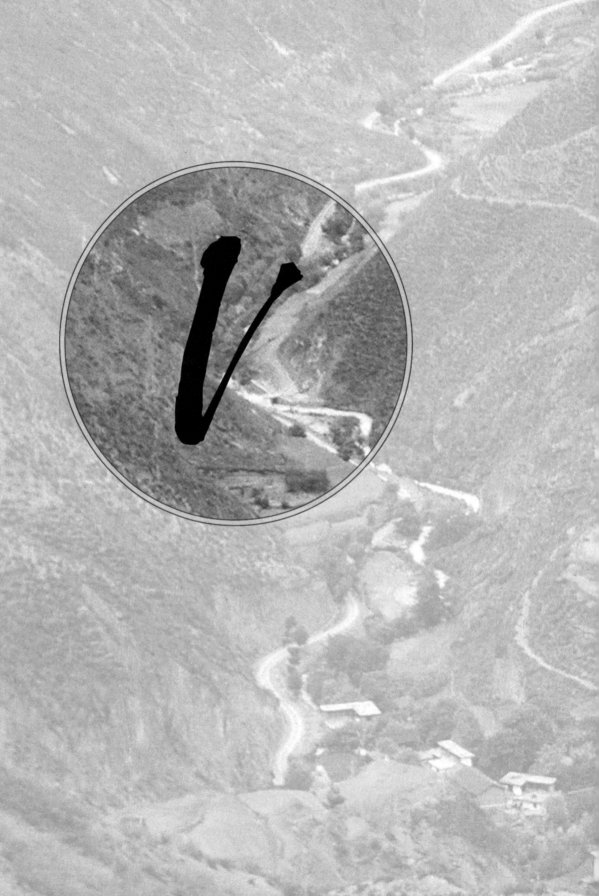

VERBIEST, Father Ferdinand

Nán Huáirén 南怀仁

1623–1688   Jesuit scientist, astronomer

One of a number of Jesuit missionaries who were sent to China from Rome in the seventeenth century, Father Ferdinand Verbiest was befriended by the K'ang-shi emperor and became one of the foremost astronomers and scientists in China.

Father Ferdinand Verbiest was born in Pittem, a small town in what is now Belgium, and from an early age he studied at the institutions of the Jesuits in Belgium and in Seville, Spain. He excelled at mathematics, science, and astronomy, as well as languages: He was fluent in Flemish, Latin, German, Italian, and Spanish. At the age of eighteen, he joined the Society of Jesus in the hope of going to work in the missions in Central and South America. But the Jesuits had other plans for him; word had come from the Far East, calling for more priests to carry on missionary work in China. Father Ferdinand at once set about to learn Manchu, gaining much fluency by the time he left for China in 1658. He was one of about thirty-five missionaries sent by the Jesuits.

The subsequent years were difficult ones. The missionaries faced varying degrees of persecution and privations, since their fates were closely tied with Chinese politics. When the Shunzhi emperor died at a young age, the affairs of the state fell into the hands of four co-regents who governed on behalf of his seven-year-old successor, K'ang-shi. The regents looked unfavorably on the influence of the Jesuits, and sought to discredit them by an old custom in which they pitted them against renowned shamans of the court. The Jesuits, led by Father Johann Adam Schall von Bell, lost the competition to a Muslim shaman, Yang Guangxian. Schall and the others were imprisoned on the charge of spreading Christianity (labeled an evil religion), and sentenced to death. They were saved by an earthquake, however, which was interpreted as a sign of heavenly displeasure. All the inmates in the prison were released, including the Jesuits. A few years later, Father Verbiest underwent a similar competition, again against Yang, but this time the Jesuits won.

In 1699 the heir to the throne came of age and took power as the K'ang-shi emperor. He, like his father, favored the Jesuits, and within the year, Father Ferdinand was placed in charge of the royal observatory and was made the overseer of the dissemination of mathematical knowledge in the kingdom.

One of his first tasks was to complete a calendar that would reform an inaccurate lunar calendar, devised by a Muslim rival of the Jesuits, which had included an extra month. The new calendar that Father Ferdinand made used solar rather than lunar calculations and was personally approved by the emperor, thus becoming the new standard across China. Thereafter he and Father Ferdinand became close friends, and the Jesuit taught the young emperor mathematics and geometry, music, and philosophy. As a result, Father Ferdinand's stature grew, and he became one of the most influential men of his time in China.

Among the things he devised for the emperor were star charts, a cannon, and even a steam-driven toy cart, which some say is the first automobile. The star charts, which became a great aid to navigation, clearly identified

Father Ferdinand Verbiest, from the manuscript *Galerie illustrée de portraits de jésuites*, by A. Hamy, 1893.

---

the various constellations and celestial bodies and located their exact position in the sky. The cannons that were cast were far superior to the ones then in use in the Chinese army, in that they could withstand prolonged use without fear of explosion from overheating. In addition, he designed and had cast six astronomical instruments in 1673, which were housed in a newly built observatory in Beijing. Replicas of these instruments may still be seen at the observatory; the original instruments were removed during the Boxer Rebellion and taken to Prussia by the Germans. Among the instruments that would prove the most beneficial were the sextant, which one could use to determine latitude; the ecliptic *armilla,* which was used to calculate ecliptical longitude and latitude of the stars and planets; and the equatorial *armilla,* which allowed for the computation of true solar time.

Father Ferdinand also wrote more than forty books on science, mechanics, astronomy, and theology. As special gifts for the emperor, he created a world map and a table of all lunar and solar eclipses for the coming two thousand years. This world map included the latest details available, and was the most complete of its time. Its impact was immeasurable in that it sought to chart the entire world from the Chinese point of view. China was the locus, from which the various points of longitude and latitude radiated.

Father Ferdinand died in 1688 after falling from his horse. He was buried in Beijing near equally renowned fellow Jesuits: Fathers Matteo Ricci and Johann Adam Schall von Bell. The emperor bestowed upon him a posthumous name; he was the only European to have been given such a royal honor. Through his work in mathematics, physics, engineering, astrology, mechanics, cartography, philosophy, and theology, Father Verbiest provided a wide-ranging and comprehensive view of Western scientific traditions to the Chinese intellectual tradition.

Nirmal DASS

Further Reading

Golvers, N. (2003). Ferdinand Verbiest, S. J. (1623–1688) and the Chinese heaven: The composition of the astronomical corpus, its diffusion and reception in the European Republic of Letters. *Louvain Chinese Studies, 12.* Leuven, Belgium: Leuven University Press.

Hardenberg, H. O. (1995). *The oldest precursor of the automobile: Ferdinand Verbiest steam turbine-powered vehicle model.* Warrendale, PA: Society of Automotive Engineers.

Masini, F. (1996). *Western humanistic culture presented to China by Jesuit missionaries (XVII–XVIII centuries): Proceedings of the conference held in Rome, Ocober. 25–27, 1993.* Rome: Institutum Historicum, S. I.

Rowbotham, A. H. (1942). *Missionary and Mandarin: The Jesuits at the court of China.* Berkeley: University of California Press.

Witek, J. W. (Ed.). (1994). *Ferdinand Verbiest (1623–1688): Jesuit missionary, scientist, engineer, and diplomat.* Nettetal, Germany: Steylar Verlag.

Vernacular Language Movement

Báihuàwén Yùndòng　白话文运动

The Vernacular Language Movement, which fostered a radical change in the writing style of Chinese composition, developed from century-long usage of a northern dialect in literature and gained momentum during the student and intellectual-led New Culture Movement (1917–1923). It won nation-wide acceptance in the 1920s and has made a lasting impact on education, communication, and literary research.

The Vernacular Language Movement began with efforts of the radical wing of the educated elite in the early twentieth century. The efforts to replace classical Chinese (*wenyan*) with spoken language (*baihua*) in nearly all written works were stimulated by a sense of national crisis in the late nineteenth century. After sporadic, short-lived attempts at the turn of the twentieth century, the movement acquired momentum in the mid-1910s when using the vernacular in writing became a major agenda in the New Culture Movement (1917–1923), a period of student and intellectual protests. By the early 1920s vernacular in written Chinese finally gained nation-wide acceptance as a reputable style in prose, poetry, and fiction and was officially designated the style for school textbooks.

The vernacular that became a national language in the 1920s was originally a northern dialect, spoken with varied local accents by people living in areas north of the Huai River. It acquired broader usage within officialdom, hence the name "Mandarin" (*guanhua*). National mobility in warfare, social advancement, and economic activities had contributed to wider usage of Mandarin Chinese since the Song dynasty (960–1279). Fiction, which came to maturity during the Song dynasty and drew inspirations from Tang dynasty (618–907 CE)*bianwen* (stories of Buddha and his disciples written in vernacular) and Tang *chuanqi* (short stories, or romance), as well as storytelling and stage performance, were written in Mandarin Chinese. By the end of the nineteenth century, fiction written in the vernacular and often intended for social criticism had national circulation. Although it was a noticeable force in literature, the vernacular remained heterodox because *wenyan* Chinese received institutional support as the normative style in the official Civil Service Examinations.

Several forces converged to propel the Vernacular Language Movement at the turn of the twentieth century. First among these, ironically, was awareness among the literati that *wenyan* Chinese restrained China's progress. Wu Rulun (1840–1903), a leading member of the Tongcheng School known for its elegant style in *wenyan* prose, was among the first who viewed *wenyan* as contributing to China's backwardness in comparison with the West. He considered a standardized form of Mandarin Chinese to be necessary for providing mass education. Huang Zunxian (1848–1905), a diplomat to Japan and an activist in political reforms, advocated the vernacular and experimented in using it to compose poetry in classical form.

Awareness of the need for a national language in the

2387

vernacular was sustained by the growing forces of nationalism and modern mass media at the turn of the twentieth century. Liang Qichao (1873–1929), the energetic political reformer and journalist, had a lasting impact on the generations after him through his promotion of "new fictions" as a means to enlightenment and national strength. Liang also wrote fiction and poetry in the vernacular that were read by many. His passionate appeal and innovative experiments inspired further attempts. Magazines that published "new fictions" written in spoken language—as well as newspapers such as *Chinese Vernacular Newspaper, Hangzhou Vernacular Newspaper, Newspaper of Anhui Dialect, Anhui Vernacular Newspaper, Ningbo Vernacular Newspaper, Chaozhou Vernacular Newspaper,* and *Citizens' Vernacular Daily*—appeared in cities along the southeast coast. These publications, however, did not last long.

In 1905 *wenyan* Chinese lost its institutional ground when the Civil Service Examinations were abolished. The reform in education gave rise to a new generation of Chinese leaders whose education in Western-style schools in China or in the West gained social legitimacy. The most vocal advocates for the vernacular then were those who were well versed in both Chinese and Western traditions. Thus, it was not accidental that the most passionate discussion of language reform first took place among Chinese students abroad, who led the Vernacular Language Movement in the 1910s.

Language Reform

Between 1915 and 1917 a small group of Chinese students pursuing graduate degrees at Cornell, Columbia, and Harvard universities engaged in an informal but serious discussion of Chinese language reform. They all supported the ongoing New Culture Movement and saw language reform as necessary for a revolution in literature. Yet, some vehemently opposed introducing the vernacular into poetry. Ren Hongjun (1886–1961) and Mei Guangdi (1890–1945) held the deepest doubt about the feasibility of the vernacular in poetry, which they viewed as ill-matched for rhythm and elegance, the key elements in the form. Hu Shi (1891–1962), however, was determined to bring the vernacular into all forms of Chinese literature and composed verses in the vernacular as a means of debate with his friends. In 1917 he published an article entitled "A Preliminary Discussion on Literature Reform" in the *New Youth,* a magazine founded by Chen Duxiu, another advocate for literature in the vernacular.

The debate about literature in the vernacular instantly became a focus of the New Culture Movement, which

These members of the New Culture Movement advocated literature written in the vernacular language of the masses. Clockwise from left: Chen Duxiu, Hu Shi, Lu Xun, Cai Yuanpei, and Li Dazhao.

made *New Youth* its major forum. Qian Xuantong and Liu Bannong, two professors at Beijing University and major leaders in the New Culture Movement, engaged in a mock debate to promote vernacular literature. It caught national attention and became a memorable episode in the movement. In 1918 the Vernacular Language Movement established yet another landmark in publishing "A Madman's Diary" by Lu Xun in *New Youth*. Other proponents, such as Zhou Zuoren, Liu Bannong, and Sheng Yinmo, also composed and published works in prose or poetry in the vernacular. By the end of the 1910s using the vernacular in written Chinese had gained acceptance beyond a small group of advocates and became a national phenomenon.

In the final phase of the vernacular's rise, defenders of classical Chinese fought three rounds of battle before giving up. The first battle, ironically, came from Lin Shu and Yan Fu, who would otherwise be viewed as pioneers in modern Chinese literature and harbingers of the New Culture Movement through the influence of their translated works from Western literature and thought. Between 1917 and 1919 Lin Shu took a public stand against the vernacular by publishing three articles and two short stories. He attacked the Vernacular Language Movement by insinuating, through his fictional characters, that Chen, Hu, and Cai Yuanpei, their supporter and chancellor of Beijing University, were three "demons." Yan Fu viewed Lin's attack as "laughable" and refrained from making public statements. But Yan did express his disdain for the advocates of the vernacular as "spring birds and autumn insects" that would go away with the season. The second battle came from some scholars gathered around *Xueheng* magazine, who were mostly U.S.-educated scholars, while some, such as Ren Hongjun and Mei Guangdi, were friends of Hu Shi. The most active opponent of the vernacular among this group was Hu Xiansu (1893?–1968), who wrote articles in debate with Hu Shi. Interestingly, the *Xueheng* group did not oppose a revolution in literature but warned against the radical tendency to abandon classical literature, a significant part of Chinese cultural heritage they cherished. The final attack came from Zhang Shizhao through the *Tiger Weekly* in 1925. By then the vernacular had been a "national language" for four years, since elementary school textbooks had been written in the vernacular in accord with an order from the Ministry of Education in 1920.

Mass Communication

The Vernacular Language Movement succeeded in incorporating the language of the masses into written works yet remained a movement of the elite. Its long-term impact can be found in education, in national communication, in writing style, and in research on Chinese literature. Using the vernacular in textbooks made education more accessible to ordinary people. The vernacular further developed and reinforced the historical practice of using Mandarin Chinese as the national language of communication. As the strict rules of composition in classical Chinese were abandoned when written Chinese took the form of the vernacular, it opened the way to importing more foreign (Japanese and Western) elements into the Chinese lexicon, grammar, and composition. In 1927 Hu Shi published *A History of Vernacular Literature*. The work provided the Vernacular Language Movement with historical justification in the Chinese context and encouraged further studies of Chinese vernacular literature in the premodern period.

LU Yan

Further Reading

Chow, T. (1960). *The May Fourth movement.* Cambridge, MA: Harvard University Press..

Gunn, E. M. (1991). *Rewriting Chinese: Style and innovation in twentieth-century Chinese prose.* Stanford, CA: Stanford University Press.

Hanan, P. (1981). *The Chinese vernacular story.* Cambridge, MA: Harvard University Press.

Hu Shi. (1917, January). Wenxu gailiang chuyi. *Xinqingnian, 1,* 5.

Hu Shi. (1923). Wushi nian lai Zhongguo zhi wenxue [Chinese literature in the past fifty years]. In *Shenbao Guan, Shenbao wushi zhounian jiniance* [A volume in commemoration of the 50th anniversary of Shenbao]. Shanghai: Shenbao.

Hu Shi. (1928). *Baihua Wenxue Shi* [A history of vernacular literature]. Shanghai: Xinyue shudian.

Sima, C. (1991). *Zhongguo Xinwenxue Shi* [A history of new literature in China]. Taipei, Taiwan: Zhuanji wenxue chubanshe.

Waley, A. (1960). *Ballads and stories from Tun-huang: An anthology.* London: G. Allen & Unwin.

Versailles Peace Conference

Bālí Hépíng Huìyì 巴黎和平会议

The Treaty of Versailles marking the end of World War I did little to resolve issues of China's national sovereignty. Japan, which fought on the side of the Allies, occupied German holdings in Asia during the war, including China's Shandong Peninsula. The treaty condoned Japan's actions, sparking Chinese nationalist protests.

The Treaty of Versailles, signed on 28 June 1919, marked the end of World War I for Europeans but did little to resolve fundamental disputes related to China's national sovereignty. Talks between world leaders began in January 1919. The most important participants were the United States, Japan, Great Britain, France, and Italy. Russia had undergone Communist revolution in 1917 and did not participate. China was represented by delegates from Duan Qirui's Beijing government, a warlord regime that actually controlled little of China. Asia was not the focus of talks, and China's concerns were not paramount.

Tokyo had been determined to use World War I to increase its influence in East Asia. Shortly after fighting broke out in Europe, Japan joined the Allies and occupied German holdings in Asia, including China's Shandong Peninsula. In early 1915 Japan presented the Twenty-One Demands to China. The demands were to give the Japanese privileges and power greater than what they had obtained through the unequal treaties, a series of agreements forced upon China by the imperialist powers since the 1840s. Yuan Shikai, leader of China until early 1916, attempted to weaken the demands and hoped to find a way to restore Chinese control in Shandong.

China entered World War I on the side of the Allies in 1917. Duan Qirui's government sought to obtain foreign loans, international legitimacy, and a voice at the postwar peace settlement. To many Chinese, joining the Allies was a way to remove Japanese influence in Shandong Province. U.S. president Woodrow Wilson's Fourteen Points, first articulated in January 1918, offered hope to Chinese Nationalists because the president called for open diplomacy, self-determination, and the creation of an organization "for the purpose of affording mutual guarantees of political independence and territorial integrity to great and small states alike" (Wilson, 1918).

Japan's effective great power diplomacy and support for the Allied cause ensured that the Europeans acquiesced to Tokyo's demands. The Lansing-Ishii Agreement of 1917 had given the Japanese confidence that the United States would not interfere with Japan's "special interests in China," while the United States assumed that Japan accepted the Open Door principle and China's territorial integrity. Weak protests from the U.S. delegation at Versailles, France, had little effect, and Wilson placed priority on enticing the European powers and Japan to support the League of Nations. Article 156 of the Treaty of Versailles ratified Japanese control of Germany's concessions in the Shandong Peninsula. Japan also obtained control over German possessions in the southwest Pacific as one of the treaty's "mandates." In short, the treaty ratified Japan's wartime imperialism.

In China and among overseas Chinese communities

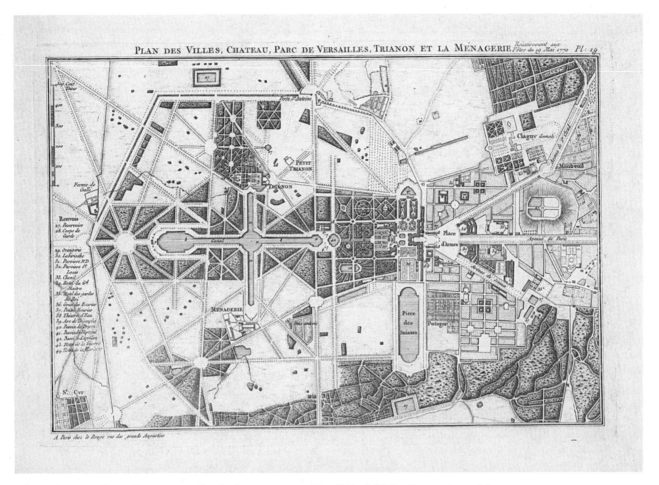

PLAN DES VILLES, CHATEAU, PARC DE VERSAILLES, TRIANON ET LA MÉNAGERIE

Plan of Versailles, the site at which the treaty ending World War I was signed in 1919.
COURTESY OF THE BEINECKE RARE BOOK AND MANUSCRIPT LIBRARY, YALE UNIVERSITY.

around the world, the Treaty of Versailles sparked outrage at the Japanese, China's warlords, and imperialism in general. The protests and strikes that resulted were known as the "May Fourth Movement." Although no longer in power, Duan was accused of being a puppet of the Japanese, as were the Chinese representatives at the peace conference. The Beijing government repudiated the Treaty of Versailles but was unable to modify Article 156 or other parts of the treaty. Many students and intellectuals were bitterly disappointed at the United States and Wilsonianism. Some of those people moved to political action by the treaty would go on to establish the Chinese Communist Party in 1921.

Steven PHILLIPS

Further Reading

Chow Tse-tsung. (1960). *The May Fourth Movement: Intellectual revolution in modern China.* Stanford, CA: Stanford University Press.

Cohen, W. (1990). *America's response to China: A history of Sino-American relations.* (3rd edition). New York: Columbia University Press.

Wilson, W. (8 January 1918). *Address to a Joint Session of Congress on the Conditions of Peace.* Retrieved December 19, 2008, from The American Presidency Project: http://www.presidency.ucsb.edu/ws/?pid=65405

Video Games

Diànzǐ yóuxì　电子游戏

Video games began to appear in China more than thirty years ago and are now ubiquitous. While this new form of entertainment has become a popular pleasure activity, especially among youths, it has also caused serious concerns among the public.

Historians generally agree that the U.S. physicist Willy Higinbotham invented the video game in 1958 when, to entertain visitors at Brookhaven National Laboratory in Long Island, New York, he demonstrated the interactive game Tennis for Two on an oscilloscope. One year later he improved this invention and displayed it on a 38-centimeter (15-inch) monitor.

Video game players use an interface device such as a paddle, joystick, mouse, or computer keys to manipulate images on a video display or television screen, and have changed quite dramatically from Higinbotham's first version. In 1971 the first video arcade games appeared. In 1972 Magnavox marketed the first home television video game. In 1973 Pong was the first commercially available video game, marketed by Atari. The Atari Video Computer System (VCS) was released in 1977 with an introductory price of $199.95. It was the most popular video game console of its day and was available until 1990, being on the market longer than any other system in history. Several hundred games were developed for it. Atari software and hardware rights were sold to Hasbro for only $5 million in 1998.

Development in China

Video games in China developed more than thirty years ago, evolving from TVs and PCs to mobile phones, and from single PCs to networks to mobile games as developers made hardware and software innovations. In the early 1980s arcade video games appeared in some children's entertainment places and adolescents' activity centers in China. By the middle of the 1980s or so, electronic video games arrived in China. In the 1990s a new type of family computer quietly entered China—Family Computer (FC) of Nintendo in Japan. With the price gradually going down, FC went into more and more homes and became an indispensable part of the recreational facilities of many families. Around 1993 a new kind of game computer—the sixteen-bit Sega MD—was introduced in China. It had brighter colors and richer game content. Sega MD and the sixteen-bit Nintendo SFC have brought Chinese game players closer to the video world.

With the popularization of the Internet in China, online games also have become more accessible to Chinese players. In June 1998 the website OurGame was established as the first website specializing in online games in China. It provides such online games as Encirclement, Chinese chess, and Chinese checkers for registered users. By May 2001 OurGame had the most game players in the world. Later companies in Taiwan and South Korea began to promote games in China. In 2001 Shanghai Shanda Interactive Entertainment Limited, an agent of the Korean online game Legend, began amassing a legendary Internet fortune in China and has become the largest online game enterprise in China. At present video games in China concentrate on these media platforms: screen machines, palm screens, home televisions, Internet bar computers, mobile phones, and home computers. With the development of technology the last two platforms may become the most popular.

Market for Online Video Games

China has a large online game market.. In 2002 players of online games outnumbered players of single computer games and arcade games. According to the *21st Report on China's Internet Development* by the China Internet Network Information Center (CNNIC), 120 million Netizens (active participants in the online community of the Internet) play online games; adolescents are the main players; 73.7 percent of Netizens under eighteen years of age have online game experience. Low age, low income, and low educational level are the three significant characteristics of online game players.

According to a 2007 survey of the Chinese game market, the scale of the Chinese electronic game industry increased considerably in 2006, and the industry's overall income in 2006 increased 68 percent over that of 2005. Online games, other types of video games, handheld game consoles, mobile phones, and the like enable players to play games at any place without any limitation. The market for mobile phone games is also large, and it is expected to reach a total value of five billion Chinese yuan in 2008, which is about 714 million U.S. dollars. The video game market in China is rapidly growing and is reinforcing the development of local original software as domestically made games increase and dominate the market in China.

The Future

The central government has placed many regulations on video games, especially for young students playing in Internet bars. On the other hand, with the popularization of the personal computer, people will tend to play video games mostly in the home. The number of younger players is also likely to increase. To cater to the tastes of those

A kiosk advertisement demonstrating cross-promotion of Chinese and Western businesses. Here, the popular Taiwanese singing group S.H.E. promotes *World of Warcraft*, the successful computer game from the United States.

younger people, the research and development departments of video game companies will focus on content and design. In China new college curriculums attract majors in animation, art design, and creation, reflecting societal needs and desires and also the potential of the consumption of video games.

Junhao HONG and Wenfa HE

Further Reading

China Internet Network Information Center (CNNIC). (2008, January 21). *21st statistical survey report on the Internet development in China*. Retrieved June 16, 2008, from http://www.cnnic.net.cn/html/Dir/2008/02/29/4999.htm

Jin Shengxi. (2005). Sony in total isolation in video game market. *IT Times Weekly, 12,* 60–61.

Sun Ping. (2007). Brief analysis on current advertisements in Chinese video games. *Modern Corporation Education, 6,* 6–47.

Vietnam-China Relations

Yuè-Zhōng wàijiāo guānxì　越中外交关系

China and Vietnam share a complicated history. Their relationship has been characterized by long periods of collaboration and shorter periods of conflicts. Currently relations and collaboration are expanding and the two countries are addressing their territorial disputes through negotiations.

*V*ietnam was a part of the Chinese empire for more than a thousand years before gaining independence in the tenth century CE. However, the independent Vietnam remained under Chinese cultural and political influence, and a tributary relationship developed. The period of French colonial rule in Vietnam during the second half of the nineteenth century and the first half of the twentieth ended this close relationship.

After Vietnam regained independence from France in 1954, relations between China and Vietnam were officially closed until the end of the Vietnam War in 1975. Thereafter, relations deteriorated further into open hostilities in early 1979, and tensions remained high for most of the 1980s. During the late 1980s relations started to improve, leading to full normalization in November 1991. The 1990s were characterized by two contradictory trends: expanding and improving relations in most fields on the one hand and recurring periods of tension relating to border disputes on the other hand. Both countries are trying to manage and eventually settle the border disputes. The early 2000s have been characterized by less tension compared with the 1990s relating to territorial issues and by expanding political and economic relations.

Background

Relations between the countries were close during the 1950s and for two decades China provided the Democratic Republic of Vietnam with extensive economic and military assistance. China sent thousands of advisers to assist in various fields. China also provided considerable assistance during the Vietnam War. However, differences between the two nations developed during the 1960s and into the first half of the 1970s because of varying perceptions of the Soviet Union and divergent views on relations with the United States. After the 1973 Paris agreement, which led to the withdrawal of U.S. troops from Vietnam and established a cease-fire in the Vietnam War, the Vietnamese claimed that Chinese leaders had advised them to diminish the level of the fighting in the south for a few years, advice perceived as aimed at keeping Vietnam divided. China rejected this claim.

Sino-Vietnamese Relations, 1975–1991

In 1975 China's allies emerged victorious in the war in Vietnam, and experts expected that relations between China and Vietnam would continue to be very close. However, relations between China and Vietnam dramatically declined from seemingly good in 1975 to war in

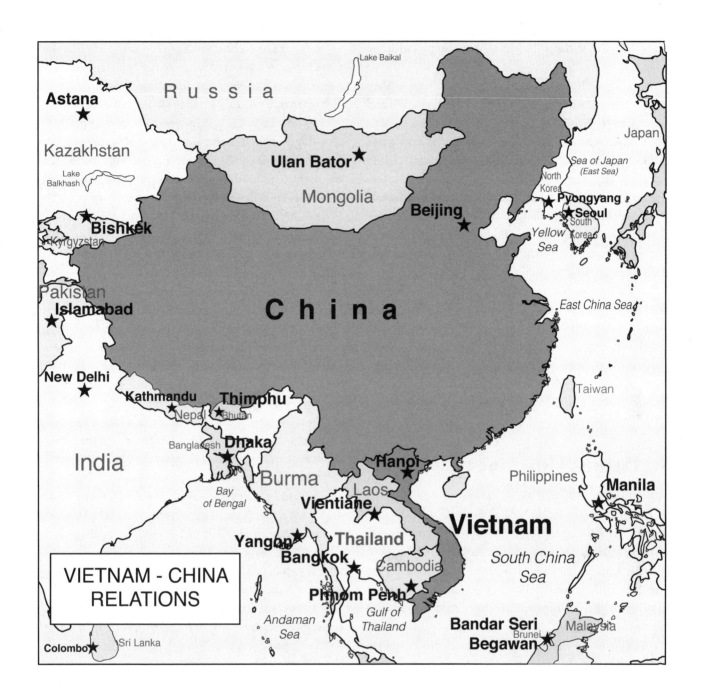

VIETNAM - CHINA
RELATIONS

1979. Relations deteriorated over several issues. First were differences in opinion concerning the Soviet Union and China's uneasiness about Vietnam's relations with that country. Second were conflicting interests in Cambodia and China's gradually increasing support for Cambodia in the conflict between Vietnam and Cambodia. Third, territorial disputes between China and Vietnam caused tension. Fourth, the way in which the ethnic Chinese in Vietnam were treated became an issue. In fact, the mass migration of ethnic Chinese from Vietnam in the spring

of 1978 officially led to the public deterioration of bilateral relations between the two countries.

The overall deterioration of relations led to a militarized conflict that escalated into China's attack on Vietnam in February and March 1979. China declared that the attack was a response to Vietnamese attacks on China. China claimed to have captured three of six provincial capitals in the bordering provinces of Cao Bang, Lang Son, and Lao Cai as well as seventeen cities and counties before announcing a withdrawal on 5 March. China announced that the withdrawal was completed by 16 March.

The normalization process between China and Vietnam began with low-level contacts in the mid-1980s and expanded to high-level meetings in early 1989. In early September 1990 a (then-secret) high-level meeting was held in China. Despite this meeting the normalization process lacked momentum on the political front. This situation prevailed until mid-1991, when the normalization process gained momentum. The increased diplomatic interaction paved the way for a high-level summit in early November 1991, when bilateral relations were officially fully normalized.

The full normalization of relations between China and Vietnam was made possible by the removal of the differences between the two countries regarding relations with the Soviet Union with the Sino-Soviet normalization of 1989 and by the formal resolution of the Cambodian conflict through the Paris agreements in October 1991, which removed two deeply dividing factors from the agenda.

Relations since 1991

After full normalization the relationship between China and Vietnam was characterized by two contradictory trends in the 1990s: expanding contacts and cooperation in many fields but tension relating to territorial disputes. The early 2000s have been characterized by continued expansion of relations and collaboration and by less tension relating to the territorial disputes as compared with the 1990s.

The positive trend in bilateral relations can be seen in the expanding political, cultural, economic, and military contacts between the two countries. Official delegations from one country regularly visit the other country to discuss ways of expanding relations in various fields. Increased economic ties since 1991 can be seen in bilateral trade, which grew from $32 million in 1991 to $1 billion in 1996 and from $10.42 billion in 2006 to $15.85 billion in 2007. The bilateral trade displays a steadily growing trade surplus for China. China has also provided loans and assistance to upgrade Chinese-built factories in northern Vietnam. In the political field the close relationship between the two ruling parties—the Chinese Communist Party (CCP) and the Communist Party of Vietnam (CPV)—expanded through a steady stream of exchange visits at various levels. The contacts between the armed forces of the two countries have also expanded through regular exchange visits.

Sharp differences relating to all the territorial disputes (that is, overlapping claims to the Paracel and Spratly archipelagos, to water and continental shelf areas in the South China Sea and in the Gulf of Tonkin, and to areas along the land border) were prevalent from May to November 1992. Differences relating to oil exploration in the South China Sea and the signing of contracts with foreign companies for exploration were prevalent during parts of 1994, 1996, and 1997. During 1998 shorter periods of tension relating to the disputes occurred.

During 1999 talks focused on reaching a settlement of the land border dispute and resulted in the Land Border Treaty on 30 December 1999. This treaty was ratified in 2000, and the demarcation process is expected to be completed before the end of 2008. The border disputes created no significant tension during 1999. During 2000 the focus was on resolving the Gulf of Tonkin dispute and led to the Agreement on the Demarcation of Waters, Exclusive Economic Zones, and Continental Shelves in the Gulf of Tonkin on 25 December 2000. On the same day the two countries signed the Agreement on Fishery Cooperation in the Tonkin Gulf and the Regulations on Preservation and Management of the Living Resources in the Common Fishery Zone in the Gulf of Tonkin. The agreement on demarcation was ratified and entered into force in 2004 after the completion of additional talks on supplementary protocol of the fishery agreement had been completed. The trend of no significant tension caused by the remaining border disputes in 1999 continued to prevail in 2000.

Since 2001 tensions relating to the disputes in the South China Sea have mainly been contained through talks at government and expert levels. However, official protests have been issued in response to a limited number of actions carried out in or in relation to the South China Sea area.

The Future

The future of relations between China and Vietnam will be determined by how successfully the two sides handle disputes. Deepening bilateral cooperation in different fields and expanding economic interaction have contributed to building a more stable bilateral relationship. The progress in managing the territorial disputes has also improved the prospect of long-term stability in the bilateral relationship.

Despite these positive developments the disputes in the South China Sea area remain a threat to a stable relationship both through the overlapping sovereignty claims to the Paracel and Spratly archipelagoes and the disputes over resources in maritime areas. Potential future challenges to bilateral relations include risks associated with economic competition and uneven trade relations as well as risks associated with developments affecting the Mekong River.

Ramses AMER

Further Reading

Amer, R. (1994). Sino-Vietnamese normalization in the light of the crisis of the late 1970s. *Pacific Affairs, 67*(3), 357–383.

Amer, R. (1999). Sino-Vietnamese relations: Past, present, and future. In C. A. Thayer & R. Amer (Eds.), *Vietnamese foreign policy in transition* (pp. 68–130). Singapore: Institute for Southeast Asian Studies; New York: St. Martin's Press.

Amer, R. (2002). *The Sino-Vietnamese approach to managing border disputes.* Durham, U.K.: University of Durham, International Boundaries Research Unit.

Amer, R. (2004). Assessing Sino-Vietnamese relations through the management of contentious issues. *Contemporary Southeast Asia, 26*(2), 320–345.

Gilks, A. (1992). The breakdown of the Sino-Vietnamese alliance, 1970–1979. *China Research Monograph No. 39.*

Thayer, C. A. (1994). Sino-Vietnamese relations: The interplay of ideology and national interest. *Asian Survey, 34*(6), 513–528.

Womak, B. (1994). Sino-Vietnamese border trade: The edge of normalization. *Asian Survey, 34*(6), 495–512.

Womak, B. (2006). *China and Vietnam: The politics of asymmetry.* Cambridge, U.K.: Cambridge University Press.

Woodside, A. (1979). Nationalism and poverty in the breakdown of Sino-Vietnamese relations. *Pacific Affairs, 52*(3), 381–409.

WANG Fuzhi

Wáng Fūzhī 王夫之

1619–1692   Ming–Qing Scholar

Wang Fuzhi (1619–1692) was one of the most important scholars of the Ming–Qing period whose pragmatic philosophies of statecraft challenged long-standing traditions, and his writings influence cultural ideas of Chinese nationalism even today.

Wang Fuzhi was one of the most important Chinese thinkers and scholars of the Ming–Qing period (1368–1912), and his philosophies influence cultural ideas of Chinese nationalism even today. He wrote more than one hundred books during his lifetime and fought against the Manchu invaders during their campaign establishing the Qing dynasty (1644–1912).

A native of Hengyang in Hunan, Wang Fuzhi passed the provincial examinations in 1642, but his political career was quickly ended by nationwide peasant rebellions and the Manchu invasion. Devoting the rest of his life to reading and writing, Wang completely withdrew from politics in 1650 after his anti-Manchu military activities failed. Wang's scholarly interests included Confucian classics, philosophy, history, textual criticism, literature, military strategies, medicine, astronomy, calendar, numerology, astrology, and Western science introduced by the Jesuits. Most of Wang's writings were unknown to the wider audience of readers before they were edited and printed beginning in the late 1830s. His most cited philosophic works include *Outer Commentary to the Book of Change, Commentary on Zhang Zai's Correction of Youthful Ignorance,* and *Record of Thoughts and Questions: Inner and Outer Sections.* Wang's main ideas on history and politics can be found in his *On Reading Comprehensive Mirror* and *On the History of the Song Dynasty.*

Wang was obsessed with rectifying the flaws he saw in Song–Ming neo-Confucian, Daoist, and Buddhist teachings and with reforming political and economic institutions, drawing lessons from history, and preserving and carrying forward Chinese culture while the alien Manchus ruled China.

Wang firmly rejected Daoism and Buddhism: He disapproved that these teachings advocated a denial of the real world in order to achieve absolute emptiness and quiescence of the mind. He criticized the Song neo-Confucian studies of *li* 理 for paying too much attention to abstract principles while overlooking human society and the material world from which these principles were derived. Wang also attacked the neo-Confucian studies of *xin* 心 (mind) for equating the concepts of the human mind (*neng* 能) with the outside world (*suo* 所), and knowledge (*zhi* 知) with practice and action (*xing* 行).

To rectify these empty and impractical teachings, Wang returned to Zhang Zai (1020–1077) and further advanced his materialistic philosophy. Wang stated that no materials can be added to or reduced from the universe and that no materials can be created from nothing; all materials follow their own *dao* (way), to be transformed from their original form, qi (material force), to what they are now. Wang discarded the idea that human nature is completely innate and never changes. To Wang, although human nature bears some innate qualities, which are the ultimate source of moral goodness, it reflects the mind's (*xin*) experiences in real human life.

2399

A Critique of Neo-Confucianism

Writing during the seventeenth century, Wang Fuzhi criticized the thinking of neo-Confucianist Zhu Xi for giving priority to principle and the Way over material-force and actual phenomena.

The world consists of nothing but actual physical phenomena or concrete things. The Way is the Way (or Ways) of actual phenomena, but one cannot describe the actual phenomena as phenomena of the Way. "When the Way is nonexistent, so is the actual phenomena" is something that anyone is capable of saying. But if the phenomena exists, why worry about its Way not existing? The sage knows what the gentleman does not, and yet ordinary men and women can do what the sage cannot. It may be that people are not clear about the Way of some particular phenomenon, and so the thing is not perfected, but the fact that it is not perfected does not mean that it does not exist. "When the actual phenomenon is nonexistent, so is its Way" is something that few people are capable of saying, but it is really and truly so.

Source: de Bary, W. T., & Lufrano, R. (2001). *Sources of Chinese tradition, vol. 2. (2nd ed.).* New York: Columbia University Press, 30.

Wang laid down a philosophical foundation for Qing pragmatic statecraft. Whereas his philosophical focus was on the material world, his political focus was on specific political and socioeconomic problems. In Wang's view, human society faces different problems in different times, and people of different historical periods should try hard to find specific solutions for their own problems. While denouncing those Song philosophers who put abstract principles above substance, Wang strongly rejected those who put general rules, particularly the ones set up by ancient statesmen, above specific institutions created for solving contemporary problems. In this regard, Wang pointed out that a specific problem that caused the Ming (1368–1644) to fall was the imbalance between the monarch and scholar-officials headed by a prime minister. Wang also vigorously defended Chinese culture against barbarism of non-Chinese nomads, causing his writings to become a cultural source of modern Chinese nationalism. The most prominent modern Chinese intellectuals and statesmen, such as Zeng Guofan, Tan Sitong, Liang Qichao, and Mao Zedong, who intensely searched for solutions for problems faced by China, were all inspired by Wang and his works.

Yamin XU

Further Reading

Black, A. H. (1989). *Man and nature in the philosophical thought of Wang Fu-chih.* Seattle: University of Washington Press.

Zhong Erju & Zhang Dainian. (1997). *Wang Fuzhi.* Changchun, China: Jilin wenshi chubanshe.

Zhang Qihui. (2001). *Quangshi daru: Wang Fuzhi* [The great Confucianist Wang Fuzhi]. Shijiazhuang, China: Hebei renmin chubanshe.

Zhou Bing. (2006). *Tian ren zhiji de lixue xinquanshi: Wang Fuzhi "Du sishu daquan shuo" sixiang yanjiu* [A new interpretation of Neo-Confucianism standing between heaven and human: A study of Wang Fuzhi's thought reflected in his "Reflections on 'The four complete books'"]. Chengdu, China: Bashu shushe.

WANG Jingwei

Wāng Jīngwèi 汪精卫

1883–1944   Rival of Chiang Kai-shek

An early and fervent supporter of Sun Zhong-shan's Chinese Nationalist revolutionary cause, Wang Jingwei became a leading rival to the Nationalist Army commander Chiang Kai-shek after Sun's death in 1925. Wang led the left wing of the Nationalist Party, but proved no match for Chiang. After war broke out with Japan in 1937 Wang lost all hope for Chiang's government in Chongqing and agreed to lead a pro-Japanese government in Nanjing.

Wang Jingwei began his political career in 1905 associated with the Tongmenghui leader Sun Zhongshan and died in 1944 as a Japanese collaborator. In between he aligned with various Nationalist Party (Guomindang) factions on both the left and right in his unsuccessful pursuit of power. The main theme of his life after 1925 became his rivalry with Nationalist Army Commander Chiang Kai-shek, who regularly bested Wang Jingwei's challenges.

Wang Jingwei was born into a poor but well-educated family in Guangdong Province. In his early twenties he studied in Japan on a Qing dynasty (1644–1912) government scholarship. In Japan he joined Sun Zhongshan's fledging revolutionary movement, Tongmenghui (Revolutionary Alliance), aimed at ending the Qing dynasty. Wang became widely known through his writings and public speaking on behalf of the Tongmenghui. In 1910 he led a plot to assassinate the Qing dynasty's Prince

Regent Caifeng by means of a roadside bomb. Authorities discovered the plot; Wang was imprisoned but not executed.

The end of the Manchu-ruled Qing dynasty did not make Sun Zhongshan and his associates leaders of the new Chinese Republic. Rather, the former Qing dynasty general Yuan Shikai became president of the new Chinese Republic and suppressed Sun Zhongshan's political supporters. In 1912 Wang Jingwei withdrew from Chinese domestic politics and married Chen Bijun, daughter of a wealthy Chinese merchant from Penang, the British-ruled island in the Malaya States. For the next few years Wang devoted himself primarily to Chinese literati pursuits.

In 1917 he rejoined Sun Zhongshan in Guangzhou (Canton), where Sun was raising forces to overthrow the northern warlords. Over the next seven years Wang became ever closer to Sun Zhongshan. Wang Jingwei followed Sun in moving toward stronger anti-imperialist views and practical cooperation with the Soviet Union. When Sun died of cancer in Beijing in 1925, Wang Jingwei was at his side.

After Sun's death Wang Jingwei advocated continued radicalization of the Nationalist Party along Soviet lines. Chiang Kai-shek, head of the Nationalist military, became a powerful opponent for leadership of the Nationalist Party. By 1929 the two men had reached open confrontation. Chiang Kai-shek, who possessed a wide range of factional supporters, repeatedly bested Wang Jingwei, who relied primarily on his personal leadership strengths. After several of these contests Wang Jingwei withdrew temporarily to Europe, only to return to China with renewed but futile hopes of gaining power. Wang

2401

Wang Jingwei circa 1930, a Chinese politician and rival of Chiang Kai-shek. Wang collaborated with the Japanese during the Second Sino-Japanese War (1937–1945).

remained a prominent Nationalist Party figure but increasingly isolated and disgruntled.

By the 1930s three Chinese positions emerged for dealing with Japan. One position, most strongly associated with the rural revolutionary leader Mao Zedong and the Chinese Communists, called for armed resistance to Japan. Chiang Kai-shek argued for grudging appeasement of Japan until the Nationalist government became strong enough to thwart Japanese aggression. Wang Jingwei, in a major shift from his position in the 1920s, became spokesperson for a third position. He now accepted Japanese leadership and Japan's dream of a new pan-Asian order from which Western capitalist colonialism would be excluded. This vision of an Asian-led anti-imperialist strategy fit with Wang's views from the 1920s. It also had considerable appeal to many Asian nationalists until the realities of World War II made Japan's own imperialist nature clear. Wang Jingwei's pro-Japanese stance had raised fierce patriotic Chinese opposition even in the mid-1930s. In 1935 an assassin seriously wounded Wang, and in 1939 while he was in Hanoi, Vietnam, another attempt on his life was made.

In 1940 Wang Jingwei left Chiang Kai-shek's Nationalist government in Chongqing and accepted leadership of a Japanese-sponsored Chinese regime at Nanjing (Nanking) that claimed the Nationalist Party mantle. Wang's government reached agreements with Japan that restored some of China's compromised sovereignty, but his government clearly served as a Japanese puppet. Wang Jingwei's health continued to decline from injuries suffered in the 1935 assassination attempt. When in November 1944 he went to Japan for treatment and died there, his reputation as a Japanese puppet and traitor to the Chinese nation already had been fixed.

David D. BUCK

Further Reading

Barrett, D. P., & Shyu, L. (Eds.). (2001). *Chinese collaboration with the Japanese, 1932–1945*. Stanford, CA: Stanford University Press.

Boorman, H. L. (Ed.). (1970). *Biographical dictionary of Republican China* (Vol. 3). New York: Columbia University Press.

Boyle, J. H. (1972). *China and Japan at war: The politics of collaboration, 1937–1945*. Stanford, CA: Stanford University Press.

WANG Mian

Wáng Miǎn 王冕

1287–1359   Yuan dynasty artist and poet

Wang Mian was a Yuan dynasty (1279–1368) painter most renowned for his *momei* (ink plum) paintings on silk and paper. In his compositions he integrated pictures and words by framing his calligraphic inscriptions with images of flowering plum branches.

Wang Mian 王冕 was a Yuan dynasty (1279–1368) artist noted for his *momei* (ink plum) paintings. He also composed poetry. He was born into a farmer's family in Zhuji, Zhejiang Province, and received his Confucian education and mastered classics. But Wang failed the civil service examinations, and he later rejected several civil appointments. After spending one year in Beijing Wang retreated to his hometown in the Guiji Mountains, where he made a living by selling his paintings.

Wang Mian's poetry, recorded in *Zhuzhai shiji* (Poetry Collection of the Bamboo Studio), conveyed his awareness of the danger and uncertainty of late Yuan society., expressed his concern for the suffering of the people, and criticized the failure of the government to protect them. During his later years Wang witnessed ethnic Han Chinese rebellions against the Mongolian court and probably even offered his advice to the rebels.

Wang painted plums on both silk and paper. He juxtaposed image and inscriptions in such a way that the image framed the inscriptions, his calligraphy enhancing the beauty of flowering plums. The organic forms and elegant, S-curved plum boughs contrast with the square, rustic, poetic or prose inscriptions and characterize the radiant beauty, self-assurance, and reclusion of Wang's plum world.

Wang's extant dated works span the period of 1346–1355. He painted the plums either in a plain style, with S-curved bough, or in a more ambitious style. In the plain style he used smooth, even brushstrokes to portray the rhythm and grace of the gentle main plum branch. The round petals of the blossoms were often rendered in several overlapping ink washes to symbolize the purity and virtual transparency of the flower. In the ambitious style the plum bough is painted in an S-curve, forming the backbone of the composition, which is often counterbalanced by blossom-bearing branchlets. Thick and thin applications of ink create varied tones that suggest the uneven texture of the branches. The main bough also defines the space where inscriptions are placed, although the inscriptions sometimes overlap with the plums. In the ambitious style massive old plum trunks and boughs meander through the painting space. The main bough gradually tapers toward the top, with secondary branches growing from the bough. The balance between the monumental old branch and the graceful, snowy petals is remarkable. The inscriptions never compete with the image in the ambitious style. Surely Wang Mian was associating himself with the old plum tree that lives a tough life but still grows younger branches with blossoming flowers. He took pride in his own perseverance, confidence, heroism, and ultimate triumph over harsh conditions. By using stylized forms and masterfully contrasted petals and boughs, Wang Mian created an idealized world of

2403

flowering plums as emblematic of the gentleman's endurance and resilience.

Wang Mian's influence on later ink plum specialists cannot be overestimated. They expanded the aesthetic scope of the ink plum genre and set a new standard that brought grandeur, intensity, scale, and visual power to later practice.

Yu JIANG

Further Reading

Bickford, M. (1996). *Ink plum: The making of a Chinese scholar-painting genre.* New York: Cambridge University Press.

Cahill, J. (1972). *Treasures of Asia, Chinese painting.* New York: Crown Publishers.

Cahill, J. (1997). The Yuan dynasty (1271–1368). In Barnhart, J. C., Yang Xin, Nie Chongzheng, J. Cahill, L. Shaojun, & W. Hung (Eds.), *Three thousand years of Chinese painting* (pp. 192–193). New Haven, CT: Yale University Press.

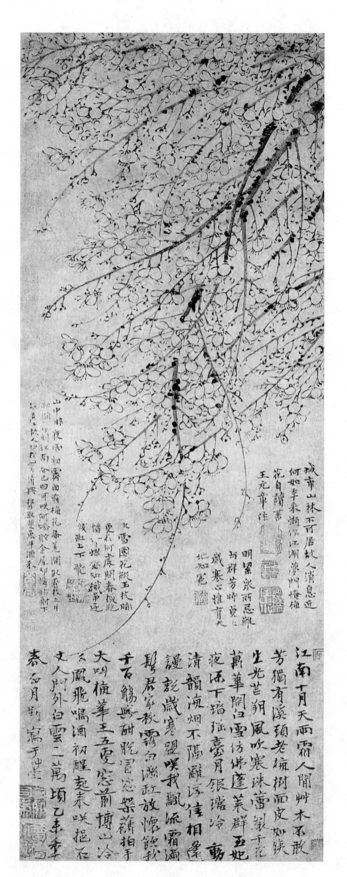

A scroll painting of a blossoming plum branch by Wang Mian, who inscribed six poems on the painting. Four of his contemporaries also added their own poems; calligraphy often served as a frame for the images or became an integral part of the composition.

WANG Wei

Wáng Wéi 王维

701–761 Tang poet and painter

Wang Wei earned himself an enduring reputation in both poetry and painting. His greatest works in both art forms involve themes of reclusion or subtly portrayed political and natural landscapes.

Wang Wei earned himself an enduring reputation in both poetry and painting. His pen name, "Mojie," was adopted from the Buddhist sutra (one of the discourses of the Buddha that constitute the basic text of Buddhist scripture) *Weimojie jing* (*Vimalakīrti-nirdeśa-sūtra*) and is emblematic of his belief in Buddhism. The synthetic Buddho-Confucian philosophy informed the style of his artwork.

Wang composed his first poem at the age of nine. When he was twenty-one he passed the national *jinshi* (advanced scholar) examination. Upon the political demise of his patron Zhang Jiuling (678–740), a result of corruption of the time, the disappointed poet began to express in verse his intention to retreat from political life. Thereafter he lived a half-reclusive life while enjoying high official positions. In 756 the rebels of An Lushan's (d. 757) stormed the Tang capital Chang'an (modern Xi'an), from where Emperor Xuanzong (reigned 712–756) fled the bloodshed to Shu (modern Sichuan Province). Wang was captured and forced to serve the rebel government. He was convicted of treason and given the death penalty when the new Tang emperor, Suzong (reigned 756–762), recovered the capital. Evidence of his loyalty to the Tang dynasty was found in a poem

composed in captivity, and his life was pardoned, but he was demoted. This peril facilitated Wang's conversion to Buddhism. Indeed, the vicissitudes in Wang's life seemed to parallel those of the high Tang dynasty (618–907 CE)in the eighth century.

Wang Wei's greatest works of painting and poetry involve themes of reclusion or subtly portrayed political and natural landscapes. In some of his early poetry he presents himself as a knight-errant or a brave soldier. His wife's premature death and his political setbacks led Wang's poetic style to a radical change, and he began to load his poetic imagery with philosophical messages. The natural scenes in his later works became more serene, and this serenity of imagery was often employed as a metaphorical presentation of meditation. In the interplay between the scene and the poet's mind lay the quintessence of his poetry.

The setting for many of Wang's most famous poems was a villa that Wang acquired in the early 740s that once belonged to the early Tang poet Song Zhiwen (d. 712). Located in the Zhongnan Mountain area in the countryside surrounding the capital, the villa provided a resort with wonderful scenery for his reclusive and artistically productive life. *Anthology of the Wang River,* a collection of poems by Wang and his friend Pei Di, was based on their excursions in the extensive villa gardens and vicinity.

Not much is known about Wang Wei's paintings because only imitations have survived. Although *The Snowy Brooks* has been regarded as representative of Wang's work, a false attribution to Wang makes no guarantee that it is at all indicative of Wang's painting style.

2405

Fu Sheng, as painted in this portrait by Tang dynasty artist and poet Wang Wei.

Su Shi's (1037–1101) famous evaluation of Wang Wei—"If one savours Mojie's [Wang Wei's] poetry, there is painting in it; if one gazes at Mojie's painting, there is poetry in it" (Yang 2007, 191)— guides us in appreciating Wang's work and provides at the highest level of Chinese poetry and painting.

Timothy Wai Keung CHAN

Further Reading

Barnstone, W., Barnstone, T., & Xu Haixin. (Trans). (1991). *Laughing lost in the mountains: Poems of Wang Wei.* Hanover, MA: University Press of New England.

Carré, P. (1989). *Les Saisons bleues: L'oeuvre de Wang Wei, poète et peintre* [The blue seasons: The works of the poet-painter Wang Wei]. Paris: Phébus.

Owen, S. (1981). Wang Wei: The artifice of simplicity. In S. Owen (Ed.), *The great age of Chinese poetry: The high T'ang* (pp. 27–51). New Haven, CT: Yale University Press.

Wagner, M. (1981). *Wang Wei.* Boston: G. K. Hall.

Yang Jingqing. (2007). *The Chan interpretations of Wang Wei's poetry: A critical review.* Hong Kong: Chinese University Press.

Yu, Pauline. (1981). *The poetry of Wang Wei: New translations and commentary.* Bloomington: Indiana University Press.

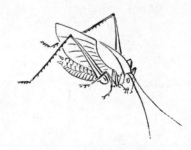

WANG Xianzhi

Wáng Xiànzhī　王献之

344–388 CE　Calligrapher

Wang Xianzhi 王献之, the youngest of Wang Xizhi's 王羲之 seven sons, was the only male in the family to follow in his father's footsteps as a calligrapher. But the style Xianzhi created, called *yibishu* 一笔书, or one-stroke writing, was unique and difficult to match, and it eventually elevated him beyond his father's fame.

Wang Xianzhi (also known as "Wang Zijing") was the seventh and youngest son of the master calligrapher Wang Xizhi (303?–379? CE); father and son are called the "two Wangs" of Chinese calligraphy. Xianzhi's ancestors lived in Shangdong Province until his grandfather relocated to Shaoxing in Zhejiang Province, where Xianzhi was born. Unlike his father, who was adept in almost all calligraphic styles, such as standard (*kai*), running (*xing*), and cursive (*cao*), the junior Wang excelled at first only in cursive script.

Xianzhi was born when his father was forty-one. When his father died, Xianzhi was seventeen. Xianzhi then followed Zhangzhi (?–361 CE) as his teacher in the art of calligraphy. By combining running and cursive scripts Xianzhi created a style for which he became famous—later critics called it *yibishu* (one-stroke writing)—in which characters connect in one brushstroke in a free-flowing style. The *yibishu* became a model for calligraphic connoisseurs and practitioners who revered Wang Xianzhi's accomplishments more than those of his father. Some of Wang Xianzhi's famous works are available to us through traced copies, stone engravings, ink rubbings, and handwritten copies. Zhao Mengfu (1254–1322 CE), a later calligrapher, described Wang's "Luoshenfu" (Song to the Goddess of the Riven Luo) in the standard script as "spirited and untrammeled, the tonality flows in motion" (Ecke, 1971). The thirteen-line fragment that survived shows a certain casualness and is less compact than the writing by Wang Xizhi.

Wang Xianzhi's "Duck Head Pill Note" (*yatouwantie*, fifteen characters reproduced on silk in the Tang dynasty [618–907 CE]) and "Mid-Autumn Note" (*zhongqiutie*, twenty-two characters), both in the cursive-running style, were described by Mi Fu (1051–1107), the famous Song calligrapher, as "natural, true, transcendental, and untrammeled" (Harriet and Fong, 1999, 51). The Qing emperor Qianlong (reigned 1736–1795) included Wang's works in his imperial collection and considered them a national treasure. The "Mad Cursive Script" (Kuangao) school, with Zhang Xu (flourished 713–740 CE) and Huaisu (737–798 CE) as its representatives, was also influenced by the work of Wang Xianzhi.

Wang Xianzhi served as secretary-general of the imperial court. Known for righteousness and integrity, Wang once refused an order by Xie An, the grand councilor, to write an inscription for a new hall. His reason was that the hall was built against the will of the people.

Legend tells that Wang had two wives and a concubine. His first wife was the daughter of his maternal uncle. They had a harmonious relationship until the Jin emperor selected Wang as his son-in-law; Wang was then compelled to divorce his wife and marry Princess Xinan. In

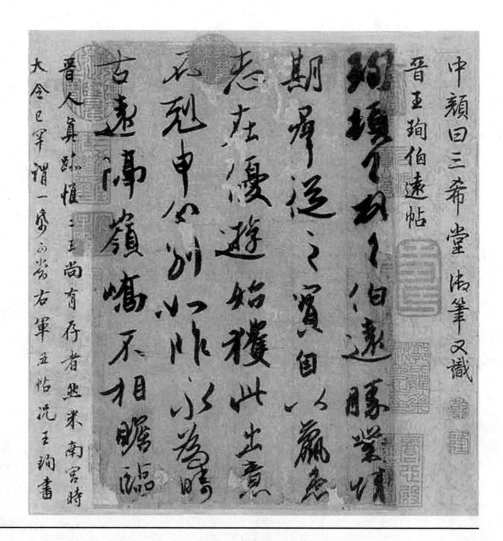

Wang Xianzhi created a unique style of calligraphy, *yibishu*, in which the characters were connected in one flowing brushstroke.

his later years he took in a concubine, Taoye, with whom he had a meaningful relationship. Their love was the subject of a song he wrote for her entitled "Song of Taoye."

Fatima WU

Further Reading

Chen Tu. (2003). *Chinese calligraphy: Cultural China series* (R. Lingjuan, Trans.). Beijing: China International Press.

Ecke, T.Y. (1971). *Chinese calligraphy*. Boston: David R. Godine Publishers.

Harrist, R. E., Jr., & Fong, W. C. (1999). *The embodied image: Chinese calligraphy from the John B. Elliott collection*. Princeton, NJ: Art Museum, Princeton University.

Wang Xianzhi. (n.d.). Retrieved January 10, 2008, from http://big5.cent.com.cn/China/surname/tribe/cw/wang-3.htm

Zhao Lengyue. (1993). *Ten calligraphers*. Taipei, Taiwan: World Cultures Publishers.

WANG Xizhi

Wang Xizhī 王羲之

303?–379? CE   Calligrapher

Wang Xizhi 王羲之, referred to as the "Saint of Calligraphy" in China, was the author of the famous *Lantingjixu* 兰亭集序 or *Preface to the Orchid Pavilion Gathering*. A rare talent who was adept to almost all calligraphic styles, Wang was an inspiration to past and present calligraphers and connoisseurs.

Wang Xizhi (also known as "Wang Shaoyi") was born during the politically chaotic Jin dynasty, (265–420 CE) part of the North and South dynasties period (220–589 CE). During this unsettled period members of the Wang family of calligraphers and literati moved from their native area in Shandong Province and relocated to Zhejiang Province in the south. Wang's father, who came from a line of respected calligraphers, was a minor court official and the first calligraphy teacher of his son.

As Wang grew he proved to be a man of character. One anecdote tells of how he was chosen to be the son-in-law of Commander Shi. The latter announced that an interview would be conducted in the prime minister's residence to select the right man for his daughter. Young men of letters flocked to the palace dressed in their best clothes. Wang, not anxious to please, arrived late in casual clothing. He managed to find a seat near a bed. Because of the heat, he untied his belt and bared his abdomen. Such behavior marked him as different from the rest, and he left an impression of spontaneity on those who were present. When Shi heard this report, he decided to give Wang his daughter's hand.

Following the Confucian tradition, Wang received a military position at court as general of the right. However, his real interest lay in art, especially the calligraphy by which he was known. When young, he had practiced calligraphy with a female master named Madam Wei (272–349 CE). Later he perfected nearly all calligraphic styles, such as standard (*kai*), running (*xing*), and cursive (*cao*), and became known as the "the saint of calligraphy." His most famous work was the "Preface to the Orchid Pavilion Gathering" (*Lantingji Xu*), done on the third day of the third month in 353 CE when he and about forty scholar friends met together in the Orchid Pavilion in Shaoxing, Zhejiang Province, to celebrate the Spring Festival. After most of his friends wrote poems for the occasion, Wang, intoxicated by alcohol, added a preface written in the running script. The calligraphy he did that day was outstanding, and the brushstrokes were often described as *"longwo hutiao"* or "Leaning Dragon and Leaping Tiger." Wang tried to copy it afterward, but he could never achieve that ease and style again. This particular work was such a treasure to connoisseurs that the Tang dynasty (618–907 CE) emperor, Li Shimin (Taizong, reigned 626–649 CE), who obtained the original after much difficulty, ordered it to be buried with him at death.

Other famous pieces by Wang include "Essay on Yue I," dated 348 CE in standard script, and "Three Passages of Calligraphy: *Pingan, Heru and Fengju*" and "Short Note of a Sunny Day after a Pleasant Snow," both in running script. Out of the thousands of Wang's calligraphic pieces, only a small fraction survived, thanks to the traced copies, stone engravings, ink rubbings, and hand copies by later calligraphy masters. For more than a thousand years Wang's

Calligraphy by Wang Xizhi, father and first teacher of master calligrapher Wang Xianzhi. Father and son were called the "two Wangs" of this revered Chinese art form.

calligraphy has been used as the example for all who practice this art. He and his son, Wang Xianzhi (344–388 CE), are called the "two Wangs" in Chinese calligraphy.

Wang, disillusioned by the political upheaval of his era, retired early at the age of forty-nine and switched to neo-Daoism to pursue a life of simplicity and peace. Three stories of his death are told. The first is that he died of an illness at age fifty-nine. Another claims that Wang was executed by the emperor when he refused to come to court. The last one, which most critics feel is valid, tells of Wang's pursuit of immortality by way of alchemy and his subsequent death by poison.

Fatima WU

Further Reading

Ecke, T. Y. (1971). *Chinese calligraphy*. Boston: David R. Godine Publishers.

Harrist, R. E., Jr., & Fong, Wen C. (1999). *The embodied image: Chinese calligraphy from the John B. Elliot collection*. Princeton, NJ: Art Museum, Princeton University.

Hsu, K.-Y. (Trans.). (n.d.). *A reproduction of the Lan-T'ing calligraphy scroll by Wang Hsi-chih (321–379)*. Taipei, Taiwan: China Color Printing.

Ou Shaoyou. (Ed.). (1990). *The biography of Wang Xizhi*. Taipei, Taiwan: Kezu Publishers.

Zhao Lengyue. (Ed.). (1993). *Ten calligraphers*. Taipei, Taiwan: World Cultures Publishers.

閒談 chat

China changes constantly, and the *Encyclopedia of China* will change and grow, too. Berkshire's authors and editors welcome questions, comments, and corrections: china.updates@berkshirepublishing.com.

Wang Yangming School

Wáng Yángmíng Xuéxiào 王阳明学校

Neo-Confucianism combined principles from the three major ancient philosophies of China—Daoism, Buddhism, and Confucianism—and the Wang Yangming school was one of its dominant and most influential movements.

The Wang Yangming school was named after the philosopher Wang Yangming (1472–1529), who began to critique the Confucian concept that material things alone are worthy of investigation. Instead, Wang advocated broadening of the definition of the "thing" to include not only materiality, but also moral precepts and ideas or thoughts.

Neo-Confucianism

The need for Confucianism to address ideas that had become established in Chinese society, namely Daoism and Buddhism, led to a synthesis of sorts during the Song Dynasty (960–1279). The pragmatic approach of the Confucians, with its concern for the here-and-now and the betterment of the individual and society, was tempered first by the Daoist view that human beings were essentially good and required institutions and a society that would permit this goodness to exert itself; and second, by the Buddhist notion that the world was both illusory and filled with suffering, and one's concern should be on being rid of this pain. These three dominant philosophies

amalgamated to fashion what is commonly known as neo-Confucianism.

One of the hallmarks of neo-Confucian thought was the explication of unity within duality, that is, a thing possesses two opposing elements, which in their dissimilarity unite as one in order to give the thing its being. Neo-Confucianism also maintained that the self can be morally constructed by way of educating and contemplating human intuition, which was innate to all people.

Neo-Confucianism focused on the investigation of material things by seeking to place the individual within his/her social context. This could only be done by cultivating the mind in order to affect change for the better upon those things that surrounded and influenced the individual, namely, society and government. A fulfilled life was one which sought to perfect the self in order to perfect society and the state.

Wang Yangming

In contrast to the contemporary neo-Confucian thought, Wang Yangming theorized that material things were in truth comprised of three elements: material reality; the idea of that reality, that is, its intellectual expression; and the moral import of the thing. For example, a friend is a person, a word, and a moral relationship (Is the friend good or bad?). Wang sought to combine materialism and idealism in order to arrive at a moral understanding of human actions. In this way, he was very much grounded in the Confucian notion that people must continually strive for betterment. But he wanted to know how to achieve this betterment; it could not be attained by merely following ancient sages and one's ancestors as Confucians would have it. Rather, Wang placed the onus on the individual: It is up to each person to construct mental moral principles, intellectual moral things that may be used as guides to a better life. Such an understanding further led Wang to define what the actions of the mind may be. He said that the life of the mind involves not only cold, hard facts, but also deep human emotions, such as joy, sadness, and empathy. The mind becomes that location where dissimilarities unite and intellectual activity merges with the emotions. The resultant unity is the surest guide to truth and a truthful life. Wang stressed the necessity of knowing the mind and the self by educating the intuition; this means that it is the moral responsibility of the individual to educate the mind so that she or he will intuitively choose the morally right action for his or her own and the good of the world.

A portrait of Wang Yangming, the philosopher who expanded the concept of the "thing" beyond materiality to embrace moral precepts and ideas.

Wang, of course, did not ignore the importance given by Confucians to right actions. But he suggested that such actions must be guided by the mind. He linked action to both knowledge and morality. Indeed, one cannot have action without knowledge, nor can one have knowledge without action; by extension, all knowledge is morality because the chief end of knowledge is to better the self, society and the state. Betterment requires a principle of morality, in that the lesser is raised to a higher level. This is more than mere tautology (needless repetition of an idea), for Wang pointed to a larger precept: the unity of all things. By this principle, humans and their actions are part of materiality, which is both action and idea, and it is through action (or the manifestation of ideas) that humans become part of the world around them and even part of the universe. Thus, that which is good for the individual is also good for society, the world at large, and the cosmos. Each component must work harmoniously within its larger context to bring about an essential unity of all creation, because all things, in fact, are one body. Each thing shares a pattern (the *li*), or a way of being, with another thing, just as we eat living things in order to live. For example, theoretical physics states that all things in the universe are constructed from an elementary particle, called the Higgs boson, or what Wang would call a pattern.

The concept that all things are united by shared patterns is an important contribution of the Wang Yangming school. With this theory, it broke free from the Confucian valorization of the family: Confucian thinkers such as Mencius (371–289 BCE) said that society and the structures of the world were versions of the family. In the place of such an analogy, Wang suggested that the relationship between things is not a familial one at all; rather, it is a far more intimate harmony of similar patterns. The universe—all of creation and reality itself—is not a family, it is a single body.

In order to know and comprehend this harmony, Wang refined the concept of the mind. First there exists the mind of the Way—which may be defined as a state of calm and lucidity, which permits the mind to apprehend universality (the Principle); that is, universality and the individual become one so that individual begins to carry out the will of heaven (the Principle)—and second there exists the human mind. The former is the mind in its purest primordial state. This is the mind in itself, while the

Historical illustration of dragons and wise men. Wang believed that despite class status or privilege wisdom was attainable for all.

human mind is that which has lost its purity by becoming ensnared in selfish desires. The object of education and of contemplation is to once again purify the mind and return it to its original state, free from all selfish entanglements, so that it might realize its essential role in, and its implicit bond with, the moral order of the self and of the universe. For Wang, such a liberated mind alone could successfully guide the individual to the good. As is obvious, Wang's debt to Buddhism was apparent in this explanation; however, he entirely negated the Buddhist self-centered ideal of purifying the soul in order to gain freedom from pain and suffering by nullifying individuality, leading the soul to escape into nothingness. For Wang, purification of the mind was not an end in itself, nor was it selfish to flee from the world. Instead, Wang described a more inclusive approach because he did not neglect the Confucian demand for a pragmatic view of action. A pure mind is the only possible guarantor of morality, because to see all things as one body is also to care for that body fully and completely. In brief, the school of thought that he established may be summarized thus: Personal morality alone saves the world and the universe. The influence of the Wang Yangming school reached its apex during the late Ming and the Qing periods. In present-day China, the influence of the school has waned, although its stress on education as a way of bettering the self and society remains as a dominant mindset.

Nirmal DASS

Further Reading

Ching, Julia & Wang, Yangming. (Ed.). (1976). *To acquire wisdom: The way of Wang Yang-ming.* New York: Columbia University Press.

Cua, A. S. (1982). *The unity of knowledge and action: A study of Wang Yang-ming's moral psychology.* Honolulu: University of Hawaii Press.

The Words of Wang Yangming

There can be little doubt that among the new trends in the Ming dynasty (1368–1644) the teachings and personal example of Wang Yangming were to have the most explosive effect.

Whenever I think of people's degeneration and difficulties I pity them and have a pain in my heart. I overlook my own unworthiness and wish to save them by this teaching. And I do not know the limits of my ability. When people see me trying to do this, they join one another in ridiculing, insulting, and cursing me as insane . . . Of course, there are cases when people see their fathers, sons, or brothers falling into a deep abyss and getting drowned. They cry, crawl, go naked and barefooted, stumble, and fall. They hang on to dangerous cliffs and go down to save them. Some gentlemen who see them behave like this . . . consider them insane because they cry, stumble, and fall as they do. Now to stand aside and make no attempt to save the drowning, while mocking those who do, is possible only for strangers who have no natural feelings of kinship, but even then they will be considered to have no sense of pity and to be no longer human beings. In the case of a father, son, or brother, because of love he will surely feel an ache in his head and a pain in his heart, run desperately until he has lost his breath, and crawl to save them. He will even risk drowning himself. How much less will he worry about whether people believe him or not?

Source: de Bary, W. T. & Bloom, I. (1999). *Sources of Chinese tradition, vol. 1.* New York: Columbia University Press, 842–843

De Bary, W. T. (1988). *The Message in the mind in Neo-Confucianism.* New York: Columbia University Press.

De Bary, W. T. (Ed.). (1970). *Self and society in Ming thought.* New York: Columbia University Press.

Ivanhoe, P. J. (2002). *Ethics in the Confucian tradition: The thought of Mengzi and Wang Yangming* Indianapolis, IN: Hackett.

Kim, H. Y. (1996). *Wang Yang-ming and Karl Barth: A Confucian-Christian dialogue.* Lanham, MD: University of America Press.

Tu Wei-Ming. (1976). *Neo-Confucian thought in action: Wang Yang-ming's youth (1472–1509).* Berkeley and Los Angeles: University of California Press.

Wang Yangming. (1916). *The philosophy of Wang Yangming.* (F. G. Henke, Trans.). Chicago: Open Court.

Wang Yangming. (1985). *Instructions for practical living and other Neo-Confucian writing s.* (Wing-Tsit Chan, Trans.). New York: Columbia University Press.

Zhang Junmai. (1962). *Wang Yang-ming: Idealist philosopher of sixteenth century China.* Jamaica, NY: St. John's University Press.

WANG Yiting

Wáng Yītíng　王一亭

1867–1938　Painter and businessman

Wang Yiting was a businessman, painter, patron, and devout Buddhist who helped found numerous art societies throughout Shanghai and was active in the relief efforts of a disastrous 1923 earthquake in Japan.

Wang Yiting was born in Shanghai and began work as an apprentice in a picture-mounting shop, later becoming a comprador (intermediary) for a Japanese company. He was successful in his business career and served as chairman of the Shanghai Chamber of Commerce.

Wang Yiting was also a generous supporter of artists and helped to found many art societies in Shanghai. He was proficient in painting historical figures, folk legends, birds with flowers, animals, and landscapes and was renowned for his Buddhist figures and dragons.

In addition to his skill and participation in China's artistic scene, Wang Yiting also volunteered his services when an earthquake on 1 September 1923 struck the region of Kanto on the Japanese island of Honshu and devastated the city of Tokyo. Leading a relief effort that involved shipping much needed materials and organizing Buddhist prayer services, Wang was a huge asset to the Japanese during the tragic event and strengthened his connections with Japan.

In later life Wang became a devout Buddhist and once was president of the Chinese Buddhist Association.

Kuiyi SHEN

Further Reading

Andrews, J., Brown, C., Fraser, D., & Shen, Kuiyi. (2000). *Between the thunder and the rain: Chinese paintings from the Opium War through the Cultural Revolution, 1840–1979.* San Francisco: Echo Rock Ventures and Asian Art Museum of San Francisco.

Katz, P. R. (n. d.). The Religious Life of a Renowned Shanghai Businessman and Philanthropist, Wang Yiting Abstract retrieved February 9, 2009, from http://www.mh.sinica.edu.tw/k/urban_history/conference/pdf/abstract09.pdf

Tsao Hsing-yuan. (1998). A forgotten celebrity: Wang Zhen (1867–1938), businessman, philanthropist, and artist. In Ju-hsi Chou (Ed.), *Art at the close of China's empire* (pp. 94–109). Phoenix, AZ: Phoebus Occasional Papers in Art History.

Warring States Period

Zhànguó 战国

475–221 BCE

The tumultuous Warring States period led to the unification of China under the Qin dynasty in 221 BCE. The period also was the foundational era of Chinese philosophy.

The Warring States (*Zhanguo*) period (475–221 BCE) was a period of Chinese history that ended with the unification of China under the first emperor of the Qin dynasty (221–206 BCE) in 221 BCE. Although scholars agree that the Warring States period ended in 221, the date of its beginning is a matter of contention: Some place it in 481, when the chronicle known as *Chunqiu* (Springs and Autumns) draws to a close; others in 453, when the state of Jin was divided into three territories; still others in 403, when each of these three new states was formally recognized by the Zhou king. For the purposes of this discussion, the Warring States period begins in 475 BCE, the first year of the reign of Viscount Xiang of Zhao, one of the three states that supplanted Jin. The Warring States period constitutes the second half of the Eastern Zhou dynasty (770–221 BCE), whereas the first half of the Eastern Zhou dynasty is known as the "Spring and Autumn period" (770–476 BCE), after the chronicle of the same name.

The Eastern Zhou kings were recognized as the heaven-ordained rulers of the terrestrial world, but they were forced over the centuries to cede more and more power to the feudal lords occupying the lands around them. During this time the most powerful of the semi-independent statelets gradually conquered and annexed their neighbors, so that by the Warring States period, only eight contenders remained: Zhou, Qin, Qi, Chu, Zhao, Wei, Han, and Yan. In 256 BCE the last Zhou king, who was by this time nothing more than a figurehead, was finally deposed, and the Chinese world awaited the final victory of the state of Qin.

Political Changes

The political landscape of the Warring States period was determined by the intensification of several interrelated geopolitical processes that began in the Spring and Autumn period: the ongoing decline of centralized power, the rise of warlike and expansionist states with their own domestic and foreign policies, and the continual diminution in the number of autonomous states as the weakest were annihilated by the strongest. By Warring States times these underlying historical forces had brought about pervasive political, economic, social, and intellectual changes that radically transformed the character of Chinese life.

"Agriculture and war" became a popular slogan as states recognized the substantial benefits of a healthy economy and a mighty army. As the stakes of battle rose, the conception of war necessarily changed from a ritualized competition between educated aristocrats (as in the Spring and Autumn period) to a lawless and bloody struggle between infantry armies as large as could be mustered.

The logistical problems associated with raising, training, and supplying a massive army induced rulers to rethink their approach to governing their territories. Those rulers who could most fully exploit their resources gained a sizable advantage in the theater of war. Thus, the demands of battle led to the restructuring of the state as a vast production ground of people and munitions, maintained by an efficient and organized administration and serving a single king, to whom the entire population owed unquestioning allegiance. Kinship ties, ritual obligations, and traditional practice, which had been significant considerations guiding human action in earlier times, were now subordinated to the material requirements of the "warring state." In this manner the imperial model of Chinese statecraft was being forged even before the establishment of the empire itself. The governments of the Qin and Han (206 BCE–220 CE) dynasties were largely based on the precedents of the Warring States.

Birth of Chinese Philosophy

The Warring States period is celebrated as the foundational era of Chinese philosophy. Historians sometimes ask why such a tumultuous and perilous time provided the context for some of the most sophisticated philosophers in Chinese history, but the reasons for this intellectual burgeoning are not obscure. The competing lords valued any resource that might aid them in their quest for world dominion, and so they were willing to listen to new ideas. The old ways, after all, were leading the Zhou dynasty to assured extinction. The demand for original thinkers resulted in the growth of a new profession: "wandering persuaders" (*youshui*), who traveled freely from state to state in search of landed patrons, earning their bread alongside diplomats, generals, diviners, and other educated specialists.

The two foremost philosophical schools in Warring States times were those of the Confucians and the Mohists. The former were followers of the ethical worldview laid down by Confucius (551–479 BCE); the latter group was founded by Mozi, or Master Mo (Mo Di, c. 480–c. 390 BCE), who preached a philosophy of "universal love" (*jian'ai*). The Confucians and Mohists were irreconcilable enemies—Confucians could never accept the Mohist tenet that one should love the father of one's neighbor as one loves one's own father—but they were alike in that their doctrines did not always coincide with the desires of the lords whom they served. Confucians, for example, believed that loyal advisers should remonstrate (*jian*)

A "money tree" sculpture from the Warring States period of the late Zhou dynasty, Chu Culture, Sichuan Provincial Museum. PHOTO BY JOAN LEBOLD COHEN.

with their lord when he is in error, and their outspoken criticism often alienated their superiors. Mohists, for their part, believed that human acquisitiveness is at the root of all suffering in the world, and they actively disrupted campaigns of conquest in the hope of deterring warlords from preying on their neighbors.

Other philosophical orientations were more amenable to the aspirations of rulers. Political philosophers such as Shan Buhai (flourished 354–340 BCE), Shen Dao (b. c. 360 BCE), and Han Fei (d. 233 BCE) formulated an ideal of statecraft (often misleadingly called "legalism") that relied on standardized laws, proto-bureaucratic administrative systems, and unfailing adherence to the protocols of reward and punishment. The political aspect of philosophy was so important that even the *Laozi* (or *Daode*

Historical illustration of Kwante, the god of war.

jing), a text whose primary purpose is to elucidate the benign cosmological notion (an idea based on a branch of metaphysics that deals with the nature of the universe) of the "way" (*dao*), takes pains to point out the political applications of its teachings.

The term *Warring States* is usually said to derive from *Stratagems of the Warring States* (*Zhanguo ce*), a collection of anecdotes about the period compiled by Liu Xiang (79–78 BCE). But the term *zhanguo* was already used in an essay by the statesman Jia Yi (201–169 BCE); this suggests that the era was known as the "Warring States" almost as soon as it had ended.

Paul R. GOLDIN

Further Reading

Graham, A. C. (1989). *Disputers of the Tao: Philosophical argument in ancient China*. La Salle, IL: Open Court.

Hsu Cho-yun. (1965). *Ancient China in transition: An analysis of social mobility, 722–222 BC*. Stanford, CA: Stanford University Press.

Lewis, M. E. (1990). *Sanctioned violence in early China*. Albany: State University of New York Press.

Lewis, M. E. (1999). *Writing and authority in early China*. Albany: State University of New York Press.

Li Xueqin. (1985). *Eastern Zhou and Qin civilizations* (K. C. Chang, Trans.). New Haven, CT: Yale University Press.

Loewe, M., & Shaughnessy, E. L. (Eds.). (1999). *The Cambridge history of ancient China: From the origins of civilization to 221 BC*. Cambridge, U.K.: Cambridge University Press.

Water Conservation

Shuǐlì 水利

Chinese practices for regulating the water supply, known as water conservation 水利 (shuili), are as old as China's civilization. The three major objectives of water conservation are irrigation, flood control, and transportation. The commitment to intensive water management has shaped Chinese history.

Access to fresh water is essential to human life. Domesticated plants also require water to survive, ideally in precisely regulated amounts. But the location, quantity, and timing of the water supply are highly variable. China's monsoon climate, its location amid the watersheds for much of the eastern Himalaya snowpack, and its ecological diversity guarantee a water supply that fluctuates dramatically from place to place and from season to season. Control of water is at the heart of farming and, indeed, civilization itself, and water engineering is one of the areas in which humans have struggled most vigorously to free themselves from constraints imposed by nature.

Turning Water to Advantage

Water conservation is known in Chinese as *shuili*, which literally means, "turning water to advantage." The objective of water conservation is to reduce the risk of flood and drought. The wet-rice agriculture of south China requires fields to be drained and flooded at different times in the life cycle of the crop. Water conservation for rice requires methods for ensuring the availability of water when needed and for letting it in and out of the fields when necessary. Historically, both drought and flood were concerns of the Chinese. Archaeologists have excavated drainage canals at the late Neolithic village of Banpo, which flourished around 7,000 years ago in the vicinity of modern-day Xi'an. And queries about rainfall and flooding are a preoccupation of the oracle bones, China's first written documents, produced from the thirteenth to the eleventh century BCE. From the emergence of their civilizations, people in China devoted substantial energy to regulating the flow of water in riverbeds and to moving water out of its natural courses and into new channels and pools that met their needs for farming, transportation, and settlement. These activities have profoundly shaped Chinese history.

Irrigation and Drainage

Irrigation is the name for the set of technologies devoted to bringing water to places where it is needed for growing crops, while *drainage systems* channel excess water out of fields. In China irrigation and drainage were practiced widely, beginning in the Neolithic era. By the time of the Song dynasty (960–1279), the world's most intensive and highly engineered agricultural economy, irrigation and drainage allowed people to grow crops where it would otherwise have been impossible, particularly in the Yangzi (Chang) delta. Irrigated and drained agriculture

Plan of an irrigation survey problem by Chin Chiu-Shao, 1247. The total length of the parallel canal is given as 118 *li* or 59 km. The irrigated fields are marked with the character *tien*, the major river dyke is called *an*, and the minor dykes *cheng*. Source: Needham, Joseph, (1959). *Science and Civilisation in China.*

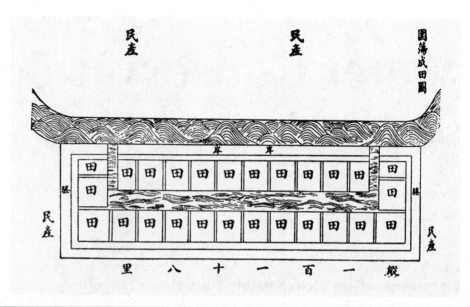

supported the commercial revolution of the Song and the population growth of that and subsequent eras.

Irrigation systems include an intake, where water enters an engineered system from its natural course, and a series of branch canals that bring water directly to fields. Many systems also include gates that control the flow of water through the branch canals. Drainage systems rely on pipes or canals that move water downhill and frequently also involve piling up earth to create fields that are raised above the water table and isolated from the surrounding marshes by bunds (embankments) and polders.

The use of polders (low-elevation fields protected by earthen dikes) appears in Chinese texts dating to the Spring and Autumn period (770–476 BCE), a millennium before their emergence in Northern Europe. During the Song dynasty, the introduction of new strains of early ripening rice made double cropping possible, and there were many important improvements in fertilization and cultivation techniques. Water conservation was an essential element of the new intensive rice agriculture of the Song; in turn the promise of high yields rewarded the massive labor that water conservation demanded. During the Northern Song (960–1126), an expansionist state directly sponsored projects to drain wetlands, fill lakes, and irrigate dry lands. By the Southern Song (1127–1279), the government and large landowners collaborated on polder construction on a massive scale that transformed the Yangzi delta into the most populous and wealthy region

of the empire and permitted intensive rice farming and commercial agriculture on the rich alluvial soil of former wetlands. The largest polders, which measured several square miles, were subdivided into smaller diked fields, demarcated by networks of natural streams and irrigation and drainage canals, and controlled by locks. Homes were situated on dikes and clustered around embankments. Boat traffic linked villages to the outside. Dikes also served as overland routes. Breaches in the earthen and stone walls would flood the villages as well as the fields. Hillsides were also leveled and diked to conserve soil, regulate water, and create terraces for wet-rice agriculture.

Water conservation initiatives often coordinated political, economic, and engineering challenges at a regional scale. Engineers had to regulate the speed, location, and timing of water flows throughout entire complex systems. It was often difficult to balance competing priorities, and individual water control projects were seldom effectively integrated. In the Yangzi delta, for instance, Song polders to the north of Lake Tai interfered with the lake's drainage, which resulted in flooding along the Grand Canal. When the canal managers drained excess water, they inundated adjacent fields, to the wrath of landowners, who built embankments to block the water. Until the fossil fuel era, irrigation systems were created and maintained by human and animal labor. According to *Song History,* one instance of restoring thirty-six silt-clogged canals around the city of Suzhou in 1158 CE required 3.3 million man-days, an equal number of strings of cash, and more than 100,000 bushels of grain. Some 6,000–7,000 farmer-solders were resettled in Suzhou to maintain the system and prevent flooding. Water engineering on the Chinese scale required abundant labor.

Coastal land reclamation deserves special mention. The Pearl River delta around modern Guangzhou and Hong Kong is a human creation, engineered by coastal farmers who learned to capture alluvial silt to create fertile agricultural land. Seawalls, which create barriers between ocean water and fresh water, have been an important feature of Chinese water conservation. The seawall that began to extend south of the Yangzi to the southern side of Hangzhou Bay in the Tang allowed a region of China larger than the Netherlands to be transformed from a land of shallow inlets, salt marshes, sandbars, and brackish creeks into a world of drained polders and navigable canals that supported population densities that were among the world's highest. Inside seawalls water becomes gradually less brackish, farmers can capture fertile sediments, and agriculture gradually overtakes salt production, fishing, and other coastal pursuits. However, like other massive waterworks, seawalls required constant attention to avert flooding and salinization. According to a 1347 description, rebuilding approximately 6 kilometers of seawall (out of a total length of 400 kilometers) required 63,000 tree trunks and close to a million cubic feet of stone.

Along with canals and polders, irrigation and drainage systems included reservoirs, pools that stored water for future use. In central and south China, where rainfall was abundant, water–storage ponds were ubiquitous from an early date. Han dynasty (206 BCE–220 CE) grave offerings, dating as early as the first century CE, include clay models that depict irrigation ponds separated from adjacent rice fields by dikes or bunds. By the Later Han (25220 CE), some historical Chinese reservoirs had become large collectively maintained structures that occupied more than 50 hectares. The Peony Dam, built under sponsorship by the state of Chu between 608 and 586 BCE, produced a great reservoir of nearly 100 kilometers in circumference that was maintained until the Tang dynasty (618–907 CE). Small reservoirs were dug by individuals who farmed fish and turtles and grew lotuses and water chestnuts at the same time that they irrigated their own rice fields. Dams and sluice gates built into watercourses controlled the flow of water in and out of reservoirs.

Flood Control

All rivers carry some load of silt, or sediment suspended in water. While silt is naturally washed into rivers through processes of erosion, its quantity is exacerbated by farming and deforestation. When rivers descend quickly, their flow is turbulent and rapid, and silt remains in suspension. But when they pass slowly across flat plains, silt is deposited on riverbeds. In the absence of human settlement, rivers periodically readjust their courses across broad alluvial plains—with fertile soils and broad, shallow waters

---

Song Ching-Chang's reconstruction of the earlier survey by Chin Chiu-Shao, paying closer attention to the reality of the geography, and adding more detail, such as the sluice-gate at the entrance to the parallel canal. The main canal runs along ½ *li* away from the river and takes 2½ *li* to reach that position. Source: Needham, Joseph, (1959). *Science and Civilisation in China*.

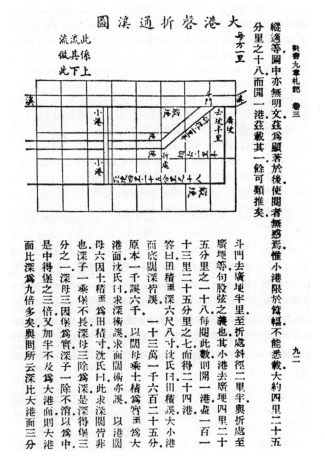

also optimized for agriculture—as their beds become full of silt and rise. The Huang (Yellow) River is the most sediment laden waterway in the world, carrying an average 1.6 billion tons of silt annually. It is an amount so great that the coastal plain at its mouth grew at a rate of 6 square kilometers per year by the 1200s and even more rapidly thereafter. Agrarian civilization emerged in the fertile loess sediment that the Huang River deposited in north China, and along with it came efforts to confine the river to a predictable course. Nevertheless, its levees, the earthen embankments that paralleled the river's course, failed more than 1,500 times beginning in the sixth century BCE. Indeed, they were sometimes breached intentionally as the court sacrificed people to the floods in order to stop invading troops or mitigate flooding elsewhere in the system. There have also been eighteen major changes of course. Death tolls from Huang River floods are among the highest associated with any natural disasters in human history. Other rivers, such as the Miju in Yunnan, also began to flood more frequently by the mid-Ming as sedimentation followed from land clearance and deforestation, and increasingly urgent regimes of dredging and levee construction thereafter, along with conflicts over property rights and land use. As the sediment-filled riverbeds rose, people constructed ever-higher levees, which eventually towered 20 feet or more over the landscape and raised the stakes of flooding as well.

When the Huang burst its dikes in the late twelfth century, it split into multiple branch streams that ran both north and south of the Shandong peninsula. Hydrologists decided to encourage this state of affairs by removing many levees to create a broader delta and a slower watercourse. While this solution reduced the likelihood of disastrous floods, it increased total sediment buildup and the overall cost of water management. In the late sixteenth century, Pan Jixun engineered the course of the river around its confluence with the Huai and the Grand Canal to eliminate the multiple channels, force the river into a single route, and constrict the channel that remained. His activities—building 1,200,000 million feet of earthen embankment, 30,000 feet of stone embankment, and four stone spillways; dredging 115,000 feet of riverbed; stopping 139 breaches; and planting 830,000 willow trees to stabilize the tops of the dikes—served to increase the velocity of the water flow and so scour out silt at this most important junction. Even after Pan Jixun's accomplishments, the maintenance work of dredging and diking in this vicinity required half a million workers and 800,000 ounces of silver annually; and sediment, simply deposited further downstream, remained a challenge.

Transportation Canals

Water transportation was about twenty times cheaper than overland transportation before the age of fossil fuels. In the lower Yangzi, natural watercourses and drainage and irrigation canals required few alterations to be used as transportation routes. But elsewhere massive earth-moving projects and innovations in hydrological engineering were required to create navigable waterways. The lure of long-distance commerce and travel made the outlay of labor that this involved a worthy investment. All of China's great natural waterways flow from west to east, and canals were the lifeline linking the distinct physiographic and cultural regions of north and south China into a single, integrated empire. In 809 an imperial official named Li Ao, traveling with his pregnant wife, conducted a nine-month trip from Luoyang to Guangzhou almost entirely by water. Canals were used for transportation, drainage, sewage, mechanical power, defense, and irrigation, aims that were sometimes in competition with one another.

Transportation canals in China have a long history. The Wild Goose Canal linked the states of Song, Zhang, Chen, Cai, Cao, and Wei during the Warring States period (475–221 BCE). By 130 BCE a 124-kilometer canal terminating in the Han capital facilitated grain shipments and was used for irrigation. But the Grand Canal was the single achievement in Chinese canal building. More than 1,000 miles long, the Grand Canal allowed rice and other products of the wealthy south to support the opulent courts of the north and the vast northern armies that confronted nomad power on the steppes. It integrated all of China into a single economy, empire, and culture. To this day it is the longest canal in the world. The Grand Canal is closely associated with Emperor Sui Yangdi, who unified China in 589 after more than 300 years of warfare. Between 605 and 609, he directed efforts to link and straighten existing canals into a single system that connected the Huai

Transportation canals of all sizes have a long history in China.

PHOTO BY JOAN LEBOLD COHEN.

to the Huang River. The Grand Canal was extended and improved during the Tang dynasty, as the court turned increasingly to the south for its supplies. When the Mongol Yuan dynasty (1279–1368) moved the capital north and east to Beijing, the canal was extended yet again. From the thirteenth to the nineteenth centuries, it remained a significant route for trade and communication, particularly the transport of the annual grain tribute from south to north. In 1793 Britain's Macartney Embassy traveled the canal to Beijing with a crew of artists and naturalists who left a vivid record of this extraordinary waterway. Nevertheless, ecological decline set in by the turn of the nineteenth century. The system collapsed altogether by the 1820s, and in 1832 troops were needed to quell an uprising of peasants who had rallied against flooding along its disintegrating course.

Maintaining the Grand Canal inspired hydrological innovation throughout the imperial era. During the Tang, Liu Yan discovered how to manage currents and earthworks to permit the Grand Canal to meet the

Huang River. Pan Jixun's efforts to reduce silt buildup in the Huang were also directed at maintaining the Grand Canal, though some other efforts to stabilize the Canal produced unintended hydrological consequences, such as sediment buildup along tributary streams. In the early 1700s, Zhang Pengge improved the canal's lock mechanisms and dredging regimes to mitigate the massive floods that plagued agricultural lands along the southern part of the canal's path.

Water Conservation and the History of China

The study of water conservation in Chinese history, at least in Western languages, is closely associated with the theories of the German-born historian and sinologist Karl Wittvogel (1896–1988), who argued that flood control was the formative activity that fostered a strong—in his words "despotic"—imperial state in China. Wittvogel overlooked many details that have become apparent to subsequent scholars. Water-control systems come in all sizes. Sometimes even the most heavily engineered of agricultural environments arose organically through centuries of small-scale collective activity with no state intervention. A great deal of water engineering was orchestrated according to local collective action, not by an authoritarian state. For instance, at the Dujiangyan waterworks in Sichuan, and at the Sangyuan polder in Guangdong, customary village associations and publicly selected representatives apportioned irrigation water among the various fields. Likewise, many constituencies needed to come together to allow the construction of Yangzi delta polders during the Song. An ambitious state in search of tax revenues, land owners seeking to increase property values, local officials seeking fame, and a growing population of civilians and military colonists eager for public works employment all played a role in water management in imperial China. All of these interests needed to be aligned for water conservation initiatives to succeed. By the Southern Song, water conservation in the lower Yangzi was funded jointly by the state and private investors, and labor was often voluntary and paid for in cash. Even the spectacular projects orchestrated from the court proceeded by trial and error, grand initiatives in one place producing unintended consequences in another.

An engineered water regime truly required not a despotic state so much as a perpetual, consultative, expensive and backbreaking commitment to the everyday maintenance of an inherently unstable and entirely artificial environment. It also required social and technological solutions for managing conflicts over priorities. The tension between the objectives of flood control, transportation, and irrigation were acute. For instance, the Huang River dikes were often breached intentionally by farmers seeking to irrigate their wheat fields. Finally, once any system was in place, it was only by dredging channels and building up earthworks that people could forestall disastrous, fatal floods. Once dense populations depended upon intensive agriculture that required water management, there was no going back.

Bracketing this critique, Wittvogel deserves credit for pioneering work on the primal role of water engineering in the development of China's empire and civilization. He and his successors have ensured that understanding the complex systems that human intervention has brought to bear on the movement of water remains a topic at the forefront of the study of imperial China. Water conservation is crucial for exploring many topics in Chinese history, including agriculture and its intensification, labor, technology, the commercial economy, environmental history, and state power.

Ruth MOSTERN

Presentation about the Water Conservancy Project at Yangzhou, 1979.
PHOTO BY JOAN LEBOLD COHEN.

Further Reading

Benn, C. (2004). *China's golden age: Everyday life in the Tang dynasty*. Oxford, U.K.: Oxford University Press.

Boserup, E. (1965). *The conditions of agricultural growth: The economics of agrarian change under population pressure*. London: G. Allen and Unwin; Chicago: Aldine.

Bray, F. (1986). *The rice economies: Technology and development in Asian societies*. Boston: Blackwell.

Elvin, M. (2004). *Retreat of the elephants: An environmental history of China*. New Haven, CT: Yale University Press.

Elvin, M. (1977). Market towns and waterways: The county of Shang-hai from 1480 to 1910. In G. W. Skinner (Ed.), *The city in late imperial China*. Palo Alto, CA: Stanford University Press.

Elvin, M., & Liu, T. (Eds.). (1998). *Sediments of time: Environment and society in Chinese history*. Cambridge, U.K.: Cambridge University Press.

Fan, I. et al. (2005). *Chinese civilization in time and space: Changes in the course of the Yellow River*. Retrieved January 31, 2008, from http://ccts.sinica.edu.tw/animation/river5.htm

Finnane, A. (2004). *Speaking of Yangzhou: A Chinese city, 1550–1850*. Cambridge, MA: Harvard University Press.

Hsu Cho-yun, Xu Zhuoyun, & Dull, J. L. (1980). *Han agriculture: The formation of early Chinese agrarian economy*. Seattle: University of Washington Press.

Leonard, J. K. (1996). *Controlling from afar: The Daoguang Emperor's management of the Grand Canal crisis, 1824–1826*. Ann Arbor: Center for Chinese Studies, University of Michigan.

Marks, R. (1997). *Tigers, rice, silk and silt: Environment and economy in late imperial south China*. Cambridge, U.K.: Cambridge University Press.

Mihelich, M. A. (1979). *Polders and the politics of land reclamation in southeast China during the Northern Sung dynasty (960–1126)*. Doctoral dissertation, Cornell University.

Needham, J., with Wang Ling & Lu Gwei-djen. (1971). *Science and civilisation in China 4. III: Civil engineering and nautics*. Cambridge, U.K.: Cambridge University Press.

Peyrefitte, A. (1993). *The collision of two civilizations: the British expedition to China in 1792–4*. (J. Rothschild, Trans.). London: Harvill.

Scarborough, V. (2003). *The flow of power: Ancient water systems and landscapes*. Santa Fe, NM: School of American Research.

Sinclair, K. (1987). *The Yellow river: A 5000 year journey through China*. Los Angeles: Knapp Press.

Strassberg, R. E. (1994). *Inscribed landscapes: Travel writing from imperial China*. Berkeley: University of California Press.

Stuermer, J. R. (1980). *Polder construction and the pattern of land ownership in the T'ai-hu basin during the Southern Sung dynasty*. Doctoral dissertation, University of Pennsylvania.

Tuo, Tuo. ([1345] 1977) *Songshi* [Song history]. Beijing: Zhonghua shuju.

Van Slyke, L. (1988). *Yangtze: Nature, history and the river*. Palo Alto, CA: Stanford University Press.

Wittvogel, K. (1957). *Oriental despotism: A comparative study of total power*. New Haven, CT: Yale University Press.

Xiong, Victor Cunrui. (2006). *Emperor Yang of the Sui dynasty: His life, times, and legacy*. Albany: State University of New York Press.

Comprehensive index starts
in volume 5, page 2667.

Water Margin

Shuǐhǔzhuàn 水浒传

One of the four Chinese classic novels of the Ming and Qing dynasties, *Shui hu zhuan* (Biographies of Water Margin) is based on historical events, but its authorship is in dispute. The complex story involves a group of 108 rebels who plot against the royal government. Some of the rebels are so vividly presented that they have since become heroes of the Chinese.

Shui hu zhuan (Biographies of Water Margin), also called *Zhongyi Shui hu zhuan* (Faithful and Just Men of Water Margin), is one of the four classic novels of the Ming and Qing dynasties (1368–1644)—the others being *Dream of the Red Chamber, Journey to the West,* and *Romance of the Three Kingdoms.* Originally named *Jianghu haoke zhuan* (Robbers of Rivers and Lakes) and *Shui hu* (Water Margin) for short, this novel was translated into English as *All Men Are Brothers* by Pearl S. Buck (later a Nobel laureate) in the late 1920s and as *Outlaws of the Marsh* by Sidney Shapiro in the 1970s. *Shui hu* literally means "waterside," a reference to Mount Liang at today's Dongping Lake, the alleged base of operations for the rebel heroes depicted in the novel.

Water Margin's authorship is disputed. Some ascribe it to Shi Nai'an, some to Luo Guanzhong, and others to both. The most accepted theory is that Shi Nai'an wrote it and Luo Guanzhong rearranged it later. The biographies of the coauthors are largely speculative; the only known fact about them is that they lived some time during the Yuan (1279–1368) or Ming (1368–1644) dynasties.

The novel tells a tragic story about 108 people of different backgrounds who were forced to become rebel leaders on the lakeside Mount Liang. The book begins with treacherous officials of the Song court (960–1279) bullying their subordinates and their families, driving them into the camp of the Mount Liang rebels led by Song Jiang. Meanwhile others join the rebels for various reasons. After many a successful battle against the government army, Song Jiang and his men surrender after the emperor made them believe that they were being offered amnesty. The emperor then dispatches them to repulse the invasion of Liao, a kingdom established by the Nuchens north of Song, and to put down a series of peasant uprisings; many of the 108 rebels die. The rest are then killed with poisoned wine "gifted" them by the emperor.

Water Margin is based on a true event that took place from 1119 to 1121, when Song Jiang led his thirty-five fellow rebels in fighting the government. Stories about the event later found their way into compilations such as *Zuiweng tanlu* (Tales of a Drunken Man) and *Dasong Xuanhe yi-shi* (Incidents of the Xuanhe Era of the Great Song). By the Yuan dynasty, all the 108 rebels of *Water Margin* had appeared in popular dramas of the time known as *zaju* (miscellaneous plays). Apparently the novel *Water Margin* was a re-creation based upon all the above creative efforts predating it.

The original text of *Water Margin* is long lost, but

The stories in *Water Margin,* documenting the adventures of 108 bandits, became wildly popular in Japan in the 1800s. This illustration, by Kuniyoshi, helped introduce the work beyond the borders of China.

different block-printed editions, both simplified and detailed, remain. The detailed editions are more popular, and better known among them are the 120-chapter edition compiled and supplemented by Yang Dingjian around 1614, the 70-chapter edition edited by Jin Shengtan (1608-1661), and the 100-chapter edition published by Guo Xun during the reign of the Jiajing Emperor (1522-1566).

Water Margin is of great literary value, being the first Chinese chapter novel written in vernacular Chinese. It seamlessly weaves multiple individual lives into an organic whole and yet manages to create distinct personalities with characters such as Lin Chong, Lu Zhishen, Li Kun, and Wu Song. Its intriguing plots are full of twists and turns and packed with action.

Water Margin has been interpreted differently by different people in different times. It has been either dismissed as advocating banditry or welcomed as singing the praises of heroism. In the 1950s the book was regarded as an ode to peasant uprisings. In the 1970s, however, Mao Zedong condemned it for setting a negative example, even though it had been one of his favorite childhood books.

The stories from *Water Margin* are so popular that many efforts have been made to adapt them into dramas, movies and TV series. The 43-episode TV series *Shui hu zhuan,* directed by Zhang Shaolin in 2003, is the most popular, and inspired by its success a new, 120-episode TV series is in production.

Haiwang YUAN

Further Reading

Lu Naiyan. (1982). Shui hu zhuan [*Water Margin*]. In Zhongguo da bai ke quan shu [The Encolopedia of China]. Beijing: Zhongguo da bai ke quan shu chu ban she [The Encyclopedia of China Publishing House].

Chu, Mike S. Y. (1979). The *Water Margin* and its reception in the English speaking world. M.A. Thesis, University of Nebraska–Lincoln.

Hsia, Chih-tsing. (1980). *The classic Chinese novel: A critical introduction.* Bloomington: Indiana University Press.

Shi, Nai'an, Guanzhong Luo, & Jackson, J. H. (1976). *Water Margin.* Hong Kong: The Commercial Press.

Youd, D. M. (1993). True or false: Seventeenth-century conceptions of self and society in *Water Margin.* Thesis (A.B., Honors in East Asian Languages and Civilizations). Harvard University., Cambridge, MA.

Water Resources

Shuǐlì zīyuán 水利资源

With the advent of frequent water-pollution incidents such as algae blooms that make the water unusable for millions, the necessity of irrigation for more than 70 percent of its grain and cash crops, and a perennial water shortage, China's water resources are at the center of one of the most important legal reforms in modern Chinese governance.

More and more people in China, including Chinese officials, are beginning to approach their country's water supply as a vulnerable resource—one that is inexorably linked to their future—rather than a free natural resource to be used without restraint and consideration. In the first decade of the twenty-first century problems contributing to China's water sustainability can be generalized in three categories: shortage, pollution, and abuse.

Shortage

With a total volume of freshwater resources of 2.8 trillion cubic meters, trailing only Brazil, Russia, and Canada, China's water resources equate to 2,220 cubic meters per capita—just one-fourth of the world's average.

These limited water resources are unevenly distributed both spatially and temporally. Some 80.5 percent of China's water resources are concentrated south of the Yangzi (Chang) River, where only 46.5 percent of the

population lives on only 35.2 percent of the country's total arable farmland. The remaining 53.5 percent of the population is in the north, living on 64.6 percent of the arable farmland, and, by contrast, they have access to merely 19.5 percent of the water resources. Because about 71 percent of the volume of water in China relies on direct recharge by precipitation, waterfalls are vital to replenishing and sustaining China's water supply. Yet the average annual precipitation in China is 648 millimeters, 19 percent less than the world average of 800 millimeters (over land). While the precipitation is mostly concentrated in the four months from June to September during the flood season, which may amount to 70 percent of the annual total, this volume ranges in magnitude from more than 2,000 millimeters in the southeastern coastal areas to less than 200 millimeters in the northwestern hinterlands. In Ningxia Hui Autonomous Region, for example, annual precipitation is around 305 millimeters, while annual evaporation is as much as 2,000 millimeters. The precipitation drops further to 50 millimeters in the Tarim and Turpan basins in Xinjiang and Chaidamu Basin in Qinghai. For comparison, average annual precipitation in the central Sahara Desert is less than 25 millimeters, while that of Scotland is approximately 1,500 millimeters.

Similarly uneven distribution is seen in groundwater, which constitutes about one-third of China's freshwater resources. Southern China claims 67.7 percent of the total groundwater, leaving merely 32.3 percent to the arid north. Because groundwater accounts for 70 percent of the drinking water supply and 40 percent of agricultural irrigation, the uneven distribution aggravates the water shortage in northern China.

With rapid economic growth and urbanization, the water shortage has become even more acute. China's absolute urban population increased from 172 million in 1978 to 562 million—or 43 percent of the total—in 2005, and the demand for water is growing accordingly. According to the Ministry of Water Resources, China has an annual shortage of water totaling 40 billion cubic meters, while 2 to 2.6 million square meters of land area suffer draught. The water shortage costs 15 to 20 billion kilograms of grain production and more than 200 billion yuan of industrial output value every year. Meanwhile, over 70 million people across China have difficulty accessing safe drinking water.

A dam near the Great Wall, Beijing, China.
PHOTO BY TOM CHRISTENSEN.

Pollution

While northern China thirsts for water, the water-affluent south has suffered ever more frequent water shortages due to pollution, although pollution is not unique to the south. Of the five-hundred sections of China's nine major river systems that are monitored for water quality, only 28 percent have water suitable for drinking, while 31 percent have water quality of limited or no functional use. The Haihe, Liaohe, Huang (Yellow), and Huaihe river systems are the worst polluted all in the north, although all the rest of China's river systems have also had high nitrogen or other pollutant concentrations to various degrees as well. In addition, more than 75 percent of China's lakes have been polluted. A sample survey reveals that 97 percent of the 118 cities investigated have groundwater that is polluted to varying degrees; 64 percent have seriously polluted groundwater (Ministry of Water Resources 2005). Lake Baiyangdian, China's largest natural lake, is a source of food and drinking water for people who live around it. Sometimes called the "kidney" of north China, the lake has had an historical role in filtering the waters of nine rivers that flow through it. It has been polluted by arsenic and mercury from sources such as coal emissions, agricultural runoff, and sewage discharge.

Water pollution is caused by increasing discharge of domestic, industrial, and agricultural wastes that often receives little treatment. Unreasonable industrial layout has seated many old, heavily polluting or toxically dangerous industries along rivers. A survey conducted by the State Environmental Protection Administration (2004) shows that, among the 7,555 chemical or petroleum projects in China, 81 percent are located in environmentally sensitive areas such as water networks or densely populated habitats. Of the 1,441 environmental incidents reported in 2004, half were related to water pollution.

Until 2000, only 24 percent of the total 62 billion tons of sewage and wastewater annually discharged in China were treated at the national standard. Along the Yangzi River, China's longest river, which meanders through eighteen provinces, municipalities, and autonomous regions, a number of pollution belts have formed out of industrial and domestic wastes discharged short of the treatment standard. These belts run 600 kilometers in total length. Pollutants include micro-organisms, oils, volatile phenols, cyanides, sulfides, mercury, cadmium, lead, chromium, and arsenic. Projects designed for flood control and alleviation of arid areas also have an detrimental impact on the quality of water in the Yangzi. The Three Gorges Dam exacerbates water pollution in the Yangzi by impounding water and reducing the velocity of the river. Impounded water submerges parts of the existing sewer system and wastewater treatment facilities. Plans to divert water from the Yangzi to arid north China will reduce the volume of the water flowing through the Yangzi and thus reduce its ability to dilute and flush toxins.

Pollution has aggravated the shortage of water in the water-scarce north, and it has caused water famines in the water-affluent south. According to the State Environmental Protection Administration, China now faces intensive outbreaks of water pollution incidents as a consequence of neglecting environmental protection over the past decades; reports of a water pollution incidents have been as frequent as every two or three days on average since the end of 2005. A sudden burst of foul algae blanketed the Taihu Lake in southern Jiangsu in late May 2007, cutting the drinking-water supply to more than 2 million people in Wuxi city, a leading economic engine house of the country, for a week. In the Pearl River delta in Guangdong, where the volume of freshwater resources averages at 330 billion cubic meters a year, rapid economic growth since the 1980s has coupled with pollution to nearly every river course in the urban areas. The pollution has resulted in a water shortage affecting 16 million people in the province (Ministry of Water Resources 2005). Nationwide, the safety of the drinking water more than 300 million people is in question.

Abuse

The Ministry of Water Resources maintains that the exploitation of water resources in China in general is not very high, at about 19.5 percent in 2000, although some experts have warned about abuses of water resources.

A traditional farming country, China's agriculture depends on irrigation: Some 90 percent of cash crops and 70 percent of grain crops are irrigated. In the nine provinces and autonomous regions along the Huang River alone, irrigated farmland increased from 1.4 million hectares in the early 1950s to nearly 5 million hectares in the late 1990s, while the water consumption by agricultural, industrial, and domestic users increased from 1 billion cubic meters a year to well over 30 billion cubic meters. Scientists believe the use of the Huang River water is excessive and beyond the capacity of China's second largest river, a river that provides water to nearly half of the nation and that cradled the origins of Chinese civilization. This excessive use was identified as one of the causes for the river running dry in its lower reaches for 226 days in 1997. That year the Huang River carried only 1.8 billion cubic meters of water into the sea, compare to an average of 20 billion cubic meters.

Groundwater is also excessively exploited at a volume of more than 9 billion cubic meters per year. This has led to ground subsidence or clefts in many areas, especially in the north, forming seventy-two depression cones across

the whole country. According to the Ministry of Land and Resources, about fifty cities in China have reported sinking ground, with the worst occurring in Shanghai, Tianjin, and Taiyuan, where sinking has averaged more than two meters per year since the early 1990s.

The pressure from population growth and economic development has affected wetlands as well. In the fifty-seven years since 1950, China's total lake area has shrunk by 16,585.36 square kilometers; an average of twenty lakes vanish each year (2007). For example, Qinghai Lake, China's largest inland saltwater lake at 4,300 square kilometers, lost more than 380 square kilometers between 1959 and 2006. Government plans to address the problems at Quinghai Lake include moving hotels, restaurants, and other tourist facilities to an area at least 3 kilometers from the bank. The Yangzi River valley alone lost 3,000 square kilometers of lake surface area during this period. The surface areas of Dongting Hu and Poyang Hu lakes, two of the major detention basins for Yangzi floods, have shrunk by 46 percent and 40 percent respectively, with their stored volume decreasing from more than 30 billion cubic meters to around 17 billion cubic meters. Hubei, once dubbed as "the province of a thousand lakes," had 1,066 lakes in the late 1950s. Now only 182 lakes are left.

In contrast to the withering of natural lakes is the construction of eighty-five thousand reservoirs of various sizes, with a total storage volume of 520 billion cubic meters (2000). The controversial Three Gorges Dam

The inner workings of the Water Conservancy Project at Yangzhou, 1979. PHOTO BY JOAN LEBOLD COHEN.

Rafts on the Yangzi River, 1980, now the source of water power at the Three Gorges Dam. PHOTO BY JOAN LEBOLD COHEN.

tops this list: it is the world's largest hydropower project, and more than 1.2 million people were displaced before it began to generate electricity in 2003. Despite the criticisms of opponents about the environmental and social impacts of the reservoirs (i.e., threats to living conditions of aquatic species, hazards to local vegetation and biodiversity, sedimentation, and induction of geological havocs), hydropower is prioritized as part of China's pursuit of new and clean energy. Figures from the Ministry of Water Resources, the leading dam builder, show that China has over 500 million kilowatts of exploitable water power, while the installed hydroelectric capacity by the end of 2005 was 117 million kilowatts, about 24 percent of the potential. The target is to boost the capacity to 180 million kilowatts by 2010 and to 300 million kilowatts in 2020. That means more river sections will be dammed for hydropower projects. Measures to meet these goals include construction of large hydroelectric power stations, such as the Xiaowan Dam on the Lancang River. Second in size to the Three Gorges Dam, this power station will be capable of generating 4.2 million kilowatts by 2013. China

is also investing in small hydroelectric power stations that generate 25 megawatts or less.

Although agriculture accounts for 70 percent of the total water consumption in China, the efficiency of irrigation trails other countries. The average efficiency of irrigation water nationwide is 0.43 (2000 estimate), meaning that 57 percent of the water fails to reach the end crops; this figure is 0.7 in advanced countries elsewhere. The reuse rate of industrial water is 55 percent compared with 75 to 85 percent in other advanced countries.

Lessons

China has enacted at least four laws concerning water, namely the Water Law, the Law on Flood Control, the Law on Water and Soil Conservation, and the Law on Water Pollution Prevention. This legislation has institutionalized the water-drawing permit, the utilization of water resources upon payment, the economic use of water resources, and has placed a penalty on polluters.

Programs have been created to conserve headwaters; to prevent and control water pollution; to make comprehensive use of various water resources including surface water, groundwater and flood water; to reduce water consumption; and to improve water efficiency. Meanwhile, surveillance of water quality has been enhanced, involving both government and nongovernmental organizations (NGOs).

Enforcement of the laws and regulations poses the largest question. While there has been much talk about enhancing modern water management, so far the chief administrator of water resources, the Ministry of Water Resources, is seen as being keener on tapping rather than protecting the water resources. Water pollution inspections are often conducted by environmental protection agencies, yet they lack the authority to really execute effective punishment because the polluters are usually protected by local governments by virtue of their "contributions" to the local revenue.

Perhaps incidents like the outbreak of foul algae in the Taihu Lake is teaching decision makers to manage pollution more effectively and is driving home the idea of protecting the water environment more immediately. The pollution control of the Taihu Lake had been conducted for more than ten years prior to the incident, but to no avail. Following the outbreak, however, the provincial government of Jiangsu recognized that controlling lake pollution is an urgent priority and began to treat it as a debt that had to be paid to nature. The Jiangsu government decided to shut down more than 2,000 small chemical plants around Taihu Lake by 2008 and to build a green shelter around the lake 1 kilometer wide. In this area some 660 hectares of cropland will be restored and replanted with trees and grass in order to reduce the discharge of agricultural waste to the lake. According to the local media, this plan is unprecedented. The provincial government pledged to clean the lake even if it is causes a 15 percent downturn in the province's GDP.

Numerous lessons have shown that it is essential to strike a harmonious relationship with nature rather than conquer it. More and more people in China, including officials at the Ministry of Water Resources, have come to see that water is not inexhaustible, but rather that it is a limited and vulnerable resource. It is not a free natural resource, but it is valuable and strategically significant.

Therefore water resources cannot be developed and used unboundedly without consideration of their sustainability. Authorities have also adopted the idea that it is more important to ration the use of water resources with high efficiency than to simply harness the water. This notion is regarded as the hope for the sustainability of water resources in China. Whatever the future in China holds, it is certain that the management of water resources is inextricably intertwined with its direction.

XIONG Lei

Further Reading

Chen, C. Y., Pickhardt, P. C., Xu, M. Q., & Folt, C. L. (2008). Mercury and arsenic bioaccumulation and eutrophication in Baiyangdian Lake, China. *Water, Air, Soil Pollution, 190,* 115–127.

Extremely high levels of mercury and arsenic found in Chinese lake. (2008). Retrieved February 3, 2009 from http://news.mongabay.com/2008/0110-china.html

Li Shijie, et al. (2007). Vicissitudes of China's lakes. *Forests and Human Beings,* 11.

Ministry of Water Resources. (2005). Annual Report of the Ministry of Water Resources, 2004–2005. Retrieved January 30, 2009, from http://www.mwr.gov.cn/english1/20060404/69725.asp

Wang Jiaquan. (2007). China's economic engine forced to face environmental deficit. Retrieved January 30, 2009, from http://www.worldwatch.org/node/5259

New plan to save Quinghai Lake. (2007, September 11). *China Daily,* p. 4. Retrieved February 3, 2009, from http://www.chinadaily.com.cn/cndy/2007-09/11/content_6095501.htm

World Bank. (2007). Water pollution emergencies in China: Prevention and response. Washington, DC: World Bank. Retrieved January 30, 2009, from http://siteresources.worldbank.org/INTEAPREGTOPENVIRONMENT/Resources/Water_Pollution_Emergency_Final_EN.pdf

World Wide Fund for Nature. (2007). Threat of Pollution in the Yangtze. Retrieved February 4, 2009, from http://www.panda.org/about_wwf/what_we_do/freshwater/problems/river_decline/10_rivers_risk/yangtze/yangtze_threats/

Yang Jianxiang. (2007). Hydropower: A viable solution for China's energy future? Retrieved February 2, 2009, from http://www.worldwatch.org/node/4908

WEN Jiabao

Wēn Jiābǎo 温家宝

b. 1942 Premier of China 2003–present

Wen Jiabao, who began his second five-year term as premier in 2008, is a respected leader because of his managerial abilities and a popular figure because of his common-man approach to political and social issues. Following the deadly Sichuan earthquake of 2008, he emerged as the compassionate face of the Chinese government.

Wen Jiabao was born of Han parentage on 15 September 1942 in Beichen, Tianjin Municipality, in northeast China. The people of Tianjin are said to be eloquent, humorous, and open, which in many ways fits Wen. He is known as the people's premier and has a common touch that has earned him the nickname "Grandpa Wen."

Wen attended Nankai High School, the same school from which Zhou Enlai (China's first premier) graduated. From 1960 to 1968, Wen studied at the Beijing Institute of Geology, where he earned a baccalaureate degree in geological surveying and a postgraduate degree in geological structure. He joined the Chinese Communist Party (CCP) in 1965.

His training and political enthusiasm helped him secure government posts. Between 1968 and 1985 he held such positions as technician and political instructor of the geomechanics team of the Gansu Provincial Geological Bureau; deputy director general of Gansu Provincial Geological Bureau; and vice minister of the Policy and Law Research Office of the Ministry of Geology and Mineral Resources. During this time Wen built his powerbase and gained standing as a strong administrator and dedicated technocrat.

In 1985 Wen was named deputy director of the General Office of the CCP Central Committee. In 1986 he was elevated to director, an office he held until 1992. During this time he held a number of other party positions, including chief of staff to general secretaries of the CCP Hu Yaobang, Zhao Ziyang, and Jiang Zemin.

Wen's career nearly ended in disgrace in 1989. A photograph of him alongside the then general secretary Zhao Ziyang visiting student demonstrators in Tiananmen Square on 19 May 1989 appeared on the front page of the *People's Daily*. To many party leaders, the photo signified their support of the students. Zhao was purged for his actions, but Wen somehow managed to escape persecution and continued to rise in power.

In 1993 Wen became a full member of the Secretariat of the CCP Central Committee. In 1997 he became a member of the Politburo. In 1998 he was appointed one of China's four vice premiers. The pinnacle of his career, to this point, came on 16 March 2003 when he was appointed to his first term as premier of the People's Republic of China. His second five-year term began on 16 March 2008.

Wen is a popular and, by most accounts, effective leader. His premiership is marked by his "people-first" policy. He has launched programs aimed at revitalizing the rural economy, restructuring the banking system, and reforming state-owned enterprises. He has held impromptu news conferences (an unheard of practice in a country with a state-controlled press), championed the

2433

2008 Beijing Olympics, and shed tears in public, especially following the 2008 Sichuan earthquake.

The quake, which struck on 12 May 2008, was one of the deadliest disasters in China's history. More than 69,000 people were killed, and more than 5 million were left homeless. Along with other structures, thousands of schools were destroyed. The total economic loss is estimated to be more then $75 billion.

A few hours after the quake hit, Wen headed for the quake zone to take charge of rescue operations. As a trained geologist, he understood the magnitude of the disaster. He was immediately named the executive director of the Earthquake Relief Efforts Committee. Media and amateur videos showed him directing rescue crews and comforting victims. In one instance, at the site of a collapsed elementary school, he introduced himself as Grandpa Wen (unwittingly earning himself a nickname) to a child pinned under debris and said, "Hang on child. We'll rescue you." His unusually sympathetic face of the Chinese government solidified his popularity and respect.

Wen's reputation and his face are now well known to the world. He appears often, in action, on Chinese television. He is seen as a man for his times. He has a profile on Facebook, the Internet social-networking site. The author of the page is unknown, but Wen and the Chinese press have welcomed the exposure. During Wen's trip to Europe in early 2009, when the world was focused on global economic woes, the prime minister garnered some attention for mentioning that he carried in his suitcase a copy of Adam Smith's *The Theory of Moral Sentiments*. Wen explained his view of the book's message, telling reporters that it is morally unsound—and a threat to stable society—if the fruits of economic development are not shared by all. The view is bound to resonate among those in China who suffer from the uneven distribution of wealth resulting from the country's own rapid growth. By emphasizing this aspect of Smith's philosophy, the *Economist* reported in March 2009, "Wen is trying to show he cares."

Wendell ANDERSON

Further Reading

A time for muscle-flexing. (2009, March 19). *Economist.com.* Retrieved March 25, 2009, from http://www.economist.com/world/asia/displaystory.cfm?story_id=13326082

Choy, L. K. (2005). *Pioneers of modern China: Understanding the inscrutable Chinese.* Singapore: World Scientific Publishing Company.

Fewsmith, J. (2001). *China since Tiananmen.* Cambridge, U.K.: Cambridge University Press.

Li, C. (2001). *China's leaders: The new generation.* Lanham, MD: Rowman & Littlefield.

Roberts, D., & Clifford, M. (2002, December 2). Who is Wen Jiabao? *Business Week Online.* Retrieved February 8, 2009, from http://www.businessweek.com/magazine/content/02_48/b3810166.htm

Why Grandpa Wen has to care. (2008, June 12). *Economist.com.* Retrieved February 8, 2009, from http://www.economist.com/world/asia/displayStory.cfm?source=hptextfeature&story_id=115413

Zhou, R. (2008, November 28). Studying the "Wen effect." *China Daily.*

Wencheng, Princess

Wénchéng Gōngzhǔ 文成公主

c. 624–680 CE   Royal symbol of unity

Princess Wencheng was the niece of the Chinese emperor Tang Taizong; she was sent to Lhasa to marry the Tibetan king Songzan Gambo. In contemporary China, she is famous as a symbol of "the unity of the nationalities" (*minzu tuanjie* 民族团结) and credited with the spread of Chinese culture among the Tibetans. She is also the subject of many Tibetan artistic and literary works.

Princess Wencheng was a Chinese princess who married a Tibetan king and became a symbol of intercultural exchange and of the unity of the two nationalities (*minzu tuanjie*). The Tibetan king Songzan Gambo (reigned 629–650 CE) is the most famous monarch of the ancient kingdom, credited with consolidating royal authority and expanding his territory. He developed a Tibetan script that survives to this day. He introduced Buddhism to Tibet, and the great Jokhang Monastery, which still stands at the center of the capital, Lhasa, dates from his reign.

King Songzan Gambo sent an envoy to the court of Li Shimin (599–649), who reigned as emperor in China from 627 to 649 under the title Tang Taizong, requesting a diplomatic marriage. In 640 Tang Taizong adopted his niece, Princess Wencheng, as his daughter and sent her to Lhasa, where she arrived early the next year.

Like a Nepalese wife whom Songzan Gambo had already married, Princess Wencheng bore him no children (he had offspring by Tibetan wives). But legend claims that a place in the great Potala Palace in Lhasa was their bridal chamber.

Princess Wencheng was a devout Buddhist and probably exerted considerable religious influence on the king. In the holiest innermost part of the Jokhang Monastery stands a statue of Sakyamuni Buddha that is said to be the only surviving Buddha statue dating from the time of Buddha himself and consecrated by him. According to tradition, Princess Wencheng brought this statue from China to Tibet.

Princess Wencheng was reputed to be talented, cultured, well mannered, and versed in divination and other branches of learning. She introduced Tibet to Chinese skills, such as those of the medical doctor and miller, calendar calculation, weaving, pottery, and paper and wine production. Her retinue from China also included thousands of craftsmen. She remained in Tibet after the king died, teaching weaving and embroidery to Tibetan women.

After her death Princess Wencheng was deified in Tibet, and statues of her are still found in Tibetan temples. She became the subject of wall paintings, folksongs, and legends. One of the eight great dramas in the Tibetan tradition is entitled *A-lca-rgya-za* (Princess Wencheng). Two Tibetan works, one dated to 1388, the other to 1643, record the story in some detail, the latter being closer to the version performed nowadays. Actually this drama is set in the Chinese capital and concerns the successful attempts of the Tibetan envoy in winning a competition for her hand against royals from elsewhere and in overcoming resistance from Tang Taizong to grant the marriage of Princess Wencheng to the Tibetan king. At the end Tang

2435

A tile mural and stele in the Memorial Hall dedicated to Princess Wencheng in Tibet.
PHOTO BY JOAN LEBOLD COHEN.

Taizong encourages her to spread Buddhism in Tibet as she leaves for Lhasa at the head of a mighty convoy.

In contemporary Chinese historiography (the writing of history) Princess Wencheng is given an important role in spreading Chinese culture to Tibet. By enhancing the close relationship between Chinese and Tibetans she symbolizes "the unity of the nationalities." Her marriage with the Tibetan king is considered by some as evidence that Tibet belongs to China.

Colin MACKERRAS

Further Reading

Princess Wencheng—Bridging the different cultures. (2004). Retrieved December 18, 2007, from http://www.wku.edu/~yuanh/China/tales/princesswencheng_b.htm

Richardson, H. (1997, Spring). Mun Sheng Kong Co and Kim Sheng Kong Co: Two Chinese princesses in Tibet. *The Tibet Journal, 22*(1), 3–11.

Wang, Yao. (Ed.). (1986). *Tales from Tibetan opera*. Beijing: New World Press.

The temple of Princess Wencheng in Tibet. Prayer flags flutter in the wind outside the temple.
PHOTO BY JOAN LEBOLD COHEN.

WEN Tingyun

Wēn Tíngyùn 温庭蕴

c. 812–866 CE   Tang lyric poet

Wen Tingyun was a lyric poet during the Tang dynasty (618–907 CE) whose innovations had a wide-ranging influence on Chinese poetry, especially during the Song dynasty (960–1279).

As with most things concerning the life of the poet Wen Tingyun, it is difficult to say exactly where he was born. Some scholars say he was a native of Taiyuan, in Shanxi. Others state that he was likely born in the Yangzi area. But there is little doubt that he was among the first to master the *ci* form, verses set to specific and well-known tunes and melodies. His poems are often concerned with themes unconventional for their time, such as anger, sexuality, and hatred. He also excelled in singing and playing the flute.

Wen was born into a family of minor court officials. He sought to become a scholar-official but to little avail, as he could never pass the civil service examinations. Many accounts attribute this failure to his self-indulgent life. One requirement of a scholar-official was high moral integrity; another, literary talent. Perhaps embittered, he began to criticize many of the court officials in his verses and songs. Even those who sought to help him were subject to his attacks.

After failing the examinations Wen set about to find a rich patron. But his attempts proved fruitless since there were not many powerful people whom he had not offended. Around 839 he was likely married and then had two children, a son named Wen Xian and a daughter. No further details about his family life are known. For the next ten years, he sought again and again to achieve a position at court, failing each time.

In 855 Wen was finally given a post far from the capital. Perhaps this was an effort to remove him from the inner circle of the court in a kindly fashion. Despite his slanderous and unpopular actions, and perhaps because of them, he was a highly recognized public figure, and his poems and songs were widely read.

In 863 he had made his way back to the capital of Yangzhou, where he had hopes of being granted a more worthwhile position. But that was not to be, and he continued in his old ways. Before long, he was severely beaten by a soldier because he had violated a curfew. He lodged a complaint, but the soldier's actions were upheld.

This incident infuriated Wen further, and he continued to attack in verse the various officials he deemed responsible for his humiliation. The result was that he was exiled once again. He would never return to Yangzhou. It is likely that he died in exile sometime after 866.

In Chinese literary tradition, Wen's poetry has been neglected because of his moral failings. Many are the anecdotes that relate his exploits in brothels. But such an approach is unfair to Wen's rather prodigious talent. Although his verses appear deceptively simple, their primary concern is the exploration of those emotions that hover around the individual in his or her interaction with the world, and with those who love him or her. Thus Wen seeks to find a balance between pleasure and the

The Poetry of Wen Tingyun

NEWS SO SELDOM COMES

Blue tail-feathers and markings of gold
   on a pair of mandarin ducks,
And tiny ripples of water stirring the blue
   of a pond in spring;
Beside the pond there stands a crabapple
   tree,
Its branches filled with pink after the
   rain.
Her figured sleeve covers a dimpled smile
As a flying butterfly lights on the mistlike
   grass.
Her window gives on all this loveliness—
And news so seldom comes from the
   Jade Pass!

Source: Minford, J., & Lau, J. S. M. (2000). *An anthology of translations: Classical Chinese literature, vol. 1.* New York: Columbia University Press, 1119.

Wen Tingyun, a Tang dynasty lyric poet whose themes were unconventional for his time—and whose verses and songs were often critical of court officials.

emotional cost of winning such enjoyment. This allows him to delve into those very things that mark and underscore life: love, suffering, pain, but also hope for better things to come.

Nirmal DASS

Further Reading

Chang Kang-i Sun. (1980). *The evolution of Chinese Tz'u poetry: From late T'ang to northern Sung.* Princeton, NJ: Princeton University Press.

Graham, A. C. (1965). *Poems of the late T'ang.* Harmondsworth, U.K.: Penguin.

Mou Huaichuan. (2003). *Rediscovering Wen Tingyun: A historical key to a poetic labyrinth.* Albany, NY: State University of New York Press.

Rouzer, P. F. (1993). *Writing another's dream. The poetry of Wen Tingyun.* Palo Alto, CA: Stanford University Press.

Wagner, M. L. (1984). *The lotus boat: The origins of Chinese Tz'u poetry in Tang popular culture.* New York: Columbia University Press.

WENG Wenhao

Wēng Wénhào　翁文灏

1889–1971　Geologist, statesman

Weng Wenhao was a leading figure in China's development of geological studies—as a student, researcher, teacher and administrator. As director of the National Resources Commission in the mid-1930s he oversaw the planning of heavy industrial reconstruction and the creation of state-run national defense industries; after the outbreak of war in 1937 he became one of China's leading statesman.

Weng Wenhao was among China's first geologists and a leading statesman during the War of Resistance against Japan (1937–1945, known outside of China as the Second Sino-Japanese War, and fought in the context of World War II) and the Civil War (1945–1949). He was also the principal architect of China's state enterprise system.

Weng was born in Qin County of Zhejiang Province. In 1903, at the age of fourteen, he passed the traditional civil service examination at the prefectural level and became a "received talent" (*xiucai*). In 1909 he went to Belgium to study physics and geology at Louvain University, where he received a doctorate in 1913. Upon returning to China the same year Weng Wenhao joined the Geological Research Institute, which was an institution of education designed to train future geologists. After the Geological Research Institute was forced to close in 1916, he transferred to the Geological Investigation Institute, which

was China's first veritable research institute in geological science. During the late 1910s and the 1920s he published several comprehensive studies that described China's mineral resources and their distribution, as well as the conditions of the Chinese mining industry. He served as the acting director of the Geological Investigation Institute from 1921 to 1926. He became the institute's director in 1926 and continued to serve in that position until 1938. Between 1928 and 1930 he was invited by the president of Qinghua University to establish a department of geography that would teach the subjects of geography, geology, and meteorology and to serve simultaneously as department chair. He also held the positions of acting president of Qinghua University in 1931.

From November 1932 to April 1935 he served as secretary-general of the newly created National Defense Planning Commission and coordinated the investigation of China's natural and human resources and the preparation of plans for national defense. After the National Defense Planning Commission was renamed National Resources Commission in April 1935, he became its director. During his tenure as director from 1935 to 1946 he oversaw the planning of heavy industrial reconstruction and the creation of national defense industries. Under his leadership the National Resources Commission established roughly 130 enterprises in energy, petroleum, iron and steel, machinery, alcohol, and electric industries and the management of those state-owned enterprises.

After the outbreak of war in 1937 and the reorganization of the central government, Weng in January 1938 became minister of the Ministry of Economic Affairs

Weng Wenhao's National Resource Commission

The Harvard scholar William C. Kirby writing on the twentieth century geologist/statesman Weng Wenhao:

The new industrial strategy. The basic goals of the plan arrived at by Weng Wenhao's commission in the years 1932–35 may be summed up as follows: the development of the state-run heavy industries and mines in a new "economic center" in central China. These would primarily serve national defense needs and be run by trained specialists according to a comprehensive plan as the initial step toward a fully "planned economy." Heavy industrialization was linked to the exploitation of raw materials and the development of new power-generating capacity, for all of which foreign investment and assistance were essential. A state monopoly on the export of certain raw materials would provide the necessary foreign exchange.

"Heavy industries constitute the main pillar of national defense," wrote Weng in 1940. "This is why progressive nations the world over have spared neither time nor effort in expanding and developing heavy industries."

Source: Kirby, W. C. (1984). *Germany and Republican China.* Stanford, CA: Stanford University Press, 95–96.

under the jurisdiction of the Executive Yuan; he assumed responsibility for directing the administration of the national economy while he continued to serve as director of the National Resources Commission. Under his watch the Ministry of Economic Affairs oversaw industry, mining, commerce, agriculture, forestry, and water conservancy. After May 1940 the Executive Yuan delegated new responsibilities of administering industrial regulation and business enterprises to the Ministry of Economic Affairs but removed agriculture, forestry, and water conservancy. Weng remained head of the Ministry of Economic Affairs until 1946. After the war he served as vice president of the Executive Yuan from June 1945 to April 1947 and president of the Executive Yuan from May to November 1948. The imminent Communist victory led Weng to travel to France and England from late 1949 to 1950. In 1951 he returned to China and joined the Communist government, serving three times as a member of the National Political Consultative Conference. He died in January 1971.

Morris L. BIAN

Further Reading

Bian, M. L. (2005). *The making of the state enterprise system in modern China: The dynamics of institutional change.* Cambridge, MA: Harvard University Press.

Li Xuetong. (2005). *Huanmie de meng: Weng Wenhao yu zhongguo zaoqi gongyehua* [Shattered dreams: Weng Wenhao and China's early industrialization]. Tianjin, China: Tianjin guji chubanshe.

Weng Wenhao. (1989). *Weng Wenhao lun jingji jianshe* [Weng Wenhao on economic reconstruction]. Beijing: Tuanjie chubanshe.

Wenzhou Model

Wēnzhōu Móshì   温州模式

Since the 1980s, business activity in and around the city of Wenzhou in Jiangsu Province has served as national model for economic development in China. The success of the model is due in large part to the traditions and spirit of the local people.

During the early stages of China's economic reforms (from 1979 to the mid-1980s), two distinctive regional development models emerged: the Wenzhou model and the Sunan model. The former is based on Wenzhou, a medium-sized coastal city in Zhejiang Province, where a market economy led by rapidly growing and vigorous private enterprises has helped the Wenzhou region to flourish economically. The latter is centered in Suzhou, a cultural and business center in the rich and populous Jiangsu Province, where collectively owned township enterprises with strong government backing has successfully generated business development.

Socialism versus Capitalism

The term *Wenzhou model* was first adopted in a special report by the *Jiefang Daily*, 12 May 1985, on Wenzhou's family industries. The report praised the Wenzhou model as an "eye-catching economic miracle" and "a model that leads to the prosperity of vast rural areas." However, from the beginning, this model attracted severe criticism from many Communist Party and government leaders at the national and provincial levels. As such, it became a focal point of a heated political debate. According to these critics, the Sunan model followed the socialist development road, whereas the Wenzhou model tried to restore capitalism, which the government then tried to repress. The socialism versus capitalism (*xing she* or *xing zi*) dispute between these two models echoed the broader debate between continuing the state-planned economy or permitting market economy and private enterprises.

One of the main elements of this debate, as demonstrated in Wenzhou, was the problem of managing and regulating private enterprises. Wenzhou people refer to the 1980s and even the early 1990s as the period of primitive accumulation of capital. During this period Wenzhou businesses would do almost anything to turn a profit, leaving quality by the wayside. The lack of sufficient supervision and regulation of private businesses led to chaotic, fraudulent practices and suicidal competition, resulting in devastating damage to the private economy. For a long time, Wenzhou was synonymous with forgery and poor quality (*jia, mao, wei, lue*). At the same time, the government worried about social control and the political consequences of a flourishing private economy. The debate lasted until Deng Xiaoping's famous tour to several southern cities in 1992, which brought a new momentum to Wenzhou's private businesses.

Entrepreneurial Roots

Unlike other regions where the collectively owned village and township economy boomed before private enterprises developed, Wenzhou's economic development grew immediately in the late 1970s from an explosion of private enterprises. These small family-based operations, in small towns in the Wenzhou region, became the foundation of Wenzhou businesses. Around the late 1970s, Wenzhou had only 6,477 businesses: 302 state owned, 4,801 collectively owned, and 1,372 private enterprises (or 21 percent) at the village and township levels. By 1996 the total number had increased to 117,829 and, of these, 112,232 (or 95 percent) were private businesses. From 1979 to 2000, Wenzhou's economy grew at an average rate of 15 percent a year, and the total industrial output increased from ¥1.12 billion (about $164 million) in 1978 to ¥203 billion (about $20 billion) in 2001. By 2007 the private sector made up 99.5 percent of Wenzhou's total number of firms, 95.5 percent of its industrial value, 95 percent of its foreign trade revenue, and 80 percent of its tax revenue.

The distinctiveness of the Wenzhou model owes much to its unique historical tradition and to more recent economic developments that shaped its culture and the traits of its people. Today, Wenzhou spans over 11,784 square kilometers (about 4,550 square miles, slightly smaller than Connecticut) and is home to 7.7 million people (2007 estimate). Surrounded by mountains, it has very limited arable land. In 1978 one-third of the land was agricultural, and the per capita land tenure was only 0.53 mu (one-tenth of an acre). As a result, on the eve of Deng Xiaoping's reforms Wenzhou had a surplus of more than a million agricultural laborers. In addition, as Wenzhou is situated on the Taiwan Straits, the prereform government considered it a military front against Taiwan and thus too risky for infrastructural investments. Between 1949 and 1978, total state investment in building Wenzhou's infrastructure was less than ¥60 million (about $9 million), only 15 percent the average national state investment in comparable cities. Thus, before 1978, the state-owned economy contributed only 36 percent to Wenzhou's industrial output value, far below the national average of 78 percent.

Wenzhou was called an ocean culture. Frequent migrations since ancient times, its dependence on ocean trade, and the lack of strong ties to any inland cultural centers nurtured an independent, diligent, creative, practical, and adventurous society. Its cultural uniqueness dates back as early as the Tang (618–907 CE) and Song (960–1279) dynasties, when Wenzhou—then known as Ou or Yongjia—was a prosperous manufacturing and commercial port in southeast China. Far from the capitals of imperial dynasties, Wenzhou enjoyed a relatively isolated cultural environment. Against the mainstream of Confucianism, the Yongjia School during the Southern Song (1127–1279) and the Three Scholars of East Ou during the late Qing (1644–1912) were well known for their advocacy of business and economic development.

Since the late 1980s, the Wenzhou model has been characterized by family-operated, low-tech, low-capital, and labor-intensive enterprises. Products have been heavily concentrated in light industries, such as lighters, glasses, garments, shoes, and small electrical appliances. The products of these hundreds and thousands of crude workshops go on to national and international markets. The phrase "small products, big market" has become the trademark of the Wenzhou model. Millions of surplus agriculture laborers entered the nonagricultural production market, and the economic conditions of their families and the region as a whole have improved profoundly. In 1980 the average income of Wenzhou villagers was 15 percent below the national level. By the beginning of the twenty-first century, the average income of Wenzhou villagers had risen to twice that of the national level. During the early stages of China's economic reforms, the Wenzhou model helped break down old conceptions of economic development and demonstrated to other regions, especially lower Yangzi (Chang) delta regions, the potential gains of a market economy. Through the Wenzhou model, Zhejiang Province has become the "headquarters of the private economy" in China. In 2007 the total industrial output, retail value, and income from foreign trade of its private businesses ranked first in the nation.

Future Challenges

Yet this model faces serious challenges from economic globalization and China's membership in the World Trade Organization. Certain innate weaknesses of family-operated businesses, from leadership to managerial mechanisms, have hindered the model's advantages. Since the late 1990s, to thrive in the increasingly

A woman weaves blankets to sell. The increase of small, local enterprises exemplifies the Wenzhou model of economic growth. PHOTO BY JOAN LEBOLD COHEN.

competitive domestic and international markets, Wenzhou's private enterprises have reorganized swiftly into large limited liability corporations and shareholding corporations. The size of individual enterprises has enlarged significantly, and the industrial structure, capital composition, and managerial model have been substantially transformed.

The question arises whether these new developments, as promoted by the corporations and valued at ¥1 billion (about $146 million), still represent the Wenzhou model. Wenzhou people believe it should. They consider the true spirit of the Wenzhou model to be people's creativity, sense of adventure and independence, diligence, and vision.

Qiusha MA

Further Reading

Yuan Peng, Sun Boyuan, & Zhang Min. (2004). Zhiu du zhuan xing, tou zi huan jing gai shan yu jian shao pin kung: Weng zhou mo shi he sun an mo shi de fa zhan jing yan [The system transformation, improvement of invest environment and poverty alleviation: Development experience of Wenzhou model and Sunan model]. Retrieved January 10, 2007, from http://www.worldbank.org.cn/Chinese/SME–case.pdf

Chen Junxian and Zhou Zengxing. (2003), Weng zhou tan mi [Understanding Wenzhou]. Beijing: People's Daily Publishing House.

Ma, Quisha. (2006). Corporatism vs. civil society. *Nongovernmental organizations in contemporary China*. London: Routledge.

White Terror

Báisè Kǒngbù 白色恐怖

The Chinese Nationalist Party's campaign of violence in Shanghai—the "White Terror"—was aimed at Communists and labor union members in 1927. The White Terror suppressed Communist activity in the city and influenced the later strategy of the Chinese Communist Party.

The White Terror was the regime of violence established by the Chinese Nationalist Party (CNP or Guomindang) after its capture of Shanghai in 1927. The violence, which drove a permanent wedge between the Nationalists (the White Party) and the Communists (the Red Party), was directed at labor unions and their leaders but evolved into extortion of Shanghai's privileged classes.

Fragmented Politics

From the time of the collapse of China's last imperial dynasty (Qing, 1644–1912) in 1911 and the establishment of Republican China (1912–1949), China's political landscape had been fragmented; by the early 1920s revolutionary leader Sun Yat-sen (1866–1925) led the CNP from its main base in Guangzhou (Canton), while Chen Duxiu (1879–1942) founded the Chinese Communist Party (CCP) in Shanghai in 1921. In 1923 Sun Yat-sen's favorable impression of the Bolshevik revolution in Russia and the Communist belief that a socialist revolution would follow a nationalist revolution led to the Chinese Communists and the Nationalists forming an uneasy alliance against the local warlords who held large parts of China. Michael Borodin (originally named "Mikhail Gruzenberg," 1884–1951), who was a Comintern (the Communist International established in 1919 and dissolved in 1943) agent in China from 1923 to 1927 and who was one of the architects of the alliance between the CCP and CNP, became one of Sun Yat-sen's special advisers. At a CNP conference in January 1924 Communist delegates accounted for fewer than 20 percent of those present, but two years later Communists and their supporters in the CNP were the majority of delegates at a conference in Guangzhou. After the death of Sun Yat-sen in 1925 Chiang Kai-shek (1887–1975), commander of the Whampoa Military Academy south of Guangzhou, soon emerged as the new leader of the CNP.

Although Guangzhou had become a Communist stronghold, powerful anti-Communist factions of the CNP existed all over China, and the pro-Soviet line was abandoned under the new CNP leadership. The tensions between the CCP and the CNP surfaced in March 1926 when Chiang Kai-shek felt provoked by the presence of a gunboat commanded by a Communist; Chiang imposed martial law in Guangzhou. Soviet advisers were arrested, and workers and Communists were disarmed. Martial law was lifted after some days, and after negotiations involving Borodin, the CNP-CCP alliance continued but with a weakened Communist position. By the end of 1926 the armies controlled by the CNP and Chiang Kai-shek had conquered most of southern China and established headquarters in Nanchang in Jiangxi Province, while the CCP and its supporters were based in Wuhan in Hubei Province.

The White Terror, a pogrom of anti-Communists in Shanghai, left scenes of devastation in areas with suspected Communist sympathies.

Shanghai in 1927

The central area of Shanghai in the 1920s was divided into a number of foreign settlements surrounded by Chinese neighborhoods. The foreign concessions were administratively and legislatively independent of China, and they could even overrule the legal system of the Chinese government. The city was booming—a center of industry and trade—and Communist leaders had been successful in organizing workers on the docks and in the factories into labor unions. In May 1925 strikes involving several hundreds of thousands of workers in Shanghai spread to the rest of China, and the riots were stopped only when Japanese and British troops opened fire and killed numerous Chinese workers.

In February 1927, as Chiang Kai-shek was contemplating a move on Shanghai, the Communist leaders in the city—Zhou Enlai (1899–1976) and Li Lisan (1899–1967)—organized a general strike that paralyzed the busy port and the city's industry. Numerous workers again were arrested and executed, but in March the strike turned into an armed rebellion against the CNP and the authorities in the Chinese part of Shanghai, and police stations and other key buildings were occupied. Chiang Kai-shek delayed his advance on Shanghai, hoping that foreign troops or Shanghai's local Chinese commander would crush the Communists, but when that hope was dashed, the CNP armies arrived on 26 March.

The Green Gang

One of Chiang Kai-shek's main goals in taking over the wealthy city of Shanghai was to gain financial support for his campaign to defeat the northern provinces, which were controlled by independent warlords. At the same time he wanted to curb the influence of the CCP headquarters in Wuhan and the strong Communist organization in Shanghai. The city's powerful businessmen, industrial leaders, foreign concessions, and underworld entrepreneurs occupied with prostitution, gambling, kidnapping, and opium trade shared Chiang's opposition to the Communists. A secret society known as the "Green Gang" (*Qingbang*) controlled the illegal activities in Shanghai. The Green Gang was led by Huang Jinrong, a senior officer in the French police. The exact nature of Chiang Kai-shek's relationship with the Green Gang remains unclear, but historians generally agree that an alliance was formed between the Nationalist occupying forces and the Green Gang to strike against labor unions and the Communists.

At 4 A.M. on 12 April, while Chiang was away trying to establish his capital in Nanjing in Jiangsu Province, a militia led by associates of Huang carried out a well-organized attack on union headquarters around Shanghai. The militia was made up of approximately one thousand men who were heavily armed and wore plain blue clothes and white armbands with the Chinese character for labor (*gong*). In several instances they were assisted by Nationalist troops. They were allowed to pass freely through the foreign settlements. Hundreds of labor unionists and Communists were shot or arrested and turned over to the Nationalist troops, who executed them. A few leaders, such as Zhou Enlai, narrowly escaped. The next day the labor unions responded with strikes and demonstrations, which were dispersed with machine guns, swords, and bayonets.

The White Terror spread to other cities controlled by the CNP, and several Communist attempts to establish city communes were suppressed. Having ended Communist activities in Shanghai, Chiang Kai-shek began to collect payment from the privileged classes for his services. Assisted by criminals of the Green Gang, the CNP forced the rich to donate money or to extend "loans" to finance its armies. Those who refused to comply were imprisoned and released only in return for huge sums of money or had their property confiscated or their children kidnapped.

The White Terror in Shanghai and other urban Communist strongholds had a large influence on the development of Communist strategy in China. Having lost its influence in the cities, the CCP concentrated its efforts on the rural areas and based its revolution on peasants rather than on industrial workers.

Bent NIELSON

Further Reading

Coble, P. M., Jr. (1980). *The Shanghai capitalists and the Nationalist government, 1927–1937.* Cambridge, MA: Harvard University Press.

Martin, B. G. (1996). *The Shanghai Green Gang: Politics and organized crime, 1919–1937.* Berkeley and Los Angeles: University of California Press.

Ruthlessness is key to a man's accomplishment.

无 毒 不 丈 夫

Wú dú bú zhàng fu

Wine Culture

Jiǔ wénhuà 酒文化

The use of alcoholic beverages in China has been continuous throughout its history. Today, with traditional customs of hospitality supplemented by the obligations of modern business practices, the ways in which beer, liquor, and wine are consumed reveal an important aspect of Chinese life—and producing these beverages has become a thriving subeconomy.

Evidence of the use of alcoholic beverages in China dates to the discovery and analysis of sediment found in nine-thousand-year-old crockery dug from cave-tombs in Henan Province. Archaeologists have documented that Chinese farmers produced grain, the basis of many alcoholic spirits, as early as seven thousand years ago. Alcoholic beverages have had a place in traditional customs and rituals throughout China's history, and do so increasingly in modern times as an important part of social and business life.

The alcoholic beverages the Chinese drink include *baijiu* (Chinese liquor), *putaojiu* (wine), *huangjiu* (rice wine), and *pijiu* (beer). Of the four, *baijiu* and *huangjiu* are indigenous and appeal to the most consumers.

Baijiu, literally "white liquor," is a colorless spirit distilled from sorghum, rice, wheat, corn, peas, or dried yams, or from a mixture of some of the grains aided by sacchariferous starters like yeast and mold. *Baijiu* has different types of bouquets and may or may not have flavoring added. Ranging from 40 to 65 percent alcohol (i.e., 80 to 130 proof), *baijiu*'s appearance is similar to that of vodka, yet its taste is distinctive and unique and perhaps a little too strong for some Western palates. Some of the most famous brands are Maotai, Fenjiu, Wuliangye, Jiannanchun, Yanghedaqu, Gujinggong, and Dongjiu. A bottle of low-quality *baijiu* may cost less than one U.S. dollar, but a bottle of Maotai that has been aged for many years can cost a few thousand.

Huangjiu (rice wine) is fermented like wine and beer but is made primarily of glutinous rice. Other grains can be used, like indica rice, black rice, millet, sorghum, buckwheat, or highland barley, and sometimes dried yams are used. Each gives *huangjiu* a unique flavor. Before modern technology *huangjiu* was manually produced in a process that soaked, steamed, and cooled the rice before fermenting it twice and sterilizing the extraction using heat. The Shaoxing *huangjiu* of Zhejiang Province, the millet *huangjiu* of Shandong Province, and the monascus (mold-fermented) *huangjiu* of Fujian Province are among the best of the country. Their prices are comparable to those of higher-end *baijiu*.

As their standard of living has improved, the Chinese have become health-conscious and concerned about their drinking habits, now preferring liquor of lower alcohol percentage. *Baijiu*, still the dominant "national drink," is being challenged by wine and beer, whose consumption is growing rapidly. While leading the world in the increase of beer drinking, China imports great volumes of top-grade wines and spirits each year. Favored in luxury hotels, bars, and nightclubs, and as fads of the newly rich, they also targeted to appeal to the average Chinese drinker.

History

In 2005 an American brewery, Dogfish Head, made headlines when it produced a new beer based on a biochemical analysis of dregs found in shards of crockery unearthed in a 9,000-year-old cave-tomb in Jiahu, Henan Province. Archeologists learned that early Chinese were already farming grains, the major component of wine, in the Yangshao culture six to seven thousand years ago. The excavation of a great variety of five-thousand-year-old drinking vessels from the Longshan culture (c. 3000–1900 BCE) testifies to the popularity of *huangjiu* at that time. The Chinese were able to produce a dozen types of yeast starters in the fourth century CE, and they understood the natural use of monascus mold for fermentation a thousand years ago.

Baijiu came later. A bronze distiller was discovered in a tomb of the Eastern Han period (25–220 CE), and records of the sixth or seventh century mention *shaojiu,* namely *baijiu,* but historians would rather place the time of its mass production in the Yuan dynasty (1279–1368). Grape wines and their fermenting techniques were imported from Central Asia during the Han (202 BCE–220 CE) or Tang (618–907 CE) dynasties. The first Chinese brewery, though, was not built until 1892 in Zhangyu, Hebei Province, which first produced beer and then wine. Tsingtao, the only Chinese beer known to Westerners today, was first manufactured in 1903 in a brewery of German propriety in Qingdao, Shandong Province.

Today China is a major liquor producer. In 2007, it produced 500,000 kiloliters of *baijiu;* 66,500,000 metric tons of *putaojiu;* 2,000,000 metric tons of *huangjiu;* and 39,313,700 kiloliters of *pijiu.* The majority of this volume was consumed domestically. In the same year, China imported more than 150,000 kiloliters of wine and 205,700 kiloliters of beer. China has become the third largest consumer of Martell cognac, following only Great Britain and the United States (Wang, 2008).

Customs

It is difficult to describe the customs of drinking in China because they vary from region to region, from ethnicity to ethnicity, and from occasion to occasion. They also vary among people of different tastes and occupations. Traditionally, women did not drink alcohol. Today most women in China still shun liquor and choose non-

alcoholic beverages. However, because business deals in China are closed more often at dinner tables than in meeting rooms, a growing number of enterprises and government agencies require that their public relations officers, mostly young women, develop a great capacity for drinking, much to the chagrin of the public. In general, older people choose *baijiu;* younger ones prefer beer; and people of middle age are fond of both. White-collar workers drink wine more than anything else.

Urging someone to drink is an important part of the Chinese tradition at large. To do so, people resort to various strategies and tactics. They may look for (or invent) a reason to make a toast. While Han Chinese use eloquent speech, ethnic minorities mostly sing their *quanjiuge* (songs that urge drinking) or *jingjiuge* (songs of toast). The idea is to show hospitality and to make sure guests are "drinking well." The Chinese, seeing straightforwardness as impolite, often take "no" for a euphemistic way of saying "yes." The only way to get a guest to drink to his heart's content, they reason, is to urge him repeatedly. In such a culture, the avoidance of overdrinking is equally important. This is usually achieved by pacing the amount one drinks over the course of a gathering or dinner. Cheating may be committed as a necessary evil by either stealthily substituting water for liquor or by covertly spitting liquor out into a napkin. Spilling some liquor "unintentionally" also does the trick. This custom of "offense" and "defense" over a drink can sometimes get out of hand and become a very annoying tug-of-war, which happens often at family and friendly gatherings in rural areas of eastern China.

Drinking can become unruly at home and in small eateries, where people play a *caiquan* (finger-guessing) game, something like the Italian *morra.* Each round involves two people. They stretch out a number of fingers from one or both hands at the same time that they shout out a number from 2 to 20. The one who shouts out a number equal to the total number of extended fingers will win. Whoever loses the game has to suffer the penalty of draining a glass full of alcohol. After guessing the number of fingers, the contestants also shout out a series of rhymes, known as *xingjiuling,* to pun on the numbers, such as "one respectful heart" for the number 1, "two brotherly friends" for 2, "three shining stars" for 3 and so on. As excitement builds, each tries to shout down the other. Upscale restaurants always ban the game.

Drinking etiquette can also require subtlety. When toasting, one has to make certain of the pecking order because a junior member of a group should never raise a cup

A table setting at the Great Hall of the People, including fluted wine glasses. Alcoholic beverage consumption in China is influenced by traditional customs of hospitality and the social protocols of modern business. PHOTO BY TOM CHRISTENSEN.

higher than a senior does. The most polite way to toast, particularly to a guest or senior, is to say, "I'll drink it up [meaning one glass], but you can drink as much as you can." At the table, one can never drink alone without initiating a toast or inviting others to drink. Otherwise people may think it rude. People often stand up to toast one another and clink their cups or glasses. When less excited, they may just sit and toast. As they cannot reach each other at a large table, they may instead gently tap the lazy Susan with the edge of the bottom of their cup or glass.

Ethnic Chinese usually observe their diverse time-honored rituals. When guests come to visit Mongolians, for example, they are invited into the yurt, presented with *kha-btags* (silk scarves of good wishes), and offered an alcoholic beverage made with horse milk. According to another Mongolian tradition, the guests must bless the earth, the heaven, and themselves before drinking by dipping a little finger in the liquor and tossing it in the air, snapping it to the ground, and daubing it on their foreheads.

To the Chinese, drinking without good food is unthinkable, so each formal dinner has at least two courses. The first, consisting of lighter dishes, is geared primarily to facilitate drinking, and is followed by the second course of heavier dishes. Today, however, Western-style bars or pubs that serve drinks without the accompaniment of a "proper" meal are mushrooming in big cities like Beijing and Shanghai, catering to foreigners and locals alike.

The popular Chinese saying "*He jiu he hou le; du bo du bo le* (Drinking brings people closer, but gambling sets people apart)" vividly signifies the role drinking plays in human relations in China. Drinking is not only an integral part of social life but is increasingly becoming a ritual in business culture. A lot of business deals are sealed at dinner tables amongst boisterous toasting and the clinking of cups and glasses.

Haiwang YUAN

Further Reading

Fu, Chunjiang, & Yao Hong Qiu. (2004). *Origins of Chinese tea and wine.* Chinese culture series. Singapore: Asiapac Books.

Heok K. E. (1987). Drinking in Chinese culture: Old stereotypes re-examined. *British Journal of Addiction.* 82(3): 224–225.

Wang, Shouguo. (1990). Jiu wen hua zhong de Zhongguo ren [The culture of wines and the Chinese people]. Zhengzhou Shi: Henan ren min chu ban she [Henan People's Press].

Wang, Xiaohui. (2008, September 10). *Madieli ruhe rong ru Zhongguuo shehui.* Retrieved January 13, 2009, from http://www.cnwinenews.com/html/200809/10/20080910083730.htm

Zinzius, B. (2004). *Doing business in the new China: A handbook and guide.* Westport, CT: Praeger Publishers.

Wokou

Wōkòu 倭寇

The *Wokou*, meaning "Japanese pirates," (although some of them were actually renegade Chinese), plagued the coasts of China and Korea from about 1200 to sometime after 1600. Their activities were brought to an end by wider permission of legal trade on the coast of China and by Japanese prohibitions of foreign voyages by their own people.

Wokou (Chinese) or *wakō* (Japanese) meaning "Japanese pirates," plagued the coasts of China and Korea from the 1200s to the end of Japanese seafaring in the 1600s. Their depredations shaped Chinese and Korean negative images of Japan and limited the possibilities for peaceful interaction among the three countries. Many of them were in fact Chinese, sometimes basing themselves in the Japanese islands, allying themselves with Japanese marauders or trade- and predation-oriented *daimyo* (territorial warlords) even using Japanese names or adopting Japanese dress. One of the earliest uses of the term is on a Korean stela dated 414 CE. An outbreak of piracy around the Japanese Inland Sea is recorded in the 930s. References to the Matsuura family and their associates, who would be prominent in piracy and maritime trade until their end in the early 1600s, marauding off the coast of Korea are found in texts from the 1200s.

Japanese piracy off the coasts of the continent reached its first peak in the 1300s. The struggle between the Northern and Southern Courts in Japan unleashed samurai predation and search for plunder in all directions. Raids reached down to the coasts of Shandong and other parts of northern China, but Korea bore the brunt of the pillage. Korean sources record 174 raids between 1376 and 1385, some of them mini-invasions that reached the outskirts of the capital. Some Japanese pirates reportedly were allied with maritime rivals of Zhu Yuanzhang, the Ming dynasty (1368–1644) founder, who responded with drastic measures, building up forces and fortifications and forbidding all but the smallest maritime voyages from the coasts of China. Japanese and other foreign rulers could trade with China only by sending tribute embassies to the imperial court. Several powerful figures in Japan responded to this disincentive by attempting to prevent the departure of pirates from their bases. These measures, China's improved maritime defenses, and agrarian and anti-commercial strategies for economic revival from the chaos of the Yuan-Ming wars were sufficient to reduce the numbers of pirate attacks on China in the 1400s. Illegal trade from the Fujian port of Yuegang and the vast legal loophole of the flourishing tribute trade of the kings of the Ryukyu Islands were other safety valves for trade that reduced maritime violence.

Treaty of 1443

The Koreans mounted stiff resistance to Japanese raids along their southern coast and negotiated with the Ashikaga shogunate and, more importantly, with local power-holders like the Ōuchi of western Kyushu and the Sō of

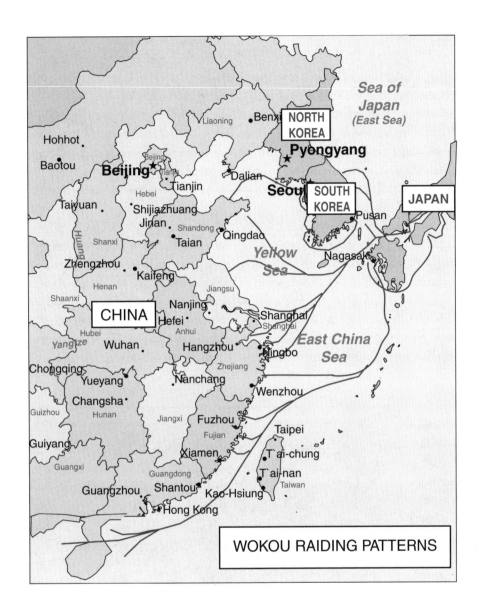

WOKOU RAIDING PATTERNS

Tsushima Island. A treaty in 1443 confirmed a regime of ship-permit quotas for various Japanese maritime powers and a very special position for the Sō; all Japanese ships were required to stop at Tsushima to have their permits checked. In 1461 Sō Shigemoto was appointed governor of Tsushima by the king of Korea. Three ports in Korea became substantial enclaves of Japanese settlement. The Japanese continually pushed the boundaries of what they were permitted under the treaty; violence declined but did not entirely cease.

Both the Chinese and the Korean solutions dissolved after 1500, as officials responded to growing volumes of trade and some increase in piracy by attempting to thoroughly enforce all the bureaucratic quotas and restrictions that had been enacted in the 1400s. Riots by Japanese in the Korean ports in 1510 were suppressed, order was restored with the cooperation of the Sō of Tsushima, and trade soon resumed. Another large-scale Japanese attack on Korea occurred in 1555, but by that time the pirates' momentum had shifted to the lower Yanzi (Chang) region. The Japanese returned to attack Korea from 1592 until 1598, employing the large and well-organized armies of Hideyoshi and his allies; their defeat owed much to Korean experience in defensive naval warfare against pirates during the preceding centuries.

Resurgence

Between 1440 and 1550 Chinese sources list only twenty-five *wokou* raids; between 1550 and 1570 they record 542. Trouble began with the strict enforcement of restrictions on foreign trade after the succession of the Jiajing emperor in 1524. A base of smugglers and pirates at the Shuangyu anchorage in the Zhoushan Archipelago off the Zhejiang coast is reported as early as 1526. Enforcement measures simply pushed well-armed Chinese maritime traders into collusion with Japanese traders, less and less under control as the chaos of Japan's Warring States period (1467–1600, *Sengoku jidai*) reached its peak. Historians differ with regard to the numbers of Chinese and Japanese involved in these *wokou* raids, and the total has remained inestimable in view of (1) the numbers of Chinese gangsters who took Japanese names or donned Japanese breechclouts to scare their countrymen, (2) the

multiple aliases used by many, and (3) the prevalence of adoption, sworn brotherhood, and other pseudo-kinship ties from Japan to Vietnam and beyond. In 1547 Zhu Wan was appointed as a special Grand Coordinator with wide authority to stamp out smuggling and piracy on the Zhejiang and Fujian coasts. In the spring of 1548 his forces occupied and devastated the Shuangyu anchorage. The number of captives taken was not large; the attack came in the season when winds favored voyages to Japan, and any sensible smuggler/pirate would have seen it coming and would have assembled his cargoes and gotten away to Japan. The maritime interests counterattacked; their gentry allies secured the execution of Zhu Wan for judicial irregularities, and their armed bands pillaged coastal areas and even made amazing thrusts inland, camping outside the gates of Wuxi and of Nanjing. The *wokou* had excellent bases in western Japan, especially in the Goto Islands, and much support from the Matsuura,

Fierce Japanese pirate raids ceased sometime around 1630, but southern coast grandmothers continued to threaten Chinese toddlers with the folklore that "the *wokou* would come get them" well into the nineteenth century.

the Shimazu, and other warrior factions. Ming forces sent in pursuit of them were no less predatory than the *wokou* toward merchants and common people. In the 1550s some astute negotiation by Ming high officials turned some of the pirates against each other and secured the surrender and execution of such important leaders as Wang Zhi. Well-trained government militias emerged under leaders like the famous Qi Jiguang. When the Portuguese were permitted to settle at Macao in 1557, they provided a growing channel for trade with Japan without legalizing either the presence of Japanese in Chinese ports or Chinese voyages to Japan. In 1567 the Ming court approved a system of legal foreign trade in Chinese shipping to all destinations except Japan; harbors on Taiwan emerged as entrepots (intermediate centers) for Sino-Japanese trade. This legalization in 1567 did more than all the military efforts had done to end the menace of the *wokou*, who went legal or far offshore into Southeast Asian waters.

Twilight of the Wokou

The *wokou* phenomenon had a long and eventful decline from 1567 until the drastic prohibitions of Japanese sea voyaging by the Tokugawa shogunate in the 1630s. Hideyoshi channeled samurai valor and pirate predation into his hugely ill-conceived invasion of Korea from 1592 until 1598. The Shimazu of Satsuma conquered the Ryukyus in 1609. From 1606 to 1608 Japanese ships heading for Southeast Asia caused rumor and panic among the Chinese people when they stopped at Macao. In the 1620s the Dutch began to settle on southern Taiwan and got into a very dangerous conflict with Japanese traders who had been there before them. The Tokugawa shogunate prohibited foreign voyages by their own people, largely in response to the dangers of Christian subversion. The Japanese were gone, but southern coast grandmothers continued to threaten Chinese toddlers with the folklore that "the *wokou* would come get them" well into the nineteenth century. Some of the *wokou* would have been peaceful traders if they had had the chance; others wanted nothing but loot and killing. They were a central aggravation, an unsolved problem in relations among Japan, Korea, and China for over four hundred years.

John E. WILLS, Jr.

Further Reading

Elisonas, J. (1991). The inseparable trinity: Japan's relations with China and Korea. In J. W. Hall (Ed.), *The Cambridge history of Japan. Vol. 4: Early modern Japan* (pp. 235–300). Cambridge, U.K.: Cambridge University Press.

Kwan Wai So. (1975). *Japanese piracy in Ming China during the 16th Century.* East Lansing: Michigan State University Press.

Wills, J. E., Jr. (1979, 1981). Maritime China from Wang Chih to Shih Lang: Themes in peripheral history. In J. D. Spence & J. E. Wills Jr. (Eds.), *From Ming to Ch'ing: Conquest, region, and continuity in seventeenth-century China* (pp. 204–238). New Haven, CT: Yale University Press.

Women, Role of

Nǚrén de dìwèi 女人的地位

Chinese women, as wives, mothers, and workers, have been central to the functioning of both state and society. In recent years they have contributed to Chinese state-building and commerce in the professions and also as soldiers and scholars, cadre commanders, and political leaders.

The Chinese expression, "women hold up half the sky," describes the important role of women throughout China's history. Confucius (551–479 BCE) believed that strong family relationships were the key to a moral society and, in turn, a moral state. Women thus contributed to state-building. In the upper-class mansions of traditional China, women managed the household and educated the young. In peasant households women worked alongside the men to shape family economies, however meager, that maintained the state.

China changed dramatically during the twentieth century. Women's roles changed as well. No longer only domestic managers and family caregivers, women were now workers and professionals, soldiers and scholars, cadre commanders and political leaders. In the twenty-first century, women remain critical to China's future economic growth and social stability.

Historical illustration of women at work. The Chinese saying, "Women hold up half the sky," reflects the importance of women's roles through history—in the family, the field, and the factory.

Confucian China

Until the twentieth century, Confucianism prescribed the roles of women from birth to death through three sets of principles. The earliest set of principles was the "four womanly virtues," set forth in *Lessons for Women*

by the woman scholar Ban Zhao during the Han dynasty (206 BCE–220 CE). The four virtues were proper virtue, proper speech, proper countenance, and proper conduct. The next important set of principles was that of the "three obediences": obedience to one's father before marriage, to one's husband when married, and to one's son if widowed. Finally, there was the principle of *bie* (separateness). Women and men held different roles in distinct spheres. Women stayed at home. Elite men ran the state and commerce in the public realm. Peasant men worked the fields. Although separate in many respects, the lives of both women and men were a public matter. Because the family was the basic political unit in the Confucian system, the state had a vested interest in the lives of women and men alike.

The Confucian moral code applied equally to women and men. One of the five basic Confucian relationships was that between wife and husband. While husbands were placed over their wives, the principle of reciprocity (*shu*) required that husbands treat their wives with respect if they expected to be obeyed. The very important Confucian virtue of filial piety (*xiao*) required sons to honor and serve both their fathers and their mothers.

Aspects of the imperial bureaucracy also provided elite women with status and power in the family. Elite boys and men spent much time studying for civil service examinations. Passing these exams qualified a man for an official position and most likely a privileged life. As a way to curtail corruption, Chinese officials were not allowed to hold office in their home province. Once a man received an official appointment, he was assigned to a post far away. In their absence wives and mothers managed the household and often the entire family estate.

Foot Binding

No discussion of women in traditional China would be complete without mentioning the custom of foot binding. Foot binding was the painful practice of wrapping young girls' feet so they would not grow. The practice has led to the stereotyping of Chinese women as victims of male subjugation and ornaments for male amusement. Yet foot binding was not condoned in orthodox Confucian literature. In actuality foot binding was an aesthetic fashion that was part of female culture.

Foot binding began during the Song dynasty (960–1279) as a fashion among courtesans. It was soon adapted by women in court circles. Tiny feet became a point of status and a mark of beauty for women in elite society. Because it was the custom in China for men to marry women of lower social standing, foot binding eventually spread across the social strata and became a means of upward mobility—or aspiration—for some families, as they would

In the twentieth century Chinese women began to take on a more prominent role in community leadership, politics, and the military.

The 1979 Women's Delegation from China to the United States at the Johnson Foundation in Racine, Wisconsin. The women also visited the Pentagon and New York City. COURTESY OF THE NATIONAL COMMITTEE ON UNITED STATES–CHINA RELATIONS AND THE JOHNSON FOUNDATION.

have their daughters' feet bound to make them more desirable to prospective husbands of a higher social status.

Foot binding was a private female ritual. Mothers bound the feet of their daughters. Young girls embroidered intricate slippers as part of their trousseau and wrote poems about their tiny feet. Bathing and rebinding feet became a lifelong part of women's daily toilet. Except for her husband, no man ever saw a woman's feet, and even he never saw his wife's feet unbound.

Women in Traditional China

The adage "men till, women weave" described gender roles in traditional China. Originally, it also described women's economic contributions to the state. In early and middle imperial China (221 BCE–1279 CE), taxes were paid in rice and woven cotton cloth; thus, women were responsible for a portion of the family tax levy. Gradually, however, the adage referred to the differentiation of men's and women's work. Elite men served in public office; peasant men labored in the fields. Both elite and peasant women worked in the domestic household.

Women's social status was based on their roles as wives and especially mothers. Producing children, especially boys, was highly valued in China's patrilineal society. The custom of revering one's ancestors made a male

heir indispensable because only he could conduct these family rituals. The virtue of filial piety required sons to care for parents in their old age. Sons brought honor, prestige, and wealth to their families if they passed their civil service examinations and were appointed to government positions. Even the lowest bureaucratic position elevated the entire family to scholar-gentry status with its many class privileges.

Even with so much emphasis on boys, girls were equally necessary for a strong society because they were the ones to produce the next generation of male heirs. From earliest childhood girls were groomed for their future roles as wives, mothers, and daughters-in-law. Marriage was a social contract between families. A bride and groom never saw each other before their wedding day. An emotional attachment may or may not have developed between a wife and husband.

A wife's primary relationship was with her mother-in-law, the ruler of the household. A woman's status within her husband's family was complicated, especially in a large extended family with many other women. Status for a woman was determined by her own age, the position of her husband in the family, and whether she produced a male heir. Her beauty, womanly virtues, and domestic skills also contributed to status, although in a minor way.

Concubines were "secondary" wives who were not legal wives; they also had little or no social standing. If a man's first wife failed to produce a male heir, law and custom allowed him to bring a second woman into the household to father his son. The son was considered legitimate, but the first wife—not the concubine—was recognized as the child's mother. While the practice of concubinage was officially condoned only as a means to secure a male heir, the practice of taking more than one concubine became a mark of wealth among the affluent.

Women in Modern China

China faced tremendous challenges over the last century and a half. Every aspect of Chinese life—social, political, and economic—changed during this time. This especially included the roles of women, who emerged from the domestic household to take an active and public role in building modern China.

A young girl dressed in soldier's garb greets a press plane landing in Beijing on 21 February 1972.

Education was the key to women's transformation. At the beginning of the twentieth century, women received educations outside of the home in missionary schools and private academies. Beginning in 1907 government-run schools began to accept women. Some women continued their studies in Japan or the United States. With the growth of higher education for women in China—through Christian union colleges for women founded between 1905 and 1915 and government-sponsored universities after 1919—women leaders were more likely to have been educated entirely in China.

Women's modern transformation was very gradual, and there were setbacks. Professions only slowly opened to women. In the 1920s women worked as doctors and educators, and in many "white-collar" jobs in stores and businesses. Gradually women entered government service. Political rights were even more elusive. Both the Nationalist and the Communist parties were essentially patriarchal. The New Life Movement, an ideological campaign launched by General Chiang Kai-shek in the early 1930s, actually emphasized the four womanly virtues and sought to curtail women's new public roles by promoting domesticity. But also in the 1930s a civil law code was finally passed that granted women many civil rights, such as the right to inheritance and property ownership.

Most of the progress women made in the first half of the twentieth century affected only women in the urban centers. In the rural countryside, where most of China's population lived, life changed slowly, if at all. Wars, rebellions, famines, floods, and a growing population drove most of China's rural populations into poverty. Infanticide, especially of girls, and the selling of girls into slavery, prostitution, and indentured servitude in factories and mills were common. The Chinese Communist Party (CCP) finally put an end to these practices when it came to power in 1949.

The creation of the People's Republic of China brought other significant changes to women. In 1949 women from various women's organizations formed the All-China Women's Federation (ACWF). A quasi-official organization, the ACWF provided Chinese women their first real opportunity to have a voice in their own affairs and those of their country. Although ideologically bound to the CCP, the ACWF is exclusively a women's organization that lobbies the government on behalf of women and helps enforce policy at the regional and local levels. In 1950 the government also enacted a series of marriage laws that, at least theoretically, made women and men equal under the law. The laws also legalized divorce and banned concubinage and the sale of brides. But women have also endured much. Political purges, ill-conceived economic reforms, and the disastrous Cultural Revolution (1966-1976) compromised or destroyed the lives of thousands if not millions.

China's rise as a world power has opened up even more possibilities for women. Educated, trained, and skilled women are helping drive China's burgeoning economy. For the first time in history, many women are delaying marriage, finding financial success, and enjoying independent lives. However, as has been true throughout Chinese history, these educated, urban professionals represent only a small fraction of Chinese women. The majority of women living in the rural areas receive only middle school educations at best and, for most, marriage remains their only option. But even women from the rural areas are testing the waters in the new industrial centers springing up across China. Whether veteran party members or young urban elites or laborers, Chinese women still hold up half the sky.

Elizabeth A. LITTELL-LAMB

Further Reading

Cong Xiaoping. (2007). *Teachers' schools and the making of the modern Chinese nation-state, 1897–1937*. Vancouver, Canada: University of British Columbia Press.

Ebrey, P. (1993). *The inner quarters, marriage and the lives of Chinese women in the Sung Period*. Berkeley: University of California Press.

Ebrey, P. (2002). *Women and the family in Chinese history*. London: Routledge.

Hershatter, G. (1997). *Dangerous pleasures: Prostitution and modernity in twentieth century Shanghai*. Berkeley: University of California Press.

Ko, Dorothy. (1994). *Teachers of the inner chambers*. Stanford, CA: Stanford University Press.

Ko, Dorothy. (2007). *Cinderella's sisters: A revisionist history of footbinding*. Berkeley: University of California Press.

Mann, S. (1997). *Precious records: Women in China's long eighteenth century*. Stanford, CA: Stanford University Press.

Spence, J. (1981). *The gate of heavenly peace: The Chinese and their revolution, 1895–1980*. New York: Penguin Books.

Tsao Hsueh-chin. (1958). *Dream of the red chamber*. New York: Anchor Books.

Wang Zheng. (1999). *Women in the Chinese enlightenment: Oral and textual histories*. Berkeley: University of California Press.

Women hold up
half the sky.

妇 女 能 顶
半 边 天

fùnǚ néng dǐng
bàn biāntiān

Word Radicals

Bùshǒu 部首

Chinese word radicals are the building blocks of most of Chinese words. Each radical conveys a certain message, be it an object or an abstract notion. Understanding of the Chinese word radicals is crucial to the appreciation of Chinese language.

A Chinese word radical (*bushou*, 部首) is a semantic marker that links certain core ideas with a word. Written Chinese words are expressed in pictograms, which are made up of certain elements, including radicals. Each element has a specific meaning. The elements collectively mold a specific object or idea into the pictogram.

The Chinese system of word radicals is the world's earliest large-scale, across-the-board classification of knowledge at the fundamental level. The system is unique in its capacity to associate a range of objects or ideas under a single umbrella. It contributes to the notion that complex matters are made up of simpler components. The system also reinforces lateral thinking and the notion of association: An object or notion should somehow be classified under a category or grouping.

Some of the word radicals exist only as components of words and have no meaning by themselves. For example, the radical 纟 (*si*) alone means nothing though it implies something related to "textile." Similarly, the radical 亻 (*ren*) is not a word in its own right though it is used for words related to "people" or "human."

Most radicals, however, have semantic importance; that is, they carry specific meaning, as the following examples show. Words related to sentiments or emotions normally have 心 or 忄 (*xin, heart*) as the radical. These include *angry, bored, forget, loyal, tolerance, fear, feeling, love, sad,* and *thought*. Most objects or concepts related to water—words such as *cool, river, stream, swamp, sweat, flow, ocean, flush, gush, soup, tears*—incorporate 水 or 氵 (*shui, water*) as the word radical. Most words for metals and minerals have the radical 钅 (*metal*). The radical 饣 (*shi, food*) is used in words related to eating and to certain types of foods. Some of the word radicals are more easily understood than others.

The number of radicals included in a particular dictionary might vary, depending on how many Chinese words that dictionary accepts. The first Chinese dictionary, shuōwéĬnjiězì, 说文解字, compiled around 100 CE, collected 9,353 characters. The most comprehensive dictionary, the Kangxi Dictionary, Kāngxīzìdiⓧn, 康熙字典 lists about 40,000 characters although, as with the entries in the Oxford English Dictionary, many are archaic or obsolete.

Examples of some of the 190 to 214 radicals commonly used are as follows:

- *Speech* (讠) found in *speech* 话; *remember* 记; *permission* 许; and *promise* 诺
- *Knife* (刀), found in *cut* 切; *distribute* 分; and *fight* for 争
- *Strength* (力), found in *add* 加; *work* 功; and *effort* 努

- Three dotted drops of *water* 氵, found in *full* 满; *river* 江; *soup* 汤; *sprinkle, pour water over* 浇; *wave* 浪; *sea* 海; and *ocean* 洋

- *Upright heart* 忄, found in *remembrance* 忆; *busy* 忙; *worry* 忧; *faint hearted* 懦; and *anger* 愤

- *Movement* 辶, found in *passing by* 过; *reach* 达; *near* 近; and *enter, advance* 进

- *Grass* 艹, found in *grass* 草; *flower* 花; and *fragrance* 芳

- *Hand* 扌, found in *hit* 打; *search* 找; *bend* 折; and *shift* 搬

- *Mouth* 口, found in *call* 叫; and *animal cry* 鸣

- *Mountain* 山, found in *peak* 峰; and *collapse* 崩

- *Food* 饣, found in *hungry* 饥; *drink* 饮; and *rice* 饭

- *Bow* 弓, found in *draw in* 引; *extend* 张; and *weak* 弱

- *Female* 女, found in *mother* 妈; *elder sister* 姐; *younger sister* 妹; and *woman* 妇

- *Child* 子, found in *grandchild* 孙; and *learn* 学

- *Horse* 马, found in *drive* 驾; *proud* 骄; and *tame* 驯

- *Fire* 火, found in *heat treatment* 炼; *heat* 炎; *cigarette, smoke* 烟; and *beacon* 烽

- *Heart* 心, found in *thoughts* 思; *tolerate* 忍; *loyal* 忠; and *love* 恋

- *Wood* 木, found in *forest* 林; *jungle* 森; *tree* 树; *plank*; 板 and *material* 材

Examples of Word Radical Combinations

The character 中 (*zhong*) refers to "middle," "central," or "center." The character depicts a line drawn through the center of a rectangle. The character 心 (*xin*) refers to "the heart." When these two characters are combined as radicals, they form the word *loyalty* 忠, the scenario whereby the heart remains central, not swayed by circumstances, giving rise to the notion of loyalty.

國　The word *nation* 國 comprises a well defined boundary or territory, as shown by the outer frame 囗. Within the territory a straight line at the bottom 一 depicts land on which people, represented by *mouth* 口, reside. Within the framework there is *spear* 戈, signifying defense of the territory. The notion of "nation" is, therefore, a territory with its land and its people who defend the associated assets and values.

愛　The word *love* 愛 incorporates the radical *heart* 心 at the core, representing emotion, feeling, or sentiment. The closest character that lies beneath the heart is *friend* 友, indicating that there are strong emotional links between friends. The sentiment and emotion is capped 冖 (enclosure above the heart), confirming that the relationship is exclusive, not open to anyone else. Finally, there is the claw component 爪 on top, implying a powerful grip, emotional or physical, on the people concerned. Such are the power and emotions involved in love.

The importance of word radicals cannot be overestimated. Radicals form an integral part of written Chinese. Until the development of phonetics, the radical was the main tool to search for words in Chinese dictionaries. An understanding of word radicals is fundamental to the study of the Chinese language.

Yit-Seng YOW

Further Reading

Theobald, U. (2000). The 214 Radicals (*bushou*). *CHINA KNOWLEDGE—a universal guide for China studies*. Retrieved October 17, 2008, from http://www.chinaknowledge.de/Literature/radicals.html

Xiandai hanyu cidian [Modern Chinese dictionary]. (1979). Beijing: Language Research Institute of the Chinese Academy of Social Science.

Yow, Yit Seng. (2006). *The Chinese dimensions: Their roots, mindset, psyche*. Selangor Darul Ehsan, Malaysia: Pelanduk Publications (M) SDN BHD.

World Expo 2010–Shanghai

2010 Nián Shànghǎi Shìbóhuì

2010 年上海世博会

World's fairs have always been a reflection of their times. Expo 2010 Shanghai China, also known as World Expo 2010, is no exception. The theme of the fair, scheduled to run 1 May to 31 October, is "Better City, Better Life." The world will converge on Shanghai to see products and to hear ideas designed to improve urban living in the twenty-first century.

Riding the success of the 2008 Beijing Olympics, China again opens its doors to the world in 2010 with Expo 2010 Shanghai China. The international event runs from 1 May to 31 October along the waterfront of the Huangpu River in downtown Shanghai. More than two hundred nations, business, and international organizations are participating, and up to 70 million visitors from around the world are expected. (If the United States participates, it will take funding from the private sector, not the government. Legislation prohibits official government funding.) The expo features exhibits, demonstrations, and symposiums centered on the theme "Better City, Better Life." Officials say the purpose of the expo is to encourage innovation for sustainable and harmonious urban living. The expo, or fair, is the first registered world exposition in a developing country and only China's second world's fair (the first was in Nanking in 1910). World's fairs and expositions have a long history in the rest of the world.

Brief History of Fairs

Fairs date back more than 2,500 years in human history. Fairs have always been a mix of cultural or religious festival and trade show. Some fairs are localized—like county fairs in the United States—and some are international. The goals of world's fairs are commercial and cultural. Besides offering products for sale, world's fairs provide an opportunity for both host and participating countries to display their capabilities, ideals, and culture. Expositions are also grand venues for amusement and entertainment: giant carnivals, essentially. As times change, expos change to fit those times.

One of the first modern trade show expositions took place in London in 1760. The Royal Society for the Encouragement of Arts, Manufacture, and Commerce organized exhibitions and offered prizes for improvements in the manufacture of tapestries, carpets, and porcelain. The first true world's fair was also held in London in 1851, the Great Exhibition of the Works of Industry of All Nations.

Between 1870 and 1940, an international exposition of some kind was held every year, mostly in Europe and North America. In 1928 the International Exhibitions Bureau was established in Paris to regulate the frequency and quality of expositions. Since the 1950s, however, the frequency and popularity of world's fairs has declined.

The first international fair in China was the Nanyang Industrial Exhibition in Nanking in 1910. Plans were laid for an American-Chinese exposition in 1920 in Shanghai, but it was never mounted. In 1957 the first

Canton Fair was held in Guangzhou. This trade fair has been held every spring and autumn since then. In 2007 it was renamed the China Import and Export Fair; it is the largest trade fair in China. The Shanghai Expo is expected to far surpass the Guangzhou trade show in attendance and the number of products displayed and business deals made.

Shanghai, the City

Shanghai, which literally means the "City on the Sea," lies in the Yangzi (Chang) River Delta. It is called in Chinese Hu for short and Shen as a nickname. The city proper covers 6,340 square kilometers (2,448 square miles). Eighteen districts and one county are under its jurisdiction. Its estimated 2007 population is nearly 19 million. Shanghai has been undergoing one of the fastest economic expansions in history and is becoming East Asia's leading business city.

Construction on infrastructure—mostly transportation—within the city and on the expo site itself began in earnest in 2007. The Shanghai Expo Park is the largest single construction project in the history of Shanghai.

Expo Park

The expo park covers 5.28 square kilometers (2 square miles). The site is divided into five zones, each averaging about 60 hectares (148 acres). Another area is a large public amusement park of about 10 hectares (25 acres). There are twenty-six clusters of pavilions. The average floor area of each pavilion cluster can accommodate forty-five exhibition areas, each covering up to 25,000 square meters (269,000 square feet). Each pavilion cluster contains cafes, shops, toilets, communication centers, nursing services, and other public facilities.

The pavilions house the main exhibits. The China Pavilion, the Expo Center, and the Performance Center are the principal structures. Other buildings include pavilions for participating countries, international organizations, corporations, and theme pavilions, including the Urban Civilization Pavilion, the Urban Exploration Pavilion, and the Urban Best Practices area. All the pavilions and exhibits reflect the expo's theme, "Better City, Better Life."

Urban Theme

Organizers of Expo 2010 Shanghai China chose the theme to represent the common wish of humankind for better living in urban environments, recognizing the trend toward urban living in China and throughout the world. The concept of the theme is meant to stimulate innovation and exploration of the full potential of urban life in the twenty-first century. This includes creating an ecofriendly society and maintaining the sustainable development of human beings, according to the organizers. The theme plays out in exhibits that display urban civilization—habitat, lifestyles, working conditions—as it is and as how it can be with progressive thinking and global cooperation. The expo's logo depicts three people representing "me, you, and him or her" holding hands to symbolize the family of humankind. Most of the events at the expo also reflect the theme.

Expo Events

Expo organizers have arranged for more than one hundred cultural and entertainment events each day during the expo's 184-day run at some thirty-five venues. Official events include the opening and closing ceremonies and China National Day. Special events include symposiums on urban issues and meetings of international organizations. Certain days, weeks, and months have been set aside to spotlight China's provinces, autonomous regions, and municipalities, as well as private and state-run enterprises.

International participants are also staging events. Along with the commercial presentations, there are designated national pavilion days on which individual countries will put on special shows highlighting their cultures. United States Day is scheduled for some time in July, if the United States participates.

Many of the national and theme pavilions will remain after the expo as part of the Huangpu Riverside

The emblem for the 2010 world expo, depicting the image of three people-you, me, him/her holding hands together, symbolizes the big family of mankind. Inspired by the shape of the Chinese character image (meaning the world), the design conveys the organizer's wish to host an Expo which is of global scale and which showcases the diversified urban cultures of the world.

城市,让生活更美好
Better City, Better Life

The motto for the World Expo in Shanghai.

Regeneration program, a project to redevelop a run-down industrial area.

After the Expo

Plans for use of the site after the expo were designed early on. Permanent buildings that will add to the skyline of Shanghai include The China Pavilion, which will serve as a cultural center; the Expo Boulevard, a semiopen structure that will serve as a large transportation and commercial center; and the Performance Center, which can be configured to accommodate between 4,000 and 18,000 audience members. In addition, for the expo Shanghai built a new tunnel under the Huangpu River, increased the number of subway trains, and generally improved the city's infrastructure. The impact of Expo 2010 Shanghai China is sure to last for many years.

Wendell ANDERSON

Further Reading

Expo 2010 Shanghai China. (n.d.). Retrieved February 13, 2009 from http://www.expo2010china.com/expo/expoenglish/index.html

Guariglia, J. (2008). *Planet Shanghai: Life in the city.* San Francisco: Chronicle Books.

Heller, A. (1999). *World's fairs and the end of progress: An insider's view* [Monograph]. Corte Madera, CA: World's Fair, Inc.

閒談
chat

China changes constantly, and the *Encyclopedia of China* will change and grow, too. Berkshire's authors and editors welcome questions, comments, and corrections: china.updates@berkshirepublishing.com.

World Heritage Sites

Shìjiè yíchǎn 世界遗产

The concept of linking nature conservation and cultural preservation was adopted in 1972 by the United Nations Educational, Scientific and Cultural Organization (UNESCO). Consequently, the World Heritage Convention authorized the designation of World Heritage sites by the World Heritage Committee.

With a history of some five thousand years China has a rich legacy of art, architecture, literature, and religion. Not until 1987, however, was China's application for its first World Heritage site, the Great Wall, granted by the United Nations Educational, Scientific and Cultural Organization (UNESCO), which has been actively engaged in endeavors to combine nature conservation with cultural preservation since 1972 .

Early Enlistees

The Great Wall (enlisted in 1987) was constructed during the Qin dynasty (221–206 BCE) to defend against invaders from the north and has been renovated throughout history. Connecting Shanghaiguan Pass in the east and Jianyuguan Pass in the west, the Great Wall stretches across Liaoning, Hebei, Shanxi, Shaanxi, Ningxia, and Gansu provinces. It is one of the seven wonders of the world and an icon of Chinese national identity.

The Peking Man Site at Zhoukoudian (enlisted in 1987) near Beijing, site of the discovery of a skullcap and teeth from a species dated broadly to 640,000–230,000 years ago engenders archaeological value in the theory of prehistoric human and evolution. The Mausoleum of the First Qin Emperor (enlisted in 1987) holds the key to the mysteries of an ancient kingdom. Complex arrays of terracotta warriors with horses, chariots, and weapons found in the excavated tombs, each differing in outfit and pose, bear great historical and cultural significance. The Tombs of the Ming and Qing Dynasties (enlisted in 2000 and 2003) signify the art of burial ingenuity, revealing traditional Chinese cosmology (a branch of metaphysics that deals with the nature of the universe), feng shui theory (involving a Chinese geomantic practice in which a structure or site is chosen or configured so as to harmonize with the spiritual forces that inhabit it), and geomancy (divination by means of figures or lines or geographic features).

Palaces and Temples

The Imperial Palace of the Ming and Qing dynasties (enlisted in 1987) in Beijing and Shenyang, the Mountain Resort in Chengde City (enlisted in 1994), the Temple of Heaven (an imperial sacrificial altar) in Beijing (enlisted in 1998), and the Imperial Summer Palace in Beijing (enlisted in 1998) are pinnacles of royal architectural art and the theory of traditional Chinese belief systems.

The Temple of Confucius, the Cemetery of Confucius, and the Kong Family Mansion in Qufu (enlisted in 1994) in Shandong Province commemorate the educator, philosopher, and politician Confucius (551–479 BCE). The cemetery containing the remains of Confucius and 100,000 of his descendants and the complex of monuments within invoke his legacy.

Potala Palace (enlisted in 1994) in Lhasa, Tibet, is a landmark atop Red Hill. The palace consists of two sections—the outer and larger White Palace, built between 1645 and 1653 as the secular administrative center and the winter residential quarters, and the sacred Red Palace of temples and spiritual buildings, built between 1690 and 1693. The complex symbolizes the central role of Buddhism in administering Tibet. Together with Jokhang Temple Monastery and the summer palace Norbulingka, the Potala Palace typifies a sanctuary of Tibetan art and architecture.

Façade of St. Paul's Cathedral, Macao. Originally built by Jesuits in the seventeenth century, St. Paul's was the largest Catholic cathedral in Asia. All but the façade was destroyed by fire during a typhoon in 1835. It remains as Macao's most famous landmark and has been designated a UNESCO World Heritage Site. PHOTO BY JOAN LEBOLD COHEN.

The ancient building complex in the Wudang Mountains (enlisted in 1994) in Hubei Province celebrates the secular and religious architectural achievements of the Yuan (1279–1368), Ming (1368–1644), and Qing (1644–1912) dynasties. The Ancient City of Pingyao (enlisted in 1997) in Shanxi Province, founded in the fourteenth century, exemplifies a well-preserved Han Chinese city with the development of its architectural style (especially of banking) and urban planning. Old Town of Lijiang (enlisted in 1997) in Yunnan Province features the blending of ethnic cultural elements through the ages with a working ancient water-supply system. The Ancient Villages in Southern Anhui Province (Xidi and Hongcun) (enlisted in 2000) embody Anhui/Huizhou architectural style of a Ming dynasty rural settlement.

Gardens and Caves

The Classical Gardens of Suzhou (enlisted in 1997) in Jiangsu Province, consisting of nine gardens dating from the eleventh to the nineteenth century, represent the best in garden design of landscape miniatures that integrate philosophical thinking into natural beauty, while Mount Qingcheng and the Dujiangyan Irrigation System (enlisted in 2000) in Sichuan Province, the birthplace of Daoism and a water-control system built in the third century BCE, bear witness to religious legacy and the ingenuity of ancient water management.

The Mogao Caves (enlisted in 1987), strategically located along the Silk Roads in Gansu Province, is also known as "Cave of Thousand Buddhas" and was carved out of sandstone cliffs over a period of eight dynasties. The caves and attached monasteries, decorated with paintings and silk wall hangings, were once a sanctuary of Buddhist art. The Longmen Grottoes (enlisted in 2000) in Henan Province feature thousands of Buddhist shrines carved on marble surfaces dating from 495 CE, after the first peak of Buddhist cave art of the Yungang Grottoes (enlisted in 2001) in Shanxi Province, with 252 caves and 51,000 statues carved out of sandstone rocks in the fifth and sixth centuries. The Dazu Rock Carvings (enlisted in 1999) of both Buddhist and secular subject matter in the city of Chongqing in Sichuan Province, dating between the ninth and the thirteenth century, culminated in the most developed Chinese art of rock carving, manifesting the spiritual harmony between Indian Buddhism and Chinese Daoist and Confucian beliefs.

Mountains

Also inscribed as World Historical sites are Mount Taishan (enlisted in 1987) in Shandong Province, Mount Huangshan (enlisted in 1990) in Anhui Province, Wulingyuan Scenic & Historic Interest Area (enlisted in 1992) in Hunan Province, Jiuzhaigou Valley Scenic & Historic Interest Area (enlisted in 1992) in Sichuan Province, Huanglong Scenic & Historic Interest Area (enlisted in 1992) in Sichuan Province, Mt. Emei Scenic Area (including Leshan Giant Buddha Scenic Area) (enlisted in 1996) in Sichuan Province, and Mount Wuyi (enlisted in 1999) in Fujian Province. Lushan National Park (enlisted in 1996) is a renowned summer resort. Many of these sites are National Natural Preservation Zones famous either for their natural beauty, historical cultural significance, or habitat for rare and endangered wildlife and plant species.

Three Parallel Rivers

Three Parallel Rivers of Yunnan Protected Areas (enlisted in 2003) host the richest biodiversity of a temperate region in China. Including the upper reaches of the three great rivers in Asia—Yangzi (Chang), Mekong, and Salween, running parallel from north to south—the areas present geological spectacles and natural beauty. The Sichuan Giant Panda Sanctuaries (enlisted in 2006), botanically the richest site in the world outside of rain forests, consist of nine scenic parks and seven nature reserves among which Wolong is the most famous. Hosting more than 30 percent of the world's endangered giant panda population, the sanctuary is also home to other endangered species, including the red panda, the snow leopard, and the clouded leopard.

Architectural Wonders

The Capital Cities and Tombs of the Ancient Koguryo Kingdom (enlisted in 2004) are tombs of three cities of the Koguryo Kingdom (37 BCE–668 CE), which ruled part of northern China and Korea. They bear witness to the kingdom's artistic and architectural ingenuity.

The Historic Centre of Macao (enlisted in 2005), a port of international trade, is an example of the fusion of Chinese and Western architectural styles and the port's colonial history after the return of its sovereignty to the Chinese government from Portugal in 1999.

Yin Xu (enlisted in 2006) in Henan Province is an archaeological site that preserves the ruins of the ancient capital city of Shang dynasty (1766–1045 BCE). It is the most culturally and historically valuable of all the royal tombs and palaces excavated. The script present on oracle bones there offers a sample of the earliest known form of written Chinese.

Kaiping Diaolou (watch tower) and Villages (enlisted in 2007) in Guangdong Province integrates defense and residence with a fusion of vernacular Chinese and Western architectural styles. It bears witness to the influence of a rich population of overseas Chinese during the Ming dynasty. Built of brick, stone, and *pise* or concrete, the multistoried Diaolou has the common defensive characteristics of narrow metal doors and windows, thick walls with gun holes, and a watch tower on the top floor equipped with defensive devices against local banditry.

The South China Karst (enlisted in 2007) has the common characteristics of a karst (an irregular limestone region with sinkholes, underground streams, and caverns) geological formation across Yunnan, Guizhou, and Guangxi provinces in south China. The karst landscape in each province, however, is different. The Shilin (Stone Forest) in Yunnan Province, for instance, presents a mountain range of exposed pinnacles with more varieties of shapes, whereas the karst landscape in Guangxi centered around Guilin typifies independent verdant hills with caves and (underground) rivers punctuated by flat pastoral fields.

As one of the world's earliest civilizations, China is endowed with more qualifying cultural and historical legacies than with the number of sites currently inscribed by the World Heritage Center. Thus the list of China's World Heritage sites seems destined to grow.

Yu Luo RIOUX

Further Reading

Bonneville, P., & Heïmono, P. (2006). *The world heritage: UNESCO's classified sites.* Saint-Hubert, Canada: Bonneville Connection.

Brockman, N. C. (1997). *Encyclopedia of sacred places.* Santa Barbara, CA: ABC-CLIO.

Ebrey, P. B. (1996). *Cambridge illustrated history of China.* Cambridge, U.K.: Cambridge University Press.

Guo Changjian & Song Jianzhi. (Eds.). (2003). *World Heritage sites in China.* Beijing: China Intercontinental Press.

Leask, A., & Fya, A. (Eds.). (2006). *Managing World Heritage sites.* Oxford, U.K., and Burlington, MA: Butterworth-Heinemann.

National Museum of Chinese Revolution History. (Eds.). (2002). *Treasures of mankind: World Heritage sites in China.* Beijing: Cultural Relics Publishing House.

Schellinger, P. E., & Salkin, R. M. (Eds.). (1996). *International dictionary of historic places: Vol. 5. Asia and Oceania.* Chicago: Fitzroy Dearborn Publishers.

United Nations Educational, Scientific and Cultural Organization (UNESCO). World Heritage list. Retrieved January 16, 2008, from http://whc.unesco.org/en/list/

United Nations Educational, Scientific and Cultural Organization & World Heritage Convention. (2007). *World heritage: Challenges for the millennium.* Paris: UNESCO World Heritage Center.

World Trade Organization

Shìjiè Màoyì Zǔzhī 世界贸易组织

China joined the World Trade Organization in 2001 after years of negotiation. The country had been keen to join the WTO given that China's economy is now highly dependent on foreign resources and markets. Joining the WTO is also a mechanism for forcing change on outdated state-owned enterprises in China.

China joined the World Trade Organization (WTO) on 11 December 2001 after years of vigorous lobbying for membership. The WTO is an international organization devoted to the reduction of trade barriers across the globe, with a view that free trade means greater overall benefit for all parties concerned. While not everyone agrees with this premise, it is widely accepted, especially in the major global economies. With the dramatic growth in international trade since World War II, the WTO is the organization primarily responsible for supporting such growth, reducing trade barriers, and helping to regulate the growth. In effect it provides the structure within which international trade can take place efficiently. As of July 2008, 153 countries were members of the WTO.

Chinese officials realized that, to make their economy grow rapidly, they needed access to foreign investment for building up industries quickly and to international markets for selling the products of these industries. In this respect joining the WTO was a logical extension of China's decision, taken in the late 1970s, to create a capitalist economy. These officials were aware that if they did not shift their economic structure away from Communism they could not modernize and regain the power they had lost during years of political and economic chaos.

China's Economy—1912–1979

China had been a great power through most of recorded history, though by the early nineteenth century the Manchu-ruled Qing dynasty (1644–1912) was beginning to fail. In the nineteenth century China failed to modernize and fell prey to Western countries that established enclaves along the East coast of China. In 1911 the Republic of China was founded, the dynasty fell (although the Qing emperor did not abdicate until 1912), and the next fifty years were characterized by political and economic chaos. Out of this chaos the Communist Party finally consolidated power in 1949 and proclaimed the creation of the People's Republic of China.

Unfortunately, China's economic policies were not effective. The Great Leap Forward of the 1950s was an attempt to rapidly catch up with the West. It was a dismal failure and led to widespread famine in China as well as the political upheaval of the Cultural Revolution (1966–1976). Mao's death in 1976 signaled the end of unworkable economic policies and the beginning of a shift to capitalism under the leadership of Deng Xiao Ping

WTO History

The WTO has a long pedigree, even though its name dates only from 1 January 1995. The organization actually began to evolve toward the end of World War II, when world leaders acknowledged they needed an economic system to replace the insularity that had led to the Great Depression of the 1930s: When major economies had faced difficulties, they turned inward with a "beggar thy neighbor" policy, imposing high tariffs, or taxes, on foreign goods to protect domestic agriculture and industry; in reality, however, they only spread and prolonged the Depression.

This situation led to the 1944 Bretton Woods Conference, at which forty-four countries produced key imperatives for postwar global economic development. Most of these Bretton Woods instruments still exist today—for example, the World Bank and the International Monetary Fund. A few years later another international meeting created the General Agreement on Tariffs and Trade (GATT), the forerunner of the WTO. GATT was rooted in compromise: On the one hand was an understanding that countries often must protect particular industries for the national good (as long as tariffs are applied multilaterally—that is, as long as there are no preferential tariffs); and on the other hand was broad support for an open trading system that would both stimulate free trade, thereby ensuring the greatest possible level of economic growth, and link economies. The underlying assumption was the belief that greater economic cooperation would mean greater political cooperation and reduce the possibility of war. The memory of Nazi Germany was strong—an insular country and economic depression had created the conditions for the rise of a totalitarian government, resulting in a terrible world war—and the signatories to the Bretton Woods agreement and GATT wanted to reduce the chances that such a government would surface again.

The Bretton Woods agreement and GATT created the conditions for the longest sustained economic boom in world history, one that lasted from the mid-1940s to the early 1970s. The members of GATT met regularly from 1948 to 1994 (eight rounds in total), in different cities. The last round of GATT talks took place in Uruguay from 1986 to 1994; at the conclusion of this round, the members decided to replace GATT by creating the WTO, essentially a more formal structure for international trade.

China and International Trade

China has the key ingredients for economic success on the international stage—a large population that includes substantial numbers of well-educated people; a reasonably good infrastructure; relatively high levels of technology, at least in the main cities; and, above all, low-cost labor. To take advantage of these factors, as well as to gain foreign access to one of the world's biggest markets, foreign investment poured into China in the 1990s, and the result was dramatic economic growth for the country.

It came as no surprise, therefore, that the Chinese government was eager to join the WTO. Joining would ensure access to world markets, especially to the markets of developed countries with so many wealthy consumers—and, therefore, would keep the economy of China booming.

The fundamental reality was that China needed international connections in order to continue rapid economic growth. Only one other country—Japan—similarly depended on international markets, and it was Japan that sponsored China's entry into the WTO. The main opposition came from the United States. In part this resistance stemmed from competitiveness: The United States was wary of letting China become too strong. In part the resistance was a matter of philosophical differences: The United States questioned whether China's political system should be supported given its view on human rights. But the major U.S. resistance concerned intellectual property. Increasingly the U.S. economy depends on its ability to create and innovate, especially in areas such as software development, biotechnology, medicine, and entertainment. After years of American research and development expenses, Chinese companies have demonstrated a predilection to copy these products, to sell them far below the cost of the American products, and to pocket the profits. Hence charges of intellectual copyright violations, or piracy as it is more commonly called, delayed China's entry into the WTO.

On the other side of the coin, the U.S. economy greatly benefited from China's entry into the WTO. One reason the American economy grew so quickly in the first years of the twenty-first century was that the flow of low-cost Chinese products into the U.S. market allowed American consumers to pay less for some products so that they could theoretically save money or spend more domestically, thereby stimulating the U.S. retail sector. Trading with China also allowed U.S. industries to source lower-cost parts. Moreover, a good number of the factories in China resulted from U.S.-China joint ventures, so the exports were actually made in part by American companies, and some of the profits from the ventures went back to the parent companies in the United States. Finally, China has replaced Japan as the greatest purchaser of U.S. Treasury Bonds, thus allowing the U.S. government to operate at a deficit while avoiding tax increases.

The WTO and Domestic Problems in China

Not all sectors of the Chinese economy benefited right away from this open trading system. One of the main victims was the state sector—state-owned enterprises, or SOEs. These large, usually inefficient producers resisted China's entry to the WTO. But it is clear that the Chinese government used the mechanism of joining the WTO to force the SOEs to change. SOEs had to initiate more efficient management, shed surplus labor and institute more effective production processes. Without this external pressure it would have been politically difficult to carry out domestic economic reform. One advantage of an authoritarian government is its power to initiate more painful economic adjustments than a democracy. That said, it is by no means easy to move China's economy into the modern era, and there have been, and continue to be, many pressures in China, such as unemployment and price increases, working against the rapid pace of economic change.

China also faces the emerging issue of becoming Asia's workshop for only less sophisticated products instead of moving up to high technology exports. This is in part because its exports are dominated by foreign companies (Wholly Foreign Owned Enterprises, or WFOEs, are permitted to register in China in cases where at least half their annual output is exported). Indeed, approximately 60 percent of China's exports overall and 80 percent of its high-tech exports, are produced by foreign companies, which are not eager to share the secrets of their success with the Chinese.

Other Challenges for the WTO and China

One of the fundamental challenges for the WTO is to address the domestic interests of its participating countries yet promote multilateral trade. For example, in Country A local representatives may not favor free trade for fear that foreign companies with lower production costs will export lower-priced versions of Country A's products to Country A, putting companies in the politicians' districts out of business. Of course, if companies in Country A are very efficient and can compete on the international scene, its politicians may support free trade. But in that case Country B's government may balk at importing products from Country A. Clearly, both political and economic factors influence international trade, making the job of the WTO complex. Demands for "level playing fields" and "free and fair" trade along with direct and indirect subsidies to producers bring the concept of free trade into question, yet it is the role of the WTO to deal with these issues and to promote the growth of international trade.

The state of a country's economy affects whether or not it wants to join the WTO. Typically a country that produces commodities inefficiently or faces many international competitors that produce the same commodities, would not support an open trading system. National prestige also affects a country's interest in the WTO. For example, the automobile industry can confer pride, even when that industry can exist only behind high tariffs—as in Australia and Malaysia. The Chinese automobile industry is posing a substantial challenge to these long-standing barriers. As barriers to trade come down the Chinese car industry will certainly be a major player in the international market. In Malaysia's case, if it dropped tariffs then Malaysia's car industry would certain have major problems.

Most countries face yet another challenge when opening their economies to international trade. There are winners and losers in any free-trading system. Inefficient producers will see their businesses fail while efficient ones will thrive. This so-called structural adjustment can produce substantial pain as the changes take place. Workers may have to retrain and move to other economic sectors, but doing so is much easier for some (generally the younger and better educated) than for others. Hence, free trade will be more welcomed by some sectors of the community than others in any particular country, and these divisions are clearly apparent in China. There is a clear employment/wealth gap between younger, more educated Chinese and older, less educated Chinese.

A concept underpinning open trade is comparative advantage. In short this means that each country will produce the goods that it is most efficient at producing. Inefficient producers will go under, and, painful though failure is, the result will be a more efficient global production system, which will, in turn, generate the highest overall global output. The argument put forward by the WTO is that there is a net gain, even though there will be losses in sectors in each country.

The charge leveled by some countries, including China, is that they are the victims of more powerful countries, typically developed countries, that have much greater resources, including a highly educated workforce, well-developed transportation and communication systems, and existing multinational companies. Therefore, meetings of the WTO often incite demonstrations, reflecting for the most part the voice of the developing world. One of the most visible anti-WTO riots took place in Seattle, Washington, on 30 November 1999.

The WTO is faced with a massive challenge—supporting free trade across the globe. The differing interests of different countries and the multiple interest groups in each country make this goal very difficult to achieve. In fact, the WTO is having problems that are reflected in the rapid growth in Free Trade Agreements (FTAs) over the past decade. Countries that strongly favor free trade are not prepared to wait for the WTO to accept them; they are striking out on their own. While this approach does promote free trade in part, it leaves behind those countries that desire a slower entry into the global trading system.

China is an important part of the global economy. It has the fourth largest economy in the world, a growth rate of about 10 percent, the world's largest current account surplus ($180 billion). It is therefore one of the great challenges of the WTO to help manage China's global trade.

Curtis ANDRESSEN

Further Reading

Bassett, R. M. (2006). *The WTO and the university: Globalization, GATTS, and American higher education.* New York: Routledge.

Berman, G. A., & Mavroidis, P. C. (Eds). (2005). *Trade and health in the World Trade Organization.* Cambridge, U.K.: Cambridge University Press.

Berman, G. A., & Mavroidis, P. C. (Eds). (2007). *WTO law and developing countries.* Cambridge, U.K.: Cambridge University Press.

Das, B. L. (2003). *The WTO and the multilateral trading system: Past, present and future.* London: Zed Books.

Ede, R., & Andressen, C. A. (2007). China's assembly-line future. *Taiwanese Journal of Australian Studies 8,* 119–144.

Feng, H. (2006). *The politics of China's accession to the World Trade Organization: The dragon goes global.* London: Routledge.

Footer, M. (2006). *An institutional and normative analysis of the World Trade Organization.* Boston: Martinus Nijhoff.

Harris, S. (1997). *The WTO and APEC: What role for China?* Canberra, Australia: Australia-Japan Research Centre.

Hoekman, B. M., & Mavroidis, P. C. (2007). *The World Trade Organization: Law, economics and politics.* New York: Routledge.

Matsushita, M. (2006). *The World Trade Organization: Law, practice and policy.* Oxford, U.K.: Oxford University Press.

Mavroidis, P. C. & Sykes, A. O. (2005). *The WTO and international trade law/dispute settlement.* Cheltenham, U.K.: Elgar.

Palmeter, D. N. (2004). *Dispute settlement in the World Trade Organization: Practice and procedure.* New York: Cambridge University Press.

Peet, R. (2003). *Unholy trinity: The IMF, World Bank and the World Trade Organization.* New York: Zed Books.

Sacerdoti, G., Yanovich, A., & Bohanes, J. (2006). *The WTO at ten: The contribution of the dispute settlement system.* Cambridge, U.K.: Cambridge University Press.

Steger, D. P. (2004). *Peace through trade: Building the World Trade Organization.* London: Cameron.

Wilkinson, R. (2006). *The WTO: Crisis and the governance of global trade.* New York: Routledge.

World Trade Organization. (2004). *Trade and environment at the WTO.* New York: Trade and Economic Division, WTO.

World Trade Organization (2008). Retrieved November 29, 2008, from http://www.wto.org

World War II in Asia

Èzhàn Yàzhōu Zhànchǎng 二战亚洲战场

Kàngrì Zhànzhēng 抗日战争

World War II in Asia was very different from World War II in Europe. The Asian war included Japanese colonial expansion into the Asian mainland, which preceded the involvement of European and North American nations, and it was also complicated by civil war in China. For some Asian nations the worldwide aspect of the war was secondary to their own conflicts with Japan.

World War II did not begin in a single place or on a single date. While the European war can be dated to the German invasion of Poland in September 1939, Germany had already annexed Austria in 1938. In Asia, the beginning of the war is said to be 7 July 1937, when Japan took military action following the Marco Polo Bridge incident 七七事变 (July Seventh Incident). But Japan had invaded Manchuria six years before. Other aspects of conflict in Asia include the Soviet Union's forced relocation of ethnic Koreans (who had fled from Japanese-occupied Korea into eastern Siberia) to Uzbekistan. In this case 190,000 Koreans were relocated to the west. Although many ethnic Russians had been relocated to the central Asian republics beginning in the 1880s, as a way to counter growing Islamic influence there, such relocations were not part of Soviet wartime relocation policy.

Expansionism by Japan

The conflict which Americans refer to as the War in the Pacific or the Second Sino-Japanese War, which the Chinese call the War of Resistance against Japan, and which the Japanese call the Japan-China War, began at different times, according to which countries were involved. To Americans, the war began with Japan's attack on Pearl Harbor on 7 December 1941. The direct conflict between Japan and China began more than four years before that. But the colonial efforts and military actions that precipitated this period began with the termination of World War I. At the end of that war Japan had acquired territories in China and the Pacific that had formerly been held by Germany. Japan's expansionist policy had begun even before World War I with acquisition of Taiwan after Japan's victory in the First Sino-Japanese War (1894–1895) and annexation of Korea in 1910. Japan's goal was strategic security, a "greater East Asia co-prosperity sphere" that stretched 1,600 kilometers from the Japanese islands and that would remove the Western powers from Asia. Western imperialism had undermined China, and Japan by the mid-1930s had begun to eliminate Western influence there by dividing China through the establishment of a puppet government in Manchuria. Armed conflict in China escalated in 1937, however, in what is known in China as the "War of Resistance against Japan."

In July of that year Japanese forces attacked Beijing; they attacked Shanghai in August. At that time Japan was fighting the army of the Chinese Nationalist Party

(Guomindang) government; the Nationalists leaned more toward the West in matters of foreign policy and trade than did the Chinese Communists, the adversaries of the Nationalists. The Nationalists, unable to stop the Japanese, retreated westward to the city of Nanking (modern Nanjing), where in December Japanese forces captured the city and massacred 300,000 civilians. The Rape of Nanking, more than any other event, created international condemnation of Japan's expansion into Asia and shaped the policies of Japan's opponents.

In southern Asia World War II came to India as a result of British rule there. When Great Britain declared war on Germany, the Indian viceroy followed suit, but the Indian congress did not support him. While war raged in East Asia and Europe, India at first was little more than a supplier of men for the African front and for the British in Singapore as well as a supply base for operations in the Middle East.

India's circumstances changed with Japanese attacks in the Pacific and on the Asian mainland. Indian soldiers who had been sent to reinforce British territories in East Asia were killed or captured by the Japanese after fighting began, causing India to return to British allegiance, at least for a short while.

Entry by the United States

The United States was still formally neutral at this time and was selling Japan oil and steel—materials that Japan needed for its military expansion. The United States had accepted Japan's annexation of the Korean peninsula, and ethnic Koreans in the United States were considered to be Japanese. The U.S. interest was on the growing war in Europe, not on Asia. While the United States provided some aid to the Nationalist Chinese, the Soviet Union provided China more operational support with aircraft and pilots until 1939, when those planes and men were recalled to fight Germany. The main U.S. support to China after that was the effort to construct the Burma Road from Lashio, Burma (Myanmar), to Kunming, China, begun in 1938 to provide a western route into China for military supplies. U.S. policy at the time was to avoid conflict in the Pacific because conflict there would divert assets

On 6 February 1945 a U.S. Army soldier and a Chinese soldier, allies in the war, each place the other's flag on the front of their respective jeeps. The first truck convoy in almost three years is just about to cross the China border en route from Ledo, India, to Kunming, China, over the Stilwell Road. NATIONAL ARCHIVES.

from the Atlantic. Only in 1940, responding to further Japanese expansion in China, did the United States begin an economic embargo of steel and oil against Japan. This embargo was expanded in mid-1941 to a complete end of all trade with Japan; after that Japan had to seize the sources of materials necessary for its strategic survival.

Japan had continued its strategy of replacing Western influence with its own in Southeast Asia. The French colonial government in Indochina (Laos, Vietnam, and Cambodia) capitulated to Japan in 1940 after France fell to Germany. Thailand accepted Japan's presence in the region as a means of recovering territory lost to Laos, Cambodia, and Malaya (Malaysia). The outbreak of war with Western forces in December 1941 led to the occupation of Burma, Malaya, and the Dutch East Indies (Indonesia) and began the conquest of the Philippines.

Although most U.S. residents view the Japanese attack on Pearl Harbor on 7 December 1941 as the beginning of World War II in Asia, this event occurred thirty-one years after the annexation of Korea, ten years after the establishment of Japanese rule in northern China, four years

A Chinese soldier guards a line of American P-40 fighter planes, painted with the shark-face emblem of the "Flying Tigers," at an airfield in China, circa 1942. NATIONAL ARCHIVES.

after the massacre at Nanking (Nanjing), and one year after much of Southeast Asia had come under Japanese domination. But to Japan the initiation of war against the United States was in response to the undeclared war that the United States had begun with its embargo of critical materials.

Early Successes by Japan

Japan's attack on Western holdings in Asia and the Pacific led to impressive early successes. U.S. military power in Hawaii was dealt a severe blow, Hong Kong fell, the Philippines and Burma were taken, and at the outer reaches of Japanese power, the Solomon Islands, the Gilbert Islands, and islands in Alaska's Aleutian chain were captured. The Solomon and Gilbert islands consolidated Japan's holdings acquired by a League of Nations mandate after World War I. By mid-1942 the Western powers were near defeat in Asia and the Pacific. But the same technological forces that had permitted Japan's quick military expansion began to work in favor of the Allies, in part because of what must be considered a stroke of luck that occurred before the attack on Pearl Harbor.

Change in Naval Strategy by the United States

U.S. naval strategy before December 1941 had been based on the use of battleships in naval combat, but after the Pearl Harbor attack, the aircraft carrier became the mainstay of U.S. naval strategy. The aircraft carrier had been an untested experiment until it was used with great success by the Japanese navy. At the time of the Japanese attack on Pearl Harbor, the U.S. Navy's three aircraft carriers were out of port, but its battleships were in port at Pearl Harbor, where they were destroyed. This circumstance forced the U.S. Navy to adopt a strategy based on the aircraft carrier for the Pacific theater of operations because the main focus of the war was still Europe, and replacements for U.S. battleships would not be available for some time. The new U.S. strategy would have to counter the advances that Japan had already made in the Pacific and would rely on U.S. industrial capacity (after it was mobilized), technological advantage, and innovative tactics.

But Japan's strategy had been one of rapid successes that would give it the advantage in establishing dominance over East Asia before the United States and other Western

Photograph of the hull damage to SS _Morrison R. Waite_ after attack by Japanese suicide planes, Leyte Gulf, Phillippine Islands, 29 January 1945.
NATIONAL ARCHIVES.

powers could retaliate. General Tojo Hideki (1884–1948), Japan's prime minister, had no misperceptions about U.S. capacity; even he recognized that a long war would work against Japan's long-term goals. As the Allies became capable of maintaining their holdings and then advancing toward the Japanese home islands, the resources available to the Allies (and denied to the Japanese), tactics, and technology swung in favor of the Allies.

Internal Battle for China

Yet on the Asian mainland Japan remained the dominant force. In China the Communists under Mao Zedong (1893–1976) and the Nationalists under Chiang Kai-shek (1887–1975) had been at odds since 1926, and at times this competition undermined Chinese efforts to defeat the Japanese. While Chinese forces avoided total defeat at Shanghai in 1932, Japan was able to establish a puppet government in Manchuria (called Manchuguo). Chiang spent the next five years strengthening his Nationalist army, while the Communists withdrew to northwest China on the Long March (1934–1935) from Jiangxi Province to Shaanxi Province—approximately 9,600 kilometers. Mao rebuilt his forces during the next year and sought a united effort of Communists and Nationalists

against the Japanese. However, Chiang wanted to defeat the Communists first, then deal with the Japanese. In late 1936 one of his own generals kidnapped Chiang while on a visit to Xi'an, and as a condition of Chiang's release he had work with the Communists to fight the Japanese. Japanese forces subsequently dramatically increased their

Camouflaged and poorly equipped Chinese soldiers repel a charge of 50,000 Japanese along the Salween River near Burma, June 1943.
NATIONAL ARCHIVES.

Mao Zedong, leader of China's Communists, addresses some of his followers, 6 December 1944. NATIONAL ARCHIVES.

efforts, leading to the Nanking Massacre and to victories at Guangzhou (Canton) and Wuhan in 1938.

Even as both Chinese factions—the Communists and the Nationalists—worked against the Japanese, each saw their efforts as a means to dominate the other. Chiang Kai-shek believed that Japan would wear down the Communists so that he would be able to deal with them after the Japanese were defeated, and Mao believed that Nationalist action against the Japanese was an opportunity for his Communist forces to rest. Both sides expanded their forces in preparation for civil war after Japan was defeated.

The United States began to support China only after years of fighting by Chinese forces, but in March 1941 the U.S. Lend-Lease Program (which had been used to support European nations fighting against German Nazi leader Adolph Hitler since 1939) was extended to China. This program and other aid were significantly increased after Japan attacked Pearl Harbor eight months later.

Expansion of the War

The Japanese attack on the U.S. naval base at Pearl Harbor dramatically changed the war for Japan. Despite Japan's early successes in late 1941 and 1942, Japan lacked the resources necessary for a protracted war. An attack on Tokyo by U.S. bombers launched from an aircraft carrier in April 1942 unsettled Japan. This raid, led by Lieutenant Colonel James Doolittle, was launched mainly for psychological reasons. For the United States the raid provided some good news after a string of defeats; for Japan the raid showed that not even Tokyo was safe.

The new U.S. aircraft carrier–based strategy, instead of being oriented exclusively against Japanese naval

Conference at Yan'an, the Chinese Communist Party headquarters, before chairman Mao Zedong left for a Chongqing meeting. Central figures are U.S. ambassador Patrick J. Hurley, Colonel I. V. Yeaton, U.S. Army observer, and Mao Zedong, 27 August 1945. NATIONAL ARCHIVES.

Franklin D. Roosevelt, Chiang Kai-shek, and Winston Churchill in Cairo, Egypt, 25 November 1943. Source: Franklin D. Roosevelt Library Public Domain Photographs, 1882–1962. NATIONAL ARCHIVES.

forces, used "island-hopping" to advance on the Japanese home islands. After the United States defeated Japanese naval forces at the Battle of Midway and the Battle of Guadalcanal in 1942, Allied forces moved through the Gilbert Islands and New Guinea in 1943 and then on to the Marianas Islands and the Philippines in 1944. The Allies, by attacking Japanese strong points that might threaten Allied operations and by seizing those islands necessary for operations while bypassing others, were able to prepare for what would have been the final assault on Japan in 1945.

Farther west the Japanese army had opened a front to invade Burma to counter British and U.S. efforts there. This front expanded in mid-1944 to an attempt to defeat the British and Indian forces in eastern India, resulting in an overextension of Japanese supply lines and the eventual destruction of the Japanese Fifteenth Army.

Also in 1944 the Flying Tigers, a volunteer corps of U.S. fliers in China, began to attack Japanese forces there. Although the Flying Tigers diverted Japanese attention from the war with Chinese forces, Chiang Kai-shek did not capitalize on the diversion, much to the anger of the senior U.S. official in China, Brigadier General Joseph Stillwell. The friction between Stillwell and Chiang soon

caused President Franklin D. Roosevelt (1882–1945) to recall Stillwell to the United States.

By 1945 a campaign of strategic bombing of Japanese cities was being waged by the United States from island bases in the Pacific. Attacks by the U.S. Air Corps targeted both Japanese cities and military forces and resulted in tens of thousands of civilian casualties and massive destruction (as had the Allied attacks on cities in Germany). For example, the firebombing of Tokyo on 9 March 1945 killed as many as 120,000 Japanese. At the time the U.S. policy was one of "total war" against the Japanese population in preparation for a final Allied push against Japan, which was to be a massive amphibious assault against the islands of Kyushu (Operation Olympic) in December 1945 and Honshu (Operation Coronet) in March 1946. For these two assaults the United States had planned to use forces made available by the defeat of Germany—forces that in many cases already were in transit to the Pacific. As many as 5 million soldiers, primarily U.S., would have taken part. The Soviet Union also would take part in the invasion of Japan.

Planning for Operation Olympic had begun in 1944 as Allied forces had moved toward Japan. By early 1945 an estimated 300,000 Japanese soldiers were on the Japanese home islands of Kyushu and Honshu; by August this estimate had risen to more than a half-million, including a considerable number of combat units. The U.S. experience in attacking islands held by the Japanese was that Japanese soldiers and civilians would fight to the death to avoid capture, leading to heavy casualties among U.S. forces. Estimates for the invasion were as high as 1 million Allied casualties and possibly three times that for Japan. The losses for Japan would include both military and civilian personnel and could have resulted in the end of Japan as a country.

The War Ends

In February 1945 at Yalta in the Crimea the leaders of the United States, the Soviet Union, and Great Britain held discussions for the Allied focus on Japan. The Yalta Conference resulted in an agreement that the Soviet Union would enter the war against Japan after Germany was defeated and that upon Japan's defeat those areas in China formerly held by Russia but captured by Japan in 1904 would be ceded to the Soviet Union. President Roosevelt kept the agreement secret from even Vice President Harry Truman (1884–1972) on his return from Yalta, but Roosevelt died within two months. The decision to proceed with the plans made earlier then fell to Truman.

President Truman met with British prime minister Winston Churchill (1875–1975) and Soviet premier Joseph Stalin (1879–1953) at Potsdam, Germany, in July 1945 to discuss further the treatment and disarmament of Japan after it had been defeated. While he was at Potsdam Truman learned of the successful test of a new weapon that might shorten the war. That weapon, of course, was the atomic bomb. Truman informed Churchill, but not Stalin, of the weapon.

The atomic bomb used against Japan eliminated the need for an invasion of Japan. A single U.S. aircraft dropped a single ten-thousand-pound (4,536-kilogram) bomb on the Japanese city of Hiroshima on 6 August 1945, resulting in an explosion equal to approximately twenty thousand metric tons of conventional explosives. Hiroshima was chosen because it was an industrial target that had not been damaged by earlier attacks, a fact that would allow estimations of the bomb's effectiveness. The bomb

United China Relief was founded in the U.S. to aid Chinese victims of war. NATIONAL ARCHIVES.

instantly killed 130,000 people, injured as many, and destroyed four-fifths of the buildings in Hiroshima. Three days later the United States dropped a second atomic bomb, this time on the Japanese city of Nagasaki. By that time the Soviet Union had declared war on Japan and had invaded Manchuria.

Although the two bombs dropped on Hiroshima and Nagasaki instantly killed approximately 200,000 people, and thousands subsequently died from injuries and radiation poisoning, these attacks were not as damaging as the combined earlier attacks on other major cities. The atomic bomb, for President Truman, was simply a weapon of war, not an element of a greater strategy. It was successful: On 14 August 1945 the Japanese government accepted the guidelines of the Potsdam Declaration. The Soviet Union refused to accept the Japanese proposal because it did not contain an order to the Japanese military to surrender; the Soviet Union accepted the official signing of the documents on 2 September 1945.

World War II cost more than 2.5 million Japanese and 11 million Chinese lives plus countless others in the occupied nations of the region. Casualties among Allied forces—the United States, Great Britain, Canada, New Zealand, Australia, and India—were relatively light; approximately 200,000 were killed in Asia, the majority of them U.S. troops.

Thomas P. DOLAN

Further Reading

Alperovitz, G. (1967). *Atomic diplomacy: Hiroshima and Potsdam.* New York: Vintage Books.

Buss, C. A. (1964). *Asia in the modern world.* New York: Macmillan.

Chang, Iris. (1997). *The rape of Nanking.* New York: Basic Books.

Dallek, R. (1979). *Franklin D. Roosevelt and American foreign policy, 1932–1943.* Oxford, U.K.: Oxford University Press.

Gallagher, M. P. (1963). *The Soviet history of World War II.* New York: Frederick A. Praeger.

Harries, M., & Harries, S. (1991). *Soldiers of the sun: The rise and fall of the Imperial Japanese Army.* New York: Random House.

Hsü, I. C. Y. (1990). *The rise of modern China* (4th ed.). New York: Oxford University Press.

Kim Young Hum. (1966). *East Asia's turbulent century.* New York: Appleton-Century-Crofts.

Lattimore, O. (1949). *The situation in Asia.* Boston: Little, Brown.

Lederer, I. J. (Ed.). (1962). *Russian foreign policy: Essays in historical perspective.* New Haven, CT: Yale University Press.

McNelly, T. (Ed.). (1967). *Sources in East Asian history and politics.* New York: Appleton-Century-Crofts.

Paterson, T. G., Clifford, J. G., Kisatsky, D., Maddock, S. J., & Hagan, K. J. (2000). *American foreign relations* (2 vols.). Boston: Houghton Mifflin.

Ulam, A. (1974). *Expansion and coexistence: Soviet foreign policy, 1917–73* (2d ed.). New York: Holt, Rinehart and Winston.

Van Alstyne, R. W. (1973). *The United States and East Asia.* New York: W. W. Norton.

A mantis stalking a cicada
is unaware of an oriole behind.

螳 螂 捕 蝉， 黄 雀 在 后

táng láng bǔ chán, huáng què zài hòu

Wound Literature

Shānghén Wénxué 伤痕文学

Wound literature, a genre appearing after the end of the Cultural Revolution, focuses on psychological and emotional damage to individuals, especially youth, from the depredations of that era. Criticized as subversive or embraced as cathartic when it first appeared, later analysis of the genre tends to focus on its literary weaknesses, including simplistic narrative and representation of character.

"Wound literature" (also known as "scar literature") refers to a body of literature that erupted onto the Chinese literary scene in the immediate wake of the Cultural Revolution 文化大革命 (1966–1976). Representative writers of this camp include Liu Xinwu 刘心武, Lu Xinhua 卢新华, Wang Meng 王蒙, Lu Yao 路遥, Gu Hua 古华, and Zhang Xianliang 张贤亮, among others. Two stories in particular are commonly referred to as the inaugurating pieces of this new literary phenomenon: "Scar" ("Shanghen" 伤痕) by Lu

Xinhua (August 1978) and "The Head Teacher" ("Banzhuren" 班主任) by Liu Xinwu (November 1977). Both stories deal with the devastation of youth caused by leftist policy and practice, but each has its own valence.

Two Examples

Authored by a then little-known freshman in the Chinese department at Fudan University and appearing first on the campus bulletin board, "Scar" tells the story of Xiaohua, who renounces her own mother after she was officially declared a "traitor." Never doubting for a second the truthfulness of the verdict, Xiaohua voluntarily and resolutely turns her back on her mother out of a sense

Woodcut depicting the smashing of the "Gang of Four." Liu Xinwu's story "The Head Teacher" (1977) stresses the psychological damage suffered by China's youth as the result of the Cultural Revolution and the notorious "Gang of Four."

of loyalty to the party and a sense of abhorrence of her mother's shameful past. But her sincere embrace of the party—which takes the form of emotional and behavioral alignment with the party ideology in every aspect of her life—is never reciprocated. The stigma of being a "traitor's daughter" follows her wherever she goes, not only denying her any chance for recognition and advancement during her years of reeducation in the countryside, but also threatening to ruin the lives of those who care about her. As she retreats further into her loneliness, disillusioned and disheartened, the news of her mother's innocence unexpectedly arrives, prompting Xiaohua to embark on a personal journey in search of reconciliation and redemption. But she is to be denied yet again: her mother dies shortly before she shows up at the hospital.

If Lu Xinhua's story highlights the deprivation of even the most basic interpersonal relationship—the mother-daughter tie in this case—visited on the politically naïve young generation, Liu Xinwu's story foregrounds the destitution of the youthful spirit as the result of the havoc wreaked on the nation by the notorious "Gang of Four." Two students occupying opposite ends of the ideological spectrum are portrayed as equal victims of the Cultural Revolution. While one is a youth league secretary with an extremely rigid mind-set, the other is a street hooligan whose mental landscape is marked largely by blankness, and occasionally by the presence of a mishmash of "feudalist" and "capitalist" ideas. In the story's narrative, only the street hooligan constitutes a problem for the head teacher, but the reader is made aware of a more urgent and daunting task on a national scale awaiting the attention of the wise educator.

Initial Motivation and Critical Reaction

As the name of this new literary genre suggests, the thematic topography of these stories focuses on the wounds inflicted by the Cultural Revolution on the individual, not so much at the physical as at the psychological level. Wound literature is therefore also sometimes referred to as "exposure literature" or "sentimental literature."

Emerging from the frenzy of the Cultural Revolution but still haunted by fresh memories of its atrocities and absurdities, the writers who eagerly embraced this genre filled a deep emotional need for collective remembering and catharsis. To a certain extent, wound literature is like "a wreath on the ruin"—it provided a platform for public airing of personal and collective grievances, so that the nation could unload the burden of its traumatic past and start the healing process. In that regard, it is analogous to a form of therapy.

When wound literature made its first appearance, the critical establishment greeted it with a great deal of caution, if not suspicion, on grounds of its perceived departure from established literary standards. Though the prestigious journal *People's Literature* 人民文学 did publish Liu Xinwu's "The Head Teacher," the editors were by no means unanimous about the decision. When Lu Xinhua submitted his work to the same journal, he received only a typed letter of rejection in return. To the mainstream literary critics, then, political correctness, social significance, and didactic function were still necessary ingredients of "good literature." Measured by these standards, wound literature, in its thematic insistence on exposing "dark problems" at both individual and societal levels, could only appear ideologically suspect, if not outright subversive.

Twenty-First-Century Perspectives

Today, the critical opinion concerning wound literature is rather mixed. Some critics contend that wound literature transcends the overly politicized narrative model of the Cultural Revolution era by bringing humanism back to the heart of literary imagination. As such, it is a narrative of emancipation and enlightenment heralding the reawakening of subjectivity. On the other hand, however, even those who are more generous in their evaluation of this literary genre recognize its inherent flaws and inevitable limits. A common criticism is that practitioners of wound literature tell an anti–Cultural Revolution story while they continue to rely on the narrative model of the Cultural Revolution era. The literary merit of wound literature is also dubious according to the genre's detractors;

not only are these works populated by characters that are heavily codified and flat, they have little to recommend for themselves in terms of narrative technique, artistic form, and aesthetic value.

Moreover, the mode of thinking that infuses wound literature is considered by some critics to be simplistic and mechanical. In their so-called indulgent and sentimental display of their wounds, writers of this genre collectively adopt a victim mentality, never bothering to explore their complex relationship—such as their own complicity—to the power system they now condemn. To the extent that the sentiments expressed in these works, from sorrow to indignation, are seen without exception as politically correct under the party's new directives in the post–Cultural Revolution period, wound literature constitutes for some not the voice of reflection and critique but ironically a device of legitimation. One critic even goes so far as to caricature writers of wound literature as "pouting children who crave their mother's attention and affection above anything else."

Jing JIANG

Further Reading

Cheng Guangwei. (2005). Shanghen wenxue de lishi juxianxing. [Historical limitations of wound literature]. *Wenyi yanjiu* [Literature and Arts Studies], 1: 18–22.

Liu Dongling. (2007). Shanghen wenxue zaisikao.[Rethinking wound literature]. *Wenyi zhengming* [Contending Views on Literature and Arts], 8, 65–67.

Liu Xinwu. (1977). Banzhuren [The head teacher]. *Renmin wenxue* [People's Literature], 11, 16–29.

Lu Xinhua. (1978, August 11). Shanghen. [Scar]. *Wenhui bao* [Wenhui Journal].

Nie Mao. (2005). Ruozhe wenhua de chuanbo zhengtu: shengming huanshi yu jingshen ziliao—shanghen wenxue de zhengzhao yuedu.[Transmitting the culture of the weak: reading the symptoms of wound literature as self-aggrandizing delusions and spiritual self-therapy]. *Wenshi bolan* [A Bird's Eye View of Literature and History], 6, 22–24.

Zhang Yesong. (2008). Dakai shanghen wenxue de lijie kongjian. [Expanding our understanding of wound literature]. *Dangdai zuojia pinglun* [Contemporary Writer Criticism], 3, 12–20.

Wu

Wúyǔ 吴语

Wu is one of the sublanguages of China, spoken primarily in the eastern provinces of Zhejiang and Jiangsu and metropolitan Shanghai. It is the second most populous language in China, after Mandarin.

An estimated 85 million people, concentrated in the provincial-level municipality of Shanghai and neighboring Zhejiang and Jiangsu provinces in China, speak the various dialects of Wu. The Wu speakers in Jiangsu Province predominantly live south of the Yangzi (Chang) River; a few enclaves of people speaking Wu reside to the north of the mouth of this river.

The Wu region is different in several ways from the other regions where the major Sinitic sublanguages are dominant. In the Wu region, there are several culture centers, whereas in the other sublanguage groups, there is one major "local" capital; this is a populous location that sets the cultural as well as linguistic pattern for the rest of the group. For example, the Yue have Guangzhou, while the Minnan of Fujian Province have Xiamen. The scattered Hakka also look to Meixian as their geographic, cultural, and linguistic center.

In comparison, the Wu people are far more diverse. Shanghai, the sublanguage's largest population center, does not really assume the role of the hub for the Wu people, because it is a new city, relatively speaking, and is subject to Western influences. Furthermore, the population in Shanghai has come from various Wu-speaking districts as well as from Nanjing and beyond. Cities such as Suzhou, Hangzhou, and Shaoxing have all played prominently in the history of the Wu, but none can truly be said to be its center.

The Wu people are also different from other Chinese because they usually do not characterize their subethnic identities in terms of their province of origin. This is because only the southern third of Jiangsu Province is Wu speaking. There is also great diversity in Zhejiang Province itself, and the people are not all Wu speakers. The Wu people of Zhejiang instead identify themselves by their native prefectures, which are subprovincial political units. The Wu people did not join the modern migration of Chinese abroad on any major scale, unlike the Yue, Hakka, and Min people to the south, and Wu speakers have only a minor representation in the overseas Chinese population.

The Wu language had its origin in Suzhou (Jiangsu Province), one of the cultural centers of the imperial period. The sociolinguistic evolution of the Wu region, however, is not well documented. From Suzhou, the language spread to regions south of the lower Yangzi River. It is a language that has gained importance because of the rise of Shanghai as an international metropolitan center and one of the treaty ports that was ceded to the Western powers—Britain, France, and Germany—in the nineteenth century.

Origins of Wu

The Chinese character for *wu* was possibly first applied to people living around the mouth of the Yangzi River who spoke a non-Sinitic language that was largely unintelligible to those speaking the various Sinitic sublanguages. The other meaning given to the word *wu*, rarely, is "clamorous" or "yelling," which might be a reference to the rather forceful and boisterous manner of the Wu people's way of speaking. To many early Han Chinese, the language also might have sounded loud and guttural. The first mention of the Wu kingdom appeared in Chinese annals around the seventh century BCE. Historical linguists have been uncertain how to classify the ancient Wu dialect, which could not be considered a Sinitic sublanguage at that time. There is a widespread assumption that the language is related to the Tai languages (of Southeast Asia), but the probability is that it is more of a Sino-Tibetan language. The kingdom of Wu began to adopt aspects of the evolving Chinese culture during the Zhou dynasty (1045–256 BCE); subsequent warfare led to the complete assimilation of the kingdom into the Sinitic political world.

Sinitic Wu culture is thought to have reached its peak during the Southern Song period (1127–1279). This would have been the time when the Wu region was at the geographical center of what was then considered to be the most highly cultured state in China, if not in the world. The Wu-speaking people left a major legacy for human civilization: The Southern Song, with its capital at present-day Hangzhou, played a significant role in disseminating Buddhism and other cultural and artistic values to neighboring countries.

Distinguishing Features of the Wu Sublanguage

Many of the archaic features found in the Wu sublanguage keenly differentiate it from modern Mandarin. Foremost among these is the continuing use in Wu of the series of voiced initial consonants that have been lost in other Sinitic sublanguages. Most forms of Wu will have *b, d, dzh, g, p,* and *z* as initial sounds. Another feature in Wu is a special voiced *h* (a bit like the guttural German *r*), which contrasts with the normal, or unvoiced, *h,* according to the linguist Leo Moser.

There are fewer diphthongs in Wu than in most other Sinitic sublanguages, and the phonetics are thought to be somewhat closer to the Old Xiang, or Laoxianghua, of Hunan Province. Wu is different from other sublanguages like the Yue, Minnan, Gan, and Hakka, particularly in the simplified endings of its syllables. While Mandarin has also simplified its endings, it has done this differently from Wu, with varying results. Hence, the ancient final syllables such as, *p, t,* and *k* appear in neither Mandarin nor Wu.

Final consonants of Wu dialects typically include only one or two nasal endings with perhaps the glottal stop. It is a pattern that more closely resembles the dialects of Minbei and some forms of Eastern Mandarin. The Wu vernaculars are characterized by complex patterns of tone sandhi in which the tone of one syllable is modified in speech by that of the syllable that falls next to it; "sandhi" is a linguistic term meaning the modification of the sound of a morpheme in certain phonetic situations or contexts. While tone sandhi in the Min-speaking areas has been deemed to be complex, it is even more so among the Wu dialects.

Wu also differs from other Sinitic sublanguages in grammatical and structural ways. In particular, the Wu dialects differ from Mandarin by putting the direct object before the indirect object when both appear in a sentence. This characteristic makes Wu similar to Cantonese, but different from the intervening Min vernacular tongues, which tend to have an ordering that more resembles that of Mandarin.

The Wu dialect tends to vary by stages over the larger region mainly as a consequence of the pluralism of standards in the sublanguage. The isoglosses (geographical boundaries that delimit the area within which a linguistic feature is found) overlap in what has been found to be a complex pattern. In spite of such variations within the region of Wu-speaking peoples, however, there is generally intercomprehensibility among the so-called Shanghai dialects, of which Suzhou Wu is one example.

One exception to the intercomprehensibility of the Wu dialects is the dialect spoken in the port city of Wenzhou, located in the south of Zhejiang Province. This Wenzhou dialect and some of the dialects spoken by people living inland from the port are considered extremely different from other Wu dialects. This has persuaded some linguists to suggest that the Wenzhou dialect should be treated and recognized as a Sinitic language that is separate from the rest of Wu.

The vernacular of Shanghai represents a fusion of various forms of Northern Wu and other dialectical influences, even including some Eastern Mandarin. Other Wu speakers have traditionally treated the Shanghai

A bustling crowd of shoppers at a Shanghai market. Wu is one of the sub languages of China, spoken primarily in the eastern provinces of Zhejiang and Jiangsu and metropolitan Shanghai.

vernacular somewhat contemptuously as a mixture of Suzhou and Ningbo dialects. Shanghainese have been portrayed as strategic, smart thinkers who are interested in both new ideas and new words to add to their language. But the Shanghainese people have long resisted the Communist government's efforts to make them speak the universally accepted Mandarin dialect.

OOI Giok Ling

Further Reading

Chao, Y. R. (1967). Contrastive aspects of the Wu dialects. *Language, 43*(1): 92–101.

Chao, Y. R. (1968). *A grammar of spoken Chinese.* Berkeley: University of California Press.

Forrest, R. A. D. (1948). *The Chinese language.* London: Faber and Faber.

Moser, L. J. (1985). *The Chinese mosaic: The peoples and provinces of China.* Boulder, CO: Westview Press.

Parker, E. H. (1884). The Wenchow Dialect. *The China Review 12,* 162–175, 377–389.

Whitaker, D. P., Shinn, R. S., Barth, H. A., Heimann, J. M., MacDonald, J. E., Martindale, K. W., et, al. (1972). *Area handbook for the People's Republic of China.* Washington, DC: U.S. Government Printing Office.

WU Changshi

Wú Chāngshí 吴昌硕

1844–1927   Twentieth-century painter and calligrapher

Wu Changshi was best known for his calligraphy in the *zhuan* (seal) and *shigu* (stone drum) scripts. Despite his commercial appeal, the ultimate ideal of literati painting—to combine poetry, calligraphy, and painting—was realized in his work.

Wu Changshi, Qing dynasty scroll. Wu brought together the conventions of painting and calligraphy in his loosely brushed artwork. Collection of Shaanxi Artists Association and Shaanxi Academy. PHOTO BY JOAN LEBOLD COHEN.

The career of Wu Changshi represents the process of evolution from the artistic patterns of late imperial China to those of the modern era. Born into a declining scholarly family in Anji, Zhejiang Province, he moved to Shanghai and became a professional painter. Wu was best known for his calligraphy in the *zhuan* (seal) and *shigu* (stone drum) scripts. His calligraphy and painting were famed for their *jinshiqi*, or antiquarian epigrapher's taste.

In his youth Wu studied briefly with Ren Yi (1840–1895) but was mostly self-taught as a painter. Although his favorite themes were usually flowers and rocks, Wu's pictures are to be seen not as images from nature but rather as arrangements of plants and rocks in an abstract space. Conventions of calligraphy and painting were brought together in his loosely brushed artwork. Thus, despite his commercial market, the ultimate ideal of literati painting—to combine poetry, calligraphy, and painting—was realized in his work.

Kuiyi SHEN

Further Reading

Andrews, J., & Kuiyi Shen. (1998). *A century in crisis: Modernity and tradition in the art of twentieth century China.* New York: Guggenheim Museum and Abrams.

Cahill, J. (1988). The Shanghai school in later Chinese painting. In Mayching Kao (Ed.), *Twentieth-century Chinese painting* (pp. 54–77). New York: Oxford University Press.

WU Zetian

Wǔ Zétiān 武则天

625–705 China's only female emperor

Wu Zetian 武则天 was the only woman to rule China as an emperor in name, declaring herself emperor after deposing her sons. She changed the composition of the ruling class by removing entrenched aristocrats from the court and enlarging the civil service examination to recruit men of merit to serve.

Wu Zetian entered the Chinese imperial court at the age of thirteen as a low-ranked concubine to Emperor Taizong (reigned 626–649) of the Tang dynasty (618–907 CE). However, after he died she became concubine and later empress to her stepson, Emperor Gaozong (reigned 650–683). After Gaozong died, Wu declared herself emperor after deposing her sons and attempting to establish her own dynasty, sometimes referred to as the Second Zhou period 周, which lasted

Tang court ladies from the tomb painting of Princess Yongtai in the Qianling Mausoleum, near Xi'an in Shaanxi Province, from the year 706. Empress Wu Zetian would also later be buried at the Qiangling Mausoleum.

2487

from 690 to 705. To legitimize her position as emperor she turned to the Buddhist establishment and also invented about a dozen characters with a new script.

The overall rule of Wu Zetian did not result in a radical break from Tang domestic prosperity and foreign prestige. However, Wu altered the composition of the ruling class by removing the entrenched aristocrats from the court and gradually enlarging the civil service examination to recruit men of merit to serve in the government. Although Wu gave political clout to some women, such as her secretary, she did not go as far as to challenge the Confucian tradition of excluding women from taking the civil service examinations. By 674 Wu had drafted twelve policy directives that ranged from encouraging agriculture to formulating social rules of conduct. She also maintained a stable economy and a moderate taxation system for the peasantry. The population increased to 60 million during her reign, and when she died her centralized bureaucracy was regulating the economic well-being and social life of her empire.

Wu Zetian was a capable ruler, but she was allegedly vicious in her personal life, murdering two sons, one daughter, and other relatives who opposed her. As a woman ruler, she challenged the traditional patriarchal dominance of power, state, monarchy, sovereignty, and political ideology. Her reign brought a reversal of the gender roles and restrictions that her society and government had constructed for her and other women. While succeeding in the male-ruled and power-focused realm, she showed traits usually attributed to men, including long-range vision, political ambition, talented organization, and hard work. Later historians have been less generous, describing her as a despotic usurper of the throne. These historians say that her reign ended in corruption and drinking, with the elderly ruler delighting in sexual relations with young men who enjoyed lavish favors. In 705 Wu Zetian was forced to abdicate, her son Zhongzong was again enthroned, and the Tang dynasty was restored.

Jennifer W. JAY

Further Reading

Jay, J. W. (1990). Vignettes of Chinese women in Tang Xi'an (618–906): Individualism in Wu Zetian, Yang Guifei, Yu Xuanji and Li Wa. *Chinese Culture, 31*(1), 78–89.

Wills, J. E., Jr. (1994). *Mountains of fame: Portraits in Chinese history.* Princeton, NJ: Princeton University Press.

Each sovereign maintains his own courtiers.

一朝天子一朝臣

Yì cháo tiān zǐ yì cháo chén

Comprehensive index starts in volume 5, page 2667.

Wulingyuan Scenic Reserve

Wǔlíngyuán Fēngjǐng Bǎohùqū

武陵源风景保护区

Known as China's Yellowstone, Wulingyuan Scenic Reserve in Hunan Province is one of the country's most spectacular and popular national parks, featuring limestone gorges, sinkholes, underground streams, and caverns. It was designated a UNESCO World Heritage Site in 1992.

Wulingyuan Scenic Reserve, known as China's Yellowstone, is a spectacular natural setting near Zhangjiajie City in northwestern Hunan Province in south central China. It also borders Guizhou Province and the province-level municipality of Chongqing. The climate of the region is subtropical, with moderate summers and mild winters with ample rainfall. Wulingyuan Scenic Reserve comprises four sections: Zhangjiajie National Forest Park, Suoxiyu Natural Resource Reserve, Tianzi Mountain Natural Resource Reserve, and the Yangjiajie Scenic Area, added in the 1990s. The reserve covers about 690 square kilometers (266 square miles), roughly the size of Zion National Park in Utah. (By comparison Yellowstone National Park covers some 8,980 square kilometers, or 3,470 square miles.)

The area is known for its *karst* topography, a type of terrain formed by the dissolving and collapse of irregular limestone, which produces gorges, fissures, sinkholes, underground streams, and caverns. The impressive sites of the reserve include more than 3,100 quartzite sandstone pillars that resemble deformed bamboo shoots, many over 200 meters (656 feet) high. There are also many ravines, streams, pools, and waterfalls; more than forty caves; and two natural bridges. The Zhoutian Dong cavern is thought to be the largest in Asia, and the Tianqia Shengkong natural bridge, the highest in the world.

The Zhangjiajie National Forest Park was established in 1982 as the first authorized forest national park in China. It covers 34 square kilometers (13 square miles). About 97 percent of the park is covered with both dense virgin forest and planted secondary growth. The forest is home to more than 3,000 species of plants, 35 of which are rare protected species. Native plants—such as the dove tree and the lobster flower, a perennial that can change color up to five times in a day—thrive in the park. A number of rare birds and animals also call the park home, including Chinese giant salamanders, Chinese water deer, Asiatic black bears, Asiatic wild dogs, and clouded leopards.

Wulingyuan is also home to a number of China's ethnic minority groups, most prominent being the Tujia, Miao, and Bai peoples. The people in these groups maintain their traditional languages, arts and crafts, costumes, foods, festivals, and music and dance. A museum dedicated to Tujia culture is in Zhangjiajie Village within the reserve. The Yangjiajie Scenic Area is said to have been settled by the famous and venerable Yang family, who moved to the region during the Song Dynasty (960–1279) to escape from continuous warfare. The name of Yang is still important in the area.

Wulingyuan received a UNESCO (United Nations Educational, Scientific, and Cultural Organization) World Heritage listing in 1992 and is a popular destination for both Chinese and foreign tourists. An admission fee of 158 yuan (about $23), which includes transportation

2489

The famous quartzite columns of Wulingyuan.
PHOTO BY YIXUAN SHUKE.

within the park, is charged for a two-day visit. Campfires and smoking are prohibited, just one of many restrictions designed to protect the reserve. There are no overnight facilities inside Wulingyuan. The nearest large town is Zhangjiajie City, a city of about 1.5 people about 33 kilometers (20 miles) from the entrance to Wulingyuan. Ample transportation is available from the city to destinations within the reserve.

Michael PRETES

Further Reading

Hunan sheng di fang zhi bian zuan wei yuan hui bian [Hunan Province Local History Editorial Committee] (1998).

Li Wenhua & Xianying Zhao (1980). *China's nature reserves.* Beijing: Foreign Languages Press.

Liu Ying. (2007). *Natural wonders in China,* (Trans. Zhou Xiaozheng). Beijing: China Intercontinental Press.

Wulingyuan feng jing zhi [Wulingyuan Scenery]. Changsha, China: Hunan ren min chu ban she.

Xia Dynasty

Xià Cháo　夏朝

2100?–1766? BCE

The Xia was the earliest Chinese dynasty (going back some two thousand years, although scholars debate the dates). Knowledge of the Xia comes from from oral tradition, ancient historical records, and archaeological research. Scholars also debate the veracity of the legends of the founding of the dynasty.

The quasi-legendary Xia, or Hsia, dynasty of China is the oldest dynasty described in ancient historical records including the *Records of the Grand Historian* (covering the period c. 2600–91 BCE and written 109–91 BCE) and *Bamboo Annals* (documenting the period from legendary times, 2497–221 BCE). Mythologically, Chinese civilization began with Pan Gu, the creator of the universe, and a succession of legendary sage-emperors and culture heroes who instructed the ancient Chinese in communication and enabled them to find sustenance and to fabricate clothing and shelter. The name *Xia* was embodied in early oral traditions but also was documented in archaeological sites and artifacts discovered in 1928. Western and Chinese scholars debate the veracity of the legends of the founding of the dynasty, particularly the accuracies of the chronologies expressed in written records such as the *Records* and *Annals,* which were composed 2,500 years after the supposed creation of the dynasty. In addition, the existing archaeological evidence does not appear to correlate with the historical records.

The Xia had villages and urban centers but were an agrarian people whose pottery and bronze implements have assisted prehistorians in developing more finite chronologies. During the Xia dynasty the major crafts included jade carving and casting bronze vessels, some of which were embellished with jade. The Xia also devised a calendar system that incorporated lunar and solar movements.

The Xia period—dating, as explained below, from the twenty-first to the sixteenth century BCE—defined a cultural stage between late neolithic cultures and the urban civilization of the Shang dynasty. Excavations in the city of Yanshi, Henan Province, uncovered what appears to have been a capital of the Xia dynasty. Although archaeological evidence (including radiocarbon dating) demonstrated that the inhabitants were the direct ancestors of the Longshan and were predecessors of the Shang, some Western scholars contend that the Xia were not a true dynasty. The two earliest of the three ancient dynasties of ancient China (Xia and Shang) are not directly known from contemporary written records, hence some scholars contend that these are mythical; however, there is agreement that the existence of the subsequent Zhou dynasty is based on historic documentation.

Xia Dates

A traditional chronology based on calculations by Liu Xin (c. 46 BCE–23 CE), an astronomer and historian, suggests that the Xia ruled from 2205 to 1766 BCE, but a chronology based on the *Bamboo Annals* dates the Xia dynasty from 1989 to 1558 BCE. The Skeptical School of early Chinese history, founded by Gu Jiegang in the 1920s, seriously questioned the traditional history, noting that through

Statue at the Yellow River Visitor's Center depicting the legendary Yu, the first ruler of the Xia Dynasty. Yu earned his title through his merit as a civil servant; he was esteemed by his people for eliminating devastating annual flooding by organizing the construction of canals and dikes along all the major rivers. PHOTO BY PAUL AND BERNICE NOLL.

time the oral history had been embellished with elements added to the earlier periods. The Xia Shang Zhou Chronology Project, a multidisciplinary effort commissioned by the People's Republic of China in 1996, involved two hundred scholars whose task was to determine precisely the chronology and geographic locations of the Xia, Shang, and Zhou dynasties. The report, published in 2000, determined that the Xia dynasty dated from 2070 to 1600 BCE. Scholars such as Sarah Allen contend that aspects of the Xia are the opposite of traits emblematic of the Shang, and she argues that the Zhou dynasty justified their conquest of the Shang by pointing out that the Shang had supplanted the Xia.

Xia Rulers

Traditional Chinese histories contend that the Xia dynasty was founded by Yu and ultimately had seventeen rulers. (See table 1.) According to the traditional history, the dynasty was founded when Shun, following the abdication system (which chose leaders according to their ability) ceded his throne to his minister Yu, whom Shun viewed as the "perfect civil servant." Yu was esteemed by his people for eliminating devastating annual flooding by organizing the construction of canals and dikes along all the major rivers. But before his death Yu passed power to his son, Qi, setting the precedent for dynastic rule, or the hereditary system, which began a period of family and clan political and economic control. The rulers often performed as shamans, communicating with spirits for guidance, and the ruling families employed elaborate and dramatic rituals to confirm their political power.

Continuing with the hereditary system, fifteen descendants of Qi succeeded him after his death. Several,

TABLE 1 **The Xia emperors in order of succession**

EMPEROR	RELATIONSHIP	REIGN (in years)
Xiayu	or Dayu; family name: Si; given name: Wenming	45
Qi	son of Xiayu; established the hereditary system	29
Taikang	son of Qi	29
Zhongkang	younger brother of Taikang	13
Xiang	son of Zhongkang	28
Shaokang	posthumous child of Xiang	21
Zhu	son of Shaokang	17
Huai	son of Zhy	44
Mang	son of Huai	18
Xie	son of Mang	21
Bujiang	son of Xie	59
Jiong	younger brother of Bujiang	21
Jin	son of Jiong	21
Kongjia	son of Bujiang	31
Gao	son of Kongjia	11
Fa	son of Gao	11
Jie	son of Fa	52

such as Shaokang and Huai, made important contributions to Chinese society, but three were tyrannical emperors: Taikang, Kongjia, and Jie. The Xia dynasty ended under the reign of Jie, whose dictatorial and extravagant ways caused a popular revolt under the leadership of T'ang (the leader of the Shang tribe), who overthrew the Xia and established the Shang dynasty. Liu Xin's calculations give the Shang dynasty a reign of 1766–1122 BCE; the chronology from the *Bamboo Annals* dates it 1556–1046 BCE; and the Xia Shang Zhou Chronology Project places it 1600–1046 BCE.

Charles C. KOLB

Further Reading

Allan, S. (1991). *The shape of the turtle: Myth, art and cosmos in early China. SUNY Series in Chinese Philosophy and Culture.* Albany: State University of New York Press.

Allan, S. (2007). Erlitou and the formation of Chinese civilization: Toward a new paradigm. *Journal of Asian Studies 66,* 461–496.

Fairbank, J. K., & Goldman, M. (2006). *China: A new history* (2nd enl. ed). Cambridge, MA: Belknap Press of Harvard University Press.

Gernet, J. (1996). *A history of Chinese civilization* (2nd ed.). Cambridge, U.K.: Cambridge University Press.

Institute of East Asiatic Studies, University of California. (1952–1968). *Chinese dynastic histories translations.* Berkeley: University of California Press.

Liu, L., & Xiu, H. (2007). Rethinking Erlitou: legend, history and Chinese archaeology. *Antiquity 81*(314), 886–901.

Needham, J. et al. (Eds.). (1954–2005). *Science and civilisation in China.* (Vols.1– 7). Cambridge, U.K.: Cambridge University Press.

Underhill, A. P. (2002). *Craft production and social change in northern China.* New York: Kluwer Academic/Plenum Publishers.

Wilkinson, E. (2000). *Chinese history: A manual.* (Rev. and enl. Ed.). Cambridge, MA: Harvard University Asia Center for the Harvard-Yenching Institute.

Xi'an

Xī'ān 西安

7.64 million est. 2007 pop.

Xi'an is the modern capital of Shaanxi Province, but the Xi'an area has a legacy dating back thousands of years—most notably as the capital of China's first imperial dynasty, the Qin (221–206 BCE), as well as of the Han and Tang dynasties. The terracotta soldiers from the burial tomb of the Qin emperor Shi Huangdi are located about 30 kilometers from the city.

Xi'an is the capital of Shaanxi Province in central China. The city, which is the largest in the province, is situated in the central part of Shaanxi in the Wei River valley north of the Qinling range. The area around Xi'an has been inhabited for thousands of years; the remains of a well-established village from around 5000 BCE have been found at Banpo. The Xi'an area was also chosen as the capital of the Zhou dynasty (1045–256 BCE), of China's first imperial dynasty, the Qin (221–206 BCE), and also of the Han (206 BCE–220 CE) and the Tang dynasties (618–907 CE). The city was then known as "Chang'an." The renowned terracotta soldiers—a life-size army of some 8,000 troops that was commissioned by the first emperor of the Qin dynasty (Shi Huangdi) as part of his tomb—are located about 30 kilometers east of the city. Many other archaeological sites dot the area.

For hundreds of years Xi'an was the gateway to the Silk Roads to central Asia, and during the Tang dynasty

The Bell Tower in the center of Xi'an, entered through an underpass on the north side. It was originally built in the fourteenth century, but was rebuilt at the present location in 1739 during the Qing dynasty. A large iron bell in the tower is used to mark the time each day. PHOTO BY PAUL AND BERNICE NOLL.

it was the largest and most cosmopolitan city in the world. The Big Wild Goose Pagoda, which was completed in 709, still stands 64 meters tall, and the old part of Xi'an, with the drum tower, the bell tower, and a mosque dating to the eighteenth century, is surrounded by one of the best-preserved city walls in China. The walls date to the fourteenth century and were originally 14 kilometers long and measured 12 meters in height and 18 meters in width. The modern city has a major textile industry and some electrical industries, and food processing factories are located in a rich agricultural region in the river valley. Tourism is a major source of income. Xi'an is also home to several important colleges.

Bent NIELSEN

Further Reading

Bonavia, J. (Rev. by Baumer, C.). (2004). *The Silk Road: From Xi'an to Kashgar*. New York: W. W. Norton.

Xiang Yang. (1992). *Xi'an, ancienne capitale de la Chine* [Xi'an, ancient capital of China]. Beijing: Editions en langue étrangères.

Xi'an City Wall

Xī'ān chéngqiáng 西安城墙

The Xi'an City Wall is one of the last remaining ancient battlement sites of North China, and one of the largest military defense systems in the world.

The Xi'an City Wall is a major tourist site at the center of Xi'an, capital of Shaanxi Province in the northcentral part of the country. Xi'an is also the site of the famous terracotta entombed warriors, along with museums, pagodas, and other sites of historical interest. Xi'an has been referred to as China's eternal city because of its ancient heritage. In the Xi'an area the capitals of the Chinese dynasties from Zhou (1045–256 BCE) to Tang (618–907 CE) were established.

The city wall was first built in the Sui dynasty (581–618 CE) and rebuilt in the third year of the reign of Zhu Yuanzhang, the first emperor of the Ming dynasty (1368–1644). It then went through three major renovations. The first took place in 1568 under the supervision of Zhang Zhi, then governor of Shaanxi. The second started in 1781 under the supervision of another Shaanxi governor, Bi Yuan. The last renovation was in 1983 when the Shaanxi government launched its ambitious project to renovate it and restore the parts that had been destroyed.

The Xi'an city wall. The words read: "The working class must lead all." PHOTO BY JOAN LEBOLD COHEN.

Sections of the city wall of Xi'an, originally built of rammed earth, underwent their last renovation in 1983. PHOTO BY JOAN LEBOLD COHEN.

An attractive circular park has been built along the wall, with trees, shrubs, and flowers enhancing the beauty of the traditional Chinese architecture.

The Xi'an City Wall is an imposing presence around the city. Its north side is 3,241 meters (10,633 feet) long; its south side, 3,442 meters (11,291 feet); its east side, 2,590 meters (8,497 feet); and its west side, 2631 meters (8,633 feet). The base is 18 meters (59 feet) wide, tapering to 15 meters (49 feet) at the top, which is as wide as a four-lane superhighway. The wall has a perimeter of 13.74 kilometers (8.5 miles). Originally built of rammed earth, it is now sided with large gray bricks.

A watchtower (*jiaolou*) sits at each corner of the wall. A rampart (*ditai*) projects from the top of the wall every 120 meters (394 feet). All together, there are ninety-eight *ditai*, each having a sentry (*dilou*) built upon it. A gate opens in each side: Far-Reaching Tranquility (*Anyuan*) in the north, Eternal Peace (*Yongning*) in the south, Everlasting Joy (*Changle*) in the east, and Security and Stability (*Anding*) in the west. Each gate consists of three gate towers. Central tower (*zhenglou*) is the inner tower sitting over the main entrance. Lock tower (*zhalou*) is the outer tower controlling the suspension bridge connecting to the entrance. Arrow tower (*jianlou*) is a watchtower lying between the other towers. Joining the three towers is an enclosure for defense known as jar city (*wengcheng*), where soldiers were stationed to guard the gate. From jar city to the top of the wall, there are passages with gradually ascending steps, which allowed war horses to travel up and down. There are altogether eleven horse passages on all sides.

The top of the city wall is paved with three layers of gray bricks. Battlements with a total of 5,984 crenels, or indentations, skirt the outer edge of the wall. Parapets (*nü'erqiang*) line the inner edge of the wall. While the battlements were used for defense, the parapets served as lookout posts.

"Build high walls and store up provisions" has been an important guiding principle of Chinese monarchs in history. Well known for the construction of the Great Wall, the ancient Chinese built walls around every city. When the People's Republic of China was established in 1949, the Xi'an City Wall was one of many surviving city walls, but today it is the only one left in its entirety. The others were demolished to make way for modern traffic.

Now the Xi'an City Wall is not only the pride of the Xi'an citizens but also a mecca for Chinese and foreign tourists. Many festivities and reenactments happen at or on the wall. When President Clinton visited Xi'an in 1998 he was given a royal reception at the wall's Yongning Gate. The Xi'an City Wall International Marathon has been held yearly since 1993. The wall is popular with hikers, bicyclists, and tai chi practitioners.

Haiwang YUAN

Further Reading

Hou, Guangqian, & Huichuan Jing. (1990). *Xi'an cheng qiang* [Xi'an City Wall]. Xi'an: Shanxi lu you chu ban she [Shanxi Tourism Press].

Shi, Yi, Chonghui Shi, Ruiyong Zhao, & Zhong Cheng. (2005). *Zhongguo gu cheng qiang* [China's ancient city walls]. Shantou, China: Shantou hai yang yin xiang chu ban she [Shantou Ocean Sound and Picture Publishing House].

Steinhardt, N. S. (1990). *Chinese imperial city planning.* Honolulu: University of Hawaii Press.

Yu, Maohong, Xuebin Zhang, & Dongping Fang. (1994). *Xi'an gu cheng qiang yan jiu: Jian zhu jie gou he kang zhen* [Studies of the ancient Xi'an City Wall: Its earthquake-proof structures]. Xian Shi, China: Xi'an jiao tong da xue chu ban she [Xi'an Communications Press].

Lure a tiger out of its mountain.

调 虎 离 山

Diào hǔ lís hān

Xi'an Incident

Xī'ān Shìbìan　西安事变

The Xi'an Incident of 1936 is often considered a turning point in Chinese history. As a result of the incident, in which two Nationalist generals, Zhang Xueliang and Yang Hucheng, arrested President Chiang Kai-shek, the Chinese Communist Party (CCP) won breathing room from the Nationalists who wanted to destroy the CCP and at the same time gained popular support for their strong opposition to Japanese aggression.

The Xi'an Incident (December 1936) occurred when two Chinese Nationalist generals, Zhang Xueliang and Yang Hucheng, arrested President Chiang Kai-shek while he was in Xi'an to assist the Nationalist campaign against the Chinese Communists. Chiang was taken captive on 12 December and released on 25 December, partly at the urging of the Chinese Communists. Chiang might have been assassinated while a prisoner, but he won his freedom with a promise to undertake strong united resistance to the Japanese aggression in China.

Nevertheless, the Xi'an Incident seriously weakened Chiang Kai-shek by undermining his strategy for first suppressing the Communists and then resisting the Japanese. As a result of the Xi'an Incident the Chinese Communists won breathing room from the Nationalists who were determined to destroy the CCP; at the same time they gained heightened popularity for their strong opposition to Japanese aggression. The Japanese took the apparent Nationalist-Communists rapprochement as evidence that armed conflict was inevitable. The Japanese invasion of China took place a scant seven months after the Xi'an Incident.

Until the Xi'an Incident Chiang Kai-shek's strategy against the Communists appeared to be succeeding. In October 1934 Nationalist armies had driven the Chinese Communists out of their base in Jiangxi, forcing the 100,000 Communists to undertake the fabled Long March. The Long March decimated the Communists and ended a year later in October 1935 in a remote and poor area of Shaanxi Province where a small base existed at Yan'an. From Yan'an Red Army leader Mao Zedong took up the new United Front policy against fascism of the Soviet Comintern (the Communist International established in 1919 and dissolved in 1943) and argued that Chinese should not be fighting one another but rather must resist the Japanese.

In 1936 Chiang Kai-shek had charged Yang Hucheng and Zhang Xueliang to carry out the final extermination of the weakened Communists at Yan'an. Yang Hucheng. a former bandit, led an army of questionable quality; Zhang Xueliang, the young cosmopolitan commander of the warlord army of Manchuria, commanded a stronger force. With Japanese encroachments in north China continuing, officers and men from both armies thought the threat from Japan was greater than from the Chinese Communists. Chiang Kai-shek, hoping to bolster the resolve of his armies, made two trips by airplane in late 1936 to Xi'an. His kidnapping occurred a few days after he began his second visit.

An actor portraying Chiang Kai-shek in a play about the Xi'an Incident, during which Chiang was kidnapped by overzealous Nationalist Party generals. PHOTO BY JOAN LEBOLD COHEN.

Initially the Communists urged Generals Yang and Zhang to kill Chiang Kai-shek but quickly altered their policy by sending Zhou Enlai to advocate the sparing Chiang if he agreed to an anti-Japanese united front. Hoping to free Chiang, both his wife, Song Meiling, and his brother-in-law, Song Ziwen, flew to Xi'an to help negotiate a solution. After Chiang agreed with the terms he was released. The promised cooperation between the Chinese Nationalists and the Chinese Communists never could be realized. Their enmity proved so great that even all-out Japanese invasion in June 1937 could not bring them to a truly united resistance.

The fates of the two kidnappers are a fascinating sidelight to the Xi'an Incident. When released at Xi'an Chiang

This scene from a play about the 1936 Xi'an Incident shows Mao Zedong in Yan'an, the headquarters of Chinese Communists at that time. PHOTO BY JOAN LEBOLD COHEN.

Actors portraying Zhou Enlai and Chiang Kai-shek. Zhou persuaded the Nationalist generals not to kill Chiang in return for Chiang's promise to provide a Nationalist/Communist united front against the Japanese. PHOTO BY JOAN LEBOLD COHEN.

Kai-shek convinced Yang Hucheng and Zhang Xueliang to accompany him on his return to Nanjing. Once in Nanjing, Chiang had them placed under house arrest. Then, as the Nationalists retreated in 1949 to Taiwan, Chiang Kai-shek had Yang Hucheng executed. Zhang Xueliang was spared but remained under house arrest until 1991. After the deaths of both Chiang Kai-shek and his son, Chiang Ching-kuo (Jiang Jingguo), Zhang Xueliang was released. Zhang, who had become a devout Christian during his long imprisonment, moved to Hawaii and lived there until his death in 2001 at the age of one hundred.

The Xi'an Incident revealed Chiang Kai-shek's questionable control over his supposedly allied Chinese armies while enhancing the Chinese Communists' identification with patriotic national resistance to Japan. It marked a renewed but futile attempt at cooperation between the Chinese Nationalists and the Chinese Communists. By heightening the anti-Japanese sentiment in China, it set the stage for open but undeclared war between Japan and China in July 1937. The War of Resistance against Japan, 1937–1945, and known outside China as the Second Sino-Japanese War, was later fought in context of World War II in Asia.

David D. BUCK

Further Reading

Snow, E. (1968). *Red star over China* (Rev. ed.). New York: Grove Press.

Wu Tien-Wei. (1976). *The Sian Incident: A pivotal point in modern Chinese history*. Ann Arbor: University of Michigan Press.

Wu Tien-Wei. (1984, January). New materials on the Xi'an Incident. *Modern China, 10*(1), 115–141.

Xiang

Xiāng 湘

Xiang is the name of the people and local sub-language of the central southeastern province of Hunan. The Xiang people are one of three subgroups of Han Chinese that settled south of Mandarin-speaking Chinese; their language is complex with many dialects.

The name *Xiang* is derived from the older literary name of Hunan. It is estimated that more than 34 million Chinese (most of them living in Hunan Province) speak Xiang today. Several early leaders of the Chinese Communist Party (most notably Mao Zedong) came from Hunan, and the linguistic influence of people thinking in Xiang or in Xiang-accented Mandarin appears to have influenced the forms chosen to simplify the characters used in the Chinese language.

Along with the Gan and Wannan, the Xiang are one of the three subgroups of Han Chinese who settled inland and to the south of the Mandarin-speaking people in China. The sublanguage (a division of the main language) spoken by the Xiang has not been regarded as significant as the Mandarin forms spoken in the north, and the Xiang have not contributed in a major way to Chinese migration overseas. The Xiang, like the Gan and Wannan, generally have been considered to be Chinese who speak Mandarin, but with very poor pronunciation.

Xiang is a complex language with many dialects. While it shares similarities with Mandarin, it differs from other sublanguages of Han Chinese mainly because of the way the dialects and subdialects relate to each other. The dialects that have similarities with Mandarin are grouped together as the New Xiang or the Xinxianghua. Local histories suggest that the complexity in the Xiang sublanguage may be due in part to the fact that most of the population now living in Hunan Province originated in other provinces. Migration has thus contributed greatly to the complex pattern of Xiang subgroups in Hunan Province.

Linguists find it easier to divide the sublanguage chronologically into New Xiang and Old Xiang, rather than describing the geographical distinctions of the various forms. Old Xiang, or Laoxianghua, has been described as a conservative form of the Xiang sublanguage and therefore much closer to the Middle Chinese of the Tang dynasty (618–907 CE) than New Xiang. Some linguists have suggested that there are ties between Old Xiang and the Wu dialects of the region around Shanghai. It is not surprising that Old Xiang is spoken only in the more isolated rural districts and some of the smaller cities of central Hunan Province. New Xiang, on the other hand, is spoken mainly in most of the larger cities and towns, where people from other regions and provinces have settled.

New Xiang

Linguists point out that New Xiang has evolved much further from the Middle Chinese norm than has Old Xiang. The development of New Xiang generally has paralleled that of southwestern Mandarin. Indeed, this form of Mandarin is supposed to have been the strongest influence on New Xiang, partly because southwestern Mandarin is spoken in Hubei Province, which is located directly to the north of Hunan Province. New Xiang is therefore much closer phonetically to Standard Mandarin than is Old Xiang. Yet both Old and New Xiang have been in use together and coexist in many towns. Complicating the geographical distribution of the speakers of Old and New Xiang are generational divisions: Elderly speakers usually speak Old Xiang, while their younger family members speak New Xiang.

Speakers of New Xiang in Changsha, the capital of Hunan Province, typically do not pronounce the initial sounds b-, d-, dz-, dzh-, and gh-, as they do the other surrounding forms, sounds that are added or part of Han Chinese. Because these initials have been retained in the Old Xiang spoken in the smaller Hunanese city of Shuangfeng, linguists consider Old Xiang an island of linguistic conservatism. New Xiang is expected to change Old Xiang in time, bringing it more into conformity with Standard Mandarin and Mandarin-like speech forms.

The nature of spoken New Xiang can be examined in a list of words used in the provincial capital of Changsha. In New Xiang subdialects, the personal pronouns are similar to those used in Mandarin. Hence, "him" or "he" (t'a), is pronounced similarly in both New Xiang and Mandarin. Likewise, "you" (ni) is pronounced the same in New Xiang and Mandarin. According to scholar Leo Moser, the Changsha vernacular as described in the reference text *Hanyu Fangyan Cihui* can be compared with Standard Mandarin in several ways. First, it has no retroflex series of consonants. Second, there are no words ending in -ng, although some people in Changsha do use retroflex consonants as well as some syllables ending in -ng. Third, there are words beginning with -ng and z-. Fourth, there are six tones rather than four. Fifth, there are nasalized vowels and, sixth, a pattern of consonant liaison that may modify medial sounds in two-syllable phrases. Finally, there are different grammatical particles somewhat differently employed. Words in the Changsha subdialect can also start with an h- and an f-. These characteristics make the Changsha subdialect different from other forms of Xiang. (See table 1.)

In northern Hunan Province, the Yiyang subdialect is another form of New Xiang. It shares many characteristics

TABLE 1 Corresponding Terms in English, Standard Chinese, and New Xiang (Changsha)

ENGLISH	STANDARD CHINESE	NEW XIANG (CHANGSHA)
tomorrow	mingtian	min-zi
this year	jinnian	chin-nie
we	women	ngo-men
this	zhege	ko-ko
what	shenme	mo-tsi
cold	leng	len
person	ren	zen

Source: Moser (1985).

with the Changsha subdialect but has five tones and words ending in ng- . The subdialect has also developed a pattern of inserting l-like sounds in many words.

Linguists have concluded that the Xiang sublanguage differs from most other Sinitic sublanguages. Hunanese do not appear to take pride in their local dialect, since there does not seem to be uniform pronunciation of the name *Changsha,* for example, even within the city itself.

Old Xiang

Linguists consider the Shuangfeng dialect a good example of Laoxianghua, or Old Xiang. The vernacular of Shuangfeng lacks the f- and the initial j-, although there are the initial consonants n-, ng-, and the voiced h or gh-. According to Wade-Giles Standard Chinese, the word *liang* (two, a couple), is *niang* in Shuangfeng, while *jou* (meat) becomes *niu.* The tendency to use old forms with voiced consonants and other ancient language habits has led to the comparison of Old Xiang and the Wu dialects.

Pronouns in Shuangfeng differ widely from Standard Chinese in both sound and formation. Several pronouns do not share the pluralizing element *men* in Standard Chinese. (See table 2.)

In the far south of Hunan Province, a zone of eleven counties, the Southern Xiang, or Xiangnan, dialect is spoken. Some have assumed that this dialect was influenced by Cantonese, the sublanguage spoken to the south, but in

TABLE 2 **Corresponding Pronouns in English, Standard Chinese, Old Xiang, and New Xiang**

ENGLISH (AND STANDARD CHINESE)	OLD XIANG (SHUANGFENG)	NEW XIANG (CHANGSHA)
I, me (wo)	ang	ngo
we, us (wo-men)	ang-nga	ngo-men
he, him (ta)	to	ta

Source: Moser (1985)

fact the pronunciation shows a heavy influence of southwestern Mandarin.

OOI Giok Ling

Further Reading

Chao, Yuen Ren. (1968). *A grammar of spoken Chinese.* Berkeley and Los Angeles: University of California Press.

Ho, Ping-Ti. (1959). *Studies on the population of China, 1368–1953.* Cambridge, MA: Harvard University Press.

Moser, L. J. (1985). *The Chinese mosaic: The peoples and provinces of China.* Boulder, CO and London: Westview Press.

Whitaker, D. P., Shinn, R. S., Barth, H.A., Heimann, J. M., MacDonald, J. E., Martindale, et. al. (1972). *Area handbook for the People's Republic of China.* Washington, DC: U.S. Government Printing Office.

Xiang Dialects

Xiāng fāngyán　湘方言

Mandarin 普通话 (*putonghua*, literally "commoner's language") is the standard Chinese language. Apart from Mandarin, there are other languages and dialects spoken in China. Xiang 湘 is one of the ten main Chinese Han 汉 dialects, and is spoken primarily throughout Hunan Province.

The Xiang dialect group is one of the recognized ten dialect groups of spoken Chinese. Some 34 million people throughout Hunan Province speak one of the Xiang dialects. Speakers are also found in Sichuan and Guangxi provinces.

The Xiang dialect group is further divided into New Xiang (spoken in the north) and Old Xiang (spoken in the south). Within these classifications are three further sub-dialect groups and an unclassified number of subgroups. There are some distinctive features between New Xiang and Old Xiang at the grammatical and sound levels. However, both the Old Xiang and New Xiang dialects have more features in common than differences. The representative of New Xiang is the Changsha dialect, which is spoken in the capital city of Hunan, and the representative of Old Xiang is the Shuangfeng dialect. Communications between speakers of New Xiang and Old Xiang are not always possible.

Origins of Xiang Dialects

The name *Xiang* comes from the major river in Hunan. Modern Xiang evolved from the language of the Chu kingdom, which was established in the third century CE, but it was greatly influenced by northern Chinese (Mandarin) at various times. The Chu kingdom occupied modern Hubei and Hunan provinces. Some records of the vocabulary used in the Chu kingdom areas can be found in *Fangyan*, compiled by Yang Xiong (53 BCE–18 CE), and *Shuowen jiezi*, compiled by Xu Shen in 100 CE. Both works give the impression that the dialect spoken in the Chu kingdom had some strong local features.

The dialects spoken in Chu were influenced strongly by northern Chinese migrants. The first group of migrants came into Hunan in 307–312 CE. Most of them came from Henan and Shanxi provinces and occupied Anxiang, Huarong, and Lixian in Hunan. In the mid-Tang dynasty, a large group of northern people came to Hunan following the Yuan River into western Hunan. The third wave of migrants arrived at the end of the Northern Song dynasty (960–1126). Most migrants came to areas in northern Hunan, such as Changde and Lixian. The Xiang dialects today are surrounded by Mandarin in the north, west, and south, and by Gan and Hakka in the east. The different dialects spoken by migrants have had a great effect on the Xiang dialects.

Official government policy since the 1920s, and especially since 1955, has encouraged the use of standard Mandarin (*putonghua*, literally "Commoner's language). All aspects of the Xiang dialects have felt the effects of this policy. For example, in Changsha, there are three speech codes: spoken Changsha, the local regional dialect used to communicate in everyday life; reading Changsha, a dialect system of literary pronunciation used solely for reading aloud, dictating newspapers or letters, and performing

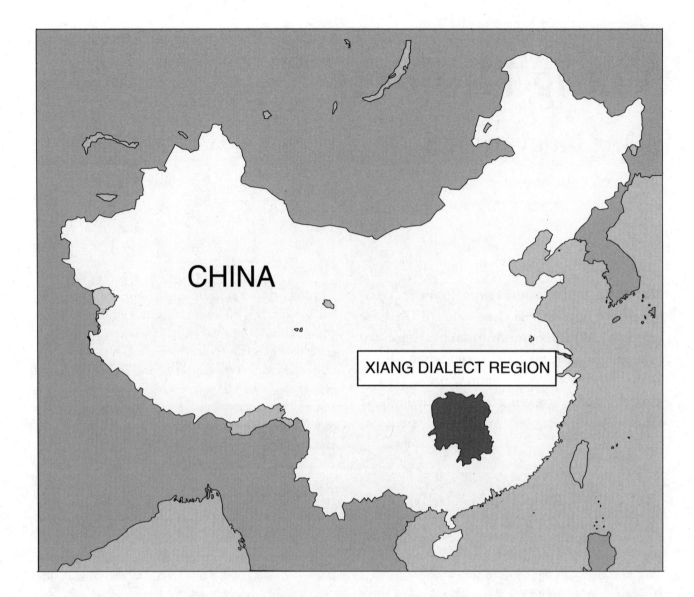

local operas and plays; and *suliao putonghua,* or "plastic Mandarin," an expression used by people in Changsha to mock the fact that they are not native speakers of Mandarin and their Mandarin does not sound natural. Plastic Mandarin can be heard in schools and at some formal events, such as conferences. Generally speaking, the code of reading Changsha acts as a bridge for new sounds and new words from Mandarin into the Changsha dialect. In the twentieth century, the sound system of the Changsha dialect underwent a lot of changes because of the influence of Mandarin. For example, there are four tones in Mandarin but six in the Changsha dialect. The words *dòng* 冻 and *dòng* 洞 share the same sound in Mandarin but differ in the Changsha dialect: 冻 *dòng* has a high rising

tone while 洞 *dòng* has a low falling tone. In the twentieth century, many words with a falling tone shifted to a rising tone. In other words, *dòng* 冻 and *dòng* 洞 have become homophones, as they are in Mandarin. It is possible that the Changsha dialect eventually will lose the low falling tone and go from six tones to five.

Sound System Features

Although different in some respects, in general, the Xiang dialects have some of the same phonological (speech system) features. For instance, most Xiang dialects possess five or six tones. The Middle Chinese (a term for historical

Chinese phonology, which refers to Chinese spoken from the sixth to tenth centuries) *rù* 入 tone is retained as one tonal category in the Xiang dialects. For example, the numbers *yi* 一 "one," *shi* 十 "ten," *bai* 百 "hundred," and *liu* 六 "six" belong to *rù* 入 tone category in Middle Chinese. In the Xiang dialect, these four words still share a rising tone while in Mandarin the word "one" has a level tone, "ten" a rising tone, "hundred" a falling-rising tone, and "six" a falling tone.

The most significant feature of the Xiang dialects is the retention of the contrast between Middle Chinese voiced and voiceless consonants (just like the difference between the English /b/ and /p/ in "bet" and "pet"), since this contrast has been lost in most other Chinese dialects.

Morphological Features

Morphemes are the smallest meaningful units used to form words. In Xiang about 15 percent of morphemes have no correspondences in Mandarin. For example, in Mandarin the verb "to lie" is *pian* 骗 while in the Xiang dialect, it is [co] with a rising tone. *Pian* 骗 does not have a phonological correspondence with [co]. We don't know its written form. We don't know where the word [co] comes from. It might be a borrowed from some other language, or it might be an independent development of the Xiang dialect itself. Linguists have been trying to find the etymology of these words from early dictionaries and documents, but, so far, only a small proportion has been identified.

There are three main types of word formations for words of more than two morphemes in Chinese. They are compounds, such as *fùmǔ* 父母 (father + mother) "parents"; reduplications, such as *māma* 妈妈 (mother + mother) "mother"; and affixations such as *lǎohǔ* 老虎 (prefix + tiger) "tiger"; or *zhuōzi* 桌子 (table + suffix) "table." In the Xiang dialects, affixation is much more common than it is in Mandarin, but reduplication is not commonly employed. In the twentieth century, some new morphemes were borrowed into Xiang. For example, the local kinship terms and Mandarin kinship terms coexist in the Changsha dialect: *yé* 爷 and *niáng* 娘 are local terms for father and mother; *bàba* 爸爸 and *māma* 妈妈 are borrowed terms. The borrowed terms have brought not only new morphemes (words) into Xiang but also the reduplicative formation.

Grammatical Features

There are many features of grammar in the Xiang dialects that distinguish them from Mandarin and other Chinese dialects or languages.

In Mandarin, there is no distinction between the attributive particle and nominalized particle. For example, in the expressions *wǒ de shû* 我的书, "my book" (*de* = attributive particle) and *shû shì wǒ de* 书是我的, "the book belongs to me" (*de* = nominalized particle), both the attributive and nominalized particle is *de* 的. In New Xiang both particles are cognates of *de* 的 while in Old Xiang they are cognates with *ge* 个 (scholars are still debating the lexical source of *ge* 个). In some localities of Old Xiang—such as Qiyang, Qidong, and Xinhua—however, there is a distinction between the two particles. In the Qiyang dialect, the attributive is [ke] while the nominalized is [kau]. That is to say, *wǒ de shû* 我的书, "my book," in the Qiyang dialect would be *wǒ* [ke] *shû my book* 我的书 ([ke] = attributive particle) while *shû shì wǒ de* 书是我的, "the book belongs to me," would be *shû shì wǒ* [kau] ([kau] = nominalized particle). This type of distinction occurred before the Qin dynasty (221–206 BCE) but disappeared in Mandarin as well as in most Xiang localities.

In written language the passive construction first appeared before the Warring States period (475–221 BCE) while disposal constructions first appeared in the Tang dynasty (618–907 CE). In Mandarin the passive marker derived from a verb with a passive meaning (*bèi* 被, "to be covered, to suffer," as used in *Bēizi bèi mèimei dǎ pò le* 杯子被妹妹打破了 [glass + passive marker + younger sister + to hit + complement + aspectual marker] "The glass was broken by (my) sister") or while the disposal marker derived from a verb with an active meaning (*pǎ* 把, "to hold," as used in *Mèimei bǎ bçizi dǎ pò le* 妹妹把杯子打破了 [younger sister + disposal marker + glass + to hit + complement + aspectual marker] "(My) sister broke the cup"). In Xiang, however, both passive markers and disposal markers derived from active verbs meaning "to give" or "to take," such as *pǎ* 把, "to hold, to give"; *dé* 得, "to gain, to give"; or *ná* 拿, "to take." More interestingly, there are even some localities such as Lengshuijiang, where both passive and disposal constructions share the same marker: *ná* 拿, "to take." The sentence *Zhang San na Lisi sa le* 张三拿李四杀了 in the Lengshuijiang dialect can have two readings: "Zhang San killed Lisi" and "Zhang San was killed by Lisi." In addition, in Xiang dialects, these two constructions are not as active as they are in Mandarin. Instead of forming a request as in "to open the door," (*bǎ mén dǎ kā* 把门打开 [disposal marker + door + to open + complement]), in Mandarin a direct order is more likely to be heard (*kāi kai mén* 开开门 [to open + complement + door] "open the door"). Now the Mandarin passive markers and disposal markers have come into the local system. In many localities, the local forms and the borrowed forms coexist.

Word order is very important to meaning in many languages. The most distinctive feature of Xiang word order is the position of the object. In Mandarin the word order for double objects is [verb + indirect object + direct object], for example *gěi tâ shû* 给他书 [to give + he + book] "give him a book"; but in Xiang it is [verb + direct object + indirect object] *gěi shû tâ* 给书他 [to give + book + he] "give a book to him."

In Mandarin if a verb takes both an object and a complement, the word order is [verb + complement + object], such as in *gǎn shàng chç le* 赶上车了 [to catch + complement + bus + particle] "have caught up to the bus." In Xiang positive sentences share the same order as Mandarin, but negative sentences have a different order [verb + object + complement]: *gǎn bú shàng chç* 赶不上车 [to catch + no + complement + bus] "unable to catch the bus" or *gǎn chç bú dào* 赶车不到 [to catch + bus + no + complement] "unable to catch the bus". If a verb indicates a common action in everyday life, such as "wish to eat, wish to drink, or wish to sleep," the construction in Mandarin is [*xiǎng* 想 "to wish" + verb + object]. The word order in the Changsha dialect is [*xiǎng* 想 "to wish" + object + verb]: *xiǎng chī fàn* 想吃饭 [to wish + to eat + rice] "(I) want to eat (now)" in Mandarin but *xiǎng fàn chī* 想饭吃 [to wish + rice + to eat] in the Xiang dialects. All of these Mandarin constructions have come into Xiang and coexist with the local constructions.

Studies of Xiang Dialects

There have been three general surveys of dialects spoken in Hunan. All three include the Xiang dialects. The first survey covered seventy-five localities and was conducted by a team under the leadership of Chao Yuenren in 1935. The results were not published until 1974, by Yang Shifeng. The second was conducted by the Chinese department of Hunan Normal University between 1956 and 1959 (and published in 1960) and covered eighty-one localities. The third survey started in 1987 and was conducted by a team led by Li Yongming and Bao Houxing. It covered 102 localities of which twenty-two were studied in detail. Since the late 1990s, much work has been done on different aspects of the Xiang dialects, especially grammar, which had been overlooked in the past.

A five-volume series with descriptions of phonology, vocabulary, and grammar of the Xiang dialects, edited by Bao Houxing, was launched at the first International Conference of the Xiang Dialects held in Changsha in 2006. Scholars working in the Xiang dialects are very active. More important, more and more postgraduate students are engaged in the research of the Xiang dialects.

Most research in the Xiang dialects so far has been descriptive work on contemporary dialects. More detailed descriptions of different localities of Xiang, especially the localities in the remote areas, are needed. But studies from historical and comparative points of view also are important. There is a need to put Xiang on the big map of universal linguistics, in the interests of linguistic studies in general.

Yunji WU

Further Reading

Bao Houxing. (Ed.). (2006). *Xiang fangyan yanjiu congshu* [Series on the research of Xiang] (Vols. 1–5). Changsha, China: Hunan Normal University Press.

Bao Houxing, Chen Lizhong & Peng Zerun. (2000). Ershishiji Hunan fangyan yanjiu gaishu [On the research on the Hunan dialects in the twentieth century] *Fangyan 1*, 47–54.

Chappell, H. (Ed.). (2001). *Sinitic grammar: Synchronic and diachronic perspectives*. Oxford, U.K.: Oxford University Press.

Heine, B. & Kuteva, K. (2002). *World lexicon of grammaticalization*. Cambridge, U.K.: Cambridge University Press.

Hunan Normal University. (1960). *Hunan hanyu fangyan pucha zongjie baogao* [Report of an investigation into the Hunan dialects]. Changsha, China: Author.

Li, Rong. (Ed.). (1991). *Language atlas of China*. Hong Kong: Longman.

Li Yongming & Bao Hongxing. (2001). *Hunan shengzhi: Fangyan zhi* [Gazetteer of Hunan: Records on the dialects]. Changsha, China: Hunan Renmin Chubanshe.

Peng Fengshu. (1999). *Xiang fangyan kaoshi* [Research on the etymology of words in the Xiang dialects]. Changsha, China: Hunan Normal University Press.

Wu, Yunji. (1999). *The development of aspectual systems in Chinese-Xiang dialects.* Paris: École des Hautes Etudes en Sciences Sociales, Centre de Recherches Linguistiques sur l'Asie Orientale.

Wu, Yunji. (2005). *A synchronic and diachronic study of the grammar of the Chinese Xiang dialects.* Berlin: Mouton de Gruyter.

Wu, Yunji. (1996–2006). *Hunan fangyan yufa xilie* [Hunan grammar series] (Vols. 1–5). Changsha, China: Hunan Normal University Press.

Wu Qizhu. (Ed.). (1998–1999). *Hunan fangyan yanjiu congshu* [A series of research on the Hunan dialects] (Vols. 1–15). Changsha, China: Hunan Jiaoyu Chubanshe.

Yang Shifeng. (1974). *Hunan fangyan diaocha baogao* [Report of a survey on the Hunan dialects]. Taipei, Taiwan: Institute of History and Philology, Academia Sinica Press.

Yang Shuda. (1983). Changsha fangyan kao [A study of the etymology of characters in the Changsha dialect]. In *Jiweiju xiaoxue jinshi luncong* [Essays on philology and phonology] (pp. 155–171). Beijing: Zhonghua Shuju. (Original work published 1931)

Yang Shuda. (1983). Changsha fangyan xu kao [A further study on the etymology of characters in the Changsha dialect]. In *Jiweiju xiaoxue jinshi luncong* [Essays on philology and phonology] (pp. 172–189). Beijing: Zhonghua Shuju.

Zhou Zhenhe & You Rujie. (1986). *Fangyan yu Zhongguo wenhua* [Chinese dialects and culture]. Shanghai: Shanghai Renmin Chubanshe.

He who stays near vermilion gets stained red; he who stays near ink gets stained black.

近朱者赤，近墨者黑

Jìn zhū zhě chì, jìn mò zhě hēi

XIE Jin

Xiè Jìn 谢 晋

1923–2008 Film director and writer

One of the best-known Chinese film directors of the twentieth century, Xie Jin blended Confucian morality with melodrama into more than twenty films—from state-sanctioned evaluations of Chinese history or bleak portrayals of the Mao years to wildly popular features.

Xie Jin occupies a complex, vitally important position in the history of Chinese cinema. A director of celebrated talents, his *Stage Sisters* (1964) and *Hibiscus Town* (1986) have gained reputations as examples of some of the finest filmmaking to emerge from the People's Republic of China during the twentieth century. At the same time, Xie's cultural authority has become institutionalized through his close ties to state studios and artistic organizations. He served as a vice chairman of the national committee of the China Federation of Literary and Art Circles, and was a standing committee member of the Eighth and Ninth Chinese People's Political Consultative Conferences, an advisory body to the PRC government. Nonetheless, the "Xie Jin school" of filmmaking, supposedly based on the melding of melodrama with Confucian morality, has been both emulated and challenged by Chinese filmmakers during the post-Mao era.

A native of Shangyu, Zhejiang Province, Xie's directorial training began in Sichuan during the 1940s, when he attended a public dramatic arts institute near Chengdu. As a consequence of wartime migration, this institution boasted several cultural luminaries as teachers, including both dramatists (Cao Yu, Hong Shen) and directors (Huang Zuolin, Zhang Junxiang). Xie followed several of these mentors to Chongqing in 1943, essentially working as a fulltime understudy.

Xie Jin recommenced his studies at the Nanjing National Theater Institute in 1946, and began work as an assistant director for the Datong Film Company two years later. After another period of political training at the Huabei (North China) People's Revolutionary University in 1950, he entered the Shanghai film world at a time when the transition to a state-run system left very few opportunities for new arrivals. Xie distinguished himself, however, and by 1954 was already directing his own films. *Woman Basketball Player No. 5* (1957), recognized at the Fourth World Youth Assembly in Moscow, constituted his first notable success. A series of cheaply made films promoting the state's Great Leap Forward production-policies followed, after which Xie released a series of well-received features, including the wildly popular *Red Detachment of Women* (1961).

By this time, several patterns in Xie Jin's filmmaking method had already emerged. First, he developed a reputation for directing films centered on female characters and for launching the careers of relatively unknown actresses such as Xiaoqing (now an infamous subject of tabloid gossip) and Siqin Gaowa (a recent recipient of the Hong Kong Film Award), with whom he often worked. Second, Xie's films proved capable of attaining both domestic popularity and international acclaim—his masterpiece, *Two Stage Sisters* (1965), remains a classic of melodramatic social realism. Third, Xie was able to maintain this level of quality within a variety of political environments, as attested to by the fact that he was one of a handful of directors picked to transform "model operas" (a mode of "proletarian" theater devised by Mao Zedong's wife, Jiang Qing) into films during the Cultural Revolution (1966–1976).

Xie Jin's popularity during the 1980s and 1990s was often overshadowed by the international success of Fifth Generation directors such as Zhang Yimou and Chen Kaige. (Xie, whose career began after World War II, belongs to the Third Generation.) Yet Xie proved as durable as any of his famous successors. *Legend of Tianyun Mountain* (1980) and *Hibiscus Town* (1986) earned him plaudits for bleakly realistic portrayals of the Mao years, while subsequent films such as *The Opium War* (1997) wedded big-budget aesthetics with an officially sanctioned take on China's colonial past.

Xie was a member of numerous professional film associations in the PRC and abroad. While his final works were directed mainly toward domestic markets, during these years he also acted as the state's official ambassador as vice-chairman of the China Federation of Literary and Art Circles to cinematic and scholarly communities worldwide. Xie died in Shangyu in 2008.

Matthew JOHNSON

Further Reading

Berry, M. (2005). *Speaking in images: Interviews with contemporary Chinese filmmakers.* New York: Columbia University Press.

Brown, N., Pickowicz, P. G., Sobchack, V., & Yau, E. (Eds.). (1994). *New Chinese cinemas: Forms, identities, politics.* Cambridge, U.K.: Cambridge University Press.

Lu, Sheldon Hsiao-peng (Ed.) (1997). *Transnational Chinese cinemas: Identity, nationhood, gender.* Honolulu: University of Hawaii Press.

Silbergeld, J. (1999). *China into film: Frames of reference in contemporary Chinese cinema.* London: Reaktion Books.

XIN Qiji

Xīn Qìjí   辛棄疾

1140–1270   Song dynasty lyric writer, poet, and military leader

Xin Qiji, the most prolific lyric writer of the Southern Song dynasty, devoted his life to seeing that the former Northern Song territories captured by Jurchen Jin forces would be returned to Chinese rule. Ultimately Xin's heroic recovery mission failed; in his retirement he wrote unabashed lyrics that expressed the frustrations of his thwarted ambitions.

The conflict that raged within the heart of Xin Qiji, one of the most important lyric writers of the Southern Song dynasty (1127–1279), reflects the major political dilemma of his time—the division and competition between the reconstituted Song dynasty in the South and the conquering Jurchen Jin dynasty (1125–1234) in the north. He is known for his forthright and martial personality, and his song lyrics were characterized by the term "heroic and unrestrained" (*haofang*) during his own lifetime, even though the broad stylistic range in his lyrics often belies the simplicity of this label. Over 670 of his song lyrics have been preserved, making Xin Qiji the most prolific song lyric writer of the Song dynasty.

The central concern of his entire life, fueled by patriotism and reinforced by homesickness for a homeland unoccupied by alien invaders, was his determination to recover the Song empire's lost territory. In 1126 the Northern Song dynasty (960–1126) capital of Kaifeng was sacked by the Jurchen Jin dynasty army, forcing the last heir to the throne to flee south of the Huai River and reestablish the capital in Hangzhou. Xin Qiji was born in the occupied north in the city of Licheng (modern Jinan in Shandong Province). In 1161, when Xin Qiji was twenty-one, he organized an uprising and joined forces with Geng Jing. On Geng Jing's orders Xin Qiji led his forces to join the court in the south. He met Emperor Gaozong (reigned 1131–1162) in Jiankang (modern Nanjing) on an inspection tour and was granted an audience and an official title. Despite this promising reception, Xin Qiji received no support for his plans to retake captured northern territories. When Geng was murdered by a subordinate who had gone over to the Jurchen Jin, Xin rode into the enemy camp and returned with the traitor for execution. Afterward Xin relocated to the south for good. There he tirelessly advocated a policy of retaking the occupied northern territories, submitting to the throne his "Ten Discourses of an Ignorant Rustic" sometime between 1165 and 1168 and nine essays to a newly appointed pro-war grand councilor in 1170. Although Xin Qiji served ably in a series of provincial appointments in various parts of the Yangzi (Chang) River delta, he was frustrated by repeated misinterpretations of his actions and by downright slander from his political opponents. In 1182 Xin retired to a villa of eccentric design called "Ribbon Lake" in Jiangxi Province and, after this villa burned down, to a second villa called "Calabash Spring." It was during his twenty years of retirement that he composed over nine-tenths of his song lyrics.

Xin Qiji failed in his ambition to become the heroic leader who recovered the northern half of his country. Instead he became the greatest songwriter of the Southern Song dynasty and poured his pent-up feelings into his lyrics. The lyrics of Xin Qiji have often been compared

A Chinese Lady Under the Escort of the Mongols, ink and color on silk, unknown artist.
This Song dynasty painting depicts a Han beauty crossing a northern river inside a camel-
drawn carriage. She is to be given as a gift to a tribal ruler, most likely of the Khitan,
Jurchen, or Mongol peoples. Xin Qiji wrote lyrics with themes that reflect the political
upheaval of his time: fierce competition between dynasties of the north and south.

with those of his literary predecessor Su Shi (1037–1101).
In reality they are quite different in tone and technique.
The late Qing dynasty (1644–1912) critic Wang Guo-
wei (1877–1927) aptly distinguished the tone of the two

writers, calling Su Shi's lyrics "expansive" (*kuang*) and
Xin Qiji's "heroic" (*hao*). The one main similarity of the
two poets is their interest in experimenting across genres.
Like Su Shi, Xin Qiji further elevated the lyric by using it

The Poetry of Xin Qiji

SUNG TO THE TUNE
"THE PARTRIDGE SKY"

In my prime, beneath my flag were ten
thousand warriors.
My horseman, in brocaded uniforms,
burst across the river.
At night the northern soldiers held fast to
their silver quivers.
At dawn our archers let fly their golden
arrows.

Thinking back on those events,
I sigh over my present circumstances.
The spring wind will not darken my
graying beard.
I've traded my ten-thousand word
treatise on military strategy
For my neighbor's book on planting trees.

Source: Ebrey, P. B. (1981). *Chinese civilization: A source-book.* New York, The Free Press, 170.

to write about his public ambitions, a topic typically associated with *shi* poetry. In technique Xin surpassed Su Shi's efforts as well—by incorporating quotations from old-style prose and by combining classical prose with colloquial phrases from the spoken language.

Benjamin RIDGWAY

Further Reading

Cheang, A. (Ed.). (2003). *A silver treasury of Chinese lyrics.* Hong Kong: Chinese University of Hong Kong.

Hightower, J. R., & Yeh, F. Chia-ying. (1998). *Studies in Chinese poetry.* Cambridge, MA: Harvard University Asia Center.

Lian, Xinda. (1999). *The wild and the arrogant: Expressions of self in Xin Qiji's song lyrics.* New York: Peter Lang Publishing.

Sargeant, S. (2001). Tz'u. In V. Mair (Ed.), *The Columbia history of Chinese literature* (pp. 320–321). New York: Columbia University Press.

Yan, Bai. (2005). *The political and military thought of Xin Qiji, 1140–1207, with a translation of his ten discussions.* Lewiston, NY: Edwin Mellon Press.

Xinhua News Agency

Xīnhuá Tōngxùnshè　新华通讯社

Established in 1931 as Red China News Agency, Xinhua News Agency, as it has been known since 1937, is the official state news agency of China and the largest news and information-gathering and distribution center in the country. Xinhua disseminates all information about government policies through its thirty-two branches in China, as well as its branches in more than one hundred countries.

As the official state news agency of China, and the country's largest news organization, Xinhua News Agency 新华社 is the primary source for information about government policies, resolutions, and viewpoints throughout the country. Established in 1931 as Red China News Agency and renamed "Xinhua" in 1937, the agency has undergone steady growth since the founding of the People's Republic of China in 1949, and especially since China's economic reforms and opening-up drive began in 1978. Xinhua today has more than seven thousand employees working in news coverage (domestic, international, and sports), management and operation, and technical support.

Xinhua operates a head office in Beijing; thirty-two domestic branches in China's provinces and autonomous regions, including Hong Kong and Macao (but excluding Taiwan), as well as reporters substations in some fifty cities; and overseas branches in more than one hundred countries. Five regional offices authorized to release news include: an Asia-Pacific regional office headquartered in Hong Kong, the Latin American regional office in Mexico City, the African regional office in Nairobi, the Middle East regional office in Cairo, and the French regional office in Paris.

Domestically the agency releases daily news to newspapers and radio and TV stations at the county, prefecture, and provincial levels. Overseas it releases news in Chinese, English, French, Spanish, Russian, Arabic, and Portuguese. It also releases economic information daily to Chinese and foreign clients. It offers special reports and news features to more than 130 countries. It has cooperation agreements on news exchange with news agencies or media organizations in nearly one hundred countries. The Xinhua Audio and Video Center, established in 1993, provides news and special programs for TV stations and audio and video customers.

Xinhua publishes nearly forty newspapers and magazines, including *Xinhua Daily Telegraph*, *News Bulletin of the Xinhua News Agency* (in English, French, Spanish, Arabic, and Russian), *Reference News* (daily), *Economic Information Daily*, *China Securities* (daily), *Shanghai Securities* (daily), *Sports Express* (weekly), *Outlook* (weekly), *China Comment* (fortnightly), *Globe* (monthly), *Chinese Reporters* (monthly), *Photography World* (monthly), *Great Rural World* (monthly), *Securities Investment Weekly*, *China Photo* (quarterly), and *China Yearbook* (in Chinese and English). The Xinhua Publishing House, an affiliate, annually publishes four hundred books titles on current affairs and politics.

In recent years Xinhua has established more business operations such as China News Development Co., China National United Advertising Corporation, China Photo Service, Global Public Relations Co., and Hangzhou International Public Relations Co. Xinhua also operates the

2517

New China Agency to Handle Foreign and Financial News

BEIJING—China has named the State Council Information Office, a Cabinet-level agency, as the new regulator of foreign news agencies and financial information providers, replacing the official Xinhua news agency, Xinhua reported.

The announcement, which was issued Friday and took effect immediately, follows a complaint about new Xinhua regulations brought to the World Trade Organization by the U.S., the European Union and Canada last year.

The new rules would have required foreign financial information providers such as Thomson Reuters Corp., Bloomberg L. P. and Dow Jones & Co. to sell their products through an entity designated by Xinhua, and to disclose sensitive commercial information.

The complaint stated that the new rules constituted a conflict of interest since Xinhua was both a regulator and a market competitor.

In response to the complaint, China in November agreed to end Xinhua's regulatory control, to allow foreign financial information providers to sell directly to customers and to appoint an independent regulator, which wouldn't share proprietary information.

The previous Xinhua regulatory regime distinguished between foreign financial information providers, selling to financial professionals, and foreign news agencies such as the Associated Press and Agence France Presse, supplying a media market that includes newspapers, broadcasters and Web sites.

Friday's announcement made clear that both groups would now be regulated by the State Council Information Office.

It isn't clear how foreign news agencies will be allowed to conduct commercial activities under the new regulator. They are now required to distribute through Xinhua, which has long claimed a monopoly in this area.

Set up in 1991, the SCIO is a ministerial-level agency led by Minister Wang Chen.

According to its Web site, the agency's chief role is to raise awareness and understanding of China and the country's issues through media.

Source: Wu, J. R. (2009, February 2). New China agency to handle foreign and financial news. *The Wall Street Journal.* Retrieved March 23, 2009, from http://online.wsj.com/article/SB123348675730736723.html

---

News Research Institute, the World Questions Research Center, and the China School of Journalism for journalism research and professional training. Xinhua made its information available online in 1997 and in 2000 established its website, which releases news in Chinese, English, French, Spanish, Russian, and Arabic, using three domain names: xinhuanet.com, xinhua.org, and news.cn. An English-only version is also available at chinaview.cn.

YU Xuejian

Further Reading

50 years of new China's media. (2000). Beijing: China Journalism Yearbook Publishing House.

China journalism yearbook: 2006. (2006). Beijing: China Journalism Yearbook Publishing House.

China journalism yearbook: 2007. (2007). Beijing: China Journalism Yearbook Publishing House.

Xinjiang Uygur Autonomous Region

Wéiwú'ěrzú Zìzhìqū 维吾尔族自治区

20.95 million est. pop. 2007   1.6 million square km

Xinjiang Uygur Autonomous Region is the largest political unit in China but also one of the least populated. Muslim Uygurs make up Xinjiang's largest ethnic population (although several other minorities reside there as well). CCP authorities have had a policy of settling Han (China's majority ethnicity) in the region in an attempt to solidify government rule.

Xinjiang Uygur Autonomous Region, located in northwestern China, is bordered by Russia to the north, Mongolia to the northeast, the Chinese provinces of Gansu and Qinghai to the east, Tibet (Xizang) Autonomous Region to the southeast, Afghanistan and India to the south and southwest, and Kyrgyzstan, Kazakhstan, and Tajikistan to the west. Xinjiang Uygur Autonomous Region is the largest political unit in China, covering 1.6 million square kilometers: slightly smaller than Iran. However, despite its size, Xinjiang is one of the least-populated regions of China. Its geography and climate help explain its low population density: Much of the southern half of the region is covered by the vast Taklimakan Desert, whereas the center is dominated by the uninhabitable Tian Shan range.

Xinjiang has long been China's gateway to central Asia. As far back as the Han (206 BCE–220 CE) and

View of the Tian Shan range, Xinjiang's most scenic mountains. PHOTO BY JOAN LEBOLD COHEN.

2519

XINJIANG

CHINA

• Karamay
Urumqi ◉
Korla • Hami •
• Kashi
Xinjiang
• Hotan • Qiemo

Tang (618–907 CE) dynasties, the oasis towns scattered throughout Xinjiang were the backbone of the great Silk Roads, a highway over which merchants carried luxury goods from the Chinese empire to the Arab empires of the Middle East and the kingdoms of central Asia. Despite its strategic location, Xinjiang retained considerable independence during much of its history. The region's current name, which in Chinese means "new frontier," can be traced to the conquest of the region by the Manchu armies of the Qing dynasty (1644–1912) during the mid-eighteenth century. Even after 250 years of Chinese control, however, Xinjiang retains much of its traditional culture. The region's largest ethnic group continues to be the Muslim Uygurs, although several other minority nationalities, including Uzbeks, Kazakhs, and Tajiks, also have sizable populations. The "minority" population of Xinjiang in 1997 was 10.58 million (61.6 percent of the region's total population). This population figure is all the

View of a lake amid the snow-capped mountains in Xinjiang.

PHOTO BY JOAN LEBOLD COHEN.

more noteworthy because, since 1949 when the Chinese Communist Party took over the governance of Xinjiang, central authorities have had a policy of settling Han (ethnic Chinese) in the region in an attempt to solidify their rule.

This policy, together with the arrival of hundreds of thousands of Chinese economic migrants from the eastern provinces and the growth of Islamic fundamentalism in central Asia, has resulted in the development of a separatist movement among Xinjiang's Muslims since the mid-1980s. During the 1990s movement extremists began a terrorist campaign against local authorities in Xinjiang's capital city of Urumqi and symbols of the Chinese "occupation" throughout the region. The Chinese government, in an attempt to keep the separatists from acquiring external support, during the late 1990s negotiated a number of agreements with neighboring states to jointly develop the region's natural resources and to promote trade. Authorities in Beijing hoped to suppress support for Uygur nationalists by promising economic prosperity to the Islamic nations of central Asia.

When world attention was on pro-Tibet protests along the Olympic torch relay route prior to the Summer Olympics in Beijing in 2008, Uygur separatist groups staged demonstrations in several countries. The East Turkestan Islamic Movement (ETIM) is an Uygur group that advocates creation of the Islamic state of East Turkestan in Xinjiang. On 4 August 2008, four days before the Olympics, suspected ETIM members rammed a dump truck into a patrol station in Xinjiang, killing or wounding thirty-two Chinese police officers.

Xinjiang Uygur Autonomous Region is to be a central element of China's Developing the West program, which was announced by Premier Jiang Zemin in 2000.

Robert John PERRINS

Iron Discovery in Xinjiang

The China scholar Joseph Needham discusses the origins of iron-smelting technology in the Xinjiang region of China.

In Xinjiang, in the far northwest of modern China, some surprisingly early dates for iron have been published in recent years. Iron is found in graves which for the most part show no sign at all of Chinese influence and which have surprisingly early radiocarbon dates. The most important early iron artifact type appears to be a small knife.... Archaeological material available ... suggests that iron technology came to Xinjiang from the Chust culture of the Ferghana Valley, in modern Uzbekistan. Here iron appears at the beginning of the –1st millennium [BCE], and there is solid evidence of mutual influence between this culture and several cultures of southern Xinjiang.

Farther east, in the Russian Maritime Province, some scholars believe that the use of iron was much earlier, perhaps as early as the –12th century [BCE]. This claim seems to be based on a single radiocarbon date, and should therefore be treated with extreme caution until such a time as more solid evidence becomes available.

It seems reasonable to conclude that the technology of iron smelting came to Xinjiang from further west. Given the present state of Inner Eurasian archaeology, however, further speculation concerning the precise route by which this transmission took place would probably be unwise. On the other hand, transmission to the Central Plain from Xinjiang through Gansu seems uncontroversial.

Source: Needham, J., and Wagner, D. B. (Eds.). (2008). *Science & civilisation in China, Vol. V: 11.* Cambridge, U. K.: Cambridge University Press, 91, 97.

Further Reading

Besson, L., Rudelson, J., & Toops, S. W. (1994). *Xinjiang in the twentieth century.* Washington, DC: Woodrow Wilson International Center for Scholars.

Bovingdon, G., & Gladney, D. C. (2000). *Inner Asia: Special issue—Xinjiang.* Cambridge, MA: White Horse Press.

Dillon, M. (1995). *Xinjiang: Ethnicity, separation, and control in Chinese central Asia.* Durham, U.K.: University of Durham, Department of East Asian Studies.

Kirk, M. (Ed.). (2009). *China by numbers 2009.* Hong Kong: China Economic Review Publishing.

McMillen, D. H. (1979). *Chinese communist power and policy in Xinjiang, 1949–1977.* Boulder, CO: Westview Press.

State Statistical Bureau. (1998). *China statistical yearbook.* Beijing: China Statistical Publishing House.

Weng Weiquan. (1986). *Xinjiang, the Silk Road: Islam's overland route to China.* New York: Oxford University Press.

Xixia

Xīxià Wángcháo 西夏王朝

Xixia was a flourishing regional state in northwest China eventually destroyed by the Mongols. Before its downfall, Xixia was ruled by the Tanguts, a group of uncertain ethnic origin, although they were probably Sino-Tibetan.

Xixia (western Xia), named after an ancient Chinese dynastic name dating to 2100 BCE, existed in northwest China from the late tenth century until extinguished by the Mongols in 1227. The core population was composed of Tanguts, a culturally mixed group variously identified but most likely Sino-Tibetan, with many other elements present, including: the Altaic Tuoba, who had played a major role in northern China prior to the reunification of the Sui dynasty (581–618 CE); local Turkic speakers, in the Ordos; Chinese; and even a few Mongols. Considered the real founder of the state was Li Yixing (d. 967), whose surname was a gift for services rendered from the Tang (618–907 CE). He and his successors, ruling a small state—wedged at first between Khitan Liao Dynasty (960–1125) and Northern Song (960–1126), and later between the even more powerful Jurchen Jin dynasty (1125–1234) and Southern Song (1127–1279)—had to tread carefully to survive, taking full advantage of a remote position in the northwest surrounded by natural barriers and large, well-fortified cities in a relatively well-populated region. Nonetheless, thanks to a successful military, Xixia did survive and, by the eleventh century, occupied a substantial strip of territory, including the Ordos, the Alashan Desert, and the Gansu corridor, an area

A mural fragment from the Xixia (western Xia) dynasty, which existed in northwest China from the late tenth century until defeated by the Mongols in 1227.

once well connected to China but, by the time of the Tang dynasty, heavily influenced by non-Chinese cultures. Contributing to Xixia's survival was not only the power and skill of its military and leaders, but also its position as the third party in a balanced rivalry between the Chinese north and south, one that was to persist for almost three hundred years. Neither the north nor the south was able to conquer the other and reunify China, and Xixia carefully positioned itself to upset the balance of forces at any one time, if one of its rivals grew too powerful.

Mongol Invasions

Xixia managed this quite successfully, and the end came for Xixia not due to an attack by one of its immediate rivals, but rather from an entirely new direction, the steppe, where the Mongol world had been united under the house of Chinggis Khan (often referred to as Genghis Khan, reigned 1206–1227). Even before his official rise, Chinggis Khan had sent some of his troops to raid Xixia domains in 1205. The raids continued until 1210, when, after a deep penetration to threaten the Xixia capital of Eriqaya (in what is now Ningxia Province), the then Xixia ruler, Li Anquan (reigned 1206–1211), agreed to submit to the Mongols. Making the Tangut position insecure was the Mongol acquisition of the realm of the White Tatar, or Ongud, positioned in the Ordos and inland toward Jurchen Jin domains and providing Mongol armies with easy access not only to the Jurchens themselves, but to Xixia. In any case, Xixia's submission eased the Mongol military position by eliminating one potential enemy, on their left flank, allowing a concentration of forces to attack the Jin in a series of major advances between 1211 and 1214. In 1215, the Jin government abandoned much of its territory and fled to what was seen as more security south of the Huang (Yellow) River.

After the Mongols turned their attentions west, Xixia seemed secure, except that its government had gained

Members of a Tibetan minority traverse the hills once inhabited centuries ago by the Tanguts of the Xixia dynasty, a state that flourished in northwest China before being taken over by Mongols.

the enmity of Chinggis Khan by refusing to support his invasion of Turkistan. This invasion absorbed Mongol energies for a number of years thereafter, but on his return to Mongolia, Chinggis Khan began planning the complete subjugation and destruction of Xixia. After carefully mobilizing troops, the advance began in 1226, the Xixia strong points being reduced one after the other. By this time, the Mongols possessed a substantial siege train and substantial ability to reduce even the most heavily fortified cities. In the end, the last Xixia ruler, Li Xian (reigned 1226–1227), had no choice but to surrender his capital. The Mongols, enraged by his last-ditch resistance and by the death of Chinggis Khan probably weeks after the final Xixia submission, executed Li Xian and all of his family as well as large masses of his subjects.

Surviving Records of Xixia Culture

Despite the ferocity of the final war of conquest, and what seems to have been an intentional genocide, at least among the Tangut elite, the culture did survive, although the surviving Tanguts were not numerous enough to leave behind a recognizable society persisting until today. Some Tanguts were given to Mongol potentates as booty, and some Mongol groups may trace all or some of their origins back to them. Others were drafted into Mongol service and served in civil and even military capacities. Also surviving, for a short time at least, was the complex Tangut script. This script, based on Chinese characters but lacking their pictographic basis, provided a large number of complex symbols to write Tangut words, without any of the visual clues associated with the Chinese script. Long unreadable, this script is slowly being deciphered, and along with it, the Tangut language, but this work is still far from completion, and it will be decades before the existing corpus of documents can be understood to its fullest. Of course, Chinese was also in use in Tangut domains, and much of what we know about Xixia history comes from Chinese sources, principally those written by Xixia enemies.

The Tanguts, as far as can be determined, were devout Buddhists, and a good deal of their surviving literature, mostly manuscript fragments, but some nearly complete texts as well, is composed of Buddhist literature. Texts are not always the same as those circulating under the same names elsewhere, a fact having an adverse impact on reading them as Rosetta stones to decipher Tangut. Because of its Buddhism, Xixia maintained active connections with other Buddhist cultures, including with Tibetans, who established direct connections with Xixia from an early date and later used the Tangut domains as a jumping off point for converting Mongols.

Paul D. BUELL

Further Reading

Buell, P. D. (2003). *Historical dictionary of the Mongolian world empire*. Lanham, MD, and Oxford, U.K.: The Scarecrow Press.

Dunnell, R. W. (1996). *The great state of white and high: Buddhism and state formation in eleventh century Xia*. Honolulu: University of Hawaii Press.

Kychanov, E. I. (1968). *Ocherki Istorii Tangutskogo Gosudarstva*. Moscow: Nauka.

XU Beihong

Xú Bēihóng 徐悲鴻

1895–1953   Artist and educator

Xu Beihong was an important figure in introducing Western ideas to modern Chinese painting. He trained and exhibited in Europe, and held important teaching posts in China. Xu's work combined traditional Chinese heroic subjects with Western realism. He is best known for his monochrome ink paintings of galloping horses, which integrated Chinese brushwork with Western foreshortening and realism.

Xu Beihong was one of the most important figures in the introduction of Western ideas to Chinese painting in the first half of the twentieth century. He trained in Europe, exhibited abroad, and held a succession of important teaching posts in his home country. His huge canvases combined traditional Chinese heroic subjects with Western realism and were seen as ushering in a new era in Chinese painting. Xu Beihong's best-known works are his monochrome ink paintings of galloping horses, which integrated Chinese brushwork with Western foreshortening and realism and brought him enduring fame.

Xu Beihong was born in Yixing, Jiangsu Province. His father, a farmer and self-taught artist, was also Xu's first teacher. Xu showed talent at an early age—he and his father made their livings as itinerant portrait painters—and at the age of seventeen he began to teach painting at a local school. In May 1917 Xu received financial support to study abroad in Tokyo. He returned at the end of the year and was given a position at the Society for the Study of Painting Technique at Beijing University by Cai Yuanpei (1868–1940), who was a strong advocate of the New Culture Movement that sought to rejuvenate China's arts.

In 1919 Xu left to study art in Paris on a government scholarship at the École Nationale Supérieure des Beaux-Arts, where he also participated in salon exhibitions. In 1920 he met and studied under the French realist painter Pascal-Adolphe-Jean Dagnan-Bouveret (1852–1929), a strong antimodernist known for his meticulous attention

In his masterful paintings of galloping horses, Xu Beihong used principles of foreshortening introduced from Western art. PHOTO BY JOAN LEBOLD COHEN.

2526

Xu Beihong's galloping horses, the dominant theme of his work after 1941, earned him enduring fame. PHOTO BY JOAN LEBOLD COHEN.

to detail. From Dagnan-Bouveret Xu learned the importance of technique. For Dagnan-Bouveret drawing was the foundation of painting; he valued precision and transmitted these standards to his students.

Xu returned to China in 1927 and taught at the Nanguo Art College before being appointed by Cai Yuanpei as the head of the art department of National Central University. He began painting his large canvases of heroic and patriotic subjects that united Chinese brushwork and themes with Western realism. At this time he began working with the horse as subject, first seen in *Jiufang Gao* of 1930. This would lead to the large work, *Galloping Horse* (1941), a theme he used for the rest of his life and for which he became internationally known. Xu Beihong continued to exhibit in solo shows and group exhibitions. In 1933 he organized a successful exhibition of Chinese painting that traveled throughout Europe and the Soviet Union. After 1949 Xu Beihong was named president of the Central Academy of Fine Arts and president of the Chinese Association of Workers in the Arts. In 1951 a stroke paralyzed him, and he died in 1953. In 1954 the Xu Beihong Memorial House was established at his residence in Beijing.

In the end Xu Beihong's importance lies not in his abilities as a painter but rather in his dedication and passion as an art educator. His interest in European academic realism and firm belief that strong technique and discipline are the necessary foundations for a painter shaped generations of Chinese artists in the twentieth century.

Catherine PAGANI

Further Reading

Fong, W. C. (2001). *Between two cultures: Late-nineteenth-and twentieth-century Chinese paintings from the Robert H. Ellsworth collection in the Metropolitan Museum of Art.* New York: Metropolitan Museum of Art.

Sullivan, M. (1996). *Art and artists of twentieth-century China.* Berkeley and Los Angeles: University of California Press.

XU Guangqi

Xú Guāngqǐ 徐光启

1562–1633   Official and scholar

Xu Guangqi, with missionary Matteo Ricci, translated Western texts into Chinese during the Ming dynasty. Their translation of Euclid's *Elements* exerted great influence on Chinese mathematics. Xu became a high official in the Ming court.

Xu Guangqi (1562–1633), born in Shanghai, was baptized by Italian Jesuit missionary Matteo Ricci in 1603, taking the name "Paul." For the next three years Xu and Ricci collaborated in translating Western texts on astronomy, mathematics, and geography into Chinese. Their most famous translation was the Greek geometer Euclid's *Elements,* which exerted a great influence on Chinese mathematics. Xu also wrote original works on trigonometry and agriculture, most notably the *Book of Agriculture,* which advocated the adoption of Western agricultural practices such as mapping, surveying, and irrigation. His interest in practical subjects was a departure from the dominance of neo-Confucian thought. After Xu became a high official in the Ming dynasty (1368–1644) court, he sponsored the Jesuit missionaries in China.

Xu believed that Western scholarship, particularly geometry, could complement Confucianism and replace Buddhism by undermining the tendency toward vague speculation. In 1629 Xu demonstrated the use of Western science in predicting solar eclipses and other astrological events. When the Manchus invaded China in 1630, Xu

The Italian Jesuit Matteo Ricci (left) and the Chinese mathematician Xu Guangqi (徐光啟) (right) in an image from Athanasius Kircher's *China Illustrata,* published in 1667. The Chinese edition of *Euclid's Elements* (幾何原本) was printed in 1607.

Xu Guangqi's "Preface" to the Chinese translations of Euclid's *Elements*

During the times of the Tang and Yu there already were Xi and He who took care of the calendar, as well as the Minister of Works, the Minister of Agriculture, the Forester, and the Director of Ritual Music—if those five Offices would have been deprived of Measures and Numbers, it would have been impossible to fulfill their tasks. Mathematics is one of the Six Arts mentioned in the *Offices of Zhou*, and the (other) five could not have led to any results without the use of Measures and Numbers . . . Therefore I have said that far back, during the period of the Three Dynasties, those who applied themselves to this calling were immersed in a rock-solid tradition of learning that was passed on from master to pupil—but that has in the end perished in the flames of the Ancestral Dragon. Since the Han dynasty there have been many who haphazardly groped to fine their way, like a blind man aiming at a target, vainly shooting in the air without effect; others followed their own judgments, based on outward appearances, like one who lights up an elephant with a candle, and, by the time he gets hold of its head has lost sight of its tail. That in our days the Way has completely disappeared, was that not unavoidable?! The *Jihe Yuanben* is the Ancestor of Measure and Numbers it is that by which one exhausts all the aspects of the square, the round, the plane, and the straight, and by which one completely covers the use of compasses, carpenter's square, water-level and measuring rope . . . Starting from what is clearly perceptible, [this work] penetrates into what is most subtle; from what is doubtful certainly is obtained. Is not that utility of what is useless, the basis of all what is useful?! In truth it can be called "the pleasure-garden of the myriad forms, the Erudite Ocean of the Hundred Schools [of philosophy]." Although it actually has not yet been completed, yet, with it as a reference, it is already possible to discuss the other books . . .

Source: Katz, V. J. (2007). *The Mathematics of Egypt, Mesopotamia, China, India, and Islam: A sourcebook*. Princeton, NJ: Princeton University Press, 372–373.

persuaded the emperor to use Western armaments to defend the capital.

Daniel OAKMAN

Further Reading

Engelfriet, P. (1998). *Euclid in China: The genesis of the first Chinese translation of Euclid's Elements, books I–VI (Jihe yuanben, Beijing, 1607) and its reception up to 1723.* Boston: E. J. Brill.

Jami, C., Engelfriet, P., & Blue, G. (2001). *Statecraft and intellectual renewal in late Ming China: The cross-cultural synthesis of Xu Guangqi, 1562–1633.* Boston: E. J. Brill.

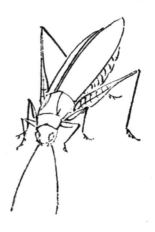

XU Haifeng

Xǔ Hǎifēng 许海峰

b. 1957   Olympic sharpshooter and coach

Xu Haifeng was the first athlete to win an Olympic gold medal for the People's Republic of China. After retiring from his career as a champion sharpshooter, during which he won a number of golds in international competition, Xu went on to become a dedicated coach.

In taking the first gold medal of the 1984 Summer Olympics in Los Angeles with a steely performance, sharpshooter Xu Haifeng also became a Chinese icon. He was not simply a winner, but the first winner of gold for his country since its return to the Olympic Games after a thirty-two-year absence due to controversy over the recognition of Taiwan. Hailed as a national hero upon his return for his timely victory in a sport demanding discipline and concentration, he went on to win many more titles and then to mentor younger champions, earning recognition not only as a top-tier athlete but also as a coach with a golden touch.

Xu was an unlikely Olympic hero; he'd been training in the sport for just two years, becoming a champion sharpshooter in Anhui Province in 1982 and winning his first national title in 1983. His only previous formal experience at shooting consisted of a week of military training in high school—although he reputedly was a crack shot with a slingshot during his childhood in Fujian Province.

Before joining the national shooting team (which was coached by Xu's former high school teacher), Xu had been farming and selling chemical fertilizer in rural Anhui Province. Xu went to Los Angeles as the rookie on a team of six, expecting merely "to take part," he later said. In the pistol events, attention gradually shifted from the Swedish world champion, Ragnar Skanaker, to the focused young man from China. Xu's victory in the 50-meter free pistol shooting final, at age twenty-seven, changed his life.

Juan Antonio Samaranch, then president of the International Olympic Committee, called the occasion "a great day for China's sports." The absence of strong contenders from Eastern Europe due to the Eastern Bloc's boycott of the Los Angeles Games certainly worked to the advantage of unknowns like Xu, but his win was no fluke, and he went on to prove his mettle in subsequent world competitions. In 1988, he won a bronze medal at the Summer Olympics in Seoul. Other wins accumulated over the years, including three golds at the 1986 Asian Games in Seoul, four golds at the 1990 Asian Games in Beijing, and five golds at the Seventh Asian Championships in 1991.

Xu Haifeng's Los Angeles feat was commemorated in a Chinese television play, *Shots over Prada*—a reference to the name of the city's Olympic shooting range. He donated that first Olympic gold medal to China's National Museum. Retiring from competition in 1994, Xu became the coach of the Chinese national women's shooting team; one of his charges, Li Duihong, won a gold in Atlanta in 1996, and another, Tao Luna, took a gold in Sydney in 2000. He was head coach of the shooting team at the Athens Games in 2004, which won golds in three men's events and one women's event. In anticipation of the 2008 Beijing Summer Games, Xu took over supervision of China's modern pentathlon team. When the Games opened, Xu was listed as deputy team leader for pentathlon, at which Chinese

Xu Haifeng receiving the first gold medal for China in the 1984 Los Angeles Olympics.

the opening ceremony, carrying the Olympic torch as it neared the end of its journey from Athens.

China's State Sports Commission awarded Xu a National Sports Medal of Honor in 1984, and he was named one of the nation's top ten athletes twice, in 1984 and 1986. *Newsweek* magazine's assertion that, "Posterity will forget that a Chinese fertilizer salesman won the first gold medal of the 1984 Summer Games" was wrong: A quarter century since the event that catapulted him to fame, Xu Haifeng remains a household name in China.

Judy POLUMBAUM

came in fifth and tenth among the women and fourth for the men—noteworthy in this European-dominated event. Xu's most prominent role at the 2008 Olympics, however, was his appearance in the main stadium during

Further Reading

Brownell, S. (2008). *Beijing's Games: What the Olympics mean to China*. Lanham, MD: Rowman & Littlefield.

Gao Dianmin. (1984, July 29). The moment when China's Olympic zero is broken. Xinhua News Agency.

Morris, A. (2004). *Marrow of the nation: A history of sport and physical culture in Republican China*. Berkeley: University of California Press.

XU Zhimo

Xú Zhìmó 徐志摩

1895–1931 Modernist poet

Xu Zhimo was a modernist poet who actively sought to break Chinese poetry from its traditional roots and align it to Western poetic models, especially those found in the Romantic poets.

Xu Zhimo, the poet renowned for introducing Western poetic forms and techniques that allowed tradition-bound Chinese verse to acquire a freer form of expression, was born in the town of Xiashi, Sichuan Province, 15 January 1895. Xu was a precocious child who showed at an early age a delight in nature, a delight that would continue to hold sway in his poetry. His early education was in Hanzhou Secondary School, where he met and befriended Yu Da Fu, the future story writer and poet.

Shortly after graduating at the age of twenty in 1915, Xu entered an arranged marriage, according to the dictates of traditional Chinese society. His bride was Zhang Youyi. But the marriage was a failure from the outset, and, perhaps to escape it, Xu enrolled in Tianjin University, where he soon came under the influence of the reformer Liang Qichao, who encouraged Xu to continue his education in the West. Xu applied to Clark University in Worcester, Massachusetts, to study history and came to the United States in 1918. The next year he transferred to Columbia University, where he took up the study of economics. Before long, he came to feel that the United States was a place where he could not obtain the type of education that he wished to receive. He left for Great Britain in 1920, where he was accepted into the London School of Economics. Eventually he would enter Cambridge University, which at last suited his sensibilities, for it was there that he discovered the works of the English Romantics, as well as the French Symbolists. Xu felt an immediate affinity for their work.

Picture of a young Xu Zhimo, a poet renowned for introducing Western poetic forms and techniques that allowed tradition-bound Chinese verse to acquire a freer form of expression.

The Poetry of Xu Zhimo

LOVE'S INSPIRATION

For a long time I have been gazing at death
  itself.
Since the day the bond of love was sealed in
  my heart
I have been gazing at death—
That realm of perpetual beauty; to death
I happily surrendered myself because
It is the birth of the brilliant and the free.
From that moment on I scorned my body
And even less did I care
For the floating glory of this life;
I longed to trust my breath to time
Even more infinite than it.
Then my eyes would urn into the glittering
  starts,

And my glistening hair, the clouds that are
  draped
All over the sky. Buffeting winds would
Whirl in front of my chest, before my eyes;
Waves would lap at my ankles, their sacred
  luster
Surging with each breaker!
My thoughts would be lightning
That whips up a dance of dragons and snakes
    on the horizon;
My voice would thunder, suddenly awakening
The Spring and awakening life. Ah!
Beyond imagination, beyond compare
Is love's inspiration, love's power.

Source: Lau, J. S. M., & Goldblatt, H. (Eds.). (1995.). *The Co-lumbia anthology of modern Chinese literature*. (Kai-yu Hsu, Trans.). New York, Columbia University Press, 504.

His Cambridge years can be termed his transformative years, for he not only discovered a form of poetry to which he felt an innate attraction but also met and fell in love with Lin Huiyin, who was only sixteen at the time and a student at Saint Mary's College in London. He quickly obtained a divorce from his wife so he could marry Lin. It was an effort in vain, however. Lin returned to China with her father in 1922. Distraught at the outcome of events, Xu also headed back home and tried to find Lin. But she had already married Liang Sicheng. Thereafter Xu devoted himself entirely to poetry and worked intensely to change Chinese poetry radically by aligning it with Western traditions.

His first collection, titled simply *Zhimo's Poems,* appeared in 1925. The poems were heavily influenced by the English Romantics, especially Keats, Shelley, and Wordsworth. Xu soon befriended like-minded poets, also Western educated, such as Wen Yiduo, and became the founding member of the Crescent Moon Society, which was established in 1927. The society published the influential journal *Xinyue (Crescent Moon)*. Xu's next collections, *A Night in Florence* (1927), *Fierce Tiger* (1928), and *Love's Inspiration* (1930) showed a further refinement of expression in which the Western elements become more thoroughly blended with his own sensibilities. The larger intention of his poetry was to reject the tradition-bound morality of old China so that a new China might be born, one in which the ideas of Western enlightenment would pervade. Xu's poetic experimentations were tragically cut short when he died in an airplane crash on 19 November 1931.

Nirmal DASS

Further Reading

Goldman, M., & Lee, L. O. (Eds.). (2002). *An intellectual history of modern China*. Cambridge, U.K.: Cambridge University Press.

Lau, J., & Goldblatt, H. (Eds.). (1994). *Columbia anthology of modern Chinese Literature*. New York: Columbia University Press.

Lee, L. O. (1973). *The modern generation of modern Chinese writers*. Cambridge, MA: Harvard University Press.

McDougall, B., & Kam, L. (1997). *The literature of China in the twentieth century*. New York: Columbia University Press.

Spence, J. D. (1981). *The Chinese and their revolution, 1895–1980*. New York: The Viking Press.

Xuanzang

Xuánzàng　玄藏

602?–664　Buddhist monk-scholar, pilgrim, translator

Xuanzang of the Tang dynasty was one of the most influential figures in the history of Chinese Buddhism. He is best known for his sixteen-year pilgrimage to India in search of the true Buddhist teachings, from which he brought back hundreds of scriptures. Xuanzang and his chief disciple, Kuiji, founded the Faxiang (Characteristics of the Dharmas) school.

Xuanzang 玄藏 was a Buddhist monk-scholar, pilgrim, and translator in the early Tang 唐 dynasty (618–907 CE). He traveled to India in search of the true dharma (divine law) and brought back with him hundreds of Buddhist texts. In addition to translating and commenting on the texts, he wrote *Record of the Western Regions during the Great Tang* (*Datang xiyu ji*) about his sixteen-year journey to India. His biography can be found in Zanning's (919–1001) *Song [Compiled] Biographies of Eminent Monks* (*Song gaoseng zhuan*). He and his chief disciple, Kuiji 窺基 (632–682), founded the Faxiang 法相 (Characteristics of the Dharmas) school, a Chinese version of the Indian Yogâcâra (Consciousness-only) school of thought.

Xuanzang, surnamed Chen (known as "Chen Yi"), was a native of Henan Province. His family for generations produced erudite Confucian scholar-officials. He was the youngest of four children. After the death of his father in 611, Xuanzang, under the influence of his elder brother, a Buddhist monk, joined the monastery at the age of thirteen. He became a fully ordained monk in 622.

Paper cutout of Xuanzang (602–664), a monk during the Tang dynasty who endured great troubles as he traveled to India to retrieve Buddhist scriptures. His adventures were the basis of the famous Chinese novel *Journey to the West*.

Troubled by the discrepancies and contradictions in the Chinese translations of scriptures, he began to learn Sanskrit and decided to go to India to study Buddhism.

Xuanzang sneaked out of the Tang capital of Chang'an in 629 after the imperial court refused his petition to travel westward. He crossed the Gobi Desert and took the Silk Roads route via central Asia to India. Having endured numerous hardships and escaped from life-threatening

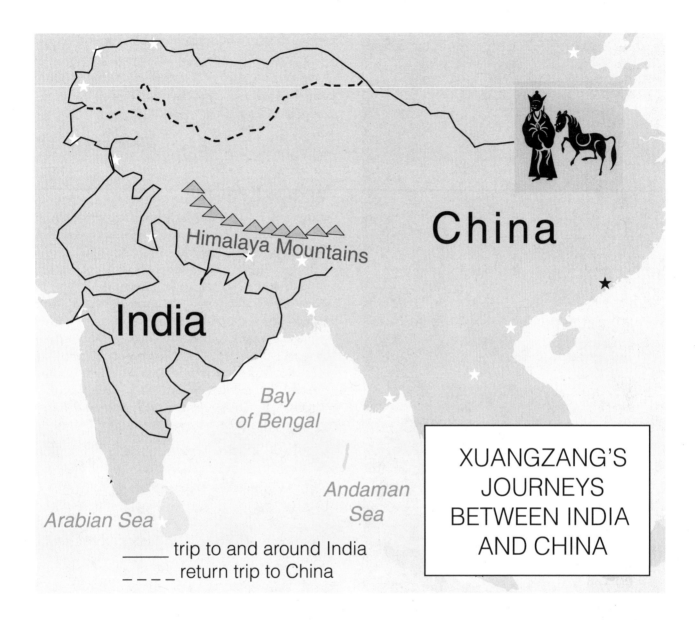

China

Himalaya Mountains

India

Bay
of Bengal

Andaman
Sea

Arabian Sea

_____ trip to and around India
_ _ _ _ return trip to China

XUANGZANG'S
JOURNEYS
BETWEEN INDIA
AND CHINA

dangers, he eventually arrived in India, where he studied with many renowned masters and visited important Buddhist centers.

Xuanzang returned to Chang'an in 645. This time he received a warm welcome from the Tang imperial court. He declined the emperor's offer of an official position, however; instead, assisted by a group of well-trained Buddhist scholars and linguistic experts, he spent the rest of his lifetime translating the texts that he had brought back from India.

Xuanzang is said to have brought back 657 items in 520 cases, and he himself translated 73 items in 1330 fascicles (divisions of a book published in parts) of scriptures into Chinese.. His scholarly efforts not only made a great

number of Mahayana scriptures and treatises available in Chinese but also contributed significantly to the Chinese understanding of Indian Buddhist doctrines and philosophies.

Xuanzang and his disciple, Kuiji, founded the Faxiang school on the basis of the Yogâcâra theory of the mind. It teaches that so-called reality is simply a result of how the mind functions; in particular, the storehouse consciousness (Sanskrit: *âlayavijñâna*) is the repository of all the mental projections and perceptions. Although the Faxiang school soon died out in China, it had a profound impact on Chinese Huayan and Chan Buddhism.

Xuanzang's *Record of the Western Regions during the Great Tang,* completed in 646, has become a valuable primary source of information about medieval central Asia and India. Based on Xuanzang's pilgrimage, Wu Cheng'en (1500–1582) of the Ming dynasty (1368–1644) wrote the novel *Journey to the West,* which is one of the most popular classics in Chinese literature.

Ding-hwa HSIEH

Further Reading

Bernstein, R. (2001). *Ultimate journey: Retracing the path of an ancient Buddhist monk who crossed Asia in search of enlightenment.* New York: Alfred A. Knopf.

Ch'en, K. K. S. (1973). *Buddhism in China: A historical survey.* Princeton, NJ: Princeton University Press.

Devahuti, D. (Ed.). (2001). *The unknown Hsuan-Tsang.* New York: Oxford University Press.

Li Rongxi (Trans.). (1995). *A biography of the Tripitaka master of the great Ci'en Monastery of the great Tang dynasty.* Berkeley, CA: Numata Center for Buddhist Translation and Research.

Wriggins, S. H. (2004). *The Silk Road journey with Xuanzang.* Boulder, CO: Westview Press.

Painting of the traveling monk Xuanzang by a Japanese artist of the Kamakura period (fourteenth century).

Xunzi

Xúnzǐ 荀子

c. 300–230 BCE *philosopher*

A key figure in Chinese philosophy, Xunzi is best known for his critique of Mencius' concept of the essential goodness of humankind and for moving beyond Confucian ideals. For Xunzi, a rigid hierarchical social structure constrained by tradition, moral education, and threat of punishment is the necessary antidote for the naturally evil tendencies of humanity.

Xunzi is both the name of one of the most important Confucian thinkers and also the name of the book containing his teachings and his writings as compiled over the years. The significance of Xunzi, the man, lies in his thorough critique of Mencius, who upheld the basic and innate goodness of human beings. For Xunzi, there was little to laud in humankind; he held humankind to be inherently evil and therefore untrustworthy if not constrained by tradition, strict guidance, and the looming threat of punishment.

Very few details of Xunzi's life are known. He lived during the Warring States Period (475–221 BCE), and he received his education in the city-state of Qi sometime in the third century BCE, after which he served in various courtly positions; he is thought to have died not long after the year 238 BCE.

Although Xunzi's philosophy is thoroughly grounded in Confucianism, in so much as it recognizes the need for ritual and duty as taught by the sages of the past, it also seeks to fill an inherent insufficiency in the ideas of Confucius and Mencius concerning the human condition.

Confucius is ambivalent; he states that there are people who are not interested in participating in the Way (the path to betterment, both of the self and the world), and such people are led into deeds of immorality. Mencius holds to the essential goodness of all people, who are only betrayed into immorality by a corrupted society. For Xunzi, both views are, at best, partial definitions of what constitutes the social makeup of the individual. If some people are not interested in following the Way, then the method of leading them is at fault because it abandons precisely those people that should be helped. Further, the Way becomes selective, picking and choosing who may follow and who may not, thereby becoming arbitrary. And if all people are inherently good, then there would not be any need for laws to govern people. But this is nowhere evident in human society; all people abide by rules and laws. This leads Xunzi to observe that human nature is evil and must be continually taught to become good, even if provisionally; the evidence for this evil is found in the manifestation of desire. People, if unchecked by regulations and prohibitions, would live solely to satisfy their desires, no matter what the cost to those around them or to society, and even the world. Hence the need for government, leaders, religion, rituals, rules and laws, all of which work in concert to retrain the natural, and therefore destructive, human tendencies. For this reason that which has been established by the ancient sages must be dutifully followed because such precepts have been put in place in order to guide the individual into correct social behavior. And these rules have been put in place by those who know better, namely, the ancient sages.

Painting of Xunxi, one of the most important Confucian thinkers.

Traditions become important for Xunzi because he sees them as examples of the good which people must emulate; and this is the educational worth of tradition and ritual. Human beings need to follow examples; they need to see how they must behave and act in a moral fashion. This pedagogical turn in Xunzi's philosophy points to a rather precise definition of people's social behavior; they need good leaders. And just as examples educate men and women, so also must they be led by rulers who are learned in tradition, and therefore wise, who can explain to people the need for moral action. For Xunzi, a learned person is one that is fully adept in the tradition, so that he or she can teach those that need to be taught. And here Xunzi makes an important concession: people are inherently evil, but they have the capacity to be taught to be good and morally upright.

Thus, one of the central concepts for Xunzi is the need for education, which must continue until a person dies. Learning is not a natural process; it is not like taste or hearing, which one is born with; it is a very much an artificial process, and therefore a very human one. Learning does not lead to natural growth; rather, it leads to social and therefore moral growth. The ideal education for Xunzi consists of studying the canon, that is, books of poetry and history, as well as books dealing with rituals and observances; and he advocates the learning of music, which educates through inspiration and by providing evidence of harmony, order, and structure. And here the role of the wise teacher becomes much more essential; one cannot learn good music from a bad teacher. Only a wise teacher can lead one into the perfection that music demands.

Despite his insistence that the lowliest person from the street can be educated into wisdom, Xunzi does not abandon the need for punishment. Drawing upon the Confucian understanding that humans need to be continually perfected, Xunzi understands that this always brings about a fundamental division in society: the rulers and the ruled. Given this ongoing difference between people living within the same social structure, there must be the means available to the rulers to maintain order and negate chaos. Because human beings are forever seeking to fulfill their desires, they must be constrained by the threat of punishment, lest they willfully overthrow the fundamental structure of society, namely, its hierarchy. For Xunzi it is the structure of society that allows it to function harmoniously; and people need to be guided into being good, first through education, and then, failing that, through punishment.

One of the central shortcomings of Xunzi's ideas is his inability to identify the role of practical reason. He does not delve into how the sages of long ago came up with traditions and rituals. What criteria of judgment did they use to say this ritual was good and that was not good? The question of individual judgment is indeed entirely lacking. In addition, he cannot explain why the sages were led to seek out morality, social order, and harmony, when they, like the rest of humanity, shared in an inherently evil nature. Why would they abandon their natural instincts to forever fulfill their desires and seek to impose restrictions upon themselves and upon others? In short, Xunzi does not explain what gives him the authority to understand human nature in the way that he does. Nor does he clarify why he holds his solution of education and punishment as being proper and good.

The importance of Xunzi lies in his ability to present Confucianism as the very best possible way of living a moral life—both for the individual and for society. The moral life may only be acquired, he maintains, through a moral education, which is a lifelong endeavor, for it is

The Works of Xunzi

Xunzi, a philosopher deeply concerned with promoting learning that is relevant to the present, makes a strong case for the value of personal association with a teacher and personal involvement in ritual practice—as opposed to education based on a bookish or antiquarian absorption in the past.

The noble person says: Learning must never cease. Blue comes from the indigo plant, yet it is bluer than indigo. Ice is made from water, yet it is colder than water. Wood as straight as a plumb line may be bent into a wheel that is as round as if it were drawn with a compass, and, even after the wood has dried, it will not straighten out again because this is the way it has been bent. Thus wood marked by the plumb line will become straight, and metal that is put to the whetstone will become sharp. The noble person who studies widely and examines himself each day will become clear in his knowing and faultless in his conduct...

... Once I spent an entire day in thought, but it was not as good as a moment of study. Once I stood on tiptoe to gaze into the distance, but it was not as good as climbing to a high place to get a broad view. Climbing to a high place and waving will not make your arm any longer, but you can see from farther away. Shouting down the wind will give your voice no added urgency, but you can be heard more distinctly. By borrowing a horse and carriage you will not improve your feet, but you can cover a thousand li. By borrowing a boat and paddles you will not improve your ability in water, but you can cross rivers and seas. The noble person is by birth no different from others, but he is good at borrowing from external things.

Source: de Bary, W. T., & Bloom, I. (1999). *Sources of Chinese tradition, vol. 1.* New York: Columbia University Press, 161–162.

---

morality that ultimately refines the individual and makes of him or her a civilized human being.

Nirmal DASS

Further Reading

Cua, A. (1985). *Ethical argumentation: A study of Hsün Tzu's moral epistemology.* Honolulu: University of Hawaii Press.

Goldin, P. R. (1999). *Rituals of the Way: The philosophy of Xunzi.* Chicago: Open Court.

Hagen, K. (2007). *The philosophy of Xunzi: A reconstruction.* Chicago: Open Court.

Kline, T. C. & Ivanhoe, P. J. (2000). *Virtue, nature, and moral agency in the Xunzi.* Indianapolis, IN: Hackett Publishing.

Lee, J. (2005). *Xunzi and early Chinese naturalism.* Albany: State University of New York Press.

Liu, J. (2006). *An introduction to Chinese philosophy: From ancient philosophy to Chinese Buddhism.* Malden, MA: Blackwell.

Machle, E. J. (1993). *Nature and heaven in the Xunzi.* Albany: State University of New York Press.

Sato, M. (2003). *The Confucian quest for order: The origin and formation of the political thought of Xun Zi.* Leiden, The Netherlands, and Boston: E. J. Brill.

Stalnaker, A. (2006). *Overcoming our evil: Human nature and spiritual exercises in Xunzi and Augustine.* Washington, DC: Georgetown University Press.

Watson, B. (1963). *Hsün Tzu: Basic writings.* New York: Columbia University Press.

Yalta Agreement

Yǎ'ěrtǎ Tiáoyuē　雅尔塔条约

Planning for the post–World War II world, Winston Churchill, Joseph Stalin, and Franklin Roosevelt met at Yalta, a resort town in the Ukraine, in 1945. The agreement restored imperialist privileges in Manchuria that Russia had enjoyed in the early 1900s. In exchange the Soviets signed a treaty of friendship with Chiang Kai-shek and entered the war against Japan.

At the February 1945 conference held in Yalta, a resort town in the Ukraine, British prime minister Winston Churchill, Soviet leader Joseph Stalin, and U.S. president Franklin Roosevelt sought to plan for the defeat of Germany and Japan and to shape the post–World War II world. The results of the conference proved that China was not going to be one of great powers of the postwar era. China was not represented at the conference, and Chiang Kai-shek, leader of the Nationalist (Guomindang) government, was informed of the Yalta Agreement by the United States only after the conference's conclusion.

The final agreement concerning China, published 13 February 1945, declared that "The commercial port of Dairen shall be internationalized, the pre-eminent interests of the Soviet Union in this port being safeguarded, and the lease of Port Arthur as a naval base of the U.S.S.R. restored" and "The Chinese-Eastern Railroad and the South Manchurian Railroad, which provide an outlet to Dairen, shall be jointly operated by the establishment of a joint Soviet-Chinese company, it being understood that the pre-eminent interests of the Soviet Union shall be safeguarded and that China shall retain sovereignty in Manchuria" (Tucker et al. 1738). These terms essentially restored the imperialist privileges in Manchuria that Russia had enjoyed immediately prior to the Russo-Japanese War of 1904–1905. In exchange the Soviets signed a treaty of friendship and alliance with Chiang's government and entered the war against Japan in August 1945. The Yalta Agreement also contained plans for the disposition of other territories occupied by the Japanese, such as the temporary division of Korea.

Roosevelt hoped that tying the Soviets to the Nationalist regime would solidify two postwar relationships: cordial ties between Washington and Moscow and a coalition government in China led by the Nationalists with Communist participation. Under U.S. pressure Chiang grudgingly accepted the agreement, which he hoped would drive a wedge between Stalin and Mao Zedong's Chinese Communist Party. Mao's forces, at their own base at Yan'an in north-central China, had a shaky truce (often called the "Second United Front") with Chiang's Nationalist government during the War of Resistance against Japan. Few expected the truce to last after Japan's surrender. Stalin's actions, however, seemed to belie claims of Communist solidarity and illustrated his ambivalence toward the Chinese Communists.

The Yalta framework did not last to the end of the decade. The short-lived alliance between the Soviet Union and Nationalist China could not save Chiang's regime or deter Stalin from supporting the Communists. The

2541

The "Big Three" of the Yalta Conference: Franklin D. Roosevelt, Winston Churchill, and Joseph Stalin at the Livadia Palace, Yalta, 9 February 1945.

Soviets fulfilled their promise to withdraw from Manchuria in 1946, but they stripped the region of its industry and left behind Japanese weapons to assist the Communists. By early 1947 civil war began anew, and by 1948 the Nationalists were collapsing. Stalin threw his support behind Mao as it became evident who would win the civil war. The dream of Soviet-U.S. cooperation or a coalition government in China was dead.

Chiang would point to Yalta as an example of U.S. naiveté about Communist machinations. Within the United States Yalta became part of a heated debate over "who lost China" and a rallying cry for conservative supporters of Chiang's regime, which had retreated to Taiwan. In fact, both Mao and Chiang were bitter that the United States and Soviet Union attempted to define the international order of northeast Asia with little attention to Chinese interests—or sovereignty.

Steven PHILLIPS

Further Reading

Tang Tsou. (1963). *America's failure in China, 1941–1950.* Chicago: University of Chicago Press.

Tucker, S. C., et al. (Eds.). (2005). *World War II: A student encyclopedia. (5 Vols.).* Santa Barbara, CA: ABC-CLIO.

Zhang Zhenjiang. (2004). Yaerta mimi xieding yu Zhongguo [The secret agreements at Yalta and China]. In Niu Dayong and Shen Zhihua (Eds.). *Lengzhan yu Zhongguo de zhoubian guanxi* (pp 131–164). Beijing: Shijie zhishi chubanshe.

YAN Zhenqing

Yán Zhēnqīng 颜真卿

709–785 CE   Court scholar and calligrapher

Yan Zhenqing was a court scholar and calligrapher of the Tang dynasty (618–907 CE). He was imprisoned and strangled to death during a rebellion.

Yan Zhenqing, also known as "Yan Qingchen," lived in Shandong Province until he relocated to Xi'an in Shaanxi Province. His parents were descendants of clans whose members either held important official positions in court or were renowned scholars. For example, Yan Zhitui (531–c. 590 CE) was the author of *Home Instructions of the Yan Family (Yanshi Jiasun)*. Yan Shigu (581–645 CE), Yan Zhenqing's grandfather, was a famous calligrapher and historian during the end of the Sui dynasty (581–618 CE). Yan's maternal grandfather, Yin Zhongrong, also skilled in calligraphy, was the head secretary to Empress Wu (624–705 CE).

Yan had a difficult childhood because his father passed away when Yan was only three years old. Working hard, he passed the civil exam and became a scholar (*jinshi*) in 734. In that year he was married to the daughter of a prince. Even with these advantages, Yan's career in politics was tumultuous. Being a man of integrity and loyalty, Yan was constantly a target for his opponents in court. Every time Yan emerged from a conspiracy or slander, he was either demoted or transferred. According to historical records, Yan was instrumental in pacifying the An Lu Shan Rebellion in 755. Again, when the court faced another rebellion in 783, Yan volunteered to go into enemy territory to negotiate with the head rebel, Li Xilie, who incarcerated Yan

Calligraphy by Yan Zhengqing.

when he refused to surrender. Li, on the verge of defeat by the Tang dynasty (618–907 CE)army, ordered a eunuch to strangle Yan to death. He was seventy-six.

Yan Zhenqing's other love was calligraphy. When he was too poor to buy ink and brushes, he used a broom to write on the wall with yellow dirt. Beginning in 743 Yan deemed Zhang Xu (flourished 713–740), "the saint of cursive calligraphy," as his teacher.

Another calligrapher, the monk Huaisu (737–798), was also Yan's ally in calligraphy. Yan's calligraphic achievements began rather late, around the age of sixty. His journey to artistic success can be divided into three stages: (1) the early stage before Yan was fifty, (2) the blooming stage of running and cursive (*xing* and *cao*) scripts before he was sixty, and (3) the final stage when his standard script (*kai*) reached full maturity. Famous cursive scripts done by Yan include "Begging for Rice Note" (764), "Mourning over My Nephew" (758), and "Fighting for a Seat Note" (764). After age sixty Yan became attracted to the standard script, which he wrote on big pieces of flat stone that were later engraved. "Ancestral Temple of the Guo Family Tablet," done at age fifty-six, and "The Tablet of Songjing," done at age sixty-four, were some of his prime examples in the standard script.

Yan's unadorned calligraphic style breaks up the glamorous and formal style of the two Wangs (Wang Xizhi, 303–379? CE, and Wang Xianzhi, 344–388 CE) from the Jin dynasty (265–420 CE). (The Jin dynasty is a brief period during the North and South Dynasties in China.) His writings reflect the character of an honorable man who was righteous and magnanimous but true and simple. The imperfection and simplicity found in his works somehow manifest a form of aesthetics.

Fatima WU

Further Reading

Ecke, Tseng Yu-ho. (1971). *Chinese calligraphy*. Boston: David R. Godine.

Harrist, R. E., Jr., & Fong, Wen C. (1999). *The embodied image: Chinese calligraphy from the John B. Elliot collection*. New Haven, CT: Art Museum, Princeton University.

Masterpiece of Chinese calligraphy in the National Palace Museum supplement. (1973). Taipei, Taiwan: National Palace Museum.

Zhao Lengyue. (Ed.). (1993). *Ten calligraphers*. Taipei, Taiwan: World Cultures Publishers.

Kill **one**
to warn
a hundred.

杀一儆百

Shā yī jǐng bǎi

Yan'an Rectification Campaign

Yán'ān Zhěngfēng Yùndòng   延安整风运动

The Yan'an Rectification Campaign of 1942 established the *modus operandi* of subsequent ideological campaigns in the history of Chinese Communism. It signified the expansion of the power of the Communist leaders from political and economic realms into other spheres of life, with the result that no alternative bases existed from which political authorities could be challenged.

Kang Sheng, an official of the CCP, was closely involved in the Cultural Revolution purges during the Yanan Rectification Movement.

The Yan'an Rectification Campaign 延安整风运动 of 1942 was a significant event in the history of the Chinese Communist Party (CCP). The campaign's success in quashing the first serious challenge to CCP leader Mao Zedong's commanding position within the party, gradually acquired during the Long March, made it a prototype of later ideological campaigns; it also showed the aggressive reach of the CCP into intellectual life in Yan'an, a city in Shaanxi Province. No longer content to manage only political and economic affairs, CCP leaders would regard as their prerogative the total subjugation of literature and art to politics from this point on. As such, the campaign was a mass movement of a kind hitherto unseen in the history of the CCP, affecting not only the top echelon of the party's leadership but also the lives of people from other social strata in Yan'an.

Targets

The late 1930s and early 1940s brought a fundamental change in CCP membership as more and more people from various places arrived in Yan'an, the last stronghold of Communism in China at the time. Unlike those who had endured the hardships of the Long March, many of the new arrivals were perhaps more anti-Japanese or anti-Guomindang (Nationalist Party) than pro-Communist. Moreover, coming mostly from cosmopolitan urban centers, they had an outlook quite at odds with the nativist bent of Mao's brand of Communism, making it difficult for the party to maintain its iron discipline.

In a speech delivered on 1 February 1942, at the Central Party School at Yan'an, Mao highlighted three errors that he called upon "the masses" to correct: subjectivism, sectarianism, and party formalism. The scope of the Rectification Campaign at this stage was still rather limited, aimed as it was only at the general working style of party cadres. But when Mao's call triggered vociferous complaints from students disgruntled with life in Yan'an, the nature of the campaign began to change. A number of prominent writers associated with the *Jiefang Ribao* 解放日报 (Liberation Daily) saw an opportunity to voice criticism of the party leadership, utilizing a form of intellectual essay called the *zawen* to highlight instances of inequality that exposed the party's hypocrisy and pointedly questioning the legitimacy of the party to assume leadership in areas other than politics. Wang Shiwei, who would later become the prime target of the campaign, was particularly outspoken in asserting the role of writers and artists as social critics free from party interference. As these events unfolded, it became clear to party leaders that the campaign would have to rein in this group of wayward intellectuals and neutralize their destabilizing influence.

Modus Operandi

To lay down the ideological groundwork for the expanded scope of the Rectification Campaign, the party confronted head-on the question of art and literature in a socialist society. Mao's keynote speech on 2 May, the first day of the Yan'an Forum on Literature and Art, served this purpose. Mao argued that literature and art transcending time and class did not exist and hence that the notion that the artist could be an objective critic of society was a myth. It behooved artists and writers to ally their interests with those of the workers, farmers, and soldiers under the guidance of the CCP, Mao asserted. Any public

criticism of the party at this stage would be regarded as an act of betrayal of the larger cause of Communism and tantamount to heresies such as Trotskyism, with which Wang Shiwei was indeed later charged.

The campaign then moved to the next stage of bringing intellectuals to heel, proceeding through a number of phases that would be replicated in subsequent ideological struggles. First, a negative example was established, in this case, Wang Shiwei and people thought to be associated with him. Second, gentle pressure was applied on this group by means of private visits from leaders and friends to persuade them of the error of their ways. When this pressure failed to produce the desired results, public meetings were held at which Wang was put under hostile cross-examination. At the same time people throughout Yan'an society were instructed to study key Communist texts and documents related to Wang's case so that they could participate in the denunciation of Wang. Transcripts of these public meetings, called "struggle sessions," clearly indicate a willful distortion of Wang's position by the CCP. Despite claims of fairness, the proceedings often degenerated into name calling and other forms of intimidation. Most of Wang's associates, notably Ding Ling and Liu Xuewei, recanted at this point, but Wang remained intransigent, going so far as to threaten to withdraw from the party. Finally, trumped-up charges were brought against him for belonging to the Five-Member Anti-Party Clique, and what had begun as an ideological disagreement then turned into a punishable crime, and Wang was arrested. The goal of the campaign had been achieved at this point, even though it would be extended and would evolve into other political movements in 1943. Wang was executed in 1947 under circumstances that remain unclear to this day.

Repercussions

The Yan'an Rectification Campaign was one of the most successful attempts of the CCP to induce conformity among its ranks. The same strategies that were employed in bringing intellectuals to submission, especially the clever deployment of "the masses" against the target of the campaign, would be applied to nonparty members in later years as well and often in more thorough and violent ways.

The success of the campaign also marked an important ideological victory for Mao. With the suppression

Mao's Speech at the Yan'an Forum on Literature and Art

Political leader Mao Zedong laid out the meaning and purpose of the Yan'an Rectification Campaign in a 1942 speech at the Yan'an Forum on Literature and Art.

"Literature and art have been an important and highly effective part of the cultural front since the May Fourth [Movement]. During the Civil War the revolutionary literature and art movement showed great development, and in its overall direction was consistent with the Red Army's struggle of that period, although in actual work the two were fighting in isolation, owing to the separation of the two fraternal armies by the reactionaries. Since the War of Resistance a great number of revolutionary literature and art workers have come to Yan'an and every other anti-Japanese base. This is a very good thing. However, merely coming to these bases is not the same as identifying oneself with the people's movement in the bases. If we are to push the revolutionary work forward, we will have to make these two become completely identified with each other.

The purpose of our meeting today is to make literature and art become a constructive part of the whole revolutionary machine; to use them as powerful weapons for uniting and educating the people and for crushing and destroying the enemy, as well as to help the people wage the struggle against the enemy with one heart and one mind. What are some of the problems which must be solved in order to achieve this aim? They are the problems of standpoint, attitude, audience, work, and study."

Source: Saich, T. (1996) *The rise to power of the Chinese Communist Party.* Armonk, NY: M. E. Sharpe, 1123.

---

of cosmopolitan elements in the party, Mao was able to continue with his project of "making Marxism concretely Chinese." After the CCP's role as the sole arbiter of what was right and wrong in all spheres of society was established, no alternative bases from which its authority could be challenged existed.

King-fai TAM

Further Reading

Apter, D. (1995). Discourse as power: Yan'an and the Chinese revolution. In T. Saich & H. van de Ven (Eds.), *New perspectives on the Chinese Communist revolution* (pp. 193–234). Armonk, NY: M. E. Sharpe.

Cheek, T. (1984, January). The fading of wild lilies: Wang Shiwei and Mao Zedong's Yan'an Talks in the first CPC rectification movement. *The Australian Journal of Chinese Affairs, 11,* 25–58.

Compton, B. (1952). *Mao's China: Party reform documents, 1942–44.* Seattle: University of Washington Press.

Dai Qing. (1944). *Wang Shiwei and the wild lilies* (D. Apter & T. Cheek, Eds.; N. Liu & L. Sullivan, Trans.). Armonk, NY: M. E. Sharpe.

Goldman, M. (1967). *Literary dissent in Communist China.* Cambridge, MA: Harvard University Press.

McDougall, B. (1980). *Mao Zedong's "Talk at the Yan'an Conference on Literature and Art": a translation of the 1943 text with commentary.* Ann Arbor: Center for Chinese Studies, Univeristy of Michigan.

Selden, M. (1971). *The Yenan way in revolutionary China.* Cambridge, MA: Harvard University Press.

Seybolt, P. (1986, January). Terror and conformity: Counterespionage campaigns, rectification, and mass movements, 1942–43. *Modern China, 12*(1), 39–73.

Teiwes, F. (1979). Politics and purges in China: Rectification and the decline of party norms. Armonk, NY: M. E. Sharpe.

YANG Zhu

Yáng Zhū 杨朱

Flourished c. 450–350 BCE   Philosopher

Yang Zhu is believed to have been a hermit philosopher who advocated the importance of self-esteem and self-protection. Because his teachings countered the common call for self-sacrifice, his ideas were misrepresented and criticized by others, especially the Confucian scholar, Mencius.

Discerning who Yang Zhu was or what his philosophy advocated is difficult because no documents that he authored have survived. Scholars date Yang Zhu's life based on a passage in the *Collection of Stories* (*Shuoyuan*) by Liu Xiang (79–8 BCE), which claims that Yang had an audience with King Hui of Liang (370–319 BCE). *The Annals of Lü Buwei* (c. 238 BCE) state that Yang Zhu valued the self. Yang's philosophy was well known because the Chinese philosopher Mencius (Mengzi, flourished 371–289 BCE) claimed that the teaching of Yang Zhu and Mo Di (flourished 479–438 BCE) were popular during his time. Mencius distorted and simplified Yang's teachings, declaring him to be a hedonistic egoist, claiming that Yang would not remove one hair from his shin if he could benefit the people of the empire by doing so.

Because of the vagueness of the classical Chinese language, it is not clear whether Yang was an egoist and valued only his own person, or if he taught that each person should esteem himself. An egoist would not advocate that others should be egoists because that would not help the egoist benefit himself. Yang Zhu was not an egoist because he taught that all people should value and protect their own lives. A Daoist text, the *Liezi* (c. 300 CE), contains a chapter entitled "Yang Zhu," which advocates seeking pleasure. It contains a reasonable explanation for why Yang Zhu would not pluck out a hair to benefit the empire because one hair will not be sufficient. One hair will lead to a pound of flesh, leading to a limb, then one's life, and finally others' lives. Someone who values life will not take this path. The eclectic Daoist text, the *Huainanzi* (c. 140 BCE), outlines three basic teachings of Yang's philosophy: keeping a person's human nature intact, protecting a person's genuineness, and not allowing the body to become attached to material things. This individualistic, protect-your-life thinking began in the Spring and Autumn period (770–476 BCE) among hermits and recluses who withdrew from the dangers of public life, becoming popular during the Warring States period (475–221 BCE) for practical reasons. Through history it serves as a reminder that a person must keep the body intact to live a fulfilling life. Yang disagrees with the majority of ancient Chinese philosophies that call on the individual to sacrifice, even die, for the greater good. Five chapters in *The Annals of Lü Buwei* promote Yang's philosophy. In that book Yang's self-preservation approach is offered to the ruler for his own protection; it is not for the common people because they must be willing to die for the ruler. In the Daoist text, the *Zhuangzi*, at least four chapters advocate Yang's philosophy. In the *Zhuangzi* Yang's teachings are used to persuade any person from any social status to realize that self-preservation is the utmost principle.

James D. SELLMANN

2548

Yangist Thought

Although the philosophies of Yang Zhu are often disputed and unclear, a few accounts do exist of his teaching and thought. In The Construction of Space in China *the historian Mark Lewis discusses a passage from the* Liezi *that briefly captures Yang's theory on the central role of the body.*

The clearest demonstrations of the central role of the body in Yangist thought are assertions of the absurdity of exchanging bodily parts for external objects. One example of this, or rather a parody of it, was the passage from the *Mencius* ... in which the willingness to sacrifice bodily hairs distinguished rival philosophical traditions. A more elaborate version couched in terms favorable to the Yangist teachings appears in the fourth-century A.D. *Liezi*:

> Qin Guli asked Yang Zhu, "If you could save the whole world by giving up one hair, would you do it?" Master Yang replied, "The world could certainly not be saved by one hair." Master Qin said, "If it would be saved, would you do it?" Master Yang did not reply. Master Qin went out and spoke to Mengsun Yang. Mengsun Yang said, "You have not understood Master Yang's thoughts. Let me say them. If you could gain ten thousand in gold by having some of your skin peeled off, would you do it?" "I would." "If you could obtain a state by having one limb cut off at a joint, would you do it?" Master Qin remained silent for a while. Mengsun Yang said, "A hair is less than some skin, and some skin is less than a limb. This is plain. But if you accumulate individual hairs it forms a patch of skin and if you accumulate skin if forms a limb. Even one hair is certainly a tiny part of the body, so how could you treat it lightly?"

The relation between body and things is worked out in a set of hypothetical exchanges that mark the higher value of the former.

Source: Lewis, M. E. (2006). *The construction of space in early China*. Albany: State University of New York Press, 18.

Further Reading

Graham, A. C. (Trans.). (1960). *The book of Lieh-tzu*. London: John Murray.

Graham, A. C. (1989). *Chuang-Tzu: The inner chapters*. London: Unwin Paperbacks.

Graham, A. C. (1989). *Disputers of the Tao*. La Salle, IL: Open Court.

Knoblock, J., & Riegel, J. (2000). *The annals of Lü Buwei*. Stanford, CA: Stanford University Press.

Kushner, T. (1980). Yang Chu [Zhu]: Ethical egoist in ancient China. *Journal of Chinese Philosophy, 7*(4), 319–326.

Lau, D. C. (Trans.). (1970). *Mencius*. Middlesex, U.K.: Penguin Books.

Yangge

Yānggē 秧歌

A style of folk song and dance from northern China, *yangge* developed into theater (*yangge xi*) and was adapted by artists of the Chinese Communist Party (CCP) to create a new and revolutionary form of art.

The term *yangge* literally means "rice-seedlings song," suggesting its derivation from peasants' harvest labor. As early as the twelfth or thirteenth centuries, monks or rural laborers of various kinds put on small-scale musical performances for the amusement of villagers. Over the course of time, these developed into communal song-and-dance shows and, by the eighteenth century, into small-scale folk dramas (*yangge xi*) with two or three performers, usually a female character (*dan*) and clown (*chou*), and sometimes a male character (*sheng*) also.

Performed from the Spring Festival (Chinese New Year, the first day of the first month in the lunar calendar) until the Lantern Festival (the fifteenth day of the first month), the plays were always associated with religious rituals, which is typical of rural regional theater. The structure consisted of three parts, with song-and-dance performances surrounding a light, comic play. The content reflected rural life, and a favorite theme was courtship among young people. These were sometimes offensive to authorities bent on preserving conservative social norms: *Yangge* usually showed young people themselves, not their parents, choosing their spouses, and the plays were often quite bawdy and sometimes pornographic.

Classroom performance of *The White-Haired Girl* at Beijing's Middle School 26. PHOTO BY JOAN LEBOLD COHEN.

Yangge and the CCP

From the end of 1942 until 1946 (and beyond), the CCP, then headquartered in Yan'an in northern Shaanxi Province,

2550

sponsored its New *Yangge* Movement, which was a mass effort based on the local indigenous art form. Mao Zedong's "Talks at the Yan'an Forum on Literature and Art" of May 1942 were a major spark for using this folk art as propaganda for the revolutionary and anti-Japanese cause.

The CCP censored and politicized the *yangge* performances. They secularized the social context, sponsoring their own troupes and performance sites, though they did not prevent folk troupes from visiting temples. They forbade the more explicit sexual material and created their own plays to reflect the CCP's ideology. The most famous example, *Brother and Sister Clear Wasteland* (*Xiongmei kaihuang*), premiered in the spring of 1943 north of Yan'an; it boasted of the advantages of CCP government in a skit about peasant labor. There were two characters only, one male and one female, but the traditional sexual themes were replaced with those relevant to labor. The musical accompaniment included both traditional Chinese and Western instruments.

The increasing complexity and revolutionary nature of these CCP-inspired *yangge* plays climaxed in the large-scale opera *The White-Haired Girl* (*Baimao nü*). The opera's story—about a girl who escapes her landlord's oppression and undergoes privations serious enough to make her hair turn white but is then saved by the CCP's soldiers—is focused very explicitly on class struggle and functions as CCP propaganda. Its music combined traditional folk songs and Western-style music, with Western instruments in the orchestra. Representing an original genre, this "new opera" (*xin geju*) premiered during the CCP's Seventh Party Congress in 1945. It has retained some popularity since then and, in ballet form, became one of the "model dramas" (*yangban xi*) during the Cultural Revolution (1966–1976). While *yangge* was not generally performed outside of northern China, *baimao nu* became popular nationwide eventually. *Baimao nü* is still occasionally performed, but it is uncertain if *yangge* performances still occur. It is possible that they take place currently as folk performances in northern China.

Colin MACKERRAS

Further Reading

Chen, Jack. (1949). *The Chinese theatre*. London: Dennis Dobson.
Ho Ching-chih & Ting Yi. (1954). *The white-haired girl: An opera in five acts* (Yang Hsien-Yi & G. Yang, Trans.). Peking: Foreign Languages Press.
Holm, D. (1991). *Art and ideology in revolutionary China*. Oxford, U.K.: Clarendon Press.

Yangshao Culture

Yǎngsháo wénhuà 仰韶文化

Well known for its painted red pottery and the high status it afforded its women, the Yangshao culture is one of the best known in Chinese history. Scholars have drawn many conclusions about this Neolithic culture based on remains found at archaeological excavations and Yangshao sites, although unanswered questions and theories remain.

The Yangshao culture, dated from about 5000 to 3000 BCE, is one of the best known Chinese Neolithic (8000–5500 BCE) cultures. It is named after the Yangshao village on the southern bank of the Huang (Yellow) River in Mianchi County, Henan Province. Discovered in 1920 by local farmers, the Yangshao site was excavated a year later by Swedish geologist Johan G. Andersson (1874–1960). The relative date of the Yangshao culture was established in 1931 when Chinese archaeologist Liang Siyong (1904–1954) identified material remains of Yangshao, Longshan, and Shang cultures in three successive layers of strata at the Hougang site in Anyang, Henan. This discovery proved that the Yangshao culture is a Neolithic culture and that it predated the Longshan and Shang cultures.

Yangshao Excavation Sites

Chinese archaeologists have found more than two thousand sites of the Yangshao culture, many of which have been excavated, presenting a comprehensive picture of this society. Experts think that the Yangshao culture developed from several of the Neolithic cultures in north China, including Peiligang, Cishan, Laoguantai, and

---

Scale model village from the Yangshao culture, based on excavations at the Banpo Neolithic Village, Xi'an. PHOTO BY PAUL AND BERNICE NOLL.

Lijiacun. Centered at three major tributaries of the Huang River (the Wei, Fen, and Luo rivers in the middle Huang River basin), the Yangshao culture expanded to the areas far beyond the reaches of its ancestral cultures. It reached Gansu and Qinghai provinces in the west, the area along the Great Wall in the northwest, and the northwestern part of Hubei Province in the south.

Material remains from Yangshao sites across several regions demonstrate great variations, challenging scholars to develop better approaches to characterize the temporal and spatial differences of the Yangshao culture. Scholars have proposed several theories to establish different regional types and phases of the Yangshao culture. The most widely accepted theory defines the Yangshao culture in Shaanxi, Henan, and Hebei provinces as seven distinctive regional types: Banpo, Miaodigou, Xiwangcun, Wangwan, Dahecun, Hougang, and Dasikongcun.

The Yangshao people lived in sedentary communities consisting of semisubterranean and above-ground houses built of wood and earth. The Yangshao society engaged in a millet-based agricultural economy, supplemented by hunting, gathering, and fishing. Pigs, dogs, and sheep were domesticated. Tools for economic activities were mostly polished stone axes, adzes, and knives, accompanied by a small number of bone arrowheads, fish forks, needles, and chisels.

Burial Grounds

Our understanding of the Yangshao culture also comes from its burials. In general, adults were buried in a community cemetery of the village near the residential area. The burial sites are mostly rectangular earthen pits containing no coffin. Single adult burials were common; composite burials of individuals of both males and females at different ages were also widely seen. Popular burial goods include painted pottery such as *bo* bowls, *guan* pots, *pan* basins, and other personal ornaments. Children were treated differently in burial. They were buried in ceramic urns, often near the house or in some cases in the community cemetery.

Painted Red Pottery

The Yangshao culture was best known for its painted red pottery featuring black geometric motifs. The pottery was handmade. The most popular objects were red and brown *guan* pots, *pen* basins, *bo* bowls, and small-mouthed, pointed-based vases with painted motifs. The vessel was shaped first and then painted before it was sent to the kiln for firing. Black designs on red pots were the most characteristic of the Yangshao painted pottery. Nevertheless, red motifs against white coating on red pottery are seen as well. The most intriguing designs on the painted vessels are those featuring fish, frogs, and human faces symmetrically displayed on the interior of the painted basin. Some basins were used as covers for children's urn burials, implying that the motif might have some religious or social meanings. Some scholars hypothesize that distinctive marks found on the rim of some vessels are the precursors of Chinese writing.

Society and Community

The Yangshao society has long been regarded as an equalitarian matrilineal society in which females generally enjoyed a high social status and played significant roles in economic and political arenas. But an increasing number of scholars recently suggest that during the late period of the Yangshao culture the society was much more complex and can be defined as a patriarchal society in which males had dominant economic and political power.

Settlements at Banpo in the city of Xi'an and at Jiangzhai in the city of Lintong provide us the best insight into early Yangshao society. The Banpo site, mainly occupied between 4800 BCE and 4300 BCE, covered an area of about 30,000 square meters, which was further surrounded by trenches of 6 to 8 meters wide and 5 to 6 meters deep. Forty-six houses, mostly circular with a diameter of 4 to 6 meters, were found in two residential areas where storage pits, animal pens, and children's burial sites were also scattered. In each residential area was a large house likely to be occupied by clan leaders and used for community activities. The largest house at Banpo covered an area of about 160 square meters. Remains of six pottery kilns were located east of the residential area. A cemetery of 174 burials, mostly individual adults, was located north of the residential area.

The Jiangzhai site was 15 kilometers east of the Banpo site. It provides another good example of detailed layout of a Yangshao village. The village consisted of three components: residential area, cemetery, and kilns. The residential area, dated from 4600 to 4400 BCE by calibrated radiocarbon-14 analysis, covered an area of 50,000 square meters. It was surrounded by trenches on the east, north, and south and protected by a natural river on the southwest. A plaza situated at the center of the residential area was encircled by one hundred houses organized in five groups. Headed by a large house, each group was comprised of ten to twenty houses with their doors oriented to the central plaza. The layout of the houses at Jiangzhai indicated that several clans or families might inhabit the site. Like those at Banpo, the houses at Jiangzhai featured wattle-and-daub walls and thatched roof.

WALLED SETTLEMENT

A settlement enclosed by walls appeared in a late phase of the Yangshao culture (3300–2800 BCE) at the Xishan site in Zhengzhou, Henan Province. The Xishan site covers 100,000 square meters, with a walled settlement in the northwestern section of the site. The layout of the walled settlement is roughly circular in shape, measuring 180 meters in diameter and 345,000 square meters in area. The walls, surrounded by a moat with a maximum width of 11 meters, were built with advanced *banzhu* technique, in which earth was pounded between wooden boards. Archaeological excavations have revealed lower sections of the western and northern gates of the settlement. The northern gate was furnished with two triangular platforms, possibly watchtowers, and a protecting wall outside the entrance. The appearance of a sophisticated defensive facility in the city, together with the increasing

stratification of the burial treatment and the transition of the settlement patterns, indicates the increasing complexity of the late Yangshao society, which forecasts the emergence of regional political power in north China.

Yan SUN

Further Reading

Beijing daoxue lishixi kaogu jiaoyanshi. (1983). *Yuanjunmiao Yangshao mudi* [The cemetery of Yangshao Culture at Yuanjunmiao]. Beijing: Wenwu chubanshe.

Guojia wenwuju kaogu lingduiban. (1999). Zhengzhou Xishan Yangshao shidai chengzhi de fajue [The excavation of walled settlement remains of Yangshao Culture at Xishan]. *Wenwu* (7), 4–15.

Henansheng wenwu yanjiusuo, Changjiang liuyu guihuaban shi kaogudui Henan fendui. (1989). *Xichuan Xiaowanggang* Beijing: Wenwu chubanshe.

Xi'an Banpo bowuguan, Shaanxisheng kaogu yanjiusuo, Lintongxian bowuguan. (1988). *Jiangzhai—xinshiqi shidai yizhi fajue baogao* [The excavation report of the Neolithic site at Jiangzhai]. Beijing: Wenwu chubanshe.

Yan Wenming. (1989). *Yangshao wenhua yanjiu* [The study of Yangshao Culture]. Beijing: Wenwu chubanshe.

Zhengzhoushi wenwu kaogu yanjiusuo. (2001). *Zhengzhou Dahecun*. Beijing: Kexue chubanshe.

Zhongguo kexueyuan kaogu yanjiusuo, Shaanxisheng, Xi'an banpo bowuguan. (1963). *Xi'an Banpo*. [The settlement remains of a primitive clan society.] Beijing: Wenwu chubanshe.

Yangzi (Chang) River

Cháng Jiāng 长江

The Yangzi (Chang) River is the third-longest river in the world at 6,276 kilometers and the longest river in Asia. It rises in the Kunlun mountain range on the border of Tibet and Qinghai Province and flows south until it empties into the East China Sea near Shanghai. The Yangzi derives its name from the ancient kingdom of Yang, which settled along its banks.

The Yangzi (Chang) River, known as the "Changjiang" (Long River) in Chinese, begins in the Kunlun Mountains and flows south through the high mountain valleys in Qinghai, Tibet, and Yunnan provinces before veering northeast at Shiigu. Thence the Yangzi flows through Sichuan Province before it enters the scenic Three Gorges region. Then it crosses central China through Hubei, Hunan, Jiangxi, Anhui, and Jiangsu provinces before emptying into the East China Sea at Chongming Island, 16 kilometers north of Shanghai. The Yangzi, stretching the length of the country, has been the unofficial boundary line between north and south China. In fact, no bridge was built over the eastern stretch of the river until 1969, when the Changjiang Daqiao Bridge was constructed at Nanjing.

The Yangzi has been prominent in the development of trade and culture throughout China's history. As far back as the Neolithic period (8000–5500 BCE),

settlements existed along the lower Yangzi. Qin dynasty (221–206 BCE)founder Qin Shi Huangdi constructed canals and waterways to facilitate trade from Yangzhou to Guangzhou, a distance of 1,931 kilometers. Since that time the Yangzi has been the main transportation route across central China as it flows through many of the nation's industrial and economic centers. Since the Tang dynasty (618–907 CE) the Yangzi River delta has become a center for cultivating and shipping rice.

Almost 2,900 kilometers of the Yangzi is navigable all year. In the early 1990s the Yangzi and its major tributaries drained an area of 1.8 million square kilometers—one-quarter of China's cultivated land—in which 386 million people lived. Its network of rivers and canals carries 85 percent of China's domestic waterborne traffic and passes through many of its major cities, including Kunmin, Chongqing, Wuhan, Chengdu, Shanghai, and Nanjing. The gross value of industrial products of the areas along the Yangzi is about 40 percent of China's total.

Given its potential as an inexhaustible hydroelectric resource, the Chinese government began construction of the Three Gorges Dam in 1985 and completed it on 8 October 2008. Located in the Xilingxia gorge near Sandouping, Yichang, Hubei, the Three Gorges Dam is the largest hydroelectric power station in the world and is expected to help control the annual flooding of the Yangzi River valley. When fully operational the dam is expected to generate 22,500 megawatts of electricity that will provide 10 percent of electricity consumption in China.

The project is not without controversy. Construction of the Three Gorges Dam has displaced over 1.2 million

The Yangzi River has carved out deep gorges in China's countryside over the centuries.
PHOTO BY JOAN LEBOLD COHEN.

people, uprooted numerous villages and towns the length of the reservoir as well as flooded over important archaeological and historical sites. In addition, the project has been plagued by corruption, spiraling costs, technological problems, human rights violations and resettlement difficulties.

Keith LEITICH

Further Reading

Chetham, D. (2002). *Before the deluge: the vanishing world of the upper Yangtze River.* New York: Palgrave.

Huang, Phillip C. C. (1990). *The peasant family and rural development in the Yangzi Delta, 1350–1988.* Stanford, CA: Stanford University Press.

Jackson, S., & Sleigh, A. (2000). Resettlement for China's Three Gorges Dam: Socio-economic impact and institutional tensions. *Communist and Post-Communist Studies, 33*(2), 223–241.

Qing, D. (1998) *The river dragon has come! The Three Gorges Dam and the fate of China's Yangtze River and its people,* Armonk, NY: M.E. Sharpe.

Van Slyke, L. P. (1988). *Yangtze: Nature, history and the river.* Reading, MA: Addison-Wesley.

Wang, H. (1989) *Exploring the Yangtze: China's longest river,* San Francisco: CA: Ching Book and Periodicals Inc.

Yangzi (Chang) River Bridge at Nanjing

Nánjīng Cháng Jiāng Dàqiáo   南京长江大桥

The Yangzi (Chang) River Bridge at Nanjing is comprised of a 6.7-kilometer train deck topped by a 4.5-kilometer car deck. The bridge, completed in 1968, was a massive feat of engineering and the first to be built entirely by the Chinese; it has been a crucial element of north–south transportation as well as a source of national pride ever since.

Over the past two decades, engineers throughout the world have heralded China's construction of daringly innovative bridges that seem to defy engineering principles. Old China hands recall the pride that accompanied the completion in 1968 of the first bridge to span the Yangzi (Chang) River at Nanjing. Not only had Western engineers doubted that a major bridge could span the river at this location, many believed that China was not capable of designing any large-scale bridge without the assistance of foreign engineers. In the 1950s, preliminary design efforts were carried out with the assistance of Soviet engineers to build a monumental bridge at Nanjing, but it appeared that the sudden withdrawal of Soviet technical experts in 1960 following the Sino-Soviet rift would abort any possibility of building such a bridge. Instead, Chinese engineers worked feverishly to overcome this perceived lack of confidence by reconceptualizing the project. Completed at the end of 1968, the Yangzi River Bridge at Nanjing became the first highway and railway bridge designed and constructed by the Chinese without outside engineering assistance. Until the completion of this bridge, it was necessary for trains and trucks to be ferried across the river, requiring some two hours of time and effort.

Among the challenges in building a bridge at this site were the fact that the bedrock in the river was some 72 meters below the surface and the river banks were low. High piers were necessary to lift the decks of the bridge so as not to impede boat traffic along China's principal artery of water-borne transport. Although the river itself is only 1.5 kilometers wide in this area, the long and gradual approaches necessary for rail traffic along two lines necessitated a 6.7-kilometer structure, while the four-lane highway portion needed a 4.5-kilometers span. Nine piers embedded in the river's channel support eighteen steel trusses, each of which is 160 meters long.

For more than forty years the bridge has been an important destination for tourists visiting Nanjing. At the base of the southern approaches is an extensive park with access via elevators to a high observation platform. Constructed during the Great Proletarian Cultural Revolution (1966–1976), the bridge was adorned with the slogans of Chairman Mao in his own calligraphy as well as oversized statues and relief carvings of peasants, workers, and soldiers. Mao Yisheng, one of China's most prominent first-generation structural engineers and designer of bridges, stated that the building of the "Great Bridge ... tested and advanced the skill of Chinese bridge builders, and stimulated the growth

The two-level bridge spanning the Yangzi River at Nanjing, an engineering marvel built and designed entirely by the Chinese, symbolizes the country's independent spirit and its pride in accomplishment. PHOTO BY JOAN LEBOLD COHEN.

of many industries connected with bridge building, including steel, cement, structural parts, and construction machinery." Today, some fifty bridges span the Yangzi, but none symbolize the independence of spirit and accomplishment as clearly or as much as the Yangzi River Bridge at Nanjing.

Ronald G. KNAPP

Further Reading

Knapp, R. G. (2008). *Chinese bridges: Living architecture from China's past.* North Clarendon, VT: Tuttle Publishing.

Mao Yisheng 茅以升. (Ed.) (1986). *Zhongguo gu qiao jishu shi* 中國古橋技術史 [A technological history of ancient Chinese bridges]. Beijing: Beijing chubanshe 北京出版社.

Yangzi Delta Economic Region

Cháng Jiāng sānjiǎozhōu jīngjìqū

长江三角洲经济区

The Yangzi Delta Economic Region has the largest regional economy in China as measured in gross regional product. The area also is the most attractive location for both domestic and international investment.

The Yangzi Delta Economic Region (YDER) is located in the central part of the east coast of China. It covers an area of 109,654.2 square kilometers, only 1.14 percent of China's total area, and has a population of 83.24 million, which accounts for only 6.33 percent of China's total population. It also contains sixteen major cities, which include one provincial-level municipality (Shanghai), three subprovincial-level cities (Nanjing in Jiangsu Province and Hangzhou and Ningbo in Zhejiang Province), and twelve prefecture-level cities (Suzhou, Wuxi, Changzhou, Zhenjiang, Nantong, Yangzhou, and Taizhou in Jiangsu Province and Jiaxing, Huzhou, Shaoxing, Zhoushan, and Taizhou in Zhejiang Province).

History of the Delta

The Yangzi (Chang) River delta is the triangular alluvial tract at the month of the river, enclosed or traversed by its diverging branches. It is the biggest river delta in China. Humans moved there in two large-scale migrations to hunt and farm after the delta was formed. The first migration occurred during the South and North Dynasties (220–589 CE), and the second one occurred during the Song dynasty (960–1279). The migrants built irrigation systems (from the tenth century onward) and vibrant cities and developed local industries. The Yangzi delta became the main cultural and economic center of China and enjoyed the reputation of being a "land flowing with milk and honey." The key cities of the region in premodern times included Suzhou, Nanjing, Hangzhou, and Shaoxing. The silk manufacturing industry in this region, especially in Suzhou, became famous during the Tang (618–907 CE) and Song dynasties. Suzhou silk even made its way to Rome along the Silk Roads.

Shanghai is located near the point where the Yangzi River flows into the East China Sea. It is one of the top three seaports in the world now, the largest city in China, and the starting point of modern Chinese industry. Shanghai began to become the hub of the Yangzi delta region and even the economic center of the whole of China gradually after 1842, when China was forced to open Shanghai to British trade and residence. Many Chinese "firsts" occurred in Shanghai, such as the first textile factory, the first flour mill, the first medicine factory, and the first electric fan factory. By the 1930s Shanghai had become the center of all economic activity in Asia and the financial center of Asia, as Hong Kong later became.

After establishment of the People's Republic of China in 1949, the country finally was able to stop wars on its own territory. China's economy recovered and developed step by step, although China was still isolated from the Western world and suffered internal political troubles from time to time. Shanghai's average GRP (gross regional product) growth rate from 1952 to 1978 was 10.17 percent, higher than the country's GDP (gross domestic product) growth level, which was 6.68 percent during the period. However, the growth rate of both Zhejiang and Jiangsu provinces was lower than China's average at 6.08 percent and 5.48 percent, respectively. The total GRP created by Shanghai, Jiangsu, and Zhejiang was RMB65.68 billion (at current prices) in 1978, accounting for 17.82 percent of China's total GDP in that year. And as the economic center of China, Shanghai had a GRP of RMB27.28 billion in 1978, accounting for 7.48 percent of China's total GDP. The preceding figures reveal the delta's, and especially Shanghai's, significant position in China's economy before China's economic reform was launched in 1979.

The Pearl River delta in the southeast part of China was the most dazzling star in China in the 1980s. Benefiting from its superior geographic position (adjoining Hong Kong) and its reform and open policy, the Pearl River delta region achieved dramatic economic growth during the period and attracted the attention of the whole world. Capital and managerial experts moved into the Pearl River delta and made this region a famous business area. The average GRP growth rate of Fujian and Guangdong provinces from 1979 to 1990 was 11.61 percent and 12.83 percent, respectively, obviously higher than the country's GDP growth level of 9.08 percent during the period.

The situation in the Yangzi River delta was different from that in the Pearl River delta during this decade. The non-state-owned sector, especially the township and village enterprises (TVEs) in the Yangzi delta region achieved rapid growth, but Shanghai's performance was relatively slow. Jiangsu and Zhejiang provinces grew faster than the whole country (at 11.14 percent and 11.87 percent, respectively), but Shanghai's average GRP growth rate was only 7.49 percent from 1970 to 1990, only 58 percent of Guangdong's growth level. And Shanghai's GRP contribution to China's total GDP dropped to 4.19 percent in 1990. Compared with its share of 7.48 percent in 1978, the figure reflects the relative decrease of Shanghai's economic significance in China.

The Yangzi delta got its chance in the 1990s. With the deepening of China's economic reform, the strategic emphasis of China's economic development shifted, and the Yangzi delta region, especially Shanghai, became the focus again in the 1990s. After 1991, especially after the seminal visit of China's leader, Deng Xiaoping (1904–1997), to Shanghai in 1992, the provincial and municipal governments in the Yangzi delta began to implement far-researching reforms, and the result has been economic growth rates higher than those of other major Chinese cities as well as of most Asian "tiger" economies since 1992. Statistics show that the average annual GDP growth rate was 10.13 percent for the whole of China from 1991 to 2006, but the rate for Shanghai was 12.03 percent, the rate for Zhejiang was 14.18 percent, and the rate for Jiangsu was 13.61 percent, more than two times the growth of the four tigers (Hong Kong 6.8 percent, Taiwan 4.9 percent, Korea 4.2 percent, and Singapore 7.9 percent) during this period.

Establishment of the Economic Region

To promote economic collaboration among the cities in the Yangzi River delta and to facilitate sustainable development of the region, the Fourteen Cities Collaboration Office Director Conference was launched in 1992, including the cities of Shanghai, Nanjing, Wuxi, Changzhou, Zhenjiang, Nantong, Yangzhou, Suzhou, Hangzhou, Ningbo, Jiaxing, Huzhou, Shaoxing, and Zhoushan. After negotiation among the municipal governments of these fourteen cities and Taizhou, a new prefecture-level city in Jiangsu Province, a new regional economic institution, the Coordinating Committee of Yangzi Delta Urban Economies, was set up in 1997. Members agreed that the standing committee chairman would come from Shanghai and that the executive committee chairman would come from one of the other fifteen cities (in turn). A formal session among the members is held every two years, and a standing office is set up in Shanghai as the liaison office to deal with day-to-day administration. During the fourth session of the committee, which was held in Nanjing in 2003, another prefecture-level city, Taizhou in Zhejiang Province, was accepted as a member of the committee. At the fifth session, which was held in Shanghai in 2004, members decided that a formal session would be held every year. Hence, clearly economic collaboration in the delta is seen as important to the region's growth, and the cities' leaders are working to manage economic development together.

Economic Importance in China

The YDER is already the largest regional economy in China as measured in GRP. It and the Pearl River delta (PRD) and the Bohai-Rim Economic Circle (BREC) are China's three major industrial belts. In 2006 the YDER's GRP increased to RMB3,952.57 billion (about $503 billion), accounting for 18.88 percent of China's total GDP and equal to 57.27 percent of South Korea's GDP and more than four times the Philippines' GDP.

The per capita GRP in China in 2006 was RMB16,165. All sixteen cities in the YDER surpassed that figure. Shanghai kept its top position among China's thirty-one provinces (and provincial-level municipalities), and Zhejiang and Jiangsu ranked fourth and fifth. Among the sixteen cities in the YDER, two had a per capita GRP of more than RMB70,000, more than four times the country's average.

The YDER is the most attractive location for both domestic and international investment, and Shanghai has regained its reputation as the most important international municipality in Asia. The YDER accounts for 16.83 percent of China's total investment in fixed assets (seven of them more than RMB100 billion individually) and 47.17 percent of China's total amount of foreign capital actually used (actually used foreign capital is the amount that is definitely invested in contrast to the amount that was promised to be invested). Its contribution to China's total imports and exports was 35.55 percent in 2006. By the end of 2006, Shanghai had signed foreign direct investment contracts with foreign business people from 127 countries and regions, and the number of contracts reached 445,000 with a contracted value of $114.54 billion. More than 150 multinationals have set up their regional head offices in Shanghai, and there are 150 international investment companies and 196 foreign research and development centers. Shanghai is expected to have more multinational regional head offices than Hong Kong by 2010.

The YDER also has become an important international integrated circuits manufacturing base. China's total microcomputer output was 93.36 million units in 2006. Out of every 1,000, about 742 came from Suzhou or Shanghai. In integrated circuits the YDER's output accounted for 62.26 percent of China's total, and most of them were made in Shanghai and Wuxi, accounting for 39.33 percent of China's total output.

The automobile industry is another rising industry in the YDER. Eleven cities of the YDER have been involved in motor vehicle manufacturing and contributed 13.75 percent of China's total output in 2006. The YDER is also famous for its electronics industry. Of China's home washing machines, 61.42 percent were made in the YDER in 2006, and Ningbo's contribution to China's total output was more than 31.4 percent in that year.

Rapid economic growth has brought local people better lives. The average annual disposable income per capita of urban households in YDER in 2006 was RMB17,208 (about US$2,051), 46.34 percent higher than the country's average level (RMB11,759).

Reasons for Growth

The largest contributor to the rapid GRP growth in YDER has been the GRPS (gross regional product from secondary industry). In 2006's GRP 3.7 percent came from primary industry, 55 percent from secondary industry, and 41.3 percent from tertiary industry. From 1990 to 2006 the average annual growth rate of industry value-added was 15.15 percent in the YDER. During the same period the average annual growth rate of its GRP was 13.48 percent.

Now the driving force for the YDER's economic growth is shifting from traditional processing industries to modern manufacturing and service industries. The share of information technology increased from 4.5 percent in 1990 to 13.6 percent in 2005, and the share of the textile industry decreased from 20.1 percent to 8.8 percent during the same period. The tertiary industry's share in the GRP of Shanghai is more than 50 percent. In the other fifteen cities service industries are growing rapidly, although the share in GRP is still less than 50 percent. The YDER is upgrading from a huge processing workshop of the world to one of the most important international manufacturing bases.

The economic growth in the YDER, however, has been highly dependent on the rapid growth of investment, both domestic and international, in the area. Because of the limitation of land and other natural resources and industry duplication in many cities, this kind of growth is hard to sustain, and the increase in industry value-added and the domestic and international investment in the YDER have been going down in recent years.

The Future

In 2010 Shanghai will hold the World Exposition. The exposition will be a great chance not only for Shanghai but also the whole of the YDER. The exposition will benefit all the cities in the region as well and bring them into closer collaboration. Finally, with the improvement in the regional transportation system, the YDER is becoming a three-hour economic circle (it takes less than three hours to complete any travel from one city to another within the YDER), and more products bearing the "Made in China" label will go to the rest of the world from there.

SHU Ping

Further Reading

Cai Jianying & Liu Chengfu. (2002, November). FDI in the development strategy of Jiangsu Province. *China Report, 38*, 491–502.

Chen Xiaoyun & Jiang Luquan. (2007). *Urban economies collaboration development report 2006*. Shanghai: Shanghai Sanlian Publishing House.

Fulong Wu & Jingxing Zhang. (2007, May). Planning the competitive city-region: The emergence of strategic development plan in China. *Urban Affairs Review, 42*, 714–740.

Leman, E. (1996). *The Yangtze delta megalopolis*. Ottawa, Canada: CHREOD.

Liang Meifang. (2007). *Yangtze River delta urban commerce development report 2007*. Shanghai: Shanghai Science and Tech Literatures Publishing House.

Lu Zheng, Xu Jianguo, Han Qinghua, & Ding Yaomin. (2006). *Yangtze River delta manufacturing development report 2006*. Beijing: Economics and Management Press.

Son Linfei. (2007). *Yangtze delta's sustainable development 2006*. Beijing: Social Sciences Literatures Publishing House.

Sun Yu. (2005). *Yangtze River delta development report 2005: Economic growth and urbanization process*. Shanghai: Shanghai People's Press.

Zhang, Le-Yin. (2003, July). Economic development in Shanghai and the role of the state. *Urban Study, 40*, 1549–1572.

Zhang, Tingwei. (2006, September). From intercity competition to collaborative planning: The case of the Yangtze River delta region of China. *Urban Affairs Review, 42*, 26–56.

United Institute of Yangtze Delta. (2007). *Research on Yangtze delta*. Shanghai: Shanghai Academy of Social Sciences Press.

Victor, F. S., & Chun Yang. (1997, April). Foreign-investment-induced exo-urbanisation in the Pearl River delta, China. *Urban Study, 34*, 647–677.

Wang Ronghua. (2007). *Innovation of Changjiang delta (2007)*. Shanghai: Social Sciences Academic Press.

Wang Zhan. (2005). *Improving Shanghai's international competitiveness: Shanghai development report 2004/2005*. Shanghai: Shanghai University of Finance and Economics Press.

Xiangming Chen. (2007, April). A tale of two regions in China: Rapid economic development and slow industrial upgrading in the Pearl River and the Yangtze River deltas. *International Journal of Comparative Sociology, 48*, 167–201.

Yao

Yáozú 瑶族

The Yao are ethnic Chinese living mainly in high mountain valleys of the Guangxi Zhuang Autonomous Region of south China. Although the Yao are linguistically diverse and have a rich oral literary tradition, they had no formal written language until 1982. Yao today are known as expert weavers, dyers, and singers, and their population has doubled since 1949.

The Yao Chinese, an ethnic group numbering nearly 3 million in the 2000 Chinese census, live in humid, subtropical, densely wooded mountain valleys 1,000–2,000 meters high in south China. Historically these people were known by at least thirty names, but the name "Yao" was adopted after the founding of the People's Republic of China (PRC) in 1949. Seventy percent of the Yao people live in Guangxi Zhuang Autonomous Region and the rest in seven autonomous counties and more than two hundred small autonomous townships established from 1952 to 1963 in the provinces of Hunan, Yunnan, Guangdong, Guizhou, and Jiangxi. Another 470,000 Yao live in northern Vietnam.

The Yao spoken language traditionally is categorized as a subgroup of the Sino-Tibetan language family and is similar to the Miao language, although some Western linguists put it into its own new family. Some Yao people speak only Miao or Dong. The Yao have so much linguistic diversity that Yao from different areas cannot easily communicate with each other. Until recently they had no written language but kept records by making notches on wood or bamboo slips. However, a subgroup of twenty thousand Yao women in southern Hunan Province developed a unique system of writing based on rhomboid characters called "Nv Shu" (ant writing). In 1982 a universal writing system based on the Latin alphabet was created for the Yao people by the Guangxi Nationality Institute, approved by the Chinese Academy of Sciences, and now is used extensively.

During the Han dynasty (206 BCE–220 CE) the Yao, called "Wuling" or "Wuxi" in Chinese histories, wove tree bark fabrics, lived around Changsha (today's capital of Hunan Province), and began their migrations south into Vietnam and Thailand. Yao agriculture and distinctive handicrafts, such as iron knives and indigo-dyed cloth with delicate designs made in beeswax, developed during the Song dynasty (960–1279). Yao have been celebrated in history for their independent militancy. From 1316 to 1331 they participated in forty uprisings in the late Yuan dynasty (1279–1368). They revolted for one century against the Ming dynasty (1368–1644) and participated in the Taiping Rebellion in the second half of the 1800s during the Manchu Qing dynasty (1644–1912). Their communities were a base area for the Seventh Red Army commanded by politician Deng Xiaoping (1904–1997) in the 1930s during the Chinese civil war.

Today the Yao live in groups of ten to seventy households, ruled by hereditary headmen, in rectangular, reed thatch, peak-roofed huts. Usually the huts consist of three rooms, but some hillside houses are two-storied with the lower floor used to stable animals. The diverse Yao groups practice three types of mixed economies: hillside, irrigated agriculture and forestry; forestry-based hunting and gathering; and slash-and-burn agriculture based on

The Yao are noted for elaborately decorated turbans. PHOTO BY PAUL AND BERNICE NOLL.

communes of twenty families or fewer. In all economies hunting of boars, bears, and monkeys is important. The Yao are famous for "singing while digging" during spring planting when a young man in the fields beats a drum and leads the workers in song. Staple crops are rice, corn, sweet potatoes, and taro, usually prepared stewed or roasted. Homemade sweet wine, teas flavored with ginger or cassia, and tobacco products are popular. Among well-known Yao foods are an oily tea with tea leaves fried and boiled into a thick salty soup mixed with puffed rice or soybeans, pickled birds, insect pupae, and bacon meats. They eat many fresh fruits and dried or pickled vegetables such as pumpkins and peppers.

The Yao people's traditional religion included nature and ancestor worship and belief in Panhu, the dog tribal totem. Many of their sacrificial ceremonies are based on medieval Chinese Daoism. Some Yao converted to Buddhism and later Christianity. They are expert weavers, dyers, and embroiderers. Clothes of the Yao differ according to region but are mainly made of dyed blue or black cloth with various brocaded geometric and stylized animal and plant designs on the sleeve cuffs and trouser legs. Men curl their hair into a bun wound with red or black cloth and decorated with long pheasant feathers. They wear collarless shirts, belted jackets, and either trousers wrapped at the ankle or knickers. Women wear highly embroidered trousers, short skirts, or pleated skirts with decorative silver jewelry and silver hair ornaments in their buns or chignons. Both sexes wear black or red scarves on their heads, sometimes wrapped into fantastic turbans. Headgear for boys and girls changes in style to signal the onset of adulthood. Boys undergo trials to mark passage into full manhood, such as walking on hot coals or bricks, jumping from a 3-meter-high tower, climbing a ladder of knives, and retrieving objects from hot oil.

The Yao have a rich oral literary tradition and are famous for their romantic and historical songs. They celebrate many festivals monthly and offer sacrifices, including those dedicated to their founding ancestor and to their grandmothers. They play bamboo flutes and sing and dance with drums. Certain gongs, *suona* horns, and long waist drums are unique to the Yao. Antiphonal singing is important in courtship rituals, and bridegrooms pay bride prices in silver bars. Couples choose their own partners but obtain their parents' consent. The Yao still practice marriage by bride capture.

Since 1949 schools have been established in all villages, and small factories have been created for timber, cement, farm machinery, and chemical production. With the elimination of smallpox and cholera epidemics, the population of the Yao has doubled under the Chinese government.

Alicia CAMPI

Further Reading

Alberts, E. (2007). *A history of Daoism and the Yao people of south China.* Youngstown, NY: Cambria Press.

Faure, D. (2006). The Yao wars in mid-Ming and their impact on Yao ethnicity. In P. K. Crossley, H. F. Siu, & D. S. Sutton (Eds.), *Empire at the margins—Culture, ethnicity and frontier in early modern China* (pp. 171–189). Berkeley and Los Angeles: University of California Press.

YAO Ming

Yáo Míng 姚明

b. 1980   Professional basketball player

A member of the Chinese men's national basketball team, former player on China's Shanghai Sharks, and number one pick of the U.S. National Basketball Association draft in 2002, Yao Ming became a popular center on the Houston Rockets and China's first professional superstar athlete with global recognition.

Yao Ming may be deemed China's first crossover superstar athlete. Although Yao was not the first Chinese basketball player to play professionally in the United States, his recruitment into the National Basketball Association (NBA) was attended by far more fanfare than his predecessors'. Most fans have forgotten Wang Zhizhi and Menk Bateer, intermittent players on NBA teams from 2001 on, and the even less-known Zheng Haixia, who played for the Women's National Basketball Association Los Angeles Sparks in 1997–1998.

Son of a basketball-playing couple and groomed for the sport in state-run schools for future athletes, Yao approached his prime as a player at an opportune time. China's state-managed sports system was opening up to commercial forces, North American sports leagues were searching the world for athletic talent, and transnational corporations sought boundary-crossing spokespersons. Yao led his hometown team, the Shanghai Sharks, to the Chinese Basketball Association finals three years in a row, culminating in a championship in 2002. This helped position the 7-foot 6-inch center to be the Number 1 pick in the 2002 NBA player draft and to land lucrative corporate contracts worldwide.

Basketball star Yao Ming being interviewed.

Drafted by the Houston Rockets, Yao performed ably on the court and gained an enthusiastic following among American, Asian American, and expatriate Chinese fans. In his rookie year, he averaged 13.5 points and 8.2 rebounds per game and was among the top twenty in the league in

blocks, rebounds, and field-goal percentage. With a new influx from Chinese balloting, fans voted him to the NBA All Star team his first three seasons, and the Rockets signed him to a five-year extension lasting through the 2010–2011 season.

An ideal fit with the NBA's strategy of expanding international markets, Yao was called China's most valuable export. His appeal to multiple, multigenerational, and multinational audiences generated lucrative commercial sponsorships, negotiated by business advisers who call themselves Team Yao. He has represented the likes of Apple, Visa, Adidas, Gatorade, Pepsi, and McDonald's, and partnered with a California-based chain to open fitness clubs in China. He also lent his image to the Special Olympics, campaigns against SARS and HIV/AIDS, and other charitable causes. Yao ranked Number 6 on *Forbes* magazine's 2007 list of top-earning non–U.S. athletes, with an estimated income of nearly $27.5 million.

Along with his celebrity and wealth, Yao has retained popularity and respect among compatriots as a representative of Chinese achievement abroad with enduring loyalties to his native country. His every move became an item for the Chinese media, from setbacks due to a broken foot to plans to marry his longtime girlfriend Ye Li, a former player with China's national women's basketball team. As a member of the Chinese national team, Yao reported for training and competitions between NBA seasons, including Olympics practice and attendance. He was the obvious choice as China's final runner in the torch relay for the 2004 Athens Olympics and China's flag bearer at those games. At the 2008 Beijing Olympics he ran through the Tiananmen Gate, the ninth of 433 torch bearers, and was a logical figure in promotions for the Games.

Judy POLUMBAUM

Further Reading

Ballard, C. (2007, April 16). The evolution of Yao. *Sports Illustrated*, 46–51.

Larmer, B. (2005). *Operation Yao Ming: The Chinese sports empire, American big business, and the making of an NBA superstar.* New York: Gotham Books.

Oates, T., & Polumbaum, J. (2004, Summer). Agile big man: The flexible marketing of Yao Ming. *Pacific Affairs*, 187–210.

Rodgers, M. (2003, January 5). The tao of Yao. *Basketball Digest*, 46–51.

Approach heaven with a single stride.

一步登天

Yí bù dēng tiān

Yellow Sea

Huáng Hǎi　黄海

The Yellow Sea (Huang Hai) is the overly exploited gulf that lies between China and Korea; it is known for its omnipresent fishing vessels and oil refineries. Its name comes from yellow silt deposited in its waters by the Huang (Yellow) River.

The Yellow Sea (Huang Hai), the shallow gulf between China and Korea, is 870 kilometers long from the south to the north and 556 kilometers wide from the east to the west and covers an area of 378,600 square kilometers. The northern part comprises the inlet of Bohai Bay in the northwest, which is almost enclosed by the Liaodong Peninsula in the northeast and the Shandong Peninsula in south, and the Korea Bay in the northeast. The southern part of the Yellow Sea borders on the Shandong Peninsula in the north and the Chinese mainland in the west and meets the East China Sea where the Yangzi (Chang) River flows into the sea. In the east, it borders on Korea and the Korea Strait. The Yellow Sea, which has received its name from the yellowish silt deposited mainly by the Huang (Yellow) River, has a warm temperate climate. With an average depth of about forty meters, it is one of China's best fishing grounds.

The entire Yellow Sea, and especially its coastal regions, is presently being overexploited by Chinese, Vietnamese, Korean, and Japanese fishing vessels, and the environmental problems are critical. Important ports and fishing bases on the Chinese coast are Qingdao and Yantai in Shandong Province and Dalian on the Liaodong

The Battle of the Yellow Sea

The Battle of the Yellow Sea, which took place on 10 August 1904, is considered a critical moment of the Russo-Japanese War of 1904–1905.

The Battle of the Yellow Sea was the closest and, except for Tsushima, the most decisive naval engagement of the war. Encountering [Russian Admiral] Vitgeft's squadron in the early afternoon, [Japanese Admiral] Togo's first moves were designed to put himself between it and Port Arthur, so as to prevent its return and force a major fleet action. However when it had become clear that the Russians had no intention of going back but were making for Vladivostok, Togo was so far behind the Russian fleet that he had to waste hours in detouring around Vitgeft's weaker vessels so as to catch up with the battleships at the head of the Russian line. It was 1743 hrs when he opened fire on the leading Russian ships. From then until dusk Togo's First Division and the six Russian battleships banged away at each other on almost even terms, with *Mikasa* and *Tsarevich* sharing the brunt of the punishment.

Source: The Russo-Japanese War Research Society (n. d.). *The battle of the Yellow Sea.* Retrieved March 2, 2009, from http://www.russojapanesewar.com/bttl-yellow-sea.html

Peninsula in Liaoning Province. Bohai Bay in the northwest has been the traditional location for salt works. Large offshore petroleum deposits have been discovered there, and a number of oil refineries have been set up.

Bent NIELSEN

Further Reading

Choi, B. H. (1980). *A tidal model of the Yellow Sea and the Eastern China Sea*. Seoul: KORDI Report.

Chough, Sung Kwun, Homa J. Lee, & S. H. Yoon. (2000). *Marine geology of Korean seas*. Amsterdam: Elsevier.

Ichiye, T. (Ed.). (1986). *Japan, East China and Yellow Sea studies*. Oxford, U.K.: Pergamon Press.

Jin Xianshi. (1996). *Variations in fish community structure and ecology of major species in the Yellow/Bohai Sea*. Bergen, Norway: Universitetet i Bergen.

Morgan, J. & Valencia, M. J. (Eds.) (1992). *Atlas for marine policy in East Asian Seas*. Berkeley and Los Angeles: University of California Press.

Comprehensive index starts
in volume 5, page 2667.

YEN, Y. C. James

Yàn Yángchū 晏 阳 初

1890–1990   Educator

James Yen led the Mass Education Movement (MEM) of the May Fourth period, which coordinated local basic literacy programs for an estimated five million people. The MEM then moved to the countryside in 1926 to develop the "Ding Xian Experiment," a program of economic, political, social, and cultural village reforms that sought to pose a non-Communist alternative to revolution.

James Yen, known to his many American friends as "Jimmy," represented a patriotic Chinese liberalism that pragmatically addressed mass education and rural reconstruction.

Y. C. James Yen (Yan Yangchu 晏阳初), known to his many U.S. friends as "Jimmy," represented a patriotic Chinese liberalism that pragmatically addressed mass education and rural reconstruction. Born in the mountains of Sichuan, the young Yen was sent to mission schools, where he became, in his later words, not a "Christian" (implying membership in a foreign institution) but rather "a follower of Christ." After studying at Hong Kong University Yen graduated in 1918 from Yale University and worked under the International YMCA with the Chinese Labor Corps in France; he wrote a widely copied literacy primer that used one thousand basic characters.

Yen returned to China in 1921 to head a national mass literacy campaign under the Chinese National YMCA and to marry Alice Huie, a U.S.-born Chinese with whom he had three sons and two daughters. He wrote that "China can never become a truly representative government if the greatest masses of the people are illiterate and ignorant ... [or] expect to put a stop or check to the present prevailing corrupt and unscrupulous officialdom if there is not a public opinion formed to battle against it" (Hayford 1990). He adapted the publicity and organization techniques of the YMCA's science education campaigns and, using non-professionalized teachers in neighborhood classes

2569

scheduled with the flexibility of the traditional village school, produced a campaign (*yundong*) model used in hundreds of localities that attracted more than 5 million students (Chinese Communist Party leader Mao Zedong taught in a 1922 campaign). In 1923 Yen and leading intellectuals formed the National Association of Mass Education Movements (MEM).

For the illiterates who lived in villages, illiteracy was not their fundamental problem. In 1926 the MEM set up a village campaign in Ding Xian 定縣河北, a county some 321 kilometers south of Beijing. Rejecting the radical approach, Yen saw "farmers" in need of education and support, not "peasants" in need of class war. In 1928 Yen received an honorary graduate degree from Yale, raised a substantial endowment in the United States, and then enlisted socially conscious specialists to develop the Four Fold Program in rural reconstruction. The Ting Hsien (Ding Xian) Experiment, a kind of commune based on family farming, sponsored People's Schools, coordinated innovations ranging from breeding hybrid pigs to setting up economic cooperatives, and incorporated existing aspects of village life, like industry and the expertise of local health workers, to further benefit its residents.

By 1931 these successes excited nationwide public and government interest. Yen joined Liang Shuming and other independent reformers to form the National Rural Reconstruction Movement 鄉村建設運動 (Xiangcun jianshe yundong) comprising hundreds of organizations. The 1937 Japanese invasion drove MEM operations first to Hunan, then to Sichuan, but Yen spent much of the war in Washington, D.C. After 1945 Yen found himself increasingly at odds with the Nationalist (Guomindang) government's military preoccupation; in 1948 he persuaded the U.S. Congress to fund the independent Joint Commission on Rural Reconstruction, of which he became one of the commissioners. After 1949 Yen led the Philippines Rural Reconstruction Movement and founded the International Rural Reconstruction Movement, which he headed until his death in New York City in the autumn of 1990.

Charles W. HAYFORD

Further Reading

Hayford, C. W. (1990). *To the people: James Yen and village China*. New York: Columbia University Press.

Sun, Enrong. (Ed.). (1980). *Yan Yangchu quanji* 晏陽初全集 [Works of Yan Yangchu]. Changsha, China: Hunan Jiaoyu.

Wu, Hsiang-hsiang. (1981). *Yan Yangchu Zhuan* 晏陽初傳 [Biography of Yan Yangchu]. Taipei, Taiwan: Shi Bao.

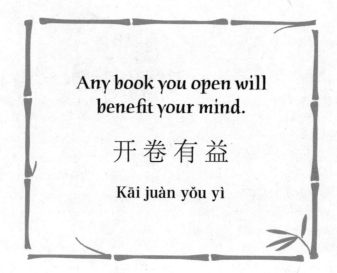

Any book you open will
benefit your mind.

开 卷 有 益

Kāi juàn yǒu yì

Yi

Yízú 彝族

As a minority nationality living in mountainous southwest China and with rich history and
distinctive culture and language, the Yi people
in modern times have abolished slavery and
made progress in agricultural economy, education, health care, and social development.

The Yi people live in southwest China, in the mountainous regions of Yunnan, Sichuan, Guizhou, and
Guangxi provinces. With 7,762,286 people (2000
census), the Yi are the fourth-largest minority nationality
in China. Yi groups in various areas described themselves
with a variety of names until the 1950s, when the Chinese
government redefined all Yi groups under one common
name, the Yi.

History

Scholars have different views about the origins of the Yi.
Some believe that the Yi originated from the ancient nomadic Qiang peoples who had lived in northwest China.
Others argue that the Yi people developed from the original inhabitants of Yunnan, as early as 10,000 years ago.

A group of Yi women,
wearing their traditional
big hats, on the road to
Tiger Leaping Gorge.
PHOTO BY JOAN LEBOLD
COHEN.

2571

Yi clothing styles developed from the tribe's own traditions and from exposure to the cultures of neighboring minority groups. PHOTO BY JOAN LEBOLD COHEN.

In either case scholars agree that starting from the early second millennium BCE, the people in central Yunnan, whether they were the original inhabitants or Qiang immigrants, migrated out of their homeland and mixed with the Han Chinese (the ethnic Chinese majority) and other minority groups. As a result the Yi are a mixed group with diverse origins.

Their migration extended along the watersheds of the six rivers in the Sichuan-Yunnan region and the Yunnan-Guizhou plateau and divided the Yi into six branches. These six branches are the origins of the six branches of the modern Yi nationality: Southern Nisu Yi, Southeastern Sani Yi, Eastern Nasu Yi, Northern Nuosu Yi, Central Yi, and Western Yi. According to a Yi legend, the Yi people originated from an ancient ceremony of tribal division, the division of six ancestors (*liu zu*).

During the Han dynasty (206 BCE–220 CE), the ethnic minority peoples inhabiting the mountainous border region of Yunnan, Sichuan, and Guizhou were first referred to as *yi* (barbarians) in Chinese records. The Yi people were part of this group. The Han government established an administrative prefecture in the region and appointed a Yi chief to rule the region with the title King of Dian. During and after this time, large clans emerged in the Yi tribes. A caste system, which not only established various social statuses in the Yi communities but also defined a large number of common people as slaves, started to dominate Yi societies.

From the Sui (581–618 CE) to the Song dynasty (960–1279), the Yi people were generally referred to in the Chinese records as *wuman* (black barbarians) and *baiman* (white barbarians). While the former exclusively designated the Yi groups in central Yunnan, the latter referred to the minority groups inhabiting the border region of Yunnan, Sichuan, and Guizhou, including some of the Yi tribes. During these centuries two independent kingdoms, Nanzhao (739–902 CE) and Dali (902–1253), ruled Yunnan, organized by the Yi and other minority peoples. Under the reign of these authorities, a distinct Yi culture—including music, dance, ancestral worship, and architectural, culinary, and clothing styles—developed from Yi tribal traditions and from contact with the cultures of neighboring groups.

The Mongols invaded southern China in 1253 and destroyed the Dali kingdom. After conquering the region, the Mongol Yuan dynasty (1279–1368) extended its administration to the Yi areas through a system of *tusi* (local chiefs). By pledging loyalty to the central government, the Yi local chiefs were allowed to govern their realms. During the Mongol period, the Yi people were referred to as *luoluo* (barbarians). Malaria and other epidemic diseases spread to the Yi areas and led to a loss of population and a setback to Yi socioeconomic development.

To consolidate its political control of Yunnan, the Ming dynasty (1368–1644) in the late fifteenth century decided to substitute for the *tusi* system a new policy whereby locals were replaced by Han Chinese officials. The process of replacing locals was not completed until the 1730s during the reign of the emperor Yongzheng of the Qing dynasty (1644–1912), and in most areas the Yi chiefs were powerful enough to maintain their rule and defy the penetration of the Chinese central government at least until the end of Republican China (1949).

The Modern Era

During the early period of the People's Republic of China, the government made efforts to redefine Yi nationality. After bringing the six branches of the Yi peoples together, the government changed their name from the barbarian term *yi* to Yi, a different Chinese word, with connotations of respect. Beginning with the founding of the Liangshan Yi Autonomous Prefecture in 1952, the government established a total of fifteen Yi independent prefectures and counties. Viewing the Yi as the only existing slave society in the world, the government implemented democratic reforms in the Yi areas between 1956 and 1958 and abolished slavery. Under the policy of the equality of all nationalities, the government trained many Yi cadres and extended its political administration into the Yi areas through these cadres. But the Cultural Revolution (1966–1976) brought chaos to all the Yi communities. Traditional Yi customs and religion became the targets of political campaigns, and former local chiefs and priests were scorned or even prosecuted.

With the beginning of reform in 1979, the government reassured the Yi of their rights and privileges as a minority nationality and promoted their equality more in terms of economic development. Since then, the Yi communities have made progress in agricultural economy, education, and health care, and many of the Yi people have become modern workers employed in the tin and coal mines in Yunnan and Guizhou. Yi trade with the outside world has developed, and modern railroads, highways, and communications have been extended through the Yi areas. Despite these developments the Yi societies, disadvantaged by their geographic locations in remote mountains, are still poor in economic terms and are far behind the Han Chinese areas.

Culture

The Yi have a long and rich cultural history. Much traditional literature is written in the distinctive script used for the old Yi language. Folk tales, epics, and songs have also been passed down orally. Yi traditional medicine has a rich variety of resources—such as *baiyao,* a white medical powder for treating hemorrhage, wounds, bruises, and similar ailments—which are widely used by all Chinese. Yi religion, based on ancestor worship and a belief in many gods, has been revived in recent years after its practices were prohibited in the 1960s and 1970s.

Yi people speak the Yi language, a linguistic branch of the Chinese-Tibetan language family, which has six sets of major dialects and many more local dialects that are not always mutually intelligible. One million members of the Yi nationality do not speak the Yi language at all. In 1975 the Chinese government attempted to formalize a unified Yi language by defining 819 standard Yi words, but the effort has not been as successful as hoped, as isolation and language barriers have prevented the Yi from establishing a commonly shared ethnic identity. The development of their independent power and the modernization of their economy and society await the future.

Yixin CHEN

Further Reading

Yi Mouyuan. (2007). *Yizu shiyao* 彝族史要 [A brief history of Yi nationality]. Beijing: Social Science Literature Press.

Li Shaoming & Feng Min. (1996). *Yizu* 彝族 [Yi nationality]. Beijing: The National Minority Press.

Harrell, S. (Ed.). (2001). *Perspectives on the Yi of southwest China.* Berkeley and Los Angeles: University of California Press.

Ma Yin. (1989). *China's minority nationalities.* Beijing: Foreign Language Press.

Yin and Yang

Yīn-Yáng 阴阳

Representing the Chinese philosophy of duality, yin and yang have a deeply rooted history in China. Developing into the School of Yin and Yang, thinkers of this concept seek to define the relationship between human and natural phenomena.

Probably no aspect of Chinese philosophy is more widely recognized in the West than the concept of yin and yang. People rightly see the two terms *yin* and *yang* as symbolic of the dualistic nature of the phenomenal world, but some incorrectly see this duality as hostile, like the moral opposition between good and evil. In the Chinese conception duality is complementary, not conflicting. Furthermore, the categories are not static but rather dynamic. Although yang may eventually overcome yin, at the point of triumph its power will immediately begin to wane. The alternation of yin and yang is thus the most indicative quality of this philosophical concept.

One of the earliest textual references to the two terms in the Chinese tradition occurs in a poem from the *Book of Songs* that recounts the founding of the Zhou dynasty (1045–256 BCE). This excerpt shows the venerable ancestor surveying the realm:

> Blessed was Chief Liu.
> He measured the breadth and length of the land;
> He measured the shadow and noted the hills,
> Observing the sunshine (*yang*) and shade (*yin*).
> (Mao *Shi* no. 250; Legge 1861, 487)

Chief Liu was measuring the shadow of the gnomon, or sundial, to determine the cardinal directions. Yang hillsides (the south slopes) and river banks (the north sides) were appropriate for human habitation because houses built there would receive the most sunshine during the winter.

Yin and Yang in Ancient Cosmology

By the time the two terms reappeared in the textual tradition, they had acquired cosmological connotations (associations relating to a branch of metaphysics that deals with the nature of the universe). In the *Zuo Commentary* to the *Spring and Autumn Annals* (written c. fifth century BCE) a passage that mentions yin and yang concerns astrological prognostication. The failure of ice to appear at the beginning of the year was blamed on Jupiter (the Year Star), whose "licentious" (retrograde) movement caused "the *yin* not to cover the *yang*" (Legge 1861, 540). Normally, the annual dominance of yin would have allowed ice to form. But Jupiter's licentious behavior (lodging in the inappropriate constellation) increased the influence of yang in the corresponding earthly realm.

During the mid-Warring States period (475–221 BCE) the function of yin and yang in literary contexts continued to have cosmological import, but now the terms were elevated to cosmogonic status (relating to a theory of the origin of the universe). The opening to the poem "Heaven Questions" from the *Songs of Chu* describes how the world came about:

In the beginning of old,
All is yet formless, no up or down.
Dark and light are a blur,
The only image is a whir.
Bright gets brighter, dark gets darker,
The *yin* couples with the *yang*—
Then is the round pattern manifold.
    (Trans. S. Field, in Major 1993, 63)

The process being narrated here is birth and generation. The whirling image is inchoate matter, what might be called "chaos" in Western mythology. In cosmogonies appearing later in the Chinese tradition, such matter would be given the term *qi*. In this poem form and light spawn from the motion of embryonic qi as yin and yang materialize. At that point they couple and generate roundness, the shape of the phenomenal world.

In the mid-second century BCE, when the philosophical treatise *Huainanzi* was compiled, the sexual connotations surrounding the cosmological terms became even more overt: "When *yin* and *yang* gather together their interaction produces thunder. Aroused, they produce lightning" (Major 1993, 65). In the mythical version of this passage, instead of abstract yin and yang interacting in a vacuum the coupling of two dragons is visualized, one male and one female, who leave their winter refuge, mount up to heaven, and cause the spring rains to fall. The *Huainanzi* version may simply be the philosophical refinement of vestiges of folk tradition that had always recognized in nature the same sexual groupings that govern society. Scholars therefore speculate that the original impulse for positing a yin/yang duality in the cosmos may have been the spring mating ritual in ancient China. In that ceremony sexual communion among the young people of neighboring villages was the central rite, but that union subsequently guaranteed the fecundity of all of nature: The rains arrived, the rainbow appeared, seeds sprouted, and winter gave way to spring (Granet 1975, 46–50).

School of Yin and Yang

By the end of the Warring States period, at the time of the great flowering of Chinese philosophy, the School of Yin and Yang arose, led by the thinker Zou Yan (350–270 BCE?). The Han dynasty (206 BCE–220 CE) *Records of the Grand Historian* had this to say about Zou:

> He examined deeply into the phenomena of the increase and decrease of *yin* and *yang,* and wrote essays totaling more than a hundred thousand words about their strange permutations. (Needham 1956, 232)

None of his works survives, but he is credited with proposing five categories of qi as a further elaboration of the original two forces of yin and yang. This is the concept of *wuxing,* or the "five elements" of wood, fire, earth, metal, and water. The "strange permutations" mentioned earlier are the so-called enumeration orders whereby the elements successively conquer (or produce) each other. Thus, earth dams water, water quenches fire, fire melts metal, metal cuts wood, and wood saps earth, and so forth. Such thinking, based as it was on the empirical observation of nature, was an early attempt at a scientific view of the world. Zou Yan and his followers subsequently built a correlative universe based on these categories and their orders. For example, when the five internal organs (spleen, lungs, heart, kidney, liver) are correlated with

The yin and yang symbol from Daoism, which represents a complementary, rather than a hostile, duality.

Heaven Questions

> … Bright gets brighter, dark gets darker,
>
> The yin couples with the yang—
>
> Then is the round pattern manifold.

Source: Field, S. (1992). Cosmos, cosmograph, and the inquiring poet: New answers to the "heaven questions." *Early China* 17, 83–110.

the five elements, wood governs the liver. When the five grains (rice, millet, barley, wheat, legumes) are correlated with the five elements, legumes belong to the element water. In the production order of the elements water nourishes wood, so a diet rich in soybeans can be beneficial to the liver.

In seeking proto-scientific correspondences between human and natural phenomena the thinkers of the School of Yin and Yang sought to control human civilization by aligning it with natural cycles and patterns. Their theories inspired great thinkers in the Han dynasty and continued to influence Chinese philosophy until the Song dynasty (960–1279). At that time the cosmology of Zou Yan was integrated with Confucian metaphysics by Zhou Dunyi (1017–1073), who composed the treatise, "Explanation of the Diagram of the Supreme Ultimate." That diagram, the *taiji*, is considered to be the precursor of the familiar circular symbol of yin and yang.

Stephen FIELD

Further Reading

Field, S. (1992). Cosmos, cosmograph, and the inquiring poet: New answers to the "heaven questions." *Early China* 17, 83–110.

Granet, M. (1975). *The religion of the Chinese people* (M. Freedman, Trans. & Ed.). New York: Harper and Row.

Legge, J. (Trans.). (1861–1872). *The Chinese Classics,* 5 vols. (Vol. 4, *The She King* [Classic of odes], Vol. 5, *The Ch'un Ts'ew, with the Tso Chuen* [Spring and autumn annals with the Zuo commentary]). Hong Kong and London: Oxford University Press.

Major, J. S. (Trans.). (1993). *Heaven and Earth in early Han thought: Chapters three, four, and five of the* Huainanzi. Albany: State University of New York Press.

Needham, J. (1956). *Science and civilisation in China: Vol. 2. History of scientific thought.* Cambridge, UK: Cambridge University Press.

Waley, A. (Trans.). (1937). *The book of songs.* London: George Allen and Unwin.

Yin Ruins (Yinxu)

Yīnxū 殷墟

The structures and artifacts excavated from Yinxu reveal much about the religion, social organization, and technology of the last phase of the Shang dynasty (1766–1045 BCE). The square architectural design of royal tombs reflects an image of the cosmos as having four corners, for example, and the number and quality of bronze vessels indicates an advanced technology and artistic vision.

The Shang dynasty (1766–1045 BCE) was the second dynastic period of China (although some scholars consider the Xia dynasty [2100–1766 BCE] to be only legendary, thus making the Shang the first) and the first central power of East Asia. Yinxu, located near the modern city of Anyang in Henan Province, was the site of the last capital of the Shang dynasty (sometimes known as the Yin dynasty). Occupied from about 1300 to 1045 BCE, the city was abandoned right after the Zhou people conquered the Shang. Excavation of the Yin Ruins, ongoing since 1928, reveals that it was the greatest of the Bronze Age cultures of China.

The archaeological excavations have uncovered 300,000 square meters of this site, which measure about 6 kilometers from east to west and 5 kilometers from north to south. However, its original boundary has not been defined. Architectural remains, cemeteries, and workshops have been mapped, and thousands of ritual bronze artifacts, mostly vessels, along with jades, stones, carved bones, inscribed oracle bones, and a great amount of pottery have been found. These materials have informed modern onlookers about the social organization, belief system, religious practice, science and technology, artistic invention, life styles of the people, and natural environment of the time.

Discovery and Excavation

The early period of archaeological excavation, from 1928 to 1937, was led by archaeologists Li Chi, Liang Siyong, Dong Zuobin, Shi Zhangru, and Gao Quxun of the Institute of Philology and Histology, Central Academia Sinica. They performed fifteen excavations of around 46,000 square meters and discovered the core of this site: the temple-palace complex at Xiaotun village and the royal cemetery at Houjiazhuang, along with their respective oracle inscriptions and ritual bronzes.

Excavation was resumed in 1950, and the archaeological findings continue to update our knowledge of this civilization. In 1976, the first undisturbed royal tomb, the tomb of Lady Hao, was excavated. It contained more than one thousand ritual bronzes, some seven hundred jade artifacts, and five hundred bone artifacts. Lady Hao can be clearly identified as the third queen of King Wu Ding; about two hundred pieces of oracle inscriptions talk about her as a military commander, mother, and a wife. There were rare goods and tribute goods in her tombs, which came through long-distance trade or from other nations and groups.

The bronze castings of the ritual vessels indicate the advanced technology and social organization of Lady

Hao's time. From mining to casting of ores and artifacts, and from design to distribution and usage, no other nation or people at the time in East Asia or nearby regions reached such an advanced level in the making and use of bronze as the Yin/Shang.

Cosmology of the Shang

With the exception of the tomb of the Lady Hao, all the large royal tombs were looted in antiquity, but the architectural form revealed by the scale and design of the tombs discloses much about the image of the cosmos as conceived by the Shang people. The tombs of eleven of the royals were about 40 square meters each. More than one thousand human sacrificial pits were well arranged in rows next to these tombs. The ramps were not functional but rather were ritualistic in their construction and in their numbers; the number of ramps indicated the social and political rank of the royals buried there. All pits contained four corners that indicated the four directions of the square-shaped universe. The design of the tombs formed a three-dimensional image that some scholars believed was the Shang people's image of the cosmos. These spatial arrangements are consistent with square-shaped universes with upper and lower worlds that have characterized Chinese belief throughout history.

Human Sacrifice

The way human bodies were treated in the royal tombs reveals the hierarchical nature of the Shang society: gods, king, elites, commoners, slaves, and captives, in that order, from top to bottom. A thousand human sacrificial pits in a neat pattern were located next to the royal tombs. Each pit contained a group of human remains; some had only bodies while their heads were in the royal tombs. Inside the royal tombs (e.g., in tomb HPKM1001), there were remains of more than 100 human sacrifices even after the looting of the tombs. Six lacquered coffins were buried in tomb HPKM1550. These sacrifices were consorts of the king and were elaborately decorated with jade, bone hairpins, and had ritual bronzes buried with them.

An entire army with foot soldiers and chariots was buried in the southwest area of the complex, displayed as in a battlefield with center with left and right wings. Individual human sacrificial pits and sites have been excavated as well. The oracle inscriptions record activities of offerings of human sacrifice, sometimes in great numbers. Most of the human victims were healthy and handsome young men.

The Shang's ancestors enjoyed offerings along with the gods who decided all matters of the nation, from war to harvest, from giving birth to tooth pain. The living king was a medium between the supernatural and the living worlds, and he reigned above all.

Gender Roles

The choice of sacrificial victims in Yinxu shows that gender was a complicated issue in the Shang dynasty. Both elite and common women could be buried with weapons, and men could be buried with weaving tools or even make-up. Queen Lady Hao had led the Shang army and had conquered some nations. The elite females were in charge of important rituals such as preparing oracle materials, the ceremony of harvesting, and they joined in hunting expeditions. Yet the king had many consorts, and the queens had to wait their turn to receive their offerings in death after their husbands had passed on. Women and children were not used for sacrifices until the last fifty years of Yinxu, indicating that the choice of sacrificial gifts for the gods and the ancestors was a highly selective process in the Shang dynasty.

Perspectives on Shang Culture

The Yin Ruins disclose the nature of the Shang culture, which was one of the most advanced in East Asia. Its complicated social structure, sophisticated religion, innovative art, science, and technology present a level of civilization with well-developed ideology and thought and richness of material production. Yet the ruins also hint at a dictatorial and hierarchical system with strict social, political, economic, and even spiritual boundaries.

WANG Ying

Further Reading

Chang, K. C. (1980). *Shang civilization.* New Haven, CT: Yale University Press.

Keightley, D. N. (2000). *The ancestral landscape: Time, space, and community in late Shang China, ca. 1200–1045*

The Tomb of Lady Fu Hao, Yin ruins, China. PHOTO BY CHRIS GYFORD.

B.C. Berkeley: University of California Institute of East Asian Studies.

Keightley, D. N. (1989). Craft and culture: Metaphors of governance in early China. *Proceedings of the 2nd International Conference on Sinology. Section on History and Archaeology,* 31–70.

Li Chi. (1977). *Anyang: A chronicle of the discovery, excavation, and reconstruction of the ancient capital of the Shang dynasty.* Seattle: University of Washington Press.

Li Chi. (1957). *The beginnings of Chinese civilization: Three lectures illustrated with finds at Anyang.* Seattle: University of Washington Press.

Thorp, R. L. (2005). *China in the early Bronze Age: Shang civilization.* Philadelphia: University of Pennsylvania Press.

閒談
chat

China changes constantly, and the *Encyclopedia of China* will change and grow, too. Berkshire's authors and editors welcome questions, comments, and corrections: china.updates@berkshirepublishing.com.

Yin-Yang Theory

Yīnyángjiā　阴阳家

Yin–yang theory, embodying the most basic forces in nature, is an important component of Chinese philosophy, medicine, divination, and feng shui. It unites the Confucian emphasis on virtue with the Daoist emphasis on harmony with nature.

Yin–yang theory, originally referring to the shady and sunny parts of gorges and mountains, is integral to Chinese philosophy, medicine, divination, and geomancy (feng shui). The term came to embody the most basic forces in nature, such as male/female, night/ day, and old/young.

First used in the fourteenth century BCE, yin–yang theory was able to unite the Confucian focus on virtue and the Daoist concern for living in harmony with nature within its naturalistic philosophy. The character *yin* referred to the shady, northern side of a mountain or the southern side of a gorge, and *yang* to the sunny, southern side of a mountain or the northern side of a gorge.

By the Spring and Autumn period (770–476 BCE) yin and yang were beginning to take on cosmological significance as two of the six forms of material force (qi), namely, shady-yin, sunny-yang, wind, rain, dark, and light. It was believed that success/health and disaster/illnesses are related to an excess or deficiency of shady-yin and sunny-yang. During the Warring States period (475–221 BCE) yin and yang began to take on a more encompassing philosophical meaning as the most basic forces and, by extension, the most general categories for classifying all things in existence. The concepts *yin* and *yang* are used as philosophical categories in the naturalistic philosophies of the Daoist texts *Laozi* and *Zhuangzi* and the Confucian book *Xunzi*. As philosophical categories yin and yang are understood to be two opposing yet interconnected forces; they are not a duality. Yin contains yang, and yang contains yin. When one extreme is exhausted the other force comes into play. They are similar to the negative and positive charges in the electro-magnetic spectrum. The following list depicts some of the major correlations associated with them:

Yin	Yang
Earth	Heaven
Autumn	Spring
Night	Day
Small states	Large states
Rest	Action
Below	Above
Younger	Elder
Female	Male

Zou Yan (c. 305–240 BCE) was the founder of the yin– yang five-phases school. He associated yin and yang with the five phases (*wuxing*), namely, wood, fire, earth, metal, and water, creating a more dynamic explanation for the processes of change. Wood and fire are associated with yang; metal, earth, and water are yin. The five phases first appeared in the "Grand Norm" chapter of the *Classic of Documents,* a book comprising fifty-eight chapters with documents and records relating to the ancient history of China. Rubin

The eight trigrams, each representing a compass point, surround the yin–yang symbol.

argues that Zou Yan transformed the static categories of the five phases into a dynamic and temporal system by connecting it to the undulating pulsations of yin and yang. Scholars debate whether Zou and his school should be classified as a naturalist philosophy or as diviners and geomancers. The yin–yang philosophy is closely related to both natural philosophy and divination because by being aware of the natural processes of change a person is in a better position to predict the future. *The Annals of Lü Buwei* (c. 240 BCE) contains the following passage that describes the application of the five phases theory in political philosophy.

When ever an emperor or king is about to arise, Heaven is certain to manifest good omens to the people below. At the time of the Yellow Emperor, Heaven first caused giant mole crickets and earthworms to appear. The Yellow Emperor announced, "The ethers of Earth are in ascendance." Since the ethers of Earth were ascendant, he honored the color yellow and modeled his activities on Earth. When it came to the time of Yu, Heaven first caused trees and grasses to appear that did not wither in autumn and winter. Yu Proclaimed, "The ethers of Wood are in ascendance." Since the ethers of Wood were ascendant, he honored

the color green and modeled his affairs on Wood. When it came to the time of Tang, Heaven first caused metal blades to appear coming froth from Water. Tang proclaimed, "The ethers of Metal are in ascendance." Since the ethers of Metal were ascendant, he honored the color white and modeled his affairs on Metal. When it came to the time of King Wen, Heaven first caused a fiery-red crow to appear and alight on the altars of Zhou, holding in its beak a document written in cinnabar. King Wen proclaimed, "The ethers of Fire are in ascendance." Since the ethers of Fire were ascendant, he honored the color vermilion and modeled his affairs on Fire. (modifying Knoblock & Riegel 2000, 283)

The preceding passage depicts the rise and fall of dynasties according to the conquest cycle of the five phases, in which water extinguishes fire, fire melts metal, metal cuts wood, wood breaks up earth, and earth obstructs water. A ruler could influence state affairs with this model by advocating that his form of government was aligned with the cosmic forces. For example, the state of Qin vanquished the house of Zhou in 256 BCE, but not until the unification of the empire, in 221 BCE, did the first emperor of Qin adopt the color black and model his affairs on water. He justified his rule by adopting the five phases theory. During the Han dynasty (206 BCE–220 CE) court officials continued to debate which one of the five phases was ascending and what color and emblem the state should institute as its model. If the natural cycles of yin, yang, and the five phases could be used to determine the rise and fall of states, then they should have application to all sorts of endeavors. During the Han dynasty yin–yang theory was used to explain natural phenomena, human activities, health, and wealth.

Besides the conquest cycle for the five phases, there is a cycle of generation in which earth grows wood, wood fuels fire, fire's ash produces earth, earth produces metal, and metal precipitates water. During the early Han dynasty (206 BCE–220 CE) the yin–yang and five phases were expanded into a comprehensive classification system such that everything was classified as being predominantly yin or yang and further linked to one of the five phases. This comprehensive approach paved the way for yin–yang theory to influence the practice of traditional Chinese medicine, divination, and geomancy. For example, the following chart links the phases to the five colors, directions, seasons, internal organs, and numbers.

The Five Phases

WOOD	FIRE	EARTH	METAL	WATER
Green	Red	Yellow	White	Black
East	South	Center	West	North
Spring	Summer	Late Summer	Autumn	Winter
Liver	Heart	Spleen	Lungs	Kidneys
Eight	Seven	Five	Nine	Six

Each of the five phases also correlates with any number of natural phenomena. By understanding the relationships between the five phases and other natural phenomena and whether or not the generation or destruction cycle is at work, a person can predict what phenomena will arise next. The alleged diagnostic and predictive powers of the yin–yang five phases theory naturally influenced the practice of Chinese medicine and divination.

Medicine

Traditional Chinese medicine pays close attention to environmental influences on people's health. It has always been concerned about the influences of cold/heat, damp/dry climate, and light/dark on a person's health. By the beginning of the Han dynasty when yin–yang theory was taking shape, traditional Chinese medicine was being formalized. Yin–yang theory's influence on traditional Chinese medicine is seen in the early medical texts, namely, *The Spiritual Pivot* and *The Yellow Emperor's Classic of Internal Medicine*. All health-related phenomena are associated with yin, yang, and the five phases. At conception each individual is bestowed an allotment of prenatal-energy qi, composed of yin and yang. When yin, yang, and the five phases operate in harmony there is health. Illness develops when they are imbalanced. The physiology, pathology, diagnosis, and treatment of illness in Chinese medicine are described in terms of yin–yang theory. All symptoms and physiological processes are analyzed according to the yin–yang five phases theory. There are basically four treatment modalities: to tonify yin or yang and to eliminate excess yin or yang. Chinese medicine employs the dynamic transformations of yin and yang in accounting for the processes of health and illness. As opposites yin and yang are interdependent, contain each other, and mutually consume each other. Bodily parts and structures are assigned yin–yang associations. Yin is associated with structure and yang with function. The lower extremities, interior, and front are yin. The upper extremities, exterior, and back are yang. So all of the yang channels flow through the back and begin or end at the head. The yin channels flow through the abdomen and chest and begin or end below the waist. Likewise, pathogenic factors follow the yin–yang pattern. So the upper body is affected by yang factors such as wind and summer heat. The lower body is affected by dampness and cold.

Bodily organs are also classified according to yin and yang. The yin organs store energy; the yang organs digest and excrete food to generate energy. Through the bodily openings the yang organs such as the stomach, intestines, and bladder are in contact with the exterior. Like the yang force, the yang organs are active constantly filling, emptying, and digesting food. The yin organs are tranquil and store the energy and vital substances, such as qi, blood, and other bodily fluids within the body. Because yin and yang are never separated, all organs have them. Yin correlates to an organ's structure and yang to its function. Like yin and yang, structure and function are interconnected and codependent. For example, the spleen's yang function is to transform food into blood, which is the yin structure of the spleen. Blood-and-energy qi form a bipolar relationship: Blood nourishes and moistens, like yin; energy qi is warming, protecting, and transforming, like yang. Defensive and nutritive energy follow the paradigm. Defensive energy circulates in the skin and muscles and is yang. Nutritive energy is yin, circulating in the internal organs.

Yin–yang theory forms the basic character of all symptoms and signs in Chinese medicine. The basic qualities that direct clinical practice are assigned the following correlations:

YIN	YANG
Water	Fire
Cold	Hot
Quiet	Restless
Wet	Dry
Soft	Hard
Inhibited	Excited
Slow	Rapid

Water is associated with the kidneys; fire with the heart. Maintaining a balance between water and fire is most important for health. Water moistens and nourishes the body; fire heats the body and fuels the metabolic processes. Fire in the heart helps maintain emotional well-being. Its warming energy allows the spleen to produce blood, facilitating the small intestine's digestion and the bladder's ability to excrete fluids. The major clinical manifestations correlate as follows:

Yin	Yang
Chronic disease	Acute disease
Gradual onset	Rapid onset
Lingering disease	Rapid changes
Cold	Hot
Sleepy	Insomnia
Likes bed covers	Throws off covers
Curls up	Lies stretched out
Pale face	Red face
Prefers hot drinks	Prefers cold drinks
Weak voice	Loud voice
Shallow breathing	Coarse breathing
No thirst	Thirst
Profuse, pale urine	Scanty, dark urine
Loose stools	Constipated
Pale tongue	Red tongue
Empty pulse	Full pulse

Yin–yang theory forms the foundation for an understanding of the clinical manifestations of symptoms. The yin–yang correlations must be integrated with the eight principles and the theory of internal organ patterns to be used successfully in diagnosing illnesses.

Divination

Divination has always played a role in Chinese culture. In the Shang dynasty (1766–1045 BCE) oracle bones were employed for this purpose. The bones were prepared and heated, and when the bone cracked, the lines were "read" for divination. The *I Ching* (*Yijing, Classic of Changes*), the Confucian text of divination, is dated to the early Zhou dynasty (1045–256 BCE). Although the terms *yin* and *yang* to do not appear within the main body of the *Classic of Changes*, the text has been interpreted according to those categories. The appendix to the *Changes* defines the dao as one yin and one yang. The method of divination developed in the *Changes* is based on symbolic images depicted

by solid and broken lines. The broken line is associated with yin and the solid line with yang. The following figures depict the progression.

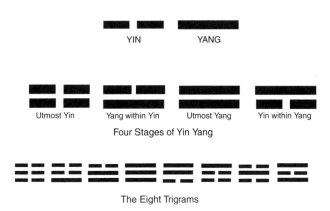

YIN　　　　YANG

Utmost Yin　　Yang within Yin　　Utmost Yang　　Yin within Yang

Four Stages of Yin Yang

The Eight Trigrams

The first chapter of the *Changes* is "Qian," represented by three solid lines arranged vertically. It is associated with pure yang, heaven, and light. The second chapter of the *Changes* is "Kun," represented by three broken lines. Kun is associated with pure yin, earth, and darkness. There are eight different possible permutations combining solid and broken lines. These are known as the "Eight Trigrams" (*Bagua*). They are combined into the sixty-four hexagrams that comprise the chapters of the *Changes*. The Eight Trigrams are typically arranged around the eight compass points, giving them a spatial orientation. The trigrams especially represent temporal changes and are correlated with the seasons, the phases of the moon, the days of the week, and the hours of the day. The traditional Chinese calendar is a hybrid of both lunar and solar calendars. The four seasons are subdivided into three moons or months consisting of three ten-day weeks. The day is divided into twelve two-hour periods. Yin and yang are associated with the year, month, week, day, and hour. These time periods are also associated with a hexagram. The time of day or the day of the week can be used to find a hexagram to determine whether that time is auspicious or not. Because yin–yang theory and the principles of divination both focus on the process of change, it is natural that the two systems merged together.

Feng Shui: The Art of Placement

Feng shui literally means "wind and water." It is the ancient art, science, and magic of geomancy. It is employed in both ancient and modern architecture. Because wind and water are two of the most powerful natural forces that shape the landscape and pose a threat to human habitation, the art of living in harmony with the forces of nature came to be referred to as *feng shui*. Until recently feng shui was dismissed as mere superstition and an appeal to magic. In part feng shui practices are concerned with promoting good luck and avoiding bad luck, but they also have a practical and an aesthetic aspect. Some feng shui practices have artistic appeal and are based on sound observations. Feng shui is the art of placement that promotes both aesthetic and ecological values. Modern people recognize the aesthetic value of feng shui practices, especially in arranging a Chinese-, Korean-, or Japanese-style garden. Feng shui practices promote building homes and other structures in such a manner that they take advantage of the natural surrounding, allowing natural light and heat to enter the building in the winter and cool breezes in the summer. The aesthetic and ecological advantages of feng shui have revitalized people's interest in it.

Yin–yang theory plays an important role in the ancient art of placement. Any human structure, whether it is a farm, a garden, a building, a home, or a grave, will impose itself on the natural surrounding. It will have to withstand the forces of nature and adjust to the changes of the seasons and climate, so it will have to be in harmony with those forces, which are governed by yin and yang. Daoist priests are traditionally the master practitioners of feng shui. They use a *loban,* or feng shui compass. The compass has a magnetic north-south needle in the center, which is surrounded by concentric circles containing other information such as the seventy-two dragon veins, the twenty-eight constellations, the 360 degrees of the compass, the sixty points of good and bad luck, the eight trigrams, the auspicious river directions, and good and bad burial positions. The eight major compass points are associated with the eight treasures as follows: Fame is associated with the south; wealth with the southeast; education with the east; children with the northeast;

relationships with the north; friends with the northwest; pleasure with the west; and health with the southwest. The direction the front door of a person's home faces will determine which one of the eight treasures is most benefited in that person's life. For example, if someone seeks to improve her relationships, then she should move into a house with a front door that faces north, so that her comings and goings take her through the relationship area. Because feng shui assists people in determining the aesthetic and practical value of the art of placing objects in the home and within the natural environment, feng shui continues to inspire architects and common people.

Yin–yang theory has its roots in ancient political philosophy. Through the syncretic approach of Han dynasty philosophy, the yin–yang five phases theory was integrated into other aspects of natural philosophy, medicine, divination, and the art of placement.

James D. SELLMANN

Further Reading

Craze, R. (1997). *Practical feng shui: The Chinese art of living in harmony with your surroundings.* New York: Lorenz Books.

Graham, A. C. (1986). Yin–yang and the nature of correlative thinking. *Occasional paper and monograph series, 6.* Singapore: Institute of East Asian Philosophies.

Graham, A. C. (1989). *Disputers of the Tao.* La Salle, IL: Open Court.

Jarrett, L. S. (1998). *Nourishing destiny: The inner tradition of Chinese medicine.* Stockbridge, MA: Spirit Path Press.

Knoblock, J., & Riegel, J. (2000). *The annals of Lü Buwei.* Stanford, CA: Stanford University Press.

Maciocia, G. (1989). *The foundations of Chinese medicine: A comprehensive text for acupuncturists and herbalists.* New York: Churchill Livingstone.

Rubin, V. A. (1982). The concepts of wu-hsing and yin–yang. *Journal of Chinese Philosophy, 9*(2), 131–158.

Wilhelm, R. (1978). *The I ching* (C. F. Baynes, Trans.). Princeton, NJ: Princeton University Press.

Yokohama Specie Bank

Héngbīn Zhèngjīn Yínháng 横滨正金银行

The Yokahama Specie Bank Limited originally was a private commercial bank which became a Japanese official overseas bank in the 1890s. The bank issued and circulated Japanese military notes during Sino-Japanese war periods, and was closed in 1945 after World War II.

The Yokohama Specie Bank was established on 28 February 1880 in Yokohama, Japan, to engage in foreign trade and discount trade bills. The bank was originally private but soon became the quasi-official bank of Japan because of the capital that the Meiji (1868–1912) government had injected into the bank during its financial crisis in early years. The government also granted the Yokohama bank a charter to handle foreign exchange reserves and to issue government notes. To expand foreign trade and share the sphere of influence in China, the bank opened its first China branch in Shanghai in 1893.

In the later nineteenth century Japan used a multi-metallic currency system based on gold, silver, and copper cash. This complex currency system contributed to fluctuations in transactions of foreign trade and foreign exchange. As a result of China's loss in the Sino-Japanese War in 1895, Japan received a large quantity of gold as war

The Dalian Branch of the Yokohama Specie Bank. Photo taken around 1915.

indemnity from China and used it as reserves to establish a gold standard in 1897. As the first Japanese national overseas bank, the Yokohama Specie Bank handled transactions involving the indemnity and also used part of the gold as reserves to issue bank notes in China.

Since many Japanese firms in China conducted their business with other countries solely through the Yokohama Specie Bank, the bank gained a strong national prestige within Japan. With its privileged relationship with most Japanese trading firms and benefits from government, which included being granted a deep discount rate and low tariffs, the Yokohama Specie Bank became a strong competitor of other foreign banks in China. From 1880 to 1926 the bank's capital increased from an initial ¥3 million to ¥100 million.

From 1893 to 1945 the Yokohama Specie Bank opened thirty-four branches in China and built a large banking and financial network, especially in northeast China. During this period the Yokohama bank acted as the Japanese central bank in issuing banknotes, which were linked with Japanese yen in the currency circulation of northeast China. In addition, this bank gained a special right to finance the construction of Manchou railways, controlled regional foreign trade, and acted as the de facto Japanese treasury to receive Maritime Customs revenue in northeast China. After the outbreak of the World War II in the Pacific in December 1941 the Yokohama Specie Bank replaced the British Hong Kong and Shanghai Banking Corporation in handling China's Maritime Customs revenue. The bank's major wartime financial activity was issuing military notes to finance Japanese military activities in China.

After Japan's unconditional surrender in August 1945 the Yokohama Specie Bank was closed. It was reorganized into the Bank of Tokyo in 1947.

JI Zhaojin

Further Reading

Fu Wenling, Xu Guobing, Wang Zhenlin, Ren Hongxiu, Hao Shumin, & Kuang Houjun. (Eds.). (1992). *Riben Hengbinzhengjin Yinhang Zaihuahuodong Shiliao.* [The historical materials of Japan's Yokahama Specie Bank in China]. Beijing: Zhongguo Jinrong Chubanshe.

Hijikata, S. (1980). Yokohama Shokin Ginko [The Yokohama Specie Bank]. *Rekishi Shinsho, Nihon Shi,* [Japanese History], *146.*

Hong Jiaguan, Ye Schichang, Zhang Guohui, Kong Xiangyi, Xu Huijun, Yuan Yuanfu, Yu Tao, & Hong Qinguan. (1993). *Zhongguo Jinrongshi* [A history of Chinese finance]. Chengdu, China: Xinan Caijing Daxue Chubanshe.

Tamagna, F. M. (1942). *Banking and finance in China.* New York: Institute of Pacific Relations.

Wang Jingyu. (1999). *Weiguo Ziben zai Jindai Zhongguo de Jingrong Huodong* [Foreign capital in modern China's financial activities]. Beijing: Renmin Chubanshe.

Yongle Dadian

Yŏnglè Dà Diăn　永乐大典

Yongle dadian 永乐大典 is a massive, imperially-commissioned encyclopedia compiled in 1408 and composed of thousands of excerpts from all across the Chinese textual tradition. Most of the encyclopedia was destroyed in the wars of the nineteenth and early twentieth centuries.

The *Yongle dadian*, or *Great Compendium of the Yongle Reign*, was a massive literary encyclopedia completed in 1408. The work had 22,877 chapters in 11,095 volumes. The table of contents alone was sixty chapters long. In 1900 most of the last known copy of the *Yongle dadian* was largely destroyed in a fire started during the suppression of the Boxer Rebellion, an uprising of a Chinese secret society called Righteous and Harmonious Fists against foreign influence in trade, politics, religion, and technology. The *New York Times* mourned the loss as "perhaps the greatest tragedy in the history of literature," noting that the encyclopedia was "the most colossal literary work ever carried out by man" (8 February 1914).

The *Yongle dadian* was commissioned at the behest of Emperor Yongle (reigned 1402–1424) shortly after he usurped the throne from his nephew, the Jianwen emperor (reigned 1398–1402). In 1403 the new emperor ordered one of his leading advisors to direct the project. A staff of 147 scholars was drafted, and the project was completed the following year. The emperor, however, was dissatisfied with the result, complaining that it was too limited in scope. He recommissioned the project on a grander scale, insisting that it include material from all philosophical, technical, and literary fields. The staff of compilers, editors, and scribes was expanded to include over two thousand scholars. When the compendium was completed in 1408, Yongle declared his satisfaction and wrote the preface for it himself, boasting of the great aid this work would be to the scholars of the empire. All the information of the world, he explained, was arranged here in topical and phonetic order.

The encyclopedia was but one of many scholarly initiatives of the court at this time. Yongle ordered several other large projects, including elaborately annotated editions of each of the Confucian Five Classics and the Four Books, a large encyclopedia of neo-Confucian terms and teachings, and the full Buddhist scriptural canon, the Tripitaka. Historians generally regard these ambitious projects as an effort by Yongle to shed his image as a violent usurper and to recast his legacy as that of a cultured and benevolent ruler. Moreover, projects such as the *Yongle dadian* served to enlist officials from among the wary scholar-elite of the empire.

Imperial Precedent

In commissioning the *Yongle dadian* and other projects, Yongle followed a longstanding imperial precedent that went back at least to the third century CE. His two Ming dynasty (1368–1644) predecessors, Hongwu (reigned 1368–1398) and Jianwen, had each initiated large compilations. However, the *Yongle dadian* dwarfed all precedents. The term *encyclopedia* understates the scope of this work because it included large excerpts from a wide range of

Two pages of the Yongle Dadian, one of the first encyclopedias ever printed. This was commissioned by the Yongle Emperor, the greatest of the Ming Dynasty emperors.

texts of the Chinese tradition. Several were transcribed in their entirety. Some pieces, including literary, historical, and dramatic works, have survived only because they were reconstructed or copied from the *Yongle dadian*.

Yongle originally intended that copies of the *Yongle dadian* be printed with woodblocks and distributed to various parts of the empire for educational purposes. But this elaborate plan was later abandoned, possibly because the imperial treasuries had been strained by Yongle's other projects. The compendium was kept at the palace at Nanjing and moved to Beijing along with rest of the imperial library when Yongle relocated his capital to the north. (Some sources say an additional copy was kept in Nanjing.) The *Yongle dadian* remained on the palace grounds and apparently saw little use in the decades that followed. In 1562 it was nearly destroyed by a fire that engulfed several palace buildings. In response, the Jiajing emperor (reigned 1521–1567) ordered that two copies be made of the original manuscript. (Some scholars say only one copy was made.) This endeavor took five years, supervised by high court officials with a staff of 108 scholars. The original volumes were sent back to the southern Ming capital at Nanjing, while the two copies were kept in Beijing.

The Nanjing copy and one of the Beijing copies are believed to have been destroyed when the Ming dynasty fell in 1644. By the late eighteenth century only one dilapidated copy remained, with some sections missing. Some scholars have speculated that the original edition of the encyclopedia still survives in some hidden location. One theory is that this edition was entombed with the Jiajing emperor when he died in 1567.

Reconstruction

No subsequent Ming emperor attempted to emulate Yongle's ambitious project, but emperors of the early Qing dynasty (1644–1912) did. The Kangxi emperor (reigned 1662–1722) ordered two ambitious encyclopedic projects, although neither attained the scope of the *Yongle dadian*. In the late eighteenth century the Qianlong emperor (reigned 1736–1795) ordered his officials to comb through Yongle's encyclopedia to reconstruct texts that had been lost in the intervening centuries. Several hundred previously missing works were partially or completely reconstructed.

In 1900 the *Yongle dadian* was located in the scholarly halls of the Hanlin Academy near the British Legation and other foreign embassies. That summer as Western armies battled against Chinese forces of the Boxer Rebellion, the buildings of the academy caught on fire, destroying most of the library and nearly all of the *Yongle dadian*. Approximately 400 of the original 11,095 volumes survived. In the ensuing chaotic years individual pages and volumes of the encyclopedia found their way into private hands, and many were eventually acquired by foreigners. Hence, many of the surviving sections of the *Yongle dadian* are now held outside of China in Europe, the United States, and Japan. (Russia and East Germany returned their volumes in the 1950s.) Two hundred twenty-one of the surviving volumes are currently held in China, sixty of which are in Taiwan.

Various portions of the surviving volumes have been reprinted in modern editions. Several scholars have called for a return of the original volumes of the *Yongle dadian* to China, arguing that with the reprinted editions now available to researchers, there is no reason not to return the originals to their country of origin. In 2001 the National Central Library in Beijing began to digitize the entire surviving corpus of the encyclopedia, calling for the cooperation of holders of volumes around the globe.

Peter B. DITMANSON

Further Reading

Gu Liren 顧力仁. (1985). Yongle Dadian *ji qi jiyi shu yanjiu* 永樂大典及其輯佚書研究 [The *Yongle dian* and its compilation and loss]. Taipei, Taiwan: Wenshizhe Press.

Perseverance can reduce an iron rod to a sewing needle.

铁 杵 磨 成 针

Tiě chǔ mó chéng zhēn

Yongle, Emperor (ZHU Di)

Yŏnglè Huángdì (Zhū Dì) 永乐皇帝（朱棣）

1360–1424   Ming dynasty emperor

Zhu Di 朱棣, son of the founder of the Ming 明 dynasty, usurped the throne from his nephew in 1402 to become the Yongle 永樂 emperor. During his reign he extended the power and influence of the dynasty, commissioned naval expeditions to the Indian Ocean, moved the imperial capital to Beijing 北京, and oversaw important scholarly enterprises.

Zhu Di (reigned 1402–1424) was the son of the Hongwu emperor (reigned 1368–1398), who founded the Ming dynasty (1368–1644). Zhu, usurping the throne from his nephew, the Jianwen emperor (reigned 1398–1402), became one of the most powerful and effective emperors of the dynasty. Under his reign the empire became stabilized after the tumultuous early years of the dynasty. As a powerful military leader, Zhu Di oversaw the consolidation and expansion of Ming power.

Zhu Di claimed to be the fourth son of the founder by his primary wife, Empress Ma (1332–1382). Some later sources rumored that Zhu Di was a son by a concubine, perhaps from Korea or Mongolia. As a youth, Zhu Di was known for his military prowess, and his father entrusted him with the strategic northern fiefdom of Yan, the ancient name for the Beijing region. Zhu Di took up his post as the prince of Yan in 1380 when he was twenty years old, participating in successful military campaigns against the Mongols in 1381, 1390, and 1396.

In 1399, suspicious of the Jianwen emperor and covetous of the throne, the prince of Yan launched a civil war

against his nephew. He claimed that the court had fallen prey to evil advisors and that his intervention to "quell the difficulties" was in accord with the wishes of the founder. Zhu Di's superior military leadership and well-trained troops defeated the imperial forces, leading to the capture

---

Portrait of the Yongle Emperor Zhu Di, founder of the Ming dynasty. Ink and color on silk, by an anonymous painter.

Yongle's Preface to the *Great Compendium of the Yongle Reign* (Yongle dadian)

The Yongle emperor was so pleased with the compilation of material in this 11,095-volume encyclopedia that he gave it the eponymous title Great Compendium of the Yongle Reign. *To confirm that he was the driving force behind this historical enterprise, Yongle wrote a lengthy preface.*

Ever since I succeeded to my father's throne, I have thought about writing and publication as a means of unifying confusing systems and standardizing government regulations and social customs. But it is indeed very difficult to write introductions to the biographies of hundreds of rulers, to summarize classics from every dynasty, to record continuing events of so many centuries, and to simplify and edit so many complex topics . . . Undertaking such a task is like sifting gold from sand or searching for pearls from the sea. Nevertheless, I ordered my literati-officials to compile The Four Treasuries, to purchase lost books from the four corners of the country, to search and to collect whatever [works] they could find, to assemble and classify them according to both topical and phonetic order, and to make them into enduring classics. The fruit of their labor is this encyclopedia, which includes the breadth of the universe and all the texts from antiquity to the present time, whether they are big or small, polished or crude . . .

Source: Shih-Shan Henry Tsai. (2001). *Perpetual happiness: The Ming emperor Yongle.* Seattle: University of Washington Press, 133–134.

of Nanjing, where the Jianwen emperor apparently died in the burning palace (although rumors persisted that he had miraculously escaped).

After the bloody civil war Zhu Di ascended the throne, declaring his reign "Yongle" (Everlasting Happiness). Seeking to consolidate his rule and restore order to the realm, he restored the civil service examination system and recruited large numbers of scholars to work on several ambitious literary projects, including the giant encyclopedia, the *Yongle dadian* (*Great Compendium of the Yongle Reign*), comprehensive editions of the Confucian canon (the Five Classics and the Four Books), a large anthology of neo-Confucian terms and teachings, and the entire Buddhist canon (the Tripitaka).

The Yongle emperor had grand imperial pretensions far beyond those of his predecessors. He launched military campaigns against the Mongols to the north and affirmed the northern power of the dynasty by moving the imperial capital from Nanjing to Beijing, where he built an imposing imperial complex (the Forbidden City). To the south he sought to extend Ming military and political control over Vietnam. His most celebrated initiative was the series of voyages in the Indian Ocean from 1405 to 1433, led by the eunuch Zheng He. These expeditions asserted Ming military and economic power as far as the Persian Gulf and the coast of Africa.

Upon his death in 1424 Zhu Di was canonized with the posthumous title of Taizong (Grand Ancestor), a standard title for the second emperor of a dynasty, once again officially bypassing the Jianwen reign. In 1537 the Jiajing emperor (1521–1567) changed Zhu's posthumous title to Chengzu (Accomplished Progenitor) in recognition of his importance in the consolidation of the dynasty.

Peter B. DITMANSON

Further Reading

Shih-shan Henry Tsai. (2001). *Perpetual happiness: The Ming Emperor Yongle.* Seattle: University of Washington Press.

Shang Chuan 商傳. (1989). *Yongle huangdi* 永樂皇帝. Beijing: Beijing Publishing.

Comprehensive index starts
in volume 5, page 2667.

Yu Boya and Zhong Ziqi

Yú Bóya hé Zhōng Zǐqī 俞伯牙和钟子期

The Chinese call a close, sympathetic friend *zhiyin* (knowing the sound) or "one who truly appreciates the tune played by another." This is an allusion to a legend about two friends named Yu Boya and Zhong Ziqi.

Yu Boya refers to the actual famed musician Bo Ya who lived in the State of Chu during the Spring and Autumn Period (770–476 BCE). He demonstrated a great musical talent at an early age and later became a student of a great master *zheng* player named Cheng Lian. *Zheng* is a traditional Chinese stringed instrument of the zither family. Even though he excelled at all the techniques Master Cheng could teach him, Yu Boya was still unsatisfied, because he felt unable to express his feelings when he played. Seeing this, Cheng Lian offered to take him to his own master, who lived on an island in the East China Sea. Once there, Cheng Lian asked Yu Boya to wait for his master; he promised to pick up Yu Boya when he was done. Days passed, however, without a sign of either Cheng Lian or Cheng's master. Now Yu Boya's only companions were the birds singing in the forest. Their

This man plays a *zheng*, the instrument Yu Boya played to his friend Zhong Ziqi during the Spring and Autumn period (770–476 BCE). PHOTO BY PAUL AND BERNICE NOLL.

After the death of his friend Zhong Ziqi, Yu Boya never plucked the strings of his *zheng* again.

songs, with the backdrop of the pounding waves, sounded as melancholy as he felt. This struck a chord in his heart; with a sigh, Yu Boya began to pluck his *zheng,* and it produced the soul-stirring music he had been seeking all along. In fact, this was just what Master Cheng Lian had planned. Later, people observed that Yu Boya played so well that "even horses eating at their troughs would raise their heads and listen" (Zhu, 1998). Nevertheless, he still was not satisfied because he felt that no one really understood the beautiful music he could play.

One day, Yu Boya was traveling on a riverboat when it began to rain. He had to seek shelter at the foot of a mountain. Watching the downpour as it beat on the heaving waters of the river, Yu Boya felt the urge to play a tune in response. He was indulging himself with the emotions that his beautiful music had created when a string on his *zheng* snapped. Yu Boya raised his head and caught sight of a woodchopper sitting on the bank. The man, Zhong Ziqi by name, had been listening to Yu's music so attentively

that he was even oblivious of the rain. Deeply touched, Yu Boya invited Zhong Ziqi to his boat so he could share his music with him. As soon as Yu Boya finished a tune he had named in his own mind "High Mountains," Zhong Ziqi told him, unaware of Yu Boya's unstated title for the song, that the melody painted a picture of unbroken mountain ranges in his mind. Then, after Yu Boya performed another tune he intended to call "Flowing Waters," Zhong Ziqi commented that it seemed as if he had heard the torrent of the Yangzi (Chang) River while listening to the song. Seeing his *zhiyin* in front of him, Yu Boya's joy was boundless. Instantly they became avowed friends. Before parting, they agreed to meet again in the near future.

A few years later, Yu Boya decided to pay Zhong Ziqi a visit. Unfortunately, when he arrived at his home, he learned that Zhong Ziqi had already passed away. Yu Boya was filled with sorrow, lamenting that no one in this world would ever appreciate his music like Zhong Ziqi. Rushing to his friend's tomb, Yu Boya knelt down and started playing his *zheng.* Then, rising slowly, he crashed it to the ground. After that day, not a single tune ever came out of Yu Boya's skillful hands again.

Haiwang YUAN

Further Reading

He Lifang. (1995). *A tune of Guangdong opera Boya smashing the qin.* Guangzhou, China: Zhongguo chang pian Guangzhou gong si.

Mann, S. (2000) The male bond in Chinese history and culture. *The American Historical Review 105,5.* Retrieved October 29, 2008, from http://historycooperativepress.uiuc.edu/journals/ahr/105.5/ah001600.html

Zhu Guanfa. (1998). *Zhongguo gu dai quan xue ming pian xuan zhu (Translation and annotation of selected masterpieces on the encouragement of learning).* Shanghai: Fudan da xue chubanshe.

Yuan Drama

Yuán Cháo zájù　元朝杂剧

Growing out of a largely anonymous performance and ritual tradition of the Song and Jin periods, Yuan drama matured into a recognizable artistic form. During this first golden age of Chinese song-drama (1279–1368), individual actresses and actors, playwrights, and critics perfected performance conventions, scripts, and aesthetic criteria.

The Yuan dynasty (1279–1368) is generally regarded as the first golden age of traditional Chinese song-drama, particularly with regard to the theatrical form commonly known as "Northern-style *zaju* drama." Drama became significant enough as an aesthetic form for urban communities and their participants—authors, performers, critics, patrons—to acknowledge their contributions to the world of theater. The names of approximately one hundred *zaju* authors and the titles of more than six hundred plays attributed to them are known to us today. Similarly, the names, and in some rare cases the likenesses of individual *zaju* actors and actresses, have been transmitted through visual, poetic, and documentary sources produced by patrons, scholar-officials, other playwrights, and drama connoisseurs. In addition, a number of critics developed explicit formal criteria to evaluate the authors, the performers, and the stylistic characteristics of song-drama as well as the musically related form known as *sanqu* songs. Finally, the libretti of at least thirty *zaju* song-dramas were considered aesthetically important and linguistically demanding enough to be printed

as early as the first half of the fourteenth century, thus providing us with some of the earliest texts in the Asian theatrical repertoire.

History of the Form

All the impressive firsts of Yuan dynasty *zaju* notwithstanding, *zaju* evolved over the course of at least two hundred years before becoming a literary medium for playwrights and a star vehicle for performers. In the mid-twelfth century contemporary observers reminisced about the large commercial theaters operating in the capital of the Northern Song dynasty (960–1126), Kaifeng (modern Kaifeng), where comic duos (*fumo* and *fujing*) together with a leading man (*moni*) and an official (*zhuanggu*) role type offered humorous fare then known as "variety plays" (*zaju*). These same diarists also mentioned that various entertainments were enacted on permanent open-air stages attached to temples as well as on temporary stages erected for particular holidays. In the context of a Buddhist-inspired All Souls Festival the title of a particular *zaju* play, the Buddhist salvation story of *Mulian Rescues His Mother* [*from Hell*], first appeared. The tale was subsequently adopted into the Yuan *zaju* repertoire and remains a staple of certain regional operas to this day.

When in the 1130s the Jurchen Jin dynasty (1125–1234) assumed control over the heartland of early *zaju* performances (modern-day Henan, Shanxi, and Shaanxi provinces), the development of *zaju* continued unabated, partly because Jurchens had a strong song-and-dance tradition of their own and partly because the Jin court selectively

The last section from the Yuan drama *The Story of the Western Wing,* by playwright Wang Shifu. Calligraphy by Wang Cheng (1494–1533).

adopted Song institutions as well as Chinese literary culture more generally. Not only do later lists of comic skits about everyday life and of stories about historical figures, romance, and religions suggest a rich urban repertoire performed in the new capital of Yanjing (present-day Beijing), but also Jin dynasty stages found in smaller towns around Henan, Shanxi, and Shaanxi provinces suggest that *zaju* performance was a common feature of rural life. Furthermore, judging both from extant stages and from the replicas of stages and performers unearthed from Jin dynasty tombs, conventions of *zaju* performance were moving toward a specialized theatrical stage and the role system of a main female or male lead (*zhengdan* and *zhengmo*), both of which would become hallmarks of mature Yuan drama. Moreover, the popularity of the musically innovative Jin dynasty *chantefable* genre known as

"All Keys and Modes" (*zhugongdiao*) coincided with the final stage of the maturation of Yuan drama. Rather than simply repeating identical tunes patterns, "All Keys and Modes" welded together several melodies into song-sets, a feature that would be developed into song-suites set to different musical modes in Yuan *zaju* plays.

The Mongol defeat of the Jin in 1233 and of the Southern Song dynasty (1127–1279) did not disrupt but rather furthered the evolution of song-drama in the old capitals as well as the hinterland. The new Yuan capital, Dadu (modern Beijing), was located in the same city as the Jurchen capital of Yanjing. Not surprisingly perhaps, Dadu was the initial urban epicenter of the synthesis of the theatrical, musical, and authorial developments begun under the Song and the Jin dynasties. Most of the early dramatists hailed from Dadu, including the reputed progenitor of the genre of Yuan *zaju*, Guan Hanqing. However, the move of the Song court to Lin'an (modern-day Hangzhou), the capital of the Southern Song dynasty, had helped old-style *zaju* find a new home in the south in the 1100s, and hence mature Yuan *zaju* quickly took hold in the former Southern Song capital as well, with many of the later Yuan dramatists such as Zheng Guangzu being active in Hangzhou.

Form of Yuan Zaju Song-Drama

In its mature form Yuan *zaju* typically consisted of a melodic sequence of songs set to different musical modes, which musically delineated four distinct acts. Occasionally the four-act format was expanded with short melodic prologues or interludes known as "wedges." In rare cases such as the cross-culturally famous *The Orphan of the House of Zhao* (*Zhaoshi gu'er*), Yuan *zaju* were comprised of five rather than the standard four acts. With five books consisting of four acts each, the famous love comedy *The Story of the Western Wing* (*Xixiang ji*) adhered to the conventions of both the short *zaju* and the much longer *chuanqi* form. In general, each song-suite accommodated different sets of melodies, which were said to have connoted different emotive timbres. All songs were sung by a single role type, the main female (*zhengdan*) or male lead (*zhengmo*), the story's central locus of emotion. In most cases a single character occupied that role type, but in rare instances two characters assumed the role of the singing lead. In the exceptional *The Story of the Western Wing*, a set of four acts was principally sung by the same role, but the lead role varied across the five books of the play.

The arias alternated with dialogue spoken by all parties. The language of the arias blended both classical

Illustration for *The Story of the Western Wing*, a Yuan period play. Ink and color on silk, by Qiu Ying (active painter c. 1522–1560).

allusions and colloquial elements, which earned the genre the characterization of "being neither excessively formal nor vulgar" (*buwen busu*). In Yuan-printed texts the dialogue was sketchy rather than fully elaborated, implying that performers may have improvised those segments or that audiences needed no reading aids to follow the spoken parts. By contrast, extant Ming dynasty (1368–1644) versions of Yuan drama greatly expanded the dialogue and added set poetic recitation pieces. In *Selections of Yuan Plays* (*Yuanqu xuan,* also known as *One Hundred Yuan Plays, Yuanren baizhong qu,* 1615/16), Zang Maoxun (1550–1620) fleshed out the dialogue and edited the arias to create the definitive reading text for "Yuan drama." Cleverly claiming that the Yuan court selected the highest echelon of examination candidates through the writing of arias, Zang provided a new sheen of literary respectability for song-drama in general.

Authors and Themes

The bulk of individually attributable Chinese literature written prior to the Yuan dynasty originated with scholar-officials or aristocrats. By contrast, Yuan *zaju* was the first major body of Chinese texts to have been primarily written by relatively well-educated professional authors. Zhou Deqing (flourished 1330), the most influential contemporaneous critic, singled out Guan Hanqing, Zheng Guangzu, Bai Pu, and Ma Zhiyuan as particularly accomplished, a judgment that, with the addition of Wang Shifu, has largely withstood the vagaries of time.

Within a corpus of more than sixty known titles, Guan Hanqing was, despite the uncorroborated claim to a minor post, the professional author par excellence. The subject matter of his plays ranged widely, covering all social registers and moving from uproarious comedy to deeply felt grief. Guan's plays reworked both well-known and untapped tales about lovelorn emperors and heartbroken consorts; turned biographical bits about generals, scholar-officials, and young girls into alternately heartrending and didactic stories such as *The Jade Mirror Stand* (*Yujingtai*); adapted episodes from the well-known *The Records of the Three Kingdoms* to turn them into heroic or melancholy pieces; fashioned innovative romantic plots with few or no known precedents into vehicles for clever courtesans, maids, and widows such as *Rescuing a Coquette* (*Jiufengchen*). In the Yuan dynasty other playwrights adopted the nicknames "Little Hanqing" and "Southern Hanqing," attesting to Guan Hanqing's standing as Yuan *zaju*'s foundational author. In the twentieth century *The Injustice to Dou E* (*Dou E yuan*) was singled out and came to exemplify Guan's excellence as a writer of the then newly sinicized genre of tragedy.

Pai Pu (1226–c. 1280) ranked among the few known literati authors of Yuan drama. Hailing from Shanxi Province, Pai Pu's father, Bai Hua, had passed the highest examinations during the Jin dynasty, an honor that earned him a biography in the official *History of the Jin.* After the fall of the dynasty the family fell on hard times but eventually settled in Nanjing. Bai's song lyrics alluded to his longing for the old dynasty; given the extant attributions, his plays for the most part dealt with romance. Most famous among these was *Rain on the Pawlownia Tree* (*Wutongyu*), one of the few extant song-dramas that survived the Ming dynasty prohibition on the imperial figures in *zaju* texts and performance. *Rain* empathetically told the well-known story of Tang emperor Xuanzong's loss of his favorite consort, Yang Guifei, to political necessity from the point of view of the heartbroken emperor.

A native of Dadu, Ma Zhiyuan, may have served as a minor functionary, according to one source, but according to another, he was a member of a professional writing association. The rather bleak outlook of his songs and of his plays certainly seemed in tune with the often resentfully satirical tone associated with the Southern *xiwen* plays produced by writing guilds. Ma adapted famous episodes from the dynastic histories and from the annals of poetry to conjure melancholy meditations on loss, most notably in *Autumn in the Han Palace* (*Hanqongqiu*) and *Tears on the Official's Gown* (*Qingshan lei*). Ma is equally well known for his Dao-inspired deliverance plays that tout the rewards of renunciation in the face of an intractable and futile quest for success. Ma adopted the official patriarch of a newly popular school of Quanzhen Daoism, Lü Dongbin, as the hero of two of his deliverance plays, *The Yueyang Tower* (*Yueyanglou*) and *The Yellow Millet Dream* (*Huangliangmeng*).

Another native of Dadu, Wang Shifu, made his name largely as the author of *The Story of the Western Wing* (*Xixiang ji*), the most widely reproduced love comedy in the Chinese corpus. When literary critic Jin Shengtan (1608–1661) created an alternative, quasi-modern canon of six literary works called "books of genius," he included a highly idiosyncratic version of Wang's *Story* as the "Sixth Book of Genius." The many successive reprints and versions of Jin's version of *The Story of the Western Wing*, together with Zang Maoxun's *One Hundred Yuan Plays*, ensured that Yuan *zaju* continued to be widely disseminated as reading material long after the end of the Yuan dynasty.

Modern Impact

Although the musical form of Yuan *zaju* drama gradually died out in the sixteenth century, Ming dynasty playwrights such as Tang Xianzu (1550–1616) drew ideas from Yuan drama, and many of the stories from the Yuan corpus, such as *The Butterfly Lovers*, found their way into the regional operas of the Qing dynasty (1644–1912). Among the earliest Chinese dramatic forms to be introduced to Japan, *Xixiang ji* was translated into Japanese in the early 1800s. European translations of Yuan *zaju* plays inspired famous plays by the French writer Voltaire (1694–1778) and the German dramatist Bertolt Brecht (1898–1956).

Because of the modern academic study of Yuan drama by influential scholars such as Wang Guowei (1877–1927) and Wu Mei (1883–1939), many important modern Chinese playwrights such as Guo Moruo (1892–1978) and Tian Han (1898–1968) seized upon plays in Zang Maoxun's anthology and other Yuan dramas to address modern cultural concerns such as marriage reform. More recently other Chinese playwrights have staged Chinese and Western versions of Yuan drama side-by-side to offer political commentary. Thus, the legacy of Yuan drama continues to evolve at the crossroads of Chinese and world theater.

Patricia SIEBER

Further Reading

Shih Chung-wen. (1976). *The golden age of Chinese drama, Yuan tsa-chu*. Princeton: Princeton University Press.

Sieber, P. (2003). *Theaters of desire: Authors, readers, and the reproduction of early Chinese Song-drama, 1300-2000*. New York: Palgrave Macmillan.

West, S. H. (Ed.), & Idema, W. L. (Trans.). (1995). *The story of the western wing*. Berkeley and Los Angeles: University of California Press.

Play a harp before a cow.

对 牛 弹 琴

Duì niú tán qín

Yuan Dynasty

Yuán Cháo　元朝

1279–1368

**In the late thirteenth century the Mongols, no-
madic invaders from Central Asia, conquered
China. During their rule as the Yuan dynasty
the Mongols borrowed extensively from other
traditions, creating a uniquely multicultural
political and cultural environment. While
many aspects of Mongolian rule over China
vanished with the dynasty in 1368, some political, military and social features survived and
influenced succeeding dynasties.**

The Yuan dynasty (1279–1368) marked the first era in
Chinese history in which Central Asian invaders
succeeded in conquering all of China territorially.
Mongolian tribes, reorganized into military units by the
famed conqueror Chinggis Khan (also known as Genghis
Khan, 1162–1227), descended upon China in repeated campaigns from the early years of the thirteenth century until
the conquest process ended with the collapse of the Southern Song dynasty (1127–1279) under Chinggis's grandson,
Khubilai Khan (1215–1294). North China had been ruled by
other invaders from the north (first the Khitans, then the
Jurchens) from 916 to 1234, but the Mongols were the first
outsiders to conquer and reunify all of China.

After Chinggis Khan's death, his heirs carved out separate imperial domains (khanates) that, while connected
by trade and diplomacy, evolved into independent geopolitical units. In addition to the Yuan dynasty in China,
these units consisted of the Il-Khan dynasty in Persia,
the Golden Horde in Russia, and the Chagatai khanate
in Central Asia. The Yuan dynasty in China was directly
ruled by a branch of Chinggis Khan's descendants who
were based in the Yuan capital city of Daidu (modern
Beijing). As such, the Yuan dynasty was an independent
polity that was governed quite differently from the other
Mongolian-ruled polities in Eurasia.

The Mongols as Rulers of China

After the fall of the Yuan dynasty the new Ming rulers of
China castigated the Mongols for their inattention to the
welfare of the people and for their abuses of privilege. The
Mongols, in fact, did rule China differently than previous
dynasties had. As a pastoral nomadic people, they relied on
their traditional emphasis on military values and hereditary transmission of office. Yet the Mongols also adapted
many preexisting Chinese institutions to facilitate their
rule. The structure of the Yuan civilian bureaucracy fit the
traditional Chinese mold to a high degree, but the fact that
Mongols and Western and Central Asians (Turks, Uygurs,
Persians, and others) held the higher-level positions meant
that many Chinese scholars, accustomed to the status derived from government service, felt disenfranchised.

The Yuan rulers did not allow the traditional Chinese
civil examination system, which had determined who entered into the civilian bureaucracy in previous centuries,
to function until 1315; even then it was a minor source of
recruitment. The Mongolian emphasis on heredity and
the primacy given to the military sphere over the civilian

Gateway called Kuo-chieh-t'a ("Tower which Bestrides the Road," also known as the "Cloud Terrace"), in Hebei Province. Inscribed with date corresponding to 1345, during the Yuan dynasty. PHOTO BY JOAN LEBOLD COHEN.

sphere made government service less accessible and even unpalatable for many Chinese.

However, the Chinese viewed the Yuan dynasty as a legitimate dynasty that had won the Mandate of Heaven and had reunified the empire. Khubilai Khan was largely responsible for winning Chinese acceptance of Mongolian rule. In 1272, Khubilai gave the dynasty its Chinese name, Yuan, and employed several prominent Chinese scholars as advisers at his court in Daidu (Dadu). Khubilai also selected this site (modern-day Beijing) in 1260 as the dynasty's capital, thereby moving the symbolic center of Mongolian rule from Mongolia into China proper.

Khubilai also employed Tibetan Buddhist monks and Central Asian Muslim financiers as his court advisers. A multiethnic, multilingual entourage gave the Yuan court a cosmopolitan aura. Yet, from the point of view of contemporary Chinese observers, the Tibetans at the Yuan court were seen as arrogantly interfering with the administration of justice and claiming privileged status for themselves; Muslim financial advisers were criticized for imposing too severe a tax burden on the Chinese people and were accused of usury and embezzlement. While such criticisms may have been exacerbated by the factions at the Yuan court, it is true that the Tibetans and Central Asians rarely displayed any philosophical interest in Confucianism and its values of frugality and loyal, selfless service to one's ruler. Tensions ran high among the different ethnic groups that served the Yuan court during Khubilai's reign and in later Yuan times.

Culture and Society

Blocked from government service and alienated from their Mongolian rulers, some Chinese literati turned to the arts as an outlet for their untapped energies and talents. Popular drama, a genre that had existed in China for at least two centuries prior to the Mongolian invasion, benefited from the elite's participation in the writing of new plays. Displaced from their usual roles as scholar-officials, the Chinese elite developed Yuan drama, known as *zaju*, which exposed social problems of the era, thus allowing modern readers precious insights into everyday life. At least 160 Yuan plays are extant. The Yuan era also produced many great Chinese painters, some of whom, like Zhao Mengfu (1254–1322), served the Yuan court in official capacities. Since the Yuan rulers for the most part did not scrutinize or censor artistic themes, Chinese painting of this era flourished both stylistically and thematically, one example being the new focus on horse painting.

While Confucianism as a philosophy and way of life was never directly threatened with suppression by the Mongolian rulers of China, competing philosophies were encouraged in the Yuan period. Uygurs reintroduced Islam, Tibetans promoted Buddhism, and Central Asian monks revived Nestorian Christianity. The Mongol rulers practiced religious toleration in China and elsewhere throughout Eurasia; they exempted the clergy of all religions from taxation and from military conscription. As long as clerics did not foment or support anti-Mongolian sentiments, their churches, temples, and mosques were left untouched. In spite of the coexistence of a variety of religions in China in the thirteenth and fourteenth centuries, however, the Chinese elite remained strongly bonded to their own Confucian tradition. Overall during the Yuan, Confucianism, Daoism, Buddhism, Islam, and the Mongols' own shamanistic beliefs managed to weather the inevitable strains and mutual antagonisms of a multiethnic empire, giving the Yuan a rather unique cultural profile in Chinese history.

Trade, Transport, and the Economy

The Mongols, like other pastoral nomadic peoples of Eurasia, saw trade with neighboring sedentary peoples as an acceptable method to obtain needed goods to supplement the products of their own economy. Trade and raids coexisted in the frontier history of China and Central Asia. Chinggis Khan had employed Muslim merchants in long-distance trading ventures as early as 1218 in western Central Asia. By the generation of his grandson, Khubilai, the Yuan imperial family was experienced in world trade. Investing silver in Central Asian Muslim merchant companies that financed trade caravans to distant lands and loaned funds within China at usurious rates, Khubilai and his successors reaped enormous profits. Maritime trade also flourished in Yuan times, and the government treasury was enriched by trade taxes.

Within China itself, trade and communications were facilitated by the more than 1,400 government postal stations which allowed authorized officials and merchants to cover great distances in a short span of time, with fresh mounts supplied at each station. Using some 3 million conscripted laborers and an enormous expenditure of government funds, Khubilai Khan extended the Grand Canal so that grain from the Yangzi (Chang) River region could be shipped north to the Yuan capital at Daidu. Both land and inland waterway transport routes were improved in the Yuan era.

Paper currency had been in circulation to varying degrees in China before the Yuan dynasty, but during Khubilai Khan's reign it became more widespread than ever. Taxes were paid in paper money, and merchants saw the advantages of the new currency. The Yuan court, however, never completely resisted the temptation to print more money when revenue demands generated by military campaigns of expansion and by fiscal mismanagement arose. Ultimately, inflation was one of the economic factors that contributed to the collapse of the dynasty in 1368.

Decline

During Khubilai's reign, the Mongols continued their campaigns outward from China, successfully subjugating Korea. Their naval attacks upon Japan in 1274 and 1281, however, were defeated. Mongolian military expeditions into Southeast Asia in the 1270s and 1280s also met stiff resistance. After Khubilai's reign, the Yuan rulers abandoned further expansionist campaigns. The dynasty fell into decline during the course of the fourteenth century because the once-powerful military could not suppress widespread popular revolts after 1350. The last decades of the Yuan dynasty were marred by major floods, droughts, and epidemics, creating a confluence of natural disasters that would have undermined any dynasty, whether foreign or Chinese in origin. The Mongols fled their capital city of Daidu and returned to Mongolia in 1368, escaping before the arrival of the armies of Zhu Yuanzhang, a rebel leader who founded the Ming dynasty (1368–1644). Although a short-lived dynasty, the Yuan left a strong imprint upon Chinese society, military practices, and politics as evidenced by the post-Yuan continuation of hereditary household occupational registration, the continuation of aspects of military organization, and ultimately an expanded notion of what constituted "China" territorially.

Elizabeth ENDICOTT

Further Reading

Franke, H. & Twitchett, D. (Eds.). (1994). *The Cambridge history of China. Volume 6. Alien regimes and border states.* Cambridge, U.K.: Cambridge University Press.

Langlois, J. D., Jr. (Ed.) (1981). *China under Mongol rule.* Princeton, NJ: Princeton University Press.

Latham, R. (Trans.) (1980). *The travels of Marco Polo.* New York: Penguin.

Rossabi, M. (1988). *Khubilai Khan. His life and times.* Berkeley and Los Angeles: University of California Press.

Ruthlessness is key to a man's accomplishment.

无 毒 不 丈 夫

Wú dú bú zhàng fu

YUAN Shikai

Yuán Shìkǎi 袁世凯

1859–1916   *First president of the Chinese Republic*

Yuan Shikai became the first president of the Chinese Republic in 1913 at the behest of both the Qing court and the provisional government. By 1915 he had become the supreme dictator, dissolving parliament and outlawing the Nationalist Party. But for rebellion in the southern provinces, Yuan would have had himself declared emperor before his death in 1916.

Yuan Shikai 袁世凯 was born in 1859 in Xiangcheng, Henan Province, and was adopted. He joined the Qing army in 1880, and from 1885 to 1894 he was the Chinese commissioner of commerce in Korea. He was appointed governor of Shandong Province in 1899, where he suppressed the Boxer Rebellion. In 1901 Yuan Shikai was made governor-general of Zhili Province and the high commissioner for the Northern Ocean (Beiyang Dachen), a position which put him in charge of foreign and military affairs in North China. He directed various reform programs from 1901 to 1908, including the establishment of a modern army, the creation of military schools, the organization of the police system, and the inauguration of modern industry.

With the outbreak of the revolution in 1911, Yuan was placed in charge of the Imperial troops and of negotiations with the revolutionaries, a position of immense military power. He used his position to promote his own interests by clever manipulation of the negotiations, and, as a result, both the Qing court and the provisional government of the Chinese Republic appointed Yuan the president of the first Chinese Republic in February 1912. He assumed

Yuan Shikai, first president of the Republic of China, 1915. HARRIS & EWING COLLECTION, LIBRARY OF CONGRESS PRINTS AND PHOTOGRAPHS DIVISION WASHINGTON, D.C.

the formal presidency in 1913, and in the next two years he outlawed the Nationalist Party, dissolved the parliament, and attained dictatorial control. Yuan prepared to assume the title of emperor in late 1915, announcing that his imperial title, Hong Xian, would be used beginning 1 January

2603

Yuan Shikai's Work

Of the many reform programs led by Yuan Shikai, the reorganization of the indigenous banking industry in Tianjin proved to be particularly difficult, though successful in the end.

When Yuan Shikai took over administration of Tianjin from the foreigners in 1902, he immediately moved to prohibit the discounting of paper currency issued by indigenous banks. This resulted in a second round of failures. Between 1900 and 1902, 90 percent of Tianjin's three hundred indigenous banks closed. With the indigenous bank industry in ruins, Yuan was left with the task of creating his own financial institutions. Together with Zhou Xuexi and Sun Duoxin, Yuan founded the Tianjin Mint (Yinyuan Ju), which turned out a new eight of copper coin based on the yuan, not the tael. Machine-minted, the new copper coins were difficult to forge or debase, and thus found wide acceptance, making a substantial profit.

Source: Sheehan, B. (2003). *Trust in troubled times.* Cambridge, MA: Harvard University Press, 33.

1916. But southern provinces rebelled, and the ceremony was cancelled. He died of natural causes on 6 June 1916. Yuan Shikai's military might and political prowess during the formative transition between the Qing dynasty and the Republic of China have established his sometimes controversial position in Chinese history.

CHEN Shiwei

Further Reading

Mackinnon, S. (1980). *Power and politics in late Imperial China: Yuan Shi-kai in Beijing and Tianjin, 1901–1908.* Berkeley and Los Angeles: University of California Press.

Young, E. (1977). *The presidency of Yuan Shih-k'ai: Liberalism and dictatorship in early Republican China.* Ann Arbor: University of Michigan Press.

Yuanming Yuan, Ruins of

Yuánmíngyuán fèixū　圆明园废墟

A famous imperial park outside of Beijing, Yuanming Yuan is known for its expansive compound of gardens, lakes, and temples. While once a truly beautiful Summer Palace for the Qing court, damages incurred during the Boxer Rebellion and the Cultural Revolution have left much of Yuanming Yuan in ruins.

Thanks to its well-documented and tragic history, the Summer Palace Yuanming Yuan (Garden of Perfect Brightness) is one of the most famous imperial parks worldwide. This vast complex of gardens, lakes, pavilions, temples, and hills is located only 10 kilometers from the walls of Beijing in Haidian, in the vicinity of the prestigious Peking and Qinghua universities. Since this was the preferred residence of five Qing emperors, Chinese historians have viewed the founding, enlargement, and destruction of the palatial complex as an illustration of the growth, extravagance, and decline of the Qing dynasty (1644–1912).

The name "Summer Palace" is misleading because until 1820 the Qing court spent most of the summer away from Beijing, in the cooler hills of Chengde. Yuanming Yuan became known in Europe in 1743 when a Jesuit

The Summer Palace of Yuanming Yuan is one of the most famous imperial parks worldwide. This vast complex of gardens, lakes, pavilions, temples, and hills is located only 10 kilometers from the walls of Beijing in Haidian, in the vicinity of the prestigious Peking and Qinghua universities.

Detail of the Summer Palace of Yuanming Yuan.

missionary employed at Qianlong's court, the painter Jean-Denis Attiret, mailed an account of his visit in a letter to his correspondent in Paris. His description of the beauty of Chinese items and themes in the gardens helped change the history of landscape design and the design of contemporary European gardens. Parks in the Yuanming Yuan complex include the parks of the Kangxi emperor (1654–1722) and the Qianlong emperor (1711–1799), and Yihe Yuan (Garden of Concord and Peace), renamed by the Cixi dowager empress (1835–1908) in 1888. Xiyang Lou is a European baroque-style section that Qianlong commissioned in the northeast corner of his residence. Cixi decided to restore the western park of the Summer Palace after a French-British military expedition plundered and burnt to the ground the entire complex during the Second Opium War (1856–1960). Within its present limits, Cixi's Yihe Yuan consists of Kunming Lake and Wanshou Hill, whose massive Buddhist temple dominates the site.

The Summer Palace was further damaged during the Boxer Rebellion (1899–1901) and the Cultural Revolution (1966–1976). Kangxi and Qianlong's gardens in Yuanming Yuan have not been rebuilt because the Chinese government wants to preserve the site as a symbol of the depredations of foreign imperialism and as a reminder of the humiliations the Qing monarchs brought to China. The Summer Palace is on the United Nations Educational, Scientific, and Cultural Organization (UNESCO) World Heritage List, and the melancholic ruins and ponds of Yuanming Yuan and the placid waters of Kunming Lake in Yihe Yuan attract today nearly as many domestic and foreign tourists as the Forbidden City does.

Philippe FORÊT

Further Reading

Chiu Che Bing. (2000). *Yuanming Yuan: Le Jardin de la Clarté Parfaite* [Yuanming Yuan: The Garden of Perfect Brightness]. Paris: Les Editions de l'Imprimeur.

Malone, C. B. (1934). *History of the Peking Summer Palaces under the Ch'ing Dynasty.* Champaign: University of Illinois Press.

Wong Young-tsu. (2001). *A paradise lost: The imperial garden Yuanming Yuan.* Honolulu, HI: University of Hawaii Press.

YUNG Wing

Róng Hóng 容闳

1828–1912   Educator and diplomat

Yung Wing was the first Chinese person to graduate from an American university (Yale, class of 1854). Enthusiastic about his education, he persuaded the Qing government to send the Chinese Educational Mission to preparatory schools and colleges in the United States (1872–1881). He also championed the cause of better treatment of Chinese overseas laborers.

Yung Wing 容闳, (also known as Rong Hong) the first Chinese to graduate from a North American college (Yale, 1854), was born into a farming family in the village of Namping, Guangdong Province, now part of the south Chinese city of Zhuhai. The village was only a few miles from the Portuguese colony of Macao, and at the age of seven Yung Wing became the youngest pupil in its foreign-run school. After the First Opium War (1839–1842) the school, now the Morrison Education Society School, moved to Britain's newly acquired colony, Hong Kong. This early start gave Yung a remarkable fluency in English, part of the explanation for the achievements of his later life.

In Hong Kong, when a missionary teacher sought student volunteers to take back to the United States, Yung's autobiography recalled, "I was the first one on my feet!" (Yung 1909, 18) He sailed for the United States in January 1847, his destination being Monson Academy in Massachusetts, where he spent three years on English-language skills and the Latin, Greek, and mathematics required for college entrance. He began his freshman year at Yale in 1850.

Finances were a problem. Funding was available provided that after graduation he would return to China as a missionary, but although he had become an enthusiastic Christian, he declined, deciding: "I wanted the utmost freedom of action to avail myself of every opportunity to do the greatest good in China …. (Yung 1909, 35–36). He found others willing to help him and took paid jobs waiting tables, singing in the choir, and working in the library.

Yung Wing was so delighted with his Yale experience that he appealed to the Chinese government to replicate it for other Chinese boys. In 1871 the government organized the Chinese Educational Mission to the United States, with a preparatory school in Shanghai and competitive examinations. The plan was for students to remain in the United States for fifteen years, first studying English in southern New England homes, where they were lodged, then attending local grammar and high schools, and finally entering U.S. colleges, preferably to gain an education in technical subjects that would be useful in public service. Over the course of four years the program sent 120 boys in four groups of thirty. Although China recalled the students after only nine years, some had already received a good education. Mission members later became well known in China: One was foreign minister, another served as prime minister in the new republic, and one became the first Chinese to direct a railroad-building project in China; such projects had before than been directed by Westerners.

Midway in supervising the mission students, Yung Wing was appointed deputy at the newly opened Chinese legation in Washington, D.C. The duties of this post soon involved an investigation of the treatment of Chinese laborers in Peru and Cuba. In Peru Yung surreptitiously

2607

Photograph of Yung Wing, the first Chinese man to graduate from an American university. His positive experience at Yale spurred his later advocacy of Western education for Chinese young men.

photographed the whiplash marks on the backs of Chinese workers. The eventual report provoked China into ending the infamous coolie trade.

In 1876 Yung Wing married a U.S. citizen, Mary Louise Kellogg. They had two sons. His final years were devoted to writing his autobiography. He died in Hartford, Connecticut.

Beatrice S. BARTLETT

Further Reading

Gao Zonglu. (Trans.). (1982). *Zhongguo youtong liu Mei shi* [History of the Chinese educational mission in America]. Taipei, Taiwan: Zhuanji wenxue chubanshe.

Jeme, T. Y. (1974, October). The man who laid the tracks from Peiping to Kalgan. *Echo of Things Chinese, 4*(9), 21–33.

LaFargue, T. E. (1987). *China's first hundred: Educational mission students in the United States, 1872–1881.* Pullman: Washington State University Press. (Original work published 1942)

Leung, E. P. (1988, October). The first Chinese college graduate in America: Yung Wing and his educational experiences. *Asian Profile, 16*(5), 453–458.

Worthy, E. (1965, August). Yung Wing in America. *Pacific Historical Review, 134*(3), 265–287.

Yung Wing. (1909). *My life in China and America.* New York: Henry Holt.

Yungang Caves

Yúngǎng Shíkū 云岗石窟

The cave temples at Yungang date to the fifth and sixth centuries and are considered the earliest surviving Buddhist monuments in China. The forty-five extant caves that stretch nearly a kilometer were built between 460 and 524 CE. Work was sponsored by the Northern Wei 北魏 rulers and by local elites and officials. The largest Buddha at the site is nearly 56 feet in height.

The fifth and sixth century cave temples at Yungang are considered to be the earliest surviving Buddhist monuments in China. Located ten miles west of the present-day city of Datong (formerly the Northern Wei capital of Pingcheng), the cave temples were cut into a sandstone ridge that stretches nearly a kilometer along the Wuzhou River. The forty-five extant caves were built in three phases from 460 to 524 CE, and include both imperially-sponsored caves and those financed by local elites and court officials. The site contains thousands of carvings of Buddhist figures ranging in height from less than one inch to nearly fifty-six feet (2.5 centimeters to 17 meters).

Buddhism was adopted as the state religion by the non-Chinese Tuoba from Central Asia who ruled in north China as the Northern Wei dynasty (386–534). However, not all of the Northern Wei rulers were ardent followers of Buddhism. Taiwu Di (r. 424–452), the third emperor of the period, at first supported Buddhism, but on advice

The big statue of Buddha on the exterior of the Yungang caves. PHOTO BY JOAN LEBOLD COHEN.

Statues of Buddha in niches on the exterior of the Yungang caves. PHOTO BY JOAN LEBOLD COHEN.

from Confucian and Daoist court bureaucrats who saw the religion as a threat, instituted a severe anti-Buddhist persecution that lasted from 446 until 452.

In 460, Tanyao, a monk and the head of the Buddhist church, petitioned the emperor. Wencheng Di, to cut five large caves from the stone cliff at Yungang as an act of expiation. These caves, known today as the Tanyao Caves and numbered 16 through 20, each contain a colossal Buddha said to honor—and perhaps represent—the first five Northern Wei emperors, with the Buddha in Cave 16 representing Wencheng Di himself. These caves were made between 460 and 465 or 467. The technique of carving cave temples into cliffs has earlier precedents in India and Central Asia. Indeed, these Buddha figures are an amalgam of foreign and native styles. The colossal Buddha of

Cave 20, at 46 feet (14 meters) high, is considered to be the epitome of Northern Wei stone sculpture. These caves are simple and austere in their program of design.

A second phase of construction began around 470 and ended when emperor Xiaowu Di (reigned 471–499) moved the capital south to Luoyang. These imperially-sponsored caves are more Chinese in style. They are more elaborate, show more variation, and contain more inscriptions than the caves of phase I. The colossal Buddhas were replaced by numerous smaller figures. These included the paired caves 1 and 2, 5 and 6, 7 and 8, and 9 and 10, along with caves 11, 12, and 13. The paired caves may relate to the pairings of ruler and consort. Often the Buddha is dressed in the robes of a Chinese scholar. Xiaowen Di decreed in 486 that official court dress would be the traditional dress of the Chinese scholar class, and these Buddhas likely reflect court practice.

After the capital was moved, work continued at the site until 524. During this third phase, Caves 21 to 45 were constructed, along with a number of smaller caves and niches that stretched westward from the Tanyao Caves. With imperial patronage over, support came from local officials, and the work was done on a much smaller scale.

Over time, wind, rain, pollution, and the activities of looters have taken their toll. In 1988, researchers from the Getty Institute joined the Chinese in working to preserve the site. The cultural importance of the Buddhist Yungang caves has been recognized by UNESCO, which named Yungang a World Heritage Site in 2001.

Catherine PAGANI

Further Reading

Caswell, J. O. (1988). *Written and unwritten: A new history of the Buddhist caves at Yungang.* Vancouver: University of British Columbia Press.

Caswell, J. O. (1996 September–October). Buddhas of Cloud Hill. *Archaeology (49)*5, 60-65.

Harrington, S. P. (1996, September–October). An endangered sanctuary. *Archaeology (49)*5, 64-65.

Seiichi, M., & Nagashiro, T. (1952–1956). *Yun-kang (Unkô-sekkutsu): The Buddhist cave-temples of the fifth century A.D. in North China; A detailed report of the archaeological survey carried out by the mission of the Tohobunka Kenkyosho 1938-45.* Kyoto, Japan: Kyoto University.

Yunnan Province

Yúnnán Shěng 云南省

45.14 million est. 2007 pop.   394,000 square km

Covering an area about the size of the state of California, Yunnan Province in the south of China is a mountainous region whose climate ranges from temperate to subtropical to tropical. About a third of its over 45 million people belong to one of China's fifty-five officially recognized minority groups; twenty-two minority groups are represented, with the Yi being the largest.

The southern province of Yunnan (*Yun nan*, the cloudy south) borders in the west on Myanmar (Burma) and the Tibet (Xizang) Autonomous Region, in the north on Sichuan Province, in the east on Guizhou Province and the Guangxi Zhuang Autonomous Region, and in the south on Vietnam and Laos. The province covers 394,000 square kilometers (152,124 square miles) of mountains and plateaus. The northwestern section features the Hengduan mountain range, traversed by several big rivers and with peaks reaching over 4,000

Ho-nhi and other Tribes in the Department of Lin-ngan in S. Yun-nan (supposed to be the Anin country of Marco Polo). (From Garnier's Work

Historical illustration from an edition of *The Travels of Marco Polo*. The original caption reads: "Ho-nhi and other Tribes in the Department of Lin-ngan in S. Yun-nan (supposed to be the Anin country of Marco Polo)."

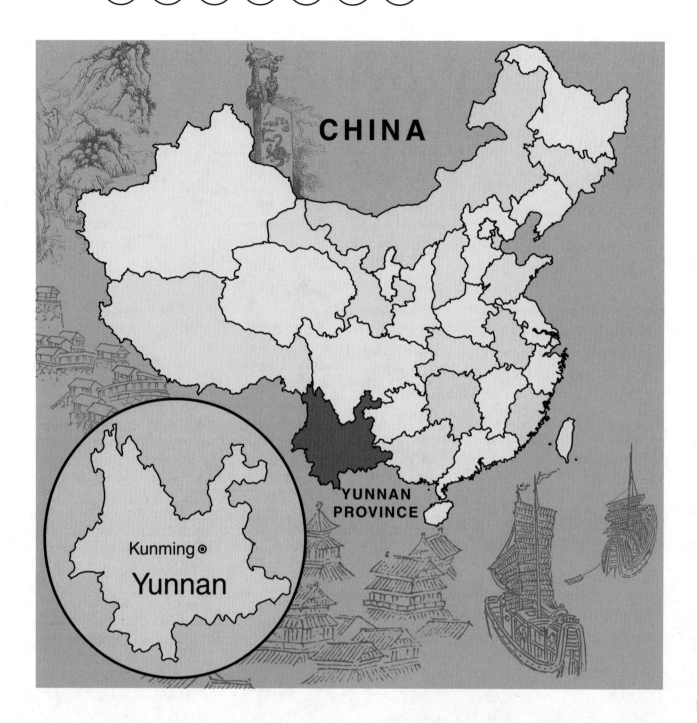

CHINA

YUNNAN PROVINCE

Kunming ◉

Yunnan

meters (13,123 feet). The eastern and southeastern sections form a lower plateau. The diversity of Yunnan's topography means there are three climate zones: temperate in the mountains and subtropic and tropic to the south. The rainy season between May and October accounts for about 80 percent of the annual precipitation, which averages above 1,000 millimeters (39 inches).

Yunnan has a population of over 45 million, of which about a third belong to twenty-two officially recognized minority peoples, the Yi being the largest. The Han Chinese, who constitute about 70 percent of the population, are mainly concentrated on the eastern plateau, where the capital, Kunming (2007 est. pop. 6.19 million), is located.

Yunnan was loosely incorporated into the Chinese Empire during the Han dynasty (206 BCE–220 CE). It was the center of the independent Nanzhao and Dali kingdoms from the eighth to the thirteenth centuries and was reincorporated as a Chinese frontier area under the Yuan dynasty (1267–1368). During the Ming dynasty (1368–1644), the Chinese government encouraged Chinese immigration into Yunnan, and during the Qing dynasty (1644–1912) the province was repeatedly the seat of rebellion against the Manchu government. In the nineteenth century British and French colonial powers in Southeast Asia extended their activities into Yunnan, and the French built a railway connecting Kunming with Vietnam. During the Japanese occupation of eastern China, the Chinese Nationalist Party (Guomindang) moved the government and various industries to the western provinces of Sichuan and Yunnan, and Yunnan became a stronghold against further Japanese advance.

Kunming developed into an important industrial center in the southwest, a position it still retains. Yunnan has one of the largest reserves of tin in the world, and the principal industries are tin and copper mining. Heavy industry, such as iron and steel works, is concentrated in the area around Kunming. The province is an important manufacturer of textiles, chemicals, processed foods, and various light industrial products, and a major producer of tea, cigarettes, and sugar.

Bent NIELSEN

Further Reading

Arvidsson, S. S. (2001). *Ethnicity and economic development in Yunnan.* Uppsala, Sweden: Uppsala University Department of Economic History.

Hall, J. C. S. (1976). *The Yunnan provincial faction, 1927–1937.* Canberra: Australian National University Department of Far Eastern History.

Hansen, M. H. (1999). *Lessons in being Chinese: Minority education and ethnic identity in southwest China.* Seattle: University of Washington Press.

Sutton, D. S. (1980). *Provincial militarism and the Chinese republic: The Yunnan army, 1905–25.* Ann Arbor: University of Michigan Press.

Wang Jianping. (1996). *Concord and conflict: The Hui communities of Yunnan society in a historical perspective.* Lund, Sweden: Lund Studies in African and Asian Religions.

Comprehensive index starts
in volume 5, page 2667.

ZENG Guofan

Zēng Guófán 曾国藩

1811–1872   Qing government official

Zeng Guofan was a leading government official during the mid-nineteenth century who initiated the decentralization of power and the rise in influence of regional officials that took place during the final decades of the Qing dynasty (1644–1912). He is best known for his role in suppressing the Taiping Rebellion (1850–1864) and for his efforts to modernize China's military and improve its industrial capabilities.

Zeng Guofan (Tseng Kuo-fan) was born in Xiangxiang, Hunan Province. He received the *jinshi* (advanced scholar) degree at the age of twenty-seven (1838) and was appointed to the prestigious Hanlin Academy in Beijing. He served on various boards in the capital during the next fourteen years and was promoted to the position of junior vice president of the Board of Ceremonies. In 1852 Zeng returned to his home province as commissioner for local defense, charged with the task of suppressing the Taiping rebels. He raised a province-wide militia, the Hunan Braves (later known as the "Hunan Army" or "Xiang Army"), personally selecting the officers and insisting on Confucian discipline among the troops. In August 1860 the emperor appointed Zeng governor-general of Jiangsu and Jiangxi provinces (*liang Jiang*) and granted him the political authority and fiscal independence he needed to coordinate the military campaign against the Taiping rebels. Together with the armies of Li Hongzhang and Zuo Zongtang, Zeng captured the city on 19 July 1864, bringing to an end the devastating rebellion. For his role in suppressing the Taiping rebels, Zeng Guofan was awarded the title of "marquis of the first class." He was the first civil official to receive this honor.

After the Taiping Rebellion Zeng returned to Nanjing to take up his post as governor-general. He initiated a number of policies aimed at inspiring obedience to local and central authorities. He opened printing offices to republish classical Confucian texts and reinstated the provincial examinations at Nanjing. In 1865 he established the Jiangnan Arsenal in Shanghai to produce modern weapons and gunboats. In addition to manufacturing rifles, ammunition, cannons, and steamships, it housed a school for training technicians and translators. In 1867 Zeng was appointed grand secretary and the next year was made governor-general of Zhili Province. In 1870 he was ordered to negotiate a settlement with the French over the Tianjin Massacre (21 June 1870). His conciliatory approach to foreign demands during these negotiations conflicted with the hard-line position of many officials in Beijing. He was replaced by Li Hongzhang and reassigned to Nanjing, where he died.

Zeng Guofan's importance in late Qing history is undeniable. He was instrumental in preserving the dynasty during the Taiping Rebellion. The reforms he enacted after the rebellion helped to stabilize and strengthen the country. His arsenals provided modern weapons

Photograph of Zeng Guofeng, a leading Qing official during the mid-nineteenth century. He is best known for suppressing the Taiping Rebellion (1850–1864) and for his efforts to stabilize and strengthen the country.

to protect the nation's sovereignty. Perhaps most significantly, however, Zeng's career symbolized a turning point in late Qing political affairs. His ability to independently raise, train, finance, and command the Hunan Army indicated a shift in power from Beijing to the provinces. From this time onward provincial officials would most often take the lead in introducing new technologies, modern industries, and advanced educational systems.

Daniel J. MEISSNER

Further Reading

Chen Qitian. (1961). *Zeng Guofan: Pioneer promoter of the steamship in China.* New York: Paragon Book Gallery.

Guo Yingjie. (2004). *Cultural nationalism in contemporary China: The search for national identity under reform.* New York: Routledge.

Hail, W. (1964). *Tseng Kuo-fan and the Taiping Rebellion: With a short sketch of his later career.* New York: Paragon Book Reprint Corp.

He Baogang. (2000). *Nationalism, national identity, and democratization in China.* New York: Ashgate.

Porter, J. (1972). *Tseng Kuo-Fan's private bureaucracy.* Berkeley and Los Angeles: University of California Press.

Make a decision when a decision is called for. Hesitation only brings disaster.

当 断 不 断

Dāng duàn bú duàn

Comprehensive index starts
in volume 5, page 2667.

ZHANG Daqian

Zhāng Dàqiān　张大千

1899–1983　Modernist painter, collector, and forger

Zhang Daqian was one of the great modernist painters of the twentieth century. Along with a mastery of styles, techniques, and innovative methods, he is also known for his convincing copies and forgeries, many of which found their way into museum and private collections. In his sixty-year career, Zhang Daqian produced around thirty thousand paintings, five thousand of which are extant.

rest of his life. He had a colorful youth: In 1916, when he was captured by bandits and held for one hundred days, Zhang managed to convince the leader to make him his

---

Drinking and Singing at the Foot of a Precipitous Mountain **was supposedly a tenth century work attributed to the painter Guan Tong, now believed to be a master forgery by Zhang Daqian. The forgery includes seals of supposed past owners to create a false history.**

Although he considered himself a traditionalist painter, Zhang Daqian was one of the great modernists of the twentieth century. He combined a mastery of a broad range of styles and techniques with innovative methods of using ink splashes and color splashes to produce bold, semiabstract compositions that also evoked works of the past. Zhang's command of the styles of the great masters also allowed him to make convincing copies and forgeries, many of which found their way into both museum and private collections. A well-traveled artist, Zhang was also a prolific one: Estimates put his total output during a sixty-year career at around thirty thousand paintings, five thousand of which are extant.

Zhang Daqian was born in Neijiang, Sichuan Province, to a large, well-to-do family. His given name was "Zhengchuan," but in 1919 a Buddhist abbot gave him the name "Dai-chien," which he preferred and used for the

Zambian collectible stamps featuring paintings by Zhang Daqian.

personal secretary. In 1917 Shang traveled to Kyoto with his brother, Shanzi, where he studied textile weaving and dyeing for two years. This time in Japan was influential for Zhang: He was introduced to Western styles of art, Japanese-style painting, Japanese woodblock prints, and Chinese works by the Southern Song dynasty (1127–1279) Zen Buddhist artists.

Upon his return to China in 1919 Zhang briefly entered a Buddhist monastery. He then studied calligraphy in Shanghai under the celebrated masters Zeng Xi and Li Ruiqing. Soon Zhang showed an impressive ability to copy the works of others. He gained a reputation for his imitations, and from 1941 to 1943 he used this talent to copy the wall paintings in the Mogao Caves at Dunhuang. With the Communist takeover of China in 1949 Zhang left for India, Hong Kong, Argentina, Brazil, the United States, and eventually Taiwan, where he retired. He never returned to China.

Zhang's best-known works are his abstract ink-splashed paintings that utilized rich, dark tones and brilliant mineral-based colors, a technique he started in the late 1950s. He poured ink and colors onto the paper or silk so that they produced random, ambiguous forms to which he added small details—a figure or a tree—to give concreteness to the painting. This combination of traditional Chinese brushwork and abstract expressionism created powerful and dramatic works unlike anything seen before. Although the splashing technique itself is quick, some paintings were years in the making because Zhang had to wait for one application of ink to dry before he could pour on another.

Zhang was also an art collector and connoisseur. He felt that in order to paint well an artist needs to copy the works of the best artists. He traveled widely, viewing paintings in private collections and acquiring works for his own. Three aspects of his career—as an innovative artist, as a connoisseur and collector of all genres of Chinese art, and as a masterful forger—were the focus of a 2008 exhibition at the Boston Museum of Fine Arts, to which Zhang, upon visiting there in 1953 and finding not a single one of his works in the museum's collection, bequeathed a painting of a mountain scene in Sichuan. One of the highlights of the exhibit was a Zhang forgery the museum acquired in 1957, believing it to be an authentic tenth-century landscape by the Five Dynasties master Guan Tong.

Upon his death in 1983 Zhang left his collection to the National Palace Museum in Taipei, Taiwan. With his innovative use of color and his firm rooting in ancient styles, Zhang Daqian is remembered as both China's last great literati artist and also as its first great abstractionist.

Catherine PAGANI

Further Reading

Fong, W. C. (2001). *Between two cultures: Late-nineteenth-and twentieth-century Chinese paintings from the Robert H. Ellsworth collection in the Metropolitan Museum of Art.* New York: Metropolitan Museum of Art.

Fu, S. C. Y. (1991). *Challenging the past: The paintings of Chang Dai-chien.* Washington, DC: Arthur M. Sackler Gallery.

Sullivan, M. (1996). *Art and artists of twentieth-century China.* Berkeley and Los Angeles: University of California Press.

Zhang Daqian: Painter, Collector, Forger. Retrieved January 7, 2009, from www.mfa.org/exhibitions/sub.asp?key=15&subkey=5340

ZHANG Yimou

Zhāng Yìmóu 张艺谋

b. 1951   Film, stage, and 2008 Olympics opening ceremonies director

Zhang Yimou is one of China's most celebrated and commercially successful film directors. His martial arts blockbusters since 2002 contrast with films from the early part of his career that focused on China's tumultuous history. An acclaimed stage director, Zhang has directed operas, ballets, folk musicals, and the spectacular opening ceremonies to the 2008 Summer Olympics in Beijing.

Born in Xi'an on November 14, 1951, Zhang Yimou has been one of China's most celebrated and commercially successful filmmakers since the 1980s. Zhang graduated from the Beijing Film Academy in 1978 and was assigned to work as a cinematographer in the Guangxi Film Studio in 1982. Founded in 1958 and located in the southwestern city of Nanning, this studio is one of the major state-owned film and television studios in China. Zhang served as the cinematographer for *Yellow Earth* (1984), which was directed by classmate Chen Kaige. The film's stark shots, sparse dialogue, and politically ambiguous message marked a radical change from the revolutionary themes and socialist realist style of films made during the Maoist era (1949–1976).

His directorial debut *Red Sorghum* (1987) received notable international acclaim for its rich imagery and powerful narrative about a rural winery's opposition to the Japanese occupation of northeast China. *Ju Dou* (1990) and *Raise the Red Lantern* (1991) provide an oblique critique on contemporary society by adopting the theme of traditional society's oppression of women.

To Live (1994) reminds audiences of the tumult of China's twentieth history while affirming the universal theme of the struggle to survive and maintain dignity despite hardship and tragedy. Zhang's new cinematic language combined with social and historical critique launched his international stardom and established Zhang as one of the key representatives of the fifth generation of filmmakers in China.

Between 1992 and 2000 Zhang experimented with a range of cinematic styles, especially neo-realism. Whereas

Gong Li, in a scene from the film *Red Sorghum*, Zhang Yimou's first film to become a major hit. Zhang Yimou filmed it at Xi'an Studio. PHOTO COURTESY OF JOAN LEBOLD COHEN.

his earlier films featured stories from China's past, *The Story of Qiu Ju* (1992), *The Road Home* (1999), and *Not One Less* (2000) are set in recent China and address contemporary social issues such as legal rights, universal education, and family values. The latter two films represent a shift away from a critique of China to a call for audiences to assist in China's social development. These films moved Zhang closer to the government and shaped the trajectory of his future career.

Following on the heels of the success of Ang Lee's *Crouching Tiger, Hidden Dragon,* Zhang sought to create a Chinese blockbuster and capture global box office receipts by appealing to the international audience's interest in an exotic, mythical China and the Chinese audience's taste for historical costume dramas and martial arts. *Hero* (2002) is an action-packed and visually mesmerizing film about a failed assassination attempt on China's first emperor. *House of Flying Daggers* (2003) and *Curse of the Golden Flower* (2007) feature increased budgets and star-studded casts, and despite their unconvincing plots, achieved success at the box office.

The spectacle of Zhang's films are also presented on stage as ballets, operas, theatre, and pageantry. Zhang directed Puccini's opera *Turandot* in Italy (1997) and in an historically unprecedented performance in Beijing's Forbidden City (1998), he adapted *Raise the Red Lantern* into a ballet (2001), and directed *The First Emperor* at the Metropolitan Opera in New York (premiered in 2007). He has also directed the outdoor folk music spectaculars *Third Sister Liu* (since 2003) in southwestern China and *Impression Lijiang* in scenic Yunnan Province (since 2006).

After having directed the 2001 short film to promote Beijing's Olympic bid and China's eight-minute performance at the closing ceremonies of the 2004 summer Olympics in Athens, Zhang was selected to direct the opening ceremonies of the 2008 Summer Olympics in Beijing. The nearly four-hour show, described by many as dazzling, was held in the Bird's Nest, China's newly built and iconic national stadium. It was attended by an unprecedented eighty world leaders and viewed by 1 billion

A scene from the film *Red Sorghum*, by Zhang Yimou. PHOTO COURTESY OF JOAN LEBOLD COHEN.

people on television. The spectacular show included a display of 35,000 fireworks, designed by acclaimed artist Cai Guo-qiang, and 15,000 performers of acrobatics, martial arts, and a variety of musical performances, including the countdown performed by 2,008 drummers. The magnificent performance represented China's global prominence and symbolically displayed the Chinese government's emphasis upon solidarity, harmony, and technological progress.

Jonathan NOBLE

Further Reading

Clark, P. (2006). *Reinventing China: A generation and its films.* Hong Kong: The Chinese University Press.

Gateward, F. (Ed.). (2001). *Zhang Yimou: Interviews.* Jackson: University of Mississippi.

Zhen Ni (2002). *Memoirs from the Beijing Film Academy: The genesis of Chinas fifth generation.* Durham, NC: Duke University Press.

ZHANG Zhidong

Zhāng Zhīdòng 张之洞

1837–1909   Confucian scholar-official

Zhang Zhidong was a Confucian scholar-official of the late nineteenth century who was closely associated with China's Self-Strengthening Movement. Appointed by the Qing government as viceroy of Liangjiang, Zhang Zhidong promoted Western-style industrialization through the establishment of a modern coal and steel complexes in the lower Yangzi River region.

Zhang Zhidong, born in Nanpi in Zhili (modern-day Hebei) Province, was a Confucian scholar-official who was closely associated with China's Self-Strengthening Movement. His service in the Qing dynasty (1644–1912) government began in 1863 when he passed the highest-level civil service exam and earned the *jinshi* (presented scholar) degree. He then held several supervisory posts related to the Confucian examination system and education in Sichuan, Zhejiang, and Hubei provinces from 1867 to 1877. Zhang was known for his promotion of scholarship and exemplary rectitude in administrative affairs during this time. In 1879 he was admitted to the Imperial Academy. There he earned a reputation as a commentator on Chinese political reform and foreign relations.

Zhang became governor of Shanxi Province in 1882. This was the first of several administrative posts that culminated in his tenure as governor-general of Hubei and Hunan provinces. During his eighteen years as governor-

Zhang Zhidong, a Confucian scholar-official of the late Qing dynasty, advocated a philosophy of modernizing reform: "Chinese learning as the essence, Western learning for practical development."

Zhang Zhidong's View of the Examination System

Wendy Larson, a scholar of Chinese literature, film, and theory, writing on Zhang Zhidong:

One of the most forceful attacks on the examination system was engineered by Qing reformer Zhang Zhidong, who felt the exam was too literary and did not test candidates in a sufficient scope of affairs. His suggestion, similar to that of Ouyang Xiu in 1044, was to emphasize the dissertation and discussion in essays on the *shi* and *fu* poetry and to abandon the *bagu* writing style. He also petitioned to have the test of small formal calligraphy eliminated. Symbolic of an interpretation of writing as form equal to or more important than content, calligraphy is often mentioned by critics of the examination as one type of uselessly applied textual effort.... When the abolition of the examination system was announced and took place in 1905, however, Zhang Zhidong began to develop plans to establish a School for the Preservation of Antiquity; he petitioned the throne to establish this school on July 9, 1907, and it was opened August 28 of the same year. The school was to concentrate on Chinese subjects, emphasizing national literature, both prose and poetry, as well as the spoken and written language.

Zhang obviously perceived the value of the examination system as a unifying influence in the spiritual and conceptual realm of Chinese though and realized that while its abolition would allow China to progress in previously undeveloped ways, a chaotic spiritual gap may result from the lack of guiding and unifying ideology.

Source: Larson, W. (1991). *Literary authority and the modern Chinese writer.* Durham, NC: Duke University Press, 33

general Zhang was known as a political reformer and modernizer even as he remained devoted to Confucianism and the Qing dynastic order. Zhang's philosophy of reform was *Zhongxue wei ti, Xixue wei yong* (Chinese learning as the essence, Western learning for practical development).

The Qing court in 1901 appointed Zhang viceroy of Liangjiang in Guangxi Zhuang. He promoted development of railways and sponsored the Han-Ye-Ping iron and steelworks in the lower Yangzi River region to strengthen the Chinese state and economy. In addition he founded an institute of higher learning that was the foundation of modern University of Nanjing.

Michael C. LAZICH

Further Reading

Ayers, W. (1971). *Chang Chih-tung and educational reform in China.* Cambridge, MA: Harvard University Press.

Bays, D. H. (1978). *China enters the twentieth century: Chang Chih-tung and the issues of a new age, 1895–1909.* Ann Arbor: University of Michigan Press.

ZHAO Mengfu

Zhào Mèngfǔ 赵孟頫

1254–1322   *Yuan dynasty painter and calligrapher*

Zhao Mengfu 赵孟頫 was a poet and musician and a highly distinguished painter and calligrapher of the Yuan dynasty (1279–1368). His painting was marked with a return to archaism and covered a wide range of subjects, while his calligraphic scripts, called the "Zhao style," were elegantly structured and rigorously controlled.

Zhao Mengfu, born in Huzhou, Zhejiang Province, as a descendant of the founding Northern Song dynasty (960–1126) emperor, was a painter, calligrapher, poet, and musician of the Yuan dynasty (1279–1368). His father, who excelled in poetry, was a high local official during the Southern Song dynasty (1127–1279), and Zhao thus benefited from his family's rich literary collections. After the collapse of the Song dynasty Zhao Mengfu accepted an offer of an official post from Yuan emperor Khubilai Khan. This acceptance provoked bitter feelings among many ethnic Han Chinese scholars who regarded Zhao's service in the Mongolian court as a dishonorable collaboration. Zhao later held many other high posts, including the governorship in two provinces and the directorship of the imperial Hanlin Academy.

Zhao Mengfu painted a wide range of subjects, including landscape, human figures, birds and flowers, bamboos and rocks, humans and horses, and goats and sheep. The techniques he used also varied, ranging from finely detailed colored paintings to pictures done with broad, spontaneous brushstrokes that express symbolic messages. One of Zhao's most famous paintings, *Autumn Colors on the Que and Hua Mountains* (handscroll, ink and color on paper, 1296, National Museum, Taipei, Taiwan), is based on his visit to the two mountains in Shandong Province. Arranged on the two sides of the painting, the two greenish mountains rise abruptly in the background. The middle and front distances of the picture are filled with cottages, trees, boats, reeds, and human figures. Stylistically, this painting is far from naturalistic. The mountains in the back are too small in scale compared with the houses and trees in front of them. Light brushstrokes moving left to right by the lakefront establish the different levels of perspective in the painting but somehow impede the sense of space receding into the picture plane. Such discontinuities and anomalies deliberately refer and pay tribute to the ancient masters such as Gu Kaizhi (active fourth century), who experimented with spatial relations among human figures, trees, rocks, and flowers. Zhao's return to archaism marked a decisive move from the naturalism of Song painting technique and was followed by many artists in the same spirit.

Another famous painting by Zhao, *Elegant Rocks and Sparse Trees* (handscroll, ink on paper, Palace Museum, Beijing), uses broad and cursive brushstrokes to depict the rocks and tree boughs in a typical calligraphic style. His own inscription on the painting states that "Rocks as in flying white (script), trees as in seal script" and "calligraphy and painting have always been the same" (Cahill 1997, 187). Indeed, Zhao was one of the four great masters of the formal scripts in China with Ouyang Xun (557–641), Yan Zhenqing (709–785), and Liu Gongquan (778–865). His calligraphy, called the "Zhao style," is elegantly

Horse and Groom in the Wind, **a painting by master painter and calligrapher Zhao Mengfu (1254–1322). Ink on paper.**

structured and rigorously controlled. The official *History of the Yuan Dynasty* (composed in the fourteenth century) judged Zhao's skills in different kinds of scripts as having no rival.

Yu JIANG

Further Reading

Cahill, J. (1997). The Yuan dynasty (1271–1368). In R. Barnhart, Yang Xin, Nie Chongzheng, J. Cahill, Lang Shaojun, & Wu Hung (Eds.), *Three thousand years of Chinese painting* (pp. 138–195). New Haven, CT: Yale University Press.

Fong, Wen C. (1992). *Beyond representation, Chinese painting and calligraphy 8th–14th century.* New Haven, CT: Yale University Press.

Loehr, M. (1980). *The great painters of China.* New York: Harper & Row.

Wu Hung. (1997). The origins of Chinese painting (Paleolithic period to Tang dynasty). In R. Barnhart, Yang Xin, Nie Chongzheng, J. Cahill, Lang Shaojun, & Wu Hung (Eds.), *Three thousand years of Chinese painting* (pp. 79–81). New Haven, CT: Yale University Press.

ZHAO Ziyang

Zhào Zǐyáng 赵紫阳

1919–2005 *Chinese Communist Party leader and economic reformer*

Zhao Ziyang was a leading economic reformer of the People's Republic of China in the 1970s. He rapidly rose through the ranks of the Chinese Communist Party (CCP), becoming premier and party general secretary in the 1980s. His opposition to the crackdown on the 1989 protests in Tiananmen Square in Beijing resulted in his dismissal from office.

Zhao Ziyang was born as Zhao Xiusheng in Huaxian County, Henan Province in 1919. His father was a local landlord. He attended primary school in his native town and middle schools in Kaifeng and Wuhan. He joined the Communist Youth League in 1932 and the Chinese Communist Party (CCP) in 1938. By 1940 he was the party secretary of the Third Special District in the Hebei-Shandong Border Region. After the end of World War II in Asia, he occupied himself with rural reform work in the Hebei-Shandong-Henan Border Region. He also served as the party secretary of Luoyang District in Henan from 1948 to 1949.

After the establishment of the People's Republic of China (PRC), Zhao served in numerous positions in Guangdong Province. He was elected a member of the People's Council of Guangdong in 1955, was appointed secretary of the Guangdong Province Communist Party in 1957, and rose to the position of provincial first party secretary in 1965. He played an instrumental role in consolidating CCP control and implementing land reform policies.

During the Cultural Revolution, Zhao was accused of being a follower of unpopular figures such as Tao Zhu and Liu Shaoqi. During the late 1960s, he was publicly denounced, stripped of office, and paraded through the streets of Guangzhou (Canton) in a dunce cap. In 1971, he was sent to what amounted to internal exile as a party secretary in Inner Mongolia.

In the dying days of the Cultural Revolution, Zhao was rehabilitated by Zhou Enlai (1899–1976) and assigned as provincial first party secretary in Sichuan Province in 1976. He proceeded to address the province's economic stagnation that resulted from the Cultural Revolution. He allowed up to 15 percent of land in communes to be worked privately. He also permitted both farmers and workers to engage in a wide range of small-scale private economic activities. The results were impressive: grain production grew by 24 percent and industrial production rose by 80 percent in the period from 1976 to 1979.

Due to his success in Sichuan, Zhao was rapidly promoted by China's paramount leader Deng Xiaoping (1904–1997). Zhao was appointed alternate member of the Politburo in 1977, a full member of the Politburo in 1979, a member of the Politburo's Standing Committee in 1980, and vice-premier in the same year. Six months later, he replaced Hua Guofeng as premier. He was appointed to the post of CCP general secretary in January of 1987.

In positions of nationwide power and influence, Zhao continued to advocate market-style reforms and a more open policy toward the outside world, particularly the West. He also implemented measures to streamline the bloated bureaucracy and called for the gradual separation of the CCP from both government administration and industrial management. While many of his reforms were praised, his economic liberalization program was blamed for the rising inflation of the late 1980s.

Zhao's most important moment and his political downfall came with the student protests in Tiananmen Square in May and June of 1989. Many of the student demonstrators felt that Zhao would be more sympathetic to their demands for reform than many of Zhao's more hard-line colleagues. This was borne out in secret meetings of China's top leaders, where Zhao consistently opposed the use of force against the demonstrators. When Deng Xiaoping declared that "I have the army behind me" in a tumultuous 17 May 1989 Politburo meeting, Zhao reportedly retorted, "But I have the people behind me. You have nothing." But as the students became increasingly strident in their criticism of the government, emboldened by worldwide media coverage and joined by over one million residents in Beijing, averting the ultimate repression of the demonstrations proved impossible for the state. Zhao's personal visit to Tiananmen Square to urge students to end their hunger strike had no effect; "I came too late; I came too late," he lamented to student leaders. After the declaration of martial law and the bloody clearing of Tiananmen Square by military troops, Zhao was removed from office and replaced by Jiang Zemin. He was also placed under house arrest. He remained a member of the CCP but was almost completely absent from public life until his death.

Zhao died in January 2005 at the age of eighty-five. The PRC government acknowledged Zhao's death but kept memorials to a bare minimum, perhaps in fear that widespread mourning of Zhao's passing might lead to anti-government demonstrations as had previously happened in the cases of Zhou Enlai and Hu Yaobang. Zhao was survived by his second wife, Liang Boqi, five children, and several grandchildren.

Kirk W. LARSEN

Further Reading

Cheng Chu-yuan. (1990). *Behind the Tiananmen massacre.* Boulder, CO: Westview Press.

Liang Zhang, Nathan, A., & Link, P. (Eds.). (2001). *The Tiananmen papers.* New York: Public Affairs.

Shambaugh, D. (1984). *The making of premier Zhao Ziyang's provincial career.* Boulder, CO: Westview Press.

Vogel, E. (1969). *Canton under Communism.* Cambridge, MA: Harvard University Press.

Many events have been held in the world's largest public square, but it is the student protests of June 1989, when Zhao Ziyang supported and then tried to calm those camped in the Square, that continue to resonant. PHOTO BY JOAN LEBOLD COHEN.

Zhaozhou Bridge

Zhàozhōu Qiáo 赵州桥

The Zhaozhou Bridge, built between 595 and 605 CE, is the world's first large segmental arch bridge, making possible a near-level span of a broad river in North China. The innovation of open spandrels—arch-shaped openings—in the triangular area below the deck on both ends of the bridge did not appear in the West until the nineteenth century.

Among China's contributions to world architecture and engineering, no bridge has received more acclaim than the Zhaozhou Bridge, in Zhaoxian County, Hebei Province. Constructed between 595 and 605 CE in the middle of the Sui dynasty, the structure is the world's first large segmental arch bridge, a daringly innovative form that broke with the tradition of using a semicircle for the arched shape of a bridge. By using a segment of a circle, thus flattening the curve of the arch, it was possible to meet the seemingly conflicting demands for both a single long span with gentle approaches *and* one that was high enough to permit boat traffic beneath. In addition, the incorporation of two pairs of open spandrels—arch-shaped cavities—in the triangular area below the deck on both ends of the bridge was an innovation not used in the West until the nineteenth century. The open spandrels not only lessen the weight of the bridge, thus reducing the outward thrusts on the abutments, but also facilitate the passage of periodic flood waters that might impact the bridge. Unlike most old bridges whose construction can only be attributed to anonymous builders, the design of the Zhaozhou Bridge—also called the Anji [Safe Crossing] Bridge—is credited to Li Chun, a historical figure who also organized the masons who crafted it.

Approximately 65 meters long with an open span of nearly 37 meters, the low-lying bridge rises only some 7 meters above the water below. The full circle, of which the arch is but a segment, has a radius of 27.7 meters along the west side and 27.3 meters along the east side. Viewed from beneath, it's apparent how the bridge was constructed using twenty-eight parallel sets of stone voussoirs (wedge-shaped stones forming the curved part of an arch) that run the length of each segmental ring. While these parallel voussoirs produce a stone structure of great flexibility, the need to stabilize the bridge led to the use of reinforcing stone rods, stone hooks, and dovetailed iron keys, as well as a slight inward camber. The elegant geometry and sophisticated mathematics of the superstructure were enhanced with profuse stone carvings along the balustrades and posts. These carvings include a variety of dragons and protective amulets in animal form.

With tall sails providing propulsion, boat traffic along the Xiao River continued well into the middle of the twentieth century. In time, because of diminished water flow and increased road traffic, the Zhaozhou Bridge, like numerous other bridges on the North China Plain, fell into disrepair. In the 1980s, major efforts were made to restore the bridge to its original state. The Zhaozhou Bridge

The segmented open spandrels (arches) that support the Zhaozhou Bridge, built during the Sui dynasty, were a Chinese innovation. Such engineering allowed the bridge to span a wide river and accommodate boat traffic.

today is preserved within a park-like setting, and an admission ticket is required to cross it. In this in situ outdoor museum, exhibits focus on the technical aspects of the bridge's structure as well as the historical circumstances that gave rise to its construction. Although graceful open-spandrel, segmental masonry bridges are ubiquitous today throughout the world—and are usually considered to be modern since they are constructed of reinforced cement rather than blocks of stone—it is important to remember that their design had its origins in China more than thirteen centuries ago.

Ronald G. KNAPP

Further Reading

Knapp, R. G. (2008). *Chinese bridges: Living architecture from China's past.* Singapore: Tuttle Publishing.

Knapp, R. G. (1988). Bridge on the River Xiao. *Archaeology, 41*(1), 48–54.

Liang Ssu-ch'eng [Liang Sicheng] 梁思成. (1938). Open spandrel bridges in ancient China—1: The An-chi Ch'iao at Chao Chou, Hopei. *Progressive Architecture: Pencil Points, 19,* 25–32.

Tang Huancheng 唐寰澄 & Lu Jiaxi 卢嘉锡. *Zhongguo kexue jishushi: Qiaoliang juan* 中国科学技术史. 桥梁卷 [History of China's science and technology: Bridges]. Beijing : Kexue chubanshe 科学出版社.

Zhejiang Province

Zhéjiāng Shěng 浙江省

49 million est. 2006 pop.   101,800 square km

Zhejiang, on China's southeastern coast, is one of the nation's wealthiest and most fertile provinces. Since the tenth century Zhejiang has been a leading producer of silk, porcelain, tea, and paper. It also is the home of many of China's political and intellectual elite. Its 101,800 square kilometers, which make it comparable in size to Iceland, include 3,061 off-shore islands.

Zhejiang, one of the wealthiest and most fertile provinces in China, lies on the southeastern coast south of the Yangzi (Chang) River delta and China's largest city, Shanghai. Zhejiang is bordered on the north by Jiangsu Province, on the south by Fujian Province, and on the west by Anhui and Jiangxi provinces. It covers 101,800 square kilometers (about the size of Iceland), including 3,061 offshore islands. About one-third of Zhejiang consists of rivers, lakes, and plains, whereas the other two-thirds is mountainous.

The capital is Hangzhou, which was China's capital during the Southern Song dynasty (1127–1279). The Venetian traveler Marco Polo in his travels described Hangzhou as "the finest and most splendid city in the world" (Polo 1986, 213) in the world. The province has forty-one counties, twenty-three cities, and twenty-three county-level towns. In 2008, about 300,000 people in Zhejiang were categorized as ethnic minorities, the largest being the She and Hui nationalities.

Zhejiang Province historically has been in the forefront of China's cultural and economic development since the early Han dynasty (206 BCE–220 CE). During the seventh century its emergence as a major grain producer resulted in the extension of the Grand Canal to Hangzhou. Since the tenth century Zhejiang also has been a leading producer of silk, porcelain, tea, and paper and a center of commerce and trade. When the Southern Song dynasty established its capital in Hangzhou in 1127, Zhejiang also became the cultural and political center of China. It continues to be the home of many of China's political and intellectual elite. Two of the greatest modern Chinese writers—Mao Dun and Lu Xun—were from Zhejiang, as

An aerial view of Hangzhou, capital of Zhejiang Province, with its fertile fields. The province has been a center for commerce and trade since the tenth century. PHOTO BY JOAN LEBOLD COHEN.

are nearly one-fifth of the members of the Chinese Academy of Sciences. Zhejiang also produced two of China's best-known contemporary leaders: Chiang Kai-shek, president of the Republic of China on Taiwan from 1949 to 1975, and Zhou En-lai, premier of the People's Republic of China from 1949 to 1976.

Zhejiang Province has been a prime beneficiary of China's current economic reforms. The province's economy since 1978 has grown faster than the national average, thanks in part to the rapid growth of collective and private firms. Zhejiang is one of the wealthiest of China's provinces and ranked among the top four or five on various economic indicators along with economic powerhouses such as Guangdong and Jiangsu. In addition to its traditional industries, Zhejiang has concentrated on developing its machinery, chemical, electronics, and pharmaceutical industries. Foreign tourism, trade, and investment also have flourished, especially in the coastal cities of Ningbo, Hangzhou, and Wenzhou.

Shawn SHIEH

Further Reading

Polo, M. ([1320] 1986). *The travels of Marco Polo* (R. Latham, Trans.). New York: Penguin Books.

Rankin, M. B. (1986). *Elite activism and political transformation in China: Zhejiang Province 1865–1911.* Stanford, CA: Stanford University Press.

Schoppa, K. R. (1982). *Chinese elites and political change: Zhejiang Province in the early twentieth century.* Cambridge, MA: Harvard University Press.

ZHENG Chenggong

Zhèng Chénggōng 郑 成 功

1624–1662 Maritime leader

Zheng Chenggong (1624–1662) built on the structure of commerce and naval power established by his father, Zheng Zhilong, to support a Ming loyalist regime in Fujian, and after the dynasty's collapse in 1644 he continued to oppose the Qing. He expelled the Dutch from Taiwan in 1661–1662 and died shortly thereafter.

Zheng Chenggong 鄭成功 was known to Europeans as "Coxinga," from the Chinese word *Guoxingye* (Lord of the Imperial Surname), reflecting his high favor under the Ming dynasty (1368–1644) loyalist court at Fuzhou, his continued championing of the Ming loyalist cause after the fall of that court, and perhaps his tacit move toward claiming the Ming succession for himself in the last months of his short life. He was the heir to a maritime power structure built by his father, Zheng Zhilong 鄭芝龍, who drew on a web of connections among the Fujian ports, Macao, Manila, Taiwan (then not yet heavily settled by Chinese or under Chinese administration), and Japan. Zhilong's most important base was at Hirado, Japan, where he was a leading subordinate

Zheng Chenggong (1624–1662 CE), an heir to the maritime power structure built by his father Zheng Zhilong, successfully expelled the Dutch from Taiwan three months before his death.

2631

of the "captain" of all Chinese in Japan, Li Dan. Zheng Chenggong was born in Hirado; his mother was a Japanese woman from a respected family.

In 1624 Li Dan and Zheng Zhilong brokered the withdrawal of Dutch invaders from the Penghu Islands in the Taiwan Strait, which were Ming territory, to the south coast of Taiwan, which was not. This withdrawal gave the Zheng family some kind of claim to control of Taiwan, which Zheng Chenggong would assert when he expelled the Dutch thirty-eight years later. From 1624 to 1635 Zheng Zhilong fought off rival maritime leaders, made himself indispensable to the tottering Ming dynasty, and maintained his network of fleets and lines of trade as a naval officer of the Ming dynasty. Merchants under his control or paying taxes to him dominated Chinese trade with Japan and with the Dutch on Taiwan and sailed as far as the Malay Peninsula.

When the Manchu Qing took Beijing in 1644, Zheng forces gave at best ambivalent support to the Ming loyalist court at Nanjing, then dominated another loyalist regime at Fuzhou on the Fujian coast. Zheng Chenggong, who had studied with some of the great literati of the late Ming dynasty in Nanjing, attracted the notice of the loyalist emperor at Fuzhou, who bestowed on Zheng the Ming imperial surname Zhu. However, Zheng Zhilong saw no future in resistance, negotiated with the Qing dynasty (1644–1912), and was taken away to end his life in house arrest in Beijing. Several Zheng relatives sought to preserve the maritime power structure; Chenggong won the struggle among them and in the 1650s built a powerful fleet and tightly controlled trade operations centered on his capital at Xiamen on the Fujian coast.

Under increasing pressure from Qing armies and trade embargoes, Zheng Chenggong launched a desperate and unsuccessful attack on Nanjing in 1659, then turned to invade Taiwan and expel the Dutch, only to die in 1662 a few months after their final withdrawal. His son and grandson and their generals maintained power on Taiwan until 1683, when Qing forces commanded by Shi Lang, who had defected from Zheng thirty years before, took control of Taiwan.

John E. WILLS Jr.

Further Reading

Struve, L. A. (1984). *The southern Ming, 1644–1662*. New Haven, CT: Yale University Press.

Struve, L. A. (1993). *Voices from the Ming-Qing cataclysm: China in tiger's jaws*. New Haven, CT: Yale University Press.

Wills, J. E., Jr. (1981). Maritime China from Wang Chih to Shih Lang: Themes in peripheral history. In J. D. Spence & J. E. Wills Jr. (Eds.), *From Ming to Ch'ing: Conquest, region, and continuity in seventeenth-century China* (pp. 204–238). New Haven, CT: Yale University Press.

ZHENG He

Zhèng Hé 郑 和

1371–1433 *Ming era mariner and eunuch*

Zheng He was a diplomat, explorer, and fleet admiral who, between 1405 and 1433, made seven voyages to the Indian Ocean. His expeditions and four naval and land battles brought more than thirty kingdoms into the Chinese economic sphere.

Zheng He 鄭和 was born Ma He in Yunnan Province (southwest China bordering Burma, Laos, and Vietnam.) He was a sixth-generation son of the Ma family, descended from devout Turko-Persian Muslims originally from Bukhara in Central Asia (present-day Uzbekistan).

In 1381 a Ming dynasty army came to Yunnan to quell a revolt. Ma He was taken captive, castrated, and trained as a servant for the imperial court where he became a confidant of the Prince of Yan (1360–1424), fourth son of Hongwu (1328–1398), the first Ming emperor. Yan became Yongle, the third Ming emperor. Ma He, renamed Zheng He on 11 February 1404, was director of palace servants and held the highest rank among eunuchs.

Yongle began major shipbuilding in 1403, shortly after he assumed the throne, and orderd Zheng to command a naval expedition combining exploration and the extension of the tribute system to the Western (Indian) Ocean. Zheng ultimately made seven voyages:

- First voyage (1405–1407) to Champa (a kingdom in South Vietnam), Java, Malacca, Sumatra, Ceylon, Cochin, and Calicut (southwest coast of India)

- Second voyage (1407–1409) to Champa, Java, Siam, Sumatra, and Calicut

- Third voyage (1409–1411) to Champa, Calicut, Coimbatore (southern India), and Puttanpur (western India)

- Fourth voyage (1412–1415) to Champa and Calicut, Hormuz (Persian Gulf), the Maldives, and Sumatra

- Fifth voyage (1416–1419) to Champa and Calicut, the Maldives, Hormuz, Aden, Mogadishu and Malindi (both coastal East Africa)

- Sixth voyage (1421–1422) separate squadrons sailed to Champa and Calicut, Ceylon and the Maldives, Hormuz, the Arabian peninsula, East Africa, and Sumatran states (Lambri, Aru, and Semudera)

- Seventh voyage (1431–1433) followed the route to Hormuz

From 1424 to 1430, Zheng commanded the garrison at Nanking, and the fleet remained there until the new emperor, Xuande (1398–1435) sent him on his seventh and last exploration. Zheng He died during this voyage and was buried at sea.

For all but the fifth voyage, contemporary records (*Mingshi*, Ming History) document the numbers of ships and personnel. For instance, on the first voyage, Zheng commaned 62 treasure ships, 255 other vessels, and 27,800 armed troops and mariners; other voyages were comparable. Later historians listed the treasure ships as nine-masted junks about 127 meters (416 feet) long

Woodcut of an ocean-going ship from the time of Admiral Zheng He. Ink on paper. From the book *Wu-pei chih* by Mao Yuan-i, 1626.

and 52 meters (170 feet) wide and capable of carrying up to 1,500 tons. By comparison Columbus's were about 17 meters (55 feet) long and carried 700–1,000 tons; a modern ship of 60 meters (200 feet) long carries 1,200 tons. Zheng's treasure ships would have been the largest wooden ships ever built, a claim many historians now dispute.

Zheng He's fleet consisted of treasure ships, horse ships, troop transports, and supply ships as well as auxiliary craft such as patrol boats and water tankers; overall, 1,476 wooden ships were constructed during his administration; the first voyage alone consisted of 252 vessels. The improbable sizes of the largest ships are questioned because of varying measurements given in *zhang* (141 inches) and *chi* (14.1 inches) which varied through time. Keel-less, bark-rigged treasure vessels had up to nine masts and twelve sails, and archaeological specimens suggest lengths of 164.5–183 meters (538–600 feet), while Chinese documentary accounts indicate lengths of up to 117–136 meters (385–440) feet and beams of 48–55 meters (157.5–180 feet).

Zheng's seven expeditions and four naval and land battles brought more than thirty kingdoms into the Chinese economic sphere. During Zheng He's tenure, China expanded its maritime exploration and seagoing trade, established and enhanced tribute systems, and embarked on territorial conquests in the north, especially present-day Mongolia, and the south into Vietnam. His seven voyages served to establish the wealth and political power and technical sophistication of China. Subsequently, China withdrew from the sea and focused on land conquests, and Ming dynasty naval efforts diminished dramatically primarily due to the costs of maintaining the fleet and financial pressures to maintain armies fighting in Mongolia.

Charles C. KOLB

Further Reading

Dreyer, E. L. (2007). *Zheng He: China and the oceans in the early Ming Dynasty, 1405–1433.* New York: Pearson-Longman.

Hvistendahl, M. (2008). Rebuilding a treasure ship. *Archaeology, 61*(2), 40–45.

Levathes, L. (1997). *When China ruled the seas: The treasure fleet of the Dragon Throne, 1405–1433.* Oxford, U.K.: Oxford University Press.

Ma Huan (G. Mills, trans.). (1434/1970). *Yingyai Shenglan* [Overall survey of the Star Raft]. Cambridge, U.K.: Cambridge University Press.

Menzies, G. (2003). *1421: The year the China discovered the world.* New York: Morrow.

Zhong Yong (Doctrine of the Mean)

Zhōngyōng 中庸

One of Confucianism's sacred texts, the **Zhong Yong** serves as a guide to achieving harmony—personal, social, and political—through a mind and self in a state of perfect equilibrium. Translated as *The Doctrine of the Mean*, it embodies many of the central themes of Confucianism.

The Doctrine of the Mean (the *Zhong Yong*) comprises two chapters in the *Classic of Rites* (*Li Ji*), one of the sets of books that form the canon of Confucian thought. During the early period of the Song dynasty (960–1279), it came to be regarded as a single text worthy of investigation and study on its own. Tradition maintains that it was written by Zisi (Kong Ji), who was the grandson of Confucius (551–479 BCE). The date of its composition is likely around 450 BCE.

The intellectual concerns of the Song period included, for the most part, an engagement with Buddhism, which advocated the understanding of the relationship that existed not between human beings but between human beings and the cosmos. This idea profoundly changed Song China, and more importantly, it forced the thinkers of the day to go back and reexamine traditional Chinese works of philosophy to see if they could find in them native traditions that also addressed the relationship vaunted by Buddhism. Thus, the *Zhong Yong* was read as a spiritual text first and foremost and only afterwards as a guide for bringing about a better and just society.

The work is written in an aphoristic style, with a student posing questions and a sage providing the answers. At first glance, these aphorisms seem to be unrelated, but a closer examination reveals that they address specific spiritual and philosophical themes, all of which seek to elucidate the spiritual content of Chinese culture, and not only its pragmatic concerns.

The larger aspect of externality is the cosmos, or heaven, and this too is linked with spiritual internality. Both heaven and the individual share the same reality; that is, perfection. But, whereas heaven does not deviate from its true reality, an individual does. This causes disharmony and strife, which devastate not only the individual but also society. A corrupt ruler corrupts those whom he rules, and a corrupt individual corrupts those that live with him in the community. It is only after intense struggle to attain moral rectitude (the state of perfection) that the harmony between heaven and the individual can once more be reestablished, and thus strife and disharmony are destroyed. Self-perfection, therefore, reaches outwards; first it perfects society, and then it joins with the eternal perfection that is contained in heaven. In effect, perfection is a virtue of heaven, which is also placed inside the individual; the task of the individual is to find and highlight this virtue in his or her own life.

The *Zhong Yong* thus offers a far more profound evaluation of perfectibility than that found in Buddhism. The goal is not solipsistic; it does not stay focused on the self; it is not, and never should be, an isolated event. Rather, the demand is for a person to become sincere so that she or he might know that his or her own perfectibility is an immense force for change, and for the better. And this

From *The Doctrine of the Mean*

What Heaven has endowed is called the nature. Following the nature is called the Way. Cultivating the Way is called instruction.

The Way cannot be departed from for so much as an instant. If it were possible to depart from, it would not be the Way.

Source: de Bary, W T. & Bloom, I. (1999). *Sources of Chinese tradition, Vol. 1.* New York: Columbia University Press, 334.

perfectibility is made manifest in moral rectitude, which creates and then sustains a perfected self living within a perfected community, all governed by the laws of a perfect cosmos. And this state of harmony is also the place where truth and justice easily endure.

In the *Zhong Yong*, Chinese intellectual culture found a thorough and complete system of personal and social life, which went farther than Buddhist tenets. For this reason, it became a central text for later Confucian thinkers who, throughout the breadth of Chinese history, turned to it again and again as a guide and methodology to attain and retain the Way of Confucianism.

Nirmal DASS

Further Reading:

Ames, R. T., & Hall, D. L. (2001). *Focusing the familiar: A translation and philosophical interpretation of the Zhongyong.* Honolulu: University of Hawaii Press.

Cheng, Chung-Ying. (1991). *New dimensions of Confucian and neo-Confucian philosophy.* Albany: State University of New York Press.

Franke, H. (1976). *Sung biographies.* Wiesbaden, Germany: Franz Steiner Verlag.

Fung, Yu-lan. (1952). *History of Chinese philosophy. Vol. 1: The period of the philosophers.* Princeton, NJ: Princeton University Press.

Hughes, E. R. (1943). *The Great Learning and the mean-in-action.* New York: E. P. Dutton.

Legge, J. (1960). *The Chinese classics. Vol. 1: Confucian analects, the great learning, and the doctrine of the mean.* Hong Kong: Hong Kong University Press. (Original work published 1871)

Roetz, H. (1993). *Confucian ethics of the axial age.* Albany: State University of New York Press.

Rosemont, H., Jr. (Ed.). (1991). *Chinese texts and philosophical contexts: Essays dedicated to Angus C. Graham.* LaSalle, IL: Open Court.

Tu Wei-ming. (1976). Centrality and commonality: An essay on Chung-yung. In *Monographs of the Society for Asian and Comparative Philosophy, 3.* Honolulu: The University of Hawaii Press.

Twitchett, D., & Loewe, M. (1986). *The Cambridge history of China. Vol. 1: The Ch'in and Han empires, 221 B.C.–A.D. 220.* Cambridge, U.K.: Cambridge University Press.

Zhou Dynasty

Zhōu Cháo　周朝

Western Zhou period: 1045–771 BCE; Eastern Zhou period 770–221 BCE

The Zhou dynasty covered two time periods: the Western Zhou and the Eastern Zhou. The former was characterized by the hegemonic rule of Zhou lineage over a number of tribute states. The Eastern Zhou period, when the Zhou family was forced eastward out of their western homeland, was characterized by the rise of former Zhou and non-Zhou states who competed for control and moral authority.

The Zhou dynasty covered two time periods: the Western Zhou period (1045–771 BCE) and the Eastern Zhou period (770–221 BCE). During the Western Zhou period the Zhou lineage ruled from the capital, Zongzhou, which was located near the lineage's ancestral burial grounds (near modern-day Xi'an in Shaanxi Province). In 771 BCE the Zhou elite fled east to the city of Chengzhou (located near modern-day Luoyang in Henan Province). During the Eastern Zhou period former Zhou tribute states competed for power under the guise of upholding Zhou traditional moral authority. The Zhou royal descendants themselves were puppets of neighboring states.

Origins

The original Zhou nation developed in the Wei River valley in Shaanxi. Shang dynasty (1766–1045 BCE) oracle-bone records dating from 1200–1000 BCE suggest that the Shang considered the Zhou alternately as an enemy and as a tribute-paying subject. By the middle of the eleventh century BCE the Zhou had built a coalition of partners, including former Shang subjects in northern Henan, and destroyed Shang hegemony (influence). In texts compiled centuries later this power shift was attributed to the will of heaven and called the "Mandate of Heaven" (*tianming*). In Zhou bronze texts the term referred to the will of ancestral spirits, perhaps manifested as astral phenomena (in religious philosophy, occurrences held to be next in refinement above those in the tangible world). But by the Eastern Zhou period the power shift was mythologized as a heroic military conquest commanded by heaven and executed by King Wu (representing "martial" reckoning against immoral leaders), who was the son of King Wen, the founder of the Zhou nation (who represented "humane" treatment of inferiors and a system of utopian agrarian government). By the Han dynasty (206 BCE–220 CE) the Mandate of Heaven clearly signified shifts in a system of natural forces, much closer to the five phases system (*wuxing*) that was popular by the third century BCE. The Mandate of Heaven theory became a permanent part of political thought and was used by later Chinese reformers to frighten defiant rulers, as well as by those who took up arms against the government to justify their rebellion.

After the shift of influence from the Shang in the east to the Zhou in the west, Zhou rulers spent the next two centuries consolidating their power by military coercion and trade. They concentrated on control over resources that were essential to their economic system of gift giving and award—a system inherited from the Shang and

2637

The sophistication of Zhou carved jades, bronze vessels, and musical instruments points to control over resources and production in regions beyond the Zhou homeland. At the height of Zhou influence, during the late tenth to the late ninth centuries BCE, the Zhou controlled a network that reached west into Gansu Province, northeast to Beijing, southwest into Sichuan Province, east into Shandong Province, and south into Hubei Province and beyond the Yangzi (Chang) River.

Eastern Zhou

Scholars subdivide the Eastern Zhou period into the Spring and Autumn period (770–476 BCE) and the Warring States period (475–221 BCE), the names for both periods deriving from chronicles collected that detail alliances and conflicts between former subject states of the Zhou. The entire Eastern Zhou era was characterized by larger states annexing smaller states such that by the third century BCE only a few large states remained. During the Spring and Autumn period the Zhou ruler was alternately a puppet of the states of Jin to the north, Zheng to the south, and Qi to the east, each of which took a turn as "hegemon protector" (*ba*). States on the fringes of the Zhou earlier realm rose to power and challenged the exclusionary protector system.

Powerful new players by the Warring States period included the states of Qin, located to the west in the old Zhou homeland; Yue, spreading north into the lower Huai River valley from the southeastern coastal region; Chu, spreading south and east out of the Han River valley in modern Hubei Province; and Yan, in the northeast near modern-day Beijing. In the meantime Jin (a powerful state that developed in southern Shanxi Province not far from the Zhou administrative city of Chengzhou) divided into territories run by the large lineage groups Wei, Zhao, and Han. The Han took over Zheng, but other states survived simply by allying strategically with larger groups. Examples include Lu, the birthplace of the philosopher Confucius (551–479 BCE), and nearby Song, the birthplace of the anti-Confucian thinker Mozi (470?–391? BCE).

The art of strategic alliances, known as the "Theory of Horizontal or Vertical Alliances," was advanced by itinerant "guests" (*ke*), who were members of disenfranchised

A bronze vessel from the Zhou dynasty. The Zhou were noted for the sophistication of their bronze-casting technique and design, and often rewarded their subjects with gifts of sacrificial vessels. PHOTO BY JOAN LEBOLD COHEN.

intimately tied to the spread of the worship of Zhou ancestral spirits. Cowries (a kind of seashell), jade, and bronze—all being valued in Shang religion and all requiring trade ties with distant regions—continued to be important to the Zhou. Although the Zhou initially worshiped Shang spirits, by the middle of the tenth century BCE their own Zhou ancestors had clearly become national icons. Nation building became a form of ancestor worship as the Zhou rewarded subjects with sacrificial vessels, wines, ritual clothing, and agricultural land (for food production) to advance the Zhou ritual system. Recipients used these gifts to present mortuary feasts to ancestral spirits, often including the names of their Zhou benefactors and their ancestors in the inscribed prayers.

artisan and elite families who had studied under masters of military, technical, and ritual arts. By the Warring States period literacy and text production, as well as occult or technical expertise, spread with the guest masters and their disciples from one site of patronage to another. The many new text types and ritual items discovered in Warring States tombs, especially those associated with the southern state of Chu, attest to a cross-fertilization of practices and ideas over great geographical distances. This cross-fertilization no doubt was perpetuated not only by the roving guests but also by the migrations of peoples, states, and armies. The guests took the cultural fabric once identified as Zhou and rewove it, introducing ideologies that better fit the economic and cultural realities of their far-flung patron rulers. They used tales about former Zhou-period rulers to cajole and warn cajole regional leaders. Founding kings Wen and Wu were cast as paragons of honesty and humility, and—most important to enhancing the uncertain position of these guest advisers—the wise minister Zhou Gong (regent for Wu's son and cult founder of the state of Lu) was cast as vital to the foundation of a strong Zhou state. Zhou Gong assumed rule while the king was weak, gave speeches about morality, repressed remnant Shang rebels, established an administration, and politely retired when the king came of age.

Drastic Social Changes

A comparison of the Warring States and early Western Zhou economies shows drastic social changes. The economic network that was expanded by the Zhou from the eleventh through the ninth centuries BCE collapsed under its own ideological weight (a collapse that continued through the Spring and Autumn period). The rigid link to Zhou kinship through mortuary ritual and a gift-giving system was not sustainable. In contrast, the major states during the Warring States period established their own monetary systems and individualized religious systems that incorporated both local practices and elements of the archaic but prestigious Zhou rhetoric. Lesser states participated in the expanded networks of the larger states. Markets were common in every city. The export of mass-produced trade goods and the import of exotic goods thrived. The network of interstate relationships was often multilateral, involving trade, warfare, marriage, and political agreements. Until the Qin dynasty (221–206 BCE) conquered the entire region and attempted unification, early China was a complex social web of mingled social classes, competing philosophies, and people from different cultural backgrounds. Amid this cultural fluidity individual states promoted their own calendar systems, musical styles, artistic styles, script styles, and occult practices.

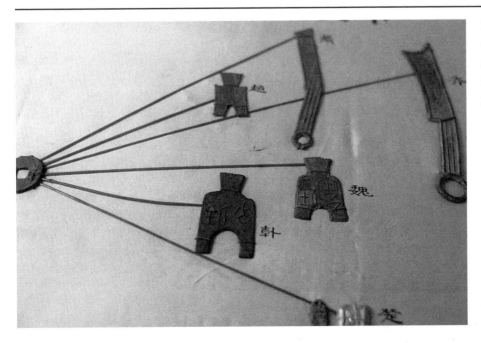

Zhou dynasty "ax-head" coins used during a period of thriving interstate trade. PHOTO BY JOAN LEBOLD COHEN.

Bronze bells, also called *bianzhong*, from the Zhou dynasty.
PHOTO BY JOAN LEBOLD COHEN.

The Warring States period was the end of the Bronze Age period (when human culture was characterized by the use of bronze, beginning between 4000 and 3000 CE and ending with the advent of the Iron Age) in Zhou culture. Philosophers and writers of this and later periods would use an increasingly idealized vision of Zhou ritual and government as a rhetorical foil against which to criticize the political chaos of their own periods.

Constance A. COOK

Further Reading

Cook, C. (1997). Wealth and the Western Zhou. *Bulletin of the School of Oriental and African Studies, 60*(2), 253–294.

Cook, C., & Major, J. (1999). *Defining Chu: Image and reality in ancient China*. Honolulu: University of Hawaii Press.

Hsu Cho-yun & Linduff, K. M. (1988). *Western Chou civilization*. New Haven, CT: Yale University Press.

Li Feng. (2006). *Landscape and power in early China: The crisis and fall of the Western Zhou 1045–771 BC*. Cambridge, U.K.: Cambridge University Press.

Li Xueqin. (1985). *Eastern Zhou and Qin civilizations* (Kwang-chih Chang, Trans.). New Haven, CT: Yale University Press.

Loewe, M., & Shaughnessy, E. L. (1999). *The Cambridge history of ancient China: From the origins of civilization to 221 BC*. Cambridge, U.K.: Cambridge University Press.

ZHOU Enlai

Zhōu Ēnlái　周恩来

1898–1976　First premier of the People's Republic of China

Considered one of the most important politicians in the Communist revolution, Zhou Enlai was the first premier of the People's Republic of China and chief diplomat for Chinese Communist Party leader Mao Zedong. Zhou's less ideological approach was pivotal in determining the future of Communism in China.

One of the towering figures of China's Communist revolution, Zhou Enlai was premier of the People's Republic of China (PRC) from 1949 until his death in 1976, chief diplomat for Chinese Communist Party (CCP) leader Mao Zedong, and mentor to CCP general secretary Deng Xiaoping, among others. Zhou Enlai is typically remembered as the revolution's second-most important politician. He was the functionary who made Chairman Mao's policies operational. Serving the Communist Party for a half-century in both international and domestic affairs, Zhou played a critical role in China's rise to power in the twentieth century.

True to the meaning of his given name "Enlai" ("Coming of Grace"), Zhou excelled at resolving logistical problems and mediating between opposing groups. He is known for his negotiations with U.S. secretary of state Henry Kissinger that culminated in the signing of the Shanghai Communique in 1972, the agreement that struck a compromise on the thorny issue of Taiwan and culminated in the reestablishment of normal relations between the People's Republic of China and the United States. In 1964 and again in 1975 Zhou urged the adoption of the Four Modernizations, a new policy direction emphasizing investment in advanced technology and economic construction that set the stage for Deng Xiaoping's Second Revolution in the post–Cultural Revolution (1966–1976) period.

Zhou Enlai rose quickly to a leadership position during the so-called United Front phase of Chinese politics (1924–1927), when his interpersonal skills were particularly useful for mediating between the Chinese Nationalist Party (Guomindang), China's Communist Party, and the Soviet Union's Communist International. Zhou first entered politics as a student activist and journalist in Tianjin during the May Fourth Movement of 1919. Exposed to Marxist ideas for the first time while studying in Japan, Zhou grew increasingly committed to Communist ideology after he was jailed for six months in Tianjin for participating in street protests. In 1920 he joined the wave of Chinese youth traveling to Europe to participate in work-study opportunities. He became known among the overseas Chinese community in France as an energetic and resourceful revolutionary organizer and publicist. Returning to China in 1924, Zhou was appointed secretary of the Communist Party of the Guangdong-Guangxi region and political director of the Whampoa Military Academy in Guangzhou (Canton), a position that allowed him to earn the trust of revolutionary military officers.

Zhou would continue to be admired by a variety of constituencies both inside and outside the Communist Party because he was perceived to be a force for moderation and openness. Zhou personally handled all of Chairman Mao's foreign policy initiatives throughout the half-century of their political partnership. Mao himself

2641

rarely traveled abroad and typically left the details of his policies to others. Even in the rare instances when Mao met personally with a head of state, such as his historic meeting with Soviet leader Joseph Stalin in Moscow to cement the Sino-Soviet Agreement of 1950 or with U.S. president Richard Nixon in Beijing to open up relations with the United States in 1972, the chairman relied on Zhou to initiate and finalize all arrangements. Thus, it is hard to distinguish the degree to which Zhou should be credited with the substance, as opposed to the mere execution, of these momentous shifts in policies.

Some analysts portray Zhou as a mere appendage of Mao, a skilled implementer of another man's strategic vision, whereas others portray Zhou as an independent force in his own right, a self-effacing figure who discretely shaped and expanded the broad field of action that Mao afforded him. The specifics of each case must be sorted out before an informed evaluation of Zhou's significance can be determined. Regarding the 1972 opening of relations with the United States, for example, not Zhou but rather his foreign minister, Marshall Chen Yi, first advocated the conceptual shift toward détente with the United States in a strategic report submitted to Mao in 1969. Zhou could never have acted on Chen Yi's recommendation to improve relations with the United States without Mao's explicit endorsement. Yet, after Mao gave approval for this broad policy shift and granted the request of the U.S. Ping Pong team to visit Beijing, Zhou orchestrated the complex preparations leading up to Nixon's visit with intelligence and finesse.

A Symbiotic Pair

Retrospectively, Zhou has won praise from those who see him as representing a more benign and cosmopolitan alternative to the Chinese Communism championed by Mao. Considering the calamitous result of Mao's Great Leap Forward and Cultural Revolution, Zhou does seem to stack up favorably by comparison. However, comparing the first and second most important Chinese revolutionaries like this presumes that their careers can be disentangled from one another. This is only partially true. Although they began as rivals, the two men became an indissoluble symbiotic pair after Zhou subordinated himself to Mao's leadership over the course of the Long

March (1934–1935). Actually their personal relationship was always strained, but they managed to forge a potent political partnership despite their contrasting personalities. Zhou was by nature a prudent and tolerant team player, whereas Mao was an uncompromising rebel, polarizing and overbearing. Mao was the brains of the dyad, and Zhou, its arms and legs. Their careers became so intertwined that Zhou must be considered accountable, at least to some degree, for all of Mao's destructive policies. He was the technocrat who enabled them to be implemented. If Zhou had sided with the leaders trying to restrain Mao rather than constantly aligning himself with Mao, the immense human suffering caused by the Great Leap Forward and the Cultural Revolution might have been limited considerably. Zhou Enlai may be credited with having mitigated some of the destructiveness of the Red Guard movement by stationing guards, for example, to defend valuable cultural properties like the Forbidden City, but he also prolonged the Cultural Revolution in that his willingness to modify the excesses of the movement kept it operational and seemingly palatable.

Although his real opinions were often shrouded in secrecy, Zhou disagreed with Mao on the critical issue of how to pace and structure China's economic development. Zhou expressed disagreement with Mao's so-called Little Leap in 1956, the precursor to the more extreme Great Leap Forward campaign that Mao devised in 1958. Zhou thought the targets for growth that Mao was advocating were overambitious and recommended scaling them back. Mao became angry at Zhou for suggesting a slower timetable and forced Zhou to recant his views before a large meeting of party delegates. A few years later, when Minister of Defense Peng Dehuai urgently sought to convince Mao to halt the Great Leap Forward, Zhou did not support Peng's petition but rather remained cowed and neutral. This was also the case in February 1967 when several military officers challenged Mao's Cultural Revolution policies. Zhou agreed with the officers' complaint that the Cultural Revolution should be curtailed and order restored, but again he remained neutral, unwilling to risk detaching himself from Mao. Thus, Zhou failed to defend the public interest when it really counted, that is, when his support for constraining Mao might have decisively blunted Mao's power.

According to the memoirs of Mao's personal physician, Zhou behaved surprisingly obsequiously in Mao's presence, tasting his food to make sure that it was not poisoned and crawling at his feet to show him maps as if Zhou were a eunuch serving the emperor. In private Mao referred to Zhou dismissively as "his housekeeper." Apparently, the servile way in which Zhou related to Mao was partially a strategy for assuaging Mao's ego and easing his paranoia and partially a relic of feudal habits and arrangements. An important watershed in cementing Zhou's partnership with Mao in the early years was Zhou's convincing apology during the Yan'an Rectification Movement of 1943. Zhou had been singled out for special criticism at Yan'an for his role in pushing Mao out of power at the Ningdu Conference of 1932. Zhou outranked Mao prior to the Long March and had sided with the Soviet-backed majority against Mao's guerilla warfare strategy.

"Self-Rectification"

Over the course of the Long March, Zhou had switched his allegiance to Mao. To persuade Mao that he could be trusted, Zhou put on a consummate performance at Yan'an, chastising himself bitterly for ever having doubts about Mao and declaring his complete loyalty going forward. In subsequent years Zhou would be called upon

repeatedly to demean himself like this, most notably near the end of his life when Mao's wife Jiang Qing and her allies accused the ailing Zhou of being a closet Confucian and arranged for Zhou to endure a "self-rectification" before hundreds of officials within the Great Hall of the People in 1974.

In the aftermath of heir-apparent Lin Biao's seeming betrayal of Mao in 1971 and his subsequent death in a plane crash, the need to establish a credible successor to Mao loomed heavily in the minds of both Zhou and Mao. By 1972 the Cultural Revolution's ideological extremism was sputtering, and in this new circumstance the contrasting approaches of Zhou and Mao seemed more contradictory than complementary. By 1972 Zhou had sprung into action, restoring normal governmental functions, rehabilitating party veterans, and putting the economy back on solid footing. Mao and his radical allies, on the other hand, seemed anxious to keep these "rightist" tendencies in check and to salvage some positive legacy for the Cultural Revolution. Because both Zhou and Mao were chronically ill, Zhou with cancer and Mao with Lou Gehrig's disease, a sense of urgency infused their decision making. The subtle rivalry between Mao and Zhou, long suppressed by the self-effacing Zhou, flared up as they both sought to leave their personal stamp on the future

Photograph of President Richard Nixon and Premier Zhou Enlai on 21 February 1972; Nixon's visit to China marked the opening of relations between China and the United States. Chairman Mao relied on Zhou to initiate and formalize much of the arrangements between the countries. NATIONAL ARCHIVES.

direction of the revolution to which they had dedicated their lives. What was at stake was whether the party machinery would be left in capable hands. Zhou was determined to pass on his position as premier to Deng Xiaoping and to secure Mao's endorsement for it. Mao respected Deng's abilities as an administrator, and he gave Zhou the approval he sought to return Deng to power and make him acting premier despite the objections of the radicals. But Mao remained ambivalent about Deng as a successor because he wanted the ultimate decision maker to be someone whose ideology he trusted would remain purely revolutionary, such as Wang Hongwen or Hua Guofeng, his choices for successors. Mao did not want to see ideological objectives diminished or buried. Mao suspected that Deng was ultimately "a capitulationist," that is, one who would eventually forgo revolutionary aspirations and "go down the capitalist road" were he not properly kept in check by a genuine revolutionary like himself.

By January 1976, when Zhou succumbed to cancer, Mao's credibility was on the wane because of his lingering support for ideological extremists such as his wife, Jiang Qing. On the other hand, Zhou's reputation had been enhanced. His conspicuous role in restoring governmental functions and rehabilitating persecuted intellectuals and party veterans since 1971 was widely appreciated. Deng was seen as the one few cadres capable of continuing Zhou's work in his absence. The intense outpouring of grief accompanying news of Zhou's death unsettled Mao and his allies and spurred them to make a decisive move to curtail public mourning for Zhou and to remove Deng Xiaoping from power for a second time.

Demonstration Suppressed

On 4 April 1976, coinciding with the Qingming Festival to honor the dead, thousands gathered at Tiananmen Square in Beijing in defiance of strictures, laying wreaths, poems, and flowers in tribute to Zhou at the Monument to the People's Heroes. The gathering threatened to escalate into a demonstration against Mao himself as some wall posters denounced him as a cruel Qin Shi Huang Di, the despotic first emperor famous in history for "burning the books and burying the scholars." The CCP sent public security forces during the night of 4–5 April to remove the offerings from the monument and cordoned

off the area in an effort to keep the throngs of mourners at bay. The radicals responded by accusing Deng Xiaoping of orchestrating a conspiracy, and troops were sent in to suppress the demonstration on the night of 5 April. After Mao's died in September and the Gang of Four was arrested, mourning for Zhou was again permitted. Deng Xiaoping was exonerated of conspiracy charges, and the verdict on the so-called Tiananmen Incident of 1976 was reversed after Deng replaced Mao's appointed successor, Hua Guofeng, as paramount leader in a peaceful transfer of power that began in 1979 and was formally consolidated in 1981.

The dramatic events after Zhou's death suggest that Zhou ultimately won the footrace with Mao over the succession issue in the manner of the tortoise overtaking the hare. Some might even go so far as to say that Zhou finally stepped out from under the shadow of Mao to contend with him, albeit in his self-effacing way, during the final years of his life. Decades later we see that Zhou's more moderate, less ideological approach proved pivotal in determining the future of communism in China. Mao's choice of successor, the ideologue Hua Guofeng, could not compete with Zhou's candidate, the seasoned pragmatist and team player, Deng Xiaoping.

Zhou's rigorous work schedule, interrupted by only a few hours of sleep a night, epitomized the self-sacrifice and industriousness implied by Mao's slogan, "Serve the People," a motto that Zhou wore pinned to his lapel every day.

Shelley Drake HAWKS

Further Reading

Barnouin, B., & Yu Changgen. (2006). *Zhou Enlai: A political life.* Hong Kong: Chinese University of Hong Kong.

Chang, David W. (1984). *Zhou Enlai and Deng Xiaoping in the Chinese leadership succession crisis.* Lanham, MD: University Press of America.

Chen Wu. (2004, February). Review of Gao Wenqian's *Zhou Enlai's later years. China Analysts Group Monthly Journal, 1,* 47.

Collins Associates. (Eds.). (1973). *Quotations from premier Chou En-lai.* New York: Thomas Y. Crowell.

Gao Wenqian. (2003). *Wannian Zhou Enlai* [Zhou Enlai in his later years]. New York: Mingjing chubanshe.

Dance and Politics

The political beliefs of Zhou Enlai can be explained by observing his behavior and performance on the dance floor.

Zhou's handling of his political life can be understood by analogy to his behavior on the dance floor. Both Mao and Zhou enjoyed ballroom dancing. For Mao, dance parties were occasions for reveling in the adulation of a harem of young ladies. Ever anxious not to upstage the chairman, Zhou Enlai always left the dance floor the moment Mao arrived, although dancing, along with table tennis, was one of the few pastimes he permitted himself. But Zhou absented himself from the limelight in deference to Mao because Zhou wished to preserve harmonious relations with Mao. Within that ruler-minister relationship, Zhou had to display his junior status conspicuously.

This was the secret of Zhou's ability to survive so many purges: Mao could rely on him because he trusted that Zhou would never plot against him.

A radical Maoist once quipped that Zhou Enlai always swung his dance partner to the right. Apparently this was true—but not because Zhou consciously swung the ladies in the direction of his politics, as his critic was suggesting, but because an arm injury limited his range of motion. Nevertheless, the joke is in fact suggestive of who Zhou really was and how he was understood during his final years. By the early 1970s, Zhou was clearly a pragmatist, or a moderate, surviving in a sea of radicals. He was their tool, but he was not one of them, and they knew it.

Source: Hawks, S. D. (2007, January). Zhou Enlai and Mao Zedong. *Guanxi: The China letter* 1(9), 5–7.

Goldstein, S. M. (1983, December). Zhou Enlai and China's revolution: A selective view. *The China Quarterly, 96,* 720–730.

Hammond, E. (1980). *Coming of grace: An illustrated biography of Zhou Enlai.* Berkeley, CA: Lancaster-Miller.

Han Suyin. (1994). *Eldest son: Zhou Enlai and the making of modern China, 1898–1976.* New York: Hill and Wang.

Kampen, T. (2000). *Mao Zedong, Zhou Enlai and the evolution of the Chinese Communist leadership.* Copenhagen, Denmark: Nordic Institute of Asian Studies.

Keith, R. C. (1989). *The diplomacy of Zhou Enlai.* New York: St. Martin's Press.

Lee Chae-Jin. (1994). *Zhou Enlai: The early years.* Stanford, CA: Stanford University Press.

Liu Wusheng & Xu Xiaohong. (Eds.). (2006). *Ping shuo Wannian Zhou Enlai* [Critical response to Zhou Enlai's late years]. Beijing: Zhonggongdangshi chubanshe.

MacFarquhar, R., & Schoenhals, M. (2006). *Mao's last revolution.* Cambridge, MA: Belknap Press of Harvard University.

Short, P. (1999). *Mao: A life.* New York: Henry Holt.

Wilson, D. (1984). *Zhou Enlai: A biography.* New York: Viking.

Zhisui Li. (1994). *The private life of Chairman Mao* (Tai Hung-Chao, Trans.). New York: Random House.

ZHOU Xuexi

Zhōu Xuéxī 周学熙

1866–1947   *Qing and Republican official*

Zhou Xuexi was an official in the late Qing dynasty (1644–1912) and early Republic of China (1912–1949). After retiring from public service he championed north China's industrial development, rivaling the reputation of Zhang Jian, another magnate who operated his industrial conglomerate at Nantong near Shanghai.

Zhou Xuexi was born in Nanjing, although his father, Zhou Fu, a noted provincial governor in the Self-Strengthening Movement (a period of institutional reforms during the Qing dynasty), kept an ancestral home at Zhide (now Dongzhi) in Anhui Province. In 1886 the younger Zhou began his bureaucratic career as an attaché at the Bureau of Irrigation and Transportation in the Ministry of Works and became a *juren* (provincial graduate; the official designation granted a passer of a provincial examination) in 1893 under somewhat controversial circumstances. After futile attempts at the coveted *jinshi* degree (presented scholar; a degree conferred on successful candidates in the highest-level Civil service examination), he purchased official titles qualifying him to serve at various provincial posts until he found a patron in Yuan Shikai (who later succeeded Sun Yat-sen as president of the Republic of China). Rising quickly through the ranks, Zhou was instrumental in the establishment of state-supervised enterprises such as the Chee-Hsin Cement Co. (1900), Beiyang Mint (1902),

the Lan-chou Official Mining Co. (1907, merged with the Kaiping Colliery to form the Kailian Mining Administration in 1912), and the Beijing Waterworks (1908). Into the republican period he served as Yuan's chief aide in economic affairs and as minister of finance (1912–1913, 1915–1916). He joined the Nationalist Party (Guomindang) briefly to push through the controversial Reorganization Loan, a £25,000,000 political loan granted in 1913–1914 from England, France, Germany, Russia and Japan in support of Yuan Shikai.

However, Zhou's resistance to Yuan Shikai's monarchial bid and Beijing's factional politics soon forced his resignation. Although subsequently he received appointments such as national director of the Cotton Development Administration (1919), he increasingly pursued private industrial development and investment, beginning with the Guangqin Spinning and Weaving Mill in Wuxi in 1917. Amid charges of misappropriating state property, he privatized the Huaxin Cotton Spinning Mill (Tianjin), which soon branched out to Qingdao in 1918. To ensure a steady supply of raw material and financing, he organized the Xinghua Capital Corp. and Xingji cotton brokerage. Successes led to the launching in 1919 of branch mills at Tangshan and Weihui in Henan Province and formation of the Huaxin Corporation. Capitalized at 10 million yuan, the corporation was to coordinate the activities of the mills, although each retained its own board of directors and accounting independence. Profits from the Kailian mines provided the initial capital for the Yaohua Mechanical Glass Co., Ltd. (1921), a joint venture with Banque d'Outremer Consortium Industriel Belge,

Vanishing Owners and Melting Spindles

The rise and ultimate demise of the cotton mills in Tianjin are indicative of the unpredictable growth and development of industry in China. Zhou Xuexi worked toward repairing such unsteady conditions, which were often exacerbated by lax government policies.

The absence of a stable group of industrialists, a problem both caused and compounded by the political instability of North China, meant that local industry grew in erratic fits and starts. Nowhere is this more clear than in the case of Tianjin's largest mechanized industry, cotton spinning. In its bid to become a cotton center of national stature, Tianjin had several advantages: a local class of moneyed investors, access to raw materials, and a large market. Changes in the political scene brought in new entrepreneurs and gave the mills at least three opportunities to flourish—during World War I, in the late 1930s, and immediately after the Allied victory in World War II. But in each case chronic warfare, as well as government policies that sometimes verged on the cannibalistic, ultimately made it impossible for industry to prosper.

In the year after World War I, most of the Tianjin cotton mills were founded with the sponsorship of specific official or warlord cliques. Four of the mills were built at the southeastern edge of the concessions; two were north of the old city. Cao Kun, of the Fengtian warlord clique, was a major investor in the Heng Yuan Mill. The Yu Yuan Mill was dominated by the Anfu warlord clique. Its largest single stockholder was Ni Sichong (1.1 million yuan), and its original Board of Directors included Ni, Duan Qirui, and various high officials. Zhou Xuexi's Hua Xin Mill and the Yu Da Mill were other attractive targets for warlord investment.

Source: Hershatter, G. (1986). *The workers of Tianjin, 1900–1949.* Stanford, CA: Stanford University Press, 34.

which held the patent on the Fourcault process of making flat glass. To maintain control of these far-flung industries, Zhou established the Huaxin central office in 1922 (dissolved 1931) to oversee the four cotton mills, supported by the Huaxin Bank (flourished 1923, dissolved 1931). Declining reappointments to various companies, he attempted to retain control through his Industrial Office in 1924 but soon retired from active management of the group. At the height of his industrial career he controlled assets estimated at over 40 million yuan.

In retirement Zhou dedicated himself to philanthropic work, establishing lineage halls to commemorate the Zhou family lineage and schools and charitable estates at Wuhu, Zhide, and Tianjin. He also compiled and financed the publication of works on neo-Confucianism, although he became a practicing Buddhist and vegetarian in 1929. He was buried in Beijing.

Kwan Man BUN

Further Reading

Chunfu. (1978). Zhou Xuexi yu Beiyang siye [Zhou Xuexi and industrial development in North China]. *Tianjin wenshi ziliao Zuanji, 1,* 1–28.

Hao Qingyuan. (1991). *Zhou Xuexi chuan (A biography of Zhou Xuexi).* Tianjin, China: Tianjin Renmin chubanshe.

Zhou, Xuexi. (Comp.). (1997). *Zhou Xuexi chuanji huibian (Collected biographies on Zhou Xuexi).* Lanzhou, China: Gansu Wenhua chubanshe.

ZHOU *Zuoren*

Zhōu Zuōrén　周作人

1884–1967　Essayist

Zhou Zuoren, a leading essayist and social-cultural critic, influenced the development of modern Chinese literature by advocating "Human Literature" (its focus on humanistic as opposed to imperialist values), and by experimenting with styles that blend the unpretentious of the vernacular with the elegance of the classical.

Zhou Zuoren, a leading essayist of the twentieth century, was one of the major leaders in the New Culture Movement, a cultural critic, and a controversial writer. Born into a scholar-official family whose fortune was in sharp decline after centuries of social prestige, Zhou Zuoren grew up in Shaoxing County, Zhejiang Province, and received a traditional education in Chinese classics. After failing entry-level civil service examinations between 1898 and 1900, Zhou was ready for change and decided in 1901 to enroll in Nanjing's Jiangnan Naval Academy; there he studied English, mathematics, natural sciences, and military and naval history.. In 1906 Zhou went to Japan on a government scholarship intended to support his study of architecture. Zhou instead turned his energy to studying language. In 1910 he returned to China without earning a degree but with language skills in Japanese, English, Russian, and Greek.

Zhou's return to China coincided with the 1911 Revolution, an event that marked not only the beginning of Republican China (1912–1949) but also decade-long chaos

that would stimulate the New Culture Movement. In 1917 he accepted a professorship in the College of Arts at Beijing University, a tenure that Zhou retained until 1945. In 1925 Zhou was instrumental in expanding the curriculum in literature to establish the Department of Eastern Literature in Beijing University. From the 1920s to the 1940s he also taught at Yenching University and Beijing Normal University as a guest professor.

Already an experienced and published translator of Western literature, Zhou entered his most productive and innovative years as a writer in Beijing. He contributed regularly to the magazine *New Youth* with translations of literature from Russia, Japan, Poland, Hungary, and the United States. He was co-translator and co-compiler with Lu Xun (the pseudonym of Zhou Shuren, Zhou Zuoren's elder brother), of *Yuwai xiaoshuo ji* (Short Stories from Abroad), China's first such publication. Most important to his growing influence was his article, "Ren de wenxue" (Human Literature), published in *New Youth* in 1918 and viewed by his contemporaries as the article that conceptualized a goal of the rising literary revolution, as the literary experiments in the May Fourth era began to be called then. Between 1919 and 1920 he was active in promoting the "New Village" in China, a utopian experiment that was initiated by the Japanese Shirahaba School and influenced Chinese youth with anarchist idealism. He was one of the founding members of the Literary Research Association when it was established in Beijing in 1921. He also was one of the founders of an influential literary weekly, *Yusi* (Threads of Talk), when it was launched in 1924 and remained, in practice, its editor-in-chief. Throughout the 1920s Zhou contributed regularly to the literary supplement of *Jing Bao,* one of the major newspapers in north China.

Experiments with the Essay

Beyond his "Human Literature," Zhou's enduring contribution to modern Chinese literature lies in his experiments with the essay. His knowledge of traditional as well as foreign literature and languages evidently influenced his choice of style and genre. Yet his attention to style was also a direct reaction to the politicization of the May Fourth Movement, which turned some literary pursuits into propaganda. Zhou, an outspoken advocate for vernacular reform, took the view that the best style should be presented in the vernacular yet be inclusive of the elegance of the classical. He praised the style of the natural and the unpretentious and valued "taste," "simplicity," and even "austerity" in essay composition. His own essays, which were published and compiled into thirty volumes during his life, reflected such values. At Beijing University, Xie Bingxin, Xu Dishan, and Yu Pingbo were among those the best-known writers whose style was influenced by Zhou.

Although he held the position of a radical iconoclast against Confucian tradition in his national debut in *New Youth,* Zhou took a more inclusive attitude toward Chinese literature by the mid-1920s when he turned to writing *biji,* essays based on informal notes and musings he made while reading. His writing subjects during the 1920s ranged from literature to folklore, religion, sexology, women, and current affairs, and his sympathy always went to the weak and the oppressed. In the late 1930s and early 1940s he even made use of writings in Confucian tradition to expound his ideas. Seemingly a dramatic change, Zhou's approach to China's cultural legacies initially resulted from his disillusionment over the government controlled by the Guomindang (Chinese Nationalist Party) in 1928, which used violence to suppress radical youth and the Communists. During the War of Resistance against Japan (1937–1945, known primarily outside China as the Second Sino-Japanese War, which was fought in the larger context of World War II beginning in 1939), Zhou again used his comments on the humanism in the Confucian tradition as a masked criticism of Japan's invasion.

A proponent of cosmopolitanism toward foreign cultures, Zhou had been known as a Japanophile because of

Zhou Zuoren in 1912. Zhou was part of the New Culture Movement whose writings championed humanistic over imperial values and the vernacular over classical language.

his writings and public activities in promoting Chinese understanding of Japan and Japanese culture since the 1920s. Yet through these writings he made a clear distinction between Japanese politics of his time, which angered him, and Japanese culture, which he admired. Many of his friends were disappointed that he chose to remain in Beijing when Japan invaded, and many more denounced him when he served as the minister of education of the North China Political Council in occupied Beijing. Testimony by underground resisters later revealed that he had been persuaded by them to take the job in order to prevent an energetic collaborator from stepping into this influential position. Zhou's own writings that criticized in masked language the Japanese brutality during the war also provided corroborative evidence. Regardless of the solid evidence against the accusation of his collaboration,

Zhou was sentenced to a ten-year jail term in the charged political climate after the war. He was released in early 1949 when the Nationalist government collapsed. Zhou chose to return to Beijing; he was able to publish essays, memoirs, and translated works from Japanese and Greek literature only under pseudonyms. He died in 1967 after being beaten and abused for months by the Red Guards.

Revival of Interest

In the 1980s the Chinese people renewed their interest in Zhou's writings and life in what was termed "Zhou Zuoren Fever." Not only were his works reprinted, but also hundreds of scholarly articles and several biographies were published. Although his literary accomplishments and his contributions to the literature revolution were appreciated, his service to a collaboration regime under Japanese occupation remained controversial as critics under the influence of nationalism refused to accept his failed "national character." The revived interest in Zhou attests to both his importance as a writer in the modern Chinese literary movement and to the enduring difficulty of separating politics and culture in modern Chinese history.

LU Yan

Further Reading

Gunn, E. M. (1980). *Unwelcome muse: Chinese literature in Shanghai and Peking, 1937–1945.* New York: Columbia University Press.

Kiyama Hideo. (1978). *Pekin Kujoan Ki: Nitchu senso jidai no Shu Sakujin* [About the Living-in-Bitterness Studio in Beijing: Zhou Zuoren during the Sino-Japanese War]. Tokyo: Chikuma shobo.

Lu Yan. (2004). *Re-understanding Japan: Chinese perspectives, 1895–1945.* Honolulu: University of Hawaii Press.

Pollard, D. (1973). *A Chinese look at literature: The literary values of Chou Tso-jen in relation to the tradition.* Berkeley and Los Angeles: University of California Press.

Qian Liqun. (1990). *Zhou Zuoren zhuan* [A biography of Zhou Zuoren]. Beijing: Beijing shiyue wenyi chubanshe.

Zhang Juxiang & Zhang Tierong. (2000). *Zhou Zuoren nianpu* [A chronological biography of Zhou Zuoren]. Tianjin, China: Nankai daxue chubanshe.

Zhou Zuoren. (1974). *Zhitang huixianglu* [Reminiscences of Zhitang]. Kowloon, China: Sanyu tushu wenju gongsi.

Zhou Zuoren. (2002). *Zhou Zuoren zibian wenji* [Essay collections edited by Zhou Zuoren] (36 vols.). Shijiazhuang, China: Hebei jiaoyu chubanshe.

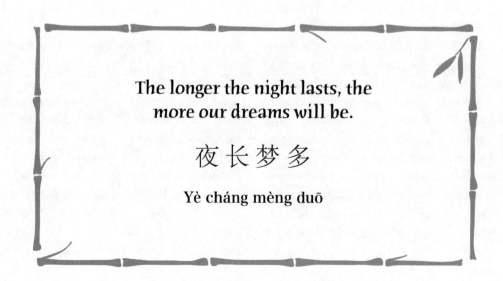

The longer the night lasts, the more our dreams will be.

夜长梦多

Yè cháng mèng duō

ZHU De

Zhū Dé 朱德

1886–1976   Founder of Chinese Communist army

Zhu De founded the Red Army. Under his command the Red Army undertook the Long March to Shaanxi Province. During the War of Resistance against Japan (1937–1945, known outside China as the Second Sino-Japanese War) Zhu commanded the Red Army's northern forces.

Zhu De (Chu Teh), the man who would found the Chinese Communist army, was the son of a poor tenant farmer. After Zhu graduated from Yunnan Military Academy in 1911, he participated in anti-Manchu activities in Yunnan and Sichuan provinces between 1912 and 1916. In 1922 he went to Europe on a work-study program and participated in Communist Party activities. Zhu returned to China in 1926 and became involved in the army of the Chinese Nationalist Party (Guomindang). After the Nanchang Uprising failed in 1927 Zhu led his troops to Hunan Province, where he joined with Chinese Communist Party (CCP) leader Mao Zedong (1893–1976). In Hunan Province they developed an effective military force that would become the Red Army. The Red Army, under Zhu's command, defended the Jiangxi soviet (the headquarters of the CCP) undertook the 9,656-kilometer Long March to Shaanxi Province.

During the War of Resistance against Japan (1937–1945, known outside China as the Second Sino-Japanese War) Zhu commanded the Red Army's northern forces. After Japan surrendered Zhu was commander of the People's Liberation Army (PLA) until 1955, when he became a PLA marshal. He later became chairman of the National People's Congress Standing Committee and continually was listed in many high positions, although he was not actively involved in politics after 1954.

Keith A. LEITICH

Further Reading

Gelder, G. S. (Ed.). (1946). *The Chinese Communists.* London: V. Gollancz.
Smedley, A. (1992). *The great road: The life and times of Chu Teh.* New York: Monthly Review Press.

Portrait of Marshal Zhu De, one of the leaders of the Long March. COURTESY OF PAUL AND BERNICE NOLL.

ZHU Xi

Zhū Xī 朱熹

1130–1200   Synthesizer of neo-Confucianism

Zhu Xi was perhaps the greatest neo-Confucian philosopher. His *Collected Commentaries on the Four Books* became the basis of the civil service examinations in 1315 until they were abolished in 1905; twenty-first-century Confucian scholars remain deeply influenced by Zhu's interpretations.

Zhu Xi, born in Youzi in Fukien Province, was perhaps the greatest neo-Confucian philosopher. He developed and clarified the metaphysics of two earlier philosophers, Cheng Yi (1033–1107) and brother Cheng Hao (1032–1085). According to their view, everything in the universe has two aspects, *li* (principle) and qi. *Li* is a structuring principle that accounts for both the way a thing is and the way it ought to be. Although the *li* is completely present in each and every thing, things are distinguished by having different endowments of qi. Qi is a sort of self-moving ethereal substance, which has varying degrees of turbidity or clarity. Inanimate objects have the most turbid qi, with plants, animals, and humans having increasingly clearer qi.

Because the *li* is one, everything is part of a potentially harmonious whole. Consequently, a good person has

---

Zhu Xi's writings on neo-Confucianism became the foundation of China's civil service exams for nearly six hundred years, and thus were the focus of study for generations of hopeful scholar-officials.

Philosophy of Zhu Xi

While Zhu Xi, also known as Chu Hsi, is best known for his work Collected Commentaries on the Four Books *and its contributions to Neo-Confucianism; he wrote on many topics, as seen below in his work on Heaven and Earth.*

In the beginning of the universe there was only material force [ch'i] consisting of yin and yang. This force moved and circulated, turning this way and that. As this movement gained speed, a mass of sediment was pushed together and, since there was no outlet for this, it consolidated to form the earth in the center of the universe. The clear part of material force formed the sky, the sun and moon, the starts and zodiacal spaces. It is only on the outside that the encircling movement perpetually goes on. The earth exists motionless in the center of the system, not at the bottom.

In the beginning of the universe, when it was still in a state of undifferentiated chaos, I imagine there were only water and fire. The sediment from water formed the earth. If today we climb the high mountains and look around, we will see ranges of mountains in the shape of waves. This is because the water formed them like this, though we do not know at what period they solidified. This solidification was at first very soft, but in time it became hard.

Question: I imagine it is like the tide rushing upon and making waves in the save. [Is that right?]

Answer: Yes. The most turbid water formed the earth and the purest fire became wind, thunder, lightening, starts, and the like.

Further Question: Can the universe be destroyed?

Answer: It is indestructible. But in time man will lose all moral principles and everything will be thrown together in a chaos. Man and things will all die out, and then there will be a new beginning.

Source: McNeill, W. H., & Sedlar, J. W. (Eds.). (1971). China, India, and Japan: The middle period. In *Readings in World History, Vol. 7.* Oxford, U.K. Oxford University Press, 83.

concern for everything that exists. Because the qi differentiates things, people have greater obligations to those tied to them by particular bonds such as the five principal relationships: ruler and subject; father and son; elder brother and younger brother; husband and wife; friend and friend. The clearer one's endowment of qi, the easier it is to appreciate one's obligations.

Relying on one's own moral sense without education is dangerous because selfish desires obscure the *li* within people. Instead, people should study the classic texts under a wise teacher because the texts provide partial abstractions of the *li* from its particular embodiments in qi.

Prior to Zhu Xi, Confucian education emphasized the Five Classics: the *Odes*, the *Documents*, the *Spring and Autumn Annals*, the *Record of Rites*, and the *I Ching* (*Yijing*). These works had been central to Confucian education since the Han dynasty (206 BCE–220 CE). Zhu Xi proposed a new curriculum based on what came to be known as the "Four Books." His *Collected Commentaries on the Four Books*, which gives a synthetic interpretation of these texts in the light of neo-Confucian metaphysics, became the basis of the Chinese civil service examinations in 1315 and was committed to memory by generations of scholars until the examinations were abolished in 1905. In the early twenty-first century the views of the majority of Confucians in East Asian communities, including the "new Confucian" philosophers, are deeply influenced by Zhu Xi's interpretations.

Bryan W. VAN NORDEN

Further Reading

Chan Wing-tsit. (Ed.). (1986). *Chu Hsi and neo-Confucianism.* Honolulu: University of Hawaii Press.

Gardner, D. K. (1990). *Chu Hsi: Learning to be a sage.* Berkeley and Los Angeles: University of California Press.

Graham, A. C. (1992). *Two Chinese philosophers* (2nd ed.). Chicago: Open Court Press.

ZHU Yuanzhang

Zhū Yuánzhāng 朱元璋

1328–1398   Founder of the Ming Dynasty

Zhu Yuanzhang 朱元璋 was the founding emperor of the Ming 明 dynasty (1368–1644). He rose from a life of suffering and adversity to become one of the most powerful and autocratic emperors in Chinese history.

Little is known of Zhu Yuanzhang's childhood except that he suffered many hardships. When most of his family died during an epidemic in 1344, he sought refuge at a Buddhist temple, where he spent several years as a novice monk, begging for food and basic supplies for the temple and learning to read and write from some of the monks. In 1352, after the temple was attacked and burned by the Yuan 元 military, he joined the Red Turban movement, part of the secret Buddhist-inspired White Lotus Society, which interpreted the floods, starvation, and chaos of the time as signs that the Buddha of the future, Maitreya, was about to appear and that the Mongols had lost the Mandate of Heaven and should be overthrown. The Mandate of Heaven, cited by every dynasty since the Zhou in 1045 BCE, refers to the belief that a benevolent Heaven bestowed the right to rule on every virtuous ruler.

Zhu was tall, physically imposing, intelligent, and fearless in battle. He quickly rose through the ranks and soon had troops under his command. He married his commander's adopted daughter, and when his commander was killed in battle in 1355, Zhu seemed the natural choice to take his place. In 1356 his troops occupied the important regional city of Nanjing, which had been the seat of several southern kingdoms. He had gained the allegiance of several learned and experienced men, and rather than simply loot and plunder, he and his forces began to administer the territory surrounding Nanjing and to impose peace and order in areas that had been in chaos for over a decade.

He formally broke with the Red Turbans in 1366, and within two years he had eliminated his rivals among the Red Turban commanders. He then declared the founding of a new dynasty, the Ming (meaning "bright" or "light") and sent his largest army in 1368 to invade and take over the former Yuan capital, which he renamed Beiping, "the north pacified." The name was changed to Beijing, "the Northern Capital," in the early fifteenth century.

The new emperor took the reign title Hongwu 明宏武 (Abundantly Martial), and he is also known in history as Ming Taizu 名太 (the Grand Progenitor of the Ming). He was energetic, smart, dedicated, and determined to ensure that the people of China would never have to suffer as he and his family had suffered. He ordered an empire-wide land and population survey, kept central government expenses low, and placed the dynasty on a firm financial footing. He put out many pleas, from 1368 on, for men of talent and dedication to come forward and aid him in the great enterprise of governing the empire. But after the empire was fully in his hands, he found it increasingly difficult to trust his officials and subordinates as implicitly as he had during his rise to power.

Whether from some deep character flaws, the insecurities of his youth, or the corruptions of power itself,

大明太祖高皇帝

A portrait of Zhu Yuanzhang, the imposing and often paranoid first emperor of the Ming dynasty, painted during his reign. Ink and color on silk.

he became a paranoid emperor who ultimately tried to control his officials through the blunt use of force and terror. In 1376 he ordered the execution of up to a thousand officials for having "prestamped" tax documents, which he took as a sign of corruption. In 1380 he turned on his prime minister, abolished his position, and had him killed along with another fifteen thousand officials. He ordered that his own Confucian admonitions and teachings be read aloud monthly at every village in the empire, so that the entire population could be taught the virtues of Confucian filial piety and loyalty to the emperor.

After his wife, Empress Ma, died in 1382 the emperor became even more paranoid and continued to order purge after purge, leaving the Confucian bureaucracy terrified and demoralized. Some have estimated that one hundred thousand people were executed by order of the "Abundantly Martial" emperor during his thirty years on the throne. Seldom has so much success and so much failure been combined in one life.

Paul ROPP

Further Reading

Dardess, J. W. (1983). *Confucianism and autocracy.* Berkeley and Los Angeles: University of California Press.

Farmer, E. (1995). *Zhu Yuanzhang and early Ming legislation: The reordering of Chinese society following the era of Mongol rule.* Leiden, The Netherlands: E. J. Brill.

Hucker, C. O. (1978). *The Ming dynasty: Its origins and evolving institutions.* Ann Arbor: University of Michigan, Center for Chinese Studies.

Mazur, M. (1997). The four Zhu Yuanzhangs: A succession of biographies of the Ming founder. *Ming Studies, 38,* 63–85.

Mote, F. W., & Twitchett, D. (Eds.). (1988). *The Cambridge history of China: Vol. 7. The Ming dynasty, 1368–1644. Part I.* Cambridge, U.K.: Cambridge University Press.

Zhuang

Zhuàngzú 壮族

The Zhuang (or Bouxcueng) tribal people of the southeast have contributed greatly to the history of southern China. They now are the largest of China's fifty-five officially recognized ethnic minority groups.

The Zhuang is the largest officially recognized minority ethnic group in China. (The Chinese government recognizes one majority group, the Han, and fifty-five minority groups.) They are very tribal and locality-oriented and traditionally have not considered themselves as one nationality. According to the 2000 census of the People's Republic of China, the Zhuang population was about 18 million.

Home

More than 90 percent of the Zhuang people live in the Guangxi Zhuang Autonomous Region in the southeast, bordering Vietnam and the Gulf of Tonkin. The remainder live in Yunnan, Guangdong, Guizhou, and Hunan provinces and often reside in areas populated with other south Chinese minority groups. A small population of Zhuang also lives in Vietnam. The tourist city of Guilin, with its famous nearby karst limestone landscape, is in a Zhuang-inhabited area. The Zhuang live in hamlets of twenty to thirty households, in brick and wood houses, often on stilts, in rain-forested mountainous regions known for straight high peaks, grottoes, and subterranean rivers.

The climate of Guangxi is mild in winter and tropical in summer. The mountains of Guangxi are heavily forested and rich in tea plantations. Minerals such as iron, coal, gold, copper, aluminum, zinc, and petroleum are abundant. Abundant rainfall flows through traditional bamboo pipes to nurture Zhuang rice paddies that can rise 1,000 meters (3,280 feet). The Zhuang also raise yams, corn, sugar cane, mangos, bananas, mushrooms, special medicinal plants, and fennel.

History

The Zhuang have a long recorded history, although the name "Zhuang" appeared only about 1,000 years ago. Their community sites came under Han Chinese control in 221 BCE under the first emperor of the Qin dynasty (221–206 BCE). Frescoes dating back more than 2,000 years have been discovered on numerous cliffs over the Zuojiang River in southwest Guangxi, which portray scenes in the life of the early Zhuang people. Powerful land-owning clans emerged in Zhuang areas of Guangxi and established Chinese-influenced kingdoms called Nan Yue (south) and Nan Han.

During the Tang dynasty (618–907 CE) and Song dynasty (960–1279), irrigated rice paddies, animal raising, and cloth manufacturing spread to the Zhuang people. Zhuang social classes included heredity landowners, tenant farmers, and servants, all ruled by headmen. Known for their martial spirit, they repulsed the Annamese (Vietnamese) invasions of south China in the 1070s and also defeated Japanese pirates in the sixteenth century.

Throughout the last thousand years the Zhuang and Yao minorities often fought each other. When the Taiping Rebellion (1851–1864) peasant uprising broke out in southwest China, many Zhuang became important leaders in its army. Zhuang and Han Chinese forces in Guangxi combined to stop invading French armies near Hanoi, Vietnam, in 1873 and in 1882.

Ethnic Zhuang played key roles in Dr. Sun Yat-sen's revolutionary organization in the early twentieth century, but Zhuang efforts to become autonomous were crushed under Chiang Kai-shek in 1929. Zhuang guerrillas fought along side the communists against the Japanese in World War II, but after the foundation of the People's Republic of China in 1949, Zhuang land was confiscated from traditional property owners and redistributed.

Under the communists, handicraft cooperatives were established and timber output increased greatly. More than twenty universities and colleges were established in Zhuang regions; the most famous is Guangxi Ethnic Institute. Infectious diseases that used to be rampant among the Zhuang—such as malaria, cholera, smallpox, and snail fever—have been wiped out.

Culture and Customs

The Zhuang language belongs to the Thai group of the Sino-Tibetan language family and has two main dialects. (Mandarin, the best known Chinese language, belongs to the Sinitic branch of Sino-Tibetan family. Zhuang and Mandarin are only distantly related, and speakers of one language do not understand speakers from the other.) The Zhuang developed their own written characters during the Song Dynasty (960–1279), but later Han Chinese characters were used for writing until in 1957, when the

China's ethnic Zhuang people and their costumes, Guangnan County, Yunnan Province. PHOTO BY JIALIANG GAO.

government helped to create a new writing system based on the Latin alphabet.

The Zhuang are polytheists, worshipping and making sacrifices to giant rocks, old trees, mountains, animals, and their human ancestors. Since the Tang dynasty, Daoism has strongly influenced their religious rites.

The Zhuang have a rich folk literature of legends, fairy tales, stories, and songs. Songfests are a common feature of social life and a means of choosing marriage partners. Common Zhuang musical instruments include the double-reed oboe (suona) bronze drum, cymbal, gong, Chinese windpipe (sheng), vertical bamboo flute, and horse-bone fiddle. Typical bronze drums of unclear purpose but reflecting skill in relief decorations have been unearthed and date back over 2,000 years. Zhuang dances are full of forceful and quick steps with humorous gestures. Their dance forms include dancing on wooden stilts, masked dances, and dancing with horse images. Zhuang opera, which combines folk literature, music, and dance, originated from Tang dynasty religious rituals. The Zhuang people also have their own form of puppet dramas.

Zhuang brocade originated in the Tang dynasty and is noted for its beautiful, colorful velour designs and tie-dyeing. There are regional clothing customs but, in general, men wear clothing similar to Han Chinese. However, the women in northwest Guangxi wear collarless, blue or black embroidered jackets buttoned to the left, with loose, wide trousers or pleated skirts with embroidered belts. Zhuang women in southwest Guangxi wear black collarless jackets buttoned to the left, with black square scarf headbands and loose black trousers. Women wear several large silver loop necklaces and other silver ornaments.

Tattooing on the face is still in practice among the Zhuang. Chewing betel nuts and drinking homemade wines remain common. Zhuang also make lacquerware similar to that found in Burma.

The Zhuang have three special festivals. On the Devil Festival, usually in August, every family prepares chicken, duck, wine, candy, and five-colored glutinous rice to offer as sacrifices to ancestors and ghosts. During the Cattle Soul Festival, after spring plowing, families carry a basket of steamed five-colored glutinous rice and a fresh grass bundle to the previously bathed cattle. They feed this mixture to the cattle to restore the souls they lost when whipped during the plowing. The Feasting Festival is celebrated by Zhuang near the Vietnamese border. It pays tribute to the Zhuang soldiers who gave up their traditional Spring Festival to repel the French invaders in the nineteenth century.

Many of the Zhuang people are surnamed Wei and trace their descent from a Han dynasty general, Han Xing. After the general's execution, a close friend took his son to south China and revised the writing of his surname Han to create the new name of Wei. Zhuang descendants of this Wei ancestor include Wei Baqun, who in 1894 led peasant uprisings in western Guanxi Province against the Manchus. These guerrilla activities developed into the Communist-inspired Baise uprising in the 1920s, which later was praised by Mao Zedong as an attempt to establish Soviet-style control in Zhuang territory. The most powerful leader in Guanxi after the communist revolution was the Zhuang tribal boss, Wei Guoqing, who was attacked and removed in the Cultural Revolution. Another famous Zhuang historical figure was Nong Zhigao, who is remembered for his declaration of independence from the Song Dynasty (960–1279) for his Zhuang clan in 1041.

Alicia CAMPI

Further Reading

Fan Qix & Qin Naicheng. (Eds.). (1993), *Zhuangzu baike cidian* [*Zhuang Encyclopedia*]. Nanning, China: Guangxi renmin chubanshe.

Palmer Kaup, K. (2000). *Creating the Zhuang: Ethnic politics in China*. Boulder, CO: Lynne Riennner.

Mackerras, C. (1994). *China's minorities: Integration and modernization in the twentieth century*. Hong Kong: Oxford University Press.

Zodiac

Shǔxiàng 属相

In China the zodiac is based on a calendrical system rather than on the stars. In a repeating sixty-year cycle twelve earthly "branches" operate in conjunction with ten heavenly "stems." Each earthly branch has an animal associated with it; each stem is associated with one of the two primordial, complementary forces of Chinese cosmology.

Whereas the Western zodiac is determined by the constellations that travel through the plane of the Earth's orbit against the celestial sphere, the Chinese zodiac is connected more closely with the Chinese calendrical system than with the stars. An ancient Chinese system of measuring time made use of a repeating sixty-year cycle whose component years combined ten heavenly "stems" and twelve earthly "branches." Each of the earthly branches has an animal associated with it—hence, the twelve animals of the Chinese zodiac.

The first earthly branch is symbolized by the rat (or mouse). The second is symbolized variously by the ox, the cow, or the water buffalo. The third is symbolized by the tiger. The fourth is symbolized by the rabbit (or the cat). The fifth earthly branch is usually symbolized by the dragon. The sixth earthly branch is symbolized by the snake; the seventh by the horse; the eighth by the goat or sheep; the ninth by the monkey; the tenth by the chicken (cock); the eleventh by the dog; and the twelfth by the pig. Stories explain how the various animals became zodiac

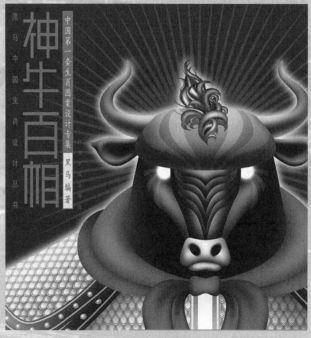

The ox, not surprisingly a symbol of hard work and dependability, can also be stubborn. The year 2009 is the Year of the Ox. From the Kailun Zodiac Collection of books. BERKSHIRE PUBLISHING.

animals and why they appear in the order they do. One story explains how the cat came to be left out of the zodiac (it was because of trickery on the part of the rat) and explains the mortal enmity between the two. Interestingly enough, in Vietnam the cat takes the rabbit's place in the zodiac.

A Chinese Horoscope of the 14th Century

The following is an excerpt from China scholar Joseph Needham's entry on the Chinese zodiac, referring to the diagram at right.

A Chinese horoscope of the 14th century. The nineteenth of a series of 39 sample horoscopes indicating all kinds of fortunes in life; here a person who is destined to achieve fame. . . . Favorable features of the horoscope are shown in the top right hand box, unfavorable ones opposite on the left. Immediately underneath and at the bottom corners are shown the celestial influences governing 42 different aspects of life and health. . . . The outer ring of the disc itself gives constellation names, the third gives *hsiu*, and the seventh cyclical characters. Segment significances are defined by the fifth ring. They concern, counting counterclockwise from the right (at half-past two), fate (i.e., longevity), wealth, brothers, landed property, sons, servants, marriage and women, illness, travel, official position, happiness, and bodily constitution. The order and nature of these twelve segments show at once that they are none other than the twelve houses or cusps (*loci, topoi*) of Hellenistic astrology. . . . The houses were so many immobile divisions of the celestial sphere, and horoscopes were cast according to the positions occupied by zodiacal constellations, planets, and certain stars at the time of the individual's birth.

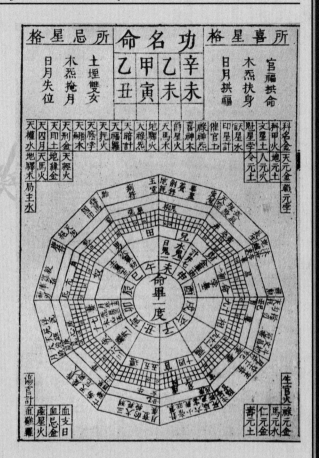

Source: Adapted from Needham, J., & Ling Wang. (1956). *Science & civilisation in China: History of scientific thought, Vol. II.* London and New York: Cambridge University Press, 352.

These twelve earthly branches operate in conjunction with the ten heavenly stems. The stems are divided into the two basic, primordial, complementary forces of Chinese cosmology (a branch of metaphysics that deals with the nature of the universe): yin (hot, dry, masculine, etc.) and yang (cold, wet, feminine, etc.), which are further modified by each of the five Chinese elements. (The ancient Greeks thought of four fundamental elements—earth, air, fire, and water—but the ancient Chinese thought in terms of five: fire, water, wood, metal, and earth.) The stems combine with the branches in six cycles of stems and five cycles of

branches, for a total of sixty years in the overarching cycle.

The way the stems and branches combine is such that each animal in the Chinese zodiac is either always yin or always yang: The rat, tiger, dragon, horse, monkey, and dog are yang; the ox, rabbit, snake, sheep (or goat), chicken (cock), and pig are yin. The animals are also divided into four groups of three: the rat, dragon, and monkey; the ox, snake, and chicken (cock); the tiger, horse, and dog; and the rabbit, sheep (goat), and pig. Each group shares similar strengths, weaknesses, and other characteristics, although the characteristics of a zodiac animal in any given year will also be modified by the element for the year—so that, for instance, the fire horse is said to be a particularly potent horse.

Thus, a year has a yin or yang designation, an elemental designation, and an animal designation. Most of 2000, for example, was a yang metal dragon year. This style of designation can also be used for days or months—and, indeed, can be related to (or used to represent) stars, directions, seasons of the year, landscape features, foods, flavors, parts of the body, and many other things. The zodiac is thus linked to astrology, geomancy (divination by means of figures or lines or geographic features), health, diet, selection of a marriage partner, and the best (or worst) time to travel, begin building a house, or perform certain religious rituals.

The Editors

Further Reading

Aslaksen, H. (2006). *The mathematics of the Chinese calendar.* Singapore: Department of Mathematics, National University of Singapore.

Walters, D. (1998). *The Chinese astrology workbook: How to calculate and interpret Chinese horoscopes.* Wellingborough, U.K: Aquarian Press.

Walters, D. (2005). *The complete guide to Chinese astrology.* London: Watkins Publishing.

Zuglakang Monastery

Dàzhāo Sì 大昭寺

Zuglakang Monastery in Lhasa is the most sacred Buddhist site in Tibet. It houses a statue of the Buddha said to date from his lifetime (c. 566–486 BCE).

Regarded as the most sacred Buddhist site in Tibet, Zuglakang Monastery has been closely linked with the historical development of Lhasa as a city and of Tibet as a nation. Zuglakang is one of the primary places of pilgrimage for Tibetan Buddhists because it contains a revered statue—that of Jowo (the Buddha at the age of twelve)—said to date from the lifetime of the Buddha (c. 566–486 BCE). Also, the name of the city, "Lhasa" (place of the gods) is an appellative for "Zuglakang."

Legends relate that the Yarlung king, Songsten Gampo (605–649 CE), began construction of the monastery in the year 639 in accordance with the wishes of his wife Bhrikuti, a princess of Nepal who had brought, as part of her dowry, statues of the Buddha that she wished to house in a suitable temple; she had noted that Tibet possessed no Buddhist temple. Songsten Gampo himself is said to have worked alongside the laborers in erecting Zuglakang.

The king had a second, Chinese wife, Wencheng Kongjo, of the Tang dynasty (618–907 CE) royal house. She, too, was a Buddhist and had brought with her the Jowo statue; she also required a temple for it. Wencheng is said to have practiced geomancy (divination by means of figures or lines or geographic features), and thereby she located the site where a temple would not be harmed by malignant forces. Zuglakang was built at that site.

Much of Zuglakang's design is based on Indian Buddhist architecture, with a strong, but later, admixture of Nepalese and Tang elements. Indeed, the structure itself may well be the oldest extant example of Indian religious structural design because similar buildings in India have long vanished, given the fact that Buddhism did not endure in the subcontinent. The monastery also contains many carved pillars, ornamented shrines, and adorned ceilings; it once had many paintings on stucco, but many of these have been destroyed, most during the Cultural Revolution (1966–1976).

When the Yarlung dynasty was overthrown in the middle of the ninth century, Zuglakang fell into disrepair, given the anti-Buddhist fervor of Repachen, the new ruler. However, subsequent kings began to demonstrate their piety and to show their legitimacy by undertaking elaborate restorations of the monastery. Thus, by the eighteenth century Zuglakang had become an expansive complex with chapels, residential apartments for the Dalai and Panchen Lamas, dormitories for monks, kitchens, storage facilities, government offices, service buildings, and large courtyards.

However, Zuglakang's symbolic significance as the first Buddhist temple in Tibet has allowed it to become intimately interwoven with Tibetan history. Thus, it has become the emblem of Tibetan identity. The sacred quality of the monastery depends on the legends that surround it, which ultimately speak of the

2662

process through which the message of the Buddha was brought to Tibet and then firmly rooted there. Zuglakang, then, is much more than a monastic complex: It is the soul of Tibet because through it Tibetans have constructed their identity, and within its walls they have historically placed their cultural, political, and religious aspirations.

Nirmal DASS

Tibetan monks at morning prayer. PHOTO BY YIXUAN SHUKE.

Further Reading

Alexander, A. (2005). *The temples of Lhasa: Tibetan Buddhist architecture from the 7th to the 21st centuries.* Chicago: Serindia Publications.

Beckwith, C. (1987). *The Tibetan empire of central Asia.* Princeton, NJ: Princeton University Press.

Haarh, E. (1969). *The Yar-lun dynasty.* Copenhagen, Denmark: G. E. C. Gad's Forlag.

Snellgrove, D. (2002). *Indo-Tibetan Buddhism: Indian Buddhists and their Tibetan successors.* Boston: Shambhala Publications.

Vitali, R. (1990). *Early temples of central Tibet.* London: Serindia Publications.

Present Buddha with
borrowed flowers.

借花献佛

Jiè huā xiàn fó

ZUO Zongtang

Zuǒ Zōngtáng 左宗棠

1812–1885   Chinese military leader and statesman

Zuo Zongtang was a renowned military leader of nineteenth-century China; he led the Chinese military in the suppression of the Muslim and Nian rebellions (1868–1880), negotiated with the Russians, and led the war against the French in 1884–1885.

Zuo Zongtang 左宗棠 (1812–1885) was born to a scholarly family in Hunan Province; in his early years he studied works in the fields of history, classics, geography, and agriculture. In 1852 he joined the military in the campaign against the Taiping Rebellion and soon displayed his military ability and wisdom. He was promoted to governor-general of Fujian and Zhejiang provinces in 1863 and remained in this position until 1866. Zuo founded China's first modern dockyard and naval school in Fuzhou during this period. In 1866 Zuo was appointed governor-general of Shaanxi and Gansu provinces to suppress the Muslim rebels there. Between 1868 and 1880, Zuo suppressed Nian rebels in Shandong Province and the Muslim rebels in the northwestern China and consolidated China's northwestern frontier. He militarily sustained China's negotiation with Russia in recovering Yili, a Chinese territory occupied by Russia during the Muslim rebellion. He also carried out several important economic reforms, including the encouragement

Portrait of General Tso (Zuo Zongtang), by Pavel Piassetsky, 1875. Zuo Zongtang, a Chinese statesman, served during China's fourteen-year-long Taiping Rebellion.

of the cotton industry in Xinjiang and the mobilization of soldiers to farm unused land. In 1881 Zuo was appointed to serve in the Grand Council of the central government. Later, in 1884, he was once again put in

The Art of War

The numerous successes in Zuo Zongtang's military career show his deep understanding of military knowledge and strategy, the foundations of which were laid out by Sunzi (also spelled Sun Tzu) in The Art of War, *thought to date from the fourth century BCE:*

ATTACK BY STRATAGEM

1 Sun Tzu said: In the practical art of war, the best thing of all is to take the enemy's country whole and intact; to shatter and destroy is not so good. So, too, it is better to recapture an army entire than to destroy it, to capture a regiment, a detachment or a company entire than to destroy them.

2 Hence to fight and conquer in all your battles is not supreme excellence; supreme excellence consists in breaking the enemy's resistance without fighting.

3 Thus the highest form of generalship is to balk the enemy's plans; the next best is to prevent the junction of the enemy's forces; the next in order is to attack the enemy's army in the field; and the worst policy of all is to besiege walled cities.

4 The rule is, not to besiege walled cities if it can possibly be avoided. The preparation of mantlets [a shield used to protect besieging soldiers], movable shelters, and various implements of war, will take up three whole months; and the piling up of mounds over against the walls will take three months more.

5 The general, unable to control his irradiation, will launch his men to the assault like swarming ants, with the result that one-third of his men are slain, while the town still remains untaken. Such are the disastrous effects of a siege.

6 Therefore the skillful leader subdues the enemy's troops without any fighting; he captures their cities without laying siege to them; he overthrows their kingdom without lengthy operations in the field.

7 With his forces intact he will dispute the mastery of the Empire, and thus, without losing a man, his triumph will be complete. This is the method of attacking by stratagem.

Source: Sun Tzu. (2007). *The art of war.* (Lionel Giles, Trans.). Charleston, SC: Forgotten Books, pp. 7–8. (Original translation published in 1910; original work thought to date from fourth century BCE).

charge of all military affairs of China during the Sino-French War (1884–1885). After a settlement between China and France was reached, Zuo Zongtang died on 5 September 1885. Zuo Zongtang's success in putting down rebellions shaped the military prowess and unity of China in the nineteenth century.

CHEN Shiwei

Further Reading

Chu, Wen-chang. (1966). *The Moslem Rebellion in Northwest China, 1862–1878: A Study of Government Minority Policy.* The Hague, The Netherlands: Mouton de Gruyter.

Wright, M. C. (1957). *The Last Stand of Chinese Conservatism: The T'ung-chih Restoration, 1862–1874.* Stanford, CA: Stanford University Press.

Image Sources

Photographers

Berkshire Publishing Staff
Burner, J. Samuel
Eaton, Robert
Gahn, Larry
Harcourt, Tim
Jensen, Derek
Lackinger, Helmut
Lebold Cohen, Joan
Mackerras, Colin
Massand, Rikki N.
McMasters, N. H.
Noll, Paul and Bernice
    (www.paulnoll.com)
Pulver Family
Shen, Rico
Wang, Jeff
Wang Ying
Wen Bo
Ye Yang, Oliver
Yixuan Shuke

Institutions and Organizations

American Chamber of Commerce in Shanghai
Australian Trade Commission
Beinecke Rare Books and Manuscripts Library,
    Yale University
Freer and Sackler Galleries of Washington, D.C.
IISH Stefan R. Landsberger Collection
    (www.iisg.nl/~landsberger)
Library of Congress Prints and Photographs Division,
    Washington, D.C.
Marxists Internet Archive
Museum of Far Eastern Antiquities, Stockholm.
Museum of Fine Arts, Boston
National Archives (U.S.)
National Committee for United States–China Relations
National Palace Museum, Taipei
Palace Museum, Beijing
Shanghai Museum
Smithsonian Photography Initiative
University of Rhode Island Historic Textile and
    Costume Collection

PHOTO BY JOAN LEBOLD COHEN

A

A

Notes: 1) **Bold** entries and page numbers denote encyclopedia entries;
2) The bold numbers preceeding the page numbers denote the volumes
(1–5) where the page numbers can be found

A

B

Notes: 1) **Bold** entries and page numbers denote encyclopedia entries;
2) The bold numbers preceeding the page numbers denote the volumes (1–5) where the page numbers can be found

B

Notes: 1) **Bold** entries and page numbers denote encyclopedia entries;
2) The bold numbers preceding the page numbers denote the volumes
(1–5) where the page numbers can be found

C

C

Notes: 1) **Bold** entries and page numbers denote encyclopedia entries;
2) The bold numbers preceeding the page numbers denote the volumes
(1–5) where the page numbers can be found

arts and, 1:101, 1:399–400, 2:644, 2:691–693, 2:892, 3:1528, 4:1653, 4:1658, 5:2550–2551

bipartisanship in, 3:1283

cadre system, 1:255–256

campaigns (*See* Campaigns)

Chen Yun in, 1:312–313, 4:1869–1870

Christianity and, 1:392–393

creative economy supported by, 1:514

Ding Lingo in, 2:610

founding of, 1:305, 3:1390, 3:1433–1434, 3:1592, 5:2391

Guo Moruo in, 2:967–968

Hu Yaobang in, 2:1082

human rights position of, 3:1112–1115

Iron Rice Bowl, 3:1183–1184, 4:1872

journalism, control of, 3:1219–1220

Korean War, role in, 3:1249–1250

legal system, influence on, 1:516, 3:1295

Li Dazhao, founder, 3:1311–1312

Liu Shaoqi in, 3:1342–1343

local secretaries, power of, 2:908

Mao's legacy and, 3:1397–1399, 3:1401

marriage and family system, reform of, 3:1405–1406

minorities and, 2:767–769, 2:773–775, 3:1279–1281

Nationalist Party, alliance with, 1:192–193, 1:354–265, 3:1311–1312, 3:1346, 4:2134

"New Democracy" transition period, 1:355

newspapers, 3:1610–1612

People's Daily, 4:1745–1746

political participation, 4:1778–1779

post-Mao, 1:356–359 (*See also* **Reforms since 1978-1979**)

propaganda, 1:99, 1:457, 5:2213

religious policies and practices, 1:116–117, 4:1881–1885

Soviet support for forces of, 1:411–413

sports, support for, 4:2089–2090

television programming, control of, 5:2213

United Nations and, 5:2345

United States and, 5:2354–2355 (*See also* **United States—China relations**)

Xi'an Incident, role in, 5:2501–2503

Youth League, 1:460–461

Notes: 1) **Bold** entries and page numbers denote encyclopedia entries;
2) The bold numbers preceeding the page numbers denote the volumes
(1–5) where the page numbers can be found

Zhao Ziyang in, 5:2625–2626

Chinese Construction Bank, 1:154–155, 1:360–361

Chinese domain names, 3:1181–1182

Chinese Eastern Railway, 2:1004, 3:1380, 4:1914, 5:2541

Chinese Educational Mission to the United States, 5:2607

Chinese Exclusion Act, 1:349, 4:1676

Chinese Export-Import Bank, 1:21

Chinese-Foreign Joint Venture Income Tax, 2:727–728, 5:2199, 5:2201

Chinese language, 1:328, 2:982–983, 4:1993. *See also* **Cantonese (Yue); Hakka languages; Mandarin; Sino-Tibetan languages; Vernacular language movement**

ancient language, Gu Yanwu's study of, 2:940

classical, 1:368–372, 2:897, 5:2387–2389

dialects, 2:897

foreign language, learning as, 1:343, 1:495

Han, languages spoken by, 2:772

Min, 2:772, 3:1471–1473

Modern Standard Chinese, 1:371, 2:983, 3:1385–1387

Northern Chinese, 3:1388

popular music, used in, 3:1529

Premodern Chinese, 3:1388–1389

translation of books, 4:1807–1808

Tujia, 5:2330

word radicals, 5:2459–2460

written language (*See* **Calligraphy;** Written language)

Wu, 5:2483–2485

Xiang, 5:2504–2510

Yao, 5:2563

Chinese Language Council International, 1:343, 1:495

Chinese naming system, 3:1541–1543

Chinese NASDAQ, 2:1028

Chinese Nationalist Party, 1:337–338, 1:362–367, 2:967–968, 5:2339. *See also* **Chiang Ching-kuo; Chiang Kai-shek; Civil War 1945-1949;** Republic of China (1912-1949); **Sun Yat-sen;** Taiwan

alliance with Communist Party, 1:192–193, 1:354–355, 3:1311–1312, 3:1346, 4:2134

baojia, use of, 1:159–160

black gold politics, 1:178

Blue Shirts Society, 1:183–184, 1:365

C

C

C

tal Bonds and Five Constant Virtues; Zhong Yong (Doctrine of the Mean)

ancestor worship, **1**:57–58, **4**:1889–1890

art influenced by, **4**:1682

atheism and, **1**:115

Buddhism and (*See* **Buddhism**)

Christianity and, **3**:1584, **4**:1897

civil service examination requirements, **2**:695–698, **3**:1578

Communist Party attacks on, **1**:481

contemporary, **4**:1880

Daoism and, **1**:478, **2**:564–565, **2**:569, **2**:570, **2**:574, **2**:995, **3**:1116, **3**:1576

education, **1**:468, **2**:637, **2**:872, **3**:1127–1128, **3**:1332, **3**:1484, **3**:1578, **4**:1679, **4**:2055

Evidential Inquiry study of, **2**:940–941

folk religion and, **4**:1873

geographical concepts, **2**:1030–1031

governance principles (*See* **Governance principles**)

Han Chinese and, **2**:983–984

Han dynasty, **1**:328, **1**:478, **1**:494, **2**:635–637, **2**:940, **2**:986, **4**:1890

humor and, **3**:1116–1117

legalism and, **1**:478, **3**:1276, **3**:1300, **3**:1301

literature, **3**:1223, **3**:1332, **3**:1333, **3**:1627–1628, **4**:1775

May Fourth Movement and, **3**:1432–1433, **5**:2649

Ming dynasty, **1**:479, **3**:1486, **3**:1488, **3**:1578

Mohist school as alternative, **3**:1301, **3**:1525, **5**:2417

New Confucianism, 20th Century, **1**:410, **1**:480–481

New Culture Movement and, **3**:1588–1591

People's Republic of China government, sponsored by, **1**:483, **1**:491

printing of classics, **2**:829

Qin dynasty, **4**:1829, **4**:1831

Qing dynasty, **1**:479–480, **3**:1092–1093, **3**:1578–1579, **4**:1833, **4**:1835, **4**:1836

regional interdependence and, **2**:734

rituals, importance of, **4**:2021

rock carvings and cave paintings, **2**:588, **3**:1507

sacred mountains, **3**:1518

social order and, **1**:516

Song dynasty, **1**:478–479, **1**:494, **3**:1576–1578, **4**:1886, **4**:2039, **4**:2042–2044

sports, attitude toward, **4**:2079, **4**:2080

strangers, solidarity with, **1**:489–490

Tang dynasty, **1**:478, **2**:995–996, **4**:1890

textile designs, reflected in, **5**:2241

tribute system, **3**:1328–1329

Vietnam, influence in, **4**:2055

Warring States period, **1**:478, **3**:1127, **5**:2417

women, role of, **5**:2260–2263, **5**:2454–2455

yin-yang theory, **5**:2580, **5**:2583

Yuan dynasty, **5**:2600, **5**:2601

Confucianism—revival, 1:482–492, 4:2008

Confucius, 1:467–468, 1:477–478, 1:493–494, 3:1127, 4:2024

Confucius Institutes, 1:458, 1:495, 4:1679

Constitutional monarchy, **4**:1835

Consumer goods, **2**:594, **2**:595, **3**:1162, **5**:2306–2308

Consumerism, 1:496–500

Consumption taxes, **5**:2199–2200

Contemporary music, **3**:1527–1530

Content providers, **4**:1808

Continental Bank, **4**:2064

Coolies, **4**:1676, **5**:2313, **5**:2607–2608

Cooperative Medical System, **2**:1006–1008

Cooperatives, agricultural, **1**:26–32, **2**:586

Copyrights, **3**:1168–1171, **4**:1809–1810

Corporate social responsibility, 1:501–503

Corporate sponsorships of sports, **4**:2082–2086

Correctional institutions, **1**:517, **1**:519–520

Corrections on the Errors of Medical Works, **3**:1439

Correctness. *See* Yi

Corruption, 1:504–505

black gold politics, **1**:178–179

criminal justice system, **1**:527

Five-Anti Campaign, **2**:837–838

Green Gang, **2**:938–939

guanxi *vs.*, **2**:955

Nationalists, art critiquing, **1**:99

Cosco Group, 1:506–508

Cosmograph, **2**:810–811

Cosmology

Daoism, **2**:566, **2**:573, **5**:2417–2418 (*See also* **Dao (the Way)**)

of the Shang, **5**:2578

Notes: 1) **Bold** entries and page numbers denote encyclopedia entries; 2) The bold numbers preceeding the page numbers denote the volumes (1–5) where the page numbers can be found

Notes: 1) **Bold** entries and page numbers denote encyclopedia entries;

2) The bold numbers preceeding the page numbers denote the volumes

(1–5) where the page numbers can be found

Note: **Bold** entries and page numbers denote encyclopedia entries.

D

Notes: 1) **Bold** entries and page numbers denote encyclopedia entries;
2) The bold numbers preceeding the page numbers denote the volumes
(1–5) where the page numbers can be found

D

Decentralization, **2**:670, **2**:911, **5**:2303, **5**:2359–2360

Decollectivization, **2**:670, **2**:929

Decoration. *See* Crafts and decoration

Defense industry, 2:593–597, 3:1560

Deforestation, **1**:42, **2**:732–733, **2**:736, **2**:738–740, **2**:753–754, **2**:934, **2**:936

Democracy, Chinese, **1**:358, **2**:605–606, **3**:1282–1283, **3**:1398–1399, **3**:1589, **3**:1591, **4**:1869–1870, **5**:2271

"Democracy Wall" movement, **3**:1618

Democratic Progressive Party, 1:309, 1:366–367, 2:598–601

Democratic Republic of Vietnam. *See* Vietnam

Deng Lijun, **3**:1529

Deng Pufang, **2**:603, **2**:613, **2**:615

Deng Xiaoping, 2:591, 2:602–604, 2:622. *See also* **Reforms since 1978-1979**

Anti-Spiritual Pollution Campaign, **1**:68–70, **4**:1686

Chen Yun and, **1**:312–313

Cultural Revolution and, **2**:539, **2**:541, **2**:542, **2**:603, **3**:1401, **5**:2357

Great Leap Forward, reforms after, **2**:539, **2**:602, **3**:1357

Jiang Zemin and, **3**:1207–1208

in Long March, **3**:1348

Mao, relationship with, **2**:602–603, **4**:1869

Mao's legacy and, **3**:1397–1399, **3**:1401

military and, **4**:1747–1748

opera supported by, **4**:1658

selection as CCP leader, **4**:1868

Soviet Union, relations with, **4**:1915

Zhou Enlai and, **5**:2641, **5**:2644

Deng Xiaoping's Southern Tour, 2:604, 2:605–607

Deng Zihui, **1**:29

Denggao Jie, **1**:383

Desertification, **1**:42, **2**:739, **2**:741, **2**:865, **2**:922, **3**:1164, **4**:2036–2037

Detention houses, **1**:519–520, **1**:524

Developing the West program, **4**:1974, **5**:2521

Development zones, 2:608–609

Dewey, John, **1**:340

Di, King, **4**:1673

Di Baio, **3**:1608–1609

Di er ci ya pian zhan zheng. *See* **Opium War, Second**

Di guo de hun yin, **3**:1410–1412

Di guo de si fa. *See* **Law, imperial**

Di guo jun dui. *See* **Military, imperial**

Di li. *See* **Geography**

Di tu xue, **1**:282–285

Di yi ci ya pian zhan zheng. *See* **Opium War, First**

Diamond Sutra, **2**:657

Dian dang hang, **4**:1724–1726

Dian nao kong jian, **2**:552–553. *See also* **Internet use**

Dian shi. *See* **Television**

Dian ying yuan. *See* **Cinema**

Diaoyu Islands, **2**:666

"Diary of a Madman," **3**:1353–1354, **3**:1433, **5**:2389

Dictionaries, 2:702–703

Di'er ci shi jie da zha zai ya zhou. *See* **World War II in Asia**

Diet therapy, **3**:1438–1439

Difang xi, **4**:1655–1659. *See also* **Kunqu; Opera, Beijing**

Diji zhu, **4**:1877

Dili. *See* **Geography**

Ding Ling, 2:610–611, 3:1590

Ding ware, **4**:1786

Ding wei liang, **3**:1417–1418

Ding Wenjiang, **1**:81

Ding Xian rural reconstruction project, **4**:1909–1910, **5**:2570

Dingcun culture, **4**:1711

Dinghushan Nature Reserve, **3**:1563

Dingling mausoleum, **5**:2250

Dingzhenlian, **2**:652

Diplomats (Warring States), **3**:1130

Disability, 2:612–616, 2:687–690, 3:1621

Disasters, 1:339, 2:617–629, 2:745, 2:906–907, 2:1015–1016. *See also* **Tangshan Earthquake, Great**

Dismissal of Hai Rui, **2**:973–974

Distributed denial of service (DDOS) attacks, **3**:1173

Divination, 1:409, 2:630–632, 2:1042, 3:1141, 3:1375, 4:1942–1943, 5:2581, 5:2583

Divine immortals, **2**:572

Divorce, **3**:1408, **3**:1411

Dizang Pusa, **1**:232

DNS tampering, **3**:1173

Notes: 1) **Bold** entries and page numbers denote encyclopedia entries; 2) The bold numbers preceeding the page numbers denote the volumes (1–5) where the page numbers can be found

E

Notes: 1) **Bold** entries and page numbers denote encyclopedia entries; 2) The bold numbers preceeding the page numbers denote the volumes (1–5) where the page numbers can be found

E

E

F

by Lu Xun, **3**:1353–1355
Fifth-generation cinema, **1**:403
Fifth-generation leaders, **3**:1283, **3**:1284
Fighting in Northern Shaanxi, **1**:101
Filial piety, **1**:468, **2**:619, **2**:813–815, **3**:1127, **3**:1605,
　　4:1890
　aging population and, **1**:486, **2**:815, **4**:1644
　in *Analects,* **1**:53
　ancestor worship and, **1**:57
　Cultural Revolution, effect of, **2**:815
　May Fourth Movement, effect of, **2**:814–815
Film. *See* **Cinema**
Filmmakers
　Chen Kaige, **1**:306–307, **1**:403, **4**:2015
　Chen Yifei, **1**:310
　Lee Ang, **3**:1287–1288, **3**:1530
　Xie Jin, **1**:399–400, **5**:2512–2513
　Zhang Yimou, **1**:403, **5**:2619–2620
　Zheng Shichuan, **1**:396
Finches and Bamboo, **4**:1694
Fireworks and firecrackers, **1**:103, **2**:816–819, **2**:965
First Automotive Group Corporation (FAW),
　　1:124–128, **3**:1159, **3**:1214, **3**:1625, **5**:2246
First Emperor, The, **3**:1530
First Opium War. *See* **Opium War, First**
First Sino-Japanese War. *See* **Sino-Japanese War, First**
First United Front, **3**:1312
Fish. *See also* Carp
　breeding/farming, **1**:73–79, **2**:820–822, **2**:903
　cultural significance of, **2**:904–905
　goldfish, **2**:903–905
Fishing industry, **2**:742, **2**:820–823, **3**:1569
　aquaculture, **1**:73–79
　Hongze Lake, **2**:1060
　Hunan Province, **3**:1119
　international fisheries agreements, **2**:824–825
　Kao-hsiung, **3**:1240
　Liaoning Province, **3**:1324
Fishing industry—Taiwan, **2**:824–826
Five-Anti Campaign, **2**:538, **2**:837–838, **5**:2251

Five Classics. *See* **Four Books and Five Classics of Confucianism**
Five Constant Virtues. *See* **Three Fundamental Bonds and Five Constant Virtues**
Five Dynasties and Ten Kingdoms Period, **2**:588,
　　2:827–830, **2**:986
　painting, **4**:1689, **4**:1693, **4**:1702
　poets, **4**:2047
　Quan Tangshi, **4**:1859–1860
Five elements, the, **2**:573, **2**:575, **2**:811–812, **2**:831–833,
　　4:1929–1931, **5**:2575–2576, **5**:2580–2582
Five Principles of Peaceful Coexistence, **2**:834–836,
　　4:2010
Five Terraces Mountain, **1**:230–231
Five-year plans
　2001-2005, **3**:1163
　current, **5**:2320
　first, **1**:35–36, **2**:668, **3**:1159, **3**:1368–1369, **4**:1959,
　　5:2371–2372
　second, **1**:36
　Third Front policy (*See* **Third Front policy**)
Five–yuan system, **2**:839–841
Flood control, **5**:2422–2423
Floods, **2**:620–621, **2**:731, **2**:736–738, **2**:741–742,
　　3:1087–1088
Flower and bird painting, **4**:1693–1696,
　　5:2403–2404
Flowers in the Mirror, **3**:1481
Fo jiao. *See* **Buddhism**
Fogong Monastery, **1**:92
Folk painting, **4**:1697–1700
Folk religion, **4**:1873–1879
Folk songs, **3**:1532
Follow Closely Our Great Leader Chairman Mao, **1**:101
Food. *See also* Agriculture; **Cuisines;** Famine
　agro-geography, influenced by, **1**:40–42
　bamboo, **1**:138
　Chinese self-sufficiency, **4**:1870
　health and nutrition issues, **2**:1010–1012
　tofu, **5**:2293
Food safety, **1**:73–79, **2**:742, **2**:842–845
Foot-binding, **1**:439, **1**:445, **1**:448, **2**:846–847, **3**:1405,
　　5:2455–2456
Forbidden City, The, **1**:93, **1**:165–167, **2**:848–851, **3**:1486
　gardens in, **2**:890, **2**:891
　as World Heritage site, **1**:167, **2**:848, **5**:2464

Notes: 1) **Bold** entries and page numbers denote encyclopedia entries;
2) The bold numbers preceeding the page numbers denote the volumes
(1–5) where the page numbers can be found

F

Fowliang (Jingdezhan), 3:1212, 3:1216–1217

France. *See also* **Opium War, Second;** Vietnam

    Boxer Rebellion, troops used in, 1:198

    Chinese immigration to, 4:1677

    missionaries, 3:1498–1499

    radicals, Chinese religion adopted by, 1:336

    Sino-French War, 3:1313–1314

    trade relations, 4:1647–1649

Free-supply system, 2:927–928

Free trade agreements. *See* Trade agreements

Friends of the Way of Tranquility and Purity, 2:938

Fu prose-poetry, 2:991–994, 3:1332–1333, 4:1774–1775, 4:1983–1984

Fu symbols, 1:440, 5:2240

Fu (trousers), 1:437–438, 1:440–442

Fubing system, 2:874–875

Fudan University, 2:876–877

Fujian Province, 1:420–421, 2:878–879, 4:2074

    cuisine, 1:41, 1:534

    ethnic groups, 2:979, 2:980

    foreign investment in, 2:855, 3:1161

    foreign trade, 2:878

    migration rank of, 3:1459

    Min dialect group, 3:1471–1473

    Wuyishan National Nature Reserve, 3:1564

Fujian ship (*fuchan*), 2:785, 5:2311

Funai ju, 2:991–992

Fuzhou, 2:608

Fuzhou dialect, 3:1471–1472

G

Gambling, 2:881–883, 3:1176

Games. *See* **Sports**

Gan ba Zhi du, 1:255–256

Ganchang. See **Three Fundamental Bonds and Five Constant Virtues**

Gang of Four, 2:542, 2:622, 2:884–886, 3:1398

    arrests and trials of, 1:356, 1:504, 2:886, 4:1868

    artifacts, destruction of, 1:108

Notes: 1) **Bold** entries and page numbers denote encyclopedia entries;
2) The bold numbers preceeding the page numbers denote the volumes
(1–5) where the page numbers can be found

Gangsters, 1:66, 1:178–179, 1:320, 2:938–939

Gansu Province, 1:91, 1:97–98, 1:421, 2:887–889, 3:1106, 5:2288. *See also* **An Lushan (An Shi) Rebellion; Dunhuang Caves**

Gansu-Xinjiang region, agrogeography of, 1:44

Gao deng jiao yu, 5:2359–2361

Gao E, 1:276

Gao lao jian cha zhi du, 4:2141–2145

Gao Ming, 3:1335

Gao xin ji shu kai fa qu, 2:1022–1029, 4:1815. *See also* **Internet industry; Mobile communications**

Gao Zu, 2:986

Gaoxiong, 3:1240

Gaozong, 4:2181

Gaozu, 4:2180

Gardens, 1:90, 1:176–177, 2:890–892, 5:2466

Gate towers, 1:91

Ge Hong, 2:572, 2:574–575, 3:1437, 4:1879

Ge ming. *See* **Revolutions**

Ge xuan, 2:574

Geary Act, 5:2352–2353

Gelao people, 2:775

Gelugpa, 1:241–242

Gender issues, 4:2017–2018. *See also* **Women, role of**

General Treatise on the Cause and Symptoms of Disease, 3:1437–1438

Generation Y, 4:2012

Genghis Khan. *See* Chinggis Khan

Geography, 2:893–898. *See also* **Climate and vegetation;** Environmental issues; **Grasslands;** Mountain ranges; Rivers; specific provinces

    administrative, 2:897–898

    cartography, 1:282–285

    economic, 2:921–922

    historical, 2:1030–1035

    human, 2:895–897, 2:919–920

    mineral resources, distribution of, 3:1477–1478

    physical, 2:893–895, 2:918–919

    Sino-Swedish Expedition, 4:1991–1992

    as study, 2:896–897

    urban, 5:2363–2368

    Western influences, 2:1032–1035

Geomancy. *See* **Divination; Feng shui**

Geothermal energy, 2:723

Germany, 1:198, 2:595, 4:1647

Geyi, 1:220–221

G

Notes: 1) **Bold** entries and page numbers denote encyclopedia entries;

2) The bold numbers preceeding the page numbers denote the volumes (1–5) where the page numbers can be found

H

H

Notes: 1) **Bold** entries and page numbers denote encyclopedia entries; 2) The bold numbers preceeding the page numbers denote the volumes (1–5) where the page numbers can be found

H

Household responsibility system, 1:36–37, **2:**671, **2:**1066–1072, **4:**1870

Housing, urban, **4:**1970–1971, **5:**2363, **5:**2365, **5:**2367–2368. *See also* **Hutong**

HSBC (Hongkong and Shanghai Banking Corporation), **1:**155, **2:**1058–1059

Hsieh, Frank, **2:**601

Hsu Hsin-liang, **2:**600

Hu bi lie da han. *See* **Khubilai Khan**

Hu Die, 2:1073–1074

Hu fu, **1:**437–438

Hu Hanmin, **1:**24, **2:**840–841

Hu Jintao, 2:591, **2:**1075–1077, **3:**1280, **4:**2009–2010, **4:**2023

Hu lian wang chan ye. *See* **Internet industry**

Hu lian wang nei rong guo lu, **3:**1172–1174, **3:**1181. *See also* Censorship

Hu lian wang shi yong. *See* **Internet use**

Hu Sanxing, **2:**1032

Hu Shi, 1:304, **1:**305, **1:**370, **2:**1078–1080, **3:**1111, **3:**1432–1433, **3:**1589–1592, **5:**2388–2389

Hu Yaobang, 2:1081–1083, **3:**1398, **3:**1399, **3:**1513, **4:**1870–1871

Hu Yuan, **3:**1576

Hua. See **Painting**

Hua Guofeng, **1:**356, **2:**603, **2:**622, **3:**1398, **4:**1868, **4:**1869

Hua jiao, **1:**241–242

Hua mei Xie jin she, **1:**340–341

Hua niao hua, **4:**1693–1696, **5:**2403–2404

Hua qiao (hua ren). *See* **Overseas Chinese**

Hua Tao, **3:**1437

Huahu, theory of, **1:**220–221

Huai River, 1:61–62, **2:**624–626, **3:**1084–1085

Huajian ji, **4:**2047

Huaju. See **Drama**

Huan jing wen ti yan jiu, **2:**752–758

Huan jing yun Dong, **2:**747–751

Huang Binghong, **1:**97

Huang Chao, **4:**2039, **4:**2182

Huang dao dai, **5:**2659–2661

Huang Hai, **1:**421, **5:**2567–2568

Huang Hsin-chieh, **2:**600

Huang jiao, **1:**241–242

Huang lan, **2:**699

Huang-Lo Daoism, **2:**568–569

Huang Quan, **4:**1693

Huang Shan, 3:1089–1091

Huang (Yellow) River, 2:630, **2:**863, **3:**1086–1088, **5:**2319

dikes, maintenance of, **2:**738, **3:**1238

floods, **2:**620–621, **2:**738, **3:**1087–1088, **5:**2422

Grand Canal and, **2:**915–916

in Heshang, **4:**1903–1904

limited flow of, **2:**744, **2:**894, **5:**2430

pollution of, **2:**744

silt in, **1:**328

Huang (Yellow) River area, **1:**421–422

agro-geography of, **1:**40, **1:**43

paintings of, **4:**1702

paleontological surveys, **1:**82

Huang Zongxi, 3:1092–1093

Huangdi Neijing, 3:1094–1095, **3:**1435, **3:**1437

Huangdi (Yellow Emperor), **1:**259, **2:**568–569, **2:**573, **2:**642

Huangjiu, **5:**2447–2448

Huanglongsi, 3:1096–1097

Huangmei Opera (Huangmei xi), **4:**1657

Huangpu Military Academy, **1:**183

Huangshan (Mount Huang), **1:**62–63

Huanguan, **2:**778–780, **3:**1487, **4:**2182

Huapao, **1:**103, **2:**816–819, **2:**965

Huaqiao. See **Overseas Chinese**

Huaren. See **Overseas Chinese**

Huating school of painting, **2:**633

Huawei, 3:1098–1099

Huayan Buddhism, 1:222–223, **3:**1100–1102, **5:**2535

Huayi Tu, **1:**282–283

Hubei Province, 1:86, **1:**420, **3:**1103, **3:**1103–1104, **3:**1447, **3:**1459. *See also* **Mount Wudang; Three Gorges Dam**

Hui, 2:764–765, **3:**1105–1107. *See also* **Ningxia Hui Autonomous Region**

Anhui Province, **1:**61

Heibei Province, **2:**1015

Heilongjiang province, **2:**1017

Henan Province, **2:**1019

leadership by, **3:**1279, **3:**1280

Notes: 1) **Bold** entries and page numbers denote encyclopedia entries;
2) The bold numbers preceeding the page numbers denote the volumes
(1–5) where the page numbers can be found

I

Notes: 1) **Bold** entries and page numbers denote encyclopedia entries; 2) The bold numbers preceeding the page numbers denote the volumes (1–5) where the page numbers can be found

J

J

Notes: 1) **Bold** entries and page numbers denote encyclopedia entries;

2) The bold numbers preceeding the page numbers denote the volumes

(1–5) where the page numbers can be found

J

Notes: 1) **Bold** entries and page numbers denote encyclopedia entries; 2) The bold numbers preceeding the page numbers denote the volumes (1–5) where the page numbers can be found

Notes: 1) **Bold** entries and page numbers denote encyclopedia entries;
2) The bold numbers preceeding the page numbers denote the volumes
(1–5) where the page numbers can be found

L

L

M

L
M

Notes: 1) **Bold** entries and page numbers denote encyclopedia entries; 2) The bold numbers preceeding the page numbers denote the volumes (1–5) where the page numbers can be found

M

Notes: 1) **Bold** entries and page numbers denote encyclopedia entries;

2) The bold numbers preceeding the page numbers denote the volumes (1–5) where the page numbers can be found

M

M

Notes: 1) **Bold** entries and page numbers denote encyclopedia entries;
2) The bold numbers preceeding the page numbers denote the volumes
(1–5) where the page numbers can be found

M

N

N

N

Notes: 1) **Bold** entries and page numbers denote encyclopedia entries;
2) The bold numbers preceeding the page numbers denote the volumes
(1–5) where the page numbers can be found

O

Opium War, Second, 1:65, 3:1470, 3:1498, 4:1663, 4:1667, 4:1669–1671, 5:2352. *See also* **Treaty of Tianjin**

Oracle bones, 1:84–85, 1:262, 1:325, 1:371, 2:630, 4:1672–1674, 4:1942–1943

Organization Department of the Party, 2:912

Oroqen, 2:936–937, 2:1017

OurGame, 5:2392

Outer Mongolia, 1:335, 4:1833, 4:1914

Outlaws of the Marshes, 3:1480, 5:2426

Overseas Chinese, 4:1675–1679

    Africa, 1:20–23, 4:1676

    Chinatowns established by, 1:348–350, 2:775

    East Asia, 2:660

    employment in China of, 2:856, 2:1027–1029, 3:1454

    from Guangzhou, 2:952–953

    Hakka, 2:979, 2:980

    Han, 2:982

    Hui, 3:1106

    investment in China by, 1:20, 2:591, 2:879, 2:947, 2:953, 3:1161, 3:1274, 4:1677–1678

    Mexico, 3:1272

    New Year celebrated by, 3:1607

    from Pearl River delta, 4:1733

    Qing dynasty, 4:1836, 5:2313

    returnees, 3:1283, 4:1678, 4:1869

    Southeast Asia, 4:1675–1678, 4:2053–2054, 4:2056, 5:2311

    Sun Yat-sen, organized by, 4:2133–2134

    Taiwan, 3:1151

    United States, 1:248, 1:348–349, 4:1675–1676, 5:2352–2353

    Vietnam, 3:1154

Ownership, foreign, 2:852–859, 3:1161. *See also* **Foreign investment;** Joint ventures

P

Pagodas, 1:91–92

Pai Pu, 5:2597

Painting, 4:1681–1687. *See also* **Calligraphy**

    Buddhist art and, 1:331, 4:1682, 4:1683

    contemporary, 1:94–96

    Dong Qichang, 2:633–634

    guohua (national-style), 2:969–971

    Mi Fu, 3:1445–1446

    Peace Reigns over the River, 4:1727–1730

    Tang Yin, 4:2190–2191

    Wang Wei, 5:2405–2406

    Western art, influence of, 4:1692, 5:2526–2527

    Wu Changshi, 5:2486

    Wu School, 2:892, 4:1684, 4:2190–2191

    Yuan dynasty, 5:2601

Painting—court, 4:1688–1692, 4:2041, 4:2109, 5:2601, 5:2623–2624

Painting—flower and bird, 4:1693–1696, 5:2403–2404

Painting—folk, 4:1697–1700

Painting, landscape, 4:1701–1703. *See also* **Dong Qichang**

Pakistan—China relations, 1:297, 2:836, 4:1704–1708, 5:2348–2349

Palaces

    Daoist Trinity Palace, 3:1507

    National Palace Museum, 1:107

    Potala Palace, 4:1788–1789, 4:1880, 5:2465

    Shenyang Imperial Palace, 4:1960–1961, 5:2464

    Summer Palace of Yiheyuan, 4:2129–2130, 5:2464

    World Heritage sites, 5:2464–2466

Paleolithic era, 4:1709–1713

Paleontology. *See* **Archaeology and paleontology**

Pan Tianshou, 1:98

Panama, 3:1272, 3:1274, 4:1676

Panax ginseng, 2:899–900

Panchen Lama, 1:240

Panda, 3:1096, 4:1714–1715, 4:1855

Pang Xunqin, 1:98

Paozhu (paozhang), 2:816

Paper cutting, 4:1716–1718

Paper money, 4:2040, 5:2601

Papermaking and printing, 2:780, 4:1719–1723

Paralympics, Beijing, 2008, 2:615

Parks, imperial. *See* Imperial China, gardens and parks

Passenger vehicles, 5:2373

Patents, 3:1168–1171

Patriarchal marriage and family system, 3:1404–1405, 3:1408–1409

Notes: 1) **Bold** entries and page numbers denote encyclopedia entries; 2) The bold numbers preceeding the page numbers denote the volumes (1–5) where the page numbers can be found

P

Notes: 1) **Bold** entries and page numbers denote encyclopedia entries; 2) The bold numbers preceeding the page numbers denote the volumes (1–5) where the page numbers can be found

P

P

P

Q

Notes: 1) **Bold** entries and page numbers denote encyclopedia entries;
2) The bold numbers preceeding the page numbers denote the volumes
(1–5) where the page numbers can be found

Q

Notes: 1) **Bold** entries and page numbers denote encyclopedia entries;

2) The bold numbers preceeding the page numbers denote the volumes (1–5) where the page numbers can be found

Q
R

R

Rhee, Syngman, **3**:1249, **3**:1253

Ri ben he Zhong guo de guan xi. *See* **Japan—China relations**

Riben, **2**:662. *See also* Japan

Ricci, Matteo, **1**:364, **1**:388–389, **2**:907, **3**:1385, **3**:1488, **3**:1497, **4**:1888, **4**:1897–1899, **5**:2528

Rice, as cuisine staple, **1**:529, **1**:531, **1**:532

Rice, as currency, **2**:661

Rice production, **1**:327–328, **1**:331–332, **2**:731, **2**:733–734, **3**:1119, **5**:2420. *See also* Grain production

Richard, Timothy, **2**:619, **4**:1900–1901

Richwin software, **2**:1024

Rickshaw Boy, **3**:1269

Ridgway, Matthew, **3**:1241–1252

Righteousness or rightness. *See Yi* (righteousness)

Rites, Board of, **3**:1328

Rites Controversy, **1**:389, **1**:392, **4**:2030

Ritsu Buddhist rite, **3**:1204

Ritual action. *See Li*

River Elegy (Heshang), **4**:1902–1904

Rivers, **2**:744, **2**:894, **2**:915. *See also* specific rivers

Rizhi lu, **2**:940

Roads, **2**:737–738, **3**:1164, **4**:1706–1707, **5**:2317–2318. *See also* Silk Roads

ROC. *See* Republic of China (1912-1949)

Roman Catholicism. *See* Catholicism

Romance of Three Kingdoms, **3**:1479–1480, **4**:1699, **4**:1905–1906, **4**:2137

Romances, **3**:1335

Rong Hong, **5**:2607–2608

Roosevelt, Franklin D., **5**:2541–2542

Root-Takahira Agreement, **3**:1266

Ru He River, **2**:624–626

Ru jia dao de. *See* **Confucian ethics**

Ru ware (celadon), **1**:293

Ru xue fu xing, **1**:482–492, **4**:2008

Ruan, **3**:1537

Ruan Ji, **2**:569

Ruan Lingyu, **4**:1907–1908

Rubbings, **4**:1720

Ruggieri, Michele, **1**:388

Ruler, importance to governance of, **2**:907–908

Rulin waishi, **3**:1481

Rural areas. *See also* **Agricultural cooperatives movement; Agriculture; Famine; Great Leap Forward; Household responsibility system;** Land reform; **Township and village enterprises**

CCP in, **1**:355

cunguan program, **2**:545–546

decollectivization, **2**:670, **2**:929

dense population resulting from rice production, **1**:327, **1**:332

disabled people, **2**:612, **2**:614

economic growth, effect of, **1**:45

economic inequalities, **2**:738, **2**:742, **4**:2016–2017, **4**:2019, **4**:2148–2149

education system, **2**:675–677

familiy system, **3**:1408–1409

forest preservation. importance of, **2**:864–865

health care, **2**:1006–1008

industrialization of, **3**:1211, **4**:2019

labor data and surveys, **3**:1459–1460

life expectancy, 1929-1931, **3**:1405

Mao's work in, **3**:1390–1392, **4**:1699

New Rural Reconstruction Movement, **3**:1598–1601

NGOs, involvement of, **3**:1600–1601, **3**:1621

one-child policy in, **2**:741, **4**:1644, **4**:2147–2148

pensions, **3**:1183–1184

Qin dynasty, **4**:1827

rustication movement, **5**:2372 (*See also* Cultural Revolution)

Rural Reconstruction Movement, **4**:1909–1911, **5**:2570

Rural-urban migration, **2**:740, **2**:947–948, **3**:1452–1454, **3**:1456–1461, **5**:2366, **5**:2368, **5**:2370, **5**:2371

Russia—China relations, **3**:1475, **4**:1912–1917. *See also* **Opium War, Second;** Soviet Union

Central Asia, treaties covering, **1**:295–296

Chinese immigration to Russia, **4**:1676

Chinese military modernization and, **3**:1462–1463

Dalian, control of, **2**:558–559

Jilin chemical plant explosion, effect of, **2**:626–627

Kangxi, relations with, **3**:1237–1238

Manchuria, rights in (*See* **Manchuria**)

military equipment sales, Russia to China, **2**:593, **4**:1915–1916

Notes: 1) **Bold** entries and page numbers denote encyclopedia entries; 2) The bold numbers preceeding the page numbers denote the volumes (1–5) where the page numbers can be found

R

Notes: 1) **Bold** entries and page numbers denote encyclopedia entries; 2) The bold numbers preceeding the page numbers denote the volumes (1–5) where the page numbers can be found

S

S

Notes: 1) **Bold** entries and page numbers denote encyclopedia entries; 2) The bold numbers preceeding the page numbers denote the volumes (1–5) where the page numbers can be found

S

S

Notes: 1) **Bold** entries and page numbers denote encyclopedia entries; 2) The bold numbers preceeding the page numbers denote the volumes (1–5) where the page numbers can be found

S

S

S

T

Notes: 1) **Bold** entries and page numbers denote encyclopedia entries;

2) The bold numbers preceeding the page numbers denote the volumes

(1–5) where the page numbers can be found

T

Notes: 1) **Bold** entries and page numbers denote encyclopedia entries; 2) The bold numbers preceding the page numbers denote the volumes (1–5) where the page numbers can be found

T

T

Notes: 1) **Bold** entries and page numbers denote encyclopedia entries;
2) The bold numbers preceding the page numbers denote the volumes
(1–5) where the page numbers can be found

T

T

Notes: 1) **Bold** entries and page numbers denote encyclopedia entries; 2) The bold numbers preceeding the page numbers denote the volumes (1–5) where the page numbers can be found

U

V

W

Notes: 1) **Bold** entries and page numbers denote encyclopedia entries;

2) The bold numbers preceding the page numbers denote the volumes (1–5) where the page numbers can be found

W

W

Notes: 1) **Bold** entries and page numbers denote encyclopedia entries; 2) The bold numbers preceeding the page numbers denote the volumes (1–5) where the page numbers can be found

X

Notes: 1) **Bold** entries and page numbers denote encyclopedia entries;
2) The bold numbers preceeding the page numbers denote the volumes
(1–5) where the page numbers can be found

Y

Y

Z

Za zhi. *See* **Magazines**

Zai xian she hui wang luo, 4:2012–2015

Zaihuang. See **Famine**

Zaji, 1:6–8

Zaju. *See* **Yuan drama**

Zambia, 1:20, 1:21

Zan shang zhi du. *See* **Tribute system**

Zang. *See* **Tibetans (Zang)**

Zang Maoxun, 5:2597, 5:2598

Zang zu de Fo jiao. *See* **Buddhism, Tibetan**

Zao Wuo-ki, 4:1703

Zao zhi xue he yin shua ye, 2:780, 4:1719–1723

Zaoshen, 4:1877

Zdansky, Otto, 4:1735

Zen Buddhism. *See* **Buddhism, Chan**

Zeng bells, 1:174

Zeng Guofan, 4:2165–2166, 5:2615–2616

ZGC companies, 2:1024

Zhan guo. *See* **Warring States Period**

Zhan Wan, 1:105

Zhang Ailing, 3:1288

Zhang Caoyang, 2:1024–1025

Zhang Chunqiao, 2:541, 2:884, 2:886

Zhang Daqian, 1:97–98, 4:1703, 5:2617–2618

Zhang Guodao, 3:1347

Zhang Heng, 2:993

Zhang Huan, 1:103

Zhang Jiaao, 1:149

Zhang Ling, 2:569, 2:573

Zhang Peilei, 1:102–103

Zhang Ruimin, 2:975–976

Zhang Shiyi, 3:1386

Zhang Weibang, 4:1695

Zhang Xiaogang, 1:103–104

Zhang Xuan, 4:1689

Zhang Xueliang, 1:321, 3:1383–1384, 5:2501–2503

Zhang Yimou, 1:403, 5:2619–2620

Zhang Zai, 3:1577

Zhang Zeduan, 4:1691, 4:1727–1730

Zhang Zhidong, 5:2621–2622

Zhang Zhongjing, 3:1437

Zhang Zuolin, 3:1311, 3:1312, 3:1382–1383

Zhanguo ce, 2:991

Zhanguo period. *See* **Warring States Period**

Zhangzong, 3:1231

Zhanjiang, 2:608

Zhanpao, 1:447

Zhao Gao, 2:779, 4:1828

Zhao jin fo, 1:233–235, 1:243–244

Zhao Kuangyin, 4:2041

Zhao Mengfu, 4:1684, 4:1702, 5:2601, 5:2623–2624

Zhao Yanwang, 2:1054

Zhao Ziyang, 1:356–358, 2:591, 5:2625–2626

Zhaozhou Bridge, 5:2627–2628

Zhejiang Industrial Bank, 4:2063–2064

Zhejiang Province, 1:420, 3:1458–1459, 4:1660–1661,
4:1712, 5:2559–2560, **5:2629–2630**

Zhejiang University, 2:999–1000

Zhen ci liao fa. *See* **Acupuncture**

Zheng (musical instrument), 3:1535, 5:2592–2593

Zheng (Qin ruler), 4:1827–1831

Zheng Chenggong, 4:2174, 5:2631–2632

Zheng He, 1:334, 2:780, 2:784–786, 3:1486–1487,
3:1490–1493, 5:2591, **5:2633–2634**

Zheng Pengqun, 3:1111–1112

Zheng Shichuan, 1:396

Zheng yi, 4:1968

Zheng Zhengiu, 1:396

Zheng zhi can yu, 4:1778–1782

Zhengton daozang, 2:572–573

Zhenguan zhengyao, 4:2186

Zhenwu, 3:1521

Zhenzhou, 2:1019–1020

Zhi, 1:469, 3:1127, 3:1442, 5:2252, 5:2254, 5:2261

Zhi shi chan quan, 3:1168–1171, 5:2469

Zhi wai fa quan. *See* **Extraterritoriality**

Zhiqing, 2:546

Zhiqu Weihushan, 2:691–692

Zhiyi, 1:222–223, 5:2277–2278

Zhong guo cheng, 1:348–350, 2:775

Zhong guo chu kou shang pin jiao yi hui, 1:267–270,
2:953

Zhong guo de jing ji zhi du, 2:668–672

Zhong guo Fo jiao xie hui, 1:225, 1:243–244, 4:1883

Notes: 1) **Bold** entries and page numbers denote encyclopedia entries;
2) The bold numbers preceeding the page numbers denote the volumes
(1–5) where the page numbers can be found

Z

Notes: 1) **Bold** entries and page numbers denote encyclopedia entries;
2) The bold numbers preceeding the page numbers denote the volumes
(1–5) where the page numbers can be found

Z